P9-CSC-261

SELECTED POETRY

OF

WILLIAM WORDSWORTH

SELECTED POETRY

OF

WILLIAM
WORDSWORTH

Edited by Mark Van Doren

Introduction by David Bromwich

Notes by Michele Turner Sharp
EAST CAROLINA UNIVERSITY

THE MODERN LIBRARY

NEW YORK

2002 Modern Library Paperback Edition

Biographical note copyright © 2001 by Random House, Inc.
Introduction copyright © 2001 by David Bromwich
Notes copyright © 2002 by Random House, Inc.

All rights reserved under International and Pan-American
Copyright Conventions. Published in the United States by
Modern Library, an imprint of The Random House Publishing
Group, a division of Random House, Inc., New York, and simultaneously
in Canada by Random House of Canada Limited, Toronto.

MODERN LIBRARY and the TORCHBEARER Design are registered trademarks
of Random House, Inc.

LIBRARY OF CONGRESS CATALOGING-IN-PUBLICATION DATA

Wordsworth, William, 1770–1850.
[Poems. Selections]
Selected poetry of William Wordsworth / edited by Mark Van Doren; introduction by
David Bromwich; notes by Michele Turner Sharp.— Modern Library paperback ed.
p.   cm.
Includes index.
ISBN 0-375-75941-7
I. Van Doren, Mark, 1894–1972.   II. Title.

PR5852 .V3 2002
821'.7—dc21
2001056297

Modern Library website address: www.modernlibrary.com

Printed in the United States of America

4   6   8   9   7   5

WILLIAM WORDSWORTH

William Wordsworth was born in the small Lake District town of Cockermouth on April 7, 1770, the second of five children of John Wordsworth, a law agent, and Ann Cookson. While William received little formal education as a child, his father taught him to memorize the works of the great English poets, including Shakespeare, Milton, and Spenser. From a very early age, William was especially close to his younger sister Dorothy, born in 1771; after a more or less continuous separation while Wordsworth attended school and traveled throughout Europe (they were temporarily reunited in the summer of 1787 after an initial nine-year separation), the siblings were permanently reunited in 1794 and spent the rest of their lives cohabitating.

In 1779, a year after his mother died, Wordsworth was sent to a grammar school in the secluded Lake District village of Hawkshead, a place that remained beloved to him and inspired his early poems of rural life. Lodging with a local family, he spent many days exploring the landscape on walks and adventures. It was here that he began studying the Greek and Roman classics and made his first attempts at verse.

In 1787 he was admitted to Cambridge University, but proved to be a mediocre student. His first major poem, *An Evening Walk*, a survey of Lake District life, was written here in 1788. On a long vacation in the summer of 1790, Wordsworth took a tour, largely on foot, of the European Alps, inspiring the poem *Descriptive Sketches*, which was written soon after. Both *An Evening Walk* and *Descriptive Sketches* were published in 1793.

Traveling to France in 1791, he became a supporter of the French

Revolution; he wrote prolifically about his political views, but his radical writings were never published in his lifetime. While in France, he fathered an illegitimate daughter, Anne-Caroline, to Annette Vallon, the daughter of an Orléans surgeon, but he was forced to return to England in the late fall of 1792 after his family cut off his income, leaving Annette and his daughter behind. War broke out between England and France in February 1793, and Wordsworth would not be able to return to France until 1802, when, in an effort to settle things between himself and Annette before his planned marriage in the fall of that year to an old schoolmate, he and Dorothy would spend four weeks with Caroline and Annette (he would see them both together only one more time, in 1820, at the Louvre).

After receiving a couple of small legacies in 1795, Wordsworth moved with Dorothy into Racedown Lodge in Dorsetshire near Crewkerne, where he wrote some of the poems that would appear in *Lyrical Ballads*, as well as *The Ruined Cottage*, which would eventually become a part of *The Excursion*. In August of that year in Bristol, he met Samuel Taylor Coleridge, who had been very impressed with *An Evening Walk* and *Descriptive Sketches* when they were first published in 1793 (though Wordsworth didn't know that at the time). Over the next two years they became good friends, and eventually an extended visit from Coleridge in the early summer of 1797 resulted in the siblings' move to Alfoxden House, near the elder poet's home at Nether Stowey in Somersetshire. It was here that Wordsworth wrote some of his greatest poems, including "Lines Left upon a Seat in a Yew-tree," "We Are Seven," "The Idiot Boy," and "Tintern Abbey." These early poems were collected with Coleridge's verse, including "The Rime of the Ancient Mariner," in their 1798 collaborative volume, *Lyrical Ballads*.

In the fall of 1798, right before *Lyrical Ballads* was to be published, Dorothy and William set off with Coleridge on a long trip to Germany, during which time Wordsworth began work on his magnum opus, *The Prelude* (*The Prelude* was meant to be just that, a prelude to another poem, *The Recluse*, about the solitary life of the poet; *The Recluse*, however, was never completed, and *The Prelude* ended up supplanting it). William and Dorothy, unhappy in Germany, returned to England in May of 1799, and by December were settled at Dove Cottage in Grasmere in the Lake District.

Wordsworth's return to the Lakes, the setting of his idyllic childhood, inspired him to complete what would be the first of several incarnations of his great autobiographical poem, *The Prelude,* in 1799 (which was not, however, published until 1850, after Wordsworth had died). In 1800, he published an expanded edition of *Lyrical Ballads,* adding a preface that outlined his theories and opinions about poetry and called for a return to the subject matter of simple, unaffected rustic life, and including several new poems such as "Nutting," "There Was a Boy," "Michael," and the Lucy poems. Following the publication of the second edition of *Lyrical Ballads,* Wordsworth continued to work on *The Recluse.* He also continued to revise and rearrange chapters of *The Prelude,* expanding it from a two-part poem to a thirteen-chapter book in 1805.

Wordsworth's family and personal life proved tumultuous during the course of the new century's first decade. On October 4, 1802, he married Mary Hutchinson, a childhood friend and schoolmate. The couple had five children between the years of 1803 and 1810, two of whom died in 1812. Another tragedy had struck in 1805, when Wordsworth's favorite brother, John, a sailor, was drowned at sea when his ship sank. Also, by as early as 1808 relations with Coleridge had become strained, with a final rupture occurring in 1810 when offhanded remarks Wordsworth made about Coleridge's character came to the attention of the elder poet. Though they would eventually reconcile, their relationship would never be the same.

Dorothy continued to live with Mary and William in a small cottage in Grasmere, assisting with the raising of the children. The growing size of his family forced Wordsworth to move to a larger house. After a series of unsatisfactory temporary residences, the extended family finally settled at Rydal Mount in Grasmere, where Wordsworth was to live for the rest of his life. In 1813, Wordsworth accepted the government position of tax collector for neighboring regions, which provoked criticism from the next generation of Romantic poets, including Byron and Shelley.

In a outpouring of creative energy between December 1801 and the spring of 1807, Wordsworth produced a substantial part of the first two books of *The Excursion* and most of the poems that were ultimately published in May of 1807 in *Poems in Two Volumes,* including the "Ode: Intimations of Immortality," "Resolution and Independence," "The Solitary Reaper," and sonnets such as "Composed upon Westminster Bridge" and "London, 1802." The reviews *Poems in Two Volumes* received were on the whole negative, a response which so pained Wordsworth that he gave up further revision on *The Prelude* and put aside a new poem he'd been working on called *The White Doe of Rylstone*. He would not publish another poem for seven years.

Wordsworth finally completed *The Excursion*, conceived originally as the middle part of the uncompleted and unpublished *Recluse*, and published it in 1814; the book was critically and commercially unsuccessful. Over the next three decades, Wordsworth continued to write and publish major poems, including the series of sonnets *The River Duddon* (1820); *Ecclesiastical Sonnets*, published in 1822; and "Yarrow Revisited" (1831), which was published in *Yarrow Revisited and Other Poems* in 1835. He also continued to revise *The Prelude*. His last separate volume of poems, *Memorials of a Tour in Italy*, which he composed during a trip to Italy in 1837, was published in 1842. Meanwhile, the reputation of his early work steadily grew, transforming Rydal Hall into something of a tourist attraction. He received such illustrious visitors as Ralph Waldo Emerson and made the acquaintance of a younger generation of poets, including John Keats and Matthew Arnold. He also received an honorary doctorate from the University of Durham in 1838 and from Oxford in 1839, and was made Poet Laureate in 1843.

Family tragedies, however, persisted, and in 1835 Dorothy succumbed to early senile dementia and remained an invalid until her death in 1855. William Wordsworth died at Rydal Mount on April 13, 1850, and is buried at Grasmere Churchyard. After his death his fame continued to grow, and his poetry continued to influence and inspire new generations of poets. "I firmly believe," wrote Matthew Arnold in 1879, "that the poetical performance of Wordsworth is, after that of Shakespeare and Milton, undoubtedly the most considerable in our language from the Elizabethan age to the present time."

CONTENTS

1802–1807

1814

1815

1817–1833

INTRODUCTION

David Bromwich

Wordsworth's poetry divides us into believers and doubters. The power
to create so fierce a response is not a necessary or perhaps a usual quality
of great poets. But Wordsworth begins his career by raising the stakes. A
poet should address his readers, he says in the Preface to *Lyrical Ballads*, as
"a man speaking to men." The assertion is as obvious as it is unprece-
dented. A peculiar and radical sense must be given to the words "man,"
"speaking," and "men" to explain the poet's belief that by descending to
the common he has touched the sublime. Wordsworth soon goes further.
The pleasure that he uniquely gives will be "a homage paid to the native
and naked dignity of man." His poems will be found to show that "the
human mind is capable of being excited without the application of gross
and violent stimulants," because he draws his words not from a special
poetic diction but "the real language of men in a state of vivid sensation."
The case for the realness, the vividness, the elementary strength of po-
etry has never been put more uncompromisingly, and it may seem cap-
tious that so large a quantity of the debate about his achievement has
always centered on the question how far Wordsworth's language typifies
the speech of anyone but himself. Readers who can admire freely when
he writes "I had no human fears," often will not extend the same gen-
erosity to a line like "Himself he propped, limbs, body, and pale face."

The dramatic rightness of Wordsworth's language can be trusted to
vindicate itself—with the reminder that some quite individual expres-
sions may be suitable chiefly to a poet. A larger challenge remains con-
cerning his preoccupation with the importance of having a moral

purpose. His admirer John Keats was a skeptic on this point: "we hate poetry that has a palpable design upon us." The challenge is fair and the criticism has found many echoes. Yet even the most appreciative contemporaries underrated the originality of Wordsworth's design. The truth is that he does not aim to catch hidden lights and shadows in the life of social man. His poetry tends to show instead that man is not essentially a social creature. That is the meaning of his saying that his subject is "The pleasure which there is in life itself." It is also the meaning of his praise of the energy and anarchy of childhood—"An appetite; a feeling and a love, / That had no need of a remoter charm / By thought supplied." Poetry exists for the sake of a recollection of feeling, and feeling is valued for its impression of sheer contact with life. By the compositional process of "emotion recollected in tranquillity," which Wordsworth speaks of in his Preface, the tranquillity of the poet "gradually disappears," and something akin to the original feeling returns "and does itself actually exist in the mind." *Does itself actually exist.* No poet or philosopher has believed more plainly in the substantial reality of thoughts and feelings. This stubborn insistence may account for the hold Wordsworth continues to have on readers without denomination or expertise. He is loved for a sense of radical sufficiency in the fact that life *is*—the faith of many people who espouse a religion without a name. Wordsworth writes of a human nature that is not to be judged by the utility of some goods over others, the propriety of some behaviors, or the reasonableness of getting and spending as the market teaches getting and spending. The life his poetry describes cannot be reduced to a series of preferable and less preferable options. We learn its deeper claim in the presence of suffering and joy, in suffering not less than in joy.

The connection of the poet's mission with the recorded life of a child born in 1770 of the smaller rural gentry, who lost his mother and father when young and grew up among four siblings, the most remarkable of whom, Dorothy, would become his closest friend and "second self": all this remains a mystery, as it must be in the effort to understand a poet. But in Wordsworth a knot of motives keeps returning—a cause of perplexity and a spur to the self-imagining he makes us share. In the summer of 1790, on vacation from Cambridge, he had set out on a walking tour in Europe accompanied by a friend, and met on his way the French Revolution. Wordsworth shared the deeper democratic and egalitarian impulses of the time. He saw close up, in a year of residence in France that started in late 1791, the accidents and treachery by which revolutionary hope was crushed and "the radiance which was once so bright" turned from possibility to memory. Gradually, and at a cost to his own aspirations, he decided that the renewal he sought for human feeling was not to be found in politics. His poetry came to be addressed to individual readers, and to readers not without some salutary fear of themselves. When he returned to England, he had left in France his lover and their child.

Few of the men and women in Wordsworth's poems embody directly the moral good the poet aims to inculcate. On the contrary, his typical characters, in the early poems especially, are convicts, vagrants, beggars, the impotent and the incontinent and the mad. They inhabit his work with a prosaic density that has not been equaled by any poetry before or since. No poet has been less eager, by his choice of subject and treatment, to solicit an understanding that he himself belongs among the respectable. Of the scandalized reception of the *Lyrical Ballads*—published in 1798 by Wordsworth and his friend and collaborator Samuel Taylor Coleridge—the leveling aesthetic of the poetry and its touches of primitivism were doubtless the leading cause. But the attacks exposed Wordsworth, at a vulnerable moment, to what would become the usual fate of the avant-garde artist, and the reverberations can be traced far into his career. *The Excursion*—the long poem written during the Napoleonic wars and published in 1814, by which a larger public finally came to recognize him—offered the dutiful gestures of community and piety that had been missed in his earlier work. Meanwhile, his great autobiographical poem, *The Prelude,* with its new subject, "the growth of a poet's mind," was suppressed by Wordsworth during his lifetime, parts of it anxiously revised or canceled. His life reveals a similar pattern of growing prudence and economy of enterprise. He married and had children, moved from the tiny cottage in Grasmere, called Town-End, where his experiments in "vivid sensation" were written, to the stately Rydal Mount, which would become a place of pilgrimage for squadrons of readers in search of counsel or a glimpse of the distinguished man. By the age of sixty, he had become the first of the Victorian sages. But his greatest poetry had borne witness to a faith less reconciled.

He remains, at his most exuberant, the prophet of a purposeless attention to nature for its own sake, a listening that can hardly be distinguished from reflection. This is the posture of the child in "There Was a Boy" who blows his mimic hooting at the owls across a lake:

> Then, sometimes, in that silence, while he hung
> Listening, a gentle shock of mild surprise
> Has carried far into his heart the voice
> Of mountain-torrents; or the visible scene
> Would enter unawares into his mind
> With all its solemn imagery, its rocks,
> Its woods, and that uncertain heaven received
> Into the bosom of the steady lake.

The pause of the child foreshadows the pause of an adult. When the routine or custom of ordinary life somehow relaxes its grip, an intimation of thought may "enter unawares." It can happen in reading a book or meeting a person, or in a flicker of self-knowledge where a life is glimpsed under a new aspect.

Wordsworth still draws a good many readers by a process of accidental discovery. You find the book in your hands and start to read; some process of enchantment works, and you read on. A list of poems may be helpful to sort out and begin to organize the odd and miscellaneous impression these poems are bound to make. Almost the first to be written were the ballads (in this volume, roughly the poems of 1798 and 1799), and the first part of Wordsworth's life is chronicled in *The Prelude*, but neither is the right place to start. Rather, begin with the lyrics that touch on ecstatic and meditative moments of experience: "A Night-Piece," "Lines Written in Early Spring," "There Was a Boy," "Nutting," "Yew-trees." Close behind should come the sonnets on liberty that deal with human memory and commemoration, especially "To Toussaint L'Ouverture" and "It Is a Beauteous Evening, Calm and Free." Then the poems of fortuitous and quite arbitrary human encounters, which form so arresting a ground note of Wordsworth's genius—"Resolution and Independence" and "The Solitary Reaper"—along with two poems about children, "Anecdote for Fathers" and "We Are Seven." To Wordsworth, a child is as strange a being as a singer in a foreign tongue or a laborer bent double by age and toil.

Turn next to the poet's inquest into the natural history of his own mind, in "Lines Composed a Few Miles above Tintern Abbey," "Ode: Intimations of Immortality," the "Ode to Duty," and the "Elegiac Stanzas" on Peele Castle, with its poignant retraction of hope after the death at sea of the poet's brother John:

A power is gone, which nothing can restore;
A deep distress hath humanised my Soul.

That deep distress may humanize is a paradox of psychology which
Wordsworth did as much as anyone to discover. His exactingness on this
modern theme can be felt in *The Prelude*, whose final books deal explicitly
with imagination "impaired and restored." When, in the autobiographical
poem itself, one has felt from within how his balance is restored in the
later 1790s, one may appreciate the peculiar sense of human loneliness
and solidarity from which he undertook to write the *Lyrical Ballads*. Per-
haps the most fully achieved of these, in the startling turns they give to
stories that could easily lend themselves to tragedy or melodrama, are
"The Thorn," "The Idiot Boy," "The Old Cumberland Beggar," and
"Michael." There is nothing else like them in literature.

Many readers have said of Wordsworth that he changed their lives. For
a modern poet, this is an exceptional compliment, but also an ambiguous
one. Is changing a life what we should expect or want from a writer? John
Stuart Mill, the political theorist of liberty, credited the poetry of
Wordsworth with having restored his sense of purpose and continuity at
a time of profound self-doubt. The poetry, said Mill, seemed to impart
"the very culture of the feelings, which I was in quest of," and all the
more effectively as Wordsworth was "the poet of unpoetical natures." In
framing his description, Mill did Wordsworth an unconscious disservice
and paid him a delicate homage. The disservice lay in the choice of
words—as if feelings were merely another walk of "culture" with their
own forms of mastery and therapy; as if, once the poetic devices have
been cleared away, what is left is the "unpoetic" subject matter to operate
at last without obstruction. Wordsworth's program had actually declared
an opposite faith: that there is no such thing as a subject by its nature po-
etic, and no specialized domain of taste and sensibility. And yet Mill's
genuine homage may be felt in the praise he meant but could not speak.
He had begun reading Wordsworth when assailed by loss of belief in sys-
tematic projects of reform; and at that moment he found Wordsworth's
poetry did for him what the hope of universal progress could not do: it
gave back or, simply, gave what had never been there, a sentiment of the
good in life itself. This was indeed the attachment Wordsworth sought to
convey—attachment to "the very world, which is the world / Of all of
us,—the place where, in the end, / We find our happiness, or not at all!"

Was he ever tempted to surrender the quest? He certainly feared that he himself might falter. He once regretted the requirement that poetry should give pleasure to the reader, on the ground that fulfilling this expectation might distract the poet from "the image of things." In his own case, Wordsworth's fear was misjudged. No poet has come closer to the image of things.

—

DAVID BROMWICH is a professor of English at Yale University and the author of numerous books, including, most recently, *Disowned by Memory: Wordsworth's Poetry of the 1790s.*

SELECTED POETRY
OF
WILLIAM WORDSWORTH

1787-89

An Evening Walk

ADDRESSED TO A YOUNG LADY

*General Sketch of the Lakes — Author's regret of his youth which was
passed amongst them —Short description of Noon — Cascade —
Noontide Retreat — Precipice and sloping Lights — Face of Nature as the
Sun declines — Mountain-farm, and the Cock — Slate-quarry —
Sunset — Superstition of the Country connected with that
moment — Swans — Female Beggar — Twilight-sounds —
Western Lights — Spirits — Night — Moonlight — Hope —
Night-sounds — Conclusion.*

Far from my dearest Friend, 'tis mine to rove
Through bare grey dell, high wood, and pastoral cove;
Where Derwent rests, and listens to the roar
That stuns the tremulous cliffs of high Lodore;
Where peace to Grasmere's lonely island leads,
To willowy hedge-rows, and to emerald meads;
Leads to her bridge, rude church, and cottaged grounds,
Her rocky sheepwalks, and her woodland bounds;
Where, undisturbed by winds, Winander sleeps
'Mid clustering isles, and holly-sprinkled steeps;   10
Where twilight glens endear my Esthwaite's shore,
And memory of departed pleasures, more.
    Fair scenes, erewhile, I taught, a happy child,
The echoes of your rocks my carols wild:
The spirit sought not then, in cherished sadness,
A cloudy substitute for failing gladness.
In youth's keen eye the livelong day was bright,
The sun at morning, and the stars at night,
Alike, when first the bittern's hollow bill
Was heard, or woodcocks roamed the moonlight hill.   20

In thoughtless gaiety I coursed the plain,
And hope itself was all I knew of pain;
For then, the inexperienced heart would beat
At times, while young Content forsook her seat,
And wild Impatience, pointing upward, showed,
Through passes yet unreached, a brighter road,
Alas! the idle tale of man is found
Depicted in the dial's moral round;
Hope with reflection blends her social rays
To gild the total tablet of his days;   30
Yet still, the sport of some malignant power,
He knows but from its shade the present hour.
    But why, ungrateful, dwell on idle pain?
To show what pleasures yet to me remain,
Say, will my Friend, with unreluctant ear,
The history of a poet's evening hear?
    When, in the south, the wan noon, brooding still,
Breathed a pale steam around the glaring hill,
And shades of deep-embattled clouds were seen,
Spotting the northern cliffs with lights between;   40
When crowding cattle, checked by rails that make
A fence far stretched into the shallow lake,
Lashed the cool water with their restless tails,
Or from high points of rock looked out for fanning gales:
When school-boys stretched their length upon the green;
And round the broad-spread oak, a glimmering scene,
In the rough fern-clad park, the herded deer
Shook the still-twinkling tail and glancing ear;
When horses in the sunburnt intake stood,
And vainly eyed below the tempting flood,   50
Or tracked the passenger, in mute distress,
With forward neck the closing gate to press—
Then, while I wandered where the huddling rill
Brightens with water-breaks the hollow ghyll
As by enchantment, an obscure retreat
Opened at once, and stayed my devious feet.
While thick above the rill the branches close,
In rocky basin its wild waves repose,
Inverted shrubs, and moss of gloomy green,

Cling from the rocks, with pale wood-weeds between; 60
And its own twilight softens the whole scene,
Save where aloft the subtle sunbeams shine
On withered briars that o'er the crags recline;
Save where, with sparkling foam, a small cascade
Illumines, from within, the leafy shade;
Beyond, along the vista of the brook,
Where antique roots its bustling course o'erlook,
The eye reposes on a secret bridge
Half grey, half shagged with ivy to its ridge;
There, bending o'er the stream, the listless swain 70
Lingers behind his disappearing wain.
—Did Sabine grace adorn my living line,
Blandusia's praise, wild stream, should yield to thine!
Never shall ruthless minister of death
'Mid thy soft glooms the glittering steel unsheath;
No goblets shall, for thee, be crowned with flowers,
No kid with piteous outcry thrill thy bowers;
The mystic shapes that by thy margin rove
A more benignant sacrifice approve—
A mind, that, in a calm angelic mood 80
Of happy wisdom, meditating good,
Beholds, of all from her high powers required,
Much done, and much designed, and more desired,—
Harmonious thoughts, a soul by truth refined,
Entire affection for all human kind.

Dear Brook, farewell! To-morrow's noon again
Shall hide me, wooing long thy wildwood strain;
But now the sun has gained his western road,
And eve's mild hour invites my steps abroad.

While, near the midway cliff, the silvered kite 90
In many a whistling circle wheels her flight;
Slant watery lights, from parting clouds, apace
Travel along the precipice's base;
Cheering its naked waste of scattered stone,
By lichens grey, and scanty moss, o'ergrown;
Where scarce the foxglove peeps, or thistle's beard;
And restless stone-chat, all day long, is heard,
How pleasant, as the sun declines, to view

The spacious landscape change in form and hue!
Here, vanish, as in mist, before a flood   100
Of bright obscurity, hill, lawn, and wood;
There, objects, by the searching beams betrayed,
Come forth, and here retire in purple shade;
Even the white stems of birch, the cottage white,
Soften their glare before the mellow light;
The skiffs, at anchor where with umbrage wide
Yon chestnuts half the latticed boat-house hide,
Shed from their sides, that face the sun's slant beam,
Strong flakes of radiance on the tremulous stream:
Raised by yon travelling flock, a dusty cloud   110
Mounts from the road, and spreads its moving shroud;
The shepherd, all involved in wreaths of fire,
Now shows a shadowy speck, and now is lost entire.

 Into a gradual calm the breezes sink,
A blue rim borders all the lake's still brink;
There doth the twinkling aspen's foliage sleep,
And insects clothe, like dust, the glassy deep:
And now, on every side, the surface breaks
Into blue spots, and slowly lengthening streaks;
Here, plots of sparkling water tremble bright   120
With thousand thousand twinkling points of light;
There, waves that, hardly weltering, die away,
Tip their smooth ridges with a softer ray;
And now the whole wide lake in deep repose
Is hushed, and like a burnished mirror glows,
Save where, along the shady western marge,
Coasts, with industrious oar, the charcoal barge.

 Their panniered train a group of potters goad,
Winding from side to side up the steep road;
The peasant, from yon cliff of fearful edge   130
Shot, down the headlong path darts with his sledge;
Bright beams the lonely mountain-horse illume
Feeding 'mid purple heath, 'green rings,' and broom;
While the sharp slope the slackened team confounds,
Downward the ponderous timber-wain resounds;
In foamy breaks the rill, with merry song,
Dashed o'er the rough rock, lightly leaps along;

From lonesome chapel at the mountain's feet,
Three humble bells their rustic chime repeat;
Sounds from the water-side the hammered boat;   140
And *blasted* quarry thunders, heard remote!

    Even here, amid the sweep of endless woods,
Blue pomp of lakes, high cliffs, and falling floods,
Not undelightful are the simplest charms,
Found by the grassy door of mountain-farms.

    Sweetly ferocious, round his native walks,
Pride of his sister-wives, the monarch stalks;
Spur-clad his nervous feet, and firm his tread;
A crest of purple tops the warrior's head.
Bright sparks his black and rolling eye-ball hurls   150
Afar, his tail he closes and unfurls;
On tiptoe reared, he strains his clarion throat,
Threatened by faintly-answering farms remote:
Again with his shrill voice the mountain rings,
While, flapped with conscious pride, resound his wings.

    Where, mixed with graceful birch, the sombrous pine
And yew-tree o'er the silver rocks decline;
I love to mark the quarry's moving trains,
Dwarf panniered steeds, and men, and numerous wains;
How busy all the enormous hive within,   160
While Echo dallies with its various din!
Some (hear you not their chisels' clinking sound?)
Toil, small as pigmies in the gulf profound;
Some, dim between the lofty cliffs descried,
O'erwalk the slender plank from side to side;
These, by the pale-blue rocks that ceaseless ring,
In airy baskets hanging, work and sing.

    Just where a cloud above the mountain rears
An edge all flame, the broadening sun appears;
A long blue bar its ægis orb divides,   170
And breaks the spreading of its golden tides;
And now that orb has touched the purple steep
Whose softened image penetrates the deep.
'Cross the calm lake's blue shades the cliffs aspire,
With towers and woods, a 'prospect all on fire;'
While coves and secret hollows, through a ray

Of fainter gold, a purple gleam betray.
Each slip of lawn the broken rocks between
Shines in the light with more than earthly green:
Deep yellow beams the scattered stems illume,   180
Far in the level forest's central gloom:
Waving his hat, the shepherd, from the vale,
Directs his winding dog the cliffs to scale,—
The dog, loud barking, 'mid the glittering rocks,
Hunts, where his master points, the intercepted flocks.
Where oaks o'erhang the road the radiance shoots
On tawny earth, wild weeds, and twisted roots;
The druid-stones a brightened ring unfold;
And all the babbling brooks are liquid gold;
Sunk to a curve, the day-star lessens still,   190
Gives one bright glance, and drops behind the hill.
    In these secluded vales, if village fame,
Confirmed by hoary hairs, belief may claim;
When up the hills, as now, retired the light,
Strange apparitions mocked the shepherd's sight.
    The form appears of one that spurs his steed
Midway along the hill with desperate speed;
Unhurt pursues his lengthened flight, while all
Attend, at every stretch, his headlong fall.
Anon, appears a brave, a gorgeous show   200
Of horsemen-shadows moving to and fro;
At intervals imperial banners stream,
And now the van reflects the solar beam;
The rear through iron brown betrays a sullen gleam.
While silent stands the admiring crowd below,.
Silent the visionary warriors go,
Winding in ordered pomp their upward way
Till the last banner of the long array
Has disappeared, and every trace is fled
Of splendour—save the beacon's spiry head   210
Tipt with eve's latest gleam of burning red.
    Now, while the solemn evening shadows sail,
On slowly-waving pinions, down the vale;
And, fronting the bright west, yon oak entwines
Its darkening boughs and leaves, in stronger lines;

'Tis pleasant near the tranquil lake to stray
Where, winding on along some secret bay,
The swan uplifts his chest, and backward flings
His neck, a varying arch, between his towering wings:
The eye that marks the gliding creature sees   220
How graceful pride can be, and how majestic, ease.
While tender cares and mild domestic loves
With furtive watch pursue her as she moves,
The female with a meeker charm succeeds,
And her brown little-ones around her leads,
Nibbling the water lilies as they pass,
Or playing wanton with the floating grass.
She, in a mother's care, her beauty's pride
Forgetting, calls the wearied to her side;
Alternately they mount her back, and rest   230
Close by her mantling wings' embraces prest.
       Long may they float upon this flood serene;
Theirs be these holms untrodden, still, and green,
Where leafy shades fence off the blustering gale,
And breathes in peace the lily of the vale!
Yon isle, which feels not even the milkmaid's feet,
Yet hears her song, "by distance made more sweet,"
Yon isle conceals their home, their hut-like bower;
Green water-rushes overspread the floor;
Long grass and willows form the woven wall,   240
And swings above the roof the poplar tall.
Thence issuing often with unwieldy stalk,
They crush with broad black feet their flowery walk;
Or, from the neighbouring water, hear at morn
The hound, the horse's tread, and mellow horn;
Involve their serpent-necks in changeful rings,
Rolled wantonly between their slippery wings,
Or, starting up with noise and rude delight,
Force half upon the wave their cumbrous flight.
Fair Swan! by all a mother's joys caressed,   250
Haply some wretch has eyed, and called thee blessed;
When with her infants, from some shady seat
By the lake's edge, she rose—to face the noontide heat;
Or taught their limbs along the dusty road

A few short steps to totter with their load.
    I see her now, denied to lay her head,
On cold blue nights, in hut or straw-built shed
Turn to a silent smile their sleepy cry,
By pointing to the gliding moon on high.
—When low-hung clouds each star of summer hide,   260
And fireless are the valleys far and wide,
Where the brook brawls along the public road
Dark with bat-haunted ashes stretching broad,
Oft has she taught them on her lap to lay
The shining glow-worm; or, in heedless play,
Toss it from hand to hand, disquieted;
While others, not unseen, are free to shed
Green unmolested light upon their mossy bed.

    Oh! when the sleety showers her path assail,
And like a torrent roars the headstrong gale;   270
No more her breath can thaw their fingers cold,
Their frozen arms her neck no more can fold;
Weak roof a cowering form two babes to shield,
And faint the fire a dying heart can yield!
Press the sad kiss, fond mother! vainly fears
Thy flooded cheek to wet them with its tears;
No tears can chill them, and no bosom warms,
Thy breast their death-bed, coffined in thine arms!

    Sweet are the sounds that mingle from afar,
Heard by calm lakes, as peeps the folding star,   280
Where the duck dabbles 'mid the rustling sedge,
And feeding pike starts from the water's edge,
Or the swan stirs the reeds, his neck and bill
Wetting, that drip upon the water still;
And heron, as resounds the trodden shore,
Shoots upward, darting his long neck before.

    Now, with religious awe, the farewell light
Blends with the solemn colouring of night;
'Mid groves of clouds that crest the mountain's brow,
And round the west's proud lodge their shadows throw,   290
Like Una shining on her gloomy way,
The half-seen form of Twilight roams astray;

Shedding, through paly loop-holes mild and small,
Gleams that upon the lake's still bosom fall;
Soft o'er the surface creep those lustres pale
Tracking the motions of the fitful gale.
With restless interchange at once the bright
Wins on the shade, the shade upon the light.
No favoured eye was e'er allowed to gaze
On lovelier spectacle in faery days;   300
When gentle Spirits urged a sportive chase,
Brushing with lucid wands the water's face:
While music, stealing round the glimmering deeps,
Charmed the tall circle of the enchanted steeps.
—The lights are vanished from the watery plains:
No wreck of all the pageantry remains.
Unheeded night has overcome the vales:
On the dark earth the wearied vision fails;
The latest lingerer of the forest train,
The lone black fir, forsakes the faded plain;   310
Last evening sight, the cottage smoke, no more,
Lost in the thickened darkness, glimmers hoar;
And, towering from the sullen dark-brown mere,
Like a black wall, the mountain-steeps appear.
—Now o'er the soothed accordant heart we feel
A sympathetic twilight slowly steal,
And ever, as we fondly muse, we find
The soft gloom deepening on the tranquil mind.
Stay! pensive, sadly-pleasing visions, stay!
Ah no! as fades the vale, they fade away: 320
Yet still the tender, vacant gloom remains;
Still the cold cheek its shuddering ear retains.
     The bird, who ceased, with fading light, to thread
Silent the hedge or steamy rivulet's bed,
From his grey re-appearing tower shall soon
Salute with gladsome note the rising moon,
While with a hoary light she frosts the ground,
And pours a deeper blue to Æther's bound;
Pleased, as she moves, her pomp of clouds to fold
In robes of azure, fleecy-white, and gold.   330

Above yon eastern hill, where darkness broods
O'er all its vanished dells, and lawns, and woods;
Where but a mass of shade the sight can trace,
Even now she shews, half-veiled, her lovely face:
Across the gloomy valley flings her light,
Far to the western slopes with hamlets white;
And gives, where woods the chequered upland strew,
To the green corn of summer, autumn's hue.

Thus Hope, first pouring from her blessed horn
Her dawn, far lovelier than the moon's own morn,   340
Till higher mounted, strives in vain to cheer
The weary hills, impervious, blackening near;
Yet does she still, undaunted, throw the while
On darling spots remote her tempting smile.

Even now she decks for me a distant scene,
(For dark and broad the gulf of time between)
Gilding that cottage with her fondest ray,
(Sole bourn, sole wish, sole object of my way;
How fair its lawns and sheltering woods appear!
How sweet its streamlet murmurs in mine ear!)   350
Where we, my Friend, to happy days shall rise,
Till our small share of hardly-paining sighs
(For sighs will ever trouble human breath)
Creep hushed into the tranquil breast of death.

But now the clear bright Moon her zenith gains,
And, rimy without speck, extend the plains:
The deepest cleft the mountain's front displays
Scarce hides a shadow from her searching rays;
From the dark-blue faint silvery threads divide
The hills, while gleams below the azure tide;   360
Time softly treads; throughout the landscape breathes
A peace enlivened, not disturbed, by wreaths
Of charcoal-smoke, that o'er the fallen wood,
Steal down the hill, and spread along the flood.

The song of mountain-streams, unheard by day,
Now hardly heard, beguiles my homeward way.
Air listens, like the sleeping water, still,
To catch the spiritual music of the hill,
Broke only by the slow clock tolling deep,

Or shout that wakes the ferry-man from sleep, 370
The echoed hoof nearing the distant shore,
The boat's first motion—made with dashing oar;
Sound of closed gate, across the water borne,
Hurrying the timid hare through rustling corn;
The sportive outcry of the mocking owl;
And at long intervals the mill-dog's howl;
The distant forge's swinging thump profound;
Or yell, in the deep woods, of lonely hound.

1791-92

DESCRIPTIVE SKETCHES

Happiness (if she had been to be found on earth) among the charms of Nature — Pleasures of the pedestrian Traveller — Author crosses France to the Alps — Present state of the Grande Chartreuse — Lake of Como — Time, Sunset — Same Scene, Twilight — Same Scene, Morning; its voluptuous Character; Old man and forest-cottage music — River Tusa — Via Mala and Grison Gipsy — Sckellenen-thal — Lake of Uri — Stormy sunset — Chapel of William Tell — Force of local emotion — Chamois-chaser — View of the higher Alps — Manner of life of a Swiss mountaineer, interspersed with views of the higher Alps — Golden age of the Alps — Life and views continued — Ranz des Vaches, famous Swiss Air — Abbey of Einsiedlen and its pilgrims — Valley of Chamouny — Mont Blanc — Slavery of Savoy — Influence of liberty on cottage-happiness — France — Wish for the Extirpation of Slavery — Conclusion.

Were there, below, a spot of holy ground
Where from distress a refuge might be found,
And solitude prepare the soul for heaven;
Sure, nature's God that spot to man had given
Where falls the purple morning far and wide
In flakes of light upon the mountain side;
Where with loud voice the power of water shakes

The leafy wood, or sleeps in quiet lakes.
　　Yet not unrecompensed the man shall roam,
Who at the call of summer quits his home, 10
And plods through some wide realm o'er vale and height,
Though seeking only holiday delight;
At least, not owning to himself an aim
To which the sage would give a prouder name.
No gains too cheaply earned his fancy cloy,
Though every passing zephyr whispers joy;
Brisk toil, alternating with ready ease,
Feeds the clear current of his sympathies.
For him sod-seats the cottage-door adorn;
And peeps the far-off spire, his evening bourn! 20
Dear is the forest frowning o'er his head,
And dear the velvet green-sward to his tread:
Moves there a cloud o'er mid-day's flaming eye?
Upward he looks—"and calls it luxury:"
Kind Nature's charities his steps attend;
In every babbling brook he finds a friend;
While chastening thoughts of sweetest use, bestowed
By wisdom, moralise his pensive road.
Host of his welcome inn, the noon-tide bower,
To his spare meal he calls the passing poor; 30
He views the sun uplift his golden fire,
Or sink, with heart alive like Memnon's lyre;
Blesses the moon that comes with kindly ray,
To light him shaken by his rugged way.
Back from his sight no bashful children steal;
He sits a brother at the cottage-meal;
His humble looks no shy restraint impart;
Around him plays at will the virgin heart.
While unsuspended wheels the village dance,
The maidens eye him with enquiring glance, 40
Much wondering by what fit of crazing care,
Or desperate love, bewildered, he came there.
　　A hope, that prudence could not then approve,
That clung at Nature with a truant's love,
O'er Gallia's wastes of corn my footsteps led;
Her files of road-elms, high above my head

In long-drawn vista, rustling in the breeze;
Or where her pathways straggle as they please
By lonely farms and secret villages.
But lo! the Alps ascending white in air,   50
Toy with the sun and glitter from afar.

    And now, emerging from the forest's gloom,
I greet thee, Chartreuse, while I mourn thy doom.
Whither is fled that Power whose frown severe
Awed sober Reason till she crouched in fear?
That Silence, once in deathlike fetters bound,
Chains that were loosened only by the sound
Of holy rites chanted in measured round?
—The voice of blasphemy the fane alarms,
The cloister startles at the gleam of arms.   60
The thundering tube the aged angler hears,
Bent o'er the groaning flood that sweeps away his tears.
Cloud-piercing pine-trees nod their troubled heads,
Spires, rocks, and lawns a browner night o'erspreads;
Strong terror checks the female peasant's sighs,
And start the astonished shades at female eyes.
From Bruno's forest screams the affrighted jay,
And slow the insulted eagle wheels away.
A viewless flight of laughing Demons mock
The Cross, by angels planted on the aërial rock.   70
The "parting Genius" sighs with hollow breath
Along the mystic streams of Life and Death.
Swelling the outcry dull, that long resounds
Portentous through her old woods' trackless bounds,
Vallombre, 'mid her falling fanes, deplores,
For ever broke, the sabbath of her bowers.
    More pleased, my foot the hidden margin roves
Of Como, bosomed deep in chestnut groves.
No meadows thrown between, the giddy steeps
Tower, bare or sylvan, from the narrow deeps.   80
—To towns, whose shades of no rude noise complain,
From ringing team apart and grating wain—
To flat-roofed towns, that touch the water's bound.
Or lurk in woody sunless glens profound,
Or, from the bending rocks, obtrusive cling,

And o'er the whitened wave their shadows fling—
The pathway leads, as round the steeps it twines;
And Silence loves its purple roof of vines.
The loitering traveller hence, at evening, sees
From rock-hewn steps the sail between the trees;   90
Or marks, 'mid opening cliffs, fair dark-eyed maids
Tend the small harvest of their garden glades;
Or stops the solemn mountain-shades to view
Stretch o'er the pictured mirror broad and blue,
And track the yellow lights from steep to steep,
As up the opposing hills they slowly creep.
Aloft, here, half a village shines, arrayed
In golden light; half hides itself in shade;
While, from amid the darkened roofs, the spire,
Restlessly flashing, seems to mount like fire: 100
There, all unshaded, blazing forests throw
Rich golden verdure on the lake below.
Slow glides the sail along the illumined shore,
And steals into the shade the lazy oar;
Soft bosoms breathe around contagious sighs,
And amorous music on the water dies.

   How blest, delicious scene! the eye that greets
Thy open beauties, or thy lone retreats;
Beholds the unwearied sweep of wood that scales
Thy cliffs; the endless waters of thy vales;   110
Thy lowly cots that sprinkle all the shore,
Each with its household boat beside the door;
Thy torrents shooting from the clear-blue sky;
Thy towns, that cleave, like swallows' nests, on high;
That glimmer hoar in eve's last light, descried
Dim from the twilight water's shaggy side,
Whence lutes and voices down the enchanted woods
Steal, and compose the oar-forgotten floods;
Thy lake, that, streaked or dappled, blue or grey,
'Mid smoking woods gleams hid from morning's ray   120
Slow-travelling down the western hills, to enfold
Its green-tinged margin in a blaze of gold;
Thy glittering steeples, whence the matin bell
Calls forth the woodman from his desert cell,

And quickens the blithe sound of oars that pass
Along the steaming lake, to early mass.
But now farewell to each and all—adieu
To every charm, and last and chief to you,
Ye lovely maidens that in noontide shade
Rest near your little plots of wheaten glade;   130
To all that binds the soul in powerless trance,
Lip-dewing song, and ringlet-tossing dance;
Where sparkling eyes and breaking smiles illume
The sylvan cabin's lute-enlivened gloom.
—Alas! the very murmur of the streams
Breathes o'er the failing soul voluptuous dreams,
While Slavery, forcing the sunk mind to dwell
On joys that might disgrace the captive's cell,
Her shameless timbrel shakes on Como's marge
And lures from bay to bay the vocal barge.   140
  Yet are thy softer arts with power indued
To soothe and cheer the poor man's solitude.
By silent cottage doors, the peasant's home
Left vacant for the day, I loved to roam.
But once I pierced the mazes of a wood
In which a cabin undeserted stood;
There an old man an olden measure scanned
On a rude viol touched with withered hand.
As lambs or fawns in April clustering lie.
Under a hoary oak's thin canopy,   150
Stretched at his feet, with stedfast upward eye,
His children's children listened to the sound;
—A Hermit with his family around!
  But let us hence; for fair Locarno smiles
Embowered in walnut slopes and citron isles:
Or seek at eve the banks of Tusa's stream,
Where, 'mid dim towers and woods, her waters gleam.
From the bright wave, in solemn gloom, retire
The dull-red steeps, and, darkening still, aspire
To where afar rich orange lustres glow   160
Round undistinguished clouds, and rocks, and snow:
Or, led where Via Mala's chasms confine
The indignant waters of the infant Rhine,

Hang o'er the abyss, whose else impervious gloom
His burning eyes with fearful light illume.
   The mind condemned, without reprieve, to go
O'er life's long deserts with its charge of woe,
With sad congratulation joins the train
Where beasts and men together o'er the plain
Move on—a mighty caravan of pain: 170
Hope, strength, and courage, social suffering brings,
Freshening the wilderness with shades and springs.
—There be whose lot far otherwise is cast:
Sole human tenant of the piny waste,
By choice or doom a gipsy wanders here,
A nursling babe her only comforter;
Lo, where she sits beneath yon shaggy rock,
A cowering shape half hid in curling smoke!
   When lightning among clouds and mountain-snows
Predominates, and darkness comes and goes,   180
And the fierce torrent, at the flashes broad
Starts, like a horse, beside the glaring road—
She seeks a covert from the battering shower
In the roofed bridge; the bridge, in that dread hour,
Itself all trembling at the torrent's power.
   Nor is she more at ease on some *still* night,
When not a star supplies the comfort of its light;
Only the waning moon hangs dull and red
Above a melancholy mountain's head,
Then sets. In total gloom the Vagrant sighs,   190
Stoops her sick head, and shuts her weary eyes;
Or on her fingers counts the distant clock,
Or, to the drowsy crow of midnight cock,
Listens, or quakes while from the forest's gulf
Howls near and nearer yet the famished wolf.
   From the green vale of Urseren smooth and wide
Descend we now, the maddened Reuss our guide;
By rocks that, shutting out the blessed day,
Cling tremblingly to rocks as loose as they;
By cells upon whose image, while he prays,   200
The kneeling peasant scarcely dares to gaze;
By many a votive death-cross planted near,

And watered duly with the pious tear,
That faded silent from the upward eye
Unmoved with each rude form of peril nigh;
Fixed on the anchor left by Him who saves
Alike in whelming snows, and roaring waves.
    But soon a peopled region on the sight
Opens—a little world of calm delight;
Where mists, suspended on the expiring gale,   210
Spread rooflike o'er the deep secluded vale,
And beams of evening slipping in between,
Gently illuminate a sober scene:—
Here, on the brown wood-cottages they sleep,
There, over rock or sloping pasture creep.
On as we journey, in clear view displayed,
The still vale lengthens underneath its shade
Of low-hung vapour: on the freshened mead
The green light sparkles;—the dim bowers recede.
While pastoral pipes and streams the landscape lull,   220
And bells of passing mules that tinkle dull,
In solemn shapes before the admiring eye
Dilated hang the misty pines on high,
Huge convent domes with pinnacles and towers,
And antique castles seen through gleamy showers.
    From such romantic dreams, my soul, awake!
To sterner pleasure, where, by Uri's lake,
In Nature's pristine majesty outspread,
Winds neither road nor path for foot to tread:
The rocks rise naked as a wall, or stretch   230
Far o'er the water, hung with groves of beech;
Aërial pines from loftier steeps ascend,
Nor stop but where creation seems to end.
Yet here and there, if mid the savage scene
Appears a scanty plot of smiling green,
Up from the lake a zigzag path will creep
To reach a small wood-hut hung boldly on the steep,
—Before those thresholds (never can they know
The face of traveller passing to and fro,)
No peasant leans upon his pole, to tell   240
For whom at morning tolled the funeral bell;

Their watch-dog ne'er his angry bark foregoes,
Touched by the beggar's moan of human woes;
The shady porch ne'er offered a cool seat
To pilgrims overcome by summer's heat.
Yet thither the world's business finds its way
At times, and tales unsought beguile the day,
And *there* are those fond thoughts which Solitude,
However stern, is powerless to exclude.
There doth the maiden watch her lover's sail   250
Approaching, and upbraid the tardy gale;
At midnight listens till his parting oar,
And its last echo, can be heard no more.

    And what if ospreys, cormorants, herons, cry
Amid tempestuous vapours driving by,
Or hovering over wastes too bleak to rear
That common growth of earth, the foodful ear;
Where the green apple shrivels on the spray,
And pines the unripened pear in summer's kindliest ray;
Contentment shares the desolate domain   260
With Independence, child of high Disdain.
Exulting 'mid the winter of the skies,
Shy as the jealous chamois, Freedom flies,
And grasps by fits her sword, and often eyes;
And sometimes, as from rock to rock she bounds
The Patriot nymph starts at imagined sounds,
And, wildly pausing, oft she hangs aghast,
Whether some old Swiss air hath checked her haste
Or thrill of Spartan fife is caught between the blast.

    Swoln with incessant rains from hour to hour,   270
All day the floods a deepening murmur pour:
The sky is veiled, and every cheerful sight:
Dark is the region as with coming night;
But what a sudden burst of overpowering light!
Triumphant on the bosom of the storm,
Glances the wheeling eagle's glorious form!
Eastward, in long perspective glittering, shine
The wood-crowned cliffs that o'er the lake recline;
Those lofty cliffs a hundred streams unfold,
At once to pillars turned that flame with gold: 280

Behind his sail the peasant shrinks, to shun
The *west,* that burns like one dilated sun,
A crucible of mighty compass, felt
By mountains, glowing till they seem to melt.
  But, lo! the boatman, overawed, before
The pictured fane of Tell suspends his oar;
Confused the Marathonian tale appears,
While his eyes sparkle with heroic tears.
And who, that walks where men of ancient days
Have wrought with godlike arm the deeds of praise,   290
Feels not the spirit of the place control,
Or rouse and agitate his labouring soul?
Say, who, by thinking on Canadian hills,
Or wild Aosta lulled by Alpine rills,
On Zutphen's plain; or on that highland dell,
Through which rough Garry cleaves his way, can tell
What high resolves exalt the tenderest thought
Of him whom passion rivets to the spot,
Where breathed the gale that caught Wolfe's happiest sigh,
And the last sunbeam fell on Bayard's eye;   300
Where bleeding Sidney from the cup retired,
And glad Dundee in "faint huzzas" expired?
  But now with other mind I stand alone
Upon the summit of this naked cone,
And watch the fearless chamois-hunter chase
His prey, through tracts abrupt of desolate space,
Through vacant worlds where Nature never gave
A brook to murmur or a bough to wave,
Which unsubstantial Phantoms sacred keep;
Thro' worlds where Life, and Voice, and Motion sleep;   310
Where silent Hours their deathlike sway extend,
Save when the avalanche breaks loose, to rend
Its way with uproar, till the ruin, drowned
In some dense wood or gulf of snow profound,
Mocks the dull ear of Time with deaf abortive sound.
—'Tis his, while wandering on from height to height,
To see a planet's pomp and steady light
In the least star of scarce-appearing night;
While the pale moon moves near him, on the bound

Of ether, shining with diminished round,   320
And far and wide the icy summits blaze,
Rejoicing in the glory of her rays:
To him the day-star glitters small and bright,
Shorn of its beams, insufferably white,
And he can look beyond the sun, and view
Those fast-receding depths of sable blue
Flying till vision can no more pursue!
—At once bewildering mists around him close,
And cold and hunger are his least of woes;
The Demon of the snow, with angry roar   330
Descending, shuts for aye his prison door.
Soon with despair's whole weight his spirits sink;
Bread has he none, the snow must be his drink;
And, ere, his eyes can close upon the day,
The eagle of the Alps o'ershades her prey.

    Now couch thyself where, heard with fear afar,
Thunders through echoing pines the headlong Aar;
Or rather stay to taste the mild delights
Of pensive Underwalden's pastoral heights.
—Is there who 'mid these awful wilds has seen   340
The native Genii walk the mountain green?
Or heard, while other worlds their charms reveal,
Soft music o'er the aërial summit steal?
While o'er the desert, answering every close,
Rich steam of sweetest perfume comes and goes.
—And sure there is a secret Power that reigns
Here, where no trace of man the spot profanes,
Nought but the *chalets,* flat and bare, on high
Suspended 'mid the quiet of the sky;
Or distant herds that pasturing upward creep,   350
And, not untended, climb the dangerous steep.
How still! no irreligious sound or sight
Rouses the soul from her severe delight.
An idle voice the sabbath region fills
Of Deep that calls to Deep across the hills,
And with that voice accords the soothing sound
Of drowsy bells, for ever tinkling round;
Faint wail of eagle melting into blue

Beneath the cliffs, and pine-woods' steady *sugh*;
The solitary heifer's deepened low;   360
Or rumbling, heard remote, of falling snow.
All motions, sounds, and voices, far and nigh,
Blend in a music of tranquillity;
Save when, a stranger seen below, the boy
Shouts from the echoing hills with savage joy.

    When, from the sunny breast of open seas,
And bays with myrtle fringed, the southern breeze
Comes on to gladden April with the sight
Of green isles widening on each snow-clad height;
When shouts and lowing herds the valley fill,   370
And louder torrents stun the noon-tide hill,
The pastoral Swiss begin the cliffs to scale,
Leaving to silence the deserted vale;
And like the Patriarchs in their simple age
Move, as the verdure leads, from stage to stage:
High and more high in summer's heat they go,
And hear the rattling thunder far below;
Or steal beneath the mountains, half-deterred,
Where huge rocks tremble to the bellowing herd.

    One I behold who, 'cross the foaming flood,   380
Leaps with a bound of graceful hardihood;
Another, high on that green ledge;—he gained
The tempting spot with every sinew strained;
And downward thence a knot of grass he throws,
Food for his beasts in time of winter snows.
—Far different life from what Tradition hoar
Transmits of happier lot in times of yore!
Then Summer lingered long; and honey flowed
From out the rocks, the wild bees' safe abode:
Continual waters welling cheered the waste,   390
And plants were wholesome, now of deadly taste:
Nor Winter yet his frozen stores had piled,
Usurping where the fairest herbage smiled:
Nor Hunger driven the herds from pastures bare,
To climb the treacherous cliffs for scanty fare.
Then the milk-thistle flourished through the land,
And forced the full-swoln udder to demand,

Thrice every day, the pail and welcome hand.
Thus does the father to his children tell
Of banished bliss, by fancy loved too well.   400
Alas! that human guilt provoked the rod
Of angry Nature to avenge her God.
Still, Nature, ever just, to him imparts
Joys only given to uncorrupted hearts.

    'Tis morn: with gold the verdant mountain glows
More high, the snowy peaks with hues of rose.
Far-stretched beneath the many-tinted hills,
A mighty waste of mist the valley fills,
A solemn sea! whose billows wide around
Stand motionless, to awful silence bound: 410
Pines, on the coast, through mist their tops uprear,
That like to leaning masts of stranded ships appear.
A single chasm, a gulf of gloomy blue,
Gapes in the centre of the sea—and, through
That dark mysterious gulf ascending, sound
Innumerable streams with roar profound.
Mount through the nearer vapours notes of birds,
And merry flageolet; the low of herds,
The bark of dogs, the heifer's tinkling bell,
Talk, laughter, and perchance a church-tower knell: 420
Think not, the peasant from aloft has gazed
And heard with heart unmoved, with soul unraised:
Nor is his spirit less enrapt, nor less
Alive to independent happiness,
Then, when he lies, out-stretched, at eventide,
Upon the fragrant mountain's purple side:
For as the pleasures of his simple day
Beyond his native valley seldom stray,
Nought round its darling precincts can he find
But brings some past enjoyment to his mind;   430
While Hope, reclining upon Pleasure's urn,
Binds her wild wreaths, and whispers his return.

    Once, Man entirely free, alone and wild,
Was blest as free—for he was Nature's child.
He, all superior but his God disdained,
Walked none restraining, and by none restrained

Confessed no law but what his reason taught,
Did all he wished, and wished but what he ought.
As man in his primeval dower arrayed
The image of his glorious Sire displayed,   440
Even so, by faithful Nature guarded, here
The traces of primeval Man appear;
The simple dignity no forms debase;
The eye sublime, and surly lion-grace:
The slave of none, of beasts alone the lord,
His book he prizes, nor neglects his sword;
Well taught by that to feel his rights, prepared
With this "the blessings he enjoys to guard."
    And, as his native hills encircle ground
For many a marvellous victory renowned,   450
The work of Freedom daring to oppose,
With few in arms, innumerable foes,
When to those famous fields his steps are led,
An unknown power connects him with the dead:
For images of other worlds are there;
Awful the light, and holy is the air.
Fitfully, and in flashes, through his soul,
Like sun-lit tempests, troubled transports roll;
His bosom heaves, his Spirit towers amain,
Beyond the senses and their little reign.   460
    And oft, when that dread vision hath past by,
He holds with God himself communion high,
There where the peal of swelling torrents fills
The sky-roofed temple of the eternal hills;
Or when, upon the mountain's silent brow
Reclined, he sees, above him and below,
Bright stars of ice and azure fields of snow;
While needle peaks of granite shooting bare
Tremble in ever-varying tints of air.
And when a gathering weight of shadows brown   470
Falls on the valleys as the sun goes down;
And Pikes, of darkness named and fear and storms,
Uplift in quiet their illumined forms,
In sea-like reach of prospect round him spread,
Tinged like an angel's smile all rosy red—

Awe in his breast with holiest love unites,
And the near heavens impart their own delights.
    When downward to his winter hut he goes,
Dear and more dear the lessening circle grows;
That hut which on the hills so oft employs   480
His thoughts, the central point of all his joys.
And as a swallow, at the hour of rest,
Peeps often ere she darts into her nest,
So to the homestead, where the grandsire tends
A little prattling child, he oft descends,
To glance a look upon the well-matched pair;
Till storm and driving ice blockade him there.
There, safely guarded by the woods behind,
He hears the chiding of the baffled wind,
Hears Winter calling all his terrors round,   490
And, blest within himself, he shrinks not from the sound.
    Through Nature's vale his homely pleasures glide,
Unstained by envy, discontent, and pride;
The bound of all his vanity, to deck,
With one bright bell, a favourite heifer's neck;
Well pleased upon some simple annual feast,
Remembered half the year and hoped the rest,
If dairy-produce, from his inner hoard,
Of thrice ten summers dignify the board.
—Alas! in every clime a flying ray   500
Is all we have to cheer our wintry way;
And here the unwilling mind may more than trace
The general sorrows of the human race;
The churlish gales of penury, that blow
Cold as the north-wind o'er a waste of snow,
To them the gentle groups of bliss deny
That on the noon-day bank of leisure lie.
Yet more;—compelled by Powers which only deign
That *solitary* man disturb their reign,
Powers that support an unremitting strife   510
With all the tender charities of life,
Full oft the father, when his sons have grown
To manhood, seems their title to disown;
And from his nest amid the storms of heaven

Drives, eagle-like, those sons as he was driven;
With stern composure watches to the plain—
And never, eagle-like, beholds again!
  When long-familiar joys are all resigned,
Why does their sad remembrance haunt the mind?
Lo! where through flat Batavia's willowy groves,   520
Or by the lazy Seine, the exile roves;
O'er the curled waters Alpine measures swell,
And search the affections to their inmost cell;
Sweet poison spreads along the listener's veins,
Turning past pleasures into mortal pains;
Poison, which not a frame of steel can brave,
Bows his young head with sorrow to the grave.
  Gay lark of hope, thy silent song resume!
Ye flattering eastern lights, once more the hills illume!
Fresh gales and dews of life's delicious morn,   530
And thou, lost fragrance of the heart, return!
Alas! the little joy to man allowed
Fades like the lustre of an evening cloud;
Or like the beauty in a flower installed,
Whose season was, and cannot be recalled.
Yet, when opprest by sickness, grief, or care,
And taught that pain is pleasure's natural heir,
We still confide in more than we can know;
Death would be else the favourite friend of woe.
  'Mid savage rocks, and seas of snow that shine,   540
Between interminable tracts of pine,
Within a temple stands an awful shrine,
By an uncertain light revealed, that falls
On the mute Image and the troubled walls.
Oh! give not me that eye of hard disdain
That views, undimmed, Einsiedlen's wretched fane.
While ghastly faces through the gloom appear,
Abortive joy, and hope that works in fear;
While prayer contends with silenced agony,
Surely in other thoughts contempt may die   550
If the sad grave of human ignorance bear
One flower of hope—oh, pass and leave it there!
  The tall sun, pausing on an Alpine spire,

Flings o'er the wilderness a stream of fire:
Now meet we other pilgrims ere the day
Close on the remnant of their weary way;
While they are drawing toward the sacred floor
Where, so they fondly think, the worm shall gnaw no more.
How gaily murmur and how sweetly taste
The fountains reared for them amid the waste!   560
Their thirst they slake:—they wash their toil-worn feet
And some with tears of joy each other greet.
Yes, I must see you when ye first behold
Those holy turrets tipped with evening gold;
In that glad moment will for you a sigh
Be heaved, of charitable sympathy;
In that glad moment when your hands are prest
In mute devotion on the thankful breast!

    Last, let us turn to Chamouny that shields
With rocks and gloomy woods her fertile fields: 570
Five streams of ice amid her cots descend,
And with wild flowers and blooming orchards blend;—
A scene more fair than what the Grecian feigns
Of purple lights and ever-vernal plains;
Here all the seasons revel hand in hand:
'Mid lawns and shades by breezy rivulets fanned,
They sport beneath that mountain's matchless height
That holds no commerce with the summer night.
From age to age, throughout his lonely bounds
The crash of ruin fitfully resounds;   580
Appalling havoc! but serene his brow,
Where daylight lingers on perpetual snow;
Glitter the stars above, and all is black below.

    What marvel then if many a Wanderer sigh,
While roars the sullen Arve in anger by,
That not for thy reward, unrivalled Vale!
Waves the ripe harvest in the autumnal gale;
That thou, the slaves of slaves, art doomed to pine
And droop, while no Italian arts are thine,
To soothe or cheer, to soften or refine.   590

    Hail Freedom! whether it was mine to stray,
With shrill winds whistling round my lonely way,

On the bleak sides of Cumbria's heath-clad moors,
Or where dank sea-weed lashes Scotland's shores;
To scent the sweets of Piedmont's breathing rose,
And orange gale that o'er Lugano blows;
Still have I found, where Tyranny prevails,
That virtue languishes and pleasure fails,
While the remotest hamlets blessings share
In thy loved presence known, and only there;   600
Heart-blessings—outward treasures, too, which the eye
Of the sun peeping through the clouds can spy,
And every passing breeze will testify.
There, to the porch, belike with jasmine bound
Or woodbine wreaths, a smoother path is wound;
The housewife there a brighter garden sees,
Where hum on busier wing her happy bees;
On infant cheeks there fresher roses blow;
And grey-haired men look up with livelier brow,—
To greet the traveller needing food and rest;   610
Housed for the night, or but a half-hour's guest.
        And oh, fair France! though now the traveller sees
Thy three-striped banner fluctuate on the breeze;
Though martial songs have banished songs of love,
And nightingales desert the village grove,
Scared by the fife and rumbling drum's alarms,
And the short thunder, and the flash of arms;
That cease not till night falls, when far and nigh,
Sole sound, the Sourd prolongs his mournful cry!
—Yet, hast thou found that Freedom spreads her power   620
Beyond the cottage-hearth, the cottage-door:
All nature smiles, and owns beneath her eyes
Her fields peculiar, and peculiar skies.
Yes, as I roamed where Loiret's waters glide
Through rustling aspens heard from side to side,
When from October clouds a milder light
Fell where the blue flood rippled into white;
Methought from every cot the watchful bird
Crowed with ear-piercing power till then unheard;
Each clacking mill, that broke the murmuring streams,   630
Rocked the charmed thought in more delightful dreams;

Chasing those pleasant dreams, the falling leaf
Awoke a fainter sense of moral grief;
The measured echo of the distant flail
Wound in more welcome cadence down the vale;
With more majestic course the water rolled,
And ripening foliage shone with richer gold.
—But foes are gathering—Liberty must raise
Red on the hills her beacon's far-seen blaze;
Must bid the tocsin ring from tower to tower!— 640
Nearer and nearer comes the trying hour!
Rejoice, brave Land, though pride's perverted ire
Rouse hell's own aid, and wrap thy fields in fire:
Lo, from the flames a great and glorious birth;
As if a new-made heaven were hailing a new earth!
—All cannot be: the promise is too fair
For creatures doomed to breathe terrestrial air:
Yet not for this will sober reason frown
Upon that promise, nor the hope disown;
She knows that only from high aims ensue 650
Rich guerdons, and to them alone are due.

    Great God! by whom the strifes of men are weighed
In an impartial balance, give thine aid
To the just cause; and, oh! do thou preside
Over the mighty stream now spreading wide:
So shall its waters, from the heavens supplied
In copious showers, from earth by wholesome springs,
Brood o'er the long-parched lands with Nile-like wings!
And grant that every sceptred child of clay
Who cries presumptuous, "Here the flood shall stay," 660
May in its progress see thy guiding hand,
And cease the acknowledged purpose to withstand;
Or, swept in anger from the insulted shore,
Sink with his servile bands, to rise no more!

    To-night, my Friend, within this humble cot
Be scorn and fear and hope alike forgot
In timely sleep; and when, at break of day,
On the tall peaks the glistening sunbeams play,
With a light heart our course we may renew,
The first whose footsteps print the mountain dew. 670

1791-94

Guilt and Sorrow

or, incidents upon salisbury plain

I

A traveller on the skirt of Sarum's Plain
Pursued his vagrant way, with feet half bare;
Stooping his gait, but not as if to gain
Help from the staff he bore; for mien and air
Were hardy, though his cheek seemed worn with care
Both of the time to come, and time long fled:
Down fell in straggling locks his thin grey hair;
A coat he wore of military red
But faded, and stuck o'er with many a patch and shred.

II

While thus he journeyed, step by step led on,   10
He saw and passed a stately inn, full sure
That welcome in such house for him was none.
No board inscribed the needy to allure
Hung there, no bush proclaimed to old and poor
And desolate, "Here you will find a friend!"
The pendent grapes glittered above the door;—
On he must pace, perchance 'till night descend,
Where'er the dreary roads their bare white lines extend.

III

The gathering clouds grow red with stormy fire,
In streaks diverging wide and mounting high;   20
That inn he long had passed; the distant spire,
Which oft as he looked back had fixed his eye,
Was lost, though still he looked, in the blank sky,
Perplexed and comfortless he gazed around,
And scarce could any trace of man descry,
Save cornfields stretched and stretching without bound;
But where the sower dwelt was nowhere to be found.

IV

No tree was there, no meadow's pleasant green,
No brook to wet his lip or soothe his ear;
Long files of corn-stacks here and there were seen,   30
But not one dwelling-place his heart to cheer.
Some labourer, thought he, may perchance be near;
And so he sent a feeble shout—in vain;
No voice made answer, he could only hear
Winds rustling over plots of unripe grain,
Or whistling thro' thin grass along the unfurrowed plain.

V

Long had he fancied each successive slope
Concealed some cottage, whither he might turn
And rest; but now along heaven's darkening cope
The crows rushed by in eddies, homeward borne.   40
Thus warned he sought some shepherd's spreading thorn
Or hovel from the storm to shield his head,
But sought in vain; for now, all wild, forlorn,
And vacant, a huge waste around him spread;
The wet cold ground, he feared, must be his only bed.

VI

And be it so—for to the chill night shower
And the sharp wind his head he oft hath bared;
A Sailor he, who many a wretched hour
Hath told; for, landing after labour hard,
Full long endured in hope of just reward,   50
He to an armed fleet was forced away
By seamen, who perhaps themselves had shared
Like fate; was hurried off, a helpless prey,
'Gainst all that in *his* heart, or theirs perhaps, said nay.

VII

For years the work of carnage did not cease,
And death's dire aspect daily he surveyed,
Death's minister; then came his glad release,
And hope returned, and pleasure fondly made
Her dwelling in his dreams. By Fancy's aid
The happy husband flies, his arms to throw   60

Round his wife's neck; the prize of victory laid
In her full lap, he sees such sweet tears flow
As if thenceforth nor pain nor trouble she could know.

VIII

Vain hope! for fraud took all that he had earned.
The lion roars and gluts his tawny brood
Even in the desert's heart; but he, returned,
Bears not to those he loves their needful food.
His home approaching, but in such a mood
That from his sight his children might have run.
He met a traveller, robbed him, shed his blood; 70
And when the miserable work was done
He fled, a vagrant since, the murderer's fate to shun.

IX

From that day forth no place to him could be
So lonely, but that thence might come a pang
Brought from without to inward misery.
Now, as he plodded on, with sullen clang
A sound of chains along the desert rang;
He looked, and saw upon a gibbet high
A human body that in irons swang,
Uplifted by the tempest whirling by; 80
And, hovering, round it often did a raven fly.

X

It was a spectacle which none might view,
In spot so savage, but with shuddering pain;
Nor only did for him at once renew
All he had feared from man, but roused a train
Of the mind's phantoms, horrible as vain.
The stones, as if to cover him from day,
Rolled at his back along the living plain;
He fell, and without sense or motion lay;
But, when the trance was gone, feebly pursued his way. 90

XI

As one whose brain habitual phrensy fires
Owes to the fit in which his soul hath tossed
Profounder quiet, when the fit retires,

Even so the dire phantasma which had crossed
His sense, in sudden vacancy quite lost,
Left his mind still as a deep evening stream.
Nor, if accosted now, in thought engrossed,
Moody, or inly troubled, would he seem
To traveller who might talk of any casual theme.

XII

Hurtle the clouds in deeper darkness piled,   100
Gone is the raven timely rest to seek;
He seemed the only creature in the wild
On whom the elements their rage might wreak;
Save that the bustard, of those regions bleak
Shy tenant, seeing by the uncertain light
A man there wandering, gave a mournful shriek,
And half upon the ground, with strange affright,
Forced hard against the wind a thick unwieldy flight.

XIII

All, all was cheerless to the horizon's bound;
The weary eye—which, wheresoe'er it strays,   110
Marks nothing but the red sun's setting round,
Or on the earth strange lines, in former days
Left by gigantic arms—at length surveys
What seems an antique castle spreading wide;
Hoary and naked are its walls, and raise
Their brow sublime: in shelter there to bide
He turned, while rain poured down smoking on every side.

XIV

Pile of Stone-henge! so proud to hint yet keep
Thy secrets, thou that lov'st to stand and hear
The Plain resounding to the whirlwind's sweep,   120
Inmate of lonesome Nature's endless year;
Even if thou saw'st the giant wicker rear
For sacrifice its throngs of living men,
Before thy face did ever wretch appear,
Who in his heart had groaned with deadlier pain
Than he who, tempest-driven, thy shelter now would gain.

XV

Within that fabric of mysterious form,
Winds met in conflict, each by turns supreme;
And, from the perilous ground dislodged, through storm
And rain he wildered on, no moon to stream   130
From gulf of parting clouds one friendly beam,
Nor any friendly sound his footsteps led;
Once did the lightning's faint disastrous gleam
Disclose a naked guide-post's double head,
Sight which tho' lost at once a gleam of pleasure shed.

XVI

No swinging sign-board creaked from cottage elm
To stay his steps with faintness overcome;
'T was dark and void as ocean's watery realm
Roaring with storms beneath night's starless gloom;
No gipsy cowered o'er fire of furze or broom;   140
No labourer watched his red kiln glaring bright,
Nor taper glimmered dim from sick man's room;
Along the waste no line of mournful light
From lamp of lonely toll-gate streamed athwart the night.

XVII

At length, though hid in clouds, the moon arose;
The downs were visible—and now revealed
A structure stands, which two bare slopes enclose.
It was a spot, where, ancient vows fulfilled,
Kind pious hands did to the Virgin build
A lonely Spital, the belated swain
From the night terrors of that waste to shield;   150
But there no human being could remain,
And now the walls are named the 'Dead House' of the plain.

XVIII

Though he had little cause to love the abode
Of man or covet sight of mortal face,
Yet when faint beams of light that ruin showed,
How glad he was at length to find some trace
Of human shelter in that dreary place.

Till to his flock the early shepherd goes,
Here shall much-needed sleep his frame embrace. 160
In a dry nook where fern the floor bestrows
He lays his stiffened limbs,—his eyes begin to close;

XIX

When hearing a deep sigh, that seemed to come
From one who mourned in sleep, he raised his head,
And saw a woman in the naked room
Outstretched, and turning on a restless bed:
The moon, a wan dead light around her shed.
He waked her—spake in tone that would not fail,
He hoped, to calm her mind; but ill he sped,
For of that ruin she had heard a tale 170
Which now with freezing thoughts did all her powers assail;

XX

Had heard of one who, forced from storms to shroud,
Felt the loose walls of this decayed Retreat
Rock to incessant neighings shrill and loud,
While his horse pawed the floor with furious heat;
Till on a stone, that sparkled to his feet,
Struck, and still struck again, the troubled horse:
The man half raised the stone with pain and sweat,
Half raised, for well his arm might lose its force
Disclosing the grim head of a late murdered corse. 180

XXI

Such tale of this lone mansion she had learned
And, when that shape, with eyes in sleep half drowned,
By the moon's sullen lamp she first discerned,
Cold stony horror all her senses bound.
Her he addressed in words of cheering sound;
Recovering heart, like answer did she make;
And well it was that, of the corse there found,
In converse that ensued she nothing spake;
She knew not what dire pangs in him such tale could wake.

XXII

But soon his voice and words of kind intent 190
Banished that dismal thought; and now the wind

In fainter howlings told its *rage* was spent:
Meanwhile discourse ensued of various kind,
Which by degrees a confidence of mind
And mutual interest failed not to create.
And, to a natural sympathy resigned,
In that forsaken building where they sate
The Woman thus retraced her own untoward fate.

XXIII

"By Derwent's side my father dwelt—a man
Of virtuous life, by pious parents bred;   200
And I believe that, soon as I began
To lisp, he made me kneel beside my bed,
And in his hearing there my prayers I said:
And afterwards, by my good father taught,
I read, and loved the books in which I read;
For books in every neighbouring house I sought,
And nothing to my mind a sweeter pleasure brought.

XXIV

"A little croft we owned—a plot of corn,
A garden stored with peas, and mint, and thyme,
And flowers for posies, oft on Sunday morn   210
Plucked while the church bells rang their earliest chime.
Can I forget our freaks at shearing time!
My hen's rich nest through long grass scarce espied;
The cowslip-gathering in June's dewy prime;
The swans that with white chests upreared in pride
Rushing and racing came to meet me at the water-side.

XXV

"The staff I well remember which upbore
The bending body of my active sire;
His seat beneath the honied sycamore
Where the bees hummed, and chair by winter fire;   220
When market-morning came, the neat attire
With which, though bent on haste, myself I decked;
Our watchful house-dog, that would tease and tire
The stranger till its barking-fit I checked;
The red-breast, known for years, which at my casement pecked.

XXVI

"The suns of twenty summers danced along,—
Too little marked how fast they rolled away:
But, through severe mischance and cruel wrong,
My father's substance fell into decay:
We toiled and struggled, hoping for a day   230
When Fortune might put on a kinder look;
But vain were wishes, efforts vain as they;
He from his old hereditary nook
Must part; the summons came;—our final leave we took.

XXVII

"It was indeed a miserable hour
When, from the last hill-top, my sire surveyed,
Peering above the trees, the steeple tower
That on his marriage day sweet music made!
Till then, he hoped his bones might there be laid
Close by my mother in their native bowers: 240
Bidding me trust in God, he stood and prayed;—
I could not pray:—through tears that fell in showers
Glimmered our dear-loved home, alas! no longer ours!

XXVIII

"There was a Youth whom I had loved so long,
That when I loved him not I cannot say:
'Mid the green mountains many a thoughtless song
We two had sung, like gladsome birds in May;
When we began to tire of childish play,
We seemed still more and more to prize each other;
We talked of marriage and our marriage day;   250
And I in truth did love him like a brother,
For never could I hope to meet with such another.

XXIX

"Two years were passed since to a distant town
He had repaired to ply a gainful trade:
What tears of bitter grief, till then unknown!
What tender vows, our last sad kiss delayed!
To him we turned:—we had no other aid:
Like one revived, upon his neck I wept;

And her whom he had loved in joy, he said,
He well could love in grief; his faith he kept;　　　　　260
And in a quiet home once more my father slept.

xxx

"We lived in peace and comfort; and were blest
With daily bread, by constant toil supplied.
Three lovely babes had lain upon my breast;
And often, viewing their sweet smiles, I sighed,
And knew not why. My happy father died,
When threatened war reduced the children's meal:
Thrice happy! that for him the grave could hide
The empty loom, cold hearth, and silent wheel,
And tears that flowed for ills which patience might not heal.　　270

xxxi

" 'Twas a hard change; an evil time was come;
We had no hope, and no relief could gain:
But some, with proud parade, the noisy drum
Beat round to clear the streets of want and pain.
My husband's arms now only served to strain
Me and his children hungering in his view;
In such dismay my prayers and tears were vain:
To join those miserable men he flew,
And now to the sea-coast, with numbers more, we drew.

xxxii

"There were we long neglected, and we bore　　　　280
Much sorrow ere the fleet its anchor weighed;
Green fields before us, and our native shore,
We breathed a pestilential air, that made
Ravage for which no knell was heard. We prayed
For our departure; wished and wished—nor knew,
'Mid that long sickness and those hopes delayed,
That happier days we never more must view.
The parting signal streamed—at last the land withdrew.

xxxiii

"But the calm summer season now was past.
On as we drove, the equinoctial deep　　　　　290
Ran mountains high before the howling blast,

And many perished in the whirlwind's sweep.
We gazed with terror on their gloomy sleep,
Untaught that soon such anguish must ensue,
Our hopes such harvest of affliction reap,
That we the mercy of the waves should rue:
We reached the western world, a poor devoted crew.

XXXIV

"The pains and plagues that on our heads came down,
Disease and famine, agony and fear,
In wood or wilderness, in camp or town,   300
It would unman the firmest heart to hear.
All perished—all in one remorseless year,
Husband and children! one by one, by sword
And ravenous plague, all perished: every tear
Dried up, despairing, desolate, on board
A British ship I waked, as from a trance restored."

XXXV

Here paused she, of all present thought forlorn,
Nor voice nor sound, that moment's pain expressed,
Yet Nature, with excess of grief o'erborne,
From her full eyes their watery load released.   310
He too was mute; and, ere her weeping ceased,
He rose, and to the ruin's portal went,
And saw the dawn opening the silvery east
With rays of promise, north and southward sent;
And soon with crimson fire kindled the firmament.

XXXVI

"O come," he cried, "come, after weary night
Of such rough storm, this happy change to view."
So forth she came, and eastward looked; the sight
Over her brow like dawn of gladness threw;
Upon her cheek, to which its youthful hue   320
Seemed to return, dried the last lingering tear,
And from her grateful heart a fresh one drew:
The whilst her comrade to her pensive cheer
Tempered fit words of hope; and the lark warbled near.

XXXVII

They looked and saw a lengthening road, and wain
That rang down a bare slope not far remote:
The barrows glistered bright with drops of rain,
Whistled the waggoner with merry note,
The cock far off sounded his clarion throat;
But town, or farm, or hamlet, none they viewed,   330
Only were told there stood a lonely cot
A long mile thence. While thither they pursued
Their way, the Woman thus her mournful tale renewed.

XXXVIII

"Peaceful as this immeasurable plain
Is now, by beams of dawning light imprest,
In the calm sunshine slept the glittering main;
The very ocean hath its hour of rest.
I too forgot the heavings of my breast.
How quiet 'round me ship and ocean were!
As quiet all within me. I was blest,   340
And looked, and fed upon the silent air
Until it seemed to bring a joy to my despair.

XXXIX

"Ah! how unlike those late terrific sleeps,
And groans that rage of racking famine spoke;
The unburied dead that lay in festering heaps,
The breathing pestilence that rose like smoke,
The shriek that from the distant battle broke,
The mine's dire earthquake, and the pallid host
Driven by the bomb's incessant thunderstroke
To loathsome vaults, where heart-sick anguish tossed,   350
Hope died, and fear itself in agony was lost!

XL

"Some mighty gulf of separation past,
I seemed transported to another world;
A thought resigned with pain, when from the mast
The impatient mariner the sail unfurled,
And, whistling, called the wind that hardly curled

The silent sea. From the sweet thoughts of home
And from all hope I was for ever hurled.
For me—farthest from earthly port to roam
Was best, could I but shun the spot where man might come.   360

XLI

"And oft I thought (my fancy was so strong)
That I, at last, a resting-place had found;
'Here will I dwell,' said I, 'my whole life long,
Roaming the illimitable waters round;
Here will I live, of all but heaven disowned,
And end my days upon the peaceful flood.'—
To break my dream the vessel reached its bound;
And homeless near a thousand homes I stood,
And near a thousand tables pined and wanted food.

XLII

"No help I sought; in sorrow turned adrift,   370
Was hopeless, as if cast on some bare rock;
Nor morsel to my mouth that day did lift,
Nor raised by hand at any door to knock.
I lay where, with his drowsy mates, the cock
From the cross-timber of an out-house hung:
Dismally tolled, that night, the city clock!
At morn my sick heart hunger scarcely stung,
Nor to the beggar's language could I fit my tongue.

XLIII

"So passed a second day; and, when the third
Was come, I tried in vain the crowd's resort.   380
—In deep despair, by frightful wishes stirred,
Near the sea-side I reached a ruined fort;
There, pains which nature could no more support,
With blindness linked, did on my vitals fall;
And, after many interruptions short
Of hideous sense, I sank, nor step could crawl:
Unsought for was the help that did my life recall.

XLIV

"Borne to a hospital, I lay with brain
Drowsy and weak, and shattered memory;

I heard my neighbours in their beds complain   390
Of many things which never troubled me—
Of feet still bustling round with busy glee,
Of looks where common kindness had no part,
Of service done with cold formality,
Fretting the fever round the languid heart,
And groans which, as they said, might make a dead man start.

XLV

"These things just served to stir the slumbering sense,
Nor pain nor pity in my bosom raised.
With strength did memory return; and, thence
Dismissed, again on open day I gazed,   400
At houses, men, and common light, amazed.
The lanes I sought, and, as the sun retired,
Came where beneath the trees a faggot blazed,
The travellers saw me weep, my fate inquired,
And gave me food—and rest, more welcome, more desired.

XLVI

"Rough potters seemed they, trading soberly
With panniered asses driven from door to door;
But life of happier sort set forth to me,
And other joys my fancy to allure—
The bag-pipe dinning on the midnight moor   410
In barn uplighted; and companions boon,
Well met from far with revelry secure
Among the forest glades, while jocund June
Rolled fast along the sky his warm and genial moon.

XLVII

"But ill they suited me—those journeys dark
O'er moor and mountain, midnight theft to hatch!
To charm the surly house-dog's faithful bark,
Or hang on tip-toe at the lifted latch.
The gloomy lantern, and the dim blue match,
The black disguise, the warning whistle shrill,   420
And ear still busy on its nightly watch,
Were not for me, brought up in nothing ill:
Besides, on griefs so fresh my thoughts were brooding still.

XLVIII

"What could I do, unaided and unblest?
My father! gone was every friend of thine:
And kindred of dead husband are at best
Small help; and, after marriage such as mine,
With little kindness would to me incline.
Nor was I then for toil or service fit;
My deep-drawn sighs no effort could confine;   430
In open air forgetful would I sit
Whole hours, with idle arms in moping sorrow knit.

XLIX

"The roads I paced, I loitered through the fields;
Contentedly, yet sometimes self-accused.
Trusted my life to what chance bounty yields,
Now coldly given, now utterly refused.
The ground I for my bed have often used:
But what afflicts my peace with keenest ruth,
Is that I have my inner self abused,
Foregone the home delight of constant truth,   440
And clear and open soul, so prized in fearless youth.

L

"Through tears the rising sun I oft have viewed,
Through tears have seen him towards that world descend
Where my poor heart lost all its fortitude:
Three years a wanderer now my course I bend—
Oh! tell me whither—for no earthly friend
Have I."—She ceased, and weeping turned away,
As if because her tale was at an end,
She wept; because she had no more to say
Of that perpetual weight which on her spirit lay.   450

LI

True sympathy the Sailor's looks expressed,
His looks—for pondering he was mute the while.
Of social Order's care for wretchedness,
Of Time's sure help to calm and reconcile,
Joy's second spring and Hope's long-treasured smile,
'Twas not for *him* to speak—a man so tried.

Yet, to relieve her heart, in friendly style
Proverbial words of comfort he applied,
And not in vain, while they went pacing side by side.

LII

Erelong, from heaps of turf, before their sight,   **460**
Together smoking in the sun's slant beam,
Rise various wreaths that into one unite
Which high and higher mounts with silver gleam;
Fair spectacle,—but instantly a scream
Thence bursting shrill did all remark prevent;
They paused, and heard a hoarser voice blaspheme,
And female cries. Their course they thither bent,
And met a man who foamed with anger vehement.

LIII

A woman stood with quivering lips and pale,
And, pointing to a little child that lay   **470**
Stretched on the ground, began a piteous tale;
How in a simple freak of thoughtless play
He had provoked his father, who straightway,
As if each blow were deadlier than the last,
Struck the poor innocent. Pallid with dismay
The Soldier's Widow heard and stood aghast;
And stern looks on the man her grey-haired Comrade cast.

LIV

His voice with indignation rising high
Such further deed in manhood's name forbade;
The peasant, wild in passion, made reply   **480**
With bitter insult and revilings sad;
Asked him in scorn what business there he had;
What kind of plunder he was hunting now;
The gallows would one day of him be glad;—
Though inward anguish damped the Sailor's brow,
Yet calm he seemed as thoughts so poignant would allow.

LV

Softly he stroked the child, who lay outstretched
With face to earth; and, as the boy turned round
His battered head, a groan the Sailor fetched

As if he saw—there and upon that ground— 490
Strange repetition of the deadly wound
He had himself inflicted. Through his brain
At once the griding iron passage found;
Deluge of tender thoughts then rushed amain,
Nor could his sunken eyes the starting tear restrain.

LVI

Within himself he said—What hearts have we!
The blessing this a father gives his child!
Yet happy thou, poor boy! compared with me,
Suffering not doing ill—fate far more mild.
The stranger's looks and tears of wrath beguiled 500
The father, and relenting thoughts awoke;
He kissed his son—so all was reconciled.
Then, with a voice which inward trouble broke
Ere to his lips it came, the Sailor them bespoke.

LVII

"Bad is the world, and hard is the world's law
Even for the man who wears the warmest fleece;
Much need have ye that time more closely draw
The bond of nature, all unkindness cease,
And that among so few there still be peace:
Else can ye hope but with such numerous foes 510
Your pains shall ever with your years increase?"—
While from his heart the appropriate lesson flows,
A correspondent calm stole gently o'er his woes.

LVIII

Forthwith the pair passed on; and down they look
Into a narrow valley's pleasant scene
Where wreaths of vapour tracked a winding brook,
That babbled on through groves and meadows green;
A low-roofed house peeped out the trees between;
The dripping groves resound with cheerful lays,
And melancholy lowings intervene 520
Of scattered herds, that in the meadow graze,
Some amid lingering shade, some touched by the sun's rays.

LIX

They saw and heard, and, winding with the road,
Down a thick wood, they dropt into the vale;
Comfort, by prouder mansions unbestowed,
Their wearied frames, she hoped, would soon regale.
Erelong they reached that cottage in the dale:
It was a rustic inn;—the board was spread,
The milk-maid followed with her brimming pail,
And lustily the master carved the bread,   530
Kindly the housewife pressed, and they in comfort fed.

LX

Their breakfast done, the pair, though loth, must part;
Wanderers whose course no longer now agrees.
She rose and bade farewell! and, while her heart
Struggled with tears nor could its sorrow ease,
She left him there; for, clustering round his knees,
With his oak-staff the cottage children played;
And soon she reached a spot o'erhung with trees
And banks of ragged earth; beneath the shade
Across the pebbly road a little runnel strayed.   540

LXI

A cart and horse beside the rivulet stood;
Chequering the canvas roof the sunbeams shone.
She saw the carman bend to scoop the flood
As the wain fronted her,—wherein lay one,
A pale-faced Woman, in disease far gone.
The carman wet her lips as well behoved;
Bed under her lean body there was none;
Though even to die near one she most had loved,
She could not of herself those wasted limbs have moved.

LXII

The Soldier's Widow learned with honest pain   550
And homefelt force of sympathy sincere,
Why thus that worn-out wretch must there sustain
The jolting road and morning air severe.
The wain pursued its way; and following near

In pure compassion she her steps retraced
Far as the cottage. "A sad sight is here,"
She cried aloud; and forth ran out in haste
The friends whom she had left but a few minutes past.

LXIII

While to the door with eager speed they ran,
From her bare straw the Woman half upraised   560
Her bony visage—gaunt and deadly wan;
No pity asking, on the group she gazed
With a dim eye, distracted and amazed;
Then sank upon her straw with feeble moan.
Fervently cried the housewife—"God be praised,
I have a house that I can call my own;
Nor shall she perish there, untended and alone!"

LXIV

So in they bear her to the chimney seat,
And busily, though yet with fear, untie
Her garments, and, to warm her icy feet   570
And chafe her temples, careful hands apply
Nature reviving, with a deep-drawn sigh
She strove, and not in vain, her head to rear;
Then said—"I thank you all; if I must die,
The God in heaven my prayers for you will hear;
Till now I did not think my end had been so near.

LXV

"Barred every comfort labour could procure,
Suffering what no endurance could assuage,
I was compelled to seek my father's door,
Though loth to be a burthen on his age.   580
But sickness stopped me in an early stage
Of my sad journey; and within the wain
They placed me—there to end life's pilgrimage,
Unless beneath your roof I may remain;
For I shall never see my father's door again.

LXVI

"My life, Heaven knows, hath long been burthensome;
But, if I have not meekly suffered, meek

May my end be! Soon will this voice be dumb:
Should child of mine e'er wander hither, speak
Of me, say that the worm is on my cheek.— 590
Torn from our hut, that stood beside the sea
Near Portland lighthouse in a lonesome creek,
My husband served in sad captivity
On shipboard, bound till peace or death should set him free.

LXVII

"A sailor's wife I knew a widow's cares,
Yet two sweet little ones partook my bed;
Hope cheered my dreams, and to my daily prayers
Our heavenly Father granted each day's bread;
Till one was found by stroke of violence dead,
Whose body near our cottage chanced to lie; 600
A dire suspicion drove us from our shed;
In vain to find a friendly face we try,
Nor could we live together those poor boys and I;

LXVIII

"For evil tongues made oath how on that day
My husband lurked about the neighbourhood;
Now he had fled, and whither none could say,
And *he* had done the deed in the dark wood—
Near his own home!—but he was mild and good;
Never on earth was gentler creature seen;
He'd not have robbed the raven of its food. 610
My husband's lovingkindness stood between
Me and all worldly harms and wrongs however keen."

LXIX

Alas! the thing she told with labouring breath
The Sailor knew too well. That wickedness
His hand had wrought; and when, in the hour of death,
He saw his Wife's lips move his name to bless
With her last words, unable to suppress
His anguish, with his heart he ceased to strive;
And, weeping loud in this extreme distress,
He cried—"Do pity me! That thou shouldst live 620
I neither ask nor wish—forgive me, but forgive!"

LXX

To tell the change that Voice within her wrought
Nature by sign or sound made no essay;
A sudden joy surprised expiring thought,
And every mortal pang dissolved away.
Borne gently to a bed, in death she lay,
Yet still while over her the husband bent,
A look was in her face which seemed to say,
"Be blest; by sight of thee from heaven was sent
Peace to my parting soul, the fulness of content."   630

LXXI

She slept in peace,—his pulses throbbed and stopped,
Breathless he gazed upon her face,—then took
Her hand in his, and raised it, but both dropped,
When on his own he cast a rueful look.
His ears were never silent; sleep forsook
His burning eyelids stretched and stiff as lead;
All night from time to time under him shook
The floor as he lay shuddering on his bed;
And oft he groaned aloud, "O God, that I were dead!"

LXXII

The Soldier's Widow lingered in the cot,   640
And, when he rose, he thanked her pious care
Through which his Wife, to that kind shelter brought,
Died in his arms; and with those thanks a prayer
He breathed for her, and for that merciful pair.
The corse interred, not one hour he remained
Beneath their roof, but to the open air
A burthen, now with fortitude sustained,
He bore within a breast where dreadful quiet reigned.

LXXIII

Confirmed of purpose, fearlessly prepared
For act and suffering, to the city straight   650
He journeyed, and forthwith his crime declared:
"And from your doom," he added, "now I wait,
Nor let it linger long, the murderer's fate."
Not ineffectual was that piteous claim;

"O welcome sentence which will end though late,"
He said, "the pangs that to my conscience came
Out of that deed. My trust, Saviour! is in thy name!"

LXXIV

His fate was pitied. Him in iron case
(Reader, forgive the intolerable thought)
They hung not:—no one on *his* form or face   660
Could gaze, as on a show by idlers sought;
No kindred sufferer, to his death-place brought
By lawless curiosity or chance,
When into storm the evening sky is wrought,
Upon his swinging corse an eye can glance,
And drop, as he once dropped, in miserable trance.

1797

LINES

LEFT UPON A SEAT IN A YEW-TREE, WHICH STANDS NEAR THE
LAKE OF ESTHWAITE, ON A DESOLATE PART OF THE SHORE,
COMMANDING A BEAUTIFUL PROSPECT

Nay, Traveller! rest. This lonely Yew-tree stands
Far from all human dwelling: what if here
No sparkling rivulet spread the verdant herb?
What if the bee love not these barren boughs?
Yet, if the wind breathe soft, the curling waves,
That break against the shore, shall lull thy mind
By one soft impulse saved from vacancy.
                                    Who he was
That piled these stones and with the mossy sod
First covered, and here taught this aged Tree   10
With its dark arms to form a circling bower,
I well remember.—He was one who owned
No common soul. In youth by science nursed,
And led by nature into a wild scene
Of lofty hopes, he to the world went forth

A favoured Being, knowing no desire
Which genius did not hallow; 'gainst the taint
Of dissolute tongues, and jealousy, and hate,
And scorn,—against all enemies prepared,
All but neglect. The world, for so it thought,   20
Owed him no service; wherefore he at once
With indignation turned himself away,
And with the food of pride sustained his soul
In solitude.—Stranger! these gloomy boughs
Had charms for him; and here he loved to sit,
His only visitants a straggling sheep,
The stone-chat, or the glancing sand-piper:
And on these barren rocks, with fern and heath,
And juniper and thistle, sprinkled o'er,
Fixing his downcast eye, he many an hour   30
A morbid pleasure nourished, tracing here
An emblem of his own unfruitful life:
And, lifting up his head, he then would gaze
On the more distant scene,—how lovely 'tis
Thou seest,—and he would gaze till it became
Far lovelier, and his heart could not sustain
The beauty, still more beauteous! Nor, that time,
When nature had subdued him to herself,
Would he forget those Beings to whose minds,
Warm from the labours of benevolence,   40
The world, and human life, appeared a scene
Of kindred loveliness: then he would sigh,
Inly disturbed, to think that others felt
What he must never feel: and so, lost Man!
On visionary views would fancy feed,
Till his eye streamed with tears. In this deep vale
He died,—this seat his only monument.
    If Thou be one whose heart the holy forms
Of young imagination have kept pure,
Stranger! henceforth be warned; and know that pride,   50
Howe'er disguised in its own majesty,
Is littleness; that he, who feels contempt
For any living thing, hath faculties

Which he has never used; that thought with him
Is in its infancy. The man whose eye
Is ever on himself doth look on one,
The least of Nature's works, one who might move
The wise man to that scorn which wisdom holds
Unlawful, ever. O be wiser, Thou!
Instructed that true knowledge leads to love;   **60**
True dignity abides with him alone
Who, in the silent hour of inward thought,
Can still suspect, and still revere himself,
In lowliness of heart.

The Reverie of Poor Susan

At the corner of Wood Street, when daylight appears,
Hangs a Thrush that sings loud, it has sung for three
     years
Poor Susan has passed by the spot, and has heard
In the silence of morning the song of the Bird.

'Tis a note of enchantment; what ails her? She sees
A mountain ascending, a vision of trees;
Bright volumes of vapour through Lothbury glide,
And a river flows on through the vale of Cheapside.

Green pastures she views in the midst of the dale,
Down which she so often has tripped with her pail;
And a single small cottage, a nest like a dove's,
The one only dwelling on earth that she loves.

She looks, and her heart is in heaven: but they fade,
The mist and the river, the hill and the shade:
The stream will not flow, and the hill will not rise,
And the colours have all passed away from her eyes!

1798–1800

A Night-Piece

————The sky is overcast
With a continuous cloud of texture close,
Heavy and wan, all whitened by the Moon,
Which through that veil is indistinctly seen,
A dull, contracted circle, yielding light
So feebly spread, that not a shadow falls,
Chequering the ground—from rock, plant, tree, or tower.
At length a pleasant instantaneous gleam
Startles the pensive traveller while he treads
His lonesome path, with unobserving eye
Bent earthwards; he looks up—the clouds are split
Asunder,—and above his head he sees
The clear Moon, and the glory of the heavens.
There, in a black-blue vault she sails along,
Followed by multitudes of stars, that, small
And sharp, and bright, along the dark abyss
Drive as she drives: how fast they wheel away,
Yet vanish not!—the wind is in the tree,
But they are silent;—still they roll along
Immeasurably distant; and the vault,
Built round by those white clouds, enormous clouds,
Still deepens its unfathomable depth.
At length the Vision closes, and the mind,
Not undisturbed by the delight it feels,
Which slowly settles into peaceful calm,
Is left to muse upon the solemn scene.

We Are Seven

A simple Child,
That lightly draws its breath,

And feels its life in every limb,
What should it know of death?

I met a little cottage Girl:
She was eight years old, she said;
Her hair was thick with many a curl
That clustered round her head.

She had a rustic, woodland air,
And she was wildly clad:
Her eyes were fair, and very fair;
—Her beauty made me glad.

10

"Sisters and brothers, little Maid,
How many may you be?"
"How many? Seven in all," she said
And wondering looked at me.

"And where are they? I pray you tell."
She answered, "Seven are we;
And two of us at Conway dwell,
And two are gone to sea.

20

"Two of us in the church-yard lie,
My sister and my brother;
And, in the church-yard cottage, I
Dwell near them with my mother."

"You say that two at Conway dwell,
And two are gone to sea,
Yet ye are seven!—I pray you tell,
Sweet Maid, how this may be."

Then did the little Maid reply,
"Seven boys and girls are we;
Two of us in the church-yard lie,
Beneath the church-yard tree."

30

"You run about, my little Maid,
Your limbs they are alive;
If two are in the church-yard laid,
Then ye are only five."

"Their graves are green, they may be seen,"
The little Maid replied,
"Twelve steps or more from my mother's door,
And they are side by side.   40

"My stockings there I often knit,
My kerchief there I hem;
And there upon the ground I sit,
And sing a song to them.

"And often after sunset, Sir,
When it is light and fair,
I take my little porringer,
And eat my supper there.

"The first that died was sister Jane;
In bed she moaning lay,   50
Till God released her of her pain;
And then she went away.

"So in the church-yard she was laid;
And, when the grass was dry,
Together round her grave we played,
My brother John and I.

"And when the ground was white with snow,
And I could run and slide,
My brother John was forced to go,
And he lies by her side."   60

"How many are you, then," said I,
"If they two are in heaven?"
Quick was the little Maid's reply,
"O Master! we are seven."

"But they are dead; those two are dead!
Their spirits are in heaven!"
'Twas throwing words away; for still
The little Maid would have her will,
And said, "Nay, we are seven!"

ANECDOTE FOR FATHERS

I have a boy of five years old;
His face is fair and fresh to see;
His limbs are cast in beauty's mould,
And dearly he loves me.

One morn we strolled on our dry walk,
Our quiet home all full in view,
And held such intermitted talk
As we are wont to do.

My thoughts on former pleasures ran;
I thought of Kilve's delightful shore,   10
Our pleasant home when spring began,
A long, long year before.

A day it was when I could bear
Some fond regrets to entertain;
With so much happiness to spare,
I could not feel a pain.

The green earth echoed to the feet
Of lambs that bounded through the glade,
From shade to sunshine, and as fleet
From sunshine back to shade.   20

Birds warbled round me—and each trace
Of inward sadness had its charm;
Kilve, thought I, was a favoured place,
And so is Liswyn farm.

My boy beside me tripped, so slim
And graceful in his rustic dress!
And, as we talked, I questioned him,
In very idleness.

"Now tell me, had you rather be,"
I said, and took him by the arm,   30
"On Kilve's smooth shore, by the green sea,
Or here at Liswyn farm?"

In careless mood he looked at me,
While still I held him by the arm,
And said, "At Kilve I'd rather be
Than here at Liswyn farm."

"Now, little Edward, say why so:
My little Edward, tell me why."—
"I cannot tell, I do not know."—
"Why, this is strange," said I;   40

"For, here are woods, hills smooth and warm:
There surely must some reason be
Why you would change sweet Liswyn farm
For Kilve by the green sea."

At this, my boy hung down his head,
He blushed with shame, nor made reply;
And three times to the child I said,
"Why, Edward, tell me why?"

His head he raised—there was in sight,
It caught his eye, he saw it plain—   50
Upon the house-top, glittering bright,
A broad and gilded vane.

Then did the boy his tongue unlock,
And eased his mind with this reply:
"At Kilve there was no weather-cock;
And that's the reason why."

O, dearest, dearest boy! my heart
For better lore would seldom yearn,
Could I but teach the hundredth part
Of what from thee I learn.   60

The Thorn

I

"There is a Thorn—it looks so old,
In truth, you'd find it hard to say
How it could ever have been young,

It looks so old and grey.
Not higher than a two years' child
It stands erect, this aged Thorn;
No leaves it has, no prickly points;
It is a mass of knotted joints,
A wretched thing forlorn.
It stands erect, and like a stone   10
With lichens is it overgrown.

II

"Like rock or stone, it is o'ergrown,
With lichens to the very top,
And hung with heavy tufts of moss,
A melancholy crop:
Up from the earth these mosses creep,
And this poor Thorn they clasp it round
So close, you'd say that they are bent
With plain and manifest intent
To drag it to the ground;   20
And all have joined in one endeavour
To bury this poor Thorn for ever.

III

"High on a mountain's highest ridge,
Where oft the stormy winter gale
Cuts like a scythe, while through the clouds
It sweeps from vale to vale;
Not five yards from the mountain path,
This Thorn you on your left espy;
And to the left, three yards beyond,
You see a little muddy pond   30
Of water—never dry
Though but of compass small, and bare
To thirsty suns and parching air.

IV

"And, close beside this aged Thorn,
There is a fresh and lovely sight,
A beauteous heap, a hill of moss,
Just half a foot in height.

All lovely colours there you see,
All colours that were ever seen;
And mossy network too is there,   40
As if by hand of lady fair
The work had woven been;
And cups, the darlings of the eye,
So deep is their vermilion dye.

V

"Ah me! what lovely tints are there
Of olive green and scarlet bright,
In spikes, in branches, and in stars,
Green, red, and pearly white!
This heap of earth o'ergrown with moss,
Which close beside the Thorn you see,   50
So fresh in all its beauteous dyes,
Is like an infant's grave in size,
As like as like can be:
But never, never any where,
An infant's grave was half so fair.

VI

"Now would you see this aged Thorn,
This pond, and beauteous hill of moss,
You must take care and choose your time
The mountain when to cross.
For oft there sits between the heap   60
So like an infant's grave in size,
And that same pond of which I spoke,
A Woman in a scarlet cloak,
And to herself she cries,
'Oh misery! oh misery!
Oh woe is me! oh misery!'

VII

"At all times of the day and night
This wretched Woman thither goes;
And she is known to every star,
And every wind that blows;   70

And there, beside the Thorn, she sits
When the blue daylight's in the skies
And when the whirlwind's on the hill,
Or frosty air is keen and still,
And to herself she cries,
'Oh misery! oh misery!
Oh woe is me! oh misery!'

VIII

"Now wherefore, thus, by day and night,
In rain, in tempest, and in snow,
Thus to the dreary mountain-top
Does this poor Woman go?
And why sits she beside the Thorn
When the blue daylight's in the sky,
Or when the whirlwind's on the hill,
Or frosty air is keen and still,
And wherefore does she cry?—
O wherefore? wherefore? tell me why
Does she repeat that doleful cry?"

80

IX

"I cannot tell; I wish I could;
For the true reason no one knows:
But would you gladly view the spot,
The spot to which she goes;
The hillock like an infant's grave,
The pond—and Thorn, so old and grey;
Pass by her door—'tis seldom shut—
And, if you see her in her hut—
Then to the spot away!
I never heard of such as dare
Approach the spot when she is there."

90

X

"But wherefore to the mountain-top
Can this unhappy Woman go?
Whatever star is in the skies,
Whatever wind may blow?"

100

"Full twenty years are past and gone
Since she (her name is Martha Ray)
Gave with a maiden's true good-will
Her company to Stephen Hill;
And she was blithe and gay,
While friends and kindred all approved
Of him whom tenderly she loved.   110

XI

"And they had fixed the wedding day,
The morning that must wed them both;
But Stephen to another Maid
Had sworn another oath;
And, with this other Maid, to church
Unthinking Stephen went—
Poor Martha! on that woeful day
A pang of pitiless dismay
Into her soul was sent;
A fire was kindled in her breast,   120
Which might not burn itself to rest.

XII

"They say, full six months after this,
While yet the summer leaves were green,
She to the mountain-top would go,
And there was often seen.
What could she seek?—or wish to hide?
Her state to any eye was plain;
She was with child, and she was mad;
Yet often was she sober sad
From her exceeding pain.   130
O guilty Father—would that death
Had saved him from that breach of faith!

XIII

"Sad case for such a brain to hold
Communion with a stirring child!
Sad case, as you may think, for one
Who had a brain so wild!

Last Christmas-eve we talked of this,
And grey-haired Wilfred of the glen
Held that the unborn infant wrought
About its mother's heart, and brought   140
Her senses back again:
And, when at last her time drew near,
Her looks were calm, her senses clear.

XIV

"More know I not, I wish I did,
And it should all be told to you;
For what became of this poor child
No mortal ever knew;
Nay—if a child to her was born
No earthly tongue could ever tell;
And if 'twas born alive or dead,   150
Far less could this with proof be said;
But some remember well,
That Martha Ray about this time
Would up the mountain often climb.

XV

"And all that winter, when at night
The wind blew from the mountain-peak,
'Twas worth your while, though in the dark,
The churchyard path to seek!
For many a time and oft were heard
Cries coming from the mountain head: 160
Some plainly living voices were;
And others, I've heard many swear,
Were voices of the dead:
I cannot think, whate'er they say,
They had to do with Martha Ray.

XVI

"But that she goes to this old Thorn,
The Thorn which I described to you,
And sits there in a scarlet cloak
I will be sworn is true.

For one day with my telescope,   170
To view the ocean wide and bright,
When to this country first I came,
Ere I had heard of Martha's name,
I climbed the mountain's height:—
A storm came on, and I could see
No object higher than my knee.

XVII

" 'Twas mist and rain, and storm, and rain:
No screen, no fence could I discover;
And then the wind! in sooth, it was
A wind full ten times over.   180
I looked around, I thought I saw
A jutting crag,—and off I ran,
Head-foremost, through the driving rain,
The shelter of the crag to gain;
And, as I am a man,
Instead of jutting crag, I found
A Woman seated on the ground.

XVIII

"I did not speak—I saw her face;
Her face!—it was enough for me;
I turned about and heard her cry,   190
'Oh misery! oh misery!'
And there she sits, until the moon
Through half the clear blue sky will go;
And, when the little breezes make
The waters of the pond to shake,
As all the country know,
She shudders, and you hear her cry,
'Oh misery! oh misery!' "

XIX

"But what's the Thorn? and what the pond?
And what the hill of moss to her?   200
And what the creeping breeze that comes
The little pond to stir?"

"I cannot tell; but some will say
She hanged her baby on the tree;
Some say she drowned it in the pond,
Which is a little step beyond:
But all and each agree,
The little Babe was buried there,
Beneath that hill of moss so fair.

XX

"I've heard, the moss is spotted red   210
With drops of that poor infant's blood;
But kill a new-born infant thus,
I do not think she could!
Some say, if to the pond you go,
And fix on it a steady view,
The shadow of a babe you trace,
A baby, and a baby's face,
And that it looks at you;
Whene'er you look on it, 'tis plain
The baby looks at you again.   220

XXI

"And some had sworn an oath that she
Should be to public justice brought;
And for the little infant's bones
With spades they would have sought.
But instantly the hill of moss
Before their eyes began to stir!
And, for full fifty yards around,
The grass—it shook upon the ground!
Yet all do still aver
The little Babe lies buried there,   230
Beneath that hill of moss so fair.

XXII

"I cannot tell how this may be,
But plain it is the Thorn is bound
With heavy tufts of moss that strive
To drag it to the ground;

And this I know, full many a time,
When she was on the mountain high,
By day, and in the silent night,
When all the stars shone clear and bright,
That I have heard her cry,   240
'Oh misery! oh misery!
Oh woe is me! oh misery!' "

GOODY BLAKE AND HARRY GILL

A TRUE STORY

Oh! what's the matter? what's the matter?
What is 't that ails young Harry Gill?
That evermore his teeth they chatter,
Chatter, chatter, chatter still!
Of waistcoats Harry has no lack,
Good duffle grey, and flannel fine;
He has a blanket on his back,
And coats enough to smother nine.

In March, December, and in July,
'Tis all the same with Harry Gill;   10
The neighbours tell, and tell you truly,
His teeth they chatter, chatter still.
At night, at morning, and at noon,
'Tis all the same with Harry Gill;
Beneath the sun, beneath the moon,
His teeth they chatter, chatter still!

Young Harry was a lusty drover,
And who so stout of limb as he?
His cheeks were red as ruddy clover;
His voice was like the voice of three.   20
Old Goody Blake was old and poor;
Ill fed she was, and thinly clad;
And any man who passed her door
Might see how poor a hut she had.

All day she spun in her poor dwelling:
And then her three hours' work at night,

Alas! 'twas hardly worth the telling,
It would not pay for candle-light.
Remote from sheltered village-green,
On a hill's northern side she dwelt,   30
Where from sea-blasts the hawthorns lean,
And hoary dews are slow to melt.

By the same fire to boil their pottage,
Two poor old Dames, as I have known,
Will often live in one small cottage;
But she, poor Woman! housed alone.
'Twas well enough when summer came,
The long, warm, lightsome summer-day,
Then at her door the *canty* Dame
Would sit, as any linnet, gay.   40

But when the ice our stream did fetter,
Oh then how her old bones would shake!
You would have said, if you had met her,
'Twas a hard time for Goody Blake.
Her evenings then were dull and dead:
Sad case it was, as you may think,
For very cold to go to bed,
And then for cold not sleep a wink.

O joy for her! whene'er in winter
The winds at night had made a rout;   50
And scattered many a lusty splinter
And many a rotten bough about.
Yet never had she, well or sick,
As every man who knew her says,
A pile beforehand, turf or stick,
Enough to warm her for three days.

Now, when the frost was past enduring,
And made her poor old bones to ache,
Could any thing be more alluring
Than an old hedge to Goody Blake?   60
And, now and then, it must be said,
When her old bones were cold and chill,

She left her fire, or left her bed,
To seek the hedge of Harry Gill.

Now Harry he had long suspected
This trespass of old Goody Blake;
And vowed that she should be detected—
That he on her would vengeance take.
And oft from his warm fire he'd go,
And to the fields his road would take;   70
And there, at night, in frost and snow,
He watched to seize old Goody Blake.

And once, behind a rick of barley,
Thus looking out did Harry stand:
The moon was full and shining clearly,
And crisp with frost the stubble land.
—He hears a noise—he's all awake—
Again?—on tip-toe down the hill
He softly creeps—'tis Goody Blake;
She's at the hedge of Harry Gill!   80

Right glad was he when he beheld her:
Stick after stick did Goody pull:
He stood behind a bush of elder,
Till she had filled her apron full.
When with her load she turned about,
The by-way back again to take;
He started forward, with a shout,
And sprang upon poor Goody Blake.

And fiercely by the arm he took her,
And by the arm he held her fast,   90
And fiercely by the arm he shook her,
And cried, "I've caught you then at last!"
Then Goody, who had nothing said,
Her bundle from her lap let fall;
And, kneeling on the sticks, she prayed
To God that is the judge of all.

She prayed, her withered hand uprearing,
While Harry held her by the arm—

"God! who art never out of hearing,
O may he never more be warm!"   100
The cold, cold moon above her head,
Thus on her knees did Goody pray;
Young Harry heard what she had said:
And icy cold he turned away.

He went complaining all the morrow
That he was cold and very chill:
His face was gloom, his heart was sorrow.
Alas! that day for Harry Gill!
That day he wore a riding-coat,
But not a whit the warmer he: 110
Another was on Thursday brought,
And ere the Sabbath he had three.

'Twas all in vain, a useless matter,
And blankets were about him pinned;
Yet still his jaws and teeth they clatter;
Like a loose casement in the wind.
And Harry's flesh it fell away;
And all who see him say, 'tis plain,
That, live as long as live he may,
He never will be warm again.   120

No word to any man he utters,
A-bed or up, to young or old;
But ever to himself he mutters,
"Poor Harry Gill is very cold."
A-bed or up, by night or day;
His teeth they chatter, chatter still.
Now think, ye farmers all, I pray,
Of Goody Blake and Harry Gill!

HER EYES ARE WILD

I

Her eyes are wild, her head is bare,
The sun has burnt her coal-black hair;

Her eyebrows have a rusty stain,
And she came far from over the main.
She has a baby on her arm,
Or else she were alone:
And underneath the hay-stack warm,
And on the greenwood stone,
She talked and sung the woods among,   10
And it was in the English tongue.

II

"Sweet babe! they say that I am mad,
But nay, my heart is far too glad;
And I am happy when I sing
Full many a sad and doleful thing:
Then, lovely baby, do not fear!
I pray thee have no fear of me;
But safe as in a cradle, here,
My lovely baby; thou shalt be:
To thee I know too much I owe:
I cannot work thee any woe.   20

III

"A fire was once within my brain;
And in my head a dull, dull pain;
And fiendish faces, one, two, three,
Hung at my breast, and pulled at me;
But then there came a sight of joy;
It came at once to do me good;
I waked, and saw my little boy,
My little boy of flesh and blood;
Oh joy for me that sight to see!
For he was here, and only he.   30

IV

"Suck, little babe, oh suck again!
It cools my blood; it cools my brain;
Thy lips I feel them, my baby! they
Draw from my heart the pain away.
Oh! press me with thy little hand;

It loosens something at my chest;
About that tight and deadly band
I feel thy little fingers prest.
The breeze I see is in the tree:
It comes to cool my babe and me.   40

V

"Oh! love me, love me, little boy!
Thou art thy mother's only joy;
And do not dread the waves below,
When o'er the sea-rock's edge we go;
The high crag cannot work me harm,
Nor leaping torrents when they howl;
The babe I carry on my arm,
He saves for me my precious soul;
Then happy lie; for blest am I;
Without me my sweet babe would die.   50

VI

"Then do not fear, my boy! for thee
Bold as a lion will I be;
And I will always be thy guide,
Through hollow snows and rivers wide.
I'll build an Indian bower; I know
The leaves that make the softest bed:
And, if from me thou wilt not go,
But still be true till I am dead,
My pretty thing! then thou shalt sing
As merry as the birds in spring.   60

VII

"Thy father cares not for my breast,
'Tis thine, sweet baby, there to rest;
'Tis all thine own!—and, if its hue
Be changed, that was so fair to view,
'Tis fair enough for thee, my dove!
My beauty, little child, is flown,
But thou wilt live with me in love,
And what if my poor cheek be brown?

'Tis well for me, thou canst not see
How pale and wan it else would be. 70

VIII

"Dread not their taunts, my little Life;
I am thy father's wedded wife;
And underneath the spreading tree
We two will live in honesty.
If his sweet boy he could forsake,
With me he never would have stayed:
From him no harm my babe can take;
But he, poor man! is wretched made;
And every day we two will pray
For him that's gone and far away. 80

IX

"I'll teach my boy the sweetest things:
I'll teach him how the owlet sings.
My little babe! thy lips are still,
And thou hast almost sucked thy fill.
—Where are thou gone, my own dear child?
What wicked looks are those I see?
Alas! alas! that look so wild,
It never, never came from me:
If thou art mad, my pretty lad,
Then I must be for ever sad. 90

X

"Oh! smile on me, my little lamb!
For I thy own dear mother am:
My love for thee has well been tried:
I've sought thy father far and wide.
I know the poisons of the shade;
I know the earth-nuts fit for food:
Then, pretty dear, be not afraid:
We'll find thy father in the wood.
Now laugh and be gay, to the woods away!
And there, my babe, we'll live for aye." 100

SIMON LEE

THE OLD HUNTSMAN;
WITH AN INCIDENT IN WHICH HE WAS CONCERNED

In the sweet shire of Cardigan,
Not far from pleasant Ivor-hall,
An old Man dwells, a little man,—
'Tis said he once was tall.
Full five and-thirty years he lived
A running huntsman merry;
And still the centre of his cheek
Is red as a ripe cherry.

No man like him the horn could sound,
And hill and valley rang with glee   10
When Echo bandied, round and round,
The halloo of Simon Lee.
In those proud days, he little cared
For husbandry or tillage;
To blither tasks did Simon rouse
The sleepers of the village.

He all the country could outrun,
Could leave both man and horse behind;
And often, ere the chase was done,
He reeled, and was stone-blind.   20
And still there's something in the world
At which his heart rejoices;
For when the chiming hounds are out,
He dearly loves their voices!

But, oh the heavy change!—bereft
Of health, strength, friends, and kindred, see!
Old Simon to the world is left
In liveried poverty.
His Master's dead,—and no one now
Dwells in the Hall of Ivor;   30
Men, dogs, and horses, all are dead;
He is the sole survivor.

And he is lean and he is sick;
His body, dwindled and awry,
Rests upon ankles swoln and thick;
His legs are thin and dry.
One prop he has, and only one,
His wife, an aged woman,
Lives with him, near the waterfall,
Upon the village Common.   40

Beside their moss-grown hut of clay,
Not twenty paces from the door,
A scrap of land they have, but they
Are poorest of the poor.
This scrap of land he from the heath
Enclosed when he was stronger;
But what to them avails the land
Which he can till no longer?

Oft, working by her Husband's side,
Ruth does what Simon cannot do;   50
For she, with scanty cause for pride,
Is stouter of the two.
And, though you with your utmost skill
From labour could not wean them,
'Tis little, very little—all
That they can do between them.

Few months of life has he in store
As he to you will tell,
For still, the more he works, the more
Do his weak ankles swell.   60
My gentle Reader, I perceive
How patiently you 've waited,
And now I fear that you expect
Some tale will be related.

O Reader! had you in your mind
Such stores as silent thought can bring,
O gentle Reader! you would find
A tale in every thing.
What more I have to say is short,

And you must kindly take it: 70
It is no tale; but, should you think,
Perhaps a tale you 'll make it.

One summer-day I chanced to see
This old Man doing all he could
To unearth the root of an old tree,
A stump of rotten wood.
The mattock tottered in his hand;
So vain was his endeavour,
That at the root of the old tree
He might have worked for ever. 80

"You 're overtasked, good Simon Lee,
Give me your tool," to him I said;
And at the word right gladly he
Received my proffered aid.
I struck, and with a single blow
The tangled root I severed,
At which the poor old Man so long
And vainly had endeavoured.

The tears into his eyes were brought,
And thanks and praises seemed to run 90
So fast out of his heart, I thought
They never would have done.
—I 've heard of hearts unkind, kind deeds
With coldness still returning;
Alas! the gratitude of men
Hath oftener left me mourning.

LINES WRITTEN IN EARLY SPRING

I heard a thousand blended notes,
While in a grove I sate reclined,
In that sweet mood when pleasant thoughts
Bring sad thoughts to the mind.

To her fair works did Nature link
The human soul that through me ran;

And much it grieved my heart to think
What man has made of man.

Through primrose tufts, in that green bower,
The periwinkle trailed its wreaths;
And 'tis my faith that every flower
Enjoys the air it breathes.

The birds around me hopped and played,
Their thoughts I cannot measure:—
But the least motion which they made
It seemed a thrill of pleasure.

The budding twigs spread out their fan,
To catch the breezy air;
And I must think, do all I can,
That there was pleasure there.

If this belief from heaven be sent,
If such be Nature's holy plan,
Have I not reason to lament
What man has made of man?

TO MY SISTER

It is the first mild day of March:
Each minute sweeter than before
The redbreast sings from the tall larch
That stands beside our door.

There is a blessing in the air,
Which seems a sense of joy to yield
To the bare trees, and mountains bare,
And grass in the green field.

My sister! ('tis a wish of mine)
Now that our morning meal is done,   10
Make haste, your morning task resign;
Come forth and feel the sun.

Edward will come with you;—and, pray,
Put on with speed your woodland dress;

And bring no book: for this one day
We'll give to idleness.

No joyless forms shall regulate
Our living calendar:
We from to-day, my Friend, will date
The opening of the year.   20

Love, now a universal birth,
From heart to heart is stealing,
From earth to man, from man to earth:
—It is the hour of feeling.

One moment now may give us more
Than years of toiling reason:
Our minds shall drink at every pore
The spirit of the season.

Some silent laws our hearts will make,
Which they shall long obey: 30
We for the year to come may take
Our temper from to-day.

And from the blessed power that rolls
About, below, above,
We'll frame the measure of our souls:
They shall be tuned to love.

Then come, my Sister! come, I pray,
With speed put on your woodland dress;
And bring no book: for this one day
We'll give to idleness.   40

"A WHIRL-BLAST FROM BEHIND THE HILL"

A whirl-blast from behind the hill
Rushed o'er the wood with startling sound;
Then—all at once the air was still,
And showers of hailstones pattered round.
Where leafless oaks towered high above,
I sat within an undergrove

Of tallest hollies, tall and green;
A fairer bower was never seen.
From year to year the spacious floor
With withered leaves is covered o'er,
And all the year the bower is green.
But see! where'er the hailstones drop
The withered leaves all skip and hop;
There's not a breeze—no breath of air—
Yet here, and there, and everywhere
Along the floor, beneath the shade
By those embowering hollies made,
The leaves in myriads jump and spring,
As if with pipes and music rare
Some Robin Good-fellow were there,
And all those leaves, in festive glee,
Were dancing to the minstrelsy.

EXPOSTULATION AND REPLY

"Why, William, on that old grey stone,
Thus for the length of half a day,
Why, William, sit you thus alone,
And dream your time away?

"Where are your books?—that light bequeathed
To Beings else forlorn and blind!
Up! up! and drink the spirit breathed
From dead men to their kind.

"You look round on your Mother Earth,
As if she for no purpose bore you;
As if you were her first-born birth,
And none had lived before you!"

One morning thus, by Esthwaite lake,
When life was sweet, I knew not why,
To me my good friend Matthew spake,
And thus I made reply:

"The eye—it cannot choose but see;
We cannot bid the ear be still;

10

Our bodies feel, where'er they be,
Against or with our will.   20

"Nor less I deem that there are Powers
Which of themselves our minds impress;
That we can feed this mind of ours
In a wise passiveness.

"Think you, 'mid all this mighty sum
Of things for ever speaking,
That nothing of itself will come,
But we must still be seeking?

"—Then ask not wherefore, here, alone,
Conversing as I may,   30
I sit upon this old grey stone,
And dream my time away."

THE TABLES TURNED

AN EVENING SCENE
ON THE SAME SUBJECT

Up! up! my Friend, and quit your books;
Or surely you 'll grow double:
Up! up! my Friend, and clear your looks;
Why all this toil and trouble?

The sun, above the mountain's head,
A freshening lustre mellow
Through all the long green fields has spread,
His first sweet evening yellow.

Books! 'tis a dull and endless strife:
Come, hear the woodland linnet,
How sweet his music! on my life,   10
There's more of wisdom in it.

And hark! how blithe the throstle sings!
He, too, is no mean preacher:
Come forth into the light of things,
Let Nature be your teacher.

She has a world of ready wealth,
Our minds and hearts to bless—
Spontaneous wisdom breathed by health,
Truth breathed by cheerfulness.   20

One impulse from a vernal wood
May teach you more of man,
Of moral evil and of good,
Than all the sages can.

Sweet is the lore which Nature brings;
Our meddling intellect
Mis-shapes the beauteous forms of things:—
We murder to dissect.

Enough of Science and of Art;
Close up those barren leaves;   30
Come forth, and bring with you a heart
That watches and receives.

THE COMPLAINT

OF A FORSAKEN INDIAN WOMAN

I

Before I see another day,
Oh let my body die away!
In sleep I heard the northern gleams;
The stars, they were among my dreams;
In rustling conflict through the skies,
I heard, I saw the flashes drive,
And yet they are upon my eyes,
And yet I am alive;
Before I see another day,
Oh let my body die away!   10

II

My fire is dead: it knew no pain;
Yet is it dead, and I remain:
All stiff with ice the ashes lie;

And they are dead, and I will die.
When I was well, I wished to live,
For clothes, for warmth, for food, and fire;
But they to me no joy can give,
No pleasure now, and no desire.
Then here contented will I lie!
Alone, I cannot fear to die.   20

III

Alas! ye might have dragged me on
Another day, a single one!
Too soon I yielded to despair;
Why did ye listen to my prayer?
When ye were gone my limbs were stronger;
And oh, how grievously I rue,
That, afterwards, a little longer,
My friends, I did not follow you!
For strong and without pain I lay,
Dear friends, when ye were gone away.   30

IV

My Child! they gave thee to another,
A woman who was not thy mother.
When from my arms my Babe they took,
On me how strangely did he look!
Through his whole body something ran,
A most strange working did I see:
—As if he strove to be a man,
That he might pull the sledge for me:
And then he stretched his arms, how wild!
Oh mercy! like a helpless child.   40

V

My little joy! my little pride!
In two days more I must have died.
Then do not weep and grieve for me;
I feel I must have died with thee.
O wind, that o'er my head art flying
The way my friends their course did bend

I should not feel the pain of dying,
Could I with thee a message send;
Too soon, my friends, ye went away;
For I had many things to say.   50

VI

I 'll follow you across the snow;
Ye travel heavily and slow;
In spite of all my weary pain
I 'll look upon your tents again.
—My fire is dead, and snowy white
The water which beside it stood:
The wolf has come to me to-night,
And he has stolen away my food.
For ever left alone am I;
Then wherefore should I fear to die?   60

VII

Young as I am, my course is run,
I shall not see another sun;
I cannot lift my limbs to know
If they have any life or no.
My poor forsaken Child, if I
For once could have thee close to me,
With happy heart I then would die,
And my last thought would happy be;
But thou, dear Babe, art far away,
Nor shall I see another day.   70

THE LAST OF THE FLOCK

I

In distant countries have I been,
And yet I have not often seen
A healthy man, a man full grown,
Weep in the public roads, alone.
But such a one, on English ground,
And in the broad highway, I met;
Along the broad highway he came,

His cheeks with tears were wet:
Sturdy he seemed, though he was sad;
And in his arms a Lamb he had.   10

II

He saw me, and he turned aside,
As if he wished himself to hide:
And with his coat did then essay
To wipe those briny tears away.
I followed him, and said, "My friend,
What ails you? wherefore weep you so?"
—"Shame on me, Sir! this lusty Lamb,
He makes my tears to flow.
To-day I fetched him from the rock;
He is the last of all my flock.   20

III

"When I was young, a single man,
And after youthful follies ran,
Though little given to care and thought,
Yet, so it was, an ewe I bought;
And other sheep from her I raised,
As healthy sheep as you might see;
And then I married, and was rich
As I could wish to be;
Of sheep I numbered a full score,
And every year increased my store.   30

IV

"Year after year my stock it grew;
And from this one, this single ewe,
Full fifty comely sheep I raised,
As fine a flock as ever grazed!
Upon the Quantock hills they fed;
They throve, and we at home did thrive:
—This lusty Lamb of all my store
Is all that is alive;
And now I care not if we die,
And perish all of poverty.   40

V

"Six Children, Sir! had I to feed;
Hard labour in a time of need!
My pride was tamed, and in our grief
I of the Parish asked relief.
They said, I was a wealthy man;
My sheep upon the uplands fed,
And it was fit that thence I took
Whereof to buy us bread.
'Do this: how can we give to you,'
They cried, 'what to the poor is due?'   50

VI

"I sold a sheep, as they had said,
And bought my little children bread,
And they were healthy with their food,
For me—it never did me good.
A woeful time it was for me,
To see the end of all my gains,
The pretty flock which I had reared
With all my care and pains,
To see it melt like snow away—
For me it was a woeful day.   60

VII

"Another still! and still another!
A little lamb, and then its mother!
It was a vein that never stopped—
Like blood-drops from my heart they dropped.
Till thirty were not left alive
They dwindled, dwindled, one by one,
And I may say, that many a time
I wished they all were gone—
Reckless of what might come at last
Were but the bitter struggle past.   70

VIII

"To wicked deeds I was inclined,
And wicked fancies crossed my mind;

And every man I chanced to see,
I thought he knew some ill of me:
No peace, no comfort could I find,
No ease, within doors or without;
And, crazily and wearily
I went my work about;
And oft was moved to flee from home,
And hide my head where the wild beasts roam.　　　**80**

IX
"Sir! 'twas a precious flock to me
As dear as my own children be;
For daily with my growing store
I loved my children more and more.
Alas! it was an evil time;
God cursed me in my sore distress;
I prayed, yet every day I thought
I loved my children less;
And every week, and every day,
My flock it seemed to melt away.　　　**90**

X
"They dwindled, Sir, sad sight to see!
From ten to five, from five to three,
A lamb, a wether, and a ewe;—
And then at last from three to two;
And, of my fifty, yesterday
I had but only one:
And here it lies upon my arm,
Alas! and I have none;—
To-day I fetched it from the rock;
It is the last of all my flock."　　　**100**

THE IDIOT BOY

'Tis eight o'clock,—a clear March night,
The moon is up,—the sky is blue,
The owlet, in the moonlight air,

Shouts from nobody knows where;
He lengthens out his lonely shout,
Halloo! halloo! a long halloo!

—Why bustle thus about your door,
What means this bustle, Betty Foy?
Why are you in this mighty fret?
And why on horseback have you set   10
Him whom you love, your Idiot Boy?

Scarcely a soul is out of bed;
Good Betty, put him down again;
His lips with joy they burr at you;
But, Betty! what has he to do
With stirrup, saddle, or with rein?

But Betty's bent on her intent;
For her good neighbour, Susan Gale,
Old Susan, she who dwells alone,
Is sick, and makes a piteous moan   20
As if her very life would fail.

There's not a house within a mile,
No hand to help them in distress;
Old Susan lies a-bed in pain,
And sorely puzzled are the twain,
For what she ails they cannot guess.

And Betty's husband's at the wood,
Where by the week he doth abide,
A woodman in the distant vale;
There's none to help poor Susan Gale;   30
What must be done? what will betide?

And Betty from the lane has fetched
Her Pony, that is mild and good;
Whether he be in joy or pain,
Feeding at will along the lane,
Or bringing faggots from the wood.

And he is all in travelling trim,—
And, by the moonlight, Betty Foy

Has on the well-girt saddle set
(The like was never heard of yet)   40
Him whom she loves, her Idiot Boy.

And he must post without delay
Across the bridge and through the dale,
And by the church, and o'er the down,
To bring a Doctor from the town,
Or she will die, old Susan Gale.

There is no need of boot or spur,
There is no need of whip or wand;
For Johnny has his holly-bough,
And with a *hurly-burly* now   50
He shakes the green bough in his hand.

And Betty o'er and o'er has told
The Boy, who is her best delight,
Both what to follow, what to shun,
What do, and what to leave undone,
How turn to left, and how to right.

And Betty's most especial charge,
Was, "Johnny! Johnny! mind that you
Come home again, nor stop at all,—
Come home again, whate'er befall,   60
My Johnny, do, I pray you do."

To this did Johnny answer make,
Both with his head and with his hand,
And proudly shook the bridle too;
And then! his words were not a few,
Which Betty well could understand.

And now that Johnny is just going,
Though Betty's in a mighty flurry,
She gently pats the Pony's side,
On which her Idiot Boy must ride,   70
And seems no longer in a hurry.

But when the Pony moved his legs,
Oh! then for the poor Idiot Boy!

For joy he cannot hold the bridle,
For joy his head and heels are idle,
He's idle all for very joy.

And while the Pony moves his legs,
In Johnny's left hand you may see
The green bough motionless and dead:
The Moon that shines above his head   80
Is not more still and mute than he.

His heart it was so full of glee,
That till full fifty yards were gone,
He quite forgot his holly whip,
And all his skill in horsemanship:
Oh! happy, happy, happy John.

And while the Mother, at the door,
Stands fixed, her face with joy o'erflows,
Proud of herself, and proud of him,
She sees him in his travelling trim,   90
How quietly her Johnny goes.

The silence of her Idiot Boy,
What hopes it sends to Betty's heart!
He's at the guide-post—he turns right;
She watches till he's out of sight,
And Betty will not then depart.

Burr, burr—now Johnny's lips they burr,
As loud as any mill, or near it;
Meek as a lamb the Pony moves,
And Johnny makes the noise he loves,   100
And Betty listens, glad to hear it.

Away she hies to Susan Gale:
Her Messenger's in merry tune;
The owlets hoot, the owlets curr,
And Johnny's lips they burr, burr, burr,
As on he goes beneath the moon.

His steed and he right well agree;
For of this Pony there's a rumour,

That, should he lose his eyes and ears,
And should he live a thousand years,
He never will be out of humour.

But then he is a horse that thinks!
And when he thinks, his pace is slack;
Now, though he knows poor Johnny well,
Yet, for his life, he cannot tell
What he has got upon his back.

So through the moonlight lanes they go,
And far into the moonlight dale,
And by the church, and o'er the down,
To bring a Doctor from the town,
To comfort poor old Susan Gale.

And Betty, now at Susan's side,
Is in the middle of her story,
What speedy help her Boy will bring,
With many a most diverting thing,
Of Johnny's wit, and Johnny's glory.

And Betty, still at Susan's side,
By this time is not quite so flurried:
Demure with porringer and plate
She sits, as if in Susan's fate
Her life and soul were buried.

But Betty, poor good woman! she,
You plainly in her face may read it,
Could lend out of that moment's store
Five years of happiness or more
To any that might need it.

But yet I guess that now and then
With Betty all was not so well;
And to the road she turns her ears,
And thence full many a sound she hears,
Which she to Susan will not tell.

Poor Susan moans, poor Susan groans;
"As sure as there's a moon in heaven,"

110

120

130

140

Cries Betty, "he'll be back again;
They 'll both be here—'tis almost ten—
Both will be here before eleven."

Poor Susan moans, poor Susan groans;
The clock gives warning for eleven;
'Tis on the stroke—"He must be near,"
Quoth Betty, "and will soon be here,   150
As sure as there's a moon in heaven."

The clock is on the stroke of twelve,
And Johnny is not yet in sight:
—The Moon's in heaven, as Betty sees,
But Betty is not quite at ease;
And Susan has a dreadful night.

And Betty, half an hour ago,
On Johnny vile reflections cast:
"A little idle sauntering Thing!"
With other names, an endless string;   160
But now that time is gone and past.

And Betty's drooping at the heart,
That happy time all past and gone,
"How can it be he is so late?
The Doctor, he has made him wait;
Susan! they 'll both be here anon."

And Susan's growing worse and worse,
And Betty's in a sad *quandary*;
And then there's nobody to say
If she must go, or she must stay!   170
—She's in a sad *quandary*.

The clock is on the stroke of one;
But neither Doctor nor his Guide
Appears along the moonlight road;
There's neither horse nor man abroad,
And Betty's still at Susan's side.

And Susan now begins to fear
Of sad mischances not a few:

That Johnny may perhaps be drowned,
Or lost, perhaps, and never found;   180
Which they must both for ever rue.

She prefaced half a hint of this
With, "God forbid it should be true!"
At the first word that Susan said
Cried Betty, rising from the bed,
"Susan, I'd gladly stay with you.

"I must be gone, I must away:
Consider, Johnny's but half-wise;
Susan, we must take care of him,
If he is hurt in life or limb"—   190
"Oh God forbid!" poor Susan cries.

"What can I do?" says Betty, going,
"What can I do to ease your pain?
Good Susan tell me, and I'll stay;
I fear you're in a dreadful way,
But I shall soon be back again."

"Nay, Betty, go! good Betty, go!
There's nothing that can ease my pain."
Then off she hies; but with a prayer
That God poor Susan's life would spare,   200
Till she comes back again.

So, through the moonlight lane she goes,
And far into the moonlight dale;
And how she ran, and how she walked,
And all that to herself she talked,
Would surely be a tedious tale.

In high and low, above, below,
In great and small, in round and square,
In tree and tower was Johnny seen,
In bush and brake, in black and green;   210
'Twas Johnny, Johnny, every where.

And while she crossed the bridge, there came
A thought with which her heart is sore—

Johnny perhaps his horse forsook,
To hunt the moon within the brook,
And never will be heard of more.

Now is she high upon the down,
Alone amid a prospect wide;
There's neither Johnny nor his Horse
Among the fern or in the gorse;   220
There's neither Doctor nor his Guide.

"O saints! what is become of him?
Perhaps he's climbed into an oak,
Where he will stay till he is dead;
Or, sadly he has been misled,
And joined the wandering gipsy-folk.

"Or him that wicked Pony's carried
To the dark cave, the goblin's hall;
Or in the castle he's pursuing
Among the ghosts his own undoing;   230
Or playing with the waterfall."

At poor old Susan then she railed,
While to the town she posts away;
"If Susan had not been so ill,
Alas! I should have had him still,
My Johnny, till my dying day."

Poor Betty, in this sad distemper,
The Doctor's self could hardly spare:
Unworthy things she talked, and wild;
Even he, of cattle the most mild,   240
The Pony had his share.

But now she's fairly in the town,
And to the Doctor's door she hies;
'Tis silence all on every side;
The town so long, the town so wide,
Is silent as the skies.

And now she's at the Doctor's door,
She lifts the knocker, rap, rap, rap;

The Doctor at the casement shows
His glimmering eyes that peep and doze!
And one hand rubs his old night-cap.

250

"O Doctor! Doctor! where's my Johnny?"
"I 'm here, what is 't you want with me?"
"O Sir! you know I'm Betty Foy,
And I have lost my poor dear Boy,
You know him—him you often see;

"He's not so wise as some folks be:"
"The devil take his wisdom!" said
The Doctor, looking somewhat grim,
"What, Woman! should I know of him?"
And, grumbling, he went back to bed!

260

"O woe is me! O woe is me!
Here will I die; here will I die;
I thought to find my lost one here,
But he is neither far nor near,
Oh! what a wretched Mother I!"

She stops, she stands, she looks about;
Which way to turn she cannot tell.
Poor Betty! it would ease her pain
If she had heart to knock again;
—The clock strikes three—a dismal knell!

270

Then up along the town she hies,
No wonder if her senses fail;
This piteous news so much it shocked her,
She quite forgot to send the Doctor,
To comfort poor old Susan Gale.

And now she's high upon the down,
And she can see a mile of road:
"O cruel! I 'm almost threescore;
Such night as this was ne'er before,
There's not a single soul abroad."

280

She listens, but she cannot hear
The foot of horse, the voice of man;

The streams with softest sound are flowing,
The grass you almost hear it growing,
You hear it now, if e'er you can.

The owlets through the long blue night
Are shouting to each other still:
Fond lovers! yet not quite hob nob,
They lengthen out the tremulous sob,   290
That echoes far from hill to hill.

Poor Betty now has lost all hope,
Her thoughts are bent on deadly sin,
A green-grown pond she just has past,
And from the brink she hurries fast,
Lest she should drown herself therein.

And now she sits her down and weeps;
Such tears she never shed before;
"Oh dear, dear Pony! my sweet joy!
Oh carry back my Idiot Boy!   300
And we will ne'er o'erload thee more."

A thought is come into her head:
The Pony he is mild and good,
And we have always used him well;
Perhaps he's gone along the dell,
And carried Johnny to the wood.

Then up she springs as if on wings;
She thinks no more of deadly sin;
If Betty fifty ponds should see,
The last of all her thoughts would be   310
To drown herself therein.

O Reader! now that I might tell
What Johnny and his Horse are doing,
What they've been doing all this time,
Oh could I put it into rhyme,
A most delightful tale pursuing!

Perhaps, and no unlikely thought!
He with his Pony now doth roam

The cliffs and peaks so high that are,
To lay his hands upon a star,
And in his pocket bring it home.

320

Perhaps he's turned himself about,
His face unto his horse's tail,
And, still and mute, in wonder lost,
All silent as a horseman-ghost,
He travels slowly down the vale.

And now, perhaps, is hunting sheep,
A fierce and dreadful hunter he;
Yon valley, now so trim and green,
In five months' time, should he be seen,
A desert wilderness will be!

330

Perhaps, with head and heels on fire,
And like the very soul of evil,
He's galloping away, away,
And so will gallop on for aye,
The bane of all that dread the devil!

I to the Muses have been bound
These fourteen years, by strong indentures.
O gentle Muses! let me tell
But half of what to him befell;
He surely met with strange adventures.

340

O gentle Muses! is this kind?
Why will ye thus my suit repel?
Why of your further aid bereave me?
And can ye thus unfriended leave me,
Ye Muses! whom I love so well?

Who's yon, that, near the waterfall,
Which thunders down with headlong force,
Beneath the moon, yet shining fair,
As careless as if nothing were,
Sits upright on a feeding horse?

350

Unto his horse—there feeding free,
He seems, I think, the rein to give;

Of moon or stars he takes no heed;
Of such we in romances read:
—'Tis Johnny! Johnny! as I live.

And that's the very Pony, too!
Where is she, where is Betty Foy?
She hardly can sustain her fears;
The roaring waterfall she hears,   360
And cannot find her Idiot Boy.

Your Pony's worth his weight in gold:
Then calm your terrors, Betty Foy!
She's coming from among the trees,
And now all full in view she sees
Him whom she loves, her Idiot Boy.

And Betty sees the Pony too:
Why stand you thus, good Betty Foy?
It is no goblin, 'tis no ghost,
'Tis he whom you so long have lost   370
He whom you love, your Idiot Boy.

She looks again—her arms are up—
She screams—she cannot move for joy;
She darts, as with a torrent's force,
She almost has o'erturned the Horse,
And fast she holds her Idiot Boy.

And Johnny burrs, and laughs aloud;
Whether in cunning or in joy
I cannot tell; but while he laughs,
Betty a drunken pleasure quaffs   380
To hear again her Idiot Boy.

And now she's at the Pony's tail,
And now is at the Pony's head,—
On that side now, and now on this;
And, almost stifled with her bliss,
A few sad tears does Betty shed.

She kisses o'er and o'er again
Him whom she loves, her Idiot Boy;

She's happy here, is happy there,
She is uneasy every where;
Her limbs are all alive with joy.   390

She pats the Pony, where or when
She knows not, happy Betty Foy!
The little Pony glad may be,
But he is milder far than she,
You hardly can perceive his joy.

"Oh! Johnny, never mind the Doctor;
You 've done your best, and that is all:"
She took the reins, when this was said,
And gently turned the Pony's head   400
From the loud waterfall.

By this the stars were almost gone,
The moon was setting on the hill,
So pale you scarcely looked at her:
The little birds began to stir,
Though yet their tongues were still.

The Pony, Betty, and her Boy,
Wind slowly through the woody dale;
And who is she, betimes abroad,
That hobbles up the steep rough road?   410
Who is it, but old Susan Gale?

Long time lay Susan lost in thought;
And many dreadful fears beset her,
Both for her Messenger and Nurse;
And, as her mind grew worse and worse,
Her body—it grew better.

She turned, she tossed herself in bed,
On all sides doubts and terrors met her;
Point after point did she discuss;
And, while her mind was fighting thus,   420
Her body still grew better.

"Alas! what is become of them?
These fears can never be endured;

I'll to the wood."—The word scarce said,
Did Susan rise up from her bed,
As if by magic cured.

Away she goes up hill and down,
And to the wood at length is come;
She spies her Friends, she shouts a greeting;
Oh me! it is a merry meeting   **430**
As ever was in Christendom.

The owls have hardly sung their last,
While our four travellers homeward wend;
The owls have hooted all night long,
And with the owls began my song,
And with the owls must end.

For while they all were travelling home,
Cried Betty, "Tell us, Johnny, do,
Where all this long night you have been,
What you have heard, what you have seen: **440**
And, Johnny, mind you tell us true."

Now Johnny all night long had heard
The owls in tuneful concert strive;
No doubt too he the moon had seen;
For in the moonlight he had been
From eight o'clock till five.

And thus, to Betty's questions, he
Made answer, like a traveller bold,
(His very words I give to you,)
"The cocks did crow to-whoo, to-whoo,   **450**
And the sun did shine so cold!"
—Thus answered Johnny in his glory,
And that was all his travel's story.

LINES COMPOSED A FEW MILES ABOVE
TINTERN ABBEY

ON REVISITING THE BANKS OF THE WYE DURING A TOUR.
July 13, 1798

Five years have past; five summers, with the length
Of five long winters! and again I hear
These waters, rolling from their mountain-springs
With a soft inland murmur.—Once again
Do I behold these steep and lofty cliffs,
That on a wild secluded scene impress
Thoughts of more deep seclusion; and connect
The landscape with the quiet of the sky.
The day is come when I again repose
Here, under this dark sycamore, and view   10
These plots of cottage-ground, these orchard-tufts,
Which at this season, with their unripe fruits,
Are clad in one green hue, and lose themselves
'Mid groves and copses. Once again I see
These hedge-rows, hardly hedge-rows, little lines
Of sportive wood run wild: these pastoral farms,
Green to the very door; and wreaths of smoke
Sent up, in silence, from among the trees!
With some uncertain notice, as might seem
Of vagrant dwellers in the houseless woods,   20
Or of some Hermit's cave, where by his fire
The Hermit sits alone.
                              These beauteous forms,
Through a long absence, have not been to me
As is a landscape to blind man's eye:
But oft, in lonely rooms, and 'mid the din
Of towns and cities, I have owed to them
In hours of weariness, sensations sweet,
Felt in the blood, and felt along the heart;
And passing even into my purer mind,
With tranquil restoration:—feelings too   30
Of unremembered pleasure: such, perhaps,

As have no slight or trivial influence
On that best portion of a good man's life,
His little, nameless, unremembered, acts
Of kindness and of love. Nor less, I trust,
To them I may have owed another gift,
Of aspect more sublime; that blessed mood,
In which the burthen of the mystery,
In which the heavy and the weary weight
Of all this unintelligible world,   40
Is lightened:—that serene and blessed mood,
In which the affections gently lead us on,—
Until, the breath of this corporeal frame
And even the motion of our human blood
Almost suspended, we are laid asleep
In body, and become a living soul:
While with an eye made quiet by the power
Of harmony, and the deep power of joy,
We see into the life of things.
                                                 If this
Be but a vain belief, yet, oh! how oft—   50
In darkness and amid the many shapes
Of joyless daylight; when the fretful stir
Unprofitable, and the fever of the world,
Have hung upon the beatings of my heart—
How oft, in spirit, have I turned to thee,
O sylvan Wye! thou wanderer thro' the woods,
How often has my spirit turned to thee!
    And now, with gleams of half-extinguished thought,
With many recognitions dim and faint,
And somewhat of a sad perplexity,   60
The picture of the mind revives again:
While here I stand, not only with the sense
Of present pleasure, but with pleasing thoughts
That in this moment there is life and food
For future years. And so I dare to hope,
Though changed, no doubt, from what I was when first
I came among these hills; when like a roe
I bounded o'er the mountains, by the sides

Of the deep rivers, and the lonely streams,
Wherever nature led: more like a man   70
Flying from something that he dreads, than one
Who sought the thing he loved. For nature then
(The coarser pleasures of my boyish days,
And their glad animal movements all gone by)
To me was all in all.—I cannot paint
What then I was. The sounding cataract
Haunted me like a passion: the tall rock,
The mountain, and the deep and gloomy wood,
Their colours and their forms, were then to me
An appetite; a feeling and a love,   80
That had no need of a remoter charm,
By thought supplied, nor any interest
Unborrowed from the eye.—That time is past,
And all its aching joys are now no more,
And all its dizzy raptures. Not for this
Faint I, nor mourn nor murmur; other gifts
Have followed; for such loss, I would believe,
Abundant recompense. For I have learned
To look on nature, not as in the hour
Of thoughtless youth; but hearing oftentimes   90
The still, sad music of humanity,
Nor harsh nor grating, though of ample power
To chasten and subdue. And I have felt
A presence that disturbs me with the joy
Of elevated thoughts; a sense sublime
Of something far more deeply interfused,
Whose dwelling is the light of setting suns,
And the round ocean and the living air,
And the blue sky, and in the mind of man;
A motion and a spirit, that impels   100
All thinking things, all objects of all thought,
And rolls through all things. Therefore am I still
A lover of the meadows and the woods,
And mountains; and of all that we behold
From this green earth; of all the mighty world
Of eye, and ear,—both what they half create,

And what perceive; well pleased to recognise
In nature and the language of the sense,
The anchor of my purest thoughts, the nurse,
The guide, the guardian of my heart, and soul   110
Of all my moral being.

                      Nor perchance,
If I were not thus taught, should I the more
Suffer my genial spirits to decay:
For thou art with me here upon the banks
Of this fair river; thou my dearest Friend,
My dear, dear Friend; and in thy voice I catch
The language of my former heart, and read
My former pleasures in the shooting lights
Of thy wild eyes. Oh! yet a little while
May I behold in thee what I was once,   120
My dear, dear Sister! and this prayer I make,
Knowing that Nature never did betray
The heart that loved her; 'tis her privilege,
Through all the years of this our life, to lead
From joy to joy: for she can so inform
The mind that is within us, so impress
With quietness and beauty, and so feed
With lofty thoughts, that neither evil tongues,
Rash judgments, nor the sneers of selfish men,
Nor greetings where no kindness is, nor all   130
The dreary intercourse of daily life,
Shall e'er prevail against us, or disturb
Our cheerful faith, that all which we behold
Is full of blessings. Therefore let the moon
Shine on thee in thy solitary walk;
And let the misty mountain-winds be free
To blow against thee: and, in after years,
When these wild ecstasies shall be matured
Into a sober pleasure; when thy mind
Shall be a mansion for all lovely forms,   140
Thy memory be as a dwelling-place
For all sweet sounds and harmonies; oh! then,
If solitude, or fear, or pain, or grief,

Should be thy portion, with what healing thoughts
Of tender joy wilt thou remember me,
And these my exhortations! Nor, perchance—
If I should be where I no more can hear
Thy voice, nor catch from thy wild eyes these gleams
Of past existence—wilt thou then forget
That on the banks of this delightful stream   150
We stood together; and that I, so long
A worshipper of Nature, hither came
Unwearied in that service; rather say
With warmer love—oh! with far deeper zeal
Of holier love. Nor wilt thou then forget,
That after many wanderings, many years
Of absence, these steep woods and lofty cliffs,
And this green pastoral landscape, were to me
More dear, both for themselves and for thy sake!

THE OLD CUMBERLAND BEGGAR

I saw an aged Beggar in my walk;
And he was seated, by the highway side,
On a low structure of rude masonry
Built at the foot of a huge hill, that they
Who lead their horses down the steep rough road
May thence remount at ease. The aged Man
Had placed his staff across the broad smooth stone
That overlays the pile; and, from a bag
All white with flour, the dole of village dames,
He drew his scraps and fragments, one by one;   10
And scanned them with a fixed and serious look
Of idle computation. In the sun,
Upon the second step of that small pile,
Surrounded by those wild unpeopled hills,
He sat, and ate his food in solitude:
And ever, scattered from his palsied hand,
That, still attempting to prevent the waste,
Was baffled still, the crumbs in little showers

Fell on the ground; and the small mountain birds,
Not venturing yet to peck their destined meal,   20
Approached within the length of half his staff.
    Him from my childhood have I known; and then
He was so old, he seems not older now;
He travels on, a solitary Man,
So helpless in appearance, that for him
The sauntering Horseman throws not with a slack
And careless hand his alms upon the ground,
But stops,—that he may safely lodge the coin
Within the old Man's hat; nor quits him so,
But still, when he has given his horse the rein,   30
Watches the aged Beggar with a look
Sidelong, and half-reverted. She who tends
The toll-gate, when in summer at her door
She turns her wheel, if on the road she sees
The aged beggar coming, quits her work,
And lifts the latch for him that he may pass.
The post-boy, when his rattling wheels o'ertake
The aged Beggar in the woody lane,
Shouts to him from behind; and if, thus warned,
The old man does not change his course, the boy   40
Turns with less noisy wheels to the roadside,
And passes gently by, without a curse
Upon his lips, or anger at his heart.
    He travels on, a solitary Man;
His age has no companion. On the ground
His eyes are turned, and, as he moves along
They move along the ground; and, evermore,
Instead of common and habitual sight
Of fields with rural works, of hill and dale,
And the blue sky, one little span of earth   50
Is all his prospect. Thus, from day to day,
Bow-bent, his eyes for ever on the ground,
He plies his weary journey; seeing still,
And seldom knowing that he sees, some straw,
Some scattered leaf, or marks which, in one track,
The nails of cart or chariot-wheel have left
Impressed on the white road,—in the same line,

At distance still the same. Poor Traveller!
His staff trails with him; scarcely do his feet
Disturb the summer dust; he is so still   60
In look and motion, that the cottage curs,
Ere he has passed the door, will turn away,
Weary of barking at him. Boys and girls,
The vacant and the busy, maids and youths,
And urchins newly breeched—all pass him by:
Him even the slow-paced waggon leaves behind.
　　　But deem not this Man useless.—Statesmen! ye
Who are so restless in your wisdom, ye
Who have a broom still ready in your hands
To rid the world of nuisances; ye proud,   70
Heart-swoln, while in your pride ye contemplate
Your talents, power, or wisdom, deem him not
A burthen of the earth! 'Tis Nature's law
That none, the meanest of created things,
Or forms created the most vile and brute,
The dullest or most noxious, should exist
Divorced from good—a spirit and pulse of good.
A life and soul, to every mode of being
Inseparably linked. Then be assured
That least of all can aught—that ever owned   80
The heaven-regarding eye and front sublime
Which man is born to—sink, howe'er depressed,
So low as to be scorned without a sin;
Without offence to God cast out of view;
Like the dry remnant of a garden-flower
Whose seeds are shed, or as an implement
Worn out and worthless. While from door to door,
This old Man creeps, the villagers in him
Behold a record which together binds
Past deeds and offices of charity,   90
Else unremembered, and so keeps alive
The kindly mood in hearts which lapse of years,
And that half-wisdom half-experience gives,
Make slow to feel, and by sure steps resign
To selfishness and cold oblivious cares.
Among the farms and solitary huts,

Hamlets and thinly-scattered villages,
Where'er the aged Beggar takes his rounds,
The mild necessity of use compels
To acts of love; and habit does the work   100
Of reason; yet prepares that after-joy
Which reason cherishes. And thus the soul,
By that sweet taste of pleasure unpursued,
Doth find herself insensibly disposed
To virtue and true goodness.
                                        Some there are,
By their good works exalted, lofty minds
And meditative, authors of delight
And happiness, which to the end of time
Will live, and spread, and kindle: even such minds
In childhood, from this solitary Being,   110
Or from like wanderer, haply have received
(A thing more precious far than all that books
Or the solicitudes of love can do!)
That first mild touch of sympathy and thought,
In which they found their kindred with a world
Where want and sorrow were. The easy man
Who sits at his own door,—and, like the pear
That overhangs his head from the green wall,
Feeds in the sunshine; the robust and young,
The prosperous and unthinking, they who live   120
Sheltered, and flourish in a little grove
Of their own kindred;—all behold in him
A silent monitor, which on their minds
Must needs impress a transitory thought
Of self-congratulation, to the heart
Of each recalling his peculiar boons,
His charters and exemptions; and, perchance,
Though he to no one give the fortitude
And circumspection needful to preserve
His present blessings, and to husband up   130
The respite of the season, he, at least,
And 'tis no vulgar service, makes them felt.
    Yet further.—Many, I believe, there are

Who live a life of virtuous decency,
Men who can hear the Decalogue and feel
No self-reproach; who of the moral law
Established in the land where they abide
Are strict observers; and not negligent
In acts of love to those with whom they dwell,
Their kindred, and the children of their blood.   140
Praise be to such, and to their slumbers peace!
—But of the poor man, ask the abject poor;
Go, and demand of him, if there be here
In this cold abstinence from evil deeds,
And these inevitable charities,
Wherewith to satisfy the human soul?
No—man is dear to man; the poorest poor
Long for some moments in a weary life
When they can know and feel that they have been,
Themselves, the fathers and the dealers-out   150
Of some small blessings; have been kind to such
As needed kindness, for this single cause,
That we have all of us one human heart.
—Such pleasure is to one kind Being known,
My neighbour, when with punctual care, each week
Duly as Friday comes, though pressed herself
By her own wants, she from her store of meal
Takes one unsparing handful for the scrip
Of this old Mendicant, and, from her door
Returning with exhilarated heart,
Sits by her fire, and builds her hope in heaven.   160
      Then let him pass, a blessing on his head!
And while in that vast solitude to which
The tide of things has borne him, he appears
To breathe and live but for himself alone,
Unblamed, uninjured, let him bear about
The good which the benignant law of Heaven
Has hung around him: and, while life is his,
Still let him prompt the unlettered villagers
To tender offices and pensive thoughts.   170
—Then let him pass, a blessing on his head!

And, long as he can wander, let him breathe
The freshness of the valleys; let his blood
Struggle with frosty air and winter snows;
And let the chartered wind that sweeps the heath
Beat his grey locks against his withered face.
Reverence the hope whose vital anxiousness
Gives the last human interest to his heart.
May never HOUSE, misnamed of INDUSTRY,
Make him a captive!—for that pent-up din,   180
Those life-consuming sounds that clog the air,
Be his the natural silence of old age!
Let him be free of mountain solitudes;
And have around him, whether heard or not,
The pleasant melody of woodland birds.
Few are his pleasures: if his eyes have now
Been doomed so long to settle upon earth
That not without some effort they behold
The countenance of the horizontal sun,
Rising or setting, let the light at least   190
Find a free entrance to their languid orbs.
And let him, *where* and *when* he will, sit down
Beneath the trees, or on a grassy bank
Of highway side, and with the little birds
Share his chance-gathered meal; and, finally,
As in the eye of Nature he has lived,
So in the eye of Nature let him die!

ANIMAL TRANQUILLITY AND DECAY

                                    The little hedgerow birds,
That peck along the roads, regard him not.
He travels on, and in his face, his step,
His gait, is one expression: every limb,
His look and bending figure, all bespeak
A man who does not move with pain, but moves
With thought.—He is insensibly subdued
To settled quiet: he is one by whom
All effort seems forgotten; one to whom

Long patience hath such mild composure given,
That patience now doth seem a thing of which
He hath no need. He is by nature led
To peace so perfect that the young behold
With envy, what the Old Man hardly feels.

PETER BELL

A TALE
What's in a Name?

· ·

Brutus will start a Spirit as soon as Cæsar!

PROLOGUE

There's something in a flying horse,
There's something in a huge balloon;
But through the clouds I 'll never float
Until I have a little Boat,
Shaped like the crescent-moon.

And now I *have* a little Boat,
In shape a very crescent-moon:
Fast through the clouds my boat can sail;
But if perchance your faith should fail,
Look up—and you shall see me soon!   10

The woods, my Friends, are round you roaring,
Rocking and roaring like a sea;
The noise of danger's in your ears,
And ye have all a thousand fears
Both for my little Boat and me!

Meanwhile untroubled I admire
The pointed horns of my canoe;
And, did not pity touch my breast,
To see how ye are all distrest,
Till my ribs ached, I 'd laugh at you!   20

Away we go, my Boat and I—
Frail man ne'er sate in such another;
Whether among the winds we strive,
Or deep into the clouds we dive,
Each is contented with the other.

Away we go—and what care we
For treasons, tumults, and for wars?
We are as calm in our delight
As is the crescent-moon so bright
Among the scattered stars.   30

Up goes my Boat among the stars
Through many a breathless field of light,
Through many a long blue field of ether,
Leaving ten thousand stars beneath her:
Up goes my little Boat so bright!

The Crab, the Scorpion, and the Bull—
We pry among them all; have shot
High o'er the red-haired race of Mars,
Covered from top to toe with scars;
Such company I like it not!   40

The towns in Saturn are decayed,
And melancholy Spectres throng them;—
The Pleiads, that appear to kiss
Each other in the vast abyss,
With joy I sail among them.

Swift Mercury resounds with mirth,
Great Jove is full of stately bowers;
But these, and all that they contain,
What are they to that tiny grain,
That little Earth of ours?   50

Then back to Earth, the dear green Earth:—
Whole ages if I here should roam,
The world for my remarks and me
Would not a whit the better be;
I 've left my heart at home.

See! there she is, the matchless Earth!
There spreads the famed Pacific Ocean!
Old Andes thrust yon craggy spear
Through the grey clouds; the Alps are here,
Like waters in commotion;   60

Yon tawny slip is Libya's sands;
That silver thread the river Dnieper!
And look, where clothed in brightest green
Is a sweet Isle, of isles the Queen;
Ye fairies, from all evil keep her!

And see the town where I was born!
Around those happy fields we span
In boyish gambols;—I was lost
Where I have been, but on this coast
I feel I am a man.   70

Never did fifty things at once
Appear so lovely, never, never;—
How tunefully the forests ring!
To hear the earth's soft murmuring
Thus could I hang for ever!

"Shame on you!" cried my little Boat,
"Was ever such a homesick Loon,
Within a living Boat to sit,
And make no better use of it;
A Boat twin-sister of the crescent-moon!   80

"Ne'er in the breast of full-grown Poet
Fluttered so faint a heart before;—
Was it the music of the spheres
That overpowered your mortal ears?
—Such din shall trouble them no more.

"These nether precincts do not lack
Charms of their own;—then come with me;
I want a comrade, and for you
There's nothing that I would not do;
Nought is there that you shall not see.   90

"Haste! and above Siberian snows
We 'll sport amid the boreal morning;
Will mingle with her lustres gliding
Among the stars, the stars now hiding,
And now the stars adorning.

"I know the secrets of a land
Where human foot did never stray;
Fair is that land as evening skies,
And cool, though in the depth it lies
Of burning Africa.   100

"Or we'll into the realm of Faery,
Among the lovely shades of things;
The shadowy forms of mountains bare,
And streams, and bowers, and ladies fair,
The shades of palaces and kings!

"Or, if you thirst with hardy zeal
Less quiet regions to explore,
Prompt voyage shall to you reveal
How earth and heaven are taught to feel
The might of magic lore!"   110

"My little vagrant Form of light,
My gay and beautiful Canoe,
Well have you played your friendly part;
As kindly take what from my heart
Experience forces—then adieu!

"Temptation lurks among your words;
But, while these pleasures you're pursuing
Without impediment or let,
No wonder if you quite forget
What on the earth is doing.   120

"There was a time when all mankind
Did listen with a faith sincere
To tuneful tongues in mystery versed;
Then Poets fearlessly rehearsed
The wonders of a wild career.

"Go—(but the world's a sleepy world,
And 'tis, I fear, an age too late)
Take with you some ambitious Youth!
For, restless Wanderer! I, in truth,
Am all unfit to be your mate.   130

"Long have I loved what I behold,
The night that calms, the day that cheers;
The common growth of mother-earth
Suffices me—her tears, her mirth,
Her humblest mirth and tears.

"The dragon's wing, the magic ring,
I shall not covet for my dower,
If I along that lowly way
With sympathetic heart may stray,
And with a soul of power.   140

"These given, what more need I desire
To stir, to soothe, or elevate?
What nobler marvels than the mind
May in life's daily prospect find,
May find or there create?

"A potent wand doth Sorrow wield;
What spell so strong as guilty Fear!
Repentance is a tender Sprite;
If aught on earth have heavenly might,
'Tis lodged within her silent tear.   150

"But grant my wishes,—let us now
Descend from this ethereal height;
Then take thy way, adventurous Skiff,
More daring far than Hippogriff,
And be thy own delight!

"To the stone-table in my garden,
Loved haunt of many a summer hour,
The Squire is come: his daughter Bess
Beside him in the cool recess
Sits blooming like a flower.   160

"With these are many more convened;
They know not I have been so far;—
I see them there, in number nine,
Beneath the spreading Weymouth-pine!
I see them—there they are!

"There sits the Vicar and his Dame;
And there my good friend, Stephen Otter;
And, ere the light of evening fail,
To them I must relate the Tale
Of Peter Bell the Potter." 170

Off flew the Boat—away she flees,
Spurning her freight with indignation!
And I, as well as I was able,
On two poor legs, toward my stone-table
Limped on with sore vexation.

"O, here he is!" cried little Bess—
She saw me at the garden-door;
"We've waited anxiously and long,"
They cried, and all around me throng,
Full nine of them or more! 180

"Reproach me not—your fears be still—
Be thankful we again have met:—
Resume, my Friends! within the shade
Your seats, and quickly shall be paid
The well-remembered debt."

I spake with faltering voice, like one
Not wholly rescued from the pale
Of a wild dream, or worse illusion;
But, straight, to cover my confusion,
Began the promised Tale. 190

PART FIRST

All by the moonlight river side
Groaned the poor Beast—alas! in vain;
The staff was raised to loftier height,
And the blows fell with heavier weight
As Peter struck—and struck again.

"Hold!" cried the Squire, "against the rules
Of common sense you're surely sinning;
This leap is for us all too bold;
Who Peter was, let that be told,
And start from the beginning."   10

——"A Potter, Sir, he was by trade,"
Said I, becoming quite collected;
"And wheresoever he appeared,
Full twenty times was Peter feared
For once that Peter was respected.

"He, two-and-thirty years or more,
Had been a wild and woodland rover;
Had heard the Atlantic surges roar
On farthest Cornwall's rocky shore,
And trod the cliffs of Dover.   20

"And he had seen Caernarvon's towers,
And well he knew the spire of Sarum;
And he had been where Lincoln bell
Flings o'er the fen that ponderous knell—
A far-renowned alarum!

"At Doncaster, at York, and Leeds,
And merry Carlisle had he been;
And all along the Lowlands fair,
All through the bonnie shire of Ayr
And far as Aberdeen.   30

"And he had been at Inverness;
And Peter, by the mountain-rills,
Had danced his round with Highland lasses;
And he had lain beside his asses
On lofty Cheviot Hills:

"And he had trudged through Yorkshire dales,
Among the rocks and winding *scars;*
Where deep and low the hamlets lie
Beneath their little patch of sky
And little lot of stars: 40

"And all along the indented coast,
Bespattered with the salt-sea foam;
Where'er a knot of houses lay
On headland, or in hollow bay;—
Sure never man like him did roam!

"As well might Peter, in the Fleet,
Have been fast bound, a begging debtor;—
He travelled here, he travelled there;—
But not the value of a hair
Was heart or head the better.   50

"He roved among the vales and streams,
In the green wood and hollow dell;
They were his dwellings night and day,—
But nature ne'er could find the way
Into the heart of Peter Bell.

"In vain, through every changeful year,
Did Nature lead him as before;
A primrose by a river's brim
A yellow primrose was to him,
And it was nothing more.   60

"Small change it made on Peter's heart
To see his gentle panniered train
With more than vernal pleasure feeding,
Where'er the tender grass was leading
Its earliest green along the lane.

"In vain, through water, earth, and air,
The soul of happy sound was spread,
When Peter on some April morn,
Beneath the broom or budding thorn,
Made the warm earth his lazy bed.   70

"At noon, when, by the forest's edge
He lay beneath the branches high,
The soft blue sky did never melt
Into his heart; he never felt
The witchery of the soft blue sky!

"On a fair prospect some have looked
And felt, as I have heard them say,
As if the moving time had been
A thing as steadfast as the scene
On which they gazed themselves away.   80

"Within the breast of Peter Bell
These silent raptures found no place;
He was a Carl as wild and rude
As ever hue-and-cry pursued,
As ever ran a felon's race.

"Of all that lead a lawless life,
Of all that love their lawless lives,
In city or in village small,
He was the wildest far of all;—
He had a dozen wedded wives.   90

"Nay, start not!—wedded wives—and twelve!
But how one wife could e'er come near him,
In simple truth I cannot tell;
For, be it said of Peter Bell,
To see him was to fear him.

"Though Nature could not touch his heart
By lovely forms, and silent weather,
And tender sounds, yet you might see
At once, that Peter Bell and she
Had often been together.   100

"A savage wildness round him hung
As of a dweller out of doors;
In his whole figure and his mien
A savage character was seen
Of mountains and of dreary moors.

"To all the unshaped half-human thoughts
Which solitary Nature feeds
'Mid summer storms or winter's ice,
Had Peter joined whatever vice
The cruel city breeds.   110

"His face was keen as is the wind
That cuts along the hawthorn-fence;—
Of courage you saw little there,
But, in its stead, a medley air
Of cunning and of impudence.

"He had a dark and sidelong walk,
And long and slouching was his gait;
Beneath his looks so bare and bold,
You might perceive, his spirit cold
Was playing with some inward bait.   120

"His forehead wrinkled was and furred;
A work, one half of which was done
By thinking of his *'whens'* and *'hows;'*
And half, by knitting of his brows
Beneath the glaring sun.

"There was a hardness in his cheek,
There was a hardness in his eye,
As if the man had fixed his face,
In many a solitary place,
Against the wind and open sky!"   130

―――――――――

One night, (and now my little Bess!
We 've reached at last the promised Tale:)
One beautiful November night,
When the full moon was shining bright
Upon the rapid river Swale,

Along the river's winding banks
Peter was travelling all alone;—
Whether to buy or sell, or led
By pleasure running in his head,
To me was never known.   140

He trudged along through copse and brake,
He trudged along o'er hill and dale;
Nor for the moon cared he a tittle,
And for the stars he cared as little,
And for the murmuring river Swale.

But, chancing to espy a path
That promised to cut short the way,
As many a wiser man hath done,
He left a trusty guide for one
That might his steps betray.   150

To a thick wood he soon is brought
Where cheerily his course he weaves,
And whistling loud may yet be heard,
Though often buried, like a bird
Darkling, among the boughs and leaves.

But quickly Peter's mood is changed,
And on he drives with cheeks that burn
In downright fury and in wrath;—
There's little sign the treacherous path
Will to the road return!   160

The path grows dim, and dimmer still;
Now up, now down, the Rover wends,
With all the sail that he can carry,
Till brought to a deserted quarry—
And there the pathway ends.

He paused—for shadows of strange shape,
Massy and black, before him lay;
But through the dark, and through the cold,
And through the yawning fissures old,
Did Peter boldly press his way   170

Right through the quarry;—and behold
A scene of soft and lovely hue!
Where blue and grey, and tender green,
Together make as sweet a scene
As ever human eye did view.

Beneath the clear blue sky he saw
A little field of meadow ground;
But field or meadow name it not;
Call it of earth a small green plot,
With rocks encompassed round.   180

The Swale flowed under the grey rocks,
But he flowed quiet and unseen;—
You need a strong and stormy gale
To bring the noises of the Swale
To that green spot, so calm and green!

And is there no one dwelling here,
No hermit with his beads and glass?
And does no little cottage look
Upon this soft and fertile nook?
Does no one live near this green grass?   190

Across the deep and quiet spot
Is Peter driving through the grass—
And now has reached the skirting trees;
When, turning round his head, he sees
A solitary Ass.

"A Prize!" cries Peter—but he first
Must spy about him far and near;
There's not a single house in sight,
No woodman's hut, no cottage light—
Peter, you need not fear!   200

There's nothing to be seen but woods,
And rocks that spread a hoary gleam,
And this one Beast, that from the bed
Of the green meadow hangs his head
Over the silent stream.

His head is with a halter bound;
The halter seizing, Peter leapt
Upon the Creature's back, and plied
With ready heels his shaggy side;
But still the Ass his station kept.   210

Then Peter gave a sudden jerk,
A jerk that from a dungeon-floor
Would have pulled up an iron ring;
But still the heavy-headed Thing
Stood just as he had stood before!

Quoth Peter, leaping from his seat,
"There is some plot against me laid;"
Once more the little meadow-ground
And all the hoary cliffs around
He cautiously surveyed.   220

All, all is silent—rocks and woods,
All still and silent—far and near!
Only the Ass, with motion dull,
Upon the pivot of his skull
Turns round his long left ear.

Thought Peter, What can mean all this?
Some ugly witchcraft must be here!
—Once more the Ass, with motion dull,
Upon the pivot of his skull
Turned round his long left ear.   230

Suspicion ripened into dread;
Yet with deliberate action slow,
His staff high-raising, in the pride
Of skill, upon the sounding hide,
He dealt a sturdy blow.

The poor Ass staggered with the shock;
And then, as if to take his ease,
In quiet uncomplaining mood,
Upon the spot where he had stood,
Dropped gently down upon his knees: 240

As gently on his side he fell;
And by the river's brink did lie;
And, while he lay like one that mourned,
The patient Beast on Peter turned
His shining hazel eye.

'Twas but one mild, reproachful look,
A look more tender than severe;
And straight in sorrow, not in dread,
He turned the eye-ball in his head
Towards the smooth river deep and clear.   250

Upon the Beast the sapling rings;
His lank sides heaved, his limbs they stirred;
He gave a groan, and then another,
Of that which went before the brother,
And then he gave a third.

All by the moonlight river side
He gave three miserable groans;
And not till now hath Peter seen
How gaunt the Creature is,—how lean
And sharp his staring bones!   260

With legs stretched out and stiff he lay:—
No word of kind commiseration
Fell at the sight from Peter's tongue;
With hard contempt his heart was wrung,
With hatred and vexation.

The meagre beast lay still as death;
And Peter's lips with fury quiver;
Quoth he, "You little mulish dog,
I'll fling your carcase like a log
Head-foremost down the river!"   270

An impious oath confirmed the threat—
Whereat from the earth on which he lay
To all the echoes, south and north,
And east and west, the Ass sent forth
A long and clamorous bray!

This outcry, on the heart of Peter,
Seems like a note of joy to strike,—
Joy at the heart of Peter knocks;
But in the echo of the rocks
Was something Peter did not like.   280

Whether to cheer his coward breast,
Or that he could not break the chain,
In this serene and solemn hour,
Twined round him by demoniac power,
To the blind work he turned again.

Among the rocks and winding crags;
Among the mountains far away;
Once more the Ass did lengthen out
More ruefully a deep-drawn shout,
The hard dry see-saw of his horrible bray!   290

What is there now in Peter's heart?
Or whence the might of this strange sound?
The moon uneasy looked and dimmer,
The broad blue heavens appeared to glimmer,
And the rocks staggered all around—

From Peter's hand the sapling dropped!
Threat has he none to execute;
"If any one should come and see
That I am here, they'll think," quoth he,
"I 'm helping this poor dying brute."   300

He scans the Ass from limb to limb,
And ventures now to uplift his eyes;
More steady looks the moon, and clear,
More like themselves the rocks appear
And touch more quiet skies.

His scorn returns—his hate revives;
He stoops the Ass's neck to seize
With malice—that again takes flight;
For in the pool a startling sight
Meets him, among the inverted trees.   310

Is it the moon's distorted face?
The ghost-like image of a cloud?
Is it a gallows there portrayed?
Is Peter of himself afraid?
Is it a coffin,—or a shroud?

A grisly idol hewn in stone?
Or imp from witch's lap let fall?
Perhaps a ring of shining fairies?
Such as pursue their feared vagaries
In sylvan bower or haunted hall?   320

Is it a fiend that to a stake
Of fire his desperate self is tethering?
Or stubborn spirit doomed to yell
In solitary ward or cell,
Ten thousand miles from all his brethren?

Never did pulse so quickly throb,
And never heart so loudly panted;
He looks, he cannot choose but look;
Like some one reading in a book—
A book that is enchanted.   330

Ah, well-a-day for Peter Bell!
He will be turned to iron soon,
Meet Statue for the court of Fear!
His hat is up—and every hair
Bristles, and whitens in the moon!

He looks, he ponders, looks again;
He sees a motion—hears a groan;
His eyes will burst—his heart will break—
He gives a loud and frightful shriek,
And back he falls, as if his life were flown!   340

PART SECOND

We left our Hero in a trance,
Beneath the alders, near the river;
The Ass is by the river-side,
And, where the feeble breezes glide,
Upon the stream the moonbeams quiver.

A happy respite! but at length
He feels the glimmering of the moon;
Wakes with glazed eye, and feebly sighing—
To sink, perhaps, where he is lying,
Into a second swoon!   10

He lifts his head, he sees his staff;
He touches—'tis to him a treasure!
Faint recollection seems to tell
That he is yet where mortals dwell—
A thought received with languid pleasure!

His head upon his elbow propped,
Becoming less and less perplexed,
Sky-ward he looks—to rock and wood—
And then—upon the glassy flood
His wandering eye is fixed.   20

Thought he, that is the face of one
In his last sleep securely bound!
So toward the stream his head he bent,
And downward thrust his staff, intent
The river's depth to sound.

Now—like a tempest-shattered bark,
That overwhelmed and prostrate lies,
And in a moment to the verge
Is lifted of a foaming surge—
Full suddenly the Ass doth rise!   30

His staring bones all shake with joy,
And close by Peter's side he stands:
While Peter o'er the river bends,
The little Ass his neck extends,
And fondly licks his hands.

Such life is in the Ass's eyes,
Such life is in his limbs and ears;
That Peter Bell, if he had been
The veriest coward ever seen,
Must now have thrown aside his fears.   40

The Ass looks on—and to his work
Is Peter quietly resigned;
He touches here—he touches there—
And now among the dead man's hair
His sapling Peter has entwined.

He pulls—and looks—and pulls again;
And he whom the poor Ass had lost,
The man who had been four days dead,
Head-foremost from the river's bed
Uprises like a ghost!   50

And Peter draws him to dry land;
And through the brain of Peter pass
Some poignant twitches, fast and faster;
"No doubt," quoth he, "he is the Master
Of this poor miserable Ass!"

The meagre Shadow that looks on—
What would he now? what is he doing?
His sudden fit of joy is flown,—
He on his knees hath laid him down,
As if he were his grief renewing;   60

But no—that Peter on his back
Must mount, he shows well as he can:
Thought Peter then, come weal or woe,
I 'll do what he would have me do,
In pity to this poor drowned man.

With that resolve he boldly mounts
Upon the pleased and thankful Ass;
And then, without a moment's stay,
That earnest Creature turned away
Leaving the body on the grass.   70

Intent upon his faithful watch,
The Beast four days and nights had past;
A sweeter meadow ne'er was seen,
And there the Ass four days had been,
Nor ever once did break his fast:

Yet firm his step, and stout his heart;
The mead is crossed—the quarry's mouth
Is reached; but there the trusty guide
Into a thicket turns aside,
And deftly ambles towards the south.   80

When hark a burst of doleful sound!
And Peter honestly might say,
The like came never to his ears,
Though he has been, full thirty years,
A rover—night and day!

'Tis not a plover of the moors,
'Tis not a bittern of the fen;
Nor can it be a barking fox,
Nor night-bird chambered in the rocks,
Nor wild-cat in a woody glen!   90

The Ass is startled—and stops short
Right in the middle of the thicket;
And Peter, wont to whistle loud
Whether alone or in a crowd,
Is silent as a silent cricket.

What ails you now, my little Bess?
Well may you tremble and look grave!
This cry—that rings along the wood,
This cry—that floats adown the flood,
Comes from the entrance of a cave: 100

I see a blooming Wood-boy there,
And if I had the power to say
How sorrowful the wanderer is,
Your heart would be as sad as his
Till you had kissed his tears away!

Grasping a hawthorn branch in hand,
All bright with berries ripe and red,
Into the cavern's mouth he peeps;
Thence back into the moonlight creeps;
Whom seeks he—whom?—the silent dead: 110

His father!—Him doth he require—
Him hath he sought with fruitless pains,
Among the rocks, behind the trees;
Now creeping on his hands and knees,
Now running o'er the open plains.

And hither is he come at last,
When he through such a day has gone,
By this dark cave to be distrest
Like a poor bird—her plundered nest
Hovering around with dolorous moan!   120

Of that intense and piercing cry
The listening Ass conjectures well;
Wild as it is, he there can read
Some intermingled notes that plead
With touches irresistible.

But Peter—when he saw the Ass
Not only stop, but turn, and change
The cherished tenor of his pace
That lamentable cry to chase—
It wrought in him conviction strange; 130

A faith that, for the dead man's sake
And this poor slave who loved him well,
Vengeance upon his head will fall,
Some visitation worse than all
Which ever till this night befell.

Meanwhile the Ass to reach his home,
Is striving stoutly as he may;
But, while he climbs the woody hill,
The cry grows weak—and weaker still;
And now at last it dies away. 140

So with his fright the Creature turns
Into a gloomy grove of beech,
Along the shade with footsteps true
Descending slowly, till the two
The open moonlight reach.

And there, along the narrow dell,
A fair smooth pathway you discern,
A length of green and open road—
As if it from a fountain flowed—
Winding away between the fern. 150

The rocks that tower on either side
Build up a wild fantastic scene;
Temples like those among the Hindoos,
And mosques, and spires, and abbey windows,
And castles all with ivy green!

And, while the Ass pursues his way,
Along this solitary dell,
As pensively his steps advance,
The mosques and spires change countenance
And look at Peter Bell!   160

That unintelligible cry
Hath left him high in preparation,—
Convinced that he, or soon or late,
This very night will meet his fate—
And so he sits in expectation!

The strenuous Animal hath clomb
With the green path; and now he wends
Where, shining like the smoothest sea,
In undisturbed immensity
A level plain extends.   170

But whence this faintly-rustling sound
By which the journeying pair are chased?
—A withered leaf is close behind,
Light plaything for the sportive wind
Upon that solitary waste.

When Peter spied the moving thing,
It only doubled his distress;
"Where there is not a bush or tree,
The very leaves they follow me—
So huge hath been my wickedness!"   180

To a close lane they now are come,
Where, as before, the enduring Ass
Moves on without a moment's stop,
Nor once turns round his head to crop
A bramble-leaf or blade of grass.

Between the hedges as they go,
The white dust sleeps upon the lane;
And Peter, ever and anon
Back-looking, sees, upon a stone,
Or in the dust, a crimson stain.   190

A stain—as of a drop of blood
By moonlight made more faint and wan:
Ha! why these sinkings of despair?
He knows not how the blood comes there—
And Peter is a wicked man.

At length he spies a bleeding wound,
Where he had struck the Ass's head;
He sees the blood, knows what it is,—
A glimpse of sudden joy was his,
But then it quickly fled;   200

Of him whom sudden death had seized
He thought,—of thee, O faithful Ass!
And once again those ghastly pains,
Shoot to and fro through heart and reins,
And through his brain like lightning pass.

PART THIRD

I've heard of one, a gentle Soul,
Though given to sadness and to gloom,
And for the fact will vouch,—one night
It chanced that by a taper's light
This man was reading in his room;

Bending, as you or I might bend
At night o'er any pious book,
When sudden blackness overspread
The snow-white page on which he read,
And made the good man round him look.   10

The chamber walls were dark all round,—
And to his book he turned again;
—The light had left the lonely taper,
And formed itself upon the paper
Into large letters—bright and plain!

The godly book was in his hand—
And, on the page, more black than coal,
Appeared, set forth in strange array,
A *word*—which to his dying day
Perplexed the good man's gentle soul.   20

The ghostly word, thus plainly seen,
Did never from his lips depart;
But he hath said, poor gentle wight!
It brought full many a sin to light
Out of the bottom of his heart.

Dread Spirits! to confound the meek
Why wander from your course so far,
Disordering colour, form, and stature!
—Let good men feel the soul of nature,
And see things as they are.   30

Yet, potent Spirits! well I know,
How ye, that play with soul and sense,
Are not unused to trouble friends
Of goodness, for most gracious ends—
And this I speak in reverence!

But might I give advice to you,
Whom in my fear I love so well;
From men of pensive virtue go,
Dread Beings! and your empire show
On hearts like that of Peter Bell.   40

Your presence often have I felt
In darkness and the stormy night;
And, with like force, if need there be,
Ye can put forth your agency
When earth is calm, and heaven is bright.

Then, coming from the wayward world,
That powerful world in which ye dwell,
Come, Spirits of the Mind! and try
To-night, beneath the moonlight sky,
What may be done with Peter Bell!   50

—O, would that some more skilful voice
My further labour might prevent!
Kind Listeners, that around me sit,
I feel that I am all unfit
For such high argument.

I've played, I've danced, with my narration;
I loitered long ere I began:
Ye waited then on my good pleasure;
Pour out indulgence still, in measure
As liberal as ye can!   60

Our Travellers, ye remember well,
Are thridding a sequestered lane;
And Peter many tricks is trying,
And many anodynes applying,
To ease his conscience of its pain.

By this his heart is lighter far;
And, finding that he can account
So snugly for that crimson stain,
His evil spirit up again
Does like an empty bucket mount.   70

And Peter is a deep logician
Who hath no lack of wit mercurial;
"Blood drops—leaves rustle—yet," quoth he,
"This poor man never, but for me,
Could have had Christian burial.

"And, say the best you can, 'tis plain,
That here has been some wicked dealing;
No doubt the devil in me wrought;
I'm not the man who could have thought
An Ass like this was worth the stealing!"   80

So from his pocket Peter takes
His shining horn tobacco-box;
And, in a light and careless way,
As men who with their purpose play,
Upon the lid he knocks.

Let them whose voice can stop the clouds,
Whose cunning eye can see the wind,
Tell to a curious world the cause
Why, making here a sudden pause,
The Ass turned round his head, and *grinned*.   90

Appalling process! I have marked
The like on heath, in lonely wood;
And, verily, have seldom met
A spectacle more hideous—yet
It suited Peter's present mood.

And, grinning in his turn, his teeth
He in jocose defiance showed—
When, to upset his spiteful mirth,
A murmur, pent within the earth,
In the dead earth beneath the road   100

Rolled audibly! it swept along,
A muffled noise—a rumbling sound!—
'T was by a troop of miners made,
Plying with gunpowder their trade,
Some twenty fathoms under ground.

Small cause of dire effect! for, surely,
If ever mortal, King or Cotter,
Believed that earth was charged to quake
And yawn for his unworthy sake,
'Twas Peter Bell the Potter.   110

But, as an oak in breathless air
Will stand though to the centre hewn;
Or as the weakest things, if frost
Have stiffened them, maintain their post;
So he, beneath the gazing moon!—

The Beast bestriding thus, he reached
A spot where, in a sheltering cove,
A little chapel stands alone,
With greenest ivy overgrown,
And tufted with an ivy grove;   120

Dying insensibly away
From human thoughts and purposes,
It seemed—wall, window, roof and tower
To bow to some transforming power,
And blend with the surrounding trees.

As ruinous a place it was,
Thought Peter, in the shire of Fife
That served my turn, when following still
From land to land a reckless will
I married my sixth wife!   130

The unheeding Ass moves slowly on,
And now is passing by an inn
Brim-full of a carousing crew,
That make, with curses not a few,
An uproar and a drunken din.

I cannot well express the thoughts
Which Peter in those noises found;—
A stifling power compressed his frame,
While-as a swimming darkness came
Over that dull and dreary sound.   140

For well did Peter know the sound;
The language of those drunken joys
To him, a jovial soul, I ween,
But a few hours ago, had been
A gladsome and a welcome noise.

Now, turned adrift into the past,
He finds no solace in his course;
Like planet-stricken men of yore,
He trembles, smitten to the core
By strong compunction and remorse.   150

But, more than all, his heart is stung
To think of one, almost a child;
A sweet and playful Highland girl,
As light and beauteous as a squirrel,
As beauteous and as wild!

Her dwelling was a lonely house,
A cottage in a healthy dell;
And she put on her gown of green,
And left her mother at sixteen,
And followed Peter Bell.   160

But many good and pious thoughts
Had she; and, in the kirk to pray,
Two long Scotch miles, through rain or snow
To kirk she had been used to go,
Twice every Sabbath-day.

And, when she followed Peter Bell,
It was to lead an honest life;
For he, with tongue not used to falter,
Had pledged his troth before the altar
To love her as his wedded wife.   170

A mother's hope is hers;—but soon
She drooped and pined like one forlorn,
From Scripture she a name did borrow;
Benoni, or the child of sorrow,
She called her babe unborn.

For she had learned how Peter lived,
And took it in most grievous part;
She to the very bone was worn,
And, ere that little child was born,
Died of a broken heart.   180

And now the Spirits of the Mind
Are busy with poor Peter Bell;
Upon the rights of visual sense
Usurping, with a prevalence
More terrible than magic spell.

Close by a brake of flowering furze
(Above it shivering aspens play)
He sees an unsubstantial creature,
His very self in form and feature,
Not four yards from the broad highway: 190

And stretched beneath the furze he sees
The Highland girl—it is no other;
And hears her crying as she cried,
The very moment that she died,
"My mother! oh my mother!"

The sweat pours down from Peter's face,
So grievous is his heart's contrition;
With agony his eye-balls ache
While he beholds by the furze-brake
This miserable vision!   200

Calm is the well-deserving brute,
His peace hath no offence betrayed;
But now, while down that slope he wends,
A voice to Peter's ear ascends,
Resounding from the woody glade:

The voice, though clamorous as a horn
Re-echoed by a naked rock,
Comes from that tabernacle—List!
Within, a fervent Methodist
Is preaching to no heedless flock!   210

"Repent! repent!" he cries aloud,
"While yet ye may find mercy;—strive
To love the Lord with all your might;
Turn to him, seek him day and night,
And save your souls alive!

"Repent! repent! though ye have gone,
Through paths of wickedness and woe,
After the Babylonian harlot;
And, though your sins be red as scarlet,
They shall be white as snow!"   220

Even as he passed the door, these words
Did plainly come to Peter's ears;
And they such joyful tidings were,
The joy was more than he could bear!—
He melted into tears.

Sweet tears of hope and tenderness!
And fast they fell, a plenteous shower!
His nerves, his sinews seemed to melt;
Through all his iron frame was felt
A gentle, a relaxing, power!   230

Each fibre of his frame was weak;
Weak all the animal within;
But, in its helplessness, grew mild
And gentle as an infant child,
An infant that has known no sin.

'Tis said, meek Beast! that, through Heaven's grace,
He not unmoved did notice now
The cross upon thy shoulder scored,
For lasting impress, by the Lord
To whom all human-kind shall bow;   240

Memorial of his touch—that day
When Jesus humbly deigned to ride,
Entering the proud Jerusalem,
By an immeasurable stream
Of shouting people deified!

Meanwhile the persevering Ass
Turned towards a gate that hung in view
Across a shady lane; his chest
Against the yielding gate he pressed
And quietly passed through.   250

And up the stony lane he goes;
No ghost more softly ever trod;
Among the stones and pebbles, he
Sets down his hoofs inaudibly,
As if with felt his hoofs were shod.

Along the lane the trusty Ass
Went twice two hundred yards or more,
And no one could have guessed his aim,—
Till to a lonely house he came,
And stopped beside the door.   260

Thought Peter, 'tis the poor man's home!
He listens—not a sound is heard
Save from the trickling household rill;
But, stepping o'er the cottage-sill,
Forthwith a little Girl appeared.

She to the Meeting-house was bound
In hopes some tidings there to gather:
No glimpse it is, no doubtful gleam;
She saw—and uttered with a scream,
"My father! here's my father!"   270

The very word was plainly heard,
Heard plainly by the wretched Mother—
Her joy was like a deep affright:
And forth she rushed into the light,
And saw it was another!

And, instantly, upon the earth,
Beneath the full moon shining bright,
Close to the Ass's feet she fell;
At the same moment Peter Bell
Dismounts in most unhappy light.   280

As he beheld the Woman lie
Breathless and motionless, the mind
Of Peter sadly was confused;
But, though to such demands unused,
And helpless almost as the blind,

He raised her up; and, while he held
Her body propped against his knee,
The Woman waked—and when she spied
The poor Ass standing by her side,
She moaned most bitterly.   290

"Oh! God be praised—my heart's at ease—
For he is dead—I know it well!"
—At this she wept a bitter flood;
And, in the best way that he could,
His tale did Peter tell.

He trembles—he is pale as death;
His voice is weak with perturbation;
He turns aside his head, he pauses;
Poor Peter, from a thousand causes,
Is crippled sore in his narration.   300

At length she learned how he espied
The Ass in that small meadow-ground;
And that her Husband now lay dead,
Beside that luckless river's bed
In which he had been drowned.

A piercing look the Widow cast
Upon the Beast that near her stands;
She sees 'tis he, that 'tis the same;
She calls the poor Ass by his name,
And wrings, and wrings her hands.   310

"O wretched loss—untimely stroke!
If he had died upon his bed!
He knew not one forewarning pain;
He never will come home again—
Is dead, for ever dead!"

Beside the woman Peter stands;
His heart is opening more and more;
A holy sense pervades his mind;
He feels what he for human kind
Had never felt before.   320

At length, by Peter's arm sustained,
The Woman rises from the ground—
"Oh, mercy! something must be done,
My little Rachel, you must run,—
Some willing neighbour must be found.

"Make haste—my little Rachel—do,
The first you meet with—bid him come,
Ask him to lend his horse to-night,
And this good Man, whom Heaven requite,
Will help to bring the body home."   330

Away goes Rachel weeping loud;—
An Infant, waked by her distress,
Makes in the house a piteous cry;
And Peter hears the Mother sigh,
"Seven are they, and all fatherless!"

And now is Peter taught to feel
That man's heart is a holy thing;
And Nature, through a world of death,
Breathes into him a second breath,
More searching than the breath of spring.   340

Upon a stone the Woman sits
In agony of silent grief—
From his own thoughts did Peter start;
He longs to press her to his heart,
From love that cannot find relief.

But roused, as if through every limb
Had past a sudden shock of dread,
The Mother o'er the threshold flies,
And up the cottage stairs she hies,
And on her pillow lays her burning head.   350

And Peter turns his steps aside
Into a shade of darksome trees,
Where he sits down, he knows not how,
With his hands pressed against his brow,
His elbows on his tremulous knees.

There, self-involved, does Peter sit
Until no sign of life he makes,
As if his mind were sinking deep
Through years that have been long asleep
The trance is passed away—he wakes;   360

He lifts his head—and sees the Ass
Yet standing in the clear moonshine;
"When shall I be as good as thou?
Oh! would, poor beast, that I had now
A heart but half as good as thine!"

But *He*—who deviously hath sought
His Father through the lonesome woods,
Hath sought, proclaiming to the ear
Of night his grief and sorrowful fear—
He comes, escaped from fields and floods;—   370

With weary pace is drawing nigh;
He sees the Ass—and nothing living
Had ever such a fit of joy
As hath this little orphan Boy,
For he has no misgiving!

Forth to the gentle Ass he springs,
And up about his neck he climbs;
In loving words he talks to him,
He kisses, kisses face and limb,—
He kisses him a thousand times!   380

This Peter sees, while in the shade
He stood beside the cottage-door;
And Peter Bell, the ruffian wild,
Sobs loud, he sobs even like a child,
"O God! I can endure no more!"

—Here ends my Tale: for in a trice
Arrived a neighbour with his horse;
Peter went forth with him straightway;
And, with due care, ere break of day,
Together they brought back the Corse.   390

And many years did this poor Ass,
Whom once it was my luck to see
Cropping the shrubs of Leming-Lane,
Help by his labour to maintain
The Widow and her family.

And Peter Bell, who, till that night,
Had been the wildest of his clan,
Forsook his crimes, renounced his folly,
And, after ten months' melancholy,
Became a good and honest man.   400

THE SIMPLON PASS

     —Brook and road
Were fellow-travellers in this gloomy Pass,
And with them did we journey several hours
At a slow step. The immeasurable height
Of woods decaying, never to be decayed,
The stationary blasts of waterfalls,
And in the narrow rent, at every turn,
Winds thwarting winds bewildered and forlorn,
The torrents shooting from the clear blue sky,
The rocks that muttered close upon our ears,   10
Black drizzling crags that spake by the wayside
As if a voice were in them, the sick sight
And giddy prospect of the raving stream,
The unfettered clouds and region of the heavens,
Tumult and peace, the darkness and the light—
Were all like workings of one mind, the features
Of the same face, blossoms upon one tree,
Characters of the great Apocalypse,
The types and symbols of Eternity,
Of first, and last, and midst, and without end.   20

INFLUENCE OF NATURAL OBJECTS

IN CALLING FORTH AND STRENGTHENING THE IMAGINATION IN BOYHOOD AND EARLY YOUTH

Wisdom and Spirit of the universe!
Thou Soul, that art the Eternity of thought!
And giv'st to forms and images a breath
And everlasting motion! not in vain,
By day or star-light, thus from my first dawn
Of childhood didst thou intertwine for me
The passions that build up our human soul;
Not with the mean and vulgar works of Man;

But with high objects, with enduring things,
With life and nature; purifying thus   10
The elements of feeling and of thought,
And sanctifying by such discipline
Both pain and fear,—until we recognise
A grandeur in the beatings of the heart.
    Nor was this fellowship vouchsafed to me
With stinted kindness. In November days,
When vapours rolling down the valleys made
A lonely scene more lonesome; among woods
At noon; and 'mid the calm of summer nights,
When, by the margin of the trembling lake,   20
Beneath the gloomy hills, homeward I went
In solitude, such intercourse was mine:
Mine was it in the fields both day and night,
And by the waters, all the summer long.
And in the frosty season, when the sun
Was set, and visible for many a mile,
The cottage-windows through the twilight blazed,
I heeded not the summons: happy time
It was indeed for all of us; for me
It was a time of rapture! Clear and loud   30
The village-clock tolled six—I wheeled about,
Proud and exulting like an untired horse
That cares not for his home.—All shod with steel
We hissed along the polished ice, in games
Confederate, imitative of the chase
And woodland pleasures,—the resounding horn,
The pack loud-chiming, and the hunted hare,
So through the darkness and the cold we flew,
And not a voice was idle: with the din
Smitten, the precipices rang aloud;   40
The leafless trees and every icy crag
Tinkled like iron; while far-distant hills
Into the tumult sent an alien sound
Of melancholy, not unnoticed while the stars,
Eastward, were sparkling clear, and in the west
The orange sky of evening died away.
    Not seldom from the uproar I retired

Into a silent bay, or sportively
Glanced sideway, leaving the tumultuous throng,
To cut across the reflex of a star;   50
Image, that, flying still before me, gleamed
Upon the glassy plain: and oftentimes,
When we had given our bodies to the wind,
And all the shadowy banks on either side
Came sweeping through the darkness, spinning still
The rapid line of motion, then at once
Have I, reclining back upon my heels,
Stopped short; yet still the solitary cliffs
Wheeled by me—even as if the earth had rolled
With visible motion her diurnal round!   60
Behind me did they stretch in solemn train,
Feebler and feebler, and I stood and watched
Till all was tranquil as a summer sea.

THERE WAS A BOY

There was a Boy; ye knew him well, ye cliffs
And islands of Winander!—many a time,
At evening, when the earliest stars began
To move along the edges of the hills,
Rising or setting, would he stand alone,
Beneath the trees, or by the glimmering lake;
And there, with fingers interwoven, both hands
Pressed closely palm to palm and to his mouth
Uplifted, he, as through an instrument,
Blew mimic hootings to the silent owls,   10
That they might answer him.—And they would shout
Across the watery vale, and shout again,
Responsive to his call,—with quivering peals,
And long halloos, and screams, and echoes loud
Redoubled and redoubled; concourse wild
Of jocund din! And, when there came a pause
Of silence such as baffled his best skill:
Then, sometimes, in that silence, while he hung
Listening, a gentle shock of mild surprise

Has carried far into his heart the voice   20
Of mountain-torrents; or the visible scene
Would enter unawares into his mind
With all its solemn imagery, its rocks,
Its woods, and that uncertain heaven received
Into the bosom of the steady lake.

    This boy was taken from his mates, and died
In childhood, ere he was full twelve years old.
Pre-eminent in beauty is the vale
Where he was born and bred: the churchyard hangs
Upon a slope above the village-school;   30
And, through that church-yard when my way has led
On summer-evenings, I believe, that there
A long half-hour together I have stood
Mute—looking at the grave in which he lies!

NUTTING

            ——It seems a day
(I speak of one from many singled out)
One of those heavenly days that cannot die;
When, in the eagerness of boyish hope,
I left our cottage-threshold, sallying forth
With a huge wallet o'er my shoulder slung,
A nutting-crook in hand; and turned my steps
Tow'rd some far-distant wood, a Figure quaint,
Tricked out in proud disguise of cast-off weeds
Which for that service had been husbanded,   10
By exhortation of my frugal Dame—
Motley accoutrement, of power to smile
At thorns, and brakes, and brambles,—and, in truth,
More ragged than need was! O'er pathless rocks,
Through beds of matted fern, and tangled thickets,
Forcing my way, I came to one dear nook
Unvisited, where not a broken bough
Drooped with its withered leaves, ungracious sign
Of devastation; but the hazels rose
Tall and erect, with tempting clusters hung,   20

A virgin scene!—A little while I stood,
Breathing with such suppression of the heart
As joy delights in; and, with wise restraint
Voluptuous, fearless of a rival, eyed
The banquet;—or beneath the trees I sate
Among the flowers, and with the flowers I played;
A temper known to those, who, after long
And weary expectation, have been blest
With sudden happiness beyond all hope.
Perhaps it was a bower beneath whose leaves   30
The violets of five seasons re-appear
And fade, unseen by any human eye;
Where fairy water-breaks do murmur on
For ever; and I saw the sparkling foam,
And—with my cheek on one of those green stones
That, fleeced with moss, under the shady trees,
Lay round me, scattered like a flock of sheep—
I heard the murmur and the murmuring sound,
In that sweet mood when pleasure loves to pay
Tribute to ease; and, of its joy secure,   40
The heart luxuriates with indifferent things,
Wasting its kindliness on stocks and stones,
And on the vacant air. Then up I rose,
And dragged to earth both branch and bough, with crash
And merciless ravage; and the shady nook
Of hazels, and the green and mossy bower,
Deformed and sullied, patiently gave up
Their quiet being; and, unless I now
Confound my present feelings with the past;
Ere from the mutilated bower I turned   50
Exulting, rich beyond the wealth of kings,
I felt a sense of pain when I beheld
The silent trees, and saw the intruding sky—
Then, dearest Maiden, move along these shades
In gentleness of heart; with gentle hand
Touch—for there is a spirit in the woods.

"STRANGE FITS OF PASSION HAVE I KNOWN"

Strange fits of passion have I known:
And I will dare to tell,
But in the Lover's ear alone,
What once to me befell.

When she I loved looked every day
Fresh as a rose in June,
I to her cottage bent my way,
Beneath an evening-moon.

Upon the moon I fixed my eye,
All over the wide lea;
With quickening pace my horse drew nigh
Those paths so dear to me.

And now we reached the orchard-plot;
And, as we climbed the hill,
The sinking moon to Lucy's cot
Came near, and nearer still.

In one of those sweet dreams I slept,
Kind Nature's gentlest boon!
And all the while my eyes I kept
On the descending moon.

My horse moved on; hoof after hoof
He raised, and never stopped:
When down behind the cottage roof,
At once, the bright moon dropped.

What fond and wayward thoughts will slide
Into a Lover's head!
"O mercy!" to myself I cried,
"If Lucy should be dead!"

"SHE DWELT AMONG THE UNTRODDEN WAYS"

She dwelt among the untrodden ways
   Beside the springs of Dove,

A Maid whom there were none to praise
    And very few to love:

A violet by a mossy stone
    Half hidden from the eye!
—Fair as a star, when only one
    Is shining in the sky.

She lived unknown, and few could know
    When Lucy ceased to be;
But she is in her grave, and, oh,
    The difference to me!

"I TRAVELLED AMONG UNKNOWN MEN"

I travelled among unknown men,
    In lands beyond the sea;
Nor, England! did I know till then
    What love I bore to thee.

'T is past, that melancholy dream!
    Nor will I quit thy shore
A second time; for still I seem
    To love thee more and more.

Among thy mountains did I feel
    The joy of my desire;
And she I cherished turned her wheel
    Beside an English fire.

Thy mornings showed, thy nights concealed
    The bowers where Lucy played;
And thine too is the last green field
    That Lucy's eyes surveyed.

"THREE YEARS SHE GREW IN SUN AND SHOWER"

Three years she grew in sun and shower,
Then Nature said, "A lovelier flower
    On earth was never sown;
    This Child I to myself will take;

She shall be mine, and I will make
A Lady of my own.

"Myself will to my darling be
Both law and impulse: and with me
The Girl, in rock and plain,
In earth and heaven, in glade and bower,   10
Shall feel an overseeing power
To kindle or restrain.

"She shall be sportive as the fawn
That wild with glee across the lawn,
Or up the mountain springs;
And hers shall be the breathing balm,
And hers the silence and the calm
Of mute insensate things.

"The floating clouds their state shall lend
To her; for her the willow bend;   20
Nor shall she fail to see
Even in the motions of the Storm
Grace that shall mould the Maiden's form
By silent sympathy.

"The stars of midnight shall be dear
To her; and she shall lean her ear
In many a secret place
Where rivulets dance their wayward round,
And beauty born of murmuring sound
Shall pass into her face.   30

"And vital feelings of delight
Shall rear her form to stately height,
Her virgin bosom swell;
Such thoughts to Lucy I will give
While she and I together live
Here in this happy dell."

Thus Nature spake—The work was done—
How soon my Lucy's race was run!
She died, and left to me
This heath, this calm, and quiet scene;   40

The memory of what has been,
And never more will be.

"A Slumber Did My Spirit Seal"

A slumber did my spirit seal;
    I had no human fears:
She seemed a thing that could not feel
    The touch of earthly years.

No motion has she now, no force;
    She neither hears nor sees;
Rolled round in earth's diurnal course,
    With rocks, and stones, and trees.

A Poet's Epitaph

Art thou a Statist in the van
Of public conflicts trained and bred?
—First learn to love one living man;
Then may'st thou think upon the dead.

A Lawyer art thou?—draw not nigh!
Go, carry to some fitter place
The keenness of that practised eye,
The hardness of that sallow face.

Art thou a Man of purple cheer?
A rosy Man, right plump to see?   10
Approach; yet, Doctor, not too near,
This grave no cushion is for thee.

Or art thou one of gallant pride,
A Soldier and no man of chaff?
Welcome!—but lay thy sword aside,
And lean upon a peasant's staff.

Physician art thou? one, all eyes,
Philosopher! a fingering slave,
One that would peep and botanise
Upon his mother's grave?   20

Wrapt closely in thy sensual fleece,
O turn aside,—and take, I pray,
That he below may rest in peace,
Thy ever-dwindling soul, away!

A Moralist perchance appears;
Led, Heaven knows how! to this poor sod:
And he has neither eyes nor ears;
Himself his world, and his own God;

One to whose smooth-rubbed soul can cling
Nor form, nor feeling, great or small;   30
A reasoning, self-sufficing thing,
An intellectual All-in-all!

Shut close the door; press down the latch;
Sleep in thy intellectual crust;
Nor lose ten tickings of thy watch
Near this unprofitable dust.

But who is He, with modest looks,
And clad in homely russet brown?
He murmurs near the running brooks
A music sweeter than their own.   40

He is retired as noontide dew,
Or fountain in a noon-day grove;
And you must love him, ere to you
He will seem worthy of your love.

The outward shows of sky and earth,
Of hill and valley, he has viewed;
And impulses of deeper birth
Have come to him in solitude.

In common things that round us lie
Some random truths he can impart,—   50
The harvest of a quiet eye
That broods and sleeps on his own heart.

But he is weak; both Man and Boy,
Hath been an idler in the land;

Contented if he might enjoy
The things which others understand.

—Come hither in thy hour of strength;
Come, weak as is a breaking wave!
Here stretch thy body at full length;
Or build thy house upon this grave.   **60**

MATTHEW

If Nature, for a favourite child,
In thee hath tempered so her clay,
That every hour thy heart runs wild,
Yet never once doth go astray,

Read o'er these lines; and then review
This tablet, that thus humbly rears
In such diversity of hue
Its history of two hundred years.

—When through this little wreck of fame,
Cipher and syllable! thine eye   **10**
Has travelled down to Matthew's name,
Pause with no common sympathy.

And, if a sleeping tear should wake,
Then be it neither checked nor stayed:
For Matthew a request I make
Which for himself he had not made.

Poor Matthew, all his frolics o'er,
Is silent as a standing pool;
Far from the chimney's merry roar,
And murmur of the village school.   **20**

The sighs which Matthew heaved were sighs
Of one tired out with fun and madness;
The tears which came to Matthew's eyes
Were tears of light, the dew of gladness.

Yet, sometimes, when the secret cup
Of still and serious thought went round,

It seemed as if he drank it up—
He felt with spirit so profound.

—Thou soul of God's best earthly mould!
Thou happy Soul! and can it be   30
That these two words of glittering gold
Are all that must remain of thee?

THE TWO APRIL MORNINGS

We walked along, while bright and red
Uprose the morning sun;
And Matthew stopped, he looked, and said,
"The will of God be done!"

A village schoolmaster was he,
With hair of glittering grey;
As blithe a man as you could see
On a spring holiday.

And on that morning, through the grass,
And by the steaming rills,
We travelled merrily, to pass   10
A day among the hills.

"Our work," said I, "was well begun,
Then, from thy breast what thought,
Beneath so beautiful a sun,
So sad a sigh has brought?

A second time did Matthew stop;
And fixing still his eye
Upon the eastern mountain-top,
To me he made reply: 20

"Yon cloud with that long purple cleft
Brings fresh into my mind
A day like this which I have left
Full thirty years behind.

"And just above yon slope of corn
Such colours, and no other,

Were in the sky, that April morn,
Of this the very brother.

"With rod and line I sued the sport
Which that sweet season gave,   30
And, to the church-yard come, stopped short
Beside my daughter's grave.

"Nine summers had she scarcely seen,
The pride of all the vale;
And then she sang;—she would have been
A very nightingale.

"Six feet in earth my Emma lay;
And yet I loved her more,
For so it seemed, than till that day
I e'er had loved before.   40

"And, turning from her grave, I met,
Beside the church-yard yew,
A blooming Girl, whose hair was wet
With points of morning dew.

"A basket on her head she bare;
Her brow was smooth and white:
To see a child so very fair,
It was a pure delight!

"No fountain from its rocky cave
E'er tripped with foot so free;   50
She seemed as happy as a wave
That dances on the sea.

"There came from me a sigh of pain
Which I could ill confine;
I looked at her, and looked again:
And did not wish her mine!"

Matthew is in his grave, yet now,
Methinks, I see him stand,
As at that moment, with a bough
Of wilding in his hand.   60

THE FOUNTAIN

A CONVERSATION

We talked with open heart, and tongue
Affectionate and true,
A pair of friends, though I was young,
And Matthew seventy-two.

We lay beneath a spreading oak,
Beside a mossy seat;
And from the turf a fountain broke,
And gurgled at our feet.

"Now, Matthew!" said I, "let us match
This water's pleasant tune
With some old border-song, or catch
That suits a summer's noon;

"Or of the church-clock and the chimes
Sing here beneath the shade,
That half-mad thing of witty rhymes
Which you last April made!"

In silence Matthew lay, and eyed
The spring beneath the tree;
And thus the dear old Man replied,
The grey-haired man of glee:

"No check, no stay, this Streamlet fears;
How merrily it goes!
'Twill murmur on a thousand years,
And flow as now it flows.

"And here, on this delightful day,
I cannot choose but think
How oft, a vigorous man, I lay
Beside this fountain's brink.

"My eyes are dim with childish tears,
My heart is idly stirred,
For the same sound is in my ears
Which in those days I heard.

10

20

30

"Thus fares it still in our decay:
And yet the wiser mind
Mourns less for what age takes away
Than what it leaves behind.

"The blackbird amid leafy trees,
The lark above the hill,
Let loose their carols when they please,
Are quiet when they will.   40

"With Nature never do *they* wage
A foolish strife; they see
A happy youth, and their old age
Is beautiful and free:

"But we are pressed by heavy laws;
And often, glad no more,
We wear a face of joy, because
We have been glad of yore.

"If there be one who need bemoan
His kindred laid in earth,   50
The household hearts that were his own;
It is the man of mirth.

"My days, my Friend, are almost gone,
My life has been approved,
And many love me; but by none
Am I enough beloved."

"Now both himself and me he wrongs,
The man who thus complains;
I live and sing my idle songs
Upon these happy plains;   60

"And, Matthew, for thy children dead
I'll be a son to thee!"
At this he grasped my hand, and said,
"Alas! that cannot be."

We rose up from the fountain-side;
And down the smooth descent

Of the green sheep-track did we glide;
And through the wood we went;

And, ere we came to Leonard's rock,
He sang those witty rhymes   70
About the crazy old church-clock,
And the bewildered chimes.

LUCY GRAY

OR, SOLITUDE

Oft I had heard of Lucy Gray:
And, when I crossed the wild,
I chanced to see at break of day
The solitary child.

No mate, no comrade Lucy knew;
She dwelt on a wide moor,
—The sweetest thing that ever grew
Beside a human door!

You yet may spy the fawn at play,
The hare upon the green;   10
But the sweet face of Lucy Gray
Will never more be seen.

"To-night will be a stormy night—
You to the town must go;
And take a lantern, Child, to light
Your mother through the snow."

"That, Father! I will gladly do:
'Tis scarcely afternoon—
The minster-clock has just struck two,
And yonder is the moon!"   20

At this the Father raised his hook,
And snapped a faggot-band;
He plied his work;—and Lucy took
The lantern in her hand.

Not blither is the mountain roe:
With many a wanton stroke
Her feet disperse the powdery snow,
That rises up like smoke.

The storm came on before its time:
She wandered up and down;   30
And many a hill did Lucy climb:
But never reached the town.

The wretched parents all that night
Went shouting far and wide;
But there was neither sound nor sight
To serve them for a guide.

At day-break on a hill they stood
That overlooked the moor;
And thence they saw the bridge of wood,
A furlong from their door.   40

They wept—and, turning homeward, cried,
"In heaven we all shall meet;"
—When in the snow the mother spied
The print of Lucy's feet.

Then downwards from the steep hill's edge
They tracked the footmarks small;
And through the broken hawthorn hedge,
And by the long stone-wall;

And then an open field they crossed:
The marks were still the same;   50
They tracked them on, nor ever lost;
And to the bridge they came.

They followed from the snowy bank
Those footmarks, one by one,
Into the middle of the plank;
And further there were none!

—Yet some maintain that to this day
She is a living child;

That you may see sweet Lucy Gray
Upon the lonesome wild. 60

O'er rough and smooth she trips along,
And never looks behind;
And sings a solitary song
That whistles in the wind.

RUTH

When Ruth was left half desolate,
Her Father took another Mate;
And Ruth, not seven years old,
A slighted child, at her own will
Went wandering over dale and hill,
In thoughtless freedom, bold.

And she had made a pipe of straw,
And music from that pipe could draw
Like sounds of winds and floods;
Had built a bower upon the green, 10
As if she from her birth had been
An infant of the woods.

Beneath her father's roof, alone
She seemed to live; her thoughts her own;
Herself her own delight;
Pleased with herself, nor sad, nor gay;
And, passing thus the live-long day,
She grew to woman's height.

There came a Youth from Georgia's shore—
A military casque he wore, 20
With splendid feathers drest;
He brought them from the Cherokees;
The feathers nodded in the breeze,
And made a gallant crest.

From Indian blood you deem him sprung:
But no! he spake the English tongue,

And bore a soldier's name;
And, when America was free
From battle and from jeopardy,
He 'cross the ocean came.   30

With hues of genius on his cheek
In finest tones the Youth could speak:
—While he was yet a boy,
The moon, the glory of the sun,
And streams that murmur as they run,
Had been his dearest joy.

He was a lovely youth! I guess
The panther in the wilderness
Was not so fair as he;
And, when he chose to sport and play,   40
No dolphin ever was so gay
Upon the tropic sea.

Among the Indians he had fought,
And with him many tales he brought
Of pleasure and of fear;
Such tales as told to any maid
By such a Youth, in the green shade,
Were perilous to hear.

He told of girls—a happy rout!
Who quit their fold with dance and shout,   50
Their pleasant Indian town,
To gather strawberries all day long;
Returning with a choral song
When daylight is gone down.

He spake of plants that hourly change
Their blossoms, through a boundless range
Of intermingling hues;
With budding, fading, faded flowers
They stand the wonder of the bowers
From morn to evening dews.   60

He told of the magnolia, spread
High as a cloud, high over head!

The cypress and her spire;
—Of flowers that with one scarlet gleam
Cover a hundred leagues, and seem
To set the hills on fire.

The Youth of green savannahs spake,
And many an endless, endless lake,
With all its fairy crowds
Of islands, that together lie
As quietly as spots of sky   70
Among the evening clouds.

"How pleasant," then he said, "it were
A fisher or a hunter there,
In sunshine or in shade
To wander with an easy mind;
And build a household fire, and find
A home in every glade!

"What days and what bright years! Ah me!
Our life were life indeed, with thee   80
So passed in quiet bliss,
And all the while," said he, "to know
That we were in a world of woe,
On such an earth as this!"

And then he sometimes interwove
Fond thoughts about a father's love;
"For there," said he, "are spun
Around the heart such tender ties,
That our own children to our eyes
Are dearer than the sun.   90

"Sweet Ruth! and could you go with me
My helpmate in the woods to be,
Our shed at night to rear;
Or run, my own adopted bride,
A sylvan huntress at my side,
And drive the flying deer!"

"Beloved Ruth!"—No more he said,
The wakeful Ruth at midnight shed

A solitary tear:
She thought again—and did agree
With him to sail across the sea,
And drive the flying deer.   100

"And now, as fitting is and right,
We in the church our faith will plight,
A husband and a wife."
Even so they did; and I may say
That to sweet Ruth that happy day
Was more than human life.

Through dream and vision did she sink,
Delighted all the while to think   110
That on those lonesome floods,
And green savannahs, she should share
His board with lawful joy, and bear
His name in the wild woods.

But, as you have before been told,
This Stripling, sportive, gay, and bold,
And, with his dancing crest,
So beautiful, through savage lands
Had roamed about, with vagrant bands
Of Indians in the West.   120

The wind, the tempest roaring high,
The tumult of a tropic sky,
Might well be dangerous food
For him, a Youth to whom was given
So much of earth—so much of heaven,
And such impetuous blood.

Whatever in those climes he found
Irregular in sight or sound
Did to his mind impart
A kindred impulse, seemed allied   130
To his own powers, and justified
The workings of his heart.

Nor less, to feed voluptuous thought,
The beauteous forms of nature wrought,

Fair trees and gorgeous flowers;
The breezes their own languor lent;
The stars had feelings, which they sent
Into those favoured bowers.

Yet, in his worst pursuits, I ween
That sometimes there did intervene   **140**
Pure hopes of high intent:
For passions linked to form so fair
And stately, needs must have their share
Of noble sentiment.

But ill he lived, much evil saw,
With men to whom no better law
Nor better life was known;
Deliberately, and undeceived,
Those wild men's vices he received,
And gave them back his own.   **150**

His genius and his moral frame
Were thus impaired, and he became
The slave of low desires:
A Man who without self-control
Would seek what the degraded soul
Unworthily admires.

And yet he with no feigned delight
Had wooed the Maiden, day and night
Had loved her, night and morn:
What could he less than love a Maid   **160**
Whose heart with so much nature played?
So kind and so forlorn!

Sometimes, most earnestly, he said,
"O Ruth! I have been worse than dead;
False thoughts, thoughts bold and vain,
Encompassed me on every side
When I, in confidence and pride,
Had crossed the Atlantic main.

"Before me shone a glorious world—
Fresh as a banner bright, unfurled   **170**

To music suddenly:
I looked upon those hills and plains,
And seemed as if let loose from chains,
To live at liberty.

"No more of this; for now, by thee
Dear Ruth! more happily set free
With nobler zeal I burn;
My soul from darkness is released,
Like the whole sky when to the east
The morning doth return."   180

Full soon that better mind was gone;
No hope, no wish remained, not one,—
They stirred him now no more;
New objects did new pleasure give,
And once again he wished to live
As lawless as before.

Meanwhile, as thus with him it fared,
They for the voyage were prepared,
And went to the sea-shore,
But, when they thither came the Youth   190
Deserted his poor Bride, and Ruth
Could never find him more.

God help thee, Ruth!—Such pains she had,
That she in half a year was mad,
And in a prison housed;
And there, with many a doleful song
Made of wild words, her cup of wrong
She fearfully caroused.

Yet sometimes milder hours she knew,
Nor wanted sun, nor rain, nor dew,   200
Nor pastimes of the May;
—They all were with her in her cell;
And a clear brook with cheerful knell
Did o'er the pebbles play.

When Ruth three seasons thus had lain,
There came a respite to her pain;

She from her prison fled;
But of the Vagrant none took thought;
And where it liked her best she sought
Her shelter and her bread.   210

Among the fields she breathed again:
The master-current of her brain
Ran permanent and free;
And, coming to the Banks of Tone,
There did she rest; and dwell alone
Under the greenwood tree.

The engines of her pain, the tools
That shaped her sorrow, rocks and pools,
And airs that gently stir
The vernal leaves—she loved them still;   220
Nor ever taxed them with the ill
Which had been done to her.

A Barn her *winter* bed supplies;
But, till the warmth of summer skies
And summer days is gone,
(And all do in this tale agree)
She sleeps beneath the greenwood tree,
And other home hath none.

An innocent life, yet far astray!
And Ruth will, long before her day,   230
Be broken down and old:
Sore aches she needs must have! but less
Of mind, than body's wretchedness,
From damp, and rain, and cold.

If she is prest by want of food,
She from her dwelling in the wood
Repairs to a road-side;
And there she begs at one steep place
Where up and down with easy pace
The horsemen-travellers ride.   240

That oaten pipe of hers is mute,
Or thrown away; but with a flute

Her loneliness she cheers:
This flute, made of a hemlock stalk,
At evening in his homeward walk
The Quantock woodman hears.

I, too, have passed her on the hills
Setting her little water-mills
By spouts and fountains wild—
Such small machinery as she turned
Ere she had wept, ere she had mourned,
A young and happy Child!

250

Farewell! and when thy days are told,
Ill-fated Ruth, in hallowed mould
Thy corpse shall buried be,
For thee a funeral bell shall ring,
And all the congregation sing
A Christian psalm for thee.

"BLEAK SEASON WAS IT, TURBULENT AND WILD"

Bleak season was it, turbulent and wild,
When hitherward we journeyed, side by side,
Through bursts of sunshine and through flying showers,
Paced the long vales,—how long they were, and yet
How fast that length of way was left behind!—
Wensley's rich dale, and Sedberge's naked heights.
The frosty wind, as if to make amends
For its keen breath, was aiding to our steps,
And drove us onward as two ships at sea;
Or like two birds, companions in mid-air,
Parted and reunited by the blast.
Stern was the face of Nature; we rejoiced
In that stern countenance; for our souls thence drew
A feeling of their strength.
                         The naked trees,
The icy brooks, as on we passed, appeared
To question us, "Whence come ye, to what end?"

"ON NATURE'S INVITATION DO I COME"

On Nature's invitation do I come,
By Reason sanctioned. Can the choice mislead,
That made the calmest, fairest spot on earth,
With all its unappropriated good,
My own; and not mine only, for with me
Entrenched—say rather peacefully embowered—
Under yon orchard, in yon humble cot,
A younger orphan of a name extinct,
The only daughter of my parents, dwells:
Aye, think on that, my heart, and cease to stir;   10
Pause upon that, and let the breathing frame
No longer breathe, but all be satisfied.
Oh, if such silence be not thanks to God
For what hath been bestowed, then where, where then
Shall gratitude find rest? Mine eyes did ne'er
Fix on a lovely object, nor my mind
Take pleasure in the midst of happy thought,
But either she, whom now I have, who now
Divides with me that loved abode, was there,
Or not far off. Where'er my footsteps turned,   20
Her voice was like a hidden bird that sang;
The thought of her was like a flash of light,
Or an unseen companionship; a breath
Or fragrance independent of the wind.
In all my goings, in the new and old
Of all my meditations, and in this
Favourite of all, in this the most of all. . . .
Embrace me then, ye hills, and close me in.
Now in the clear and open day I feel
Your guardianship: I take it to my heart;   30
'T is like the solemn shelter of the night.
But I would call thee beautiful; for mild
And soft, and gay, and beautiful thou art,
Dear valley, having in thy face a smile,
Though peaceful, full of gladness. Thou art pleased,
Pleased with thy crags, and woody steeps, thy lake,

Its one green island, and its winding shores,
The multitude of little rocky hills,
Thy church, and cottages of mountain stone
Clustered like stars some few, but single most,   40
And lurking dimly in their shy retreats,
Or glancing at each other cheerful looks
Like separated stars with clouds between.

THE PRELUDE; OR, GROWTH OF A POET'S MIND

AN AUTOBIOGRAPHICAL POEM

BOOK FIRST

Introduction — Childhood and School-Time

Oh there is blessing in this gentle breeze,
A visitant that while it fans my cheek
Doth seem half-conscious of the joy it brings
From the green fields, and from yon azure sky.
Whate'er its mission, the soft breeze can come
To none more grateful than to me; escaped
From the vast city, where I long had pined
A discontented sojourner: now free,
Free as a bird to settle where I will.
What dwelling shall receive me? in what vale   10
Shall be my harbour? underneath what grove
Shall I take up my home? and what clear stream
Shall with its murmur lull me into rest?
The earth is all before me. With a heart
Joyous, nor scared at its own liberty,
I look about; and should the chosen guide
Be nothing better than a wandering cloud,
I cannot miss my way. I breathe again!
Trances of thought and mountings of the mind
Come fast upon me: it is shaken off,   20
That burthen of my own unnatural self,

The heavy weight of many a weary day
Not mine, and such as were not made for me.
Long months of peace (if such bold word accord
With any promises of human life),
Long months of ease and undisturbed delight
Are mine in prospect; whither shall I turn,
By road or pathway, or through trackless field,
Up hill or down, or shall some floating thing
Upon the river point me out my course?   30

    Dear Liberty! Yet what would it avail
But for a gift that consecrates the joy?
For I, methought, while the sweet breath of heaven
Was blowing on my body, felt within
A correspondent breeze, that gently moved
With quickening virtue, but is now become
A tempest, a redundant energy,
Vexing its own creation. Thanks to both,
And their congenial powers, that, while they join
In breaking up a long-continued frost,   40
Bring with them vernal promises, the hope
Of active days urged on by flying hours,—
Days of sweet leisure, taxed with patient thought
Abstruse, nor wanting punctual service high,
Matins and vespers of harmonious verse!

    Thus far, O Friend! did I, not used to make
A present joy the matter of a song,
Pour forth that day my soul in measured strains
That would not be forgotten, and are here
Recorded: to the open fields I told   50
A prophecy: poetic numbers came
Spontaneously to clothe in priestly robe
A renovated spirit singled out,
Such hope was mine, for holy services.
My own voice cheered me, and, far more, the mind's
Internal echo of the imperfect sound;
To both I listened, drawing from them both
A cheerful confidence in things to come.

Content and not unwilling now to give
A respite to this passion, I paced on   60
With brisk and eager steps; and came, at length,
To a green shady place, where down I sate
Beneath a tree, slackening my thoughts by choice
And settling into gentler happiness.
'T was autumn, and a clear and placid day,
With warmth, as much as needed, from a sun
Two hours declined towards the west; a day
With silver clouds, and sunshine on the grass,
And in the sheltered and the sheltering grove
A perfect stillness. Many were the thoughts   70
Encouraged and dismissed, till choice was made
Of a known Vale, whither my feet should turn,
Nor rest till they had reached the very door
Of the one cottage which methought I saw.
No picture of mere memory ever looked
So fair; and while upon the fancied scene
I gazed with growing love, a higher power
Than Fancy gave assurance of some work
Of glory there forthwith to be begun,
Perhaps too there performed. Thus long I mused,   80
Nor e'er lost sight of what I mused upon,
Save when, amid the stately grove of oaks,
Now here, now there, an acorn, from its cup
Dislodged, through sere leaves rustled, or at once
To the bare earth dropped with a startling sound.
From that soft couch I rose not, till the sun
Had almost touched the horizon; casting then
A backward glance upon the curling cloud
Of city smoke, by distance ruralised;
Keen as a Truant or a Fugitive,   90
But as a Pilgrim resolute, I took,
Even with the chance equipment of that hour,
The road that pointed toward the chosen Vale.
It was a splendid evening, and my soul
Once more made trial of her strength, nor lacked
Æolian visitations; but the harp

Was soon defrauded, and the banded host
Of harmony dispersed in straggling sounds,
And lastly utter silence! "Be it so;
Why think of anything but present good?"   100
So, like a home-bound labourer, I pursued
My way beneath the mellowing sun, that shed
Mild influence; nor left in me one wish
Again to bend the Sabbath of that time
To a servile yoke. What need of many words?
A pleasant loitering journey, through three days
Continued, brought me to my hermitage.
I spare to tell of what ensued, the life
In common things—the endless store of things,
Rare, or at least so seeming, every day   110
Found all about me in one neighbourhood—
The self-congratulation, and, from morn
To night, unbroken cheerfulness serene.
But speedily an earnest longing rose
To brace myself to some determined aim,
Reading or thinking; either to lay up
New stores, or rescue from decay the old
By timely interference: and therewith
Came hopes still higher, that with outward life
I might endue some airy phantasies   120
That had been floating loose about for years,
And to such beings temperately deal forth
The many feelings that oppressed my heart.
That hope hath been discouraged; welcome light
Dawns from the east, but dawns to disappear
And mock me with a sky that ripens not
Into a steady morning: if my mind,
Remembering the bold promise of the past,
Would gladly grapple with some noble theme,
Vain is her wish; where'er she turns she finds   130
Impediments from day to day renewed.

      And now it would content me to yield up
Those lofty hopes awhile, for present gifts

Of humbler industry. But, oh, dear Friend!
The Poet, gentle creature as he is,
Hath, like the Lover, his unruly times;
His fits when he is neither sick nor well,
Though no distress be near him but his own
Unmanageable thoughts: his mind, best pleased
While she as duteous as the mother dove   140
Sits brooding, lives not always to that end,
But like the innocent bird, hath goadings on
That drive her as in trouble through the groves;
With me is now such passion, to be blamed
No otherwise than as it lasts too long.

      When, as becomes a man who would prepare
For such an arduous work, I through myself
Make rigorous inquisition, the report
Is often cheering; for I neither seem
To lack that first great gift, the vital soul,   150
Nor general Truths, which are themselves a sort
Of Elements and Agents, Under-powers,
Subordinate helpers of the living mind:
Nor am I naked of external things,
Forms, images, nor numerous other aids
Of less regard, though won perhaps with toil
And needful to build up a Poet's praise.
Time, place, and manners do I seek, and these
Are found in plenteous store, but nowhere such
As may be singled out with steady choice;   160
No little band of yet remembered names
Whom I, in perfect confidence, might hope
To summon back from lonesome banishment,
And make them dwellers in the hearts of men
Now living, or to live in future years.
Sometimes the ambitious Power of choice, mistaking
Proud spring-tide swellings for a regular sea,
Will settle on some British theme, some old
Romantic tale by Milton left unsung;
More often turning to some gentle place   170

Within the groves of Chivalry, I pipe
To shepherd swains, or seated harp in hand,
Amid reposing knights by a river side
Or fountain, listen to the grave reports
Of dire enchantments faced and overcome
By the strong mind, and tales of warlike feats,
Where spear encountered spear, and sword with sword
Fought, as if conscious of the blazonry
That the shield bore, so glorious was the strife;
Whence inspiration for a song that winds   180
Through ever-changing scenes of votive quest
Wrongs to redress, harmonious tribute paid
To patient courage and unblemished truth,
To firm devotion, zeal unquenchable,
And Christian meekness hallowing faithful loves.
Sometimes, more sternly moved, I would relate
How vanquished Mithridates northward passed,
And, hidden in the cloud of years, became
Odin, the Father of a race by whom
Perished the Roman Empire: how the friends   190
And followers of Sertorius, out of Spain
Flying, found shelter in the Fortunate Isles,
And left their usages, their arts and laws,
To disappear by a slow gradual death,
To dwindle and to perish one by one,
Starved in those narrow bounds: but not the soul
Of Liberty, which fifteen hundred years
Survived, and, when the European came
With skill and power that might not be withstood,
Did, like a pestilence, maintain its hold   200
And wasted down by glorious death that race
Of natural heroes: or I would record
How, in tyrannic times, some high-souled man,
Unnamed among the chronicles of kings,
Suffered in silence for Truth's sake: or tell,
How that one Frenchman, through continued force
Of meditation on the inhuman deeds
Of those who conquered first the Indian Isles,

Went single in his ministry across
The Ocean; not to comfort the oppressed, 210
But, like a thirsty wind, to roam about
Withering the Oppressor: how Gustavus sought
Help at his need in Dalecarlia's mines:
How Wallace fought for Scotland; left the name
Of Wallace to be found, like a wild flower,
All over his dear Country; left the deeds
Of Wallace, like a family of Ghosts,
To people the steep rocks and river banks,
Her natural sanctuaries, with a local soul
Of independence and stern liberty. 220
Sometimes it suits me better to invent
A tale from my own heart, more near akin
To my own passions and habitual thoughts;
Some variegated story, in the main
Lofty, but the unsubstantial structure melts
Before the very sun that brightens it,
Mist into air dissolving! Then a wish,
My last and favourite aspiration, mounts
With yearning toward some philosophic song
Of Truth that cherishes our daily life; 230
With meditations passionate from deep
Recesses in man's heart, immortal verse
Thoughtfully fitted to the Orphean lyre;
But from this awful burthen I full soon
Take refuge and beguile myself with trust
That mellower years will bring a riper mind
And clearer insight. Thus my days are past
In contradiction; with no skill to part
Vague longing, haply bred by want of power,
From paramount impulse not to be withstood, 240
A timorous capacity, from prudence,
From circumspection, infinite delay.
Humility and modest awe, themselves
Betray me, serving often for a cloak
To a more subtle selfishness; that now
Locks every function up in blank reserve,
Now dupes me, trusting to an anxious eye

That with intrusive restlessness beats off
Simplicity and self-presented truth.
Ah! better far than this, to stray about   250
Voluptuously through fields and rural walks,
And ask no record of the hours, resigned
To vacant musing, unreproved neglect
Of all things, and deliberate holiday.
Far better never to have heard the name
Of zeal and just ambition, than to live
Baffled and plagued by a mind that every hour
Turns recreant to her task; takes heart again,
Then feels immediately some hollow thought
Hang like an interdict upon her hopes.   260
This is my lot; for either still I find
Some imperfection in the chosen theme,
Or see of absolute accomplishment
Much wanting, so much wanting, in myself,
That I recoil and droop, and seek repose
In listlessness from vain perplexity,
Unprofitably travelling toward the grave,
Like a false steward who hath much received
And renders nothing back.
                                    Was it for this
That one, the fairest of all rivers, loved   270
To blend his murmurs with my nurse's song,
And, from his alder shades and rocky falls,
And from his fords and shallows, sent a voice
That flowed along my dreams? For this, didst thou,
O Derwent! winding among grassy holms
Where I was looking on, a babe in arms,
Make ceaseless music that composed my thoughts
To more than infant softness, giving me
Amid the fretful dwellings of mankind
A foretaste, a dim earnest, of the calm   280
That Nature breathes among the hills and groves.

When he had left the mountains and received
On his smooth breast the shadow of those towers
That yet survive, a shattered monument

Of feudal sway, the bright blue river passed
Along the margin of our terrace walk;
A tempting playmate whom we dearly loved.
Oh, many a time have I, a five years' child,
In a small mill-race severed from his stream,
Made one long bathing of a summer's day;   290
Basked in the sun, and plunged and basked again
Alternate, all a summer's day, or scoured
The sandy fields, leaping through flowery groves
Of yellow ragwort; or, when rock and hill,
The woods, and distant Skiddaw's lofty height,
Were bronzed with deepest radiance, stood alone
Beneath the sky, as if I had been born
On Indian plains, and from my mother's hut
Had run abroad in wantonness, to sport
A naked savage, in the thunder shower.   300

Fair seed-time had my soul, and I grew up
Fostered alike by beauty and by fear:
Much favoured in my birthplace, and no less
In that beloved Vale to which erelong
We were transplanted;—there were we let loose
For sports of wider range. Ere I had told
Ten birth-days, when among the mountain slopes
Frost, and the breath of frosty wind, had snapped
The last autumnal crocus, 't was my joy
With store of springes o'er my shoulder hung   310
To range the open heights where woodcocks run
Along the smooth green turf. Through half the night,
Scudding away from snare to snare, I plied
That anxious visitation;—moon and stars
Were shining o'er my head. I was alone,
And seemed to be a trouble to the peace
That dwelt among them. Sometimes it befell
In these night wanderings, that a strong desire
O'erpowered my better reason, and the bird
Which was the captive of another's toil   320
Became my prey; and when the deed was done
I heard among the solitary hills

Low breathings coming after me, and sounds
Of undistinguishable motion, steps
Almost as silent as the turf they trod.

    Nor less, when spring had warmed the cultured Vale,
Moved we as plunderers where the mother-bird
Had in high places built her lodge; though mean
Our object and inglorious, yet the end
Was not ignoble. Oh! when I have hung   330
Above the raven's nest, by knots of grass
And half-inch fissures in the slippery rock
But ill sustained, and almost (so it seemed)
Suspended by the blast that blew amain,
Shouldering the naked crag, oh, at that time
While on the perilous ridge I hung alone,
With what strange utterance did the loud dry wind
Blow through my ear! the sky seemed not a sky
Of earth—and with what motion moved the clouds!

    Dust as we are, the immortal spirit grows   340
Like harmony in music; there is a dark
Inscrutable workmanship that reconciles
Discordant elements, makes them cling together
In one society. How strange, that all
The terrors, pains, and early miseries,
Regrets, vexations, lassitudes interfused
Within my mind, should e'er have borne a part,
And that a needful part, in making up
The calm existence that is mine when I
Am worthy of myself! Praise to the end!   350
Thanks to the means which Nature deigned to employ;
Whether her fearless visitings, or those
That came with soft alarm, like hurtless light
Opening the peaceful clouds; or she would use
Severer interventions, ministry
More palpable, as best might suit her aim.

    One summer evening (led by her) I found
A little boat tied to a willow tree
Within a rocky cove, its usual home.

Straight I unloosed her chain, and stepping in   360
Pushed from the shore. It was an act of stealth
And troubled pleasure, nor without the voice
Of mountain-echoes did my boat move on;
Leaving behind her still, on either side,
Small circles glittering idly in the moon,
Until they melted all into one track
Of sparkling light. But now, like one who rows,
Proud of his skill, to reach a chosen point
With an unswerving line, I fixed my view
Upon the summit of a craggy ridge,   370
The horizon's utmost boundary; far above
Was nothing but the stars and the grey sky.
She was an elfin pinnace; lustily
I dipped my oars into the silent lake,
And, as I rose upon the stroke, my boat
Went heaving through the water like a swan;
When, from behind that craggy steep till then
The horizon's bound, a huge peak, black and huge,
As if with voluntary power instinct,
Upreared its head. I struck and struck again,   380
And growing still in stature the grim shape
Towered up between me and the stars, and still,
For so it seemed, with purpose of its own
And measured motion like a living thing,
Strode after me. With trembling oars I turned,
And through the silent water stole my way
Back to the covert of the willow tree;
There in her mooring-place I left my bark,—
And through the meadows homeward went, in grave
And serious mood; but after I had seen   390
That spectacle, for many days, my brain
Worked with a dim and undetermined sense
Of unknown modes of being; o'er my thoughts
There hung a darkness, call it solitude
Or blank desertion. No familiar shapes
Remained, no pleasant images of trees,
Of sea or sky, no colours of green fields;

But huge and mighty forms, that do not live
Like living men, moved slowly through the mind
By day, and were a trouble to my dreams.   **400**

    Wisdom and Spirit of the universe!
Thou Soul that art the eternity of thought
That givest to forms and images a breath
And everlasting motion, not in vain
By day or star-light thus from my first dawn
Of childhood didst thou intertwine for me
The passions that build up our human soul;
Not with the mean and vulgar works of man,
But with high objects, with enduring things—
With life and nature—purifying thus   **410**
The elements of feeling and of thought,
And sanctifying, by such discipline,
Both pain and fear, until we recognise
A grandeur in the beatings of the heart.
Nor was this fellowship vouchsafed to me
With stinted kindness. In November days,
When vapours rolling down the valley made
A lonely scene more lonesome, among woods,
At noon and 'mid the calm of summer nights,
When, by the margin of the trembling lake,   **420**
Beneath the gloomy hills homeward I went
In solitude, such intercourse was mine;
Mine was it in the fields both day and night,
And by the waters, all the summer long.

    And in the frosty season, when the sun
Was set, and visible for many a mile
The cottage windows blazed through twilight gloom,
I heeded not their summons: happy time
It was indeed for all of us—for me
It was a time of rapture! Clear and loud   **430**
The village clock tolled six,—I wheeled about,
Proud and exulting like an untired horse
That cares not for his home. All shod with steel,
We hissed along the polished ice in games

Confederate, imitative of the chase
And woodland pleasures,—the resounding horn,
The pack loud chiming, and the hunted hare.
So through the darkness and the cold we flew,
And not a voice was idle; with the din
Smitten, the precipices rang aloud;   440
The leafless trees and every icy crag
Tinkled like iron; while far distant hills
Into the tumult sent an alien sound
Of melancholy not unnoticed, while the stars
Eastward were sparkling clear, and in the west
The orange sky of evening died away.
Not seldom from the uproar I retired
Into a silent bay, or sportively
Glanced sideway, leaving the tumultuous throng,
To cut across the reflex of a star   450
That fled, and, flying still before me, gleamed
Upon the grassy plain; and oftentimes,
When we had given our bodies to the wind,
And all the shadowy banks on either side
Came sweeping through the darkness, spinning still
The rapid line of motion, then at once
Have I, reclining back upon my heels,
Stopped short; yet still the solitary cliffs
Wheeled by me—even as if the earth had rolled
With visible motion her diurnal round!   460
Behind me did they stretch in solemn train,
Feebler and feebler, and I stood and watched
Till all was tranquil as a dreamless sleep.

      Ye Presences of Nature in the sky
And on the earth! Ye Visions of the hills!
And Souls of lonely places! can I think
A vulgar hope was yours when ye employed
Such ministry, when ye, through many a year
Haunting me thus among my boyish sports,
On caves and trees, upon the woods and hills,   470
Impressed, upon all forms, the characters

Of danger or desire; and thus did make
The surface of the universal earth,
With triumph and delight, with hope and fear,
Work like a sea?

                  Not uselessly employed,
Might I pursue this theme through every change
Of exercise and play, to which the year
Did summon us in his delightful round.

    We were a noisy crew; the sun in heaven
Beheld not vales more beautiful than ours;   480
Nor saw a band in happiness and joy
Richer, or worthier of the ground they trod.
I could record with no reluctant voice
The woods of autumn, and their hazel bowers
With milk-white clusters hung; the rod and line,
True symbol of hope's foolishness, whose strong
And unreproved enchantment led us on
By rocks and pools shut out from every star,
All the green summer, to forlorn cascades
Among the windings hid of mountain brooks.   490
—Unfading recollections! at this hour
The heart is almost mine with which I felt,
From some hill-top on sunny afternoons,
The paper kite high among fleecy clouds
Pull at her rein like an impetuous courser;
Or, from the meadows sent on gusty days,
Beheld her breast the wind, then suddenly
Dashed headlong, and rejected by the storm.

    Ye lowly cottages wherein we dwelt,
A ministration of your own was yours;   500
Can I forget you, being as you were
So beautiful among the pleasant fields
In which ye stood? or can I here forget
The plain and seemly countenance with which
Ye dealt out your plain comforts? Yet had ye
Delights and exultations of your own.
Eager and never weary we pursued

Our home-amusements by the warm peat-fire
At evening, when with pencil, and smooth slate
In square divisions parcelled out and all   510
With crosses and with cyphers scribbled o'er,
We schemed and puzzled, head opposed to head
In strife too humble to be named in verse:
Or round the naked table, snow-white deal,
Cherry or maple, sate in close array,
And to the combat, Loo or Whist, led on
A thick-ribbed army; not, as in the world,
Neglected and ungratefully thrown by
Even for the very service they had wrought,
But husbanded through many a long campaign.   520
Uncouth assemblage was it, where no few
Had changed their functions: some, plebeian cards
Which Fate, beyond the promise of their birth,
Had dignified, and called to represent
The persons of departed potentates.
Oh, with what echoes on the board they fell!
Ironic diamonds,—clubs, hearts, diamonds, spades,
A congregation piteously akin!
Cheap matter offered they to boyish wit,
Those sooty knaves, precipitated down   530
With scoffs and taunts, like Vulcan out of heaven:
The paramount ace, a moon in her eclipse,
Queens gleaming through their splendour's last decay,
And monarchs surly at the wrongs sustained
By royal visages. Meanwhile abroad
Incessant rain was falling, or the frost
Raged bitterly, with keen and silent tooth;
And, interrupting oft that eager game,
From under Esthwaite's splitting fields of ice
The pent-up air, struggling to free itself,   540
Gave out to meadow grounds and hills a loud
Protracted yelling, like the noise of wolves
Howling in troops along the Bothnic Main.

Nor, sedulous as I have been to trace
How Nature by extrinsic passion first

Peopled the mind with forms sublime or fair,
And made me love them, may I here omit
How other pleasures have been mine, and joys
Of subtler origin; how I have felt,
Not seldom even in that tempestuous time,   550
Those hallowed and pure motions of the sense
Which seem, in their simplicity, to own
An intellectual charm; that calm delight
Which, if I err not, surely must belong
To those first-born affinities that fit
Our new existence to existing things,
And, in our dawn of being, constitute
The bond of union between life and joy.

    Yes, I remember when the changeful earth,
And twice five summers on my mind had stamped   560
The faces of the moving year, even then
I held unconscious intercourse with beauty
Old as creation, drinking in a pure
Organic pleasure from the silver wreaths
Of curling mist, or from the level plain
Of waters coloured by impending clouds.

    The sands of Westmoreland, the creeks and bays
Of Cumbria's rocky limits, they can tell
How, when the Sea threw off his evening shade,
And to the shepherd's hut on distant hills   570
Sent welcome notice of the rising moon,
How I have stood, to fancies such as these
A stranger, linking with the spectacle
No conscious memory of a kindred sight,
And bringing with me no peculiar sense
Of quietness or peace; yet have I stood,
Even while mine eye hath moved o'er many a league
Of shining water, gathering as it seemed,
Through every hair-breadth in that field of light,
New pleasure like a bee among the flowers.   580

    Thus oft amid those fits of vulgar joy
Which, through all seasons, on a child's pursuits

Are prompt attendants, 'mid that giddy bliss
Which, like a tempest, works along the blood
And is forgotten; even then I felt
Gleams like the flashing of a shield;—the earth
And common face of Nature spake to me
Rememberable things; sometimes, 'tis true.
By chance collisions and quaint accidents
(Like those ill-sorted unions, work supposed   590
Of evil-minded fairies), yet not vain
Nor profitless, if haply they impressed
Collateral objects and appearances,
Albeit lifeless then, and doomed to sleep
Until maturer seasons called them forth
To impregnate and to elevate the mind.
—And if the vulgar joy by its own weight
Wearied itself out of the memory,
The scenes which were a witness of that joy
Remained in their substantial lineaments   600
Depicted on the brain, and to the eye
Were visible, a daily sight; and thus
By the impressive discipline of fear,
By pleasure and repeated happiness,
So frequently repeated, and by force
Of obscure feelings representative
Of things forgotten, these same scenes so bright,
So beautiful, so majestic in themselves,
Though yet the day was distant, did become
Habitually dear, and all their forms   610
And changeful colours by invisible links
Were fastened to the affections.
                                        I began
My story early—not misled, I trust,
By an infirmity of love for days
Disowned by memory—ere the breath of spring
Planting my snowdrops among winter snows:
Nor will it seem to thee, O Friend! so prompt
In sympathy, that I have lengthened out
With fond and feeble tongue a tedious tale.

Meanwhile, my hope has been, that I might fetch   620
Invigorating thoughts from former years;
Might fix the wavering balance of my mind,
And haply meet reproaches too, whose power
May spur me on, in manhood now mature
To honourable toil. Yet should these hopes
Prove vain, and thus should neither I be taught
To understand myself, nor thou to know
With better knowledge how the heart was framed
Of him thou lovest; need I dread from thee
Harsh judgments, if the song be loth to quit   630
Those recollected hours that have the charm
Of visionary things, those lovely forms
And sweet sensations that throw back our life,
And almost make remotest infancy
A visible scene, on which the sun is shining?

    One end at least hath been attained; my mind
Hath been revived, and if this genial mood
Desert me not, forthwith shall be brought down
Through later years the story of my life.
The road lies plain before me;—'tis a theme   640
Single and of determined bounds; and hence
I choose it rather at this time, than work
Of ampler and more varied argument,
Where I might be discomfited and lost:
And certain hopes are with me, that to thee
This labour will be welcome, honoured Friend!

BOOK SECOND
School-Time (continued)

Thus far, O Friend! have we, though leaving much
Unvisited, endeavoured to retrace
The simple ways in which my childhood walked;
Those chiefly that first led me to the love
Of rivers, woods, and fields. The passion yet
Was in its birth, sustained as might befall

By nourishment that came unsought; for still
From week to week, from month to month, we lived
A round of tumult. Duly were our games
Prolonged in summer till the daylight failed;　　　　10
No chair remained before the doors; the bench
And threshold steps were empty; fast asleep
The labourer, and the old man who had sate
A later lingerer; yet the revelry
Continued and the loud uproar: at last,
When all the ground was dark, and twinkling stars
Edged the black clouds, home and to bed we went,
Feverish with weary joints and beating minds.
Ah! is there one who ever has been young,
Nor needs a warning voice to tame the pride　　　　20
Of intellect and virtue's self-esteem?
One is there, though the wisest and the best
Of all mankind, who covets not at times
Union that cannot be;—who would not give
If so he might, to duty and to truth
The eagerness of infantine desire?
A tranquillising spirit presses now
On my corporeal frame, so wide appears
The vacancy between me and those days
Which yet have such self-presence in my mind,　　　　30
That, musing on them, often do I seem
Two consciousnesses, conscious of myself
And of some other Being. A rude mass
Of native rock, left midway in the square
Of our small market village, was the goal
Or centre of these sports; and when, returned
After long absence, thither I repaired,
Gone was the old grey stone, and in its place
A smart Assembly-room usurped the ground
That had been ours. There let the fiddle scream,　　　　40
And be ye happy! Yet, my Friends! I know
That more than one of you will think with me
Of those soft starry nights, and that old Dame
From whom the stone was named, who there had sate,

And watched her table with its huckster's wares
Assiduous, through the length of sixty years.

    We ran a boisterous course; the year span round
With giddy motion. But the time approached
That brought with it a regular desire
For calmer pleasures, when the winning forms   50
Of Nature were collaterally attached
To every scheme of holiday delight
And every boyish sport, less grateful else
And languidly pursued.
                    When summer came,
Our pastime was, on bright half-holidays,
To sweep along the plain of Windermere
With rival oars; and the selected bourne
Was now an Island musical with birds
That sang and ceased not; now a Sister Isle
Beneath the oaks' umbrageous covert, sown   60
With lilies of the valley like a field;
And now a third small Island, where survived
In solitude the ruins of a shrine
Once to Our Lady dedicate, and served
Daily with chaunted rites. In such a race
So ended, disappointment could be none,
Uneasiness, or pain, or jealousy:
We rested in the shade, all pleased alike,
Conquered and conqueror. Thus the pride of strength,
And the vain-glory of superior skill,   70
Were tempered; thus was gradually produced
A quiet independence of the heart:
And to my Friend who knows me I may add,
Fearless of blame, that hence for future days
Ensued a diffidence and modesty,
And I was taught to feel, perhaps too much,
The self-sufficing power of Solitude.

    Our daily meals were frugal, Sabine fare!
More than we wished we knew the blessing then
Of vigorous hunger—hence corporeal strength   80

Unsapped by delicate viands; for, exclude
A little weekly stipend, and we lived
Through three divisions of the quartered year
In penniless poverty. But now to school
From the half-yearly holidays returned,
We came with weightier purses, that sufficed
To furnish treats more costly than the Dame
Of the old grey stone, from her scant board, supplied.
Hence rustic dinners on the cool green ground,
Or in the woods, or by a river side   90
Or shady fountains, while among the leaves
Soft airs were stirring, and the mid-day sun
Unfelt shone brightly round us in our joy.
Nor is my aim neglected if I tell
How sometimes, in the length of those half-years,
We from our funds drew largely;—proud to curb,
And eager to spur on, the galloping steed;
And with the courteous inn-keeper, whose stud
Supplied our want, we haply might employ
Sly subterfuge, if the adventure's bound   100
Were distant: some famed temple where of yore
The Druids worshipped, or the antique walls
Of that large abbey, where within the Vale
Of Nightshade, to St. Mary's honour built,
Stands yet a mouldering pile with fractured arch,
Belfry, and images, and living trees;
A holy scene!—Along the smooth green turf
Our horses grazed. To more than inland peace,
Left by the west wind sweeping overhead
From a tumultuous ocean, trees and towers   110
In that sequestered valley may be seen,
Both silent and both motionless alike;
Such the deep shelter that is there, and such
The safeguard for repose and quietness.

Our steeds remounted and the summons given,
With whip and spur we through the chauntry flew
In uncouth race, and left the cross-legged knight,

And the stone-abbot, and that single wren
Which one day sang so sweetly in the nave
Of the old church, that—though from recent showers   120
The earth was comfortless, and, touched by faint
Internal breezes, sobbings of the place
And respirations, from the roofless walls
The shuddering ivy dripped large drops—yet still
So sweetly 'mid the gloom the invisible bird
Sang to herself, that there I could have made
My dwelling-place, and lived for ever there
To hear such music. Through the walls we flew
And down the valley, and, a circuit made
In wantonness of heart, through rough and smooth   130
We scampered homewards. Oh, ye rocks and streams,
And that still spirit shed from evening air!
Even in this joyous time I sometimes felt
Your presence, when with slackened step we breathed
Along the sides of the steep hills, or when
Lighted by gleams of moonlight from the sea
We beat with thundering hoofs the level sand.

     Midway on long Winander's eastern shore,
Within the crescent of a pleasant bay,
A tavern stood; no homely-featured house,   140
Primeval like its neighbouring cottages,
But 't was a splendid place, the door beset
With chaises, grooms, and liveries, and within
Decanters, glasses, and the blood-red wine.
In ancient times, and ere the Hall was built
On the large island, had this dwelling been
More worthy of a poet's love, a hut,
Proud of its own bright fire and sycamore shade.
But—though the rhymes were gone that once inscribed
The threshold, and large golden characters,   150
Spread o'er the spangled sign-board, had dislodged
The old Lion and usurped his place, in slight
And mockery of the rustic painter's hand—
Yet, to this hour, the spot to me is dear

With all its foolish pomp. The garden lay
Upon a slope surmounted by a plain
Of a small bowling-green; beneath us stood
A grove, with gleams of water through the trees
And over the tree-tops; nor did we want
Refreshment, strawberries and mellow cream.   160
There, while through half an afternoon we played
On the smooth platform, whether skill prevailed
Or happy blunder triumphed, bursts of glee
Made all the mountains ring. But, ere night-fall,
When in our pinnace we returned at leisure
Over the shadowy lake, and to the beach
Of some small island steered our course with one,
The Minstrel of the Troop, and left him there,
And rowed off gently, while he blew his flute
Alone upon the rock—oh, then, the calm   170
And dead still water lay upon my mind
Even with a weight of pleasure, and the sky,
Never before so beautiful, sank down
Into my heart, and held me like a dream!
Thus were my sympathies enlarged, and thus
Daily the common range of visible things
Grew dear to me: already I began
To love the sun; a boy I loved the sun,
Not as I since have loved him, as a pledge
And surety of our earthly life, a light   180
Which we behold and feel we are alive;
Nor for his bounty to so many worlds—
But for this cause, that I had seen him lay
His beauty on the morning hills, had seen
The western mountain touch his setting orb,
In many a thoughtless hour, when, from excess
Of happiness, my blood appeared to flow
For its own pleasure, and I breathed with joy.
And, from like feelings, humble though intense.
To patriotic and domestic love   190
Analogous, the moon to me was dear;
For I could dream away my purposes,
Standing to gaze upon her while she hung

Midway between the hills as if she knew
No other region, but belonged to thee,
Yea, appertained by a peculiar right
To thee and thy grey huts, thou one dear Vale!

Those incidental charms which first attached
My heart to rural objects, day by day
Grew weaker, and I hasten on to tell   200
How Nature, intervenient till this time
And secondary, now at length was sought
For her own sake. But who shall parcel out
His intellect by geometric rules,
Split like a province into round and square?
Who knows the individual hour in which
His habits were first sown, even as a seed?
Who that shall point as with a wand and say
"This portion of the river of my mind
Came from yon fountain?" Thou, my Friend, art one   210
More deeply read in thy own thoughts; to thee
Science appears but what in truth she is,
Not as our glory and our absolute boast,
But as a succedaneum, and a prop
To our infirmity. No officious slave
Art thou of that false secondary power
By which we multiply distinctions, then
Deem that our puny boundaries are things
That we perceive, and not that we have made.
To thee, unblinded by these formal arts,   220
The unity of all hath been revealed,
And thou wilt doubt, with me less aptly skilled
Than many are to range the faculties
In scale and order, class the cabinet
Of their sensations, and in voluble phrase
Run through the history and birth of each
As of a single independent thing.
Hard task, vain hope, to analyse the mind,
If each most obvious and particular thought,
Not in a mystical and idle sense,   230
But in the words of Reason deeply weighed,

Hath no beginning.
                              Blest the infant Babe.
(For with my best conjecture I would trace
Our Being's earthly progress,) blest the Babe,
Nursed in his Mother's arms, who sinks to sleep
Rocked on his Mother's breast; who with his soul
Drinks in the feelings of his Mother's eye!
For him, in one dear Presence, there exists
A virtue which irradiates and exalts
Objects through widest intercourse of sense;   240
No outcast he, bewildered and depressed:
Along his infant veins are interfused
The gravitation and the filial bond
Of nature that connect him with the world.
Is there a flower, to which he points with hand
Too weak to gather it, already love
Drawn from love's purest earthly fount for him
Hath beautified that flower; already shades
Of pity cast from inward tenderness
Do fall around him upon aught that bears   250
Unsightly marks of violence or harm.
Emphatically such a Being lives,
Frail creature as he is, helpless as frail,
An inmate of this active universe:
For, feeling has to him imparted power
That through the growing faculties of sense
Doth like an agent of the one great Mind
Create, creator and receiver both,
Working but in alliance with the works
Which it beholds.—Such, verily, is the first   260
Poetic spirit of our human life,
By uniform control of after years,
In most, abated or suppressed; in some,
Through every change of growth and of decay,
Pre-eminent till death.
                              From early days,
Beginning not long after that first time
In which, a Babe, by intercourse of touch

I held mute dialogues with my Mother's heart,
I have endeavoured to display the means
Whereby this infant sensibility,   270
Great birthright of our being, was in me
Augmented and sustained. Yet is a path
More difficult before me; and I fear
That in its broken windings we shall need
The chamois' sinews, and the eagle's wing:
For now a trouble came into my mind
From unknown causes. I was left alone
Seeking the visible world, nor knowing why.
The props of my affections were removed,
And yet the building stood, as if sustained   280
By its own spirit! All that I beheld
Was dear, and hence to finer influxes
The mind lay open to a more exact
And close communion. Many are our joys
In youth, but oh! what happiness to live
When every hour brings palpable access
Of knowledge, when all knowledge is delight,
And sorrow is not there! The seasons came,
And every season wheresoe'er I moved
Unfolded transitory qualities,   290
Which, but for this most watchful power of love,
Had been neglected; left a register
Of permanent relations, else unknown.
Hence life, and change, and beauty, solitude
More active ever than "best society"—
Society made sweet as solitude
By silent inobtrusive sympathies,
And gentle agitations of the mind
From manifold distinctions, difference
Perceived in things, where, to the unwatchful eye,   300
No difference is, and hence, from the same source,
Sublimer joy; for I would walk alone,
Under the quiet stars, and at that time
Have felt whate'er there is of power in sound
To breathe an elevated mood, by form

Or image unprofaned; and I would stand,
If the night blackened with a coming storm,
Beneath some rock, listening to notes that are
The ghostly language of the ancient earth,
Or make their dim abode in distant winds.   310
Thence did I drink the visionary power;
And deem not profitless those fleeting moods
Of shadowy exultation: not for this,
That they are kindred to our purer mind
And intellectual life; but that the soul,
Remembering how she felt, but what she felt
Remembering not, retains an obscure sense
Of possible sublimity, whereto
With growing faculties she doth aspire,
With faculties still growing, feeling still   320
That whatsoever point they gain, they yet
Have something to pursue.
                                        And not alone,
'Mid gloom and tumult, but no less 'mid fair
And tranquil scenes, that universal power
And fitness in the latent qualities
And essences of things, by which the mind
Is moved with feelings of delight, to me
Came strengthened with a superadded soul,
A virtue not its own. My morning walks
Were early;—oft before the hours of school   330
I travelled round our little lake, five miles
Of pleasant wandering.

        Happy time! more dear
For this, that one was by my side, a Friend,
Then passionately loved; with heart how full
Would he peruse these lines! For many years
Have since flowed in between us, and our minds
Both silent to each other, at this time
We live as if those hours had never been.
Nor seldom did I lift our cottage latch
Far earlier, ere one smoke-wreath had risen   340
From human dwelling, or the vernal thrush

Was audible; and sate among the woods
Alone upon some jutting eminence,
At the first gleam of dawn-light, when the Vale,
Yet slumbering, lay in utter solitude.
How shall I seek the origin? where find
Faith in the marvellous things which then I felt?
Oft in these moments such a holy calm
Would overspread my soul, that bodily eyes
Were utterly forgotten, and what I saw   350
Appeared like something in myself, a dream,
A prospect in the mind.

                    'Twere long to tell
What spring and autumn, what the winter snows,
And what the summer shade, what day and night,
Evening and morning, sleep and waking, thought
From sources inexhaustible, poured forth
To feed the spirit of religious love
In which I walked with Nature. But let this
Be not forgotten, that I still retained
My first creative sensibility;   360
That by the regular action of the world
My soul was unsubdued. A plastic power
Abode with me; a forming hand, at times
Rebellious, acting in a devious mood;
A local spirit of his own, at war
With general tendency, but, for the most,
Subservient strictly to external things
With which it communed. An auxiliar light
Came from my mind, which on the setting sun
Bestowed new splendour; the melodious birds,   370
The fluttering breezes, fountains that run on
Murmuring so sweetly in themselves, obeyed
A like dominion, and the midnight storm
Grew darker in the presence of my eye:
Hence my obeisance, my devotion hence,
And hence my transport.

                    Nor should this, perchance,
Pass unrecorded, that I still had loved

The exercise and produce of a toil,
Than analytic industry to me
More pleasing, and whose character I deem   380
Is more poetic as resembling more
Creative agency. The song would speak
Of that interminable building reared
By observation of affinities
In objects where no brotherhood exists
To passive minds. My seventeenth year was come
And, whether from this habit rooted now
So deeply in my mind, or from excess
In the great social principle of life
Coercing all things into sympathy,   390
To unorganic natures were transferred
My own enjoyments; or the power of truth
Coming in revelation, did converse
With things that really are; I, at this time,
Saw blessings spread around me like a sea.
Thus while the days flew by, and years passed on,
From Nature and her overflowing soul,
I had received so much, that all my thoughts
Were steeped in feeling; I was only then
Contented, when with bliss ineffable   400
I felt the sentiment of Being spread
O'er all that moves and all that seemeth still;
O'er all that, lost beyond the reach of thought
And human knowledge, to the human eye
Invisible, yet liveth to the heart;
O'er all that leaps and runs, and shouts and sings,
Or beats the gladsome air; o'er all that glides
Beneath the wave, yea, in the wave itself,
And mighty depth of waters. Wonder not
If high the transport, great the joy I felt,   410
Communing in this sort through earth and heaven
With every form of creature, as it looked
Towards the Uncreated with a countenance
Of adoration, with an eye of love.
One song they sang, and it was audible,

Most audible, then, when the fleshy ear,
O'ercome by humblest prelude of that strain,
Forgot her functions, and slept undisturbed.

    If this be error, and another faith
Find easier access to the pious mind,   420
Yet were I grossly destitute of all
Those human sentiments that make this earth
So dear, if I should fail with grateful voice
To speak of you, ye mountains, and ye lakes
And sounding cataracts, ye mists and winds
That dwell among the hills where I was born.
If in my youth I have been pure in heart,
If, mingling with the world, I am content
With my own modest pleasures, and have lived
With God and Nature communing, removed   430
From little enmities and low desires—
The gift is yours; if in these times of fear,
This melancholy waste of hopes o'erthrown,
If, 'mid indifference and apathy,
And wicked exultation when good men
On every side fall off, we know not how,
To selfishness, disguised in gentle names
Of peace and quiet and domestic love
Yet mingled not unwillingly with sneers
On visionary minds; if, in this time   440
Of dereliction and dismay, I yet
Despair not of our nature, but retain
A more than Roman confidence, a faith
That fails not, in all sorrow, my support,
The blessing of my life—the gift is yours,
Ye winds and sounding cataracts! 'tis yours,
Ye mountains! thine, O Nature! Thou hast fed
My lofty speculations; and in thee,
For this uneasy heart of ours, I find
A never-failing principle of joy   450
And purest passion.

                Thou, my Friend! wert reared

In the great city, 'mid far other scenes;
But we, by different roads, at length have gained
The selfsame bourne. And for this cause to thee
I speak, unapprehensive of contempt,
The insinuated scoff of coward tongues,
And all that silent language which so oft
In conversation between man and man
Blots from the human countenance all trace
Of beauty and of love. For thou hast sought   460
The truth in solitude, and, since the days
That gave thee liberty, full long desired,
To serve in Nature's temple, thou hast been
The most assiduous of her ministers;
In many things my brother, chiefly here
In this our deep devotion.
                                    Fare thee well!
Health and the quiet of a healthful mind
Attend thee! seeking oft the haunts of men,
And yet more often living with thyself,
And for thyself, so haply shall thy days   470
Be many, and a blessing to mankind.

BOOK THIRD
Residence at Cambridge

It was a dreary morning when the wheels
Rolled over a wide plain o'erhung with clouds,
And nothing cheered our way till first we saw
The long-roofed chapel of King's College lift
Turrets and pinnacles in answering files,
Extended high above a dusky grove.

   Advancing, we espied upon the road
A student clothed in gown and tasselled cap,
Striding along as if o'ertasked by Time,
Or covetous of exercise and air;   10
He passed—nor was I master of my eyes
Till he was left an arrow's flight behind.
As near and nearer to the spot we drew,

It seemed to suck us in with an eddy's force.
Onward we drove beneath the Castle; caught,
While crossing the Magdalene Bridge, a glimpse of Cam;
And at the *Hoop* alighted, famous Inn.

My spirit was up, my thoughts were full of hope;
Some friends I had, acquaintances who there
Seemed friends, poor simple schoolboys, now hung round   20
With honour and importance: in a world
Of welcome faces up and down I roved;
Questions, directions, warnings and advice,
Flowed in upon me, from all sides; fresh day
Of pride and pleasure! to myself I seemed
A man of business and expense, and went
From shop to shop about my own affairs,
To Tutor or to Tailor, as befell,
From street to street with loose and careless mind.

I was the Dreamer, they the Dream; I roamed   30
Delighted through the motley spectacle;
Gowns grave, or gaudy, doctors, students, streets,
Courts, cloisters, flocks of churches, gateways, towers:
Migration strange for a stripling of the hills,
A northern villager.
                              As if the change
Had waited on some Fairy's wand, at once
Behold me rich in monies, and attired
In splendid garb, with hose of silk, and hair
Powdered like rimy trees, when frost is keen.
My lordly dressing-gown, I pass it by,   40
With other signs of manhood that supplied
The lack of beard.—The weeks went roundly on,
With invitations, suppers, wine and fruit,
Smooth housekeeping within, and all without
Liberal, and suiting gentleman's array.

The Evangelist St. John my patron was:
Three Gothic courts are his, and in the first
Was my abiding-place, a nook obscure;
Right underneath, the College kitchens made

A humming sound, less tuneable than bees,   50
But hardly less industrious; with shrill notes
Of sharp command and scolding intermixed.
Near me hung Trinity's loquacious clock,
Who never let the quarters, night or day,
Slip by him unproclaimed, and told the hours
Twice over with a male and female voice.
Her pealing organ was my neighbour too;
And from my pillow, looking forth by light
Of moon or favouring stars, I could behold
The antechapel where the statue stood   60
Of Newton with his prism and silent face,
The marble index of a mind for ever
Voyaging through strange seas of Thought, alone.

    Of College labours, of the Lecturer's room
All studded round, as thick as chairs could stand,
With loyal students, faithful to their books,
Half-and-half idlers, hardy recusants,
And honest dunces—of important days,
Examinations, when the man was weighed
As in a balance! of excessive hopes,   70
Tremblings withal and commendable fears,
Small jealousies, and triumphs good or bad—
Let others that know more speak as they know.
Such glory was but little sought by me,
And little won. Yet from the first crude days
Of settling time in this untried abode,
I was disturbed at times by prudent thoughts,
Wishing to hope without a hope, some fears
About my future worldly maintenance,
And, more than all, a strangeness in the mind,   80
A feeling that I was not for that hour,
Nor for that place. But wherefore be cast down?
For (not to speak of Reason and her pure
Reflective acts to fix the moral law
Deep in the conscience, nor of Christian Hope,
Bowing her head before her sister Faith

As one far mightier), hither I had come,
Bear witness Truth, endowed with holy powers
And faculties, whether to work or feel.
Oft when the dazzling show no longer new   90
Had ceased to dazzle, ofttimes did I quit
My comrades, leave the crowd, buildings and groves,
And as I paced alone the level fields
Far from those lovely sights and sounds sublime
With which I had been conversant, the mind
Drooped not; but there into herself returning,
With prompt rebound seemed fresh as heretofore.
At least I more distinctly recognised
Her native instincts: let me dare to speak
A higher language, say that now I felt   100
What independent solaces were mine,
To mitigate the injurious sway of place
Or circumstance, how far soever changed
In youth, or *to* be changed in after years.
As if awakened, summoned, roused, constrained,
I looked for universal things; perused
The common countenance of earth and sky:
Earth, nowhere unembellished by some trace
Of that first Paradise whence man was driven;
And sky, whose beauty and bounty are expressed   110
By the proud name she bears—the name of Heaven.
I called on both to teach me what they might;
Or, turning the mind in upon herself,
Pored, watched, expected, listened, spread my thoughts
And spread them with a wider creeping; felt
Incumbencies more awful, visitings
Of the Upholder of the tranquil soul,
That tolerates the indignities of Time,
And, from the centre of Eternity
All finite motions overruling, lives   120
In glory immutable. But peace! enough
Here to record that I was mounting now
To such community with highest truth—
A track pursuing, not untrod, before,

From strict analogies by thought supplied
Or consciousness not to be subdued.
To every natural form, rock, fruits, or flower,
Even the loose stones that cover the highway,
I gave a moral life: I saw them feel,
Or linked them to some feeling: the great mass   130
Lay imbedded in a quickening soul, and all
That I beheld respired with inward meaning.
Add that whate'er of Terror or of Love
Or Beauty, Nature's daily face put on
From transitory passion, unto this
I was as sensitive as waters are
To the sky's influence in a kindred mood
Of passion; was obedient as a lute
That waits upon the touches of the wind.
Unknown, unthought of, yet I was most rich—   140
I had a world about me—'t was my own;
I made it, for it only lived to me,
And to the God who sees into the heart.
Such sympathies, though rarely, were betrayed
By outward gestures and by visible looks:
Some called it madness—so indeed it was,
If child-like fruitfulness in passing joy,
If steady moods of thoughtfulness matured
To inspiration, sort with such a name;
If prophecy be madness; if things viewed   150
By poets in old time, and higher up
By the first men, earth's first inhabitants,
May in these tutored days no more be seen
With undisordered sight. But leaving this,
It was no madness, for the bodily eye
Amid my strongest workings evermore
Was searching out the lines of difference
As they lie hid in all external forms,
Near or remote, minute or vast; an eye
Which, from a tree, a stone, a withered leaf,   160
To the broad ocean and the azure heavens
Spangled with kindred multitudes of stars,
Could find no surface where its power might sleep;

Which spake perpetual logic to my soul,
And by an unrelenting agency
Did bind my feelings even as in a chain.

    And here, O Friend! have I retraced my life
Up to an eminence, and told a tale
Of matters which not falsely may be called
The glory of my youth. Of genius, power,   **170**
Creation and divinity itself
I have been speaking, for my theme has been
What has passed within me. Not of outward things
Done visibly for other minds, words, signs,
Symbols or actions, but of my own heart
Have I been speaking, and my youthful mind.
O Heavens! how awful is the might of souls,
And what they do within themselves while yet
The yoke of earth is new to them, the world
Nothing but a wild field where they were sown.   **180**
This is, in truth, heroic argument,
This genuine prowess, which I wished to touch
With hand however weak, but in the main
It lies far hidden from the reach of words.
Points have we all of us within our souls
Where all stand single; this I feel, and make
Breathings for incommunicable powers;
But is not each a memory to himself,
And, therefore, now that we must quit this theme,
I am not heartless, for there's not a man   **190**
That lives who hath not known his god-like hours,
And feels not what an empire we inherit
As natural beings in the strength of Nature.

    No more: for now into a populous plain
We must descend. A Traveller I am,
Whose tale is only of himself; even so,
So be it, if the pure of heart be prompt
To follow, and if thou, my honoured Friend!
Who in these thoughts art ever at my side,
Support, as heretofore, my fainting steps.   **200**

It hath been told, that when the first delight
That flashed upon me from this novel show
Had failed, the mind returned into herself;
Yet true it is, that I had made a change
In climate, and my nature's outward coat
Changed also slowly and insensibly.
Full oft the quiet and exalted thoughts
Of loneliness gave way to empty noise
And superficial pastimes; now and then
Forced labour, and more frequently forced hopes;   210
And, worst, of all, a treasonable growth
Of indecisive judgments, that impaired
And shook the mind's simplicity.—And yet
This was a gladsome time. Could I behold—
Who, less insensible than sodden clay
In a sea-river's bed at ebb of tide,
Could have beheld—with undelighted heart,
So many happy youths, so wide and fair
A congregation in its budding-time
Of health, and hope, and beauty, all at once   220
So many divers samples from the growth
Of life's sweet season—could have seen unmoved
That miscellaneous garland of wild flowers
Decking the matron temples of a place
So famous, through the world? To me, at least,
It was a goodly prospect: for, in sooth,
Though I had learnt betimes to stand unpropped,
And independent musings pleased me so
That spells seemed on me when I was alone,
Yet could I only cleave to solitude   230
In lonely places; if a throng was near
That way I leaned by nature; for my heart
Was social, and loved idleness and joy.

Not seeking those who might participate
My deeper pleasures (nay, I had not once,
Though not unused to mutter lonesome songs,
Even with myself divided such delight,
Or looked that way for aught that might be clothed

In human language), easily I passed
From the remembrances of better things,   240
And slipped into the ordinary works
Of careless youth, unburthened, unalarmed.
Caverns there were within my mind which sun
Could never penetrate, yet did there not
Want store of leafy *arbours* where the light
Might enter in at will. Companionships,
Friendships, acquaintances, were welcome all.
We sauntered, played, or rioted; we talked
Unprofitable talk at morning hours;
Drifted about along the streets and walks,   250
Read lazily in trivial books, went forth
To gallop through the country in blind zeal
Of senseless horsemanship, or on the breast
Of Cam sailed boisterously, and let the stars
Come forth, perhaps without one quiet thought.

Such was the tenor of the second act
In this new life. Imagination slept,
And yet not utterly. I could not print
Ground where the grass had yielded to the steps
Of generations of illustrious men,   260
Unmoved. I could not always lightly pass
Through the same gateways, sleep where they had slept,
Wake where they waked, range that inclosure old,
That garden of great intellects, undisturbed.
Place also by the side of this dark sense
Of noble feeling, that those spiritual men,
Even the great Newton's own ethereal self,
Seemed humbled in these precincts, thence to be
The more endeared. Their several memories here
(Even like their persons in their portraits clothed   270
With the accustomed garb of daily life)
Put on a lowly and a touching grace
Of more distinct humanity, that left
All genuine admiration unimpaired.

Beside the pleasant Mill of Trompington
I laughed with Chaucer in the hawthorn shade;

Heard him, while birds were warbling, tell his tales
Of amorous passion. And that gentle Bard,
Chosen by the Muses for their Page of State—
Sweet Spenser, moving through his clouded heaven   280
With the moon's beauty and the moon's soft pace,
I called him Brother, Englishman, and Friend!
Yea, our blind Poet, who in his later day,
Stood almost single; uttering odious truth—
Darkness before, and danger's voice behind,
Soul awful—if the earth has ever lodged
An awful soul—I seemed to see him here
Familiarly, and in his scholar's dress
Bounding before me, yet a stripling youth—
A boy, no better, with his rosy cheeks   290
Angelical, keen eye, courageous look,
And conscious step of purity and pride.
Among the band of my compeers was one
Whom chance had stationed in the very room
Honoured by Milton's name. O temperate Bard!
Be it confest that, for the first time, seated
Within thy innocent lodge and oratory,
One of a festive circle, I poured out
Libations, to thy memory drank, till pride
And gratitude grew dizzy in a brain   300
Never excited by the fumes of wine
Before that hour, or since. Then, forth I ran
From the assembly; through a length of streets,
Ran, ostrich-like, to reach our chapel door
In not a desperate or opprobrious time,
Albeit long after the importunate bell
Had stopped, with wearisome Cassandra voice
No longer haunting the dark winter night.
Call back, O Friend! a moment to thy mind,
The place itself and fashion of the rites.   310
With careless ostentation shouldering up
My surplice, through the inferior throng I clove
Of the plain Burghers, who in audience stood
On the last skirts of their permitted ground,

Under the pealing organ. Empty thoughts!
I am ashamed of them: and that great Bard,
And thou, O Friend! who in thy ample mind
Hast placed me high above my best deserts,
Ye will forgive the weakness of that hour,
In some of its unworthy vanities,   320
Brother to many more.
                         In this mixed sort
The months passed on, remissly, not given up
To wilful alienation from the right
Or walks of open scandal, but in vague
And loose indifference, easy likings, aims
Of a low pitch—duty and zeal dismissed,
Yet Nature, or a happy course of things
Not doing in their stead the needful work.
The memory languidly revolved, the heart
Reposed in noontide rest, the inner pulse   330
Of contemplation almost failed to beat.
Such life might not inaptly be compared
To a floating island, an amphibious spot
Unsound, of spongy texture, yet withal
Not wanting a fair face of water weeds
And pleasant flowers. The thirst of living praise,
Fit reverence for the glorious Dead, the sight
Of those long vistas, sacred catacombs,
Where mighty *minds* lie visibly entombed,
Have often stirred the heart of youth, and bred   340
A fervent love of rigorous discipline.—
Alas! such high emotion touched not me.
Look was there none within these walls to shame
My easy spirits, and discountenance
Their light composure, far less to instil
A calm resolve of mind, firmly addressed
To puissant efforts. Nor was this the blame
Of others but my own; I should, in truth,
As far as doth concern my single self,
Misdeem most widely, lodging it elsewhere: 350
For I, bred up 'mid Nature's luxuries,

Was a spoiled child, and, rambling like the wind,
As I had done in daily intercourse
With those crystalline rivers, solemn heights,
And mountains, raging like a fowl of the air,
I was ill-tutored for captivity;
To quit my pleasure, and, from month to month,
Take up a station calmly on the perch
Of sedentary peace. Those lovely forms
Had also left less space within my mind,   360
Which, wrought upon instinctively, had found
A freshness in those objects of her love,
A winning power, beyond all other power.
Not that I slighted books,—that were to lack
All sense,—but other passions in me ruled,
Passions more fervent, making me less prompt
To in-door study than was wise or well,
Or suited to those years. Yet I, though used
In magisterial liberty to rove,
Culling such flowers of learning as might tempt   370
A random choice, could shadow forth a place
(If now I yield not to a flattering dream)
Whose studious aspect should have bent me down
To instantaneous service; should at once
Have made me pay to science and to arts
And written lore, acknowledged my liege lord,
A homage frankly offered up, like that
Which I had paid to Nature. Toil and pains
In this recess, by thoughtful Fancy built,
Should spread from heart to heart; and stately groves,   380
Majestic edifices, should not want
A corresponding dignity within.
The congregating temper that pervades
Our unripe years, not wasted, should be taught
To minister to works of high attempt—
Works which the enthusiast would perform with love.
Youth should be awed, religiously possessed
With a conviction of the power that waits
On knowledge, when sincerely sought and prized

For its own sake, on glory and on praise
If but by labour won, and fit to endure   390
The passing day; should learn to put aside
Her trappings here, should strip them off abashed
Before antiquity and stedfast truth
And strong book-mindedness; and over all
A healthy sound simplicity should reign,
A seemly plainness, name it what you will,
Republican or pious.

                        If these thoughts
Are a gratuitous emblazonry
That mocks the recreant age *we* live in, then   400
Be Folly and False-seeming free to affect
Whatever formal gait of discipline
Shall raise them highest in their own esteem—
Let them parade among the Schools at will,
But spare the House of God. Was ever known
The witless shepherd who persists to drive
A flock that thirsts not to a pool disliked?
A weight must surely hang on days begun
And ended with such mockery. Be wise,
Ye Presidents and Deans, and, till the spirit   410
Of ancient times revive, and youth be trained
At home in pious service, to your bells
Give seasonable rest, for 'tis a sound
Hollow as ever vexed the tranquil air;
And your officious doings bring disgrace
On the plain steeples of our English Church,
Whose worship, 'mid remotest village trees,
Suffers for this. Even Science, too, at hand
In daily sight of this irreverence,
Is smitten thence with an unnatural taint,   420
Loses her just authority, falls beneath
Collateral suspicion, else unknown.
This truth escaped me not, and I confess,
That having 'mid my native hills given loose
To a schoolboy's vision, I had raised a pile
Upon the basis of the coming time,

That fell in ruins round me. Oh, what joy
To see a sanctuary for our country's youth
Informed with such a spirit as might be
Its own protection; a primeval grove,   430
Where, though the shades with cheerfulness were filled,
Nor indigent of songs warbled from crowds
In under-coverts, yet the countenance
Of the whole place should bear a stamp of awe;
A habitation sober and demure
For ruminating creatures; a domain
For quiet things to wander in; a haunt
In which the heron should delight to feed
By the shy rivers, and the pelican
Upon the cypress spire in lonely thought   440
Might sit and sun himself.—Alas! Alas!
In vain for such solemnity I looked;
Mine eyes were crossed by butterflies, ears vexed
By chattering popinjays; the inner heart
Seemed trivial, and the impresses without
Of a too gaudy region.
                                              Different sight
Those venerable Doctors saw of old,
When all who dwelt within these famous walls
Led in abstemiousness a studious life;
When, in forlorn and naked chambers cooped   450
And crowded, o'er the ponderous books they hung
Like caterpillars eating out their way
In silence, or with keen devouring noise
Not to be tracked or fathered. Princes then
At matins froze, and couched at curfew-time,
Trained up through piety and zeal to prize
Spare diet, patient labour, and plain weeds.
O seat of Arts! renowned throughout the world!
Far different service in those homely days
The Muses' modest nurslings underwent   460
From their first childhood: in that glorious time
When Learning, like a stranger come from far,
Sounding through Christian lands her trumpet, roused

Peasant and king; when boys and youths, the growth
Of ragged villages and crazy huts,
Forsook their homes, and, errant in the quest
Of Patron, famous school or friendly nook,
Where, pensioned, they in shelter might sit down,
From town to town and through wide scattered realms
Journeyed with ponderous folios in their hands;   470
And often, starting from some covert place,
Saluted the chance comer on the road,
Crying, "An obolus, a penny give
To a poor scholar!"—when illustrious men,
Lovers of truth, by penury constrained,
Bucer, Erasmus, or Melancthon, read
Before the doors or windows of their cells
By moonshine through mere lack of taper light.

    But peace to vain regrets! We see but darkly
Even when we look behind us, and best things   480
Are not so pure by nature that they needs
Must keep to all, as fondly all believe,
Their highest promise. If the mariner,
When at reluctant distance he hath passed
Some tempting island, could but know the ills
That must have fallen upon him had he brought
His bark to land upon the wished-for shore,
Good cause would oft be his to thank the surf
Whose white belt scared him thence, or wind that blew
Inexorably adverse: for myself   490
I grieve not; happy is the gownèd youth,
Who only misses what I missed, who falls
No lower than I fell.
                I did not love,
Judging not ill perhaps, the timid course
Of our scholastic studies; could have wished
To see the river flow with ampler range
And freer pace; but more, far more, I grieved
To see displayed among an eager few,
Who in the field of contest persevered,

Passions unworthy of youth's generous heart   500
And mounting spirit, pitiably repaid,
When so disturbed, whatever palms are won.
From these I turned to travel with the shoal
Of more unthinking natures, easy minds
And pillowy; yet not wanting love that makes
The day pass lightly on, when foresight sleeps,
And wisdom and the pledges interchanged
With our own inner being are forgot.

　　Yet was this deep vacation not given up
To utter waste. Hitherto I had stood   510
In my own mind remote from social life,
(At least from what we commonly so name,)
Like a lone shepherd on a promontory,
Who lacking occupation looks far forth
Into the boundless sea, and rather makes
Than finds what he beholds. And sure it is,
That this first transit from the smooth delights
And wild outlandish walks of simple youth
To something that resembles an approach
Towards human business, to a privileged world   520
Within a world, a midway residence
With all its intervenient imagery,
Did better suit my visionary mind,
Far better, than to have been bolted forth,
Thrust out abruptly into Fortune's way
Among the conflicts of substantial life;
By a more just gradation did lead on
To higher things; more naturally matured,
For permanent possession, better fruits,
Whether of truth or virtue, to ensue.   530
In serious mood, but oftener, I confess,
With playful zest of fancy, did we note
(How could we less?) the manners and the ways
Of those who lived distinguished by the badge
Of good or ill report; or those with whom
By frame of Academic discipline
We were perforce connected, men whose sway

And known authority of office served
To set our minds on edge, and did no more.
Nor wanted we rich pastime of this kind,   540
Found everywhere, but chiefly in the ring
Of the grave Elders, men unscoured, grotesque
In character, tricked out like aged trees
Which through the lapse of their infirmity
Give ready place to any random seed
That chooses to be reared upon their trunks.

    Here on my view, confronting vividly
Those shepherd swains whom I had lately left
Appeared a different aspect of old age;
How different! yet both distinctly marked,   550
Objects embossed to catch the general eye,
Or portraitures for special use designed,
As some might seem, so aptly do they serve
To illustrate Nature's book of rudiments—
That book upheld as with maternal care
When she would enter on her tender scheme
Of teaching comprehension with delight,
And mingling playful with pathetic thoughts.

    The surfaces of artificial life
And manners finely wrought, the delicate race   560
Of colours, lurking, gleaming up and down
Through that state arras woven with silk and gold;
This wily interchange of snaky hues,
Willingly or unwillingly revealed,
I neither knew nor cared for; and as such
Were wanting here, I took what might be found
Of less elaborate fabric. At this day
I smile, in many a mountain solitude
Conjuring up scenes as obsolete in freaks
Of character, in points of wit as broad,   570
As aught by wooden images performed
For entertainment of the gaping crowd
At wake or fair. And oftentimes do flit
Remembrances, before me of old men—
Old humourists, who have been long in their graves,

And having almost in my mind put off
Their human names, have into phantoms passed
Of texture midway between life and books.

    I play the loiterer; 'tis enough to note
That here in dwarf proportions were expressed   580
The limbs of the great world; its eager strifes
Collaterally pourtrayed, as in mock fight,
A tournament of blows, some hardly dealt
Though short of mortal combat; and whate'er
Might in this pageant be supposed to hit
An artless rustic's notice, this way less,
More that way, was not wasted upon me—
And yet the spectacle may well demand
A more substantial name, no mimic show,
Itself a living part of a live whole,   590
A creek in the vast sea; for, all degrees
And shapes of spurious fame and short-lived praise
Here sate in state, and fed with daily alms
Retainers won away from solid good;
And here was Labour, his own bond-slave; Hope,
That never set the pains against the prize;
Idleness halting with his weary clog,
And poor misguided Shame, and witless Fear,
And simple Pleasure foraging for Death;
Honour misplaced, and Dignity astray;   600
Feuds, factions, flatteries, enmity, and guile,
Murmuring submission, and bald government,
(The idol weak as the idolater),
And Decency and Custom starving Truth,
And blind Authority beating with his staff
The child that might have led him; Emptiness
Followed as of good omen, and meek Worth
Left to herself unheard of and unknown.

    Of these and other kindred notices
I cannot say what portion is in truth   610
The naked recollection of that time,
And what may rather have been called to life

By after-meditation. But delight
That, in an easy temper lulled asleep,
Is still with Innocence its own reward,
This was not wanting. Carelessly I roamed
As through a wide museum from whose stores
A casual rarity is singled out
And has its brief perusal, then gives way
To others, all supplanted in their turn;   620
Till 'mid this crowded neighbourhood of things
That are by nature most unneighbourly,
The head turns round and cannot right itself;
And though an aching and a barren sense
Of gay confusion still be uppermost,
With few wise longings and but little love,
Yet to the memory something cleaves at last,
Whence profit may be drawn in times to come.

    Thus in submissive idleness, my Friend!
The labouring time of autumn, winter, spring,   630
Eight months! rolled pleasingly away; the ninth
Came and returned me to my native hills.

BOOK FOURTH
Summer Vacation

Bright was the summer's noon when quickening steps
Followed each other till a dreary moor
Was crossed, a bare ridge clomb, upon whose top
Standing alone, as from a rampart's edge,
I overlooked the bed of Windermere,
Like a vast river, standing in the sun.
With exultation, at my feet I saw
Lake, islands, promontories, gleaming bays,
A universe of Nature's fairest forms
Proudly revealed with instantaneous burst.   10
Magnificent, and beautiful, and gay.
I bounded down the hill shouting amain
For the old Ferryman; to the shout the rocks

Replied, and when the Charon of the flood
Had staid his oars, and touched the jutting pier,
I did not step into the well-known boat
Without a cordial greeting. Thence with speed
Up the familiar hill I took my way
Towards that sweet Valley where I had been reared;
'T was but a short hour's walk, ere veering round   20
I saw the snow-white church upon her hill
Sit like a thronèd Lady, sending out
A gracious look all over her domain.
You azure smoke betrays the lurking town;
With eager footsteps I advance and reach
The cottage threshold where my journey closed.
Glad welcome had I, with some tears, perhaps,
From my old Dame, so kind and motherly,
While she perused me with a parent's pride.
The thoughts of gratitude shall fall like dew   30
Upon thy grave, good creature! While my heart
Can beat never will I forget thy name.
Heaven's blessing be upon thee where thou liest
After thy innocent and busy stir
In narrow cares, thy little daily growth
Of calm enjoyments, after eighty years,
And more than eighty, of untroubled life;
Childless, yet by the strangers to thy blood
Honoured with little less than filial love.
What joy was mine to see thee once again,   40
Thee and thy dwelling, and a crowd of things
About its narrow precincts all beloved,
And many of them seeming yet my own!
Why should I speak of what a thousand hearts
Have felt, and every man alive can guess?
The rooms, the court, the garden were not left
Long unsaluted, nor the sunny seat
Round the stone table under the dark pine,
Friendly to studious or to festive hours;
Nor that unruly child of mountain birth,   50
The famous brook, who, soon as he was boxed

Within our garden, found himself at once,
As if by trick insidious and unkind,
Stripped of his voice and left to dimple down
(Without an effort and without a will)
A channel paved by man's officious care.
I looked at him and smiled, and smiled again,
And in the press of twenty thousand thoughts,
"Ha," quoth I, "pretty prisoner, are you there?"
Well might sarcastic Fancy then have whispered,   60
"An emblem here behold of thy own life;
In its late course of even days with all
Their smooth enthralment;" but the heart was full,
Too full for that reproach. My aged Dame
Walked proudly at my side: she guided me;
I willing, nay—nay, wishing to be led.
—The face of every neighbour whom I met
Was like a volume to me; some were hailed
Upon the road, some busy at their work,
Unceremonious greetings interchanged   70
With half the length of a long field between.
Among my schoolfellows I scattered round
Like recognitions, but with some constraint
Attended, doubtless, with a little pride,
But with more shame, for my habiliments,
The transformation wrought by gay attire.
Not less delighted did I take my place
At our domestic table: and, dear Friend!
In this endeavour simply to relate
A Poet's history, may I leave untold   80
The thankfulness with which I laid me down
In my accustomed bed, more welcome now
Perhaps than if it had been more desired
Or been more often thought of with regret;
That lowly bed whence I had heard the wind
Roar, and the rain beat hard; where I so oft
Had lain awake on summer nights to watch
The moon in splendour couched among the leaves
Of a tall ash, that near our cottage stood;

Had watched her with fixed eyes while to and fro   90
In the dark summit of the waving tree
She rocked with every impulse of the breeze.

    Among the favourites whom it pleased me well
To see again, was one by ancient right
Our inmate, a rough terrier of the hills;
By birth and call of nature pre-ordained
To hunt the badger and unearth the fox
Among the impervious crags, but having been
From youth our own adopted, he had passed
Into a gentler service. And when first   100
The boyish spirit flagged, and day by day
Along my veins I kindled with the stir,
The fermentation, and the vernal heat
Of poesy, affecting private shades
Like a sick Lover, then this dog was used
To watch me, an attendant and a friend,
Obsequious to my steps early and late,
Though often of such dilatory walk
Tired, and uneasy at the halts I made.
A hundred times when, roving high and low,   110
I have been harassed with the toil of verse,
Much pains and little progress, and at once
Some lovely Image in the song rose up
Full-formed, like Venus rising from the sea;
Then have I darted forwards to let loose
My hand upon his back with stormy joy,
Caressing him again and yet again.
And when at evening on the public way
I sauntered, like a river murmuring
And talking to itself when all things else   120
Are still, the creature trotted on before;
Such was his custom; but whene'er he met
A passenger approaching, he would turn
To give me timely notice, and straightway,
Grateful for that admonishment, I hushed
My voice, composed my gait, and, with the air

And mien of one whose thoughts are free, advanced
To give and take a greeting that might save
My name from piteous rumours, such as wait
On men suspected to be crazed in brain.   130

Those walks well worthy to be prized and loved—
Regretted!—that word, too, was on my tongue,
But they were richly laden with all good,
And cannot be remembered but with thanks
And gratitude, and perfect joy of heart—
Those walks in all their freshness now came back
Like a returning Spring. When first I made
Once more the circuit of our little lake,
If ever happiness hath lodged with man,
That day consummate happiness was mine,   140
Wide-spreading, steady, calm, contemplative.
The sun was set, or setting, when I left
Our cottage door, and evening soon brought on
A sober hour, not winning or serene,
For cold and raw the air was, and untuned:
But as a face we love is sweetest then
When sorrow damps it, or, whatever look
It chance to wear, is sweetest if the heart
Have fulness in herself; even so with me
It fared that evening. Gently did my soul   150
Put off her veil, and, self-transmuted, stood
Naked, as in the presence of her God.
While on I walked, a comfort seemed to touch
A heart that had not been disconsolate:
Strength came where weakness was not known to be,
At least not felt; and restoration came
Like an intruder knocking at the door
Of unacknowledged weariness. I took
The balance, and with firm hand weighed myself.
—Of that external scene which round me lay,   160
Little, in this abstraction, did I see;
Remembered less; but I had inward hopes
And swellings of the spirit, was rapt and soothed,

Conversed with promises, had glimmering views
How life pervades the undecaying mind;
How the immortal soul with God-like power
Informs, creates, and thaws the deepest sleep
That time can lay upon her; how on earth,
Man, if he do but live within the light
Of high endeavours, daily spreads abroad   170
His being armed with strength that cannot fail.
Nor was there want of milder thoughts, of love,
Of innocence, and holiday repose;
And more than pastoral quiet, 'mid the stir
Of boldest projects, and a peaceful end
At last, or glorious, by endurance won.
Thus musing, in a wood I sate me down
Alone, continuing there to muse: the slopes
And heights meanwhile were slowly overspread
With darkness, and before a rippling breeze   180
The long lake lengthened out its hoary line,
And in the sheltered coppice where I sate,
Around me from among the hazel leaves,
Now here, now there, moved by the straggling wind,
Came ever and anon a breath-like sound,
Quick as the pantings of the faithful dog,
The off and on companion of my walk;
And such, at times, believing them to be,
I turned my head to look if he were there;
Then into solemn thought I passed once more.   190

  A freshness also found I at this time
In human Life, the daily life of those
Whose occupations really I loved;
The peaceful scene oft filled me with surprise
Changed like a garden in the heat of spring
After an eight-days' absence. For (to omit
The things which were the same and yet appeared
Far otherwise) amid this rural solitude,
A narrow Vale where each was known to all,
'T was not indifferent to a youthful mind   200
To mark some sheltering bower or sunny nook

Where an old man had used to sit alone,
Now vacant; pale-faced babes whom I had left
In arms, now rosy prattlers at the feet
Of a pleased grandame tottering up and down;
And growing girls whose beauty, filched away
With all its pleasant promises, was gone
To deck some slighted playmate's homely cheek.

 Yes, I had something of a subtler sense,
And often looking round was moved to smiles   210
Such as a delicate work of humour breeds;
I read, without design, the opinions, thoughts,
Of those plain-living people now observed
With clearer knowledge; with another eye
I saw the quiet woodman in the woods,
The shepherd roam the hills. With new delight,
This chiefly, did I note my grey-haired Dame;
Saw her go forth to church or other work
Of state equipped in monumental trim;
Short velvet cloak, (her bonnet of the like),   220
A mantle such as Spanish Cavaliers
Wore in old times. Her smooth domestic life,
Affectionate without disquietude,
Her talk, her business, pleased me; and no less
Her clear though shallow stream of piety
That ran on Sabbath days a fresher course;
With thoughts unfelt till now I saw her read
Her Bible on hot Sunday afternoons,
And loved the book, when she had dropped asleep
And made of it a pillow for her head.   230

 Nor less do I remember to have felt,
Distinctly manifested at this time,
A human-heartedness about my love
For objects hitherto the absolute wealth
Of my own private being and no more;
Which I had loved, even as a blessed spirit
Or Angel, if he were to dwell on earth,
Might love in individual happiness.
But now there opened on me other thoughts

Of change, congratulation or regret,   240
A pensive feeling! It spread far and wide;
The trees, the mountains shared it, and the brooks,
The stars of Heaven, now seen in their old haunts—
White Sirius glittering o'er the southern crags,
Orion with his belt, and those fair Seven,
Acquaintances of every little child,
And Jupiter, my own belovèd star!
Whatever shadings of mortality,
Whatever imports from the world of death
Had come among these objects heretofore,   250
Were, in the main, of mood less tender: strong,
Deep, gloomy were they, and severe; the scatterings
Of awe or tremulous dread, that had given way
In later youth to yearnings of a love
Enthusiastic, to delight and hope.

      As one who hangs down-bending from the side
Of a slow-moving boat, upon the breast
Of a still water, solacing himself
With such discoveries as his eye can make
Beneath him in the bottom of the deep,   260
Sees many beauteous sights—weeds, fishes, flowers,
Grots, pebbles, roots of trees, and fancies more,
Yet often is perplexed, and cannot part
The shadow from the substance, rocks and sky,
Mountains and clouds, reflected in the depth
Of the clear flood, from things which there abide
In their true dwelling; now is crossed by gleam
Of his own image, by a sunbeam now,
And wavering motions sent he knows not whence,
Impediments that make his task more sweet;   270
Such pleasant office have we long pursued
Incumbent o'er the surface of past time
With like success, nor often have appeared
Shapes fairer or less doubtfully discerned
Than these to which the Tale, indulgent Friend!
Would now direct thy notice. Yet in spite

Of pleasure won, and knowledge not withheld,
There was an inner falling off—I loved,
Loved deeply all that had been loved before,
More deeply even than ever: but a swarm   280
Of heady schemes jostling each other, gawds,
And feast and dance, and public revelry,
And sports and games (too grateful in themselves,
Yet in themselves less grateful, I believe,
Than as they were a badge glossy and fresh
Of manliness and freedom) all conspired
To lure my mind from firm habitual quest
Of feeding pleasures, to depress the zeal
And damp those yearnings which had once been mine—
A wild, unworldly-minded youth, given up   290
To his own eager thoughts. It would demand
Some skill, and longer time than may be spared
To paint these vanities, and now they wrought
In haunts where they, till now, had been unknown.
It seemed the very garments that I wore
Preyed on my strength, and stopped the quiet stream
Of self-forgetfulness.

                              Yes, that heartless chase
Of trivial pleasures was a poor exchange
For books and nature at that early age.
'Tis true, some casual knowledge might be gained   300
Of character or life; but at that time,
Of manners put to school I took small note,
And all my deeper passions lay elsewhere.
Far better had it been to exalt the mind
By solitary study, to uphold
Intense desire through meditative peace;
And yet, for chastisement of these regrets,
The memory of one particular hour
Doth here rise up against me. 'Mid a throng
Of maids and youths, old men, and matrons staid,   310
A medley of all tempers, I had passed
The night in dancing, gaiety, and mirth,
With din of instruments and shuffling feet,

And glancing forms, and tapers glittering,
And unaimed prattle flying up and down;
Spirits upon the stretch, and here and there
Slight shocks of young love-liking interspersed,
Whose transient pleasure mounted to the head,
And tingled through the veins. Ere we retired,
The cock had crowed, and now the eastern sky   320
Was kindling, not unseen, from humble copse
And open field, through which the pathway wound,
And homeward led my steps. Magnificent
The morning rose, in memorable pomp,
Glorious as e'er I had beheld—in front,
The sea lay laughing at a distance; near,
The solid mountains shone, bright as the clouds,
Grain-tinctured, drenched in empyrean light;
And in the meadows and lower grounds
Was all the sweetness of a common dawn—   330
Dews, vapours, and the melody of birds,
And labourers going forth to till the fields.
Ah! need I say, dear Friend! that to the brim
My heart was full; I made no vows, but vows
Were then made for me; bond unknown to me
Was given, that I should be, else sinning greatly,
A dedicated Spirit. On I walked
In thankful blessedness, which yet survives.

   Strange rendezvous! My mind was at that time
A parti-coloured show of grave and gay,   340
Solid and light, short-sighted and profound;
Of inconsiderate habits and sedate,
Consorting in one mansion unreproved.
The worth I knew of powers that I possessed,
Though slighted and too oft misused. Besides,
That summer, swarming as it did with thoughts
Transient and idle, lacked not intervals
When Folly from the frown of fleeting Time
Shrunk, and the mind experienced in herself
Conformity as just as that of old   350

To the end and written spirit of God's works,
Whether held forth in Nature or in Man,
Through pregnant vision, separate or conjoined.

When from our better selves we have too long
Been parted by the hurrying world, and droop,
Sick of its business, of its pleasures tired,
How gracious, how benign, is Solitude;
How potent a mere image of her sway;
Most potent when impressed upon the mind
With an appropriate human centre—hermit,   360
Deep in the bosom of the wilderness;
Votary (in vast cathedral, where no foot
Is treading, where no other face is seen)
Kneeling at prayers; or watchman on the top
Of lighthouse, beaten by Atlantic waves;
Or as the soul of that great Power is met
Sometimes embodied on a public road,
When, for the night deserted, it assumes
A character of quiet more profound
Than pathless wastes.
                Once, when those summer months   370
Were flown, and autumn brought its annual show
Of oars with oars contending, sails with sails,
Upon Winander's spacious breast, it chanced
That—after I had left a flower-decked room
(Whose in-door pastime, lighted up, survived
To a late hour), and spirits overwrought
Were making night do penance for a day
Spent in a round of strenuous idleness—
My homeward course led up a long ascent,
Where the road's watery surface, to the top   380
Of that sharp rising, glittered to the moon
And bore the semblance of another stream
Stealing with silent lapse to join the brook
That murmured in the vale. All else was still;
No living thing appeared in earth or air,
And, save the flowing water's peaceful voice,

Sound there was none—but, lo! an uncouth shape,
Shown by a sudden turning of the road,
So near that, slipping back into the shade
Of a thick hawthorn, I could mark him well,   390
Myself unseen. He was of stature tall,
A span above man's common measure, tall,
Stiff, lank, and upright; a more meagre man
Was never seen before by night or day.
Long were his arms, pallid his hands; his mouth
Looked ghastly in the moonlight: from behind,
A mile-stone propped him; I could also ken
That he was clothed in military garb,
Though faded, yet entire. Companionless,
No dog attending, by no staff sustained,   400
He stood, and in his very dress appeared
A desolation, a simplicity,
To which the trappings of a gaudy world
Make a strange back-ground. From his lips, ere long,
Issued low muttered sounds, as if of pain
Or some uneasy thought; yet still his form
Kept the same awful steadiness—at his feet
His shadow lay, and moved not. From self-blame
Not wholly free, I watched him thus; at length
Subduing my heart's specious cowardice,   410
I left the shady nook where I had stood
And hailed him. Slowly from his resting-place
He rose, and with a lean and wasted arm
In measured gesture lifted to his head
Returned my salutation; then resumed
His station as before; and when I asked
His history, the veteran, in reply,
Was neither slow nor eager; but, unmoved,
And with a quiet uncomplaining voice,
A stately air of mild indifference,   420
He told in few plain words a soldier's tale—
That in the Tropic Islands he had served,
Whence he had landed scarcely three weeks past;
That on his landing he had been dismissed,
And now was travelling towards his native home.

This heard, I said, in pity, "Come with me."
He stooped, and straightway from the ground took up
An oaken staff by me yet unobserved—
A staff which must have dropped from his slack hand
And lay till now neglected in the grass.   430
Though weak his step and cautious, he appeared
To travel without pain, and I beheld,
With an astonishment but ill suppressed,
His ghostly figure moving at my side;
Nor could I, while we journeyed thus, forbear
To turn from present hardships to the past,
And speak of war, battle, and pestilence,
Sprinkling this talk with questions, better spared,
On what he might himself have seen or felt.
He all the while was in demeanour calm,   440
Concise in answer; solemn and sublime
He might have seemed, but that in all he said
There was a strange half-absence, as of one
Knowing too well the importance of his theme,
But feeling it no longer. Our discourse
Soon ended, and together on we passed
In silence through a wood gloomy and still.
Up-turning, then, along an open field,
We reached a cottage. At the door I knocked,
And earnestly to charitable care   450
Commended him as a poor friendless man,
Belated and by sickness overcome.
Assured that now the traveller would repose
In comfort, I entreated that henceforth
He would not linger in the public ways,
But ask for timely furtherance and help
Such as his state required. At this reproof,
With the same ghastly mildness in his look,
He said, "My trust is in the God of Heaven,
And in the eye of him who passes me!"   460

    The cottage door was speedily unbarred,
And now the soldier touched his hat once more
With his lean hand, and in a faltering voice,

Whose tone bespake reviving interests
Till then unfelt, he thanked me; I returned
The farewell blessing of the patient man,
And so we parted. Back I cast a look,
And lingered near the door a little space,
Then sought with quiet heart my distant home.

BOOK FIFTH
Books

When Contemplation, like the night-calm felt
Through earth and sky, spreads widely, and sends deep
Into the soul its tranquillising power,
Even then I sometimes grieve for thee, O Man,
Earth's paramount Creature! not so much for woes
That thou endurest; heavy though that weight be,
Cloud-like it mounts, or touched with light divine
Doth melt away; but for those palms achieved
Through length of time, by patient exercise
Of study and hard thought; there, there, it is   10
That sadness finds its fuel. Hitherto,
In progress through this Verse, my mind hath looked
Upon the speaking face of earth and heaven
As her prime teacher, intercourse with man
Established by the sovereign Intellect,
Who through that bodily image hath diffused,
As might appear to the eye of fleeting time,
A deathless spirit. Thou also, man! hast wrought,
For commerce of thy nature with herself,
Things that aspire to unconquerable life;   20
And yet we feel—we cannot choose but feel—
That they must perish. Tremblings of the heart
It gives, to think that our immortal being
No more shall need such garments; and yet man,
As long as he shall be the child of earth,
Might almost "weep to have" what he may lose,
Nor be himself extinguished, but survive,
Abject, depressed, forlorn, disconsolate.

A thought is with me sometimes, and I say,—
Should the whole frame of earth by inward throes
Be wrenched, or fire come down from far to scorch
Her pleasant habitations, and dry up
Old Ocean, in his bed left singed and bare,
Yet would the living Presence still subsist
Victorious, and composure would ensue,
And kindlings like the morning—presage sure
Of day returning and of life revived.
But all the meditations of mankind,
Yea, all the adamantine holds of truth
By reason built, or passion, which itself
Is highest reason in a soul sublime;
The consecrated works of Bard and Sage,
Sensuous or intellectual, wrought by men,
Twin labourers and heirs of the same hopes;
Where would they be? Oh! why hath not the Mind
Some element to stamp her image on
In nature somewhat nearer to her own?
Why, gifted with such powers to send abroad
Her spirit, must it lodge in shrines so frail?

    One day, when from my lips a like complaint
Had fallen in presence of a studious friend,
He with a smile made answer, that in truth
'Twas going far to seek disquietude;
But on the front of his reproof confessed
That he himself had oftentimes given way
To kindred hauntings. Whereupon I told,
That once in the stillness of a summer's noon,
While I was seated in a rocky cave
By the sea-side, perusing, so it chanced,
The famous history of the errant knight
Recorded by Cervantes, these same thoughts
Beset me, and to height unusual rose,
While listlessly I sate, and, having closed
The book, had turned my eyes toward the wide sea.
On poetry and geometric truth,

And their high privilege of lasting life,
From all internal injury exempt,
I mused; upon these chiefly; and at length,
My senses yielding to the sultry air,
Sleep seized me, and I passed into a dream.   70
I saw before me stretched a boundless plain
Of sandy wilderness, all black and void,
And as I looked around, distress and fear
Came creeping over me, when at my side,
Close at my side, an uncouth shape appeared
Upon a dromedary, mounted high.
He seemed an Arab of the Bedouin tribes:
A lance he bore, and underneath one arm
A stone, and in the opposite hand a shell
Of a surpassing brightness. At the sight   80
Much I rejoiced, not doubting but a guide
Was present, one who with unerring skill
Would through the desert lead me; and while yet
I looked and looked, self-questioned what this freight
Which the new-comer carried through the waste
Could mean, the Arab told me that the stone
(To give it in the language of the dream)
Was "Euclid's Elements," and "This," said he,
"Is something of more worth;" and at the word
Stretched forth the shell, so beautiful in shape,   90
In colour so resplendent, with command
That I should hold it to my ear. I did so,
And heard that instant in an unknown tongue,
Which yet I understood, articulate sounds,
A loud prophetic blast of harmony;
An Ode, in passion uttered, which foretold
Destruction to the children of the earth
By deluge, now at hand. No sooner ceased
The song, than the Arab with calm look declared
That all would come to pass of which the voice   100
Had given forewarning, and that he himself
Was going then to bury those two books:
The one that held acquaintance with the stars,
And wedded soul to soul in purest bond

Of reason, undisturbed by space or time;
The other that was a god, yea many gods,
Had voices more than all the winds, with power
To exhilarate the spirit, and to soothe,
Through every clime, the heart of human kind.
While this was uttering, strange as it may seem,   110
I wondered not, although I plainly saw
The one to be a stone, the other a shell;
Nor doubted once but that they both were books,
Having a perfect faith in all that passed.
Far stronger, now, grew the desire I felt
To cleave unto this man; but when I prayed
To share his enterprise, he hurried on
Reckless of me: I followed, not unseen,
For oftentimes he cast a backward look,
Grasping his twofold treasure.—Lance in rest,   120
He rode, I keeping pace with him; and now
He, to my fancy, had become the knight
Whose tale Cervantes tells; yet not the knight,
But was an Arab of the desert too;
Of these was neither, and was both at once.
His countenance, meanwhile, grew more disturbed;
And, looking backwards when he looked, mine eyes
Saw, over half the wilderness diffused,
A bed of glittering light: I asked the cause:
"It is," said he, "the waters of the deep   130
Gathering upon us;" quickening then the pace
Of the unwieldy creature he bestrode,
He left me: I called after him aloud;
He heeded not; but, with his twofold charge
Still in his grasp, before me, full in view,
Went hurrying o'er the illimitable waste,
With the fleet waters of a drowning world
In chase of him; whereat I waked in terror,
And saw the sea before me, and the book,
In which I had been reading, at my side.

    Full often, taking from the world of sleep   140
This Arab phantom, which I thus beheld,

This semi-Quixote, I to him have given
A substance, fancied him a living man,
A gentle dweller in the desert, crazed
By love and feeling, and internal thought
Protracted among endless solitudes;
Have shaped him wandering upon this quest!
Nor have I pitied him; but rather felt
Reverence was due to a being thus employed;   150
And thought that, in the blind and awful lair
Of such a madness, reason did lie couched.
Enow there are on earth to take in charge
Their wives, their children, and their virgin loves,
Or whatsoever else the heart holds dear;
Enow to stir for these; yea, will I say,
Contemplating in soberness the approach
Of an event so dire, by signs in earth
Or heaven made manifest, that I could share
That maniac's fond anxiety, and go   160
Upon like errand. Oftentimes at least
Me hath such strong entrancement overcome,
When I have held a volume in my hand,
Poor earthly casket of immortal verse,
Shakespeare, or Milton, labourers divine!

    Great and benign, indeed, must be the power
Of living nature, which could thus so long
Detain me from the best of other guides
And dearest helpers, left unthanked, unpraised,
Even in the time of lisping infancy;   170
And later down, in prattling childhood even,
While I was travelling back among those days,
How could I ever play an ingrate's part?
Once more should I have made those bowers resound,
By intermingling strains of thankfulness
With their own thoughtless melodies; at least
It might have well beseemed me to repeat
Some simply fashioned tale, to tell again,
In slender accents of sweet verse, some tale

That did bewitch me then, and soothes me now.   180
O Friend! O Poet! brother of my soul,
Think not that I could pass along untouched
By these remembrances. Yet wherefore speak?
Why call upon a few weak words to say
What is already written in the hearts
Of all that breathe?—what in the path of all
Drops daily from the tongue of every child,
Wherever man is found? The trickling tear
Upon the cheek of listening Infancy
Proclaims it, and the insuperable look   190
That drinks as if it never could be full.

    That portion of my story I shall leave
There registered: whatever else of power
Or pleasure sown, or fostered thus, may be
Peculiar to myself, let that remain
Where still it works, though hidden from all search
Among the depths of time. Yet is it just
That here, in memory of all books which lay
Their sure foundations in the heart of man,
Whether by native prose, or numerous verse,   200
That in the name of all inspired souls—
From Homer the great Thunderer, from the voice
That roars along the bed of Jewish song,
And that more varied and elaborate,
Those trumpet-tones of harmony that shake
Our shores in England,—from those loftiest notes
Down to the low and wren-like warblings, made
For cottagers and spinners at the wheel,
And sun-burnt travellers resting their tired limbs,
Stretched under wayside hedge-rows, ballad tunes,   210
Food for the hungry ears of little ones,
And of old men who have survived their joys—
'T is just that in behalf of these, the works,
And of the men that framed them, whether known
Or sleeping nameless in their scattered graves,
That I should here assert their rights, attest

Their honours, and should, once for all, pronounce
Their benediction; speak of them as Powers
For ever to be hallowed; only less,
For what we are and what we may become,   220
Than Nature's self, which is the breath of God,
Or His pure Word by miracle revealed.

    Rarely and with reluctance would I stoop
To transitory themes; yet I rejoice,
And, by these thoughts admonished, will pour out
Thanks with uplifted heart, that I was reared
Safe from an evil which these days have laid
Upon the children of the land, a pest
That might have dried me up, body and soul.
This verse is dedicate to Nature's self,   230
And things that teach as Nature teaches: then,
Oh! where had been the Man, the Poet where,
Where we had been, we two, belovèd Friend!
If in the season of unperilous choice,
In lieu of wandering, as we did, through vales
Rich with indigenous produce, open ground
Of Fancy, happy pastures ranged at will,
We had been followed, hourly watched, and noosed,
Each in his several melancholy walk
Stringed like a poor man's heifer at its feed,   240
Led through the lanes in forlorn servitude;
Or rather like a stalled ox debarred
From touch of growing grass, that may not taste
A flower till it have yielded up its sweets
A prelibation to the mower's scythe.

    Behold the parent hen amid her brood,
Though fledged and feathered, and well pleased to part
And straggle from her presence, still a brood,
And she herself from the maternal bond
Still undischarged; yet doth she little more   250
Than move with them in tenderness and love,
A centre to the circle which they make;
And now and then, alike from need of theirs

And call of her own natural appetites,
She scratches, ransacks up the earth for food,
Which they partake at pleasure. Early died
My honoured Mother, she who was the heart
And hinge of all our learnings and our loves:
She left us destitute, and, as we might,
Trooping together. Little suits it me   260
To break upon the sabbath of her rest
With any thought that looks at others' blame;
Nor would I praise her but in perfect love.
Hence am I checked: but let me boldly say,
In gratitude, and for the sake of truth,
Unheard by her, that she, not falsely taught,
Fetching her goodness rather from times past,
Than shaping novelties for times to come,
Had no presumption, no such jealousy,
Nor did by habit of her thoughts mistrust   270
Our nature, but had virtual faith that He
Who fills the mother's breast with innocent milk,
Doth also for our nobler part provide,
Under His great correction and control,
As innocent instincts, and as innocent food;
Or draws, for minds that are left free to trust
In the simplicities of opening life,
Sweet honey out of spurned or dreaded weeds.
This was her creed, and therefore she was pure
From anxious fear of error or mishap.   280
And evil, overweeningly so called;
Was not puffed up by false unnatural hopes,
Nor selfish with unnecessary cares,
Nor with impatience from the season asked
More than its timely produce; rather loved
The hours for what they are, than from regard
Glanced on their promises in restless pride.
Such was she—not from faculties more strong
Than others have, but from the times, perhaps,
And spot in which she lived, and through a grace   290
Of modest meekness, simple-mindedness,

A heart that found benignity and hope,
Being itself benign.

                        My drift I fear
Is scarcely obvious; but, that common sense
May try this modern system by its fruits,
Leave let me take to place before her sight
A specimen pourtrayed with faithful hand.
Full early trained to worship seemliness,
This model of a child is never known
To mix in quarrels; that were far beneath   300
Its dignity; with gifts he bubbles o'er
As generous as a fountain; selfishness
May not come near him, nor the little throng
Of flitting pleasures tempt him from his path;
The wandering beggars propagate his name,
Dumb creatures find him tender as a nun,
And natural or supernatural fear,
Unless it leap upon him in a dream,
Touches him not. To enhance the wonder, see,
How arch his notices, how nice his sense   310
Of the ridiculous; not blind is he
To the broad follies of the licensed world,
Yet innocent himself withal, though shrewd,
And can read lectures upon innocence;
A miracle of scientific lore,
Ships he can guide across the pathless sea,
And tell you all their cunning; he can read
The inside of the earth, and spell the stars;
He knows the policies of foreign lands;
Can string you names of districts, cities, towns,   320
The whole world over, tight as beads of dew
Upon a gossamer thread; he sifts, he weighs;
All things are put to question; he must live
Knowing that he grows wiser every day
Or else not live at all, and seeing too
Each little drop of wisdom as it falls
Into the dimpling cistern of his heart:
For this unnatural growth the trainer blame,

Pity the tree.—Poor human vanity,
Wert thou extinguished, little would be left 330
Which he could truly love; but how escape?
For, ever as a thought of purer birth
Rises to lead him toward a better clime,
Some intermeddler still is on the watch
To drive him back, and pound him, like a stray,
Within the pinfold of his own conceit.
Meanwhile old grandame earth is grieved to find
The playthings, which her love designed for him,
Unthought of: in their woodland beds the flowers
Weep, and the river sides are forlorn. 340
Oh! give us once again the wishing-cap
Of Fortunatus, and the invisible coat
Of Jack the Giant-killer, Robin Hood,
And Sabra in the forest with St. George!
The child, whose love is here, at least, doth reap
One precious gain, that he forgets himself.

These mighty workmen of our later age,
Who, with a broad highway, have overbridged
The froward chaos of futurity,
Tamed to their bidding; they who have the skill 350
To manage books, and things, and make them act
On infant minds as surely as the sun
Deals with a flower; the keepers of our time,
The guides and wardens of our faculties,
Sages who in their prescience would control
All accidents, and to the very road
Which they have fashioned would confine us down,
Like engines; when will their presumption learn,
That in the unreasoning progress of the world
A wiser spirit is at work for us, 360
A better eye than theirs, most prodigal
Of blessings, and most studious of our good,
Even in what seem our most unfruitful hours?

There was a Boy: ye knew him well, ye cliffs
And islands of Winander!—many a time

At evening, when the earliest stars began
To move along the edges of the hills,
Rising or setting, would he stand alone
Beneath the trees or by the glimmering lake,
And there, with fingers interwoven, both hands   370
Pressed closely palm to palm, and to his mouth
Uplifted, he, as through an instrument,
Blew mimic hootings to the silent owls,
That they might answer him; and they would shout
Across the watery vale, and shout again,
Responsive to his call, with quivering peals,
And long halloos and screams, and echoes loud,
Redoubled and redoubled, concourse wild
Of jocund din; and, when a lengthened pause
Of silence came and baffled his best skill,   380
Then sometimes, in that silence while he hung
Listening, a gentle shock of mild surprise
Has carried far into his heart the voice
Of mountain torrents; or the visible scene
Would enter unawares into his mind,
With all its solemn imagery, its rocks,
Its woods, and that uncertain heaven, received
Into the bosom of the steady lake.

     This Boy was taken from his mates, and died
In childhood, ere he was full twelve years old.   390
Fair is the spot, most beautiful the vale
Where he was born; the grassy church-yard hangs
Upon a slope above the village school,
And through that churchyard when my way has led
On summer evenings, I believe that there
A long half hour together I have stood
Mute, looking at the grave in which he lies!
Even now appears before the mind's clear eye
That self-same village church; I see her sit
(The throned Lady whom erewhile we hailed)   400
On her green hill, forgetful of this Boy
Who slumbers at her feet,—forgetful, too,
Of all her silent neighbourhood of graves,

And listening only to the gladsome sounds
That, from the rural school ascending, play
Beneath her and about her. May she long
Behold a race of young ones like to those
With whom I herded!—(easily, indeed,
We might have fed upon a fatter soil
Of arts and letters—but be that forgiven)—   410
A race of real children; not too wise,
Too learned, or too good; but wanton, fresh,
And bandied up and down by love and hate;
Not unresentful where self-justified;
Fierce, moody, patient, venturous, modest, shy;
Mad at their sports like withered leaves in winds;
Though doing wrong and suffering, and full oft
Bending beneath our life's mysterious weight
Of pain, and doubt, and fear, yet yielding not
In happiness to the happiest upon earth.   420
Simplicity in habit, truth in speech,
Be these the daily strengtheners of their minds;
May books and Nature be their early joy!
And knowledge, rightly honoured with that name—
Knowledge not purchased by the loss of power!

     Well do I call to mind the very week
When I was first intrusted to the care
Of that sweet Valley; when its paths, its shores,
And brooks were like a dream of novelty
To my half-infant thoughts; that very week,   430
While I was roving up and down alone,
Seeking I knew not what, I chanced to cross
One of those open fields, which, shaped like ears,
Make green peninsulas on Esthwaite's Lake:
Twilight was coming on, yet through the gloom
Appeared distinctly on the opposite shore
A heap of garments, as if left by one
Who might have there been bathing. Long I watched,
But no one owned them; meanwhile the calm lake
Grew dark with all the shadows on its breast,   440
And, now and then, a fish up-leaping snapped

The breathless stillness. The succeeding day,
Those unclaimed garments telling a plain tale
Drew to the spot an anxious crowd; some looked
In passive expectation from the shore,
While from a boat others hung o'er the deep,
Sounding with grappling irons and long poles.
At last, the dead man, 'mid that beauteous scene
Of trees and hills and water, bolt upright
Rose, with his ghastly face, a spectre shape   450
Of terror; yet no soul-debasing fear,
Young as I was, a child not nine years old,
Possessed me, for my inner eye had seen
Such sights before, among the shining streams
Of faëry land, the forest of romance.
Their spirit hallowed the sad spectacle
With decoration of ideal grace;
A dignity, a smoothness, like the works
Of Grecian art, and purest poesy.

    A precious treasure had I long possessed,   460
A little yellow, canvas-covered book,
A slender abstract of the Arabian tales;
And, from companions in a new abode,
When first I learnt, that this dear prize of mine
Was but a block hewn from a mighty quarry—
That there were four large volumes, laden all
With kindred matter, 't was to me, in truth,
A promise scarcely earthly. Instantly,
With one not richer than myself, I made
A covenant that each should lay aside   470
The moneys he possessed, and hoard up more
Till our joint savings had amassed enough
To make this book our own. Through several months,
In spite of all temptation, we preserved
Religiously that vow; but firmness failed,
Nor were we ever masters of our wish.

    And when thereafter to my father's house
The holidays returned me, there to find

That golden store of books which I had left,
What joy was mine! How often in the course   480
Of those glad respites, though a soft west wind
Ruffled the waters to the angler's wish,
For a whole day together, have I lain
Down by thy side, O Derwent! murmuring stream,
On the hot stones, and in the glaring sun,
And there have read, devouring as I read,
Defrauding the day's glory, desperate!
Till with a sudden bound of smart reproach,
Such as an idler deals with in his shame,
I to the sport betook myself again.   490

A gracious spirit o'er this earth presides,
And o'er the heart of man; invisibly
It comes, to works of unreproved delight,
And tendency benign, directing those
Who care not, know not, think not, what they do.
The tales that charm away the wakeful night
In Araby; romances; legends penned
For solace by dim light of monkish lamps;
Fictions, for ladies of their love, devised
By youthful squires; adventures endless, spun   500
By the dismantled warrior in old age,
Out of the bowels of those very schemes
In which his youth did first extravagate;
These spread like day, and something in the shape
Of these will live till man shall be no more.
Dumb yearnings, hidden appetites, are ours,
And *they must* have their food. Our childhood sits,
Our simple childhood, sits upon a throne
That hath more power than all the elements.
I guess not what this tells of Being past,   510
Nor what it augurs of the life to come;
But so it is; and, in that dubious hour—
That twilight—when we first begin to see
This dawning earth, to recognise, expect,
And, in the long probation that ensues,

The time of trial, ere we learn to live
In reconcilement with our stinted powers;
To endure this state of meagre vassalage,
Unwilling to forego, confess, submit,
Uneasy and unsettled, yoke-fellows   520
To custom, mettlesome, and not yet tamed
And humbled down—oh! then we feel, we feel,
We know where we have friends. Ye dreamers then,
Forgers of daring tales! we bless you then,
Impostors, drivellers, dotards, as the ape
Philosophy will call you: *then* we feel
With what, and how great might ye are in league,
Who make our wish, our power, our thought a deed,
An empire, a possession,—ye whom time
And seasons serve; all Faculties to whom   530
Earth crouches, the elements are potter's clay,
Space like a heaven filled up with northern lights,
Here, nowhere, there, and everywhere at once.

     Relinquishing this lofty eminence
For ground, though humbler, not the less a tract
Of the same isthmus, which our spirits cross
In progress from their native continent
To earth and human life, the Song might dwell
On that delightful time of growing youth,
When craving for the marvellous gives way   540
To strengthening love for things that we have seen;
When sober truth and steady sympathies,
Offered to notice by less daring pens,
Take firmer hold of us, and words themselves
Move us with conscious pleasure.
                                   I am sad
At thought of rapture now for ever flown;
Almost to tears I sometimes could be sad
To think of, to read over, many a page,
Poems withal of name, which at that time
Did never fail to entrance me, and are now   550
Dead in my eyes, dead as a theatre
Fresh emptied of spectators. Twice five years

Or less I might have seen, when first my mind
With conscious pleasure opened to the charm
Of words in tuneful order, found them sweet
For their own *sakes*, a passion, and a power;
And phrases pleased me chosen for delight,
For pomp, or love. Oft, in the public roads
Yet unfrequented, while the morning light
Was yellowing the hill tops, I went abroad   560
With a dear friend, and for the better part
Of two delightful hours we strolled along
By the still borders of the misty lake,
Repeating favourite verses with one voice,
Or conning more, as happy as the birds
That round us chaunted. Well might we be glad,
Lifted above the ground by airy fancies,
More bright than madness or the dreams of wine;
And, though full oft the objects of our love
Were false, and in their splendour overwrought,   570
Yet was there surely then no vulgar power
Working within us,—nothing less, in truth,
Than that most noble attribute of man,
Though yet untutored and inordinate.
That wish for something loftier, more adorned,
Than is the common aspect, daily garb,
Of human life. What wonder, then, if sounds
Of exultation echoed through the groves!
For, images, and sentiments, and words,
And everything encountered or pursued   580
In that delicious world of poesy,
Kept holiday, a never-ending show,
With music, incense, festival, and flowers!

    Here must we pause: this only let me add,
From heart-experience, and in humblest sense
Of modesty, that he, who in his youth
A daily wanderer among woods and fields
With living Nature hath been intimate,
Not only in that raw unpractised time
Is stirred to ecstasy, as others are,   590

By glittering verse; but further, doth receive,
In measure only dealt out to himself,
Knowledge and increase of enduring joy
From the great Nature that exists in works
Of mighty Poets. Visionary power
Attends the motions of the viewless winds,
Embodied in the mystery of words:
There, darkness makes abode, and all the host
Of shadowy things work endless changes,—there,
As in a mansion like their proper home,   600
Even forms and substances are circumfused
By that transparent veil with light divine,
And, through the turnings intricate of verse,
Present themselves as objects recognised,
In flashes, and with glory not their own.

BOOK SIXTH
Cambridge and the Alps

The leaves were fading when to Esthwaite's banks
And the simplicities of cottage life
I bade farewell; and, one among the youth
Who, summoned by that season, reunite
As scattered birds troop to the fowler's lure,
Went back to Granta's cloisters, not so prompt
Or eager, though as gay and undepressed
In mind, as when I thence had taken flight
A few short months before. I turned my face
Without repining from the coves and heights   10
Clothed in the sunshine of the withering fern;
Quitted, not loth, the mild magnificence
Of calmer lakes and louder streams; and you,
Frank-hearted maids of rocky Cumberland,
You and your not unwelcome days of mirth,
Relinquished, and your nights of revelry,
And in my own unlovely cell sate down
In lightsome mood—such privilege has youth
That cannot take long leave of pleasant thoughts.

The bonds of indolent society   20
Relaxing in their hold, henceforth I lived
More to myself. Two winters may be passed
Without a separate notice: many books
Were skimmed, devoured, or studiously perused,
But with no settled plan. I was detached
Internally from academic cares;
Yet independent study seemed a course
Of hardy disobedience toward friends
And kindred, proud rebellion and unkind.
This spurious virtue, rather let it bear   30
A name it now deserves, this cowardice,
Gave treacherous sanction to that over-love
Of freedom which encouraged me to turn
From regulations even of my own
As from restraints and bonds. Yet who can tell—
Who knows what thus may have been gained, both then
And at a later season, or preserved;
What love of nature, what original strength
Of contemplation, what intuitive truths
The deepest and the best, what keen research,   40
Unbiassed, unbewildered, and unawed?

The Poet's soul was with me at that time;
Sweet meditations, the still overflow
Of present happiness, while future years
Lacked not anticipations, tender dreams,
No few of which have since been realised;
And some remain, hopes for my future life.
Four years and thirty, told this very week,
Have I been now a sojourner on earth,
By sorrow not unsmitten; yet for me   50
Life's morning radiance hath not left the hills,
Her dew is on the flowers. Those were the days
Which also first emboldened me to trust
With firmness, hitherto but slightly touched
By such a daring thought, that I might leave
Some monument behind me which pure hearts

Should reverence. The instinctive humbleness,
Maintained even by the very name and thought
Of printed books and authorship, began
To melt away; and further, the dread awe   60
Of mighty names was softened down and seemed
Approachable, admitting fellowship
Of modest sympathy. Such aspect now,
Though not familiarly, my mind put on,
Content to observe, to achieve, and to enjoy.

    All winter long, whenever free to choose,
Did I by night frequent the College grove
And tributary walks; the last, and oft
The only one, who had been lingering there
Through hours of silence, till the porter's bell,   70
A punctual follower on the stroke of nine,
Rang with its blunt unceremonious voice;
Inexorable summons! Lofty elms,
Inviting shades of opportune recess,
Bestowed composure on a neighbourhood
Unpeaceful in itself. A single tree
With sinuous trunk, boughs exquisitely wreathed,
Grew there; an ash which Winter for himself
Decked out with pride, and with outlandish grace:
Up from the ground, and almost to the top,   80
The trunk and every master branch were green
With clustering ivy, and the lightsome twigs
And outer spray profusely tipped with seeds
That hung in yellow tassels, while the air
Stirred them, not voiceless. Often have I stood
Foot-bound uplooking at this lovely tree
Beneath a frosty moon. The hemisphere
Of magic fiction, verse of mine perchance
May never tread; but scarcely Spenser's self
Could have more tranquil visions in his youth,   90
Or could more bright appearances create
Of human forms with superhuman powers,
Than I beheld, loitering on calm clear nights
Alone, beneath this fairy work of earth.

On the vague reading of a truant youth
'Twere idle to descant. My inner judgment
Not seldom differed from my taste in books,
As if it appertained to another mind,
And yet the books which then I valued most
Are dearest to me now; for, having scanned,   100
Not heedlessly, the laws, and watched the forms
Of Nature, in that knowledge I possessed
A standard, often usefully applied,
Even when unconsciously, to things removed
From a familiar sympathy.—In fine,
I was a better judge of thoughts than words,
Misled in estimating words, not only
By common inexperience of youth,
But by the trade in classic niceties,
The dangerous craft, of culling term and phrase   110
From languages that want the living voice
To carry meaning to the natural heart;
To tell us what is passion, what is truth,
What reason, what simplicity and sense.

Yet may we not entirely overlook
The pleasure gathered from the rudiments
Of geometric science. Though advanced
In these enquiries, with regret I speak,
No farther than the threshold, there I found
Both elevation and composed delight: 120
With Indian awe and wonder, ignorance pleased
With its own struggles, did I meditate
On the relation those abstractions bear
To Nature's laws, and by what process led,
Those immaterial agents bowed their heads
Duly to serve the mind of earth-born man;
From star to star, from kindred sphere to sphere,
From system on to system without end.

More frequently from the same source I drew
A pleasure quiet and profound, a sense   130
Of permanent and universal sway,

And paramount belief; there, recognised
A type, for finite natures, of the one
Supreme Existence, the surpassing life
Which—to the boundaries of space and time,
Of melancholy space and doleful time,
Superior and incapable of change,
Nor touched by welterings of passion—is,
And hath the name of, God. Transcendent peace
And silence did await upon these thoughts   **140**
That were a frequent comfort to my youth.

    'Tis told by one whom stormy waters threw,
With fellow-sufferers by the shipwreck spared,
Upon a desert coast, that having brought
To land a single volume, saved by chance,
A treatise of Geometry, he wont,
Although of food and clothing destitute,
And beyond common wretchedness depressed,
To part from company and take this book
(Then first a self-taught pupil in its truths)   **150**
To spots remote, and draw his diagrams
With a long staff upon the sand, and thus
Did oft beguile his sorrow, and almost
Forget his feeling: so (if like effect
From the same cause produced, 'mid outward things
So different, may rightly be compared),
So was it then with me, and so will be
With Poets ever. Mighty is the charm
Of those abstractions to a mind beset
With images and haunted by herself,   **160**
And specially delightful unto me
Was that clear synthesis built up aloft
So gracefully; even then when it appeared
Not more than a mere plaything, or a toy
To sense embodied: not the thing it is
In verity, an independent world,
Created out of pure intelligence.

    Such dispositions then were mine unearned
By aught, I fear, of genuine desert—

Mine, through heaven's grace and inborn aptitudes.   170
And not to leave the story of that time
Imperfect, with these habits must be joined,
Moods melancholy, fits of spleen, that loved
A pensive sky, sad days, and piping winds,
The twilight more than dawn, autumn than spring;
A treasured and luxurious gloom of choice
And inclination mainly, and the mere
Redundancy of youth's contentedness.
—To time thus spent, add multitudes of hours
Pilfered away, by what the Bard who sang   180
Of the Enchanter Indolence hath called
"Good-natured lounging," and behold a map
Of my collegiate life—far less intense
Than duty called for, or, without regard
To duty, *might* have sprung up of itself
By change of accidents, or even, to speak
Without unkindness, in another place.
Yet why take refuge in that plea?—the fault,
This I repeat, was mine; mine be the blame.

In summer, making quest for works of art,   190
Or scenes renowned for beauty, I explored
That streamlet whose blue current works its way
Between romantic Dovedale's spiry rocks;
Pried into Yorkshire dales, or hidden tracts
Of my own native region, and was blest
Between these sundry wanderings with a joy
Above all joys, that seemed another morn
Risen on mid noon; blest with the presence, Friend,
Of that sole Sister, her who hath been long
Dear to thee also, thy true friend and mine,   200
Now, after separation desolate,
Restored to me—such absence that she seemed
A gift then first bestowed. The varied banks
Of Emont, hitherto unnamed in song,
And that monastic castle, 'mid tall trees,
Low standing by the margin of the stream,
A mansion visited (as fame reports)

By Sidney, where, in sight of our Helvellyn,
Or stormy Cross-fell, snatches he might pen
Of his Arcadia, by fraternal love   210
Inspired;—that river and those mouldering towers
Have seen us side by side, when, having clomb
The darksome windings of a broken stair,
And crept along a ridge of fractured wall,
Not without trembling, we in safety looked
Forth, through some Gothic window's open space,
And gathered with one mind a rich reward
From the far-stretching landscape, by the light
Of morning beautified, or purple eve;
Or, not less pleased, lay on some turret's head,   220
Catching from tufts of grass and hare-bell flowers
Their faintest whisper to the passing breeze,
Given out while mid-day heat oppressed the plains.

      Another maid there was, who also shed
A gladness o'er that season, then to me,
By her exulting outside look of youth
And placid under-countenance, first endeared;
That other spirit, Coleridge! who is now
So near to us, that meek confiding heart,
So reverenced by us both. O'er paths and fields   230
In all that neighbourhood, through narrow lanes
Of eglantine, and through the shady woods,
And o'er the Border Beacon, and the waste
Of naked pools, and common crags that lay
Exposed on the bare fell, were scattered love,
The spirit of pleasure, and youth's golden gleam.
O Friend! we had not seen thee at that time,
And yet a power is on me, and a strong
Confusion, and I seem to plant thee there.
Far art thou wandered now in search of health   240
And milder breezes,—melancholy lot!
But thou art with us, with us in the past,
The present, with us in the times to come.
There is no grief, no sorrow, no despair,
No languor, no dejection, no dismay,

No absence scarcely can there be, for those
Who love as we do. Speed thee well! divide
With us thy pleasure; thy returning strength,
Receive it daily as a joy of ours;
Share with us thy fresh spirits, whether gift   250
Of gales Etesian or of tender thoughts.

    I, too, have been a wanderer; but, alas!
How different the fate of different men.
Though mutually unknown, yea nursed and reared
As if in several elements, we were framed
To bend at last to the same discipline,
Predestined, if two beings ever were,
To seek the same delights, and have one health,
One happiness. Throughout this narrative,
Else sooner ended, I have borne in mind   260
For whom it registers the birth, and marks the growth,
Of gentleness, simplicity, and truth,
And joyous loves, that hallow innocent days
Of peace and self-command. Of rivers, fields,
And groves I speak to thee, my Friend! to thee,
Who, yet a liveried schoolboy, in the depths
Of the huge city, on the leaded roof
Of that wide edifice, thy school and home,
Wert used to lie and gaze upon the clouds
Moving in heaven; or, of that pleasure tired,   270
To shut thine eyes, and by internal light
See trees, and meadows, and thy native stream,
Far distant, thus beheld from year to year
Of a long exile. Nor could I forget,
In this late portion of my argument,
That scarcely, as my term of pupilage
Ceased, had I left those academic bowers
When thou wert thither guided. From the heart
Of London, and from cloisters there, thou camest,
And didst sit down in temperance and peace,   280
A rigorous student. What a stormy course
Then followed. Oh! it is a pang that calls
For utterance, to think what easy change

Of circumstances might to thee have spared
A world of pain, ripened a thousand hopes,
For ever withered. Through this retrospect
Of my collegiate life I still have had
Thy after-sojourn in the self-same place
Present before my eyes, have played with times
And accidents as children do with cards,   290
Or as a man, who, when his house is built,
A frame locked up in wood and stone, doth still,
As impotent fancy prompts, by his fireside,
Rebuild it to his liking. I have thought
Of thee, thy learning, gorgeous eloquence,
And all the strength and plumage of thy youth,
Thy subtle speculations, toils abstruse
Among the schoolmen, and Platonic forms
Of wild ideal pageantry, shaped out
From things well-matched or ill, and words for things,   300
The self-created sustenance of a mind
Debarred from Nature's living images,
Compelled to be a life unto herself,
And unrelentingly possessed by thirst
Of greatness, love, and beauty. Not alone,
Ah! surely not in singleness of heart
Should I have seen the light of evening fade
From smooth Cam's silent waters: had we met,
Even at that early time, needs must I trust
In the belief, that my maturer age,   310
My calmer habits, and more steady voice,
Would with an influence benign have soothed,
Or chased away, the airy wretchedness
That battened on thy youth. But thou hast trod
A march of glory, which doth put to shame
These vain regrets; health suffers in thee, else
Such grief for thee would be the weakest thought
That ever harboured in the breast of man.

    A passing word erewhile did lightly touch
On wanderings of my own, that now embraced   320
With livelier hope a region wider far.

When the third summer freed us from restraint,
A youthful friend, he too a mountaineer,
Not slow to share my wishes, took his staff,
And sallying forth, we journeyed side by side,
Bound to the distant Alps. A hardy slight,
Did this unprecedented course imply,
Of college studies and their set rewards;
Nor had, in truth, the scheme been formed by me
Without uneasy forethought of the pain,   330
The censures, and ill-omening, of those
To whom my worldly interests were dear.
But Nature then was sovereign in my mind,
And mighty forms, seizing a youthful fancy,
Had given a charter to irregular hopes.
In any age of uneventful calm
Among the nations, surely would my heart
Have been possessed by similar desire;
But Europe at that time was thrilled with joy,
France standing on the top of golden hours,   340
And human nature seeming born again.

    Lightly equipped, and but a few brief looks
Cast on the white cliffs of our native shore
From the receding vessel's deck, we chanced
To land at Calais on the very eve
Of that great federal day; and there we saw,
In a mean city, and among a few,
How bright a face is worn when joy of one
Is joy for tens of millions. Southward thence
We held our way, direct through hamlets, towns,   350
Gaudy with reliques of that festival,
Flowers left to wither on triumphal arcs,
And window-garlands. On the public roads,
And, once, three days successively, through paths
By which our toilsome journey was abridged,
Among sequestered villages we walked
And found benevolence and blessedness
Spread like a fragrance everywhere, when spring
Hath left no corner of the land untouched;

Where elms for many and many a league in files 360
With their thin umbrage, on the stately roads
Of that great kingdom, rustled o'er our heads,
For ever near us as we paced along:
How sweet at such a time, with such delight
On every side, in prime of youthful strength,
To feed a Poet's tender melancholy
And fond conceit of sadness, with the sound
Of undulations varying as might please
The wind that swayed them; once, and more than once,
Unhoused beneath the evening star we saw 370
Dances of liberty, and, in late hours
Of darkness, dances in the open air
Deftly prolonged, though grey-haired lookers on
Might waste their breath in chiding.
                     Under hills—
The vine-clad hills and slopes of Burgundy,
Upon the bosom of the gentle Saone
We glided forward with the flowing stream.
Swift Rhone! thou wert the *wings* on which we cut
A winding passage with majestic ease
Between thy lofty rocks. Enchanting show 380
Those woods and farms and orchards did present,
And single cottages and lurking towns,
Reach after reach, succession without end
Of deep and stately vales! A lonely pair
Of strangers, till day closed, we sailed along
Clustered together with a merry crowd
Of those emancipated, a blithe host
Of travellers, chiefly delegates, returning
From the great spousals newly solemnised
At their chief city, in the sight of Heaven. 390
Like bees they swarmed, gaudy and gay as bees;
Some vapoured in the unruliness of joy,
And with their swords flourished as if to fight
The saucy air. In this proud company
We landed—took with them our evening meal,
Guests welcome almost as the angels were

To Abraham of old. The supper done,
With flowing cups elate and happy thoughts
We rose at signal given, and formed a ring
And, hand in hand, danced round and round the board;   400
All hearts were open, every tongue was loud
With amity and glee; we bore a name
Honoured in France, the name of Englishmen,
And hospitably did they give us hail,
As their forerunners in a glorious course;
And round and round the board we danced again.
With these blithe friends our voyage we renewed
At early dawn. The monastery bells
Made a sweet jingling in our youthful ears;
The rapid river flowing without noise,   410
And each uprising or receding spire
Spake with a sense of peace, at intervals
Touching the heart amid the boisterous crew
By whom we were encompassed. Taking leave
Of this glad throng, foot-travellers side by side,
Measuring our steps in quiet, we pursued
Our journey, and ere twice the sun had set
Beheld the Convent of Chartreuse, and there
Rested within an awful *solitude:*
Yes; for even then no other than a place   420
Of soul-affecting *solitude* appeared
That far-famed region, though our eyes had seen,
As toward the sacred mansion we advanced,
Arms flashing, and a military glare
Of riotous men commissioned to expel
The blameless inmates, and belike subvert
That frame of social being, which so long
Had bodied forth the ghostliness of things
In silence visible and perpetual calm.
—"Stay, stay your sacrilegious hands!"—The voice   430
Was Nature's, uttered from her Alpine throne;
I heard it then and seem to hear it now—
"Your impious work forbear, perish what may,
Let this one temple last, be this one spot

Of earth devoted to eternity!"
She ceased to speak, but while St. Bruno's pines
Waved their dark tops, not silent as they waved,
And while below, along their several beds,
Murmured the sister streams of Life and Death,
Thus by conflicting passions pressed, my heart   440
Responded; "Honour to the patriot's zeal!
Glory and hope to new-born Liberty!
Hail to the mighty projects of the time!
Discerning sword that Justice wields, do thou
Go forth and prosper; and, ye purging fires,
Up to the loftiest towers of Pride ascend,
Fanned by the breath of angry Providence.
But oh! if Past and Future be the wings
On whose support harmoniously conjoined
Moves the great spirit of human knowledge, spare   450
These courts of mystery, where a step advanced
Between the portals of the shadowy rocks
Leaves far behind life's treacherous vanities,
For penitential tears and trembling hopes
Exchanged—to equalise in God's pure sight
Monarch and peasant: be the house redeemed
With its unworldly votaries, for the sake
Of conquest over sense, hourly achieved
Through faith and meditative reason, resting
Upon the word of heaven-imparted truth,   460
Calmly triumphant; and for humbler claim
Of that imaginative impulse sent
From these majestic floods, yon shining cliffs,
The untransmuted shapes of many worlds,
Cerulean ether's pure inhabitants,
These forests unapproachable by death,
That shall endure as long as man endures,
To think, to hope, to worship, and to feel,
To struggle, to be lost within himself
In trepidation, from the blank abyss   470
To look with bodily eyes, and be consoled."
Not seldom since that moment have I wished

That thou, O Friend! the trouble or the calm
Hadst shared, when, from profane regards apart,
In sympathetic reverence we trod
The floors of those dim cloisters, till that hour
From their foundation, strangers to the presence
Of unrestricted and unthinking man.
Abroad, how cheeringly the sunshine lay
Upon the open lawns! Vallombre's groves   480
Entering, we fed the soul with darkness; thence
Issued, and with uplifted eyes beheld,
In different quarters of the bending sky,
The cross of Jesus stand erect, as if
Hands of angelic powers had fixed it there,
Memorial reverenced by a thousand storms;
Yet then, from the undiscriminating sweep
And rage of one State-whirlwind, insecure.

        'Tis not my present purpose to retrace
That variegated journey step by step.   490
A march it was of military speed,
And Earth did change her images and forms
Before us, fast as clouds are changed in heaven.
Day after day, up early and down late,
From hill to vale we dropped, from vale to hill
Mounted—from province on to province swept,
Keen hunters in a chase of fourteen weeks,
Eager as birds of prey, or as a ship
Upon the stretch, when winds are blowing fair:
Sweet coverts did we cross of pastoral life,   500
Enticing valleys, greeted them and left
Too soon, while yet the very flash and gleam
Of salutation were not passed away.
Oh! sorrow for the youth who could have seen,
Unchastened, unsubdued, unawed, unraised
To patriarchal dignity of mind,
And pure simplicity of wish and will,
Those sanctified abodes of peaceful man,
Pleased (though to hardship born, and compassed round

With danger, varying as the seasons change),   510
Pleased with his daily task, or, if not pleased,
Contented, from the moment that the dawn
(Ah! surely not without attendant gleams
Of soul-illumination) calls him forth
To industry, by glistenings flung on rocks,
Whose evening shadows lead him to repose.

    Well might a stranger look with bounding heart
Down on a green recess, the first I saw
Of those deep haunts, an aboriginal vale,
Quiet and lorded over and possessed   520
By naked huts, wood-built, and sown like tents
Or Indian cabins over the fresh lawns
And by the river side.
              That very day,
From a bare ridge we also first beheld
Unveiled the summit of Mont Blanc, and grieved
To have a soulless image on the eye
That had usurped upon a living thought
That never more could be. The wondrous Vale
Of Chamouny stretched far below, and soon
With its dumb cataracts and streams of ice,   530
A motionless array of mighty waves,
Five rivers broad and vast, made rich amends,
And reconciled us to realities;
There small birds warble from the leafy trees,
The eagle soars high in the element,
There doth the reaper bind the yellow sheaf,
The maiden spread the haycock in the sun,
While Winter like a well-tamed lion walks,
Descending from the mountain to make sport
Among the cottages by beds of flowers.   540

    Whate'er in this wide circuit we beheld,
Or heard, was fitted to our unripe state
Of intellect and heart. With such a book
Before our eyes, we could not choose but read
Lessons of genuine brotherhood, the plain

And universal reason of mankind,
The truths of young and old. Nor, side by side
Pacing, two social pilgrims, or alone
Each with his humour, could we fail to abound
In dreams and fictions, pensively composed: 550
Dejection taken up for pleasure's sake,
And gilded sympathies, the willow wreath,
And sober posies of funereal flowers,
Gathered among those solitudes sublime
From formal gardens of the lady Sorrow,
Did sweeten many a meditative hour.

    Yet still in me with those soft luxuries
Mixed something of stern mood, an under-thirst
Of vigour seldom utterly allayed:
And from that source how different a sadness   560
Would issue, let one incident make known.
When from the Vallais we had turned, and clomb
Along the Simplon's steep and rugged road,
Following a band of muleteers, we reached
A halting-place, where all together took
Their noon-tide meal. Hastily rose our guide,
Leaving us at the board; awhile we lingered,
Then paced the beaten downward way that led
Right to a rough stream's edge, and there broke off;
The only track now visible was one   570
That from the torrent's further brink held forth
Conspicuous invitation to ascend
A lofty mountain. After brief delay
Crossing the unbridged stream, that road we took,
And clomb with eagerness, till anxious fears
Intruded, for we failed to overtake
Our comrades gone before. By fortunate chance,
While every moment added doubt to doubt,
A peasant met us, from whose mouth we learned
That to the spot which had perplexed us first   580
We must descend, and there should find the road,
Which in the stony channel of the stream

Lay a few steps, and then along its banks;
And, that our future course, all plain to sight,
Was downwards with the current of that stream.
Loth to believe what we so grieved to hear,
For still we had hopes that pointed to the clouds,
We questioned him again, and yet again;
But every word that from the peasant's lips
Came in reply, translated by our feelings,   590
Ended in this,—*that we had crossed the Alps.*

    Imagination—here the Power so called
Through sad incompetence of human speech,
That awful Power rose from the mind's abyss
Like an unfathered vapour that enwraps,
At once, some lonely traveller. I was lost;
Halted without an effort to break through;
But to my conscious soul I now can say—
"I recognise thy glory:" in such strength
Of usurpation, when the light of sense   600
Goes out, but with a flash that has revealed
The invisible world, doth greatness make abode,
There harbours; whether we be young or old,
Our destiny, our being's heart and home,
Is with infinitude, and only there;
With hope it is, hope that can never die,
Effort, and expectation, and desire,
And something evermore about to be.
Under such banners, militant, the soul
Seeks for no trophies, struggles for no spoils   610
That may attest her prowess, blest in thoughts
That are their own perfection and reward,
Strong in herself and in beatitude
That hides her, like the mighty flood of Nile
Poured from his fount of Abyssinian clouds
To fertilise the whole Egyptian plain.

    The melancholy slackening that ensued
Upon those tidings by the peasant given
Was soon dislodged. Downwards we hurried fast,
And, with the half-shaped road which we had missed,   620

Entered a narrow chasm. The brook and road
Were fellow-travellers in this gloomy strait,
And with them did we journey several hours
At a slow pace. The immeasurable height
Of woods decaying, never to be decayed,
The stationary blasts of waterfalls,
And in the narrow rent at every turn
Winds thwarting winds, bewildered and forlorn,
The torrents shooting from the clear blue sky,
The rocks that muttered close upon our ears,   630
Black drizzling crags that spake by the way-side
As if a voice were in them, the sick sight
And giddy prospect of the raving stream,
The unfettered clouds and region of the Heavens,
Tumult and peace, the darkness and the light—
Were all like workings of one mind, the features
Of the same face, blossoms upon one tree;
Characters of the great Apocalypse,
The types and symbols of Eternity,
Of first, and last, and midst, and without end.   640

    That night our lodging was a house that stood
Alone within the valley, at a point
Where, tumbling from aloft, a torrent swelled
The rapid stream whose margin we had trod;
A dreary mansion, large beyond all need,
With high and spacious rooms, deafened and stunned
By noise of waters, making innocent sleep
Lie melancholy among weary bones.

    Uprisen betimes, our journey we renewed,
Led by the stream, ere noon-day magnified   650
Into a lordly river, broad and deep,
Dimpling along in silent majesty,
With mountains for its neighbours, and in view
Of distant mountains and their snowy tops,
And thus proceeding to Locarno's Lake,
Fit resting-place for such a visitant.
Locarno! spreading out in width like Heaven,
How dost thou cleave to the poetic heart,

Bask in the sunshine of the memory;
And Como! thou, a treasure whom the earth   660
Keeps to herself, confined as in a depth
Of Abyssinian privacy. I spake
Of thee, thy chestnut woods, and garden plots
Of Indian corn tended by dark-eyed maids;
Thy lofty steeps, and pathways roofed with vines,
Winding from house to house, from town to town,
Sole link that binds them to each other; walks,
League after league, and cloistral avenues,
Where silence dwells if music be not there:
While yet a youth undisciplined in verse,   670
Through fond ambition of that hour I strove
To chant your praise; nor can approach you now
Ungreeted by a more melodious Song,
Where tones of Nature smoothed by learned Art
May flow in lasting current. Like a breeze
Or sunbeam over your domain I passed
In motion without pause; but ye have left
Your beauty with me, a serene accord
Of forms and colours, passive, yet endowed
In their submissiveness with power as sweet   680
And gracious, almost, might I dare to say,
As virtue is, or goodness; sweet as love,
Or the remembrance of a generous deed,
Or mildest visitations of pure thought,
When God, the giver of all joy, is thanked
Religiously, in silent blessedness;
Sweet as this last herself, for such it is.

    With those delightful pathways we advanced,
For two days' space, in presence of the Lake,
That, stretching far among the Alps, assumed   690
A character more stern. The second night,
From sleep awakened, and misled by sound
Of the church clock telling the hours with strokes
Whose import then we had not learned, we rose
By moonlight, doubting not that day was nigh,

And that meanwhile, by no uncertain path,
Along the winding margin of the lake,
Led, as before, we should behold the scene
Hushed in profound repose. We left the town
Of Gravedona with this hope; but soon   700
Were lost, bewildered among woods immense,
And on a rock sate down, to wait for day.
An open place it was, and overlooked,
From high, the sullen water far beneath,
On which a dull red image of the moon
Lay bedded, changing oftentimes its form
Like an uneasy snake. From hour to hour
We sate and sate, wondering, as if the night
Had been ensnared by witchcraft. On the rock
At last we stretched our weary limbs for sleep,   710
But *could not* sleep, tormented by the stings
Of insects, which, with noise like that of noon,
Filled all the woods: the cry of unknown birds;
The mountains more by blackness visible
And their own size, than any outward light;
The breathless wilderness of clouds; the clock
That told, with unintelligible voice,
The widely parted hours; the noise of streams,
And sometimes rustling motions nigh at hand,
That did not leave us free from personal fear;   720
And, lastly, the withdrawing moon, that set
Before us, while she still was high in heaven;—
These were our food; and such a summer's night
Followed that pair of golden days that shed
On Como's Lake, and all that round it lay,
Their fairest, softest, happiest influence.

But here I must break off, and bid farewell
To days, each offering some new sight, or fraught
With some untried adventure, in a course
Prolonged till sprinklings of autumnal snow   730
Checked our unwearied steps. Let this alone
Be mentioned as a parting word, that not

In hollow exultation, dealing out
Hyperboles of praise comparative;
Not one rich moment to be poor for ever;
Not prostrate, overborne, as if the mind
Herself were nothing, a mere pensioner
On outward forms—did we in presence stand
Of that magnificent region. On the front
Of this whole Song is written that my heart   740
Must, in such Temple, needs have offered up
A different worship. Finally, whate'er
I saw, or heard, or felt, was but a stream
That flowed into a kindred stream; a gale,
Confederate with the current of the soul,
To speed my voyage; every sound or sight,
In its degree of power, administered
To grandeur or to tenderness,—to the one
Directly, but to tender thoughts by means
Less often instantaneous in effect;   750
Led me to these by paths that, in the main,
Were more circuitous, but not less sure
Duly to reach the point marked out by Heaven.

Oh, most belovèd Friend! a glorious time,
A happy time that was; triumphant looks
Were then the common language of all eyes;
As if awakened from sleep, the Nations hailed
Their great expectancy: the fife of war
Was then a spirit-stirring sound indeed,
A blackbird's whistle in a budding grove.   760
We left the Swiss exulting in the fate
Of their dear neighbours; and, when shortening fast
Our pilgrimage, nor distant far from home,
We crossed the Brabant armies on the fret
For battle in the cause of Liberty.
A stripling, scarcely of the household then
Of social life, I looked upon these things
As from a distance; heard, and saw, and felt,
Was touched, but with no intimate concern;

I seemed to move along them, as a bird   770
Moves through the air, or as a fish pursues
Its sport, or feeds in its proper element;
I wanted not that joy, I did not need
Such help; the ever-living universe,
Turn where I might, was opening out its glories,
And the independent spirit of pure youth
Called forth, at every season, new delights,
Spread round my steps like sunshine o'er green fields.

BOOK SEVENTH
Residence in London

Six changeful years have vanished since I first
Poured out (saluted by that quickening breeze
Which met me issuing from the City's walls)
A glad preamble to this Verse: I sang
Aloud, with fervour irresistible
Of short-lived transport, like a torrent bursting,
From a black thunder-cloud, down Scafell's side
To rush and disappear. But soon broke forth
(So willed the Muse) a less impetuous stream,
That flowed awhile with unabating strength,
Then stopped for years; not audible again   10
Before last primrose-time. Belovèd Friend!
The assurance which then cheered some heavy thoughts
On thy departure to a foreign land
Has failed; too slowly moves the promised work.
Through the whole summer have I been at rest,
Partly from voluntary holiday,
And part through outward hindrance. But I heard,
After the hour of sunset yester-even,
Sitting within doors between light and dark,
A choir of redbreasts gathered somewhere near   20
My threshold,—minstrels from the distant woods
Sent in on Winter's service, to announce,
With preparation artful and benign,
That the rough lord had left the surly North

On his accustomed journey. The delight,
Due to this timely notice, unawares
Smote me, and, listening, I in whispers said,
"Ye heartsome Choristers, ye and I will be
Associates, and, unscared by blustering winds,   30
Will chant together." Thereafter, as the shades
Of twilight deepened, going forth, I spied
A glow-worm underneath a dusky plume
Or canopy of yet unwithered fern,
Clear-shining, like a hermit's taper seen
Through a thick forest. Silence touched me here
No less than sound had done before; the child
Of Summer, lingering, shining, by herself,
The voiceless worm on the unfrequented hills,
Seemed sent on the same errand with the choir   40
Of Winter that had warbled at my door,
And the whole year breathed tenderness and love.

    The last night's genial feeling overflowed
Upon this morning, and my favourite grove,
Tossing in sunshine its dark boughs aloft,
As if to make the strong wind visible,
Wakes in me agitations like its own,
A spirit friendly to the Poet's task,
Which we will now resume with lively hope,
Nor checked by aught of tamer argument   50
That lies before us, needful to be told.

    Returned from that excursion, soon I bade
Farewell for ever to the sheltered seats
Of gownèd students, quitted hall and bower,
And every comfort of that privileged ground,
Well pleased to pitch a vagrant tent among
The unfenced regions of society.

    Yet, undetermined to what course of life
I should adhere, and seeming to possess
A little space of intermediate time   60
At full command, to London first I turned,

In no disturbance of excessive hope,
By personal ambition unenslaved,
Frugal as there was need, and, though self-willed,
From dangerous passions free. Three years had flown
Since I had felt in heart and soul the shock
Of the huge town's first presence, and had paced
Her endless streets, a transient visitant:
Now, fixed amid that concourse of mankind
Where Pleasure whirls about incessantly,   70
And life and labour seem but one, I filled
An idler's place; an idler well content
To have a house (what matter for a home?)
That owned him; living cheerfully abroad
With unchecked fancy ever on the stir,
And all my young affections out of doors.

There was a time when whatsoe'er is feigned
Of airy palaces, and gardens built
By Genii of romance; or hath in grave
Authentic history been set forth of Rome,   80
Alcairo, Babylon, or Persepolis;
Or given upon report by pilgrim friars,
Of golden cities ten months' journey deep
Among Tartarian wilds—fell short, far short,
Of what my fond simplicity believed
And thought of London—held me by a chain
Less strong of wonder and obscure delight.
Whether the bolt of childhood's Fancy shot
For me beyond its ordinary mark,
'T were vain to ask; but in our flock of boys   90
Was One, a cripple from his birth, whom chance
Summoned from school to London; fortunate
And envied traveller! When the Boy returned,
After short absence, curiously I scanned
His mien and person, nor was free, in sooth,
From disappointment, not to find some change
In look and air, from that new region brought,
As if from Fairy-land. Much I questioned him;

And every word he uttered, on my ears
Fell flatter than a cagèd parrot's note,   100
That answers unexpectedly awry,
And mocks the prompter's listening. Marvellous things
Had vanity (quick Spirit that appears
Almost as deeply seated and as strong
In a Child's heart as fear itself) conceived
For my enjoyment. Would that I could now
Recall what then I pictured to myself,
Of mitred Prelates, Lords in ermine clad,
The King, and the King's Palace, and, not last,
Nor least, Heaven bless him! the renowned Lord Mayor,   110
Dreams not unlike to those which once begat
A change of purpose in young Whittington,
When he, a friendless and a drooping boy,
Sate on a stone, and heard the bells speak out
Articulate music. Above all, one thought
Baffled my understanding: how men lived
Even next-door neighbours, as we say, yet still
Strangers, not knowing each the other's name.

    Oh, wondrous power of words, by simple faith
Licensed to take the meaning that we love!   120
Vauxhall and Ranelagh! I then had heard
Of your green groves, and wilderness of lamps
Dimming the stars, and fireworks magical,
And gorgeous ladies, under splendid domes,
Floating in dance, or warbling high in air
The songs of spirits! Nor had Fancy fed
With less delight upon that other class
Of marvels, broad-day wonders permanent:
The River proudly bridged; the dizzy top
And Whispering Gallery of St. Paul's; the tombs   130
Of Westminster; the Giants of Guildhall;
Bedlam, and those carved maniacs at the gates,
Perpetually recumbent; Statues—man.
And the horse under him—in gilded pomp
Adorning flowery gardens, 'mid vast squares;
The Monument, and that Chamber of the Tower

Where England's sovereigns sit in long array,
Their steeds bestriding,—every mimic shape
Cased in the gleaming mail the monarch wore,
Whether for gorgeous tournament addressed,   140
Or life or death upon the battle-field.
Those bold imaginations in due time
Had vanished, leaving others in their stead:
And now I looked upon the living scene;
Familiarly perused it; oftentimes,
In spite of strongest disappointment, pleased
Through courteous self-submission, as a tax
Paid to the object by prescriptive right.

    Rise up, thou monstrous ant-hill on the plain
Of a too busy world! Before me flow,   150
Thou endless stream of men and moving things!
Thy every-day appearance, as it strikes—
With wonder heightened, or sublimed by awe—
On strangers, of all ages; the quick dance
Of colours, lights, and forms; the deafening din;
The comers and the goers face to face,
Face after face; the string of dazzling wares,
Shop after shop, with symbols, blazoned names,
And all the tradesman's honours overhead:
Here, fronts of houses, like a title-page,   160
With letters huge inscribed from top to toe,
Stationed above the door, like guardian saints;
There, allegoric shapes, female or male,
Or physiognomies of real men,
Land-warriors, kings, or admirals of the sea,
Boyle, Shakespeare, Newton, or the attractive head
Of some quack-doctor, famous in his day.

    Meanwhile the roar continues, till at length,
Escaped as from an enemy, we turn
Abruptly into some sequestered nook,   170
Still as a sheltered place when winds blow loud!
At leisure, thence, through tracts of thin resort,
And sights and sounds that come at intervals,
We take our way. A raree-show is here,

With children gathered round; another street
Presents a company of dancing dogs,
Or dromedary, with an antic pair
Of monkeys on his back; a minstrel band
Of Savoyards; or, single and alone,
An English ballad-singer. Private courts,   180
Gloomy as coffins, and unsightly lanes
Thrilled by some female vendor's scream, belike
The very shrillest of all London cries,
May then entangle our impatient steps;
Conducted through those labyrinths, unawares,
To privileged regions and inviolate,
Where from their airy lodges studious lawyers
Look out on waters, walks, and gardens green.

    Thence back into the throng, until we reach,
Following the tide that slackens by degrees,   190
Some half-frequented scenes, where wider streets
Bring straggling breezes of suburban air.
Here files of ballads dangle from dead walls;
Advertisements, of giant-size, from high
Press forward, in all colours, on the sight;
These, bold in conscious merit, lower down;
That, fronted with a most imposing word,
Is, peradventure, one in masquerade.
As on the broadening causeway we advance,
Behold, turned upwards, a face hard and strong   200
In lineaments, and red with over-toil.
'T is one encountered here and everywhere;
A travelling cripple, by the trunk cut short,
And stumping on his arms. In sailor's garb
Another lies at length, beside a range
Of well-formed characters, with chalk inscribed
Upon the smooth flat stones: the Nurse is here,
The Bachelor, that loves to sun himself,
The military Idler, and the Dame,
That field-ward takes her walk with decent steps.   210

    Now homeward through the thickening hubbub, where
See, among less distinguishable shapes,

The begging scavenger, with hat in hand;
The Italian, as he thrids his way with care,
Steadying, far-seen, a frame of images
Upon his head; with basket at his breast
The Jew; the stately and slow-moving Turk,
With freight of slippers piled beneath his arm!

    Enough;—the mighty concourse I surveyed
With no unthinking mind, well pleased to note   220
Among the crowd all specimens of man,
Through all the colours which the sun bestows,
And every character of form and face:
The Swede, the Russian; from the genial south,
The Frenchman and the Spaniard; from remote
America, the Hunter-Indian; Moors,
Malays, Lascars, the Tartar, the Chinese,
And Negro Ladies in white muslin gowns.

    At leisure, then, I viewed, from day to day,
The spectacles within doors,—birds and beasts   230
Of every nature, and strange plants convened
From every clime; and, next, those sights that ape
The absolute presence of reality,
Expressing, as in mirror, sea and land,
And what earth is, and what she has to show.
I do not here allude to subtlest craft,
By means refined attaining purest ends,
But imitations, fondly made in plain
Confession of man's weakness and his loves.
Whether the Painter, whose ambitious skill   240
Submits to nothing less than taking in
A whole horizon's circuit, do with power,
Like that of angels or commissioned spirits,
Fix us upon some lofty pinnacle,
Or in a ship on waters, with a world
Of life, and life-like mockery beneath,
Above, behind, far stretching and before;
Or more mechanic artist represent
By scale exact, in model, wood or clay,
From blended colours also borrowing help,   250

Some miniature of famous spots or things,—
St. Peter's Church; or, more aspiring aim,
In microscopic vision, Rome herself;
Or, haply, some choice rural haunt,—the Falls
Of Tivoli; and, high upon that steep,
The Sibyl's mouldering Temple! every tree,
Villa, or cottage, lurking among rocks
Throughout the landscape; tuft, stone scratch minute—
All that the traveller sees when he is there.

Add to these exhibitions, mute and still,   260
Others of wider scope, where living men,
Music, and shifting pantomimic scenes,
Diversified the allurement. Need I fear
To mention by its name, as in degree,
Lowest of these and humblest in attempt,
Yet richly graced with honours of her own,
Half-rural Sadler's Wells? Though at that time
Intolerant, as is the way of youth
Unless itself be pleased, here more than once
Taking my seat, I saw (nor blush to add,   270
With ample recompense) giants and dwarfs,
Clowns, conjurors, posture-masters, harlequins,
Amid the uproar of the rabblement,
Perform their feats. Nor was it mean delight
To watch crude Nature work in untaught minds;
To note the laws and progress of belief;
Though obstinate on this way, yet on that
How willingly we travel, and how far!
To have, for instance, brought upon the scene
The champion, Jack the Giant-killer: Lo!   280
He dons his coat of darkness; on the stage
Walks, and achieves his wonders, from the eye
Of living Mortal covert, "as the moon
Hid in her vacant interlunar cave."
Delusion bold! and how can it be wrought?
The garb he wears is black as death, the word
"Invisible" flames forth upon his chest.

Here, too, were "forms and pressures of the time,"
Rough, bold, as Grecian comedy displayed
When Art was young; dramas of living men,   290
And recent things yet warm with life; a sea-fight,
Shipwreck, or some domestic incident
Divulged by Truth and magnified by Fame;
Such as the daring brotherhood of late
Set forth, too serious theme for that light place—
I mean, O distant Friend! a story drawn
From our own ground,—the Maid of Buttermere,
And how, unfaithful to a virtuous wife
Deserted and deceived, the Spoiler came
And wooed the artless daughter of the hills,   300
And wedded her, in cruel mockery
Of love and marriage bonds. These words to thee
Must needs bring back the moment when we first,
Ere the broad world rang with the maiden's name,
Beheld her serving at the cottage inn;
Both stricken, as she entered or withdrew,
With admiration of her modest mien
And carriage, marked by unexampled grace.
We since that time not unfamiliarly
Have seen her,—her discretion have observed,   310
Her just opinions, delicate reserve,
Her patience, and humility of mind
Unspoiled by commendation and the excess
Of public notice—an offensive light
To a meek spirit suffering inwardly.

From this memorial tribute to my theme
I was returning, when, with sundry forms
Commingled—shapes which met me in the way
That we must tread—thy image rose again,
Maiden of Buttermere! She lives in peace   320
Upon the spot where she was born and reared;
Without contamination doth she live
In quietness, without anxiety:
Beside the mountain chapel, sleeps in earth

Her new-born infant, fearless as a lamb
That, thither driven from some unsheltered place,
Rests underneath the little rock-like pile
When storms are raging. Happy are they both—
Mother and child!—These feelings, in themselves
Trite, do yet scarcely seem so when I think   330
On those ingenuous moments of our youth
Ere we have learnt by use to slight the crimes
And sorrows of the world. Those simple days
Are now my theme; and, foremost of the scenes,
Which yet survive in memory, appears
One, at whose centre sate a lovely Boy,
A sportive infant, who, for six months' space,
Not more, had been of age to deal about
Articulate prattle—Child as beautiful
As ever clung around a mother's neck,   340
Or father fondly gazed upon with pride.
There, too, conspicuous for stature tall
And large dark eyes, beside her infant stood
The mother; but, upon her cheeks diffused,
False tints too well accorded with the glare
From play-house lustres thrown without reserve
On every object near. The Boy had been
The pride and pleasure of all lookers-on
In whatsoever place, but seemed in this
A sort of alien scattered from the clouds.   350
Of lusty vigour, more than infantine
He was in limb, in cheek a summer rose
Just three parts blown—a cottage-child—if e'er,
By cottage-door on breezy mountain-side,
Or in some sheltering vale, was seen a babe
By Nature's gifts so favoured. Upon a board
Decked with refreshments had this child been placed,
His little stage in the vast theatre,
And there he sate, surrounded with a throng
Of chance spectators, chiefly dissolute men   360
And shameless women, treated and caressed;
Ate, drank, and with the fruit and glasses played,
While oaths and laughter and indecent speech

Were rife about him as the songs of birds
Contending after showers. The mother now
Is fading out of memory, but I see
The lovely Boy as I beheld him then
Among the wretched and the falsely gay,
Like one of those who walked with hair unsinged
Amid the fiery furnace. Charms and spells   370
Muttered on black and spiteful instigation
Have stopped, as some believe, the kindliest growths.
Ah, with how different spirit might a prayer
Have been preferred, that this fair creature, checked
By special privilege of Nature's love,
Should in his childhood be detained for ever!
But with its universal freight the tide
Hath rolled along, and this bright innocent,
Mary! may now have lived till he could look
With envy on thy nameless babe that sleeps,   380
Beside the mountain chapel, undisturbed.

　　Four rapid years had scarcely then been told
Since, travelling southward from our pastoral hills,
I heard, and for the first time in my life,
The voice of woman utter blasphemy—
Saw woman as she is, to open shame
Abandoned, and the pride of public vice;
I shuddered, for a barrier seemed at once
Thrown in that from humanity divorced
Humanity, splitting the race of man   390
In twain, yet leaving the same outward form.
Distress of mind ensued upon the sight,
And ardent meditation. Later years
Brought to such spectacle a milder sadness,
Feelings of pure commiseration, grief
For the individual and the overthrow
Of her soul's beauty; farther I was then
But seldom led, or wished to go; in truth
The sorrow of the passion stopped me there.

　　But let me now, less moved, in order take   400
Our argument. Enough is said to show

How casual incidents of real life,
Observed where pastime only had been sought,
Outweighed, or put to flight, the set events
And measured passions of the stage, albeit
By Siddons trod in the fulness of her power.
Yet was the theatre my dear delight;
The very gilding, lamps and painted scrolls,
And all the mean upholstery of the place,
Wanted not animation, when the tide   410
Of pleasure ebbed but to return as fast
With the ever-shifting figures of the scene,
Solemn or gay: whether some beauteous dame
Advanced in radiance through a deep recess
Of thick entangled forest, like the moon
Opening the clouds; or sovereign king, announced
With flourishing trumpet, came in full-blown state
Of the world's greatness, winding round with train
Of courtiers, banners, and a length of guards;
Or captive led in abject weeds, and jingling   420
His slender manacles; or romping girl
Bounced, leapt, and pawed the air; or mumbling sire,
A scare-crow pattern of old age dressed up
In all the tatters of infirmity
All loosely put together, hobbled in,
Stumping upon a cane with which he smites,
From time to time, the solid boards, and makes them
Prate somewhat loudly of the whereabout
Of one so overloaded with his years.
But what of this! the laugh, the grin, grimace,   430
The antics striving to outstrip each other,
Were all received, the least of them not lost,
With an unmeasured welcome. Through the night,
Between the show, and many-headed mass
Of the spectators, and each several nook
Filled with its fray or brawl, how eagerly
And with what flashes, as it were, the mind
Turned this way—that way! sportive and alert
And watchful, as a kitten when at play,

While winds are eddying round her, among straws 440
And rustling leaves. Enchanting age and sweet!
Romantic almost, looked at through a space,
How small, of intervening years! For then,
Though surely no mean progress had been made
In meditations holy and sublime,
Yet something of a girlish child-like gloss
Of novelty survived for scenes like these;
Enjoyment haply handed down from times
When at a country-playhouse, some rude barn
Tricked out for that proud use, if I perchance 450
Caught, on a summer evening through a chink
In the old wall, an unexpected glimpse
Of daylight, the bare thought of where I was
Gladdened me more than if I had been led
Into a dazzling cavern of romance,
Crowded with Genii busy among works
Not to be looked at by the common sun.

    The matter that detains us now may seem,
To many, neither dignified enough
Nor arduous, yet will not be scorned by them, 460
Who, looking inward, have observed the ties
That bind the perishable hours of life
Each to the other, and the curious props
By which the world of memory and thought
Exists and is sustained. More lofty themes,
Such as at least do wear a prouder face,
Solicit our regard; but when I think
Of these, I feel the imaginative power
Languish within me; even then it slept,
When, pressed by tragic sufferings, the heart 470
Was more than full; amid my sobs and tears
It slept, even in the pregnant season of youth.
For though I was most passionately moved
And yielded to all changes of the scene
With an obsequious promptness, yet the storm
Passed not beyond the suburbs of the mind;

Save when realities of act and mien,
The incarnation of the spirits that move
In harmony amid the Poet's world,
Rose to ideal grandeur, or, called forth   480
By power of contrast, made me recognise,
As at a glance, the things which I had shaped,
And yet not shaped, had seen and scarcely seen,
When, having closed the mighty Shakespeare's page,
I mused, and thought, and felt, in solitude.

   Pass we from entertainments, that are such
Professedly, to others titled higher,
Yet, in the estimate of youth at least,
More near akin to those than names imply,—
I mean the brawls of lawyers in their courts   490
Before the ermined judge, or that great stage
Where senators, tongue-favoured men, perform,
Admired and envied. Oh! the beating heart,
When one among the prime of these rose up,—
One, of whose name from childhood we had heard
Familiarly, a household term, like those,
The Bedfords, Glosters, Salsburys, of old,
Whom the fifth Harry talks of. Silence! hush!
This is no trifler, no short-flighted wit,
No stammerer of a minute, painfully   500
Delivered. No! the Orator hath yoked
The Hours, like young Aurora, to his car:
Thrice welcome Presence! how can patience e'er
Grow weary of attending on a track
That kindles with such glory! All are charmed,
Astonished; like a hero in romance,
He winds away his never-ending horn;
Words follow words, sense seems to follow sense:
What memory and what logic! till the strain
Transcendent, superhuman as it seemed,   510
Grows tedious even in a young man's ear.

   Genius of Burke! forgive the pen seduced
By specious wonders, and too slow to tell

Of what the ingenuous, what bewildered men,
Beginning to mistrust their boastful guides,
And wise men, willing to grow wiser, caught,
Rapt auditors! from thy most eloquent tongue—
Now mute, for ever mute in the cold grave.
I see him,—old, but vigorous in age,—
Stand like an oak whose stag-horn branches start   520
Out of its leafy brow, the more to awe
The younger brethren of the grove. But some—
While he forewarns, denounces, launches forth,
Against all systems built on abstract rights,
Keen ridicule; the majesty proclaims
Of Institutes and Laws, hallowed by time;
Declares the vital power of social ties
Endeared by Custom; and with high disdain,
Exploding upstart Theory, insists
Upon the allegiance to which men are born—   530
Some—say at once a froward multitude—
Murmur (for truth is hated, where not loved)
As the winds fret within the Æolian cave,
Galled by their monarch's chain. The times were big
With ominous change, which, night by night, provoked
Keen struggles, and black clouds of passion raised;
But memorable moments intervened,
When Wisdom, like the Goddess from Jove's brain,
Broke forth in armour of resplendent words,
Startling the Synod. Could a youth, and one   540
In ancient story versed, whose breast had heaved
Under the weight of classic eloquence,
Sit, see, and hear, unthankful, uninspired?

    Nor did the Pulpit's oratory fail
To achieve its higher triumphs. Not unfelt
Were its admonishments, nor lightly heard
The awful truths delivered thence by tongues
Endowed with various power to search the soul;
Yet ostentation, domineering, oft
Poured forth harangues, how sadly out of place!—   550

There have I seen a comely bachelor,
Fresh from a toilette of two hours, ascend
His rostrum, with seraphic glance look up,
And, in a tone elaborately low
Beginning, lead his voice through many a maze
A minuet course; and, winding up his mouth,
From time to time, into an orifice
Most delicate, a lurking eyelet, small,
And only not invisible, again
Open it out, diffusing thence a smile   560
Of rapt irradiation, exquisite,
Meanwhile the Evangelists, Isaiah, Job,
Moses, and he who penned, the other day,
The Death of Abel, Shakespeare, and the Bard
Whose genius spangled o'er a gloomy theme
With fancies thick as his inspiring stars,
And Ossian (doubt not—'tis the naked truth)
Summoned from streamy Morven—each and all
Would, in their turns, lend ornaments and flowers
To entwine the crook of eloquence that helped   570
This pretty Shepherd, pride of all the plains,
To rule and guide his captivated flock.

    I glance but at a few conspicuous marks,
Leaving a thousand others, that, in hall,
Court, theatre, conventicle, or shop,
In public room or private, park or street,
Each fondly reared on his own pedestal,
Looked out for admiration. Folly, vice,
Extravagance in gesture, mien, and dress,
And all the strife of singularity,   580
Lies to the ear, and lies to every sense—
Of these, and of the living shapes they wear,
There is no end. Such candidates for regard,
Although well pleased to be where they were found,
I did not hunt after, nor greatly prize,
Nor made unto myself a secret boast
Of reading them with quick and curious eye;

But, as a common produce, things that are
To-day, to-morrow will be, took of them
Such willing note, as, on some errand bound   590
That asks not speed, a traveller might bestow
On sea-shells that bestrew the sandy beach,
Or daisies swarming through the fields of June.

    But foolishness and madness in parade,
Though most at home in this their dear domain,
Are scattered everywhere, no rarities,
Even to the rudest novice of the Schools.
Me, rather, it employed, to note, and keep
In memory, those individual sights
Of courage, or integrity, or truth,   600
Or tenderness, which there, set off by foil,
Appeared more touching. One will I select—
A Father—for he bore that sacred name;—
Him saw I, sitting in an open square,
Upon a corner-stone of that low wall,
Wherein were fixed the iron pales that fenced
A spacious grass-plot; there, in silence, sate
This One Man, with a sickly babe outstretched
Upon his knee, whom he had thither brought
For sunshine, and to breathe the fresher air.   610
Of those who passed, and me who looked at him,
He took no heed; but in his brawny arms
(The Artificer was to the elbow bare,
And from his work this moment had been stolen)
He held the child, and, bending over it,
As if he were afraid both of the sun
And of the air, which he had come to seek,
Eyed the poor babe with love unutterable.

    As the black storm upon the mountain top
Sets off the sunbeam in the valley, so   620
That huge fermenting mass of human-kind
Serves as a solemn back-ground, or relief,
To single forms and objects, whence they draw,
For feeling and contemplative regard,

More than inherent liveliness and power.
How oft, amid those overflowing streets,
Have I gone forward with the crowd, and said
Unto myself, "The face of every one
That passes by me is a mystery!"
Thus have I looked, nor ceased to look, oppressed   630
By thoughts of what and whither, when and how,
Until the shapes before my eyes became
A second-sight procession, such as glides
Over still mountains, or appears in dreams;
And once, far-travelled in such mood, beyond
The reach of common indication, lost
Amid the moving pageant, I was smitten
Abruptly, with the view (a sight not rare)
Of a blind Beggar, who, with upright face,
Stood, propped against a wall, upon his chest   640
Wearing a written paper, to explain
His story, whence he came, and who he was.
Caught by the spectacle my mind turned round
As with the might of waters; and apt type
This label seemed of the utmost we can know,
Both of ourselves and of the universe;
And, on the shape of that unmoving man,
His steadfast face and sightless eyes, I gazed,
As if admonished from another world.

    Though reared upon the base of outward things,   650
Structures like these the excited spirit mainly
Builds for herself; scenes different there are,
Full-formed, that take, with small internal help,
Possession of the faculties,—the peace
That comes with night: the deep solemnity
Of nature's intermediate hours of rest,
When the great tide of human life stands still:
The business of the day to come, unborn,
Of that gone by, locked up, as in the grave;
The blended calmness of the heavens and earth,   660
Moonlight and stars, and empty streets, and sounds
Unfrequent as in deserts; at late hours

Of winter evenings, when unwholesome rains
Are falling hard, with people yet astir,
The feeble salutation from the voice
Of some unhappy woman, now and then
Heard as we pass, when no one looks about,
Nothing is listened to. But these, I fear,
Are falsely catalogued; things that are, are not,
As the mind answers to them, or the heart   670
Is prompt, or slow, to feel. What say you, then,
To times, when half the city shall break out
Full of one passion, vengeance, rage, or fear?
To executions, to a street on fire,
Mobs, riots, or rejoicings? From these sights
Take one,—that ancient festival, the Fair,
Holden where martyrs suffered in past time,
And named of St. Bartholomew; there, see
A work completed to our hands, that lays,
If any spectacle on earth can do,   680
The whole creative powers of man asleep!—
For once, the Muse's help will we implore,
And she shall lodge us, wafted on her wings,
Above the press and danger of the crowd,
Upon some showman's platform. What a shock
For eyes and ears! what anarchy and din,
Barbarian and infernal,—a phantasma,
Monstrous in colour, motion, shape, sight, sound!
Below, the open space, through every nook
Of the wide area, twinkles, is alive   690
With heads; the midway region, and above,
Is thronged with staring pictures and huge scrolls,
Dumb proclamations of the Prodigies;
With chattering monkeys dangling from their poles,
And children whirling in their roundabouts;
With those that stretch the neck and strain the eyes,
And crack the voice in rivalship, the crowd
Inviting; with buffoons against buffoons
Grimacing, writhing, screaming,—him who grinds
The hurdy-gurdy, at the fiddle weaves,   700
Rattles the salt-box, thumps the kettledrum,

And him who at the trumpet puffs his cheeks,
The silver-collared Negro with his timbrel,
Equestrians, tumblers, women, girls, and boys,
Blue-breeched, pink-vested, with high-towering plumes.—
All moveables of wonder, from all parts,
Are here—Albinos, painted Indians, Dwarfs,
The Horse of knowledge, and the learned Pig,
The Stone-eater, the man that swallows fire,
Giants, Ventriloquists, the Invisible Girl,   710
The Bust that speaks and moves its goggling eyes,
The Wax-work, Clock-work, all the marvellous craft
Of modern Merlins, Wild Beasts, Puppet-shows,
All out-o'-the-way, far-fetched, perverted things,
All freaks of nature, all Promethean thoughts
Of man, his dulness, madness, and their feats
All jumbled up together, to compose
A Parliament of Monsters. Tents and Booths
Meanwhile, as if the whole were one vast mill,
Are vomiting, receiving on all sides,   720
Men, Women, three-years' Children, Babes in arms.

　　Oh, blank confusion! true epitome
Of what the mighty City is herself,
To thousands upon thousands of her sons,
Living amid the same perpetual whirl
Of trivial objects, melted and reduced
To one identity, by differences
That have no law, no meaning, and no end—
Oppression, under which even highest minds
Must labour, whence the strongest are not free.   730
But though the picture weary out the eye,
By nature an unmanageable sight,
It is not wholly so to him who looks
In steadiness, who hath among least things
An under-sense of greatest; sees the parts
As parts, but with a feeling of the whole.
This, of all acquisitions, first awaits
On sundry and most widely different modes
Of education, nor with least delight

On that through which I passed. Attention springs,   740
And comprehensiveness and memory flow,
From early converse with the works of God
Among all regions; chiefly where appear
Most obviously simplicity and power.
Think, how the everlasting streams and woods,
Stretched and still stretching far and wide, exalt
The roving Indian, on his desert sands:
What grandeur not unfelt, what pregnant show
Of beauty, meets the sun-burnt Arab's eye:
And, as the sea propels, from zone to zone,   750
Its currents; magnifies its shoals of life
Beyond all compass; spreads, and sends aloft
Armies of clouds,—even so, its powers and aspects
Shape for mankind, by principles as fixed,
The views and aspirations of the soul
To majesty. Like virtue have the forms
Perennial of the ancient hills; nor less
The changeful language of their countenances
Quickens the slumbering mind, and aids the thoughts,
However multitudinous, to move   760
With order and relation. This, if still,
As hitherto, in freedom, I may speak,
Not violating any just restraint,
As may be hoped, of real modesty,—
This did I feel, in London's vast domain.
The Spirit of Nature was upon me there;
The soul of Beauty and enduring Life
Vouchsafed her inspiration, and diffused,
Through meagre lines and colours, and the press
Of self-destroying, transitory things,   770
Composure, and ennobling Harmony.

BOOK EIGHTH
Retrospect — Love of Nature Leading to Love of Man

What sounds are those, Helvellyn, that are heard
Up to thy summit, through the depth of air
Ascending, as if distance had the power

To make the sounds more audible? What crowd
Covers, or sprinkles o'er, yon village green?
Crowd seems it, solitary hill! to thee,
Though but a little family of men,
Shepherds and tillers of the ground—betimes
Assembled with their children and their wives,
And here and there a stranger interspersed.   10
They hold a rustic fair—a festival,
Such as, on this side now, and now on that,
Repeated through his tributary vales,
Helvellyn, in the silence of his rest,
Sees annually, if clouds towards either ocean
Blown from their favourite resting-place, or mists
Dissolved, have left him an unshrouded head.
Delightful day it is for all who dwell
In this secluded glen, and eagerly
They give it welcome. Long ere heat of noon,   20
From byre or field the kine were brought; the sheep
Are penned in cotes; the chaffering is begun.
The heifer lows, uneasy at the voice
Of a new master; bleat the flocks aloud.
Booths are there none; a stall or two is here;
A lame man or a blind, the one to beg,
The other to make music; hither, too,
From far, with basket, slung upon her arm,
Of hawker's wares—books, pictures, combs, and pins—
Some aged woman finds her way again,   30
Year after year, a punctual visitant!
There also stands a speech-maker by rote,
Pulling the strings of his boxed raree-show;
And in the lapse of many years may come
Prouder itinerant, mountebank, or he
Whose wonders in a covered wain lie hid.
But one there is, the loveliest of them all,
Some sweet lass of the valley, looking out
For gains, and who that sees her would not buy?
Fruits of her father's orchard are her wares,   40
And with the ruddy produce she walks round

Among the crowd, half pleased with, half ashamed
Of, her new office, blushing restlessly.
The children now are rich, for the old to-day
Are generous as the young; and, if content
With looking on, some ancient wedded pair
Sit in the shade together; while they gaze,
"A cheerful smile unbends the wrinkled brow,
The days departed start again to life,
And all the scenes of childhood reappear,   50
Faint, but more tranquil, like the changing sun
To him who slept at noon and wakes at eve."
Thus gaiety and cheerfulness prevail,
Spreading from young to old, from old to young,
And no one seems to want his share.—Immense
Is the recess, the circumambient world
Magnificent, by which they are embraced:
They move about upon the soft green turf:
How little they, they and their doings, seem,
And all that they can further or obstruct!   60
Through utter weakness pitiably dear,
As tender infants are: and yet how great!
For all things serve them: them the morning light
Loves, as it glistens on the silent rocks;
And them the silent rocks, which now from high
Look down upon them; the reposing clouds;
The wild brooks prattling from invisible haunts;
And old Helvellyn, conscious of the stir
Which animates this day their calm abode.

   With deep devotion, Nature, did I feel,   70
In that enormous City's turbulent world
Of men and things, what benefit I owed
To thee, and those domains of rural peace,
Where to the sense of beauty first my heart
Was opened; tract more exquisitely fair
Than that famed paradise of ten thousand trees,
Or Gehol's matchless gardens, for delight
Of the Tartarian dynasty composed

(Beyond that mighty wall, not fabulous,
China's stupendous mound) by patient toil   80
Of myriads and boon nature's lavish help;
There, in a clime from widest empire chosen,
Fulfilling (could enchantment have done more?)
A sumptuous dream of flowery lawns, with domes
Of pleasure sprinkled over, shady dells
For eastern monasteries, sunny mounts
With temples crested, bridges, gondolas,
Rocks, dens, and groves of foliage taught to melt
Into each other their obsequious hues,
Vanished and vanished in subtle chase,   90
Too fine to be pursued; or standing forth
In no discordant opposition, strong
And gorgeous as the colours side by side
Bedded among rich plumes of tropic birds;
And mountains over all, embracing all;
And all the landscape, endlessly enriched
With waters running, falling, or asleep.

But lovelier far than this, the paradise
Where I was reared; in Nature's primitive gifts
Favoured no less, and more to every sense   100
Delicious, seeing that the sun and sky,
The elements, and seasons as they change,
Do find a worthy fellow-labourer there—
Man free, man working for himself, with choice
Of time, and place, and object; by his wants,
His comforts, native occupations, cares,
Cheerfully led to individual ends
Or social, and still followed by a train
Unwooed, unthought-of even—simplicity,
And beauty, and inevitable grace.   110

Yea, when a glimpse of those imperial bowers
Would to a child be transport over-great,
When but a half-hour's roam through such a place
Would leave behind a dance of images,
That shall break in upon his sleep for weeks;

Even then the common haunts of the green earth,
And ordinary interests of man,
Which they embosom, all without regard
As both may seem, are fastening on the heart
Insensibly, each with the other's help.   120
For me, when my affections first were led
From kindred, friends, and playmates, to partake
Love for the human creature's absolute self,
That noticeable kindliness of heart
Sprang out of fountains, there abounding most,
Where sovereign Nature dictated the tasks
And occupations which her beauty adorned,
And Shepherds were the men that pleased me first;
Not such as Saturn ruled 'mid Latian wilds,
With arts and laws so tempered, that their lives   130
Left, even to us toiling in this late day,
A bright tradition of the golden age;
Not such as, 'mid Arcadian fastnesses
Sequestered, handed down among themselves
Felicity, in Grecian song renowned;
Nor such as—when an adverse fate had driven,
From house and home, the courtly band whose fortunes
Entered, with Shakespeare's genius, the wild woods
Of Arden—amid sunshine or in shade
Culled the best fruits of Time's uncounted hours,   140
Ere Phœbe sighed for the false Ganymede;
Or there where Perdita and Florizel
Together danced, Queen of the feast, and King;
Nor such as Spenser fabled. True it is,
That I had heard (what he perhaps had seen)
Of maids at sunrise bringing in from far
Their May-bush, and along the streets in flocks
Parading with a song of taunting rhymes,
Aimed at the laggards slumbering within doors;
Had also heard, from those who yet remembered,   150
Tales of the May-pole dance, and wreaths that decked
Porch, door-way, or kirk-pillar; and of youths,
Each with his maid, before the sun was up,

By annual custom, issuing forth in troops,
To drink the waters of some sainted well,
And hang it round with garlands. Love survives;
But, for such purpose, flowers no longer grow:
The times, too sage, perhaps too proud, have dropped
These lighter graces; and the rural ways
And manners which my childhood looked upon   160
Were the unluxuriant produce of a life
Intent on little but substantial needs,
Yet rich in beauty, beauty that was felt.
But images of danger and distress,
Man suffering among awful Powers and Forms;
Of this I heard, and saw enough to make
Imagination restless; nor was free
Myself from frequent perils; nor were tales
Wanting,—the tragedies of former times,
Hazards and strange escapes, of which the rocks   170
Immutable, and everflowing streams,
Where'er I roamed, were speaking monuments.

    Smooth life had flock and shepherd in old time,
Long springs and tepid winters, on the banks
Of delicate Galesus; and no less
Those scattered along Adria's myrtle shores:
Smooth life had herdsman, and his snow-white herd
To triumphs and to sacrificial rites
Devoted, on the inviolable stream
Of rich Clitumnus; and the goat-herd lived   180
As calmly, underneath the pleasant brows
Of cool Lucretilis, where the pipe was heard
Of Pan, Invisible God, thrilling the rocks
With tutelary music, from all harm
The fold protecting, I myself, mature
In manhood then, have seen a pastoral tract
Like one of these, where Fancy might run wild,
Though under skies less generous, less serene:
There, for her own delight had Nature framed
A pleasure-ground, diffused a fair expanse   190

Of level pasture, islanded with groves
And banked with woody risings; but the Plain
Endless, here opening widely out, and there
Shut up in lesser lakes or beds of lawn
And intricate recesses, creek or bay
Sheltered within a shelter, where at large
The shepherd strays, a rolling hut his home.
Thither he comes with spring-time, there abides
All summer, and at sunrise ye may hear
His flageolet to liquid notes of love   200
Attuned, or sprightly fife resounding far.
Nook is there none, nor tract of that vast space
Where passage opens, but the same shall have
In turn its visitant, telling there his hours
In unlaborious pleasure, with no task
More toilsome than to carve a beechen bowl
For spring or fountain, which the traveller finds,
When through the region he pursues at will
His devious course. A glimpse of such sweet life
I saw when, from the melancholy walls   210
Of Goslar, once imperial, I renewed
My daily walk along that wide champaign,
That, reaching to her gates, spreads east and west,
And northwards, from beneath the mountainous verge
Of the Hercynian forest. Yet, hail to you
Moors, mountains, headlands, and ye hollow vales,
Ye long deep channels for the Atlantic's voice,
Powers of my native region! Ye that seize
The heart with firmer grasp! Your snows and streams
Ungovernable, and your terrifying winds,   220
That howl so dismally for him who treads
Companionless your awful solitudes!
There, 'tis the shepherd's task the winter long
To wait upon the storms: of their approach
Sagacious, into sheltering coves he drives
His flock, and thither from the homestead bears
A toilsome burden up the craggy ways,
And deals it out, their regular nourishment

Strewn on the frozen snow. And when the spring
Looks out, and all the pastures dance with lambs,   230
And when the flock, with warmer weather, climbs
Higher and higher, him his office leads
To watch their goings, whatsoever track
The wanderers choose. For this he quits his home
At day-spring, and no sooner doth the sun
Begin to strike him with a fire-like heat,
Than he lies down upon some shining rock,
And breakfasts with his dog. When they have stolen,
As is their wont, a pittance from strict time,
For rest not needed or exchange of love,   240
Then from his couch he starts; and now his feet
Crush out a livelier fragrance from the flowers
Of lowly thyme, by Nature's skill enwrought
In the wild turf: the lingering dews of morn
Smoke round him, as from hill to hill he hies,
His staff protending like a hunter's spear,
Or by its aid leaping from crag to crag,
And o'er the brawling beds of unbridged streams.
Philosophy, methinks, at Fancy's call,
Might deign to follow him through what he does   250
Or sees in his day's march; himself he feels,
In those vast regions where his service lies,
A freeman, wedded to his life of hope
And hazard, and hard labour interchanged
With that majestic indolence so dear
To native man. A rambling schoolboy, thus,
I felt his presence in his own domain,
As of a lord and master, or a power,
Or genius, under Nature, under God,
Presiding; and severest solitude   260
Had more commanding looks when he was there.
When up the lonely brooks on rainy days
Angling I went, or trod the trackless hills
By mists bewildered, suddenly mine eyes
Have glanced upon him distant a few steps,
In size a giant, stalking through thick fog,
His sheep like Greenland bears; or, as he stepped

Beyond the boundary line of some hill-shadow,
His form hath flashed upon me, glorified
By the deep radiance of the setting sun: 270
Or him have I descried in distant sky,
A solitary object and sublime,
Above all height! like an aerial cross
Stationed alone upon a spiry rock
Of the Chartreuse, for worship. Thus was man
Ennobled outwardly before my sight,
And thus my heart was early introduced
To an unconscious love and reverence
Of human nature; hence the human form
To me became an index of delight,   280
Of grace and honour, power and worthiness.
Meanwhile this creature—spiritual almost
As those of books, but more exalted far;
Far more of an imaginative form
Than the gay Corin of the groves, who lives
For his own fancies, or to dance by the hour,
In coronal, with Phyllis in the midst—
Was, for the purposes of kind, a man
With the most common; husband, father; learned,
Could teach, admonish; suffered with the rest   290
From vice and folly, wretchedness and fear;
Of this I little saw, cared less for it,
But something must have felt.
                              Call ye these appearances—
Which I beheld of shepherds in my youth,
This sanctity of Nature given to man—
A shadow, a delusion, ye who pore
On the dead letter, miss the spirit of things;
Whose truth is not a motion or a shape
Instinct with vital functions, but a block
Or waxen image which yourselves have made,   300
And ye adore! But blessèd be the God
Of Nature and of Man that this was so;
That men before my inexperienced eyes
Did first present themselves thus purified,
Removed, and to a distance that was fit:

And so we all of us in some degree
Are led to knowledge, wheresoever led,
And howsoever; were it otherwise,
And we found evil fast as we find good
In our first years, or think that it is found,   310
How could the innocent heart bear up and live!
But doubly fortunate my lot; not here
Alone, that something of a better life
Perhaps was round me than it is the privilege
Of most to move in, but that first I looked
At Man through objects that were great or fair;
First communed with him by their help. And thus
Was founded a sure safeguard and defence
Against the weight of meanness, selfish cares,
Coarse manners, vulgar passions, that beat in   320
On all sides from the ordinary world
In which we traffic. Starting from this point
I had my face turned toward the truth, began
With an advantage furnished by that kind
Of prepossession, without which the soul
Receives no knowledge that can bring forth good,
No genuine insight ever comes to her.
From the restraint of over-watchful eyes
Preserved, I moved about, year after year,
Happy, and now most thankful that my walk   330
Was guarded from too early intercourse
With the deformities of crowded life,
And those ensuing laughters and contempts,
Self-pleasing, which, if we would wish to think
With a due reverence on earth's rightful lord,
Here placed to be the inheritor of heaven,
Will not permit us; but pursue the mind,
That to devotion willingly would rise,
Into the temple and the temple's heart.

  Yet deem not, Friend! that human kind with me   340
Thus early took a place pre-eminent;
Nature herself was, at this unripe time,

But secondary to my own pursuits
And animal activities, and all
Their trivial pleasures; and when these had drooped
And gradually expired, and Nature, prized
For her own sake, became my joy, even then—
And upwards through late youth, until not less
Than two-and-twenty summers had been told—
Was Man in my affections and regards   350
Subordinate to her, her visible forms
And viewless agencies: a passion, she,
A rapture often, and immediate love
Ever at hand; he, only a delight
Occasional, an accidental grace,
His hour being not yet come. Far less had then
The inferior creatures, beast or bird, attuned
My spirit to that gentleness of love,
(Though they had long been carefully observed),
Won from me those minute obeisances   360
Of tenderness, which I may number now
With my first blessings. Nevertheless, on these
The light of beauty did not fall in vain,
Or grandeur circumfuse them to no end.

But when that first poetic faculty
Of plain Imagination and severe,
No longer a mute influence of the soul,
Ventured, at some rash Muse's earnest call,
To try her strength among harmonious words;
And to book-notions and the rules of art   370
Did knowingly conform itself; there came
Among the simple shapes of human life
A wilfulness of fancy and conceit;
And Nature and her objects beautified
These fictions, as in some sort, in their turn,
They burnished her. From touch of this new power
Nothing was safe: the elder-tree that grew
Beside the well-known charnel-house had then
A dismal look: the yew-tree had its ghost,

That took his station there for ornament: 380
The dignities of plain occurrence then
Were tasteless, and truth's golden mean, a point
Where no sufficient pleasure could be found.
Then, if a widow, staggering with the blow
Of her distress, was known to have turned her steps
To the cold grave in which her husband slept,
One night, or haply more than one, through pain
Or half-insensate impotence of mind,
The fact was caught at greedily, and there
She must be visitant the whole year through,   390
Wetting the turf with never-ending tears.
Through quaint obliquities I might pursue
These cravings; when the foxglove, one by one,
Upwards through every stage of the tall stem,
Had shed beside the public way its bells,
And stood of all dismantled, save the last
Left at the tapering ladder's top, that seemed
To bend as doth a slender blade of grass
Tipped with a rain-drop, Fancy loved to seat,
Beneath the plant despoiled, but crested still   400
With this last relic, soon itself to fall,
Some vagrant mother, whose arch little ones,
All unconcerned by her dejected plight,
Laughed as with rival eagerness their hands
Gathered the purple cups that round them lay,
Strewing the turfs green slope.
                                        A diamond light
(Whene'er the summer sun, declining, smote
A smooth rock wet with constant springs) was seen
Sparkling from out a copse-clad bank that rose
Fronting our cottage. Oft beside the hearth   410
Seated, with open door, often and long
Upon this restless lustre have I gazed,
That made my fancy restless as itself.
'Twas now for me a burnished silver shield
Suspended over a knight's tomb, who lay
Inglorious, buried in the dusky wood:

An entrance now into some magic cave
Or palace built by fairies of the rock;
Nor could I have been bribed to disenchant
The spectacle, by visiting the spot.   420
Thus wilful Fancy, in no hurtful mood,
Engrafted far-fetched shapes on feelings bred
By pure Imagination: busy Power
She was, and with her ready pupil turned
Instinctively to human passions, then
Least understood. Yet, 'mid the fervent swarm
Of these vagaries, with an eye so rich
As mine was through the bounty of a grand
And lovely region, I had forms distinct
To steady me: each airy thought revolved   430
Round a substantial centre, which at once
Incited it to motion, and controlled.
I did not pine like one in cities bred,
As was thy melancholy lot, dear Friend!
Great Spirit as thou art, in endless dreams
Of sickliness, disjoining, joining, things
Without the light of knowledge. Where the harm,
If, when the woodman languished with disease
Induced by sleeping nightly on the ground
Within his sod-built cabin, Indian-wise,   440
I called the pangs of disappointed love,
And all the sad etcetera of the wrong,
To help him to his grave? Meanwhile the man,
If not already from the woods retired
To die at home, was haply, as I knew,
Withering by slow degrees, 'mid gentle airs,
Birds, running streams, and hills so beautiful
On golden evenings, while the charcoal pile
Breathed up its smoke, an image of his ghost
Or spirit that full soon must take her flight.   450
Nor shall we not be tending towards that point
Of sound humanity to which our Tale
Leads, though by sinuous ways, if here I show
How Fancy, in a season when she wove

Those slender cords, to guide the unconscious Boy
For the Man's sake, could feed at Nature's call
Some pensive musings which might well beseem
Maturer years.
                 A grove there is whose boughs
Stretch from the western marge of Thurstonmere,
With length of shade so thick, that whoso glides   460
Along the line of low-roofed water, moves
As in a cloister. Once—while, in that shade
Loitering, I watched the golden beams of light
Flung from the setting sun, as they reposed
In silent beauty on the naked ridge
Of a high eastern hill—thus flowed my thoughts
In a pure stream of words fresh from the heart:
Dear native Regions, wheresoe'er shall close
My mortal course, there will I think on you;
Dying, will cast on you a backward look;   470
Even as this setting sun (albeit the Vale
Is no where touched by one memorial gleam)
Doth with the fond remains of his last power
Still linger, and a farewell lustre sheds,
On the dear mountain-tops where first he rose.

Enough of humble arguments; recall,
My Song! those high emotions which thy voice
Has heretofore made known; that bursting forth
Of sympathy, inspiring and inspired,
When everywhere a vital pulse was felt,   480
And all the several frames of things, like stars,
Through every magnitude distinguishable,
Shone mutually indebted, or half lost
Each in the other's blaze, a galaxy
Of life and glory. In the midst stood Man,
Outwardly, inwardly contemplated,
As, of all visible natures, crown, though born
Of dust, and kindred to the worm; a Being,
Both in perception and discernment, first
In every capability of rapture,   490

Through the divine effect of power and love;
As, more than anything we know, instinct
With godhead, and, by reason and by will,
Acknowledging dependency sublime.

Ere long, the lonely mountains left, I moved,
Begirt, from day to day, with temporal shapes
Of vice and folly thrust upon my view,
Objects of sport, and ridicule, and scorn,
Manners and characters discriminate,
And little bustling passions that eclipse,   500
As well they might, the impersonated thought,
The idea, or abstraction of the kind.

An idler among academic bowers,
Such was my new condition, as at large
Has been set forth; yet here the vulgar light
Of present, actual, superficial life,
Gleaming through colouring of other times,
Old usages and local privilege,
Was welcomed, softened, if not solemnised.
This notwithstanding, being brought more near   510
To vice and guilt, forerunning wretchedness,
I trembled,—thought, at times, of human life
With an indefinite terror and dismay,
Such as the storms and angry elements
Had bred in me; but gloomier, a dim
Analogy to uproar and misrule,
Disquiet, danger, and obscurity.

It might be told (but wherefore speak of things
Common to all?) that, seeing, I was led
Gravely to ponder—judging between good   520
And evil, not as for the mind's delight
But for her guidance—one who was to *act*,
As sometimes to the best of feeble means
I did, by human sympathy impelled:
And, through dislike and most offensive pain,
Was to the truth conducted; of this faith

Never forsaken, that, by acting well,
And understanding, I should learn to love
The end of life, and everything we know.

Grave Teacher, stern Preceptress! for at times   530
Thou canst put on an aspect most severe;
London, to thee I willingly return.
Erewhile my verse played idly with the flowers
Enwrought upon thy mantle; satisfied
With that amusement, and a simple look
Of child-like inquisition now and then
Cast upwards on thy countenance, to detect
Some inner meanings which might harbour there.
But how could I in mood so light indulge,
Keeping such fresh remembrance of the day,   540
When, having thridded the long labyrinth
Of the suburban villages, I first
Entered thy vast dominion? On the roof
Of an itinerant vehicle I sate,
With vulgar men about me, trivial forms
Of houses, pavement, streets, of men and things,—
Mean shapes on every side: but, at the instant,
When to myself it fairly might be said,
The threshold now is overpast, (how strange
That aught external to the living mind   550
Should have such mighty sway! yet so it was),
A weight of ages did at once descend
Upon my heart; no thought embodied, no
Distinct remembrances, but weight and power,—
Power growing under weight: alas! I feel
That I am trifling: 'twas a moment's pause,—
All that took place within me came and went
As in a moment; yet with Time it dwells,
And grateful memory, as a thing divine.

The curious traveller, who, from open day,   560
Hath passed with torches into some huge cave,
The Grotto of Antiparos, or the Den
In old time haunted by that Danish Witch,
Yordas; he looks around and sees the vault

Widening on all sides; sees, or thinks he sees,
Erelong, the massy roof above his head,
That instantly unsettles and recedes,—
Substance and shadow, light and darkness, all
Commingled, making up a canopy
Of shapes and forms and tendencies to shape   570
That shift and vanish, change and interchange
Like spectres,—ferment silent and sublime!
That after a short space works less and less,
Till, every effort, every motion gone,
The scene before him stands in perfect view
Exposed, and lifeless as a written book!—
But let him pause awhile, and look again,
And a new quickening shall succeed, at first
Beginning timidly, then creeping fast,
Till the whole cave, so late a senseless mass,   580
Busies the eye with images and forms
Boldly assembled,—here is shadowed forth
From the projections, wrinkles, cavities,
A variegated landscape,—there the shape
Of some gigantic warrior clad in mail,
The ghostly semblance of a hooded monk,
Veiled nun, or pilgrim resting on his staff:
Strange congregation! yet not slow to meet
Eyes that perceive through minds that can inspire.

Even in such sort had I at first been moved,   590
Nor otherwise continued to be moved,
As I explored the vast metropolis,
Fount of my country's destiny and the world's;
That great emporium, chronicle at once
And burial-place of passions, and their home
Imperial, their chief living residence.

With strong sensations teeming as it did
Of past and present, such a place must needs
Have pleased me, seeking knowledge at that time
Far less than craving power; yet knowledge came,   600
Sought or unsought, and influxes of power
Came, of themselves, or at her call derived

In fits of kindliest apprehensiveness,
From all sides, when whate'er was in itself
Capacious found, or seemed to find, in me
A correspondent amplitude of mind;
Such is the strength and glory of our youth!
The human nature unto which I felt
That I belonged, and reverenced with love,
Was not a punctual presence, but a spirit   610
Diffused through time and space, with aid derived
Of evidence from monuments, erect,
Prostrate, or leaning towards their common rest
In earth, the widely scattered wreck sublime
Of vanished nations, or more clearly drawn
From books and what they picture and record.

       'Tis true, the history of our native land—
With those of Greece compared and popular Rome,
And in our high-wrought modern narratives
Stript of their harmonising soul, the life   620
Of manners and familiar incidents—
Had never much delighted me. And less
Than other intellects had mine been used
To lean upon extrinsic circumstance
Of record or tradition; but a sense
Of what in the Great City had been done
And suffered, and was doing, suffering, still,
Weighed with me, could support the test of thought;
And, in despite of all that had gone by,
Or was departing never to return,   630
There I conversed with majesty and power
Like independent natures. Hence the place
Was thronged with impregnations like the Wilds
In which my early feelings had been nursed—
Bare hills and valleys, full of caverns, rocks,
And audible seclusions, dashing lakes,
Echoes and waterfalls, and pointed crags
That into music touch the passing wind.
Here then my young imagination found

No uncongenial element; could here   640
Among new objects serve or give command,
Even as the heart's occasions might require,
To forward reason's else too-scrupulous march.
The effect was, still more elevated views
Of human nature. Neither vice nor guilt,
Debasement undergone by body or mind,
Nor all the misery forced upon my sight,
Misery not lightly passed, but sometimes scanned
Most feelingly, could overthrow my trust
In what we 'may' become; induce belief   650
That I was ignorant, had been falsely taught,
A solitary, who with vain conceits
Had been inspired, and walked about in dreams.
From those sad scenes when meditation turned,
Lo! everything that was indeed divine
Retained its purity inviolate,
Nay brighter shone, by this portentous gloom
Set off; such opposition as aroused
The mind of Adam, yet in Paradise
Though fallen from bliss, when in the East he saw   660
Darkness ere day's mid course, and morning light
More orient in the western cloud, that drew
O'er the blue firmament a radiant white,
Descending slow with something heavenly fraught.

    Add also, that among the multitudes
Of that huge city, oftentimes was seen
Affectingly set forth, more than elsewhere
Is possible, the unity of man,
One spirit over ignorance and vice
Predominant, in good and evil hearts;   670
One sense for moral judgments, as one eye
For the sun's light. The soul when smitten thus
By a sublime 'idea', whencesoe'er
Vouchsafed for union or communion, feeds
On the pure bliss, and takes her rest with God.
Thus from a very early age, O Friend!

My thoughts by slow gradations had been drawn
To human-kind, and to the good and ill
Of human life: Nature had led me on;
And oft amid the "busy hum" I seemed   680
To travel independent of her help,
As if I had forgotten her; but no,
The world of human-kind outweighed not hers
In my habitual thoughts; the scale of love,
Though filling daily, still was light, compared
With that in which 'her' mighty objects lay.

BOOK NINTH
Residence in France

Even as a river,—partly (it might seem)
Yielding to old remembrances, and swayed
In part by fear to shape a way direct,
That would engulph him soon in the ravenous sea—
Turns, and will measure back his course, far back,
Seeking the very regions which he crossed
In his first outset; so have we, my Friend!
Turned and returned with intricate delay.
Or as a traveller, who has gained the brow
Of some aerial Down, while there he halts   10
For breathing-time, is tempted to review
The region left behind him; and, if aught
Deserving notice have escaped regard,
Or been regarded with too careless eye,
Strives, from that height, with one and yet one more
Last look, to make the best amends he may:
So have we lingered. Now we start afresh
With courage, and new hope risen on our toil.
Fair greetings to this shapeless eagerness,
Whene'er it comes! needful in work so long,   20
Thrice needful to the argument which now
Awaits us! Oh, how much unlike the past!

Free as a colt at pasture on the hill,
I ranged at large, through London's wide domain,

Month after month. Obscurely did I live,
Not seeking frequent intercourse with men,
By literature, or elegance, or rank,
Distinguished. Scarcely was a year thus spent
Ere I forsook the crowded solitude,
With less regret for its luxurious pomp,   30
And all the nicely-guarded shows of art,
Than for the humble book-stalls in the streets,
Exposed to eye and hand where'er I turned.

    France lured me forth; the realm that I had crossed
So lately, journeying toward the snow-clad Alps.
But now, relinquishing the scrip and staff,
And all enjoyment which the summer sun
Sheds round the steps of those who meet the day
With motion constant as his own, I went
Prepared to sojourn in a pleasant town,   40
Washed by the current of the stately Loire.

    Through Paris lay my readiest course, and there
Sojourning a few days, I visited
In haste, each spot of old or recent fame,
The latter chiefly; from the field of Mars
Down to the suburbs of St. Antony,
And from Mont Martre southward to the Dome
Of Geneviève. In both her clamorous Halls,
The National Synod and the Jacobins,
I saw the Revolutionary Power   50
Toss like a ship at anchor, rocked by storms;
The Arcades I traversed, in the Palace huge
Of Orleans; coasted round and round the line
Of Tavern, Brothel, Gaming-house, and Shop,
Great rendezvous of worst and best, the walk
Of all who had a purpose, or had not;
I stared and listened, with a stranger's ears,
To Hawkers and Haranguers, hubbub wild!
And hissing Factionists with ardent eyes,
In knots, or pairs, or single. Not a look   60
Hope takes, or Doubt or Fear is forced to wear,
But seemed there present; and I scanned them all,

Watched every gesture uncontrollable,
Of anger, and vexation, and despite,
All side by side, and struggling face to face,
With gaiety and dissolute idleness.

    Where silent zephyrs sported with the dust
Of the Bastille, I sate in the open sun,
And from the rubbish gathered up a stone,
And pocketed the relic, in the guise   **70**
Of an enthusiast; yet, in honest truth,
I looked for something that I could not find,
Affecting more emotion than I felt;
For 'tis most certain, that these various sights,
However potent their first shock, with me
Appeared to recompense the traveller's pains
Less than the painted Magdalene of Le Brun,
A beauty exquisitely wrought, with hair
Dishevelled, gleaming eyes, and rueful cheek
Pale and bedropped with overflowing tears.   **80**

    But hence to my more permanent abode
I hasten; there, by novelties in speech,
Domestic manners, customs, gestures, looks,
And all the attire of ordinary life,
Attention was engrossed; and, thus amused,
I stood 'mid those concussions, unconcerned,
Tranquil almost, and careless as a flower
Glassed in a green-house, or a parlour shrub
That spreads its leaves in unmolested peace,
While every bush and tree, the country through,   **90**
Is shaking to the roots: indifference this
Which may seem strange: but I was unprepared
With needful knowledge, had abruptly passed
Into a theatre, whose stage was filled
And busy with an action far advanced.
Like others, I had skimmed, and sometimes read
With care, the master pamphlets of the day;
Nor wanted such half-insight as grew wild
Upon that meagre soil, helped out by talk

And public news; but having never seen   100
A chronicle that might suffice to show
Whence the main organs of the public power
Had sprung, their transmigrations, when and how
Accomplished, giving thus unto events
A form and body; all things were to me
Loose and disjointed, and the affections left
Without a vital interest. At that time,
Moreover, the first storm was overblown,
And the strong hand of outward violence
Locked up in quiet. For myself, I fear   110
Now, in connection with so great a theme,
To speak (as I must be compelled to do)
Of one so unimportant; night by night
Did I frequent the formal haunts of men,
Whom, in the city, privilege of birth
Sequestered from the rest, societies
Polished in arts, and in punctilio versed;
Whence, and from deeper causes, all discourse
Of good and evil of the time was shunned
With scrupulous care; but these restrictions soon   120
Proved tedious, and I gradually withdrew
Into a noisier world, and thus ere long
Became a patriot; and my heart was all
Given to the people, and my love was theirs.

    A band of military Officers,
Then stationed in the city, were the chief
Of my associates: some of these wore swords
That had been seasoned in the wars, and all
Were men well-born; the chivalry of France.
In age and temper differing, they had yet   130
One spirit ruling in each heart; alike
(Save only one, hereafter to be named)
Were bent upon undoing what was done:
This was their rest and only hope; therewith
No fear had they of bad becoming worse,
For worst to them was come; nor would have stirred,

Or deemed it worth a moment's thought to stir,
In anything, save only as the act
Looked thitherward. One, reckoning by years,
Was in the prime of manhood, and erewhile   140
He had sate lord in many tender hearts;
Though heedless of such honours now, and changed:
His temper was quite mastered by the times,
And they had blighted him, had eaten away
The beauty of his person, doing wrong
Alike to body and to mind: his port,
Which once had been erect and open, now
Was stooping and contracted, and a face,
Endowed by Nature with her fairest gifts
Of symmetry and light and bloom, expressed,   150
As much as any that was ever seen,
A ravage out of season, made by thoughts
Unhealthy and vexatious. With the hour,
That from the press of Paris duly brought
Its freight of public news, the fever came,
A punctual visitant, to shake this man,
Disarmed his voice and fanned his yellow cheek
Into a thousand colours; while he read,
Or mused, his sword was haunted by his touch
Continually, like an uneasy place   160
In his own body. 'Twas in truth an hour
Of universal ferment; mildest men
Were agitated, and commotions, strife
Of passion and opinion, filled the walls
Of peaceful houses with unquiet sounds.
The soil of common life was, at that time,
Too hot to tread upon. Oft said I then,
And not then only, "What a mockery this
Of history, the past and that to come!
Now do I feel how all men are deceived,   170
Reading of nations and their works, in faith,
Faith given to vanity and emptiness;
Oh! laughter for the page that would reflect
To future times the face of what now is!"

The land all swarmed with passion, like a plain
Devoured by locusts,—Carra, Gorsas,—add
A hundred other names, forgotten now,
Nor to be heard of more; yet they were powers,
Like earthquakes, shocks repeated day by day,
And felt through every nook of town and field.   180

    Such was the state of things. Meanwhile the chief
Of my associates stood prepared for flight
To augment the band of emigrants in arms
Upon the borders of the Rhine, and leagued
With foreign foes mustered for instant war.
This was their undisguised intent, and they
Were waiting with the whole of their desires
The moment to depart.

                     An Englishman,
Born in a land whose very name appeared
To license some unruliness of mind;   190
A stranger, with youth's further privilege,
And the indulgence that a half-learnt speech
Wins from the courteous; I, who had been else
Shunned and not tolerated, freely lived
With these defenders of the Crown, and talked,
And heard their notions; nor did they disdain
The wish to bring me over to their cause.

    But though untaught by thinking or by books
To reason well of polity or law,
And nice distinctions, then on every tongue,   200
Of natural rights and civil; and to acts
Of nations and their passing interests
(If with unworldly ends and aims compared)
Almost indifferent, even the historian's tale
Prizing but little otherwise than I prized
Tales of the poets, as it made the heart
Beat high, and filled the fancy with fair forms,
Old heroes and their sufferings and their deeds;
Yet in the regal sceptre, and the pomp
Of orders and degrees, I nothing found   210

Then, or had ever, even in crudest youth,
That dazzled me, but rather what I mourned
And ill could brook, beholding that the best
Ruled not, and feeling that they ought to rule.

For, born in a poor district, and which yet
Retaineth more of ancient homeliness,
Than any other nook of English ground,
It was my fortune scarcely to have seen,
Through the whole tenor of my school-day time,
The face of one, who, whether boy or man,   220
Was vested with attention or respect
Through claims of wealth or blood; nor was it least
Of many benefits, in later years
Derived from academic institutes
And rules, that they held something up to view
Of a Republic, where all stood thus far
Upon equal ground; that we were brothers all
In honour, as in one community,
Scholars and gentlemen; where, furthermore,
Distinction open lay to all that came,   230
And wealth and titles were in less esteem
Than talents, worth, and prosperous industry.
Add unto this, subservience from the first
To presences of God's mysterious power
Made manifest in Nature's sovereignty,
And fellowship with venerable books,
To sanction the proud workings of the soul,
And mountain liberty. It could not be
But that one tutored thus should look with awe
Upon the faculties of man, receive   240
Gladly the highest promises, and hail,
As best, the government of equal rights
And individual worth. And hence, O Friend!
If at the first great outbreak I rejoiced
Less than might well befit my youth, the cause
In part lay here, that unto me the events
Seemed nothing out of nature's certain course,

A gift that was come rather late than soon.
No wonder, then, if advocates like these,
Inflamed by passion blind with prejudice,   250
And stung with injury, at this riper day,
Were impotent to make my hopes put on
The shape of theirs, my understanding bend
In honour to their honour: zeal, which yet
Had slumbered, now in opposition burst
Forth like a Polar summer: every word
They uttered was a dart, by counter-winds
Blown back upon themselves; their reason seemed
Confusion-stricken by a higher power
Than human understanding, their discourse   260
Maimed, spiritless; and, in their weakness strong,
I triumphed.
                    Meantime, day by day, the roads
Were crowded with the bravest youth of France,
And all the promptest of her spirits, linked
In gallant soldiership, and posting on
To meet the war upon her frontier bounds.
Yet at this very moment do tears start
Into mine eyes: I do not say I weep—
I wept not then,—but tears have dimmed my sight,
In memory of the farewells of that time,   270
Domestic severings, female fortitude
At dearest separation, patriot love
And self-devotion, and terrestrial hope,
Encouraged with a martyr's confidence;
Even files of strangers merely seen but once,
And for a moment, men from far with sound
Of music, martial tunes, and banners spread,
Entering the city, here and there a face,
Or person, singled out among the rest,
Yet still a stranger and beloved as such;   280
Even by these passing spectacles my heart
Was oftentimes uplifted, and they seemed
Arguments sent from Heaven to prove the cause
Good, pure, which no one could stand up against,

Who was not lost, abandoned, selfish, proud,
Mean, miserable, wilfully depraved,
Hater perverse of equity and truth.

    Among that band of Officers was one,
Already hinted at, of other mould—
A patriot, thence rejected by the rest,
And with an oriental loathing spurned,   290
As of a different caste. A meeker man
Than this lived never, nor a more benign,
Meek though enthusiastic. Injuries
Made 'him' more gracious, and his nature then
Did breathe its sweetness out most sensibly,
As aromatic flowers on Alpine turf,
When foot hath crushed them. He through the events
Of that great change wandered in perfect faith,
As through a book, an old romance, or tale
Of Fairy, or some dream of actions wrought   300
Behind the summer clouds. By birth he ranked
With the most noble, but unto the poor
Among mankind he was in service bound,
As by some tie invisible, oaths professed
To a religious order. Man he loved
As man; and, to the mean and the obscure,
And all the homely in their homely works,
Transferred a courtesy which had no air
Of condescension; but did rather seem
A passion and a gallantry, like that   310
Which he, a soldier, in his idler day
Had paid to woman: somewhat vain he was,
Or seemed so, yet it was not vanity,
But fondness, and a kind of radiant joy
Diffused around him, while he was intent
On works of love or freedom, or revolved
Complacently the progress of a cause,
Whereof he was a part: yet this was meek
And placid, and took nothing from the man   320
That was delightful. Oft in solitude
With him did I discourse about the end

Of civil government, and its wisest forms;
Of ancient loyalty, and chartered rights,
Custom and habit, novelty and change;
Of self-respect, and virtue in the few
For patrimonial honour set apart,
And ignorance in the labouring multitude.
For he, to all intolerance indisposed,
Balanced these contemplations in his mind;   330
And I, who at that time was scarcely dipped
Into the turmoil, bore a sounder judgment
Than later days allowed; carried about me,
With less alloy to its integrity,
The experience of past ages, as, through help
Of books and common life, it makes sure way
To youthful minds, by objects over near
Not pressed upon, nor dazzled or misled
By struggling with the crowd for present ends.

       But though not deaf, nor obstinate to find   340
Error without excuse upon the side
Of them who strove against us, more delight
We took, and let this freely be confessed,
In painting to ourselves the miseries
Of royal courts, and that voluptuous life
Unfeeling, where the man who is of soul
The meanest thrives the most; where dignity,
True personal dignity, abideth not;
A light, a cruel, and vain world cut off
From the natural inlets of just sentiment,   350
From lowly sympathy and chastening truth;
Where good and evil interchange their names,
And thirst for bloody spoils abroad is paired
With vice at home. We added dearest themes—
Man and his noble nature, as it is
The gift which God has placed within his power,
His blind desires and steady faculties
Capable of clear truth, the one to break
Bondage, the other to build liberty
On firm foundations, making social life,   360

Through knowledge spreading and imperishable,
As just in regulation, and as pure
As individual in the wise and good.

We summoned up the honourable deeds
Of ancient Story, thought of each bright spot,
That would be found in all recorded time,
Of truth preserved and error passed away;
Of single spirits that catch the flame from Heaven,
And how the multitudes of men will feed
And fan each other; thought of sects, how keen   370
They are to put the appropriate nature on,
Triumphant over every obstacle
Of custom, language, country, love, or hate,
And what they do and suffer for their creed;
How far they travel, and how long endure:
How quickly mighty Nations have been formed,
From least beginnings; how, together locked
By new opinions, scattered tribes have made
One body, spreading wide as clouds in heaven.
To aspirations then of our own minds   380
Did we appeal; and, finally, beheld
A living confirmation of the whole
Before us, in a people from the depth
Of shameful imbecility uprisen,
Fresh as the morning star. Elate we looked
Upon their virtues; saw, in rudest men,
Self-sacrifice the firmest; generous love,
And continence of mind, and sense of right,
Uppermost in the midst of fiercest strife.

Oh, sweet it is, in academic groves,   390
Or such retirement, Friend! as we have known
In the green dales beside our Rotha's stream,
Greta, or Derwent, or some nameless rill,
To ruminate, with interchange of talk,
On rational liberty, and hope in man,
Justice and peace. But far more sweet such toil—

Toil, say I, for it leads to thoughts abstruse—
If nature then be standing on the brink
Of some great trial, and we hear the voice
Of one devoted,—one whom circumstance   400
Hath called upon to embody his deep sense
In action, give it outwardly a shape,
And that of benediction, to the world.
Then doubt is not, and truth is more than truth,—
A hope it is, and a desire; a creed
Of zeal, by an authority Divine
Sanctioned, of danger, difficulty, or death.
Such conversation, under Attic shades,
Did Dion hold with Plato; ripened thus
For a Deliverer's glorious task,—and such   410
He, on that ministry already bound,
Held with Eudemus and Timonides,
Surrounded by adventurers in arms,
When those two vessels with their daring freight,
For the Sicilian Tyrant's overthrow,
Sailed from Zacynthus,—philosophic war,
Led by Philosophers. With harder fate,
Though like ambition, such was he, O Friend!
Of whom I speak. So Beaupuis (let the name
Stand near the worthiest of Antiquity)   420
Fashioned his life; and many a long discourse,
With like persuasion honoured, we maintained:
He, on his part, accoutred for the worst,
He perished fighting, in supreme command,
Upon the borders of the unhappy Loire,
For liberty, against deluded men,
His fellow-countrymen; and yet most blessed
In this, that he the fate of later times
Lived not to see, nor what we now behold,
Who have as ardent hearts as he had then.   430

   Along that very Loire, with festal mirth
Resounding at all hours, and innocent yet
Of civil slaughter, was our frequent walk;

Or in wide forests of continuous shade,
Lofty and over-arched, with open space
Beneath the trees, clear footing many a mile—
A solemn region. Oft amid those haunts,
From earnest dialogues I slipped in thought,
And let remembrance steal to other times,
When, o'er those interwoven roots, moss-clad,
And smooth as marble or a waveless sea,   440
Some Hermit, from his cell forth-strayed, might pace
In sylvan meditation undisturbed;
As on the pavement of a Gothic church
Walks a lone Monk, when service hath expired,
In peace and silence. But if e'er was heard,—
Heard, though unseen,—a devious traveller,
Retiring or approaching from afar
With speed and echoes loud of trampling hoofs
From the hard floor reverberated, then
It was Angelica thundering through the woods   450
Upon her palfrey, or that gentle maid
Erminia, fugitive as fair as she.
Sometimes methought I saw a pair of knights
Joust underneath the trees, that as in storm
Rocked high above their heads; anon, the din
Of boisterous merriment, and music's roar,
In sudden proclamation, burst from haunt
Of Satyrs in some viewless glade, with dance
Rejoicing o'er a female in the midst,
A mortal beauty, their unhappy thrall.   460
The width of those huge forests, unto me
A novel scene, did often in this way
Master my fancy while I wandered on
With that revered companion. And sometimes—
When to a convent in a meadow green,
By a brook-side, we came, a roofless pile,
And not by reverential touch of Time
Dismantled, but by violence abrupt—
In spite of those heart-bracing colloquies,   470
In spite of real fervour, and of that

Less genuine and wrought up within myself—
I could not but bewail a wrong so harsh,
And for the Matin-bell to sound no more
Grieved, and the twilight taper, and the cross
High on the topmost pinnacle, a sign
(How welcome to the weary traveller's eyes!)
Of hospitality and peaceful rest.
And when the partner of those varied walks
Pointed upon occasion to the site   480
Of Romorentin, home of ancient kings,
To the imperial edifice of Blois,
Or to that rural castle, name now slipped
From my remembrance, where a lady lodged,
By the first Francis wooed, and bound to him
In chains of mutual passion, from the tower,
As a tradition of the country tells,
Practised to commune with her royal knight
By cressets and love-beacons, intercourse
'Twixt her high-seated residence and his   490
Far off at Chambord on the plain beneath;
Even here, though less than with the peaceful house
Religious, 'mid those frequent monuments
Of Kings, their vices and their better deeds,
Imagination, potent to inflame
At times with virtuous wrath and noble scorn,
Did also often mitigate the force
Of civic prejudice, the bigotry,
So call it, of a youthful patriot's mind;
And on these spots with many gleams I looked   500
Of chivalrous delight. Yet not the less,
Hatred of absolute rule, where will of one
Is law for all, and of that barren pride
In them who, by immunities unjust,
Between the sovereign and the people stand,
His helper and not theirs, laid stronger hold
Daily upon me, mixed with pity too
And love; for where hope is, there love will be
For the abject multitude, And when we chanced

One day to meet a hunger-bitten girl,
Who crept along fitting her languid gait   510
Unto a heifer's motion, by a cord
Tied to her arm, and picking thus from the lane
Its sustenance, while the girl with pallid hands
Was busy knitting in a heartless mood
Of solitude, and at the sight my friend
In agitation said, " 'Tis against 'that'
That we are fighting," I with him believed
That a benignant spirit was abroad
Which might not be withstood, that poverty
Abject as this would in a little time   520
Be found no more, that we should see the earth
Unthwarted in her wish to recompense
The meek, the lowly, patient child of toil,
All institutes for ever blotted out
That legalised exclusion, empty pomp
Abolished, sensual state and cruel power
Whether by edict of the one or few;
And finally, as sum and crown of all,
Should see the people having a strong hand
In framing their own laws; whence better days   530
To all mankind. But, these things set apart,
Was not this single confidence enough
To animate the mind that ever turned
A thought to human welfare? That henceforth
Captivity by mandate without law
Should cease; and open accusation lead
To sentence in the hearing of the world,
And open punishment, if not the air
Be free to breathe in, and the heart of man
Dread nothing. From this height I shall not stoop   540
To humbler matter that detained us oft
In thought or conversation, public acts,
And public persons, and emotions wrought
Within the breast, as ever-varying winds
Of record or report swept over us;
But I might here, instead, repeat a tale,
Told by my Patriot friend, of sad events,

That prove to what low depth had struck the roots,
How widely spread the boughs, of that old tree   550
Which, as a deadly mischief, and a foul
And black dishonour, France was weary of.

    Oh, happy time of youthful lovers, (thus
The story might begin), oh, balmy time,
In which a love-knot, on a lady's brow,
Is fairer than the fairest star in Heaven!
So might—and with that prelude *did* begin
The record; and, in faithful verse, was given
The doleful sequel.

                  But our little bark
On a strong river boldly hath been launched;   560
And from the driving current should we turn
To loiter wilfully within a creek,
Howe'er attractive, Fellow voyager!
Would'st thou not chide? Yet deem not my pains lost:
For Vaudracour and Julia (so were named
The ill-fated pair) in that plain tale will draw
Tears from the hearts of others, when their own
Shall beat no more. Thou, also, there may'st read,
At leisure, how the enamoured youth was driven,
By public power abased, to fatal crime,   570
Nature's rebellion against monstrous law;
How, between heart and heart, oppression thrust
Her mandates, severing whom true love had joined,
Harassing both; until he sank and pressed
The couch his fate had made for him; supine,
Save when the stings of viperous remorse,
Trying their strength, enforced him to start up,
Aghast and prayerless. Into a deep wood
He fled, to shun the haunts of human kind;
There dwelt, weakened in spirit more and more;   580
Nor could the voice of Freedom, which through France
Full speedily resounded, public hope,
Or personal memory of his own worst wrongs,
Rouse him; but, hidden in those gloomy shades,
His days he wasted,—an imbecile mind.

BOOK TENTH
Residence in France (continued)

It was a beautiful and silent day
That overspread the countenance of earth,
Then fading with unusual quietness,—
A day as beautiful as e'er was given
To soothe regret, though deepening what it soothed,
When by the gliding Loire I paused, and cast
Upon his rich domains, vineyard and tilth,
Green meadow-ground, and many-coloured woods,
Again, and yet again, a farewell look;
Then from the quiet of that scene passed on,   10
Bound to the fierce Metropolis. From his throne
The King had fallen, and that invading host—
Presumptuous cloud, on whose black front was written
The tender mercies of the dismal wind
That bore it—on the plains of Liberty
Had burst innocuous. Say in bolder words,
They—who had come elate as eastern hunters
Banded beneath the Great Mogul, when he
Erewhile went forth from Agra or Lahore,
Rajahs and Omrahs in his train, intent   20
To drive their prey enclosed within a ring
Wide as a province, but, the signal given,
Before the point of the life-threatening spear
Narrowing itself by moments—they, rash men,
Had seen the anticipated quarry turned
Into avengers, from whose wrath they fled
In terror. Disappointment and dismay
Remained for all whose fancies had run wild
With evil expectations; confidence
And perfect triumph for the better cause.   30

The State—as if to stamp the final seal
On her security, and to the world
Show what she was, a high and fearless soul,
Exulting in defiance, or heart-stung

By sharp resentment, or belike to taunt
With spiteful gratitude the baffled League,
That had stirred up her slackening faculties
To a new transition—when the King was crushed,
Spared not the empty throne, and in proud haste
Assumed the body and venerable name   40
Of a Republic. Lamentable crimes,
'Tis true, had gone before this hour, dire work
Of massacre, in which the senseless sword
Was prayed to as a judge; but these were past,
Earth free from them for ever, as was thought,—
Ephemeral monsters, to be seen but once!
Things that could only show themselves and die.

    Cheered with this hope, to Paris I returned,
And ranged, with ardour heretofore unfelt,
The spacious city, and in progress passed   50
The prison where the unhappy Monarch lay,
Associate with his children and his wife
In bondage; and the palace, lately stormed
With roar of cannon by a furious host.
I crossed the square (an empty area then!)
Of the Carrousel, where so late had lain
The dead, upon the dying heaped, and gazed
On this and other spots, as doth a man
Upon a volume whose contents he knows
Are memorable, but from him locked up,   60
Being written in a tongue he cannot read,
So that he questions the mute leaves with pain,
And half upbraids their silence. But that night
I felt most deeply in what world I was,
What ground I trod on, and what air I breathed.
High was my room and lonely, near the roof
Of a large mansion or hotel, a lodge
That would have pleased me in more quiet times;
Nor was it wholly without pleasure then.
With unextinguished taper I kept watch,   70
Reading at intervals; the fear gone by

Pressed on me almost like a fear to come.
I thought of those September massacres,
Divided from me by one little month,
Saw them and touched: the rest was conjured up
From tragic fictions or true history,
Remembrances and dim admonishments.
The horse is taught his manage, and no star
Of wildest course but treads back his own steps;
For the spent hurricane the air provides   80
As fierce a successor; the tide retreats
But to return out of its hiding-place
In the great deep; all things have second birth;
The earthquake is not satisfied at once;
And in this way I wrought upon myself,
Until I seemed to hear a voice that cried,
To the whole city, "Sleep no more." The trance
Fled with the voice to which it had given birth;
But vainly comments of a calmer mind
Promised soft peace and sweet forgetfulness.   90
The place, all hushed and silent as it was,
Appeared unfit for the repose of night,
Defenceless as a wood where tigers roam.

        With early morning towards the Palace-walk
Of Orleans eagerly I turned: as yet
The streets were still; not so those long Arcades;
There, 'mid a peal of ill-matched sounds and cries,
That greeted me on entering, I could hear
Shrill voices from the hawkers in the throng,
Bawling, "Denunciation of the Crimes   100
Of Maximilian Robespierre;" the hand,
Prompt as the voice, held forth a printed speech,
The same that had been recently pronounced,
When Robespierre, not ignorant for what mark
Some words of indirect reproof had been
Intended, rose in hardihood, and dared
The man who had an ill surmise of him
To bring his charge in openness; whereat,

When a dead pause ensued, and no one stirred,
In silence of all present, from his seat   110
Louvet walked single through the avenue,
And took his station in the Tribune, saying,
"I, Robespierre, accuse thee!" Well is known
The inglorious issue of that charge, and how
He, who had launched the startling thunderbolt,
The one bold man, whose voice the attack had sounded,
Was left without a follower to discharge
His perilous duty, and retire lamenting
That Heaven's best aid is wasted upon men
Who to themselves are false.

       But these are things   120
Of which I speak, only as they were storm
Or sunshine to my individual mind,
No further. Let me then relate that now—
In some sort seeing with my proper eyes
That Liberty, and Life, and Death, would soon
To the remotest corners of the land
Lie in the arbitrement of those who ruled
The capital City; what was struggled for,
And by what combatants victory must be won;
The indecision on their part whose aim   130
Seemed best, and the straightforward path of those
Who in attack or in defence were strong
Through their impiety—my inmost soul
Was agitated; yea, I could almost
Have prayed that throughout earth upon all men,
By patient exercise of reason made
Worthy of liberty, all spirits filled
With zeal expanding in Truth's holy light,
The gift of tongues might fall, and power arrive
From the four quarters of the winds to do   140
For France, what without help she could not do,
A work of honour; think not that to this
I added, work of safety: from all doubt
Or trepidation for the end of things
Far was I, far as angels are from guilt.

Yet did I grieve, nor only grieved, but thought
Of opposition and of remedies:
An insignificant stranger and obscure,
And one, moreover, little graced with power
Of eloquence even in my native speech,   150
And all unfit for tumult or intrigue,
Yet would I at this time with willing heart
Have undertaken for a cause so great
Service however dangerous. I revolved,
How much the destiny of Man had still
Hung upon single persons; that there was,
Transcendent to all local patrimony,
One nature, as there is one sun in heaven;
That objects, even as they are great, thereby
Do come within the reach of humblest eyes;   160
That Man is only weak through his mistrust
And want of hope where evidence divine
Proclaims to him that hope should be most sure;
Nor did the inexperience of my youth
Preclude conviction, that a spirit strong
In hope, and trained to noble aspirations,
A spirit thoroughly faithful to itself,
Is for Society's unreasoning herd
A domineering instinct, serves at once
For way and guide, a fluent receptacle   170
That gathers up each petty straggling rill
And vein of water, glad to be rolled on
In safe obedience; that a mind, whose rest
Is where it ought to be, in self-restraint,
In circumspection and simplicity,
Falls rarely in entire discomfiture
Below its aim, or meets with, from without,
A treachery that foils it or defeats;
And, lastly, if the means on human will,
Frail human will, dependent should betray   180
Him who too boldly trusted them, I felt
That 'mid the loud distractions of the world
A sovereign voice subsists within the soul,
Arbiter undisturbed of right and wrong,

Of life and death, in majesty severe
Enjoining, as may best promote the aims
Of truth and justice, either sacrifice,
From whatsoever region of our cares
Or our infirm affections Nature pleads,
Earnest and blind, against the stern decree.   190

On the other side, I called to mind those truths
That are the commonplaces of the schools—
(A theme for boys, too hackneyed for their sires,)
Yet, with a revelation's liveliness,
In all their comprehensive bearings known
And visible to philosophers of old,
Men who, to business of the world untrained,
Lived in the shade; and to Harmodius known
And his compeer Aristogiton, known
To Brutus—that tyrannic power is weak,   200
Hath neither gratitude, nor faith, nor love,
Nor the support of good or evil men
To trust in; that the godhead which is ours
Can never utterly be charmed or stilled;
That nothing hath a natural right to last
But equity and reason; that all else
Meets foes irreconcilable, and at best
Lives only by variety of disease.

Well might my wishes be intense, my thoughts
Strong and perturbed, not doubting at that time   210
But that the virtue of one paramount mind
Would have abashed those impious crests—have quelled
Outrage and bloody power, and—in despite
Of what the People long had been and were
Through ignorance and false teaching, sadder proof
Of immaturity, and—in the teeth
Of desperate opposition from without—
Have cleared a passage for just government,
And left a solid birthright to the State,
Redeemed, according to example given   220
By ancient lawgivers.

                              In this frame of mind,

Dragged by a chain of harsh necessity,
So seemed it,—now I thankfully acknowledge,
Forced by the gracious providence of Heaven,—
To England I returned, else (though assured
That I both was and must be of small weight,
No better than a landsman on the deck
Of a ship struggling with a hideous storm)
Doubtless, I should have then made common cause
With some who perished; haply perished too, 230
A poor mistaken and bewildered offering,—
Should to the breast of Nature have gone back,
With all my resolutions, all my hopes,
A Poet only to myself, to men
Useless, and even, beloved Friend! a soul
To thee unknown!
 Twice had the trees let fall
Their leaves, as often Winter had put on
His hoary crown, since I had seen the surge
Beat against Albion's shore, since ear of mine
Had caught the accents of my native speech 240
Upon our native country's sacred ground.
A patriot of the world, how could I glide
Into communion with her sylvan shades,
Erewhile my tuneful haunt? It pleased me more
To abide in the great City, where I found
The general air still busy with the stir
Of that first memorable onset made
By a strong levy of humanity
Upon the traffickers in Negro blood;
Effort which, though defeated, had recalled 250
To notice old forgotten principles,
And through the nation spread a novel heat
Of virtuous feeling. For myself, I own
That this particular strife had wanted power
To rivet my affections; nor did now
Its unsuccessful issue much excite
My sorrow; for I brought with me the faith
That, if France prospered, good men would not long

Pay fruitless worship to humanity,
And this most rotten branch of human shame,   260
Object, so seemed it, of superfluous pains,
Would fall together with its parent tree.
What, then, were my emotions, when in arms
Britain put forth her free-born strength in league,
Oh, pity and shame! with those confederate Powers!
Not in my single self alone I found,
But in the minds of all ingenuous youth,
Change and subversion from that hour. No shock
Given to my moral nature had I known
Down to that very moment; neither lapse   270
Nor turn of sentiment that might be named
A revolution, save at this one time;
All else was progress on the self-same path
On which, with a diversity of pace,
I had been travelling: this a stride at once
Into another region. As a light
And pliant harebell, swinging in the breeze
On some grey rock—its birth-place—so had I
Wantoned, fast rooted on the ancient tower
Of my beloved country, wishing not   280
A happier fortune than to wither there:
Now was I from that pleasant station torn
And tossed about in whirlwind. I rejoiced,
Yea, afterwards—truth most painful to record!—
Exulted, in the triumph of my soul.
When Englishmen by thousands were o'erthrown,
Left without glory on the field, or driven,
Brave hearts! to shameful flight. It was a grief,—
Grief call it not, 't was anything but that,—
A conflict of sensations without name,   290
Of which *he* only, who may love the sight
Of a village steeple, as I do, can judge,
When, in the congregation bending all
To their great Father, prayers were offered up,
Or praises for our country's victories;
And, 'mid the simple worshippers, perchance

I only, like an uninvited guest
Whom no one owned, sate silent, shall I add,
Fed on the day of vengeance yet to come.

Oh! much have they to account for, who could tear,   300
By violence, at one decisive rent,
From the best youth in England their dear pride,
Their joy, in England; this, too, at a time
In which worst losses easily might wean
The best of names, when patriotic love
Did of itself in modesty give way,
Like the Precursor when the Deity
Is come Whose harbinger he was; a time
In which apostasy from ancient faith
Seemed but conversion to a higher creed;   310
Withal a season dangerous and wild,
A time when sage Experience would have snatched
Flowers out of any hedge-row to compose
A chaplet in contempt of his grey locks.

When the proud fleet that bears the red-cross flag
In that unworthy service was prepared
To mingle, I beheld the vessels lie,
A brood of gallant creatures, on the deep;
I saw them in their rest, a sojourner
Through a whole month of calm and glassy days   320
In that delightful island which protects
Their place of convocation—there I heard,
Each evening, pacing by the still sea-shore,
A monitory sound that never failed,—
The sunset cannon. While the orb went down
In the tranquillity of nature, came
That voice, ill requiem! seldom heard by me
Without a spirit overcast by dark
Imaginations, sense of woes to come,
Sorrow for human kind, and pain of heart.   330

In France, the men, who, for their desperate ends,
Had plucked up mercy by the roots, were glad

Of this new enemy. Tyrants, strong before
In wicked pleas, were strong as demons now;
And thus, on every side beset with foes,
The goaded land waxed mad; the crimes of few
Spread into madness of the many; blasts
From hell came sanctified like airs from heaven.
The sternness of the just, the faith of those
Who doubted not that Providence had times   340
Of vengeful retribution, theirs who throned
The human Understanding paramount
And made of that their God, the hopes of men
Who were content to barter short-lived pangs
For a paradise of ages, the blind rage
Of insolent tempers, the light vanity
Of intermeddlers, steady purposes
Of the suspicious, slips of the indiscreet,
And all the accidents of life—were pressed
Into one service, busy with one work.   350
The Senate stood aghast, her prudence quenched,
Her wisdom stifled, and her justice scared,
Her frenzy only active to extol
Past outrages, and shape the way for new,
Which no one dared to oppose or mitigate.

Domestic carnage now filled the whole year
With feast-days; old men from the chimney-nook,
The maiden from the bosom of her love,
The mother from the cradle of her babe,
The warrior from the field—all perished, all—   360
Friends, enemies, of all parties, ages, ranks,
Head after head, and never heads enough
For those that bade them fall. They found their joy,
They made it proudly, eager as a child,
(If like desires of innocent little ones
May with such heinous appetites be compared),
Pleased in some open field to exercise
A toy that mimics with revolving wings
The motion of a wind-mill; though the air

Do of itself blow fresh, and make the vanes   370
Spin in his eyesight, 'that' contents him not,
But with the plaything at arm's length, he sets
His front against the blast, and runs amain,
That it may whirl the faster.
                    Amid the depth
Of those enormities, even thinking minds
Forgot, at seasons, whence they had their being
Forgot that such a sound was ever heard
As Liberty upon earth: yet all beneath
Her innocent authority was wrought,
Nor could have been, without her blessed name.   380
The illustrious wife of Roland, in the hour
Of her composure, felt that agony,
And gave it vent in her last words. O Friend!
It was a lamentable time for man,
Whether a hope had e'er been his or not:
A woful time for them whose hopes survived
The shock; most woful for those few who still
Were flattered, and had trust in human kind:
They had the deepest feeling of the grief.
Meanwhile the Invaders fared as they deserved: 390
The Herculean Commonwealth had put forth her arms,
And throttled with an infant godhead's might
The snakes about her cradle; that was well,
And as it should be; yet no cure for them
Whose souls were sick with pain of what would be
Hereafter brought in charge against mankind.
Most melancholy at that time, O Friend!
Were my day-thoughts,—my nights were miserable;
Through months, through years, long after the last beat
Of those atrocities, the hour of sleep   400
To me came rarely charged with natural gifts,
Such ghastly visions had I of despair
And tyranny, and implements of death;
And innocent victims sinking under fear,
And momentary hope, and worn-out prayer,
Each in his separate cell, or penned in crowds
For sacrifice, and struggling with fond mirth

And levity in dungeons, where the dust
Was laid with tears. Then suddenly the scene
Changed, and the unbroken dream entangled me
In long orations, which I strove to plead
Before unjust tribunals,—with a voice
Labouring, a brain confounded, and a sense,
Death-like, of treacherous desertion, felt
In the last place of refuge—my own soul.

    When I began in youth's delightful prime
To yield myself to Nature, when that strong
And holy passion overcame me first,
Nor day or night, evening or morn, was free
From its oppression. But, O Power Supreme!
Without Whose call this world would cease to breathe,
Who from the fountain of Thy grace dost fill
The veins that branch through every frame of life,
Making man what he is, creature divine,
In single or in social eminence,
Above the rest raised infinite ascents
When reason that enables him to be
Is not sequestered—what a change is here!
How different ritual for this after-worship,
What countenance to promote this second love!
The first was service paid to things which lie
Guarded within the bosom of Thy will.
Therefore to serve was high beatitude;
Tumult was therefore gladness, and the fear
Ennobling, venerable; sleep secure,
And waking thoughts more rich than happiest dreams.

    But as the ancient Prophets, borne aloft
In vision, yet constrained by natural laws
With them to take a troubled human heart,
Wanted not consolations, nor a creed
Of reconcilement, then when they denounced,
On towns and cities, wallowing in the abyss
Of their offences, punishment to come;
Or saw, like other men, with bodily eyes,
Before them, in some desolated place,

410

420

430

440

The wrath consummate and the threat fulfilled;
So, with devout humility be it said,
So, did a portion of that spirit fall
On me uplifted from the vantage-ground
Of pity and sorrow to a state of being   450
That through the time's exceeding fierceness saw
Glimpses of retribution, terrible,
And in the order of sublime behests:
But, even if that were not, amid the awe
Of unintelligible chastisement,
Not only acquiescences of faith
Survived, but daring sympathies with power,
Motions not treacherous or profane, else why
Within the folds of no ungentle breast
Their dread vibration to this hour prolonged?   460
Wild blasts of music thus could find their way
Into the midst of turbulent events;
So that worst tempests might be listened to.
Then was the truth received into my heart,
That, under heaviest sorrow earth can bring,
If from the affliction somewhere do not grow
Honour which could not else have been, a faith,
An elevation, and a sanctity,
If new strength be not given nor old restored,
The blame is ours, not Nature's. When a taunt   470
Was taken up by scoffers in their pride,
Saying, "Behold the harvest that we reap
From popular government and equality,"
I clearly saw that neither these nor aught
Of wild belief engrafted on their names
By false philosophy had caused the woe,
But a terrific reservoir of guilt
And ignorance filled up from age to age,
That could no longer hold its loathsome charge,
But burst and spread in deluge through the land.   480

    And as the desert hath green spots, the sea
Small islands scattered amid stormy waves,

So *that* disastrous period did not want
Bright sprinklings of all human excellence,
To which the silver wands of saints in Heaven
Might point with rapturous joy. Yet not the less,
For those examples, in no age surpassed,
Of fortitude and energy and love,
And human nature faithful to herself
Under worst trials, was I driven to think   490
Of the glad times when first I traversed France
A youthful pilgrim; above all reviewed
That eventide, when under windows bright
With happy faces and with garlands hung,
And through a rainbow-arch that spanned the street,
Triumphal pomp for liberty confirmed,
I paced, a dear companion at my side,
The town of Arras, whence with promise high
Issued, on delegation to sustain
Humanity and right, *that* Robespierre,   500
He who thereafter, and in how short time!
Wielded the sceptre of the Atheist crew.
When the calamity spread far and wide—
And this same city, that did then appear
To outrun the rest in exultation, groaned
Under the vengeance of her cruel son,
As Lear reproached the winds—I could almost
Have quarrelled with that blameless spectacle
For lingering yet an image in my mind
To mock me under such a strange reverse.   510

      O Friend! few happier moments have been mine
Than that which told the downfall of this Tribe
So dreaded, so abhorred. The day deserves
A separate record. Over the smooth sands
Of Leven's ample estuary lay
My journey, and beneath a genial sun,
With distant prospect among gleams of sky
And clouds and intermingling mountain tops,
In one inseparable glory clad,

Creatures of one ethereal substance met   520
In consistory, like a diadem
Or crown of burning seraphs as they sit
In the empyrean. Underneath that pomp
Celestial, lay unseen the pastoral vales
Among whose happy fields I had grown up
From childhood. On the fulgent spectacle,
That neither passed away nor changed, I gazed
Enrapt; but brightest things are wont to draw
Sad opposites out of the inner heart,
As even their pensive influence drew from mine.   530
How could it otherwise? for not in vain
That very morning had I turned aside
To seek the ground where, 'mid a throng of graves,
An honoured teacher of my youth was laid,
And on the stone were graven by his desire
Lines from the churchyard elegy of Gray.
This faithful guide, speaking from his deathbed,
Added no farewell to his parting counsel,
But said to me, "My head will soon lie low;"
And when I saw the turf that covered him,   540
After the lapse of full eight years, those words,
With sound of voice and countenance of the Man,
Came back upon me, so that some few tears
Fell from me in my own despite. But now
I thought, still traversing that widespread plain,
With tender pleasure of the verses graven
Upon his tombstone, whispering to myself:
He loved the Poets, and, if now alive,
Would have loved me, as one not destitute
Of promise, nor belying the kind hope   550
That he had formed, when I, at his command,
Began to spin, with toil, my earliest songs.

As I advanced, all that I saw or felt
Was gentleness and peace. Upon a small
And rocky island near, a fragment stood,
(Itself like a sea rock) the low remains

(With shells encrusted, dark with briny weeds)
Of a dilapidated structure, once
A Romish chapel, where the vested priest
Said matins at the hour that suited those   560
Who crossed the sands with ebb of morning tide.
Not far from that still ruin all the plain
Lay spotted with a variegated crowd
Of vehicles and travellers, horse and foot,
Wading beneath the conduct of their guide
In loose procession through the shallow stream
Of inland waters; the great sea meanwhile
Heaved at safe distance, far retired. I paused,
Longing for skill to paint a scene so bright
And cheerful, but the foremost of the band   570
As he approached, no salutation given
In the familiar language of the day,
Cried, "Robespierre is dead!" nor was a doubt,
After strict question, left within my mind
That he and his supporters were fallen.

　　Great was my transport, deep my gratitude
To everlasting Justice, by this fiat
Made manifest. "Come now, ye golden times,"
Said I forth-pouring on those open sands
A hymn of triumph: "as the morning comes   580
From out the bosom of the night, come ye:
Thus far our trust is verified; behold!
They who with clumsy desperation brought
A river of Blood, and preached that nothing else
Could cleanse the Augean stable, by the might
Of their own helper have been swept away;
Their madness stands declared and visible;
Elsewhere will safety now be sought, and earth
March firmly towards righteousness and peace."—
Then schemes I framed more calmly, when and how   590
The madding factions might be tranquillised,
And how through hardships manifold and long
The glorious renovation would proceed.

Thus interrupted by uneasy bursts
Of exultation, I pursued my way
Along that very shore which I had skimmed
In former days, when—spurring from the Vale
Of Nightshade, and St. Mary's mouldering fane,
And the stone abbot, after circuit made
In wantonness of heart, a joyous band   600
Of schoolboys hastening to their distant home
Along the margin of the moonlight sea—
We beat with thundering hoofs the level sand.

BOOK ELEVENTH
France (concluded)

From that time forth, Authority in France
Put on a milder face; Terror had ceased,
Yet everything was wanting that might give
Courage to them who looked for good by light
Of rational Experience, for the shoots
And hopeful blossoms of a second spring:
Yet, in me, confidence was unimpaired;
The Senate's language, and the public acts
And measures of the Government, though both
Weak, and of heartless omen, had not power   10
To daunt me; in the People was my trust:
And, in the virtues which mine eyes had seen,
I knew that wound external could not take
Life from the young Republic; that new foes
Would only follow, in the path of shame,
Their brethren, and her triumphs be in the end
Great, universal, irresistible.
This intuition led me to confound
One victory with another, higher far,—
Triumphs of unambitious peace at home,   20
And noiseless fortitude. Beholding still
Resistance strong as heretofore, I thought
That what was in degree the same was likewise
The same in quality—that, as the worse

Of the two spirits then at strife remained
Untired, the better, surely, would preserve
The heart that first had roused him. Youth maintains,
In all conditions of society,
Communion more direct and intimate
With Nature,—hence, ofttimes, with reason too—   30
Than age or manhood, even. To Nature then,
Power had reverted: habit, custom, law,
Had left an interregnum's open space
For *her* to move about in, uncontrolled.
Hence could I see how Babel-like their task,
Who, by the recent deluge stupified,
With their whole souls went culling from the day
Its petty promises, to build a tower
For their own safety; laughed with my compeers
At gravest heads, by enmity to France   40
Distempered, till they found, in every blast
Forced from the street-disturbing newsman's horn,
For her great cause record or prophecy
Of utter ruin. How might we believe
That wisdom could, in any shape, come near
Men clinging to delusions so insane?
And thus, experience proving that no few
Of our opinions had been just, we took
Like credit to ourselves where less was due,
And thought that other notions were as sound,   50
Yea, could not but be right, because we saw
That foolish men opposed them.
                              To a strain
More animated I might here give way,
And tell, since juvenile errors are my theme,
What in those days, through Britain, was performed
To turn *all* judgments out of their right course;
But this is passion over-near ourselves,
Reality too close and too intense,
And intermixed with something, in my mind,
Of scorn and condemnation personal,   60
That would profane the sanctity of verse.

Our Shepherds, this say merely, at that time
Acted, or seemed at least to act, like men
Thirsting to make the guardian crook of law
A tool of murder; they who ruled the State—
Though with such awful proof before their eyes
That he, who would sow death, reaps death, or worse,
And can reap nothing better—child-like longed
To imitate, not wise enough to avoid;
Or left (by mere timidity betrayed)   70
The plain straight road, for one no better chosen
Than if their wish had been to undermine
Justice, and make an end of Liberty.

    But from these bitter truths I must return
To my own history. It hath been told
That I was led to take an eager part
In arguments of civil polity,
Abruptly, and indeed before my time:
I had approached, like other youths, the shield
Of human nature from the golden side,   80
And would have fought, even to the death, to attest
The quality of the metal which I saw.
What there is best in individual man,
Of wise in passion, and sublime in power,
Benevolent in small societies,
And great in large ones, I had oft revolved,
Felt deeply, but not thoroughly understood
By reason: nay, far from it; they were yet,
As cause was given me afterwards to learn,
Not proof against the injuries of the day;   90
Lodged only at the sanctuary's door,
Not safe within its bosom. Thus prepared,
And with such general insight into evil,
And of the bounds which sever it from good,
As books and common intercourse with life
Must needs have given—to the inexperienced mind,
When the world travels in a beaten road,
Guide faithful as is needed—I began
To meditate with ardour on the rule

And management of nations; what it is   100
And ought to be; and strove to learn how far
Their power or weakness, wealth or poverty,
Their happiness or misery, depends
Upon their laws, and fashion of the State.

    O pleasant exercise of hope and joy!
For mighty were the auxiliars which then stood
Upon our side, us who were strong in love!
Bliss was it in that dawn to be alive,
But to be young was very Heaven! O times,
In which the meagre, stale, forbidding ways   110
Of custom, law, and statute, took at once
The attraction of a country in romance!
When Reason seemed the most to assert her rights,
When most intent on making of herself
A prime enchantress—to assist the work,
Which then was going forward in her name!
Not favoured spots alone, but the whole Earth,
The beauty wore of promise—that which sets
(As at some moments might not be unfelt
Among the bowers of Paradise itself)   120
The budding rose above the rose full blown.
What temper at the prospect did not wake
To happiness unthought of? The inert
Were roused, and lively natures rapt away!
They who had fed their childhood upon dreams,
The play-fellows of fancy, who had made
All powers of swiftness, subtilty, and strength
Their ministers,—who in lordly wise had stirred
Among the grandest objects of the sense,
And dealt with whatsoever they found there   130
As if they had within some lurking right
To wield it;—they, too, who of gentle mood
Had watched all gentle motions, and to these
Had fitted their own thoughts, schemers more mild,
And in the region of their peaceful selves;—
Now was it that 'both' found, the meek and lofty
Did both find, helpers to their hearts' desire,

And stuff at hand, plastic as they could wish,—
Were called upon to exercise their skill,
Not in Utopia,—subterranean fields,—   140
Or some secreted island, Heaven knows where!
But in the very world, which is the world
Of all of us,—the place where, in the end,
We find our happiness, or not at all!

    Why should I not confess that Earth was then
To me, what an inheritance, new-fallen,
Seems, when the first time visited, to one
Who thither comes to find in it his home?
He walks about and looks upon the spot
With cordial transport, moulds it and remoulds   150
And is half-pleased with things that are amiss,
'Twill be such joy to see them disappear.

    An active partisan, I thus convoked
From every object pleasant circumstance
To suit my ends; I moved among mankind
With genial feelings still predominant;
When erring, erring on the better part,
And in the kinder spirit; placable,
Indulgent, as not uninformed that men
See as they have been taught—Antiquity   160
Gives rights to error; and aware, no less
That throwing off oppression must be work
As well of License as of Liberty;
And above all—for this was more than all—
Not caring if the wind did now and then
Blow keen upon an eminence that gave
Prospect so large into futurity;
In brief, a child of Nature, as at first,
Diffusing only those affections wider
That from the cradle had grown up with me,   170
And losing, in no other way than light
Is lost in light, the weak in the more strong.

    In the main outline, such it might be said
Was my condition, till with open war

Britain opposed the liberties of France.
This threw me first out of the pale of love;
Soured and corrupted, upwards to the source,
My sentiments; was not, as hitherto,
A swallowing up of lesser things in great,
But change of them into their contraries;   180
And thus a way was opened for mistakes
And false conclusions, in degree as gross,
In kind more dangerous. What had been a pride,
Was now a shame; my likings and my loves
Ran in new channels, leaving old ones dry;
And hence a blow that, in maturer age,
Would but have touched the judgment, struck more deep
Into sensations near the heart: meantime,
As from the first, wild theories were afloat,
To whose pretensions, sedulously urged,   190
I had but lent a careless ear, assured
That time was ready to set all things right,
And that the multitude, so long oppressed,
Would be oppressed no more.

                                   But when events
Brought less encouragement, and unto these
The immediate proof of principles no more
Could be entrusted, while the events themselves,
Worn out in greatness, stripped of novelty,
Less occupied the mind, and sentiments
Could through my understanding's natural growth   200
No longer keep their ground, by faith maintained
Of inward consciousness, and hope that laid
Her hand upon her object—evidence
Safer, of universal application, such
As could not be impeached, was sought elsewhere.

    But now, become oppressors in their turn,
Frenchmen had changed a war of self-defence
For one of conquest, losing sight of all
Which they had struggled for: up mounted now,
Openly in the eye of earth and heaven,   210
The scale of liberty. I read her doom.

With anger vexed, with disappointment sore,
But not dismayed, nor taking to the shame
Of a false prophet. While resentment rose,
Striving to hide, what nought could heal, the wounds
Of mortified presumption, I adhered
More firmly to old tenets, and, to prove
Their temper, strained them more; and thus, in heat
Of contest, did opinions every day
Grow into consequence, till round my mind,   220
They clung, as if they were its life, nay more,
The very being of the immortal soul.

    This was the time, when, all things tending fast
To depravation, speculative schemes—
That promised to abstract the hopes of Man
Out of his feelings, to be fixed thenceforth
For ever in a purer element—
Found ready welcome. Tempting region *that*
For Zeal to enter and refresh herself,
Where passions had the privilege to work,   230
And never hear the sound of their own names.
But, speaking more in charity, the dream
Flattered the young, pleased with extremes, nor least
With that which makes our Reason's naked self
The object of its fervour. What delight!
How glorious! in self-knowledge and self-rule,
To look through all the frailties of the world,
And, with a resolute mastery shaking off
Infirmities of nature, time, and place,
Build social upon personal Liberty,   240
Which, to the blind restraints of general laws,
Superior, magisterially adopts
One guide, the light of circumstances, flashed
Upon an independent intellect.
Thus expectation rose again; thus hope,
From her first ground expelled, grew proud once more.
Oft, as my thoughts were turned to human kind,
I scorned indifference; but, inflamed with thirst
Of a secure intelligence, and sick

Of other longing, I pursued what seemed   250
A more exalted nature; wished that Man
Should start out of his earthy, worm-like state,
And spread abroad the wings of Liberty,
Lord of himself, in undisturbed delight—
A noble aspiration! *yet* I feel
(Sustained by worthier as by wiser thoughts)
The aspiration, nor shall ever cease
To feel it;—but return we to our course.

    Enough, 'tis true—could such a plea excuse
Those aberrations—had the clamorous friends   260
Of ancient Institutions said and done
To bring disgrace upon their very names;
Disgrace, of which, custom and written law,
And sundry moral sentiments as props
Or emanations of those institutes,
Too justly bore a part. A veil had been
Uplifted; why deceive ourselves? in sooth,
'Twas even so; and sorrow for the man
Who either had not eyes wherewith to see,
Or, seeing, had forgotten! A strong shock   270
Was given to old opinions; all men's minds
Had felt its power, and mine was both let loose,
Let loose and goaded. After what hath been
Already said of patriotic love,
Suffice it here to add, that, somewhat stern
In temperament, withal a happy man,
And therefore bold to look on painful things,
Free likewise of the world, and thence more bold,
I summoned my best skill, and toiled, intent
To anatomise the frame of social life;   280
Yea, the whole body of society
Searched to its heart. Share with me, Friend! the wish
That some dramatic tale, endued with shapes
Livelier, and flinging out less guarded words
Than suit the work we fashion, might set forth
What then I learned, or think I learned, of truth,
And the errors into which I fell, betrayed

By present objects, and by reasonings false
From their beginnings, inasmuch as drawn
Out of a heart that had been turned aside   290
From Nature's way by outward accidents,
And which was thus confounded, more and more
Misguided, and misguiding. So I fared,
Dragging all precepts, judgments, maxims, creeds,
Like culprits to the bar; calling the mind,
Suspiciously, to establish in plain day
Her titles and her honours; now believing,
Now disbelieving; endlessly perplexed
With impulse, motive, right and wrong, the ground
Of obligation, what the rule and whence   300
The sanction; till, demanding formal *proof*,
And seeking it in every thing, I lost
All feeling of conviction, and, in fine,
Sick, wearied out with contrarieties,
Yielded up moral questions in despair.

    This was the crisis of that strong disease,
This the soul's last and lowest ebb; I drooped,
Deeming our blessed reason of least use
Where wanted most: "The lordly attributes
Of will and choice," I bitterly exclaimed,   310
"What are they but a mockery of a Being
Who hath in no concerns of his a test
Of good and evil; knows not what to fear
Or hope for, what to covet or to shun;
And who, if those could be discerned, would yet
Be little profited, would see, and ask
Where is the obligation to enforce?
And, to acknowledged law rebellious, still,
As selfish passion urged, would act amiss;
The dupe of folly, or the slave of crime."   320

    Depressed, bewildered thus, I did not walk
With scoffers, seeking light and gay revenge
From indiscriminate laughter, nor sate down
In reconcilement with an utter waste
Of intellect; such sloth I could not brook,

(Too well I loved, in that my spring of life,
Pains-taking thoughts, and truth, their dear reward)
But turned to abstract science, and there sought
Work for the reasoning faculty enthroned
Where the disturbances of space and time—   330
Whether in matters various, properties
Inherent, or from human will and power
Derived—find no admission. Then it was—
Thanks to the bounteous Giver of all good!—
That the beloved Sister in whose sight
Those days were passed, now speaking in a voice
Of sudden admonition—like a brook
That did but *cross* a lonely road, and now
Is seen, heard, felt, and caught at every turn,
Companion never lost through many a league—   340
Maintained for me a saving intercourse
With my true self; for, though bedimmed and changed
Much, as it seemed, I was no further changed
Than as a clouded and a waning moon:
She whispered still that brightness would return;
She, in the midst of all, preserved me still
A Poet, made me seek beneath that name,
And that alone, my office upon earth;
And, lastly, as hereafter will be shown,
If willing audience fail not, Nature's self,   350
By all varieties of human love
Assisted, led me back through opening day
To those sweet counsels between head and heart
Whence grew that genuine knowledge, fraught with peace,
Which, through the later sinkings of this cause,
Hath still upheld me, and upholds me now
In the catastrophe (for so they dream,
And nothing less), when, finally to close
And seal up all the gains of France, a Pope
Is summoned in, to crown an Emperor—   360
This last opprobrium, when we see a people,
That once looked up in faith, as if to Heaven
For manna, take a lesson from the dog
Returning to his vomit; when the sun

That rose in splendour, was alive, and moved
In exultation with a living pomp
Of clouds—his glory's natural retinue—
Hath dropped all functions by the gods bestowed,
And, turned into a gewgaw, a machine,
Sets like an Opera phantom.
                        Thus, O Friend!   370
Through times of honour and through times of shame
Descending, have I faithfully retraced
The perturbations of a youthful mind
Under a long-lived storm of great events—
A story destined for thy ear, who now,
Among the fallen of nations, dost abide
Where Etna, over hill and valley, casts
His shadow stretching towards Syracuse,
The city of Timoleon! Righteous Heaven!
How are the mighty prostrated! They first,   380
They first of all that breathe should have awaked
When the great voice was heard from out the tombs
Of ancient heroes. If I suffered grief
For ill-requited France, by many deemed
A trifler only in her proudest day;
Have been distressed to think of what she once
Promised, now is; a far more sober cause
Thine eyes must see of sorrow in a land,
To the reanimating influence lost
Of memory, to virtue lost and hope,   390
Though with the wreck of loftier years bestrewn.

    But indignation works where hope is not,
And thou, O Friend! wilt be refreshed. There is
One great society alone on earth:
The noble Living and the noble Dead.

    Thine be such converse strong and sanative,
A ladder for thy spirit to reascend
To health and joy and pure contentedness;
To me the grief confined, that thou art gone
From this last spot of earth, where Freedom now   400
Stands single in her only sanctuary;

A lonely wanderer, art gone, by pain
Compelled and sickness, at this latter day,
This sorrowful reverse for all mankind.
I feel for thee, must utter what I feel:
The sympathies erewhile in part discharged,
Gather afresh, and will have vent again:
My own delights do scarcely seem to me
My own delights; the lordly Alps themselves,
Those rosy peaks, from which the Morning looks   410
Abroad on many nations, are no more
For me that image of pure gladsomeness
Which they were wont to be. Through kindred scenes,
For purpose, at a time, how different!
Thou tak'st thy way, carrying the heart and soul
That Nature gives to Poets, now by thought
Matured, and in the summer of their strength.
Oh! wrap him in your shades, ye giant woods,
On Etna's side; and thou, O flowery field
Of Enna! is there not some nook of thine,   420
From the first play-time of the infant world
Kept sacred to restorative delight,
When from afar invoked by anxious love?

    Child of the mountains, among shepherds reared,
Ere yet familiar with the classic page,
I learnt to dream of Sicily; and lo,
The gloom that, but a moment past, was deepened
At thy command, at her command gives way;
A pleasant promise, wafted from her shores,
Comes o'er my heart: in fancy I behold   430
Her seas yet smiling, her once happy vales;
Nor can my tongue give utterance to a name
Of note belonging to that honoured isle,
Philosopher or Bard, Empedocles,
Or Archimedes, pure abstracted soul!
That doth not yield a solace to my grief:
And, O Theocritus, so far have some
Prevailed among the powers of heaven and earth,
By their endowments, good or great, that they

Have had, as thou reportest, miracles 440
Wrought for them in old time: yea, not unmoved,
When thinking on my own beloved friend,
I hear thee tell how bees with honey fed
Divine Comates, by his impious lord
Within a chest imprisoned; how they came
Laden from blooming grove or flowery field,
And fed him there, alive, month after month,
Because the goatherd, blessed man! had lips
Wet with the Muse's nectar.
                            Thus I soothe
The pensive moments by this calm fire-side, 450
And find a thousand bounteous images
To cheer the thoughts of those I love, and mine.
Our prayers have been accepted; thou wilt stand
On Etna's summit, above earth and sea,
Triumphant, winning from the invaded heavens
Thoughts without bound, magnificent designs,
Worthy of poets who attuned their harps
In wood or echoing cave, for discipline
Of heroes; or, in reverence to the gods,
'Mid temples, served by sapient priests, and choirs 460
Of virgins crowned with roses. Not in vain
Those temples, where they in their ruins yet
Survive for inspiration, shall attract
Thy solitary steps: and on the brink
Thou wilt recline of pastoral Arethuse;
Or, if that fountain be in truth no more,
Then, near some other spring—which, by the name
Thou gratulatest, willingly deceived—
I see thee linger a glad votary,
And not a captive pining for his home. 470

BOOK TWELFTH
Imagination and Taste, How Impaired and Restored

Long time have human ignorance and guilt
Detained us, on what spectacles of woe

Compelled to look, and inwardly oppressed
With sorrow, disappointment, vexing thoughts,
Confusion of the judgment, zeal decayed,
And, lastly, utter loss of hope itself
And things to hope for! Not with these began
Our song, and not with these our song must end.
Ye motions of delight, that haunt the sides
Of the green hills; ye breezes and soft airs,   10
Whose subtle intercourse with breathing flowers,
Feelingly watched, might teach Man's haughty race
How without injury to take, to give
Without offence; ye who, as if to show
The wondrous influence of power gently used,
Bend the complying heads of lordly pines,
And, with a touch, shift the stupendous clouds
Through the whole compass of the sky; ye brooks,
Muttering along the stones, a busy noise
By day, a quiet sound in the silent night;   20
Ye waves, that out of the great deep steal forth
In a calm hour to kiss the pebbly shore,
Not mute, and then retire, fearing no storm;
And you, ye groves, whose ministry it is
To interpose the covert of your shades,
Even as a sleep, between the heart of man
And outward troubles, between man himself,
Not seldom, and his own uneasy heart:
Oh! that I had a music and a voice
Harmonious as your own, that I might tell   30
What ye have done for me. The morning shines,
Nor heedeth Man's perverseness; Spring returns,—
I saw the Spring return, and could rejoice,
In common with the children of her love,
Piping on boughs, or sporting on fresh fields,
Or boldly seeking pleasure nearer heaven
On wings that navigate cerulean skies.
So neither were complacency, nor peace,
Nor tender yearnings, wanting for my good
Through these distracted times; in Nature still   40
Glorying, I found a counterpoise in her,

Which, when the spirit of evil reached its height,
Maintained for me a secret happiness.

This narrative, my Friend! hath chiefly told
Of intellectual power, fostering love,
Dispensing truth, and, over men and things,
Where reason yet might hesitate, diffusing
Prophetic sympathies of genial faith:
So was I favoured—such my happy lot—
Until that natural graciousness of mind   50
Gave way to overpressure from the times
And their disastrous issues. What availed,
When spells forbade the voyager to land,
That fragrant notice of a pleasant shore
Wafted, at intervals, from many a bower
Of blissful gratitude and fearless love?
Dare I avow that wish was mine to see,
And hope that future times *would* surely see,
The man to come, parted, as by a gulph,
From him who had been; that I could no more   60
Trust the elevation which had made me one
With the great family that still survives
To illuminate the abyss of ages past,
Sage, warrior, patriot, hero; for it seemed
That their best virtues were not free from taint
Of something false and weak, that could not stand
The open eye of Reason. Then I said,
"Go to the Poets, they will speak to thee
More perfectly of purer creatures;—yet
If reason be nobility in man,   70
Can aught be more ignoble than the man
Whom they delight in, blinded as he is
By prejudice, the miserable slave
Of low ambition or distempered love?"

In such strange passion, if I may once more
Review the past, I warred against myself—
A bigot to a new idolatry—
Like a cowled monk who hath forsworn the world,

Zealously laboured to cut off my heart
From all the sources of her former strength;   80
And as, by simple waving of a wand,
The wizard instantaneously dissolves
Palace or grove, even so could I unsoul
As readily by syllogistic words
Those mysteries of being which have made,
And shall continue evermore to make,
Of the whole human race one brotherhood.

 What wonder, then, if, to a mind so far
Perverted, even the visible Universe
Fell under the dominion of a taste   90
Less spiritual, with microscopic view
Was scanned, as I had scanned the moral world?

 O Soul of Nature! excellent and fair!
That didst rejoice with me, with whom I, too,
Rejoiced through early youth, before the winds
And roaring waters, and in lights and shades
That marched and countermarched about the hills
In glorious apparition, Powers on whom
I daily waited, now all eye and now
All ear; but never long without the heart   100
Employed, and man's unfolding intellect:
O Soul of Nature! that, by laws divine
Sustained and governed, still dost overflow
With an impassioned life, what feeble ones
Walk on this earth! how feeble have I been
When thou wert in thy strength! Nor this through stroke
Of human suffering, such as justifies
Remissness and inaptitude of mind,
But through presumption; even in pleasure pleased
Unworthily, disliking here, and there   110
Liking; by rules of mimic art transferred
To things above all art; but more,—for this,
Although a strong infection of the age,
Was never much my habit—giving way
To a comparison of scene with scene,

Bent overmuch on superficial things,
Pampering myself with meagre novelties
Of colour and proportion; to the moods
Of time and season, to the moral power,
The affections and the spirit of the place,   120
Insensible. Nor only did the love
Of sitting thus in judgment interrupt
My deeper feelings, but another cause,
More subtle and less easily explained,
That almost seems inherent in the creature,
A twofold frame of body and of mind.
I speak in recollection of a time
When the bodily eye, in every stage of life
The most despotic of our senses, gained
Such strength in *me* as often held my mind   130
In absolute dominion. Gladly here,
Entering upon abstruser argument,
Could I endeavour to unfold the means
Which Nature studiously employs to thwart
This tyranny, summons all the senses each
To counteract the other, and themselves,
And makes them all, and the objects with which all
Are conversant, subservient in their turn
To the great ends of Liberty and Power.
But leave we this: enough that my delights   140
(Such as they were) were sought insatiably.
Vivid the transport, vivid though not profound;
I roamed from hill to hill, from rock to rock,
Still craving combinations of new forms,
New pleasure, wider empire for the sight,
Proud of her own endowments, and rejoiced
To lay the inner faculties asleep.
Amid the turns and counterturns, the strife
And various trials of our complex being,
As we grow up, such thraldom of that sense   150
Seems hard to shun. And yet I knew a maid,
A young enthusiast, who escaped these bonds;
Her eye was not the mistress of her heart;

Far less did rules prescribed by passive taste,
Or barren intermeddling subtleties,
Perplex her mind; but, wise as women are
When genial circumstance hath favoured them,
She welcomed what was given, and craved no more;
Whate'er the scene presented to her view
That was the best, to that she was attuned   160
By her benign simplicity of life,
And through a perfect happiness of soul,
Whose variegated feelings were in this
Sisters, that they were each some new delight.
Birds in the bower, and lambs in the green field,
Could they have known her, would have loved; methought
Her very presence such a sweetness breathed,
That flowers, and trees, and even the silent hills,
And everything she looked on, should have had
An intimation how she bore herself   170
Towards them and to all creatures. God delights
In such a being; for, her common thoughts
Are piety, her life is gratitude.

Even like this maid, before I was called forth
From the retirement of my native hills,
I loved whate'er I saw: nor lightly loved,
But most intensely; never dreamt of aught
More grand, more fair, more exquisitely framed
Than those few nooks to which my happy feet
Were limited. I had not at that time   180
Lived long enough, nor in the least survived
The first diviner influence of this world,
As it appears to unaccustomed eyes.
Worshipping them among the depth of things,
As piety ordained, could I submit
To measured admiration, or to aught
That should preclude humility and love?
I felt, observed, and pondered; did not judge,
Yea, never thought of judging; with the gift
Of all this glory filled and satisfied.   190

And afterwards, when through the gorgeous Alps
Roaming, I carried with me the same heart:
In truth, the degradation—howsoe'er
Induced, effect, in whatsoe'er degree,
Of custom that prepares a partial scale
In which the little oft outweighs the great;
Or any other cause that hath been named;
Or lastly, aggravated by the times
And their impassioned sounds, which well might make
The milder minstrelsies of rural scenes   200
Inaudible—was transient; I had known
Too forcibly, too early in my life,
Visitings of imaginative power
For this to last: I shook the habit off
Entirely and for ever, and again
In Nature's presence stood, as now I stand,
A sensitive being, a *creative* soul.

    There are in our existence spots of time,
That with distinct pre-eminence retain
A renovating virtue, whence—depressed   210
By false opinion and contentious thought,
Or aught of heavier or more deadly weight,
In trivial occupations, and the round
Of ordinary intercourse—our minds
Are nourished and invisibly repaired;
A virtue, by which pleasure is enhanced,
That penetrates, enables us to mount,
When high, more high, and lifts us up when fallen.
This efficacious spirit chiefly lurks
Among those passages of life that give   220
Profoundest knowledge to what point, and how,
The mind is lord and master—outward sense
The obedient servant of her will. Such moments
Are scattered everywhere, taking their date
From our first childhood. I remember well,
That once, while yet my inexperienced hand
Could scarcely hold a bridle, with proud hopes
I mounted, and we journeyed towards the hills:

An ancient servant of my father's house
Was with me, my encourager and guide: 230
We had not travelled long, ere some mischance
Disjoined me from my comrade; and, through fear,
Dismounting, down the rough and stony moor
I led my horse, and, stumbling on, at length
Came to a bottom, where in former times
A murderer had been hung in iron chains.
The gibbet-mast had mouldered down, the bones
And iron case were gone; but on the turf,
Hard by, soon after that fell deed was wrought,
Some unknown hand carved the murderer's name.   240
The monumental letters were inscribed
In times long past; but still, from year to year
By superstition of the neighbourhood,
The grass is cleared away, and to this hour
The characters are fresh and visible:
A casual glance had shown them, and I fled,
Faltering and faint, and ignorant of the road:
Then, reascending the bare common, saw
A naked pool that lay beneath the hills,
The beacon on the summit, and, more near,   250
A girl, who bore a pitcher on her head,
And seemed with difficult steps to force her way
Against the blowing wind. It was, in truth,
An ordinary sight; but I should need
Colours and words that are unknown to man
To paint the visionary dreariness
Which, while I looked all round for my lost guide,
Invested moorland waste and naked pool,
The beacon crowning the lone eminence,
The female and her garments vexed and tossed   260
By the strong wind. When, in the blessèd hours
Of early love, the loved one at my side,
I roamed, in daily presence of this scene,
Upon the naked pool and dreary crags,
And on the melancholy beacon, fell
A spirit of pleasure and youth's golden gleam;
And think ye not with radiance more sublime

For these remembrances, and for the power
They had left behind? So feeling comes in aid
Of feeling, and diversity of strength   270
Attends us, if but once we have been strong.
Oh! mystery of man, from what a depth
Proceed thy honours. I am lost, but see
In simple childhood something of the base
On which thy greatness stands, but this I feel,
That from thyself it comes, that thou must give,
Else never canst receive. The days gone by
Return upon me almost from the dawn
Of life: the hiding-places of man's power
Open; I would approach them, but they close.   280
I see by glimpses now; when age comes on,
May scarcely see at all; and I would give,
While yet we may, as far as words can give,
Substance and life to what I feel, enshrining,
Such is my hope, the spirit of the Past
For future restoration.—Yet another
Of these memorials:—
                                        One Christmas-time,
On the glad eve of its dear holidays,
Feverish, and tired, and restless, I went forth
Into the fields, impatient for the sight   290
Of those led palfreys that should bear us home;
My brothers and myself. There rose a crag,
That, from the meeting-point of two highways
Ascending, overlooked them both, far stretched;
Thither, uncertain on which road to fix
My expectation, thither I repaired,
Scout-like, and gained the summit; 't was a day
Tempestuous, dark, and wild, and on the grass
I sate half-sheltered by a naked wall;
Upon my right hand couched a single sheep,   300
Upon my left a blasted hawthorn stood;
With those companions at my side, I watched,
Straining my eyes intensely, as the mist
Gave intermitting prospect of the copse

And plain beneath. Ere we to school returned,—
That dreary time,—ere we had been ten days
Sojourners in my father's house, he died;
And I and my three brothers, orphans then,
Followed his body to the grave. The event,
With all the sorrow that it brought, appeared   310
A chastisement; and when I called to mind
That day so lately past, when from the crag
I looked in such anxiety of hope;
With trite reflections of morality,
Yet in the deepest passion, I bowed low
To God, Who thus corrected my desires;
And, afterwards, the wind and sleety rain,
And all the business of the elements,
The single sheep, and the one blasted tree,
And the bleak music from that old stone wall,   320
The noise of wood and water, and the mist
That on the line of each of those two roads
Advanced in such indisputable shapes;
All these were kindred spectacles and sounds
To which I oft repaired, and thence would drink,
As at a fountain; and on winter nights,
Down to this very time, when storm and rain
Beat on my roof, or, haply, at noon-day,
While in a grove I walk, whose lofty trees,
Laden with summer's thickest foliage, rock   330
In a strong wind, some working of the spirit,
Some inward agitations thence are brought,
Whate'er their office, whether to beguile
Thoughts over busy in the course they took,
Or animate an hour of vacant ease.

BOOK THIRTEENTH
Imagination and Taste, How Impaired and Restored
(concluded)

From Nature doth emotion come, and moods
Of calmness equally are Nature's gift:

This is her glory; these two attributes
Are sister horns that constitute her strength.
Hence Genius, born to thrive by interchange
Of peace and excitation, finds in her
His best and purest friend; from her receives
That energy by which he seeks the truth,
From her that happy stillness of the mind
Which fits him to receive it when unsought.   10

    Such benefit the humblest intellects
Partake of, each in their degree; 'tis mine
To speak, what I myself have known and felt;
Smooth task! for words find easy way, inspired
By gratitude, and confidence in truth.
Long time in search of knowledge did I range
The field of human life, in heart and mind
Benighted; but, the dawn beginning now
To re-appear, 'twas proved that not in vain
I had been taught to reverence a Power   20
That is the visible quality and shape
And image of right reason; that matures
Her processes by steadfast laws; gives birth
To no impatient or fallacious hopes,
No heat of passion or excessive zeal,
No vain conceits; provokes to no quick turns
Of self-applauding intellect; but trains
To meekness, and exalts by humble faith;
Holds up before the mind intoxicate
With present objects, and the busy dance   30
Of things that pass away, a temperate show
Of objects that endure; and by this course
Disposes her, when over-fondly set
On throwing off incumbrances, to seek
In man, and in the frame of social life,
Whate'er there is desirable and good
Of kindred permanence, unchanged in form
And function, or, through strict vicissitude
Of life and death, revolving. Above all
Were re-established now those watchful thoughts   40

Which, seeing little worthy or sublime
In what the Historian's pen so much delights
To blazon—power and energy detached
From moral purpose—early tutored me
To look with feelings of fraternal love
Upon the unassuming things that hold
A silent station in this beauteous world.

    Thus moderated, thus composed, I found
Once more in Man an object of delight,
Of pure imagination, and of love;   50
And, as the horizon of my mind enlarged,
Again I took the intellectual eye
For my instructor, studious more to see
Great truths, than touch and handle little ones.
Knowledge was given accordingly; my trust
Became more firm in feelings that had stood
The test of such a trial; clearer far
My sense of excellence—of right and wrong:
The promise of the present time retired
Into its true proportion; sanguine schemes,   60
Ambitious projects, pleased me less; I sought
For present good in life's familiar face,
And built thereon my hopes of good to come.

    With settling judgments now of what would last
And what would disappear; prepared to find
Presumption, folly, madness, in the men
Who thrust themselves upon the passive world
As Rulers of the world; to see in these,
Even when the public welfare is their aim,
Plans without thought, or built on theories   70
Vague and unsound; and having brought the books
Of modern statists to their proper test,
Life, human life, with all its sacred claims
Of sex and age, and heaven-descended rights,
Mortal, or those beyond the reach of death;
And having thus discerned how dire a thing
Is worshipped in that idol proudly named
"The Wealth of Nations," *where* alone that wealth

Is lodged, and how increased; and having gained
A more judicious knowledge of the worth   80
And dignity of individual man,
No composition of the brain, but man
Of whom we read, the man whom we behold
With our own eyes—I could not but enquire—
Not with less interest than heretofore,
But greater, though in spirit more subdued—
Why is this glorious creature to be found
One only in ten thousand? What one is,
Why may not millions be? What bars are thrown
By Nature in the way of such a hope?   90
Our animal appetites and daily wants,
Are these obstructions insurmountable?
If not, then others vanish into air.
"Inspect the basis of the social pile:
Enquire," said I, "how much of mental power
And genuine virtue they possess who live
By bodily toil, labour exceeding far
Their due proportion, under all the weight
Of that injustice which upon ourselves
Ourselves entail." Such estimate to frame   100
I chiefly looked (what need to look beyond?)
Among the natural abodes of men,
Fields with their rural works; recalled to mind
My earliest notices; with these compared
The observations made in later youth,
And to that day continued.—For, the time
Had never been when throes of mighty Nations
And the world's tumult unto me could yield,
How far soe'er transported and possessed,
Full measure of content; but still I craved   110
An intermingling of distinct regards
And truths of individual sympathy
Nearer ourselves. Such often might be gleaned
From the great City, else it must have proved
To me a heart-depressing wilderness;
But much was wanting: therefore did I turn
To you, ye pathways, and ye lonely roads;

Sought you enriched with everything I prized,
With human kindnesses and simple joys.

Oh! next to one dear state of bliss, vouchsafed,   120
Alas! to few in this untoward world,
The bliss of walking daily in life's prime
Through field or forest with the maid we love,
While yet our hearts are young, while yet we breathe
Nothing but happiness, in some lone nook,
Deep vale, or anywhere, the home of both,
From which it would be misery to stir:
Oh! next to such enjoyment of our youth,
In my esteem, next to such dear delight,
Was that of wandering on from day to day   130
Where I could meditate in peace, and cull
Knowledge that step by step might lead me on
To wisdom; or, as lightsome as a bird
Wafted upon the wind from distant lands,
Sing notes of greeting to strange fields or groves,
Which lacked not voice to welcome me in turn:
And, when that pleasant toil had ceased to please,
Converse with men, where if we meet a face
We almost meet a friend, on naked heaths
With long long ways before, by cottage bench,   140
Or well-spring where the weary traveller rests.

Who doth not love to follow with his eye
The windings of a public way? the sight,
Familiar object as it is, hath wrought
On my imagination since the morn
Of childhood, when a disappearing line,
One daily present to my eyes, that crossed
The naked summit of a far-off hill
Beyond the limits that my feet had trod,
Was like an invitation into space   150
Boundless, or guide into eternity.
Yes, something of the grandeur which invests
The mariner, who sails the roaring sea
Through storm and darkness, early in my mind
Surrounded, too, the wanderers of the earth;

Grandeur as much, and loveliness far more.
Awed have I been by strolling Bedlamites;
From many other uncouth vagrants (passed
In fear) have walked with quicker step; but why
Take note of this? When I began to enquire,   160
To watch and question those I met, and speak
Without reserve to them, the lonely roads
Were open schools in which I daily read
With most delight the passions of mankind,
Whether by words, looks, sighs, or tears, revealed;
There saw into the depth of human souls,
Souls that appear to have no depth at all
To careless eyes. And—now convinced at heart
How little those formalities, to which
With overweening trust alone we give   170
The name of Education, have to do
With real feeling and just sense; how vain
A correspondence with the talking world
Proves to the most; and called to make good search
If man's estate, by doom of Nature yoked
With toil, be therefore yoked with ignorance;
If virtue be indeed so hard to rear,
And intellectual strength so rare a boon—
I prized such walks still more, for there I found
Hope to my hope, and to my pleasure peace   180
And steadiness, and healing and repose
To every angry passion. There I heard,
From mouths of men obscure and lowly, truths
Replete with honour; sounds in unison
With loftiest promises of good and fair.

There are who think that strong affection, love
Known by whatever name, is falsely deemed
A gift, to use a term which they would use,
Of vulgar nature; that its growth requires
Retirement, leisure, language purified   190
By manners studied and elaborate;
That whoso feels such passion in its strength
Must live within the very light and air

Of courteous usages refined by art.
True is it, where oppression worse than death
Salutes the being at his birth, where grace
Of culture hath been utterly unknown,
And poverty and labour in excess
From day to day pre-occupy the ground
Of the affections, and to Nature's self   200
Oppose a deeper nature; there, indeed,
Love cannot be; nor does it thrive with ease
Among the close and overcrowded haunts
Of cities, where the human heart is sick,
And the eye feeds it not, and cannot feed.
—Yes, in those wanderings deeply did I feel
How we mislead each other; above all,
How books mislead us, seeking their reward
From judgments of the wealthy Few, who see
By artificial lights; how they debase   210
The Many for the pleasure of those Few;
Effeminately level down the truth
To certain general notions, for the sake
Of being understood at once, or else
Through want of better knowledge in the heads
That framed them; flattering self-conceit with words,
That, while they most ambitiously set forth
Extrinsic differences, the outward marks
Whereby society has parted man
From man, neglect the universal heart.   220

Here, calling up to mind what then I saw,
A youthful traveller, and see daily now
In the familiar circuit of my home,
Here might I pause, and bend in reverence
To Nature, and the power of human minds,
To men as they are men within themselves.
How oft high service is performed within,
When all the external man is rude in show,—
Not like a temple rich with pomp and gold,
But a mere mountain chapel, that protects   230
Its simple worshippers from sun and shower.

Of these, said I, shall be my song; of these,
If future years mature me for the task,
Will I record the praises, making verse
Deal boldly with substantial things; in truth
And sanctity of passion, speak of these,
That justice may be done, obeisance paid
Where it is due: thus haply shall I teach,
Inspire; through unadulterated ears
Pour rapture, tenderness, and hope,—my theme   240
No other than the very heart of man,
As found among the best of those who live—
Not unexalted by religious faith,
Nor uninformed by books, good books, though few—
In Nature's presence: thence may I select
Sorrow, that is not sorrow, but delight;
And miserable love, that is not pain
To hear of, for the glory that redounds
Therefrom to human kind, and what we are.
Be mine to follow with no timid step   250
Where knowledge leads me: it shall be my pride
That I have dared to tread this holy ground,
Speaking no dream, but things oracular;
Matter not lightly to be heard by those
Who to the letter of the outward promise
Do read the invisible soul; by men adroit
In speech, and for communion with the world
Accomplished; minds whose faculties are then
Most active when they are most eloquent,
And elevated most when most admired.   260
Men may be found of other mould than these,
Who are their own upholders, to themselves
Encouragement, and energy, and will,
Expressing liveliest thoughts in lively words
As native passion dictates. Others, too,
There are among the walks of homely life
Still higher, men for contemplation framed,
Shy, and unpractised in the strife of phrase;
Meek men, whose very souls perhaps would sink
Beneath them, summoned to such intercourse: 270

Theirs is the language of the heavens, the power,
The thought, the image, and the silent joy:
Words are but under-agents in their souls;
When they are grasping with their greatest strength,
They do not breathe among them: this I speak
In gratitude to God, Who feeds our hearts
For His own service; knoweth, loveth us,
When we are unregarded by the world.

    Also, about this time did I receive
Convictions still more strong than heretofore,   280
Not only that the inner frame is good,
And graciously composed, but that, no less,
Nature for all conditions wants not power
To consecrate, if we have eyes to see,
The outside of her creatures, and to breathe
Grandeur upon the very humblest face
Of human life. I felt that the array
Of act and circumstance, and visible form,
Is mainly to the pleasure of the mind
What passion makes them; that meanwhile the forms   290
Of Nature have a passion in themselves,
That intermingles with those works of man
To which she summons him; although the works
Be mean, have nothing lofty of their own;
And that the Genius of the Poet hence
May boldly take his way among mankind
Wherever Nature leads; that he hath stood
By Nature's side among the men of old,
And so shall stand for ever. Dearest Friend!
If thou partake the animating faith   300
That Poets, even as Prophets, each with each
Connected in a mighty scheme of truth,
Have each his own peculiar faculty,
Heaven's gift, a sense that fits him to perceive
Objects unseen before, thou wilt not blame
The humblest of this band who dares to hope
That unto him hath also been vouchsafed
An insight that in some sort he possesses,

A privilege whereby a work of his,
Proceeding from a source of untaught things,   310
Creative and enduring, may become
A power like one of Nature's. To a hope
Not less ambitious once among the wilds
Of Sarum's Plain, my youthful spirit was raised;
There, as I ranged at will the pastoral downs
Trackless and smooth, or paced the bare white roads
Lengthening in solitude their dreary line,
Time with his retinue of ages fled
Backwards, nor checked his flight until I saw
Our dim ancestral Past in vision clear;   320
Saw multitudes of men, and, here and there,
A single Briton clothed in wolf-skin vest,
With shield and stone-axe, stride across the wold;
The voice of spears was heard, the rattling spear
Shaken by arms of mighty bone, in strength,
Long mouldered, of barbaric majesty.
I called on Darkness—but before the word
Was uttered, midnight darkness seemed to take
All objects from my sight; and lo! again
The Desert visible by dismal flames;   330
It is the sacrificial altar, fed
With living men—how deep the groans! the voice
Of those that crowd the giant wicker thrills
The monumental hillocks, and the pomp
Is for both worlds, the living and the dead.
At other moments—(for through that wide waste
Three summer days I roamed) where'er the Plain
Was figured o'er with circles, lines, or mounds,
That yet survive, a work, as some divine,
Shaped by the Druids, so to represent   340
Their knowledge of the heavens, and image forth
The constellations—gently was I charmed
Into a waking dream, a reverie
That, with believing eyes, where'er I turned,
Beheld long-bearded teachers, with white wands
Uplifted, pointing to the starry sky,
Alternately, and plain below, while breath

Of music swayed their motions, and the waste
Rejoiced with them and me in those sweet sounds.

This for the past, and things that may be viewed   350
Or fancied in the obscurity of years
From monumental hints: and thou, O Friend!
Pleased with some unpremeditated strains
That served those wanderings to beguile, hast said
That then and there my mind had exercised
Upon the vulgar forms of present things,
The actual world of our familiar days,
Yet higher power; had caught from them a tone,
An image, and a character, by books
Not hitherto reflected. Call we this   360
A partial judgment—and yet why? for *then*
We were as strangers; and I may not speak
Thus wrongfully of verse, however rude,
Which on thy young imagination, trained
In the great City, broke like light from far.
Moreover, each man's Mind is to herself
Witness and judge; and I remember well
That in life's every-day appearances
I seemed about this time to gain clear sight
Of a new world—a world, too, that was fit   370
To be transmitted, and to other eyes
Made visible; as ruled by those fixed laws
Whence spiritual dignity originates,
Which do both give it being and maintain
A balance, an ennobling interchange
Of action from without and from within;
The excellence, pure function, and best power
Both of the objects seen, and eye that sees.

BOOK FOURTEENTH
Conclusion

In one of those excursions (may they ne'er
Fade from remembrance!) through the Northern tracts
Of Cambria ranging with a youthful friend,

I left Bethgelert's huts at couching-time,
And westward took my way, to see the sun
Rise, from the top of Snowdon. To the door
Of a rude cottage at the mountain's base
We came, and roused the shepherd who attends
The adventurous stranger's steps, a trusty guide;
Then, cheered by short refreshment, sallied forth.   10

It was a close, warm, breezeless summer night,
Wan, dull, and glaring, with a dripping fog
Low-hung and thick that covered all the sky;
But, undiscouraged, we began to climb
The mountain-side. The mist soon girt us round,
And, after ordinary travellers' talk
With our conductor, pensively we sank
Each into commerce with his private thoughts:
Thus did we breast the ascent, and by myself
Was nothing either seen or heard that checked   20
Those musings or diverted, save that once
The shepherd's lurcher, who, among the crags,
Had to his joy unearthed a hedgehog, teased
His coiled-up prey with barkings turbulent.
This small adventure, for even such it seemed
In that wild place and at the dead of night,
Being over and forgotten, on we wound
In silence as before. With forehead bent
Earthward, as if in opposition set
Against an enemy, I panted up   30
With eager pace, and no less eager thoughts.
Thus might we wear a midnight hour away,
Ascending at loose distance each from each,
And I, as chanced, the foremost of the band;
When at my feet the ground appeared to brighten,
And with a step or two seemed brighter still;
Nor was time given to ask or learn the cause,
For instantly a light upon the turf
Fell like a flash, and lo! as I looked up
The Moon hung naked in a firmament   40

Of azure without cloud, and at my feet
Rested a silent sea of hoary mist.
A hundred hills their dusky backs upheaved
All over this still ocean; and beyond,
Far, far beyond, the solid vapours stretched,
In headlands, tongues, and promontory shapes,
Into the main Atlantic, that appeared
To dwindle, and give up his majesty,
Usurped upon far as the sight could reach.
Not so the ethereal vault; encroachment none   50
Was there, nor loss; only the inferior stars
Had disappeared, or shed a fainter light
In the clear presence of the full-orbed Moon,
Who, from her sovereign elevation, gazed
Upon the billowy ocean, as it lay
All meek and silent, save that through a rift—
Not distant from the shore whereon we stood,
A fixed, abysmal, gloomy, breathing-place—
Mounted the roar of waters, torrents, streams
Innumerable, roaring with one voice!   60
Heard over earth and sea, and, in that hour,
For so it seemed, felt by the starry heavens.

When into air had partially dissolved
That vision, given to spirits of the night
And three chance human wanderers, in calm thought
Reflected, it appeared to me the type
Of a majestic intellect, its acts
And its possessions, what it has and craves,
What in itself it is, and would become.
There I beheld the emblem of a mind   70
That feeds upon infinity, that broods
Over the dark abyss, intent to hear
Its voices issuing forth to silent light
In one continuous stream; a mind sustained
By recognitions of transcendent power,
In sense conducting to ideal form,
In soul of more than mortal privilege.

One function, above all, of such a mind
Had Nature shadowed there, by putting forth,
'Mid circumstances awful and sublime,   80
That mutual domination which she loves
To exert upon the face of outward things,
So moulded, joined, abstracted, so endowed
With interchangeable supremacy,
That men, least sensitive, see, hear, perceive,
And cannot choose but feel. The power, which all
Acknowledge when thus moved, which Nature thus
To bodily sense exhibits, is the express
Resemblance of that glorious faculty
That higher minds bear with them as their own.   90
This is the very spirit in which they deal
With the whole compass of the universe:
They from their native selves can send abroad
Kindred mutations; for themselves create
A like existence; and, whene'er it dawns
Created for them, catch it, or are caught
By its inevitable mastery,
Like angels stopped upon the wing by sound
Of harmony from Heaven's remotest spheres.
Them the enduring and the transient both   100
Serve to exalt; they build up greatest things
From least suggestions; ever on the watch,
Willing to work and to be wrought upon,
They need not extraordinary calls
To rouse them; in a world of life they live,
By sensible impressions not enthralled,
But by their quickening impulse made more prompt
To hold fit converse with the spiritual world,
And with the generations of mankind
Spread over time, past, present, and to come,   110
Age after age, till Time shall be no more.
Such minds are truly from the Deity,
For they are Powers; and hence the highest bliss
That flesh can know is theirs—the consciousness
Of Whom they are, habitually infused

Through every image and through every thought,
And all affections by communion raised
From earth to heaven, from human to divine;
Hence endless occupation for the Soul,
Whether discursive or intuitive; 120
Hence cheerfulness for acts of daily life,
Emotions which best foresight need not fear,
Most worthy then of trust when most intense.
Hence, amid ills that vex and wrongs that crush
Our hearts—if here the words of Holy Writ
May with fit reverence be applied—that peace
Which passeth understanding, that repose
In moral judgments which from this pure source
Must come, or will by man be sought in vain.

Oh! who is he that his whole life long 130
Preserved, enlarged, this freedom in himself?
For this alone is genuine liberty:
Where is the favoured being who hath held
That course unchecked, unerring, and untired,
In one perpetual progress smooth and bright?—
A humbler destiny have we retraced,
And told of lapse and hesitating choice,
And backward wanderings along thorny ways:
Yet—compassed round by mountain solitudes,
Within whose solemn temple I received 140
My earliest visitations, careless then
Of what was given me; and which now I range,
A meditative, oft a suffering, man—
Do I declare—in accents which, from truth
Deriving cheerful confidence, shall blend
Their modulation with these vocal streams—
That, whatsoever falls my better mind,
Revolving with the accidents of life,
May have sustained, that, howsoe'er misled,
Never did I, in quest of right and wrong, 150
Tamper with conscience from a private aim;
Nor was in any public hope the dupe

Of selfish passions; nor did ever yield
Wilfully to mean cares or low pursuits,
But shrunk with apprehensive jealousy
From every combination which might aid
The tendency, too potent in itself,
Of use and custom to bow down the soul
Under a growing weight of vulgar sense,
And substitute a universe of death   160
For that which moves with light and life informed,
Actual, divine, and true. To fear and love,
To love as prime and chief, for there fear ends,
Be this ascribed; to early intercourse,
In presence of sublime or beautiful forms,
With the adverse principles of pain and joy—
Evil as one is rashly named by men
Who know not what they speak. By love subsists
All lasting grandeur, by pervading love;
That gone, we are as dust.—Behold the fields   170
In balmy spring-time full of rising flowers
And joyous creatures; see that pair, the lamb
And the lamb's mother, and their tender ways
Shall touch thee to the heart; thou callest this love,
And not inaptly so, for love it is,
Far as it carries thee. In some green bower
Rest, and be not alone, but have thou there
The One who is thy choice of all the world:
There linger, listening, gazing, with delight
Impassioned, but delight how pitiable!   180
Unless this love by a still higher love
Be hallowed, love that breathes not without awe;
Love that adores, but on the knees of prayer,
By heaven inspired; that frees from chains the soul,
Lifted, in union with the purest, best,
Of earth-born passions, on the wings of praise
Bearing a tribute to the Almighty's Throne.

    This spiritual Love acts not nor can exist
Without Imagination, which, in truth,
Is but another name for absolute power   190

And clearest insight, amplitude of mind,
And Reason in her most exalted mood.
This faculty hath been the feeding source
Of our long labour: we have traced the stream
From the blind cavern whence is faintly heard
Its natal murmur; followed it to light
And open day; accompanied its course
Among the ways of Nature, for a time
Lost sight of it bewildered and engulphed;
Then given it greeting as it rose once more   200
In strength, reflecting from its placid breast
The works of man and face of human life;
And lastly, from its progress have we drawn
Faith in life endless, the sustaining thought
Of human Being, Eternity, and God.

Imagination having been our theme,
So also hath that intellectual Love,
For they are each in each, and cannot stand
Dividually.—Here must thou be, O Man!
Power to thyself; no Helper hast thou here;   210
Here keepest thou in singleness thy state:
No other can divide with thee this work:
No secondary hand can intervene
To fashion this ability; 'tis thine,
The prime and vital principle is thine
In the recesses of thy nature, far
From any reach of outward fellowship,
Else is not thine at all. But joy to him,
Oh, joy to him who here hath sown, hath laid
Here, the foundation of his future years!   220
For all that friendship, all that love can do,
All that a darling countenance can look
Or dear voice utter, to complete the man,
Perfect him, made imperfect in himself,
All shall be his: and he whose soul hath risen
Up to the height of feeling intellect
Shall want no humbler tenderness; his heart
Be tender as a nursing mother's heart;

Of female softness shall his life be full,
Of humble cares and delicate desires,   230
Mild interests and gentlest sympathies.

   Child of my parents! Sister of my soul!
Thanks in sincerest verse have been elsewhere
Poured out for all the early tenderness
Which I from thee imbibed: and 'tis most true
That later seasons owed to thee no less;
For, spite of thy sweet influence and the touch
Of kindred hands that opened out the springs
Of genial thought in childhood, and in spite
Of all that unassisted I had marked   240
In life or nature of those charms minute
That win their way into the heart by stealth
(Still to the very going-out of youth)
I too exclusively esteemed *that* love,
And sought *that* beauty, which, as Milton sings,
Hath terror in it. Thou didst soften down
This over-sternness; but for thee, dear Friend!
My soul, too reckless of mild grace, had stood
In her original self too confident,
Retained too long a countenance severe;   250
A rock with torrents roaring, with the clouds
Familiar, and a favourite of the stars:
But thou didst plant its crevices with flowers,
Hang it with shrubs that twinkle in the breeze,
And teach the little birds to build their nests
And warble in its chambers. At a time
When Nature, destined to remain so long
Foremost in my affections, had fallen back
Into a second place, pleased to become
A handmaid to a nobler than herself,   260
When every day brought with it some new sense
Of exquisite regard for common things,
And all the earth was budding with these gifts
Of more refined humanity, thy breath,
Dear Sister! was a kind of gentler spring
That went before my steps. Thereafter came

One whom with thee friendship had early paired;
She came, no more a phantom to adorn
A moment, but an inmate of the heart,
And yet a spirit, there for me enshrined   270
To penetrate the lofty and the low;
Even as one essence of pervading light
Shines, in the brightest of ten thousand stars
And the meek worm that feeds her lonely lamp
Couched in the dewy grass.

                      With such a theme,
Coleridge! with this my argument, of thee
Shall I be silent? O capacious Soul!
Placed on this earth to love and understand,
And from thy presence shed the light of love,
Shall I be mute, ere thou be spoken of?   280
Thy kindred influence to my heart of hearts
Did also find its way. Thus fear relaxed
Her overweening grasp; thus thoughts and things
In the self-haunting spirit learned to take
More rational proportions; mystery,
The incumbent mystery of sense and soul,
Of life and death, time and eternity,
Admitted more habitually a mild
Interposition—a serene delight
In closelier gathering cares, such as become   290
A human creature, howsoe'er endowed,
Poet, or destined for a humbler name;
And so the deep enthusiastic joy,
The rapture of the hallelujah sent
From all that breathes and is, was chastened, stemmed
And balanced by pathetic truth, by trust
In hopeful reason, leaning on the stay
Of Providence; and in reverence for duty,
Here, if need be, struggling with storms, and there
Strewing in peace life's humblest ground with herbs,   300
At every season green, sweet at all hours.

    And now, O Friend! this history is brought
To its appointed close: the discipline

And consummation of a Poet's mind,
In everything that stood most prominent,
Have faithfully been pictured; we have reached
The time (our guiding object from the first)
When we may, not presumptuously, I hope,
Suppose my powers so far confirmed, and such
My knowledge, as to make me capable   310
Of building up a Work that shall endure.
Yet much hath been omitted, as need was;
Of books how much! and even of the other wealth
That is collected among woods and fields,
Far more: for Nature's secondary grace
Hath hitherto been barely touched upon,
The charm more superficial that attends
Her works, as they present to Fancy's choice
Apt illustrations of the moral world,
Caught at a glance, or traced with curious pains.   320

        Finally, and above all, O Friend! (I speak
With due regret) how much is overlooked
In human nature and her subtle ways,
As studied first in our own hearts, and then
In life among the passions of mankind,
Varying their composition and their hue,
Where'er we move, under the diverse shapes
That individual character presents
To an attentive eye. For progress meet,
Along this intricate and difficult path,   330
Whate'er was wanting, something had I gained,
As one of many schoolfellows compelled,
In hardy independence, to stand up
Amid conflicting interests, and the shock
Of various tempers; to endure and note
What was not understood, though known to be;
Among the mysteries of love and hate,
Honour and shame, looking to right and left,
Unchecked by innocence too delicate,
And moral notions too intolerant,   340

Sympathies too contracted. Hence, when called
To take a station among men, the step
Was easier, the transition more secure,
More profitable also; for, the mind
Learns from such timely exercise to keep
In wholesome separation the two natures,
The one that feels, the other that observes.

Yet one word more of personal concern;—
Since I withdrew unwillingly from France,
I led an undomestic wanderer's life   350
In London chiefly harboured, whence I roamed,
Tarrying at will in many a pleasant spot
Of rural England's cultivated vales
Or Cambrian solitudes. A youth—(he bore
The name of Calvert—it shall live, if words
Of mine can give it life,) in firm belief
That by endowments not from me withheld
Good might be furthered—in his last decay
By a bequest sufficient for my needs
Enabled me to pause for choice, and walk   360
At large and unrestrained; nor damped too soon
By mortal cares. Himself no Poet, yet
Far less a common follower of the world,
He deemed that my pursuits and labours lay
Apart from all that leads to wealth, or even
A necessary maintenance insures,
Without some hazard to the finer sense;
He cleared a passage for me, and the stream
Flowed in the bent of Nature.
                                        Having now
Told what best merits mention, further pains   370
Our present purpose seems not to require,
And I have other tasks. Recall to mind
The mood in which this labour was begun,
O Friend! The termination of my course
Is nearer now, much nearer; yet even then,
In that distraction and intense desire,

I said unto the life which I had lived,
Where art thou? Hear I not a voice from thee
Which 'tis reproach to hear? Anon I rose
As if on wings, and saw beneath me stretched   380
Vast prospect of the world which I had been
And was; and hence this Song, which, like a lark,
I have protracted, in the unwearied heavens
Singing, and often with more plaintive voice
To earth attempered and her deep-drawn sighs,
Yet centring all in love, and in the end
All gratulant, if rightly understood.

    Whether to me shall be allotted life,
And, with life, power to accomplish aught of worth,
That will be deemed no insufficient plea   390
For having given the story of myself,
Is all uncertain: but, beloved Friend!
When, looking back, thou seest, in clearer view
Than any liveliest sight of yesterday,
That summer, under whose indulgent skies,
Upon smooth Quantock's airy ridge we roved
Unchecked, or loitered 'mid her sylvan combs
Thou in bewitching words, with happy heart,
Didst chaunt the vision of that Ancient Man,
The bright-eyed Mariner, and rueful woes   400
Didst utter of the Lady Christabel;
And I, associate with such labour, steeped
In soft forgetfulness the livelong hours,
Murmuring of him who, joyous hap, was found,
After the perils of his moonlight ride,
Near the loud waterfall; or her who sate
In misery near the miserable Thorn—
When thou dost to that summer turn thy thoughts,
And hast before thee all which then we were,
To thee, in memory of that happiness,   410
It will be known, by thee at least, my Friend!
Felt, that the history of a Poet's mind
Is labour not unworthy of regard;
To thee the work shall justify itself.

The last and later portions of this gift
Have been prepared, not with the buoyant spirits
That were our daily portion when we first
Together wantoned in wild Poesy,
But, under pressure of a private grief,
Keen and enduring, which the mind and heart,   420
That in this meditative history
Have been laid open, needs must make me feel
More deeply, yet enable me to bear
More firmly; and a comfort now hath risen
From hope that thou art near, and wilt be soon
Restored to us in renovated health;
When, after the first mingling of our tears,
'Mong other consolations, we may draw
Some pleasure from this offering of my love.

    Oh! yet a few short years of useful life,   430
And all will be complete, thy race be run,
Thy monument of glory will be raised;
Then, though (too weak to tread the ways of truth)
This age fall back to old idolatry,
Though men return to servitude as fast
As the tide ebbs, to ignominy and shame,
By nations, sink together, we shall still
Find solace—knowing what we have learnt to know,
Rich in true happiness if allowed to be
Faithful alike in forwarding a day   440
Of firmer trust, joint labourers in the work
(Should Providence such grace to us vouchsafe)
Of their deliverance, surely yet to come.
Prophets of Nature, we to them will speak
A lasting inspiration, sanctified
By reason, blest by faith: what we have loved,
Others will love, and we will teach them how;
Instruct them how the mind of man becomes
A thousand times more beautiful than the earth
On which he dwells, above this frame of things   450
(Which, 'mid all revolution in the hopes
And fears of men, doth still remain unchanged)

In beauty exalted, as it is itself
Of quality and fabric more divine.

THE RECLUSE

PART FIRST

Book First — Home at Grasmere

Once to the verge of yon steep barrier came
A roving school-boy; what the adventurer's age
Hath now escaped his memory—but the hour,
One of a golden summer holiday,
He well remembers, though the year be gone—
Alone and devious from afar he came;
And, with a sudden influx overpowered
At sight of this seclusion, he forgot
His haste, for hasty had his footsteps been
As boyish his pursuits; and sighing said,   10
"What happy fortune were it here to live!
And, if a thought of dying, if a thought
Of mortal separation, could intrude
With paradise before him, here to die!"
No Prophet was he, had not even a hope,
Scarcely a wish, but one bright pleasing thought,
A fancy in the heart of what might be
The lot of others, never could be his.

  The station whence he looked was soft and green,
Not giddy yet aerial, with a depth   20
Of vale below, a height of hills above.
For rest of body perfect was the spot,
All that luxurious nature could desire;
But stirring to the spirit; who could gaze
And not feel motions there? He thought of clouds
That sail on winds: of breezes that delight
To play on water, or in endless chase
Pursue each other through the yielding plain
Of grass or corn, over and through and through,

In billow after billow, evermore   30
Disporting—nor unmindful was the boy
Of sunbeams, shadows, butterflies and birds;
Of fluttering sylphs and softly-gliding Fays,
Genii, and winged angels that are Lords
Without restraint of all which they behold.
The illusion strengthening as he gazed, he felt
That such unfettered liberty was his,
Such power and joy; but only for this end,
To flit from field to rock, from rock to field,
From shore to island, and from isle to shore,   40
From open ground to covert, from a bed
Of meadow-flowers into a tuft of wood,
From high to low, from low to high, yet still
Within the bound of this huge concave; here
Must be his home, this valley be his world.
      Since that day forth the Place to him—*to me*
(For I who live to register the truth
Was that same young and happy Being) became
As beautiful to thought, as it had been
When present, to the bodily sense; a haunt   50
Of pure affections, shedding upon joy
A brighter joy; and through such damp and gloom
Of the gay mind, as ofttimes splenetic youth
Mistakes for sorrow, darting beams of light
That no self-cherished sadness could withstand;
And now 'tis mine, perchance for life, dear Vale,
Beloved Grasmere (let the wandering streams
Take up, the cloud-capt hills repeat, the Name)
One of thy lowly Dwellings is my Home.
      And was the cost so great? and could it seem   60
And act of courage, and the thing itself
A conquest? who must bear the blame? Sage man
Thy prudence, thy experience, thy desires,
Thy apprehensions—blush thou for them all.
      Yes the realities of life so cold,
So cowardly, so ready to betray,
So stinted in the measure of their grace

As we pronounce them, doing them much wrong,
Have been to me more bountiful than hope,
Less timid than desire—but that is past.   70
    On Nature's invitation do I come,
By Reason sanctioned. Can the choice mislead,
That made the calmest, fairest spot of earth
With all its unappropriated good
My own; and not mine only, for with me
Entrenched, say rather peacefully embowered,
Under you orchard, in yon humble cot,
A younger Orphan of a home extinct,
The only Daughter of my Parents dwells.
    Ay, think on that, my heart, and cease to stir,   80
Pause upon that and let the breathing frame
No longer breathe, but all be satisfied.
—Oh, if such silence be not thanks to God
For what hath been bestowed, then where, where then
Shall gratitude find rest? Mine eyes did ne'er
Fix on a lovely object, nor my mind
Take pleasure in the midst of happy thoughts,
But either She whom now I have, who now
Divides with me this loved abode, was there
Or not far off. Where'er my footsteps turned,   90
Her voice was like a hidden Bird that sang.
The thought of her was like a flash of light,
Or an unseen companionship, a breath
Of fragrance independent of the Wind.
In all my goings, in the new and old
Of all my meditations, and in this
Favourite of all, in this the most of all.
—What being, therefore, since the birth of Man
Had ever more abundant cause to speak
Thanks, and if favours of the Heavenly Muse   100
Make him more thankful, then to call on Verse
To aid him and in song resound his joy?
The boon is absolute; surpassing grace
To me hath been vouchsafed; among the bowers
Of blissful Eden this was neither given

Nor could be given, possession of the good
Which had been sighed for, ancient thought fulfilled,
And dear Imaginations realised,
Up to their highest measure, yea and more.
    Embrace me then, ye Hills, and close me in;   110
Now in the clear and open day I feel
Your guardianship; I take it to my heart;
'T is like the solemn shelter of the night.
But I would call thee beautiful, for mild,
And soft, and gay, and beautiful thou art,
Dear Valley, having in thy face a smile,
Though peaceful, full of gladness. Thou art pleased,
Pleased with thy crags and woody steeps, thy Lake,
Its one green island and its winding shores;
The multitude of little rocky hills,   120
Thy Church and cottages of mountain stone
Clustered like stars some few, but single most,
And lurking dimly in their shy retreats,
Or glancing at each other cheerful looks
Like separated stars with clouds between.
What want we? have we not perpetual streams,
Warm woods, and sunny hills, and fresh green fields,
And mountains not less green, and flocks and herds,
And thickets full of songsters, and the voice
Of lordly birds, an unexpected sound   130
Heard now and then from morn to latest eve,
Admonishing the man who walks below
Of solitude and silence in the sky?
These have we, and a thousand nooks of earth
Have also these, but nowhere else is found,
Nowhere (or is it fancy?) can be found
The one sensation that is here; 'tis here,
Here as it found its way into my heart
In childhood, here as it abides by day,
By night, here only; or in chosen minds   140
That take it with them hence, where'er they go.
—'Tis, but I cannot name it, 'tis the sense
Of majesty, and beauty, and repose,

A blended holiness of earth and sky,
Something that makes this individual spot,
This small abiding-place of many men,
A termination, and a last retreat,
A centre, come from wheresoe'er you will,
A whole without dependence or defect,
Made for itself, and happy in itself,   150
Perfect contentment, Unity entire.

    Bleak season was it, turbulent and bleak,
When hitherward we journeyed side by side
Through burst of sunshine and through flying showers;
Paced the long vales—how long they were—and yet
How fast that length of way was left behind,
Wensley's rich Vale, and Sedbergh's naked heights.
The frosty wind, as if to make amends
For its keen breath, was aiding to our steps,
And drove us onward like two ships at sea,   160
Or like two birds, companions in mid-air,
Parted and reunited by the blast.
Stern was the face of nature; we rejoiced
In that stern countenance, for our souls thence drew
A feeling of their strength. The naked trees,
The icy brooks, as on we passed, appeared
To question us, "Whence come ye, to what end?"
They seemed to say. "What would ye," said the shower,
"Wild Wanderers, whither through my dark domain?"
The sunbeam said, "Be happy." When this vale   170
We entered, bright and solemn was the sky
That faced us with a passionate welcoming,
And led us to our threshold. Daylight failed
Insensibly, and round us gently fell
Composing darkness, with a quiet load
Of full contentment, in a little shed
Disturbed, uneasy in itself as seemed,
And wondering at its new inhabitants.
It loves us now, this Vale so beautiful
Begins to love us! by a sullen storm,   180
Two months unwearied of severest storm,

It put the temper of our minds to proof,
And found us faithful through the gloom, and heard
The poet mutter his prelusive songs
With cheerful heart, an unknown voice of joy
Among the silence of the woods and hills,
Silent to any gladsomeness of sound
With all their shepherds.

                         But the gates of Spring
Are opened; churlish winter hath given leave
That she should entertain for this one day,   190
Perhaps for many genial days to come,
His guests, and make them jocund.— They are pleased,
But most of all the birds that haunt the flood,
With the mild summons: inmates though they be
Of Winter's household, they keep festival
This day, who drooped, or seemed to droop, so long;
They show their pleasure, and shall I do less?
Happier of happy though I be, like them
I cannot take possession of the sky,
Mount with a thoughtless impulse, and wheel there   200
One of a mighty multitude, whose way
Is a perpetual harmony and dance
Magnificent. Behold how with a grace
Of ceaseless motion, that might scarcely seem
Inferior to angelical, they prolong
Their curious pastime, shaping in mid-air,
And sometimes with ambitious wing that soars
High as the level of the mountain tops,
A circuit ampler than the lake beneath,
Their own domain;—but ever, while intent   210
On tracing and retracing that large round,
Their jubilant activity evolves
Hundreds of curves and circlets, to and fro,
Upwards and downwards; progress intricate
Yet unperplexed, as if one spirit swayed
Their indefatigable flight. 'Tis done,
Ten times and more I fancied it had ceased,
But lo! the vanished company again

Ascending, they approach. I hear their wings
Faint, faint at first; and then an eager sound   220
Passed in a moment—and as faint again!
They tempt the sun to sport among their plumes;
Tempt the smooth water, or the gleaming ice,
To show them a fair image,—'tis themselves,
Their own fair forms upon the glimmering plain
Painted more soft and fair as they descend,
Almost to touch,—then up again aloft,
Up with a sally and a flash of speed,
As if they scorned both resting-place and rest!
—This day is a thanksgiving, 'tis a day   230
Of glad emotion and deep quietness;
Not upon me alone hath been bestowed,
Me rich in many onward-looking thoughts,
The penetrating bliss; oh surely these
Have felt it, not the happy choirs of spring,
Her own peculiar family of love
That sport among green leaves, a blither train!
    But two are missing, two, a lonely pair
Of milk-white Swans; wherefore are the not seen
Partaking this day's pleasure? From afar   240
They came, to sojourn here in solitude,
Choosing this Valley, they who had the choice
Of the whole world. We saw them day by day,
Through those two months of unrelenting storm,
Conspicuous at the centre of the Lake
Their safe retreat, we knew them well, I guess
That the whole valley knew them; but to us
They were more dear than may be well believed,
Not only for their beauty, and their still
And placid way of life, and constant love   250
Inseparable, not for these alone,
But that *their* state so much resembled ours,
They having also chosen this abode;
They strangers, and we strangers, they a pair,
And we a solitary pair like them.
They should not have departed; many days
Did I look forth in vain, nor on the wing

Could see them, nor in that small open space
Of blue unfrozen water, where they lodged
And lived so long in quiet, side by side.   260
Shall we behold them consecrated friends,
Faithful companions, yet another year
Surviving, they for us, and we for them,
And neither pair be broken? nay perchance
It is too late already for such hope;
The Dalesmen may have aimed the deadly tube,
And parted them; or haply both are gone
One death, and that were mercy given to both.
Recall, my song, the ungenerous thought; forgive,
Thrice favoured Region, the conjecture harsh   270
Of such inhospitable penalty
Inflicted upon confidence so pure.
Ah! if I wished to follow where the sight
Of all that is before my eyes, the voice
Which speaks from a presiding spirit here,
Would lead me, I should whisper to myself:
They who are dwellers in this holy place
Must needs themselves be hallowed, they require
No benediction from the stranger's lips,
For they are blessed already; none would give   280
The greeting "peace be with you" unto them,
For peace they have; it cannot but be theirs,
And mercy, and forbearance—nay—not these—
Their healing offices a pure good-will
Precludes, and charity beyond the bounds
Of charity—an overflowing love;
Not for the creature only, but for all
That is around them; love for everything
Which in their happy Region they behold!
        Thus do we soothe ourselves, and when the thought   290
Is passed, we blame it not for having come.
—What if I floated down a pleasant stream,
And now am landed, and the motion gone,
Shall I reprove myself? Ah no, the stream
Is flowing, and will never cease to flow,
And I shall float upon that stream again.

By such forgetfulness the soul becomes,
Words cannot say how beautiful: then hail,
Hail to the visible Presence, hail to thee,
Delightful Valley, habitation fair!   300
And to whatever else of outward form
Can give an inward help, can purify,
And elevate, and harmonise, and soothe,
And steal away, and for a while deceive
And lap in pleasing rest, and bear us on
Without desire in full complacency,
Contemplating perfection absolute,
And entertained as in a placid sleep.
      But not betrayed by tenderness of mind
That feared, or wholly overlooked the truth,   310
Did we come hither, with romantic hope
To find in midst of so much loveliness
Love, perfect love: of so much majesty
A like majestic frame of mind in those
Who here abide, the persons like the place.
Not from such hope, or aught of such belief,
Hath issued any portion of the joy
Which I have felt this day. An awful voice
'Tis true hath in my walks been often heard,
Sent from the mountains or the sheltered fields,   320
Shout after shout—reiterated whoop,
In manner of a bird that takes delight
In answering to itself: or like a hound
Single at chase among the lonely woods,
His yell repeating; yet it was in truth
A human voice—a spirit of coming night;
How solemn when the sky is dark, and earth
Not dark, nor yet enlightened, but by snow
Made visible, amid a noise of winds
And bleatings manifold of mountain sheep,   330
Which in that iteration recognise
Their summons, and are gathering round for food,
Devoured with keenness, ere to grove or bank
Or rocky bield with patience they retire.
      That very voice, which, in some timid mood

Of superstitious fancy, might have seemed
Awful as ever stray demoniac uttered,
His steps to govern in the wilderness;
Or as the Norman Curfew's regular beat
To hearths when first they darkened at the knell: 340
That shepherd's voice, it may have reached mine ear
Debased and under profanation, made
The ready organ of articulate sounds
From ribaldry, impiety, or wrath,
Issuing when shame hath ceased to check the brawls
Of some abused Festivity—so be it.
I came not dreaming of unruffled life,
Untainted manners; born among the hills,
Bred also there, I wanted not a scale
To regulate my hopes; pleased with the good   350
I shrink not from the evil with disgust,
Or with immoderate pain. I look for Man,
The common creature of the brotherhood,
Differing but little from the Man elsewhere,
For selfishness and envy and revenge,
Ill neighbourhood—pity that this should be—
Flattery and double-dealing, strife and wrong.
    Yet it is something gained, it is in truth
A mighty gain, that Labour here preserves
His rosy face, a servant only here   360
Of the fireside or of the open field,
A Freeman therefore sound and unimpaired:
That extreme penury is here unknown,
And cold and hunger's abject wretchedness
Mortal to body and the heaven-born mind:
That they who want are not too great a weight
For those who can relieve; here may the heart
Breathe in the air of fellow-suffering
Dreadless, as in a kind of fresher breeze
Of her own native element, the hand   370
Be ready and unwearied without plea,
From tasks too frequent or beyond its power,
For languor or indifference or despair.
And as these lofty barriers break the force

Of winds,—this deep Vale, as it doth in part
Conceal us from the storm, so here abides
A power and a protection for the mind,
Dispensed indeed to other solitudes
Favoured by noble privilege like this,
Where kindred independence of estate   **380**
Is prevalent, where he who tills the field,
He, happy man! is master of the field,
And treads the mountains which his Fathers trod.

   Not less than halfway up yon mountain's side,
Behold a dusky spot, a grove of Firs
That seems still smaller than it is; this grove
Is haunted—by what ghost? a gentle spirit
Of memory faithful to the call of love;
For, as reports the Dame, whose fire sends up
Yon curling smoke from the grey cot below,   **390**
The trees (her first-born child being then a babe)
Were planted by her husband and herself,
That ranging o'er the high and houseless ground
Their sheep might neither want from perilous storm
Of winter, nor from summer's sultry heat,
A friendly covert; "and they knew it well,"
Said she, "for thither as the trees grew up
We to the patient creatures carried food
In times of heavy snow." She then began
In fond obedience to her private thoughts   **400**
To speak of her dead husband; is there not
An art, a music, and a strain of words
That shall be life, the acknowledged voice of life,
Shall speak of what is done among the fields,
Done truly there, or felt, of solid good
And real evil, yet be sweet withal,
More grateful, more harmonious than the breath,
The idle breath of softest pipe attuned
To pastoral fancies? Is there such a stream
Pure and unsullied flowing from the heart   **410**
With motions of true dignity and grace?
Or must we seek that stream where Man is not?

Methinks I could repeat in tuneful verse,
Delicious as the gentlest breeze that sounds
Through that aerial fir-grove—could preserve
Some portion of its human history
As gathered from the Matron's lips, and tell
Of tears that have been shed at sight of it,
And moving dialogues between this Pair
Who in their prime of wedlock, with joint hands   420
Did plant the grove, now flourishing, while they
No longer flourish, he entirely gone,
She withering in her loneliness. Be this
A task above my skill—the silent mind
Has her own treasures, and I think of these,
Love what I see, and honour humankind.
      No, we are not alone, we do not stand,
My sister here misplaced and desolate,
Loving what no one cares for but ourselves.
We shall not scatter through the plains and rocks   430
Of this fair Vale, and o'er its spacious heights,
Unprofitable kindliness, bestowed
On objects unaccustomed to the gifts
Of feeling, which were cheerless and forlorn
But few weeks past, and would be so again
Were we not here; we do not tend a lamp
Whose lustre we alone participate,
Which shines dependent upon us alone,
Mortal though bright, a dying, dying flame.
Look where we will, some human hand has been   440
Before us with its offering; not a tree
Sprinkles these little pastures, but the same
Hath furnished matter for a thought; perchance
For some one serves as a familiar friend.
Joy spreads, and sorrow spreads; and this whole Vale,
Home of untutored shepherds as it is,
Swarms with sensation, as with gleams of sunshine,
Shadows or breezes, scents or sounds. Nor deem
These feelings, though subservient more than ours
To every day's demand for daily bread,   450

And borrowing more their spirit and their shape
From self-respecting interests; deem them not
Unworthy therefore, and unhallowed—no,
They lift the animal being, do themselves
By nature's kind and ever-present aid
Refine the selfishness from which they spring,
Redeem by love the individual sense
Of anxiousness, with which they are combined.
And thus it is that fitly they become
Associates in the joy of purest minds: 460
They blend therewith congenially: meanwhile
Calmly they breathe their own undying life
Through this their mountain sanctuary; long
Oh long may it remain inviolate,
Diffusing health and sober cheerfulness,
And giving to the moments as they pass
Their little boons of animating thought
That sweeten labour, make it seen and felt
To be no arbitrary weight imposed,
But a glad function natural to man.   470

　　Fair proof of this, newcomer though I be,
Already have I gained; the inward frame,
Though slowly opening, opens every day
With process not unlike to that which cheers
A pensive stranger journeying at his leisure
Through some Helvetian Dell; when low-hung mists
Break up and are beginning to recede;
How pleased he is where thin and thinner grows
The veil, or where it parts at once, to spy
The dark pines thrusting forth their spiky heads;   480
To watch the spreading lawns with cattle grazed;
Then to be greeted by the scattered huts
As they shine out; and *see* the streams whose murmur
Had soothed his ear while *they* were hidden; how pleased
To have about him which way e'er he goes
Something on every side concealed from view,
In every quarter something visible
Half seen or wholly, lost and found again,

Alternate progress and impediment,
And yet a growing prospect in the main.   490
     Such pleasure now is mine, albeit forced,
Herein less happy than the Traveller,
To cast from time to time a painful look
Upon unwelcome things which unawares
Reveal themselves, nor therefore is my heart
Depressed, nor does it fear what is to come;
But confident, enriched at every glance,
The more I see the more delight my mind
Receives, or by reflection can create:
Truth justifies herself, and as she dwells   500
With Hope, who would not follow where she leads?
     Nor let me pass unheeded other loves
Where no fear is, and humbler sympathies.
Already hath sprung up within my heart
A liking for the small grey horse that bears
The paralytic man, and for the brute
In Scripture sanctified—the patient brute
On which the cripple, in the quarry maimed,
Rides to and fro: I know them and their ways.
The famous sheep-dog, first in all the vale,   510
Though yet to me a stranger, will not be
A stranger long; nor will the blind man's guide,
Meek and neglected thing, of no renown!
Soon will peep forth the primrose, ere it fades
Friends shall I have at dawn, blackbird and thrush
To rouse me, and a hundred warblers more!
And if those Eagles to their ancient hold
Return, Helvellyn's Eagles! with the Pair
From my own door I shall be free to claim
Acquaintance, as they sweep from cloud to cloud.   520
The owl that gives the name to Owlet-Crag
Have I heard whooping, and he soon will be
A chosen one of my regards. See there
The heifer in yon little croft belongs
To one who holds it dear; with duteous care
She reared it, and in speaking of her charge

I heard her scatter some endearing words
Domestic, and in spirit motherly,
She being herself a mother; happy Beast,
If the caresses of a human voice   530
Can make it so, and care of human hands.

  And ye as happy under Nature's care,
Strangers to me and all men, or at least
Strangers to all particular amity,
All intercourse of knowledge or of love
That parts the individual from his kind.
Whether in large communities ye keep
From year to year, not shunning man's abode,
A settled residence, or be from far
Wild creatures, and of many homes, that come   540
The gift of winds, and whom the winds again
Take from us at your pleasure; yet shall ye
Not want for this your own subordinate place
In my affections. Witness the delight
With which erewhile I saw that multitude
Wheel through the sky, and see them now at rest,
Yet not at rest upon the glassy lake:
They *cannot* rest—they gambol like young whelps;
Active as lambs, and overcome with joy
They try all frolic motions; flutter, plunge,   550
And beat the passive water with their wings.
Too distant are they for plain view, but lo!
Those little fountains, sparkling in the sun,
Betray their occupation, rising up
First one and then another silver spout,
As one or other takes the fit of glee,
Fountains and spouts, yet somewhat in the guise
Of plaything fireworks, that on festal nights
Sparkle about the feet of wanton boys.
—How vast the compass of this theatre,   560
Yet nothing to be seen but lovely pomp
And silent majesty; the birch-tree woods
Are hung with thousand thousand diamond drops
Of melted hoar-frost, every tiny knot

In the bare twigs, each little budding-place
Cased with its several beads; what myriads these
Upon one tree, while all the distant grove,
That rises to the summit of the steep,
Shows like a mountain built of silver light:
See yonder the same pageant, and again   570
Behold the universal imagery
Inverted, all its sun-bright features touched
As with the varnish and the gloss of dreams.
Dreamlike the blending also of the whole
Harmonious landscape: all along the shore
The boundary lost—the line invisible
That parts the image from reality;
And the clear hills, as high as they ascend
Heavenward, so deep piercing the lake below.
Admonished of the days of love to come   580
The raven croaks, and fills the upper air
With a strange sound of genial harmony;
And in and all about that playful band,
Incapable although they be of rest,
And in their fashion very rioters,
There is a stillness; and they seem to make
Calm revelry in that their calm abode.
Them leaving to their joyous hours I pass,
Pass with a thought the life of the whole year
That is to come: the throng of woodland flowers   590
And lilies that will dance upon the waves.
     Say boldly then that solitude is not
Where these things are: he truly is alone,
He of the multitude whose eyes are doomed
To hold a vacant commerce day by day
With Objects wanting life—repelling love;
He by the vast metropolis immured,
Where pity shrinks from unremitting calls,
Where numbers overwhelm humanity,
And neighbourhood serves rather to divide   600
Than to unite—what sighs more deep than his,
Whose nobler will hath long been sacrificed;

Who must inhabit under a black sky
A city, where, if indifference to disgust
Yield not to scorn or sorrow, living men
Are ofttimes to their fellow-men no more
Than to the forest Hermit are the leaves
That hang aloft in myriads; nay, far less,
For they protect his walk from sun and shower,
Swell his devotion with their voice in storms,   610
And whisper while the stars twinkle among them
His lullaby. From crowded streets remote,
Far from the living and dead Wilderness
Of the thronged world, Society is here
A true community—a genuine frame
Of many into one incorporate.
That must be looked for here: paternal sway,
One household, under God, for high and low,
One family and one mansion; to themselves
Appropriate, and divided from the world,   620
As if it were a cave, a multitude
Human and brute, possessors undisturbed
Of this Recess—their legislative Hall,
Their Temple, and their glorious Dwelling-place.
    Dismissing therefore all Arcadian dreams,
All golden fancies of the golden age,
The bright array of shadowy thoughts from times
That were before all time, or are to be
Ere time expire, the pageantry that stirs
Or will be stirring, when our eyes are fixed   630
On lovely objects, and we wish to part
With all remembrance of a jarring world,
—Take we at once this one sufficient hope,
What need of more? that we shall neither droop
Nor pine for want of pleasure in the life
Scattered about us, nor through want of aught
That keeps in health the insatiable mind.
—That we shall have for knowledge and for love
Abundance, and that feeling as we do
How goodly, how exceeding fair, how pure   640
From all reproach is yon ethereal vault,

And this deep Vale, its earthly counterpart,
By which and under which we are enclosed
To breathe in peace; we shall moreover find
(If sound, and what we ought to be ourselves,
If rightly we observe and justly weigh)
The inmates not unworthy of their home,
The Dwellers of their Dwelling.
                     And if this
Were otherwise, we have within ourselves
Enough to fill the present day with joy,   650
And overspread the future years with hope,
Our beautiful and quiet home, enriched
Already with a stranger whom we love
Deeply, a stranger of our Father's house,
A never-resting Pilgrim of the Sea,
Who finds at last an hour to his content
Beneath our roof. And others whom we love
Will seek us also, Sisters of our hearts,
And one, like them, a Brother of our hearts,
Philosopher and Poet, in whose sight   660
These mountains will rejoice with open joy.
—Such is our wealth! O Vale of Peace we are
And must be, with God's will, a happy Band.
    Yet 'tis not to enjoy that we exist,
For that end only; something must be done:
I must not walk in unreproved delight
These narrow bounds, and think of nothing more,
No duty that looks further, and no care.
Each Being has his office, lowly some
And common, yet all worthy if fulfilled   670
With zeal, acknowledgment that with the gift
Keeps pace a harvest answering to the seed.
Of ill-advised Ambition and of Pride
I would stand clear, but yet to me I feel
That an internal brightness is vouchsafed
That must not die, that must not pass away.
Why does this inward lustre fondly seek
And gladly blend with outward fellowship?
Why do *they* shine around me whom I love?

Why do they teach me, whom I thus revere? 680
Strange question, yet it answers not itself.
That humble Roof embowered among the trees,
That calm fireside, it is not even in them,
Blest as they are, to furnish a reply
That satisfies and ends in perfect rest.
Possessions have I that are solely mine,
Something within which yet is shared by none,
Not even the nearest to me and most dear,
Something which power and effort may impart;
I would impart it, I would spread it wide: 690
Immortal in the world which is to come—
Forgive me if I add another claim—
And would not wholly perish even in this,
Lie down and be forgotten in the dust,
I and the modest Partners of my days
Making a silent company in death;
Love, knowledge, all my manifold delights,
All buried with me without monument
Or profit unto any but ourselves!
It must not be, if I, divinely taught, 700
Be privileged to speak as I have felt
Of what in man is human or divine.

    While yet an innocent little one, with a heart
That doubtless wanted not its tender moods,
I breathed (for this I better recollect)
Among wild appetites and blind desires,
Motions of savage instinct my delight
And exaltation. Nothing at that time
So welcome, no temptation half so dear
As that which urged me to a daring feat, 710
Deep pools, tall trees, black chasms, and dizzy crags,
And tottering towers: I loved to stand and read
Their looks forbidding, read and disobey,
Sometimes in act and evermore in thought.
With impulses, that scarcely were by these
Surpassed in strength, I heard of danger met
Or sought with courage; enterprise forlorn

By one, sole keeper of his own intent,
Or by a resolute few, who for the sake
Of glory fronted multitudes in arms.   720
Yea, to this hour I cannot read a Tale
Of two brave vessels matched in deadly fight,
And fighting to the death, but I am pleased
More than a wise man ought to be; I wish,
Fret, burn, and struggle, and in soul am there.
But me hath Nature tamed, and bade to seek
For other agitations, or be calm;
Hath dealt with me as with a turbulent stream,
Some nursling of the mountains which she leads
Through quiet meadows, after he has learnt   730
His strength, and had his triumph and his joy,
His desperate course of tumult and of glee.
That which in stealth by Nature was performed
Hath Reason sanctioned: her deliberate Voice
Hath said; be mild, and cleave to gentle things,
Thy glory and thy happiness be there.
Nor fear, though thou confide in me, a want
Of aspirations that have been—of foes
To wrestle with, and victory to complete,
Bounds to be leapt, darkness to be explored;   740
All that inflamed thy infant heart, the love,
The longing, the contempt, the undaunted quest,
All shall survive, though changed their office, all
Shall live, it is not in their power to die.
      Then farewell to the Warrior's Schemes, farewell
The forwardness of soul which looks that way
Upon a less incitement than the Cause
Of Liberty endangered, and farewell
That other hope, long mine, the hope to fill
The heroic trumpet with the Muse's breath!   750
Yet in this peaceful Vale we will not spend
Unheard-of days, though loving peaceful thought,
A voice shall speak, and what will be the theme?
      On Man, on Nature, and on Human Life,
Musing in solitude, I oft perceive

Fair trains of imagery before me rise,
Accompanied by feelings of delight
Pure, or with no unpleasing sadness mixed;
And I am conscious of affecting thoughts
And dear remembrances, whose presence soothes   760
Or elevates the Mind, intent to weigh
The good and evil of our mortal state.
—To these emotions, whencesoe'er they come,
Whether from breath of outward circumstance,
Or from the Soul—an impulse to herself—
I would give utterance in numerous verse.
Of Truth, of Grandeur, Beauty, Love, and Hope,
And melancholy Fear subdued by Faith;
Of blessèd consolations in distress;
Of moral strength, and intellectual Power;   770
Of joy in widest commonalty spread;
Of the individual Mind that keeps her own
Inviolate retirement, subject there
To Conscience only, and the law supreme
Of that Intelligence which governs all—
I sing:—"fit audience let me find though few!"
    So prayed, more gaining than he asked, the Bard—
In holiest mood. Urania, I shall need
Thy guidance, or a greater Muse, if such
Descend to earth or dwell in highest heaven!   780
For I must tread on shadowy ground, must sink
Deep—and, aloft ascending, breathe in worlds
To which the heaven of heavens is but a veil.
All strength—all terror, single or in bands,
That ever was put forth in personal form—
Jehovah—with his thunder, and the choir
Of shouting Angels, and the empyreal thrones—
I pass them unalarmed. Not Chaos, not
The darkest pit of lowest Erebus,
Nor aught of blinder vacancy, scooped out   790
By help of dreams—can breed such fear and awe
As fall upon us often when we look
Into our Minds, into the Mind of Man—

My haunt, and the main region of my song
—Beauty—a living Presence of the earth,
Surpassing the most fair ideal Forms
Which craft of delicate Spirits hath composed
From earth's materials—waits upon my steps;
Pitches her tents before me as I move,
An hourly neighbour. Paradise, and groves   800
Elysian, Fortunate Fields—like those of old
Sought in the Atlantic Main—why should they be
A history only of departed things,
Or a mere fiction of what never was?
For the discerning intellect of Man,
When wedded to his goodly universe
In love and holy passion, shall find these
A simple produce of the common day.
—I, long before the blissful hour arrives,
Would chant, in lonely peace, the spousal verse   810
Of this great consummation:—and, by words
Which speak of nothing more than what we are,
Would I arouse the sensual from their sleep
Of Death, and win the vacant and the vain
To noble raptures; while my voice proclaims
How exquisitely the individual Mind
(And the progressive powers perhaps no less
Of the whole species) to the external World
Is fitted:—and how exquisitely, too—
Theme this but little heard of among men—   820
The external World is fitted to the Mind;
And the creation (by no lower name
Can it be called) which they with blended might
Accomplish:—this is our high argument.
—Such grateful haunts foregoing, if I oft
Must turn elsewhere—to travel near the tribes
And fellowships of men, and see ill sights
Of madding passions mutually inflamed;
Must hear Humanity in fields and groves
Pipe solitary anguish; or must hang   830
Brooding above the fierce confederate storm

Of sorrow, barricaded evermore
Within the walls of cities—may these sounds
Have their authentic comment; that even these
Hearing, I be not downcast or forlorn!—
Descend, prophetic Spirit! that inspir'st
The human Soul of universal earth,
Dreaming on things to come; and dost possess
A metropolitan temple in the hearts
Of mighty Poets; upon me bestow   840
A gift of genuine insight; that my Song
With star-like virtue in its place may shine,
Shedding benignant influence, and secure
Itself from all malevolent effect
Of those mutations that extend their sway
Throughout the nether sphere!—And if with this
I mix more lowly matter; with the thing
Contemplated, describe the mind and Man
Contemplating; and who, and what he was—
The transitory Being that beheld   850
This Vision;—when and where, and how he lived;
Be not this labour useless. If such theme
May sort with highest objects, then—dread Power!
Whose gracious favour is the primal source
Of all illumination—may my Life
Express the image of a better time,
More wise desires, and simpler manners;—nurse
My Heart in genuine freedom:—all pure thoughts
Be with me;—so shall thy unfailing love
Guide, and support, and cheer me to the end!   860

THE BROTHERS

"These Tourists, heaven preserve us! needs must live
A profitable life: some glance along,
Rapid and gay, as if the earth were air,
And they were butterflies to wheel about

Long as the summer lasted: some, as wise,
Perched on the forehead of a jutting crag,
Pencil in hand and book upon the knee,
Will look and scribble, scribble on and look,
Until a man might travel twelve stout miles,
Or reap an acre of his neighbour's corn.   10
But, for that moping Son of Idleness,
Why can he tarry *yonder?*—In our churchyard
Is neither epitaph nor monument,
Tombstone nor name—only the turf we tread
And a few natural graves."
                           To Jane, his wife,
Thus spake the homely Priest of Ennerdale.
It was a July evening; and he sate
Upon the long stone-seat beneath the eaves
Of his old cottage,—as it chanced, that day,
Employed in winter's work. Upon the stone   20
His wife sate near him, teasing matted wool,
While, from the twin cards toothed with glittering wire,
He fed the spindle of his youngest child,
Who, in the open air, with due accord
Of busy hands and back-and-forward steps
Her large round wheel was turning. Towards the field
In which the Parish Chapel stood alone,
Girt round with a bare ring of mossy wall,
While half an hour went by, the Priest had sent
Many a long look of wonder: and at last,   30
Risen from his seat, beside the snow-white ridge
Of carded wool which the old man had piled
He laid his implements with gentle care,
Each in the other locked; and, down the path
That from his cottage to the churchyard led,
He took his way, impatient to accost
The Stranger, whom he saw still lingering there.
    'Twas one well known to him in former days,
A Shepherd-lad; who ere his sixteenth year
Had left that calling, tempted to entrust   40
His expectations to the fickle winds

And perilous waters; with the mariners
A fellow-mariner;—and so had fared
Through twenty seasons; but he had been reared
Among the mountains, and he in his heart
Was half a shepherd on the stormy seas.
Oft in the piping shrouds had Leonard heard
The tones of waterfalls, and inland sounds
Of caves and trees:—and, when the regular wind
Between the tropics filled the steady sail,   50
And blew with the same breath through days and weeks,
Lengthening invisibly its weary line
Along the cloudless Main, he, in those hours
Of tiresome indolence, would often hang
Over the vessel's side, and gaze and gaze;
And, while the broad blue wave and sparkling foam
Flashed round him images and hues that wrought
In union with the employment of his heart,
He, thus by feverish passion overcome,
Even with the organs of his bodily eye,   60
Below him, in the bosom of the deep,
Saw mountains; saw the forms of sheep that grazed
On verdant hills—with dwellings among trees,
And shepherds clad in the same country grey
Which he himself had worn.
                              And now, at last,
From perils manifold, with some small wealth
Acquired by traffic 'mid the Indian Isles,
To his paternal home he is returned,
With a determined purpose to resume
The life he had lived there; both for the sake   70
Of many darling pleasures, and the love
Which to an only brother he has borne
In all his hardships, since that happy time
When, whether it blew foul or fair, they two
Were brother-shepherds on their native hills.
—They were the last of all their race: and now,
When Leonard had approached his home, his heart
Failed in him; and, not venturing to enquire
Tidings of one so long and dearly loved,

He to the solitary churchyard turned;   80
That, as he knew in what particular spot
His family were laid, he thence might learn
If still his Brother lived, or to the file
Another grave was added.——He had found
Another grave,——near which a full half-hour
He had remained; but, as he gazed, there grew
Such a confusion in his memory,
That he began to doubt; and even to hope
That he had seen this heap of turf before,——
That it was not another grave; but one   90
He had forgotten. He had lost his path,
As up the vale, that afternoon, he walked
Through fields which once had been well known to him:
And oh what joy this recollection now
Sent to his heart! he lifted up his eyes,
And, looking around, imagined that he saw
Strange alteration wrought on every side
Among the woods and fields, and that the rocks,
And everlasting hills themselves were changed.

By this the Priest, who down the field had come,   100
Unseen by Leonard, at the churchyard gate
Stopped short,——and thence, at leisure, limb by limb
Perused him with a gay complacency.
Ay, thought the Vicar, smiling to himself,
'Tis one of those who needs must leave the path
Of the world's business to go wild alone:
His arms have a perpetual holiday;
The happy man will creep about the fields,
Following his fancies by the hour, to bring
Tears down his cheek, or solitary smiles   110
Into his face, until the setting sun
Write fool upon his forehead.——Planted thus
Beneath a shed that over-arched the gate
Of this rude churchyard, till the stars appeared
The good Man might have communed with himself,
But that the Stranger, who had left the grave,
Approached; he recognised the Priest at once,
And, after greetings interchanged, and given

By Leonard to the Vicar as to one
Unknown to him, this dialogue ensued.   120

    Leonard. You live, Sir, in these dales, a quiet life:
Your years make up one peaceful family;
And who would grieve and fret, if, welcome come
And welcome gone, they are so like each other,
They cannot be remembered? Scarce a funeral
Comes to this churchyard once in eighteen months;
And yet, some changes must take place among you:
And you, who dwell here, even among these rocks,
Can trace the finger of mortality,
And see, that with our threescore years and ten   130
We are not all that perish.——I remember,
(For many years ago I passed this road)
There was a foot-way all along the fields
By the brook-side—'tis gone—and that dark cleft!
To me it does not seem to wear the face
Which then it had!
    Priest.   Nay, Sir, for aught I know,
That chasm is much the same—
    Leonard.   But, surely, yonder—
    Priest. Ay, there, indeed, your memory is a friend
That does not play you false.—On that tall pike
(It is the loneliest place of all these hills)   140
There were two springs which bubbled side by side,
As if they had been made that they might be
Companions for each other: the huge crag
Was rent with lightning—one hath disappeared;
The other, left behind, is flowing still.
For accidents and changes such as these,
We want not store of them;—a water-spout
Will bring down half a mountain; what a feast
For folks that wander up and down like you
To see an acre's breadth of that wide cliff   150
One roaring cataract! a sharp May-storm
Will come with loads of January snow,
And in one night send twenty score of sheep
To feed the ravens; or a shepherd dies

By some untoward death among the rocks:
The ice breaks up and sweeps away a bridge;
A wood is felled:—and then for our own homes!
A child is born or christened, a field ploughed,
A daughter sent to service, a web spun,
The old house-clock is decked with a new face;   160
And hence, so far from wanting facts or dates
To chronicle the time, we all have here
A pair of diaries,—one serving, Sir,
For the whole dale, and one for each fireside—
Yours was a stranger's judgment: for historians,
Commend me to these valleys!
    Leonard.   Yet your churchyard
Seems, if such freedom may be used with you,
To say that you are heedless of the past:
An orphan could not find his mother's grave:
Here's neither head nor foot stone, plate of brass,   170
Cross-bones nor skull,—type of our earthly state
Nor emblem of our hopes: the dead man's home
Is but a fellow to that pasture-field.
    Priest. Why, there, Sir, is a thought that's new to me!
The stone-cutters, 'tis true, might beg their bread
If every English churchyard were like ours;
Yet your conclusion wanders from the truth:
We have no need of names and epitaphs;
We talk about the dead by our firesides.
And then, for our immortal part! *we* want   180
No symbols, Sir, to tell us that plain tale:
The thought of death sits easy on the man
Who has been born and dies among the mountains.
    Leonard. Your Dalesmen, then, do in each other's thoughts
Possess a kind of second life: no doubt
You, Sir, could help me to the history
Of half these graves?
    Priest.   For eight-score winters past,
With what I've witnessed, and with what I've heard,
Perhaps I might; and, on a winter-evening,
If you were seated at my chimney's nook,   190

By turning o'er these hillocks one by one,
We two could travel, Sir, through a strange round;
Yet all in the broad highway of the world.
Now there's a grave—your foot is half upon it,—
It looks just like the rest; and yet that man
Died broken-hearted.

    Leonard.   'Tis a common case.
We 'll take another: who is he that lies
Beneath yon ridge, the last of those three graves?
It touches on that piece of native rock
Left in the churchyard wall.   200

    Priest.   That's Walter Ewbank.
He had as white a head and fresh a cheek
As ever were produced by youth and age
Engendering in the blood of hale fourscore.
Through five long generations had the heart
Of Walter's forefathers o'erflowed the bounds
Of their inheritance, that single cottage—
You see it yonder! and those few green fields.
They toiled and wrought, and still, from sire to son,
Each struggled, and each yielded as before
A little—yet a little,—and old Walter,   210
They left to him the family heart, and land
With other burthens than the crop it bore.
Year after year the old man still kept up
A cheerful mind,—and buffeted with bond,
Interest, and mortgages; at last he sank,
And went into his grave before his time.
Poor Walter! whether it was care that spurred him
God only knows, but to the very last
He had the lightest foot in Ennerdale:
His pace was never that of an old man: 220
I almost see him tripping down the path
With his two grandsons after him:—but you,
Unless our Landlord be your host to-night,
Have far to travel,—and on these rough paths
Even in the longest day of midsummer—

    Leonard. But those two Orphans!

Priest.　　　　　　　Orphans!—Such they were—
Yet not while Walter lived: for, though their parents
Lay buried side by side as now they lie,
The old man was a father to the boys,
Two fathers in one father: and if tears,　　　　　　　230
Shed when he talked of them where they were not,
And hauntings from the infirmity of love,
Are aught of what makes up a mother's heart,
This old Man, in the day of his old age,
Was half a mother to them.—If you weep, Sir,
To hear a stranger talking about strangers,
Heaven bless you when you are among your kindred!
Ay—you may turn that way—it is a grave
Which will bear looking at.
　　Leonard.　　　　　　　These boys—I hope
They loved this good old Man?—
　　　Priest.　　　　　　　They did—and truly:　　　240
But that was what we almost overlooked,
They were such darlings of each other. Yes,
Though from the cradle they had lived with Walter,
The only kinsman near them, and though he
Inclined to both by reason of his age,
With a more fond, familiar, tenderness;
They, notwithstanding, had much love to spare,
And it all went into each other's hearts.
Leonard, the elder by just eighteen months,
Was two years taller: 'twas a joy to see,　　　　　　　250
To hear, to meet them!—From their house the school
Is distant three short miles, and in the time
Of storm and thaw, when every watercourse
And unbridged stream, such as you may have noticed
Crossing our roads at every hundred steps,
Was swoln into a noisy rivulet,
Would Leonard then, when elder boys remained
At home, go staggering through the slippery fords,
Bearing his brother on his back. I have seen him,
On windy days, in one of those stray brooks,　　　　　　　260
Ay, more than once I have seen him, mid-leg deep,

Their two books lying both on a dry stone,
Upon the hither side: and once I said,
As I remember, looking round these rocks
And hills on which we all of us were born,
That God who made the great book of the world
Would bless such piety—
    Leonard.   It may be then—
    Priest. Never did worthier lads break English bread:
The very brightest Sunday Autumn saw
With all its mealy clusters of ripe nuts,   270
Could never keep those boys away from church,
Or tempt them to an hour of sabbath breach.
Leonard and James! I warrant, every corner
Among these rocks, and every hollow place
That venturous foot could reach, to one or both
Was known as well as to the flowers that grow there.
Like roe-bucks they went bounding o'er the hills;
They played like two young ravens on the crags:
Then they could write, ay and speak too, as well
As many of their betters—and for Leonard!   280
The very night before he went away,
In my own house I put into his hand
A Bible, and I 'd wager house and field
That, if he be alive, he has it yet.
    Leonard. It seems, these Brothers have not lived to be
A comfort to each other—
    Priest.   That they might
Live to such end is what both old and young
In this our valley all of us have wished,
And what, for my part, I have often prayed:
But Leonard—
    Leonard. Then James still is left among you!   290
    Priest. 'Tis of the elder brother I am speaking:
They had an uncle;—he was at that time
A thriving man, and trafficked on the seas:
And, but for that same uncle, to this hour
Leonard had never handled rope or shroud:
For the boy loved the life which we lead here;

And though of unripe years, a stripling only,
His soul was knit to this his native soil,
But, as I said, old Walter was too weak
To strive with such a torrent; when he died,   300
The estate and house were sold; and all their sheep,
A pretty flock, and which, for aught I know,
Had clothed the Ewbanks for a thousand years:—
Well—all was gone, and they were destitute,
And Leonard, chiefly for his Brother's sake,
Resolved to try his fortune on the seas.
Twelve years are past since we had tidings from him.
If there were one among us who had heard
That Leonard Ewbank was come home again,
From the Great Gavel, down by Leeza's banks,   310
And down the Enna, far as Egremont,
The day would be a joyous festival;
And those two bells of ours, which there you see—
Hanging in the open air—but, O good Sir!
This is sad talk—they'll never sound for him—
Living or dead.—When last we heard of him,
He was in slavery among the Moors
Upon the Barbary coast.—'Twas not a little
That would bring down his spirit; and no doubt,
Before it ended in his death, the Youth   320
Was sadly crossed.—Poor Leonard! when we parted,
He took me by the hand, and said to me,
If e'er he should grow rich, he would return,
To live in peace upon his father's land,
And lay his bones among us.
    Leonard.   If that day
Should come, 'twould needs be a glad day for him;
He would himself, no doubt, be happy then
As any that should meet him—
    Priest.   Happy! Sir—
    Leonard. You said his kindred all were in their graves,
And that he had one Brother—   330
    Priest.   That is but
A fellow-tale of sorrow. From his youth

James, though not sickly, yet was delicate;
And Leonard being always by his side
Had done so many offices about him,
That, though he was not of a timid nature,
Yet still the spirit of a mountain-boy
In him was somewhat checked; and, when his Brother
Was gone to sea, and he was left alone,
The little colour that he had was soon
Stolen from his cheek; he drooped, and pined, and pined— 340
    Leonard. But these are all the graves of full-grown men!
    Priest. Ay, Sir, that passed away: we took him to us;
He was the child of all the dale—he lived
Three months with one, and six months with another,
And wanted neither food, nor clothes, nor love:
And many, many happy days were his.
But, whether blithe or sad, 'tis my belief
His absent Brother still was at his heart.
And, when he dwelt beneath our roof, we found
(A practice till this time unknown to him) 350
That often, rising from his bed at night,
He in his sleep would walk about, and sleeping
He sought his brother Leonard.—You are moved!
Forgive me, Sir: before I spoke to you,
I judged you most unkindly.
    Leonard.   But this Youth,
How did he die at last?
    Priest.   One sweet May-morning,
(It will be twelve years since when Spring returns)
He had gone forth among the new-dropped lambs,
With two or three companions, whom their course
Of occupation led from height to height 360
Under a cloudless sun—till he, at length,
Through weariness, or, haply, to indulge
The humour of the moment, lagged behind.
You see yon precipice;—it wears the shape
Of a vast building made of many crags;
And in the midst is one particular rock
That rises like a column from the vale,
Whence by our shepherds it is called, THE PILLAR.

Upon its aëry summit crowned with heath,
The loiterer, not unnoticed by his comrades,   370
Lay stretched at ease; but, passing by the place
On their return, they found that he was gone.
No ill was feared; till one of them by chance
Entering, when evening was far spent, the house
Which at that time was James's home, there learned
That nobody had seen him all that day:
The morning came, and still he was unheard of:
The neighbours were alarmed, and to the brook
Some hastened; some ran to the lake: ere noon
They found him at the foot of that same rock   380
Dead, and with mangled limbs. The third day after
I buried him, poor Youth, and there he lies!
   Leonard. And that then *is* his grave!—Before his death
You say that he saw many happy years?
   Priest. Ay, that he did—
   Leonard. And all went well with him?—
   Priest. If he had one, the Youth had twenty homes.
   Leonard. And you believe, then, that his mind was easy?—
   Priest. Yes, long before he died, he found that time
Is a true friend to sorrow; and unless
His thoughts were turned on Leonard's luckless fortune,   390
He talked about him with a cheerful love.
   Leonard. He could not come to an unhallowed end!
   Priest. Nay, God forbid!—You recollect I mentioned
A habit which disquietude and grief
Had brought upon him; and we all conjectured
That, as the day was warm, he had lain down
On the soft heath,—and, waiting for his comrades,
He there had fallen asleep; that in his sleep
He to the margin of the precipice
Had walked, and from the summit had fallen headlong: 400
And so no doubt he perished. When the Youth
Fell, in his hand he must have grasped, we think,
His shepherd's staff; for on that Pillar of rock
It had been caught mid-way; and there for years
It hung;—and mouldered there.
               The Priest here ended—

The Stranger would have thanked him, but he felt
A gushing from his heart, that took away
The power of speech. Both left the spot in silence;
And Leonard, when they reached the churchyard gate,
As the Priest lifted up the latch, turned round,—   410
And, looking at the grave, he said, "My Brother!"
The Vicar did not hear the words: and now,
He pointed towards his dwelling-place, entreating
That Leonard would partake his homely fare:
The other thanked him with an earnest voice;
But added, that, the evening being calm,
He would pursue his journey. So they parted.

    It was not long ere Leonard reached a grove
That overhung the road: he there stopped short,
And, sitting down beneath the trees, reviewed   420
All that the Priest had said: his early years
Were with him:—his long absence, cherished hopes,
And thoughts which had been his an hour before,
All pressed on him with such a weight, that now,
This vale, where he had been so happy, seemed
A place in which he could not bear to live:
So he relinquished all his purposes.
He travelled back to Egremont: and thence,
That night, he wrote a letter to the Priest,
Reminding him of what had passed between them;   430
And adding, with a hope to be forgiven,
That it was from the weakness of his heart
He had not dared to tell him who he was.
This done, he went on shipboard, and is now
A Seaman, a grey-headed Mariner.

Michael

A PASTORAL POEM

If from the public way you turn your steps
Up the tumultuous brook of Greenhead Ghyll,
You will suppose that with an upright path

Your feet must struggle; in such bold ascent
The pastoral mountains front you, face to face.
But, courage! for around that boisterous brook
The mountains have all opened out themselves,
And made a hidden valley of their own.
No habitation can be seen; but they
Who journey thither find themselves alone   10
With a few sheep, with rocks and stones, and kites
That overhead are sailing in the sky.
It is in truth an utter solitude;
Nor should I have made mention of this Dell
But for one object which you might pass by,
Might see and notice not. Beside the brook
Appears a straggling heap of unhewn stones!
And to that simple object appertains
A story—unenriched with strange events,
Yet not unfit, I deem, for the fireside,   20
Or for the summer shade. It was the first
Of those domestic tales that spake to me
Of shepherds, dwellers in the valleys, men
Whom I already loved; not verily
For their own sakes, but for the fields and hills
Where was their occupation and abode.
And hence this Tale, while I was yet a Boy
Careless of books, yet having felt the power
Of Nature, by the gentle agency
Of natural objects, led me on to feel   30
For passions that were not my own, and think
(At random and imperfectly indeed)
On man, the heart of man, and human life.
Therefore, although it be a history
Homely and rude, I will relate the same
For the delight of a few natural hearts;
And, with yet fonder feeling, for the sake
Of youthful Poets, who among these hills
Will be my second self when I am gone.
    Upon the forest-side in Grasmere Vale   40
There dwelt a Shepherd, Michael was his name;

An old man, stout of heart, and strong of limb.
His bodily frame had been from youth to age
Of an unusual strength: his mind was keen,
Intense, and frugal, apt for all affairs,
And in his shepherd's calling he was prompt
And watchful more than ordinary men.
Hence had he learned the meaning of all winds,
Of blasts of every tone; and, oftentimes,
When others heeded not, He heard the South   50
Make subterraneous music, like the noise
Of bagpipers on distant Highland hills.
The Shepherd, at such warning, of his flock
Bethought him, and he to himself would say,
"The winds are now devising work for me!"
And, truly, at all times, the storm, that drives
The traveller to a shelter, summoned him
Up to the mountains: he had been alone
Amid the heart of many thousand mists,
That came to him, and left him, on the heights.   60
So lived he till his eightieth year was past.
And grossly that man errs, who should suppose
That the green valleys, and the streams and rocks,
Were things indifferent to the Shepherd's thoughts.
Fields, where with cheerful spirits he had breathed
The common air; hills, which with vigorous step
He had so often climbed; which had impressed
So many incidents upon his mind
Of hardship, skill or courage, joy or fear;
Which, like a book, preserved the memory   70
Of the dumb animals, whom he had saved,
Had fed or sheltered, linking to such acts
The certainty of honourable gain;
Those fields, those hills—what could they less? had laid
Strong hold on his affections, were to him
A pleasurable feeling of blind love,
The pleasure which there is in life itself.
    His days had not been passed in singleness.
His Helpmate was a comely matron, old—

Though younger than himself full twenty years. 80
She was a woman of a stirring life,
Whose heart was in her house: two wheels she had
Of antique form; this large, for spinning wool;
That small, for flax; and if one wheel had rest
It was because the other was at work.
The Pair had but one inmate in their house,
An only Child, who had been born to them
When Michael, telling o'er his years, began
To deem that he was old,—in shepherd's phrase,
With one foot in the grave. This only Son, 90
With two brave sheep-dogs tried in many a storm,
The one of an inestimable worth,
Made all their household. I may truly say,
That they were as a proverb in the vale
For endless industry. When day was gone,
And from their occupations out of doors
The Son and Father were come home, even then,
Their labour did not cease; unless when all
Turned to the cleanly supper-board, and there,
Each with a mess of pottage and skimmed milk, 100
Sat round the basket piled with oaten cakes,
And their plain home-made cheese. Yet when the meal
Was ended, Luke (for so the Son was named)
And his old Father both betook themselves
To such convenient work as might employ
Their hands by the fireside; perhaps to card
Wool for the Housewife's spindle, or repair
Some injury done to sickle, flail, or scythe,
Or other implement of house or field.
    Down from the ceiling, by the chimney's edge, 110
That in our ancient uncouth country style
With huge and black projection overbrowed
Large space beneath, as duly as the light
Of day grew dim the Housewife hung a lamp;
An aged utensil, which had performed
Service beyond all others of its kind.
Early at evening did it burn—and late,

Surviving comrade of uncounted hours,
Which, going by from year to year, had found,
And left, the couple neither gay perhaps   120
Nor cheerful, yet with objects and with hopes,
Living a life of eager industry.
And now, when Luke had reached his eighteenth year,
There by the light of this old lamp they sate,
Father and Son, while far into the night
The Housewife plied her own peculiar work,
Making the cottage through the silent hours
Murmur as with the sound of summer flies.
This light was famous in its neighbourhood,
And was a public symbol of the life   130
That thrifty Pair had lived. For, as it chanced,
Their cottage on a plot of rising ground
Stood single, with large prospect, north and south
High into Easedale, up to Dunmail-Raise,
And westward to the village near the lake;
And from this constant light, so regular
And so far seen, the House itself, by all
Who dwelt within the limits of the vale,
Both old and young, was named THE EVENING STAR.
    Thus living on through such a length of years,   140
The Shepherd, if he loved himself, must needs
Have loved his Helpmate; but to Michael's heart
This son of his old age was yet more dear—
Less from instinctive tenderness, the same
Fond spirit that blindly works in the blood of all—
Than that a child, more than all other gifts
That earth can offer to declining man,
Brings hope with it, and forward-looking thoughts,
And stirrings of inquietude, when they
By tendency of nature needs must fail.   150
Exceeding was the love he bare to him,
His heart and his heart's joy! For oftentimes
Old Michael, while he was a babe in arms,
Had done him female service, not alone
For pastime and delight, as is the use
Of fathers, but with patient mind enforced

To acts of tenderness; and he had rocked
His cradle, as with a woman's gentle hand.
  And, in a later time, ere yet the Boy
Had put on boy's attire, did Michael love, 160
Albeit of a stern unbending mind,
To have the Young-one in his sight, when he
Wrought in the field, or on his shepherd's stool
Sate with a fettered sheep before him stretched
Under the large old oak, that near his door
Stood single, and, from matchless depth of shade,
Chosen for the Shearer's covert from the sun,
Thence in our rustic dialect was called
The CLIPPING TREE, a name which yet it bears.
There, while they two were sitting in the shade, 170
With others round them, earnest all and blithe,
Would Michael exercise his heart with looks
Of fond correction and reproof bestowed
Upon the Child, if he disturbed the sheep
By catching at their legs, or with his shouts
Scared them, while they lay still beneath the shears.
  And when by Heaven's good grace the boy grew up
A healthy Lad, and carried in his cheek
Two steady roses that were five years old;
Then Michael from a winter coppice cut 180
With his own hand a sapling, which he hooped
With iron, making it throughout in all
Due requisites a perfect shepherd's staff,
And gave it to the Boy; wherewith equipt
He as a watchman oftentimes was placed
At gate or gap, to stem or turn the flock;
And, to his office prematurely called,
There stood the urchin, as you will divine,
Something between a hindrance and a help;
And for this cause not always, I believe, 190
Receiving from his Father hire of praise;
Though nought was left undone which staff, or voice,
Or looks, or threatening gestures, could perform.
  But soon as Luke, full ten years old, could stand
Against the mountain blasts; and to the heights,

Not fearing toil, nor length of weary ways,
He with his Father daily went, and they
Were as companions, why should I relate
That objects which the Shepherd loved before
Were dearer now? that from the Boy there came   200
Feelings and emanations—things which were
Light to the sun and music to the wind;
And that the old Man's heart seemed born again?

   Thus in his Father's sight the Boy grew up:
And now, when he had reached his eighteenth year,
He was his comfort and his daily hope.

   While in this sort the simple household lived
From day to day, to Michael's ear there came
Distressful tidings. Long before the time
Of which I speak, the Shepherd had been bound   210
In surety for his brother's son, a man
Of an industrious life, and ample means;
But unforeseen misfortunes suddenly
Had prest upon him; and old Michael now
Was summoned to discharge the forfeiture,
A grievous penalty, but little less
Than half his substance. This unlooked-for claim,
At the first hearing, for a moment took
More hope out of his life than he supposed
That any old man ever could have lost.   220
As soon as he had armed himself with strength
To look his trouble in the face, it seemed
The Shepherd's sole resource to sell at once
A portion of his patrimonial fields.
Such was his first resolve; he thought again,
And his heart failed him. "Isabel," said he,
Two evenings after he had heard the news,
"I have been toiling more than seventy years,
And in the open sunshine of God's love
Have we all lived; yet if these fields of ours   230
Should pass into a stranger's hand, I think
That I could not lie quiet in my grave.
Our lot is a hard lot; the sun himself

Has scarcely been more diligent than I;
And I have lived to be a fool at last
To my own family. An evil man
That was, and made an evil choice, if he
Were false to us; and if he were not false,
There are ten thousand to whom loss like this
Had been no sorrow. I forgive him;—but   240
'Twere better to be dumb than to talk thus.

    When I began, my purpose was to speak
Of remedies and of a cheerful hope.
Our Luke shall leave us, Isabel; the land
Shall not go from us, and it shall be free;
He shall possess it, free as is the wind
That passes over it. We have, thou know'st,
Another kinsman—he will be our friend
In this distress. He is a prosperous man,
Thriving in trade—and Luke to him shall go,   250
And with his kinsman's help and his own thrift
He quickly will repair this loss, and then
He may return to us. If here he stay,
What can be done? Where every one is poor,
What can be gained?"

                    At this the old Man paused,
And Isabel sat silent, for her mind
Was busy, looking back into past times.
There's Richard Bateman, thought she to herself,
He was a parish-boy—at the church-door
They made a gathering for him, shillings, pence   260
And halfpennies, wherewith the neighbours bought
A basket, which they filled with pedlar's wares;
And, with this basket on his arm, the lad
Went up to London, found a master there,
Who, out of many, chose the trusty boy
To go and overlook his merchandise
Beyond the seas; where he grew wondrous rich,
And left estates and monies to the poor.
And, at his birth-place, built a chapel, floored
With marble which he sent from foreign lands.   270

These thoughts, and many others of like sort,
Passed quickly through the mind of Isabel,
And her face brightened. The old Man was glad,
And thus resumed:—"Well, Isabel! this scheme
These two days, has been meat and drink to me.
Far more than we have lost is left us yet.
—We have enough—I wish indeed that I
Were younger;—but this hope is a good hope.
—Make ready Luke's best garments, of the best
Buy for him more, and let us send him forth   280
To-morrow, or the next day, or to-night;
—If he *could* go, the Boy should go tonight."
    Here Michael ceased, and to the fields went forth
With a light heart. The Housewife for five days
Was restless morn and night, and all day long
Wrought on with her best fingers to prepare
Things needful for the journey of her son.
But Isabel was glad when Sunday came
To stop her in her work: for, when she lay
By Michael's side, she through the last two nights   290
Heard him, how he was troubled in his sleep;
And when they rose at morning she could see
That all his hopes were gone. That day at noon
She said to Luke, while they two by themselves
Were sitting at the door, "Thou must not go:
We have no other Child but thee to lose—
None to remember—do not go away,
For if thou leave thy Father he will die."
The Youth made answer with a jocund voice;
And Isabel, when she had told her fears,   300
Recovered heart. That evening her best fare
Did she bring forth, and all together sat
Like happy people round a Christmas fire.
    With daylight Isabel resumed her work;
And all the ensuing week the house appeared
As cheerful as a grove in Spring: at length
The expected letter from their kinsman came,
With kind assurances that he would do

His utmost for the welfare of the Boy;
To which, requests were added, that forthwith   310
He might be sent to him. Ten times or more
The letter was read over; Isabel
Went forth to show it to the neighbours round;
Nor was there at that time on English land
A prouder heart than Luke's. When Isabel
Had to her house returned, the old Man said,
"He shall depart to-morrow." To this word
The Housewife answered, talking much of things
Which, if at such short notice he should go,
Would surely be forgotten. But at length   320
She gave consent, and Michael was at ease.
　　　Near the tumultuous brook of Greenhead Ghyll,
In that deep valley, Michael had designed
To build a Sheepfold; and, before he heard
The tidings of his melancholy loss,
For this same purpose he had gathered up
A heap of stones, which by the streamlet's edge
Lay thrown together, ready for the work.
With Luke that evening thitherward he walked:
And soon as they had reached the place he stopped,   330
And thus the old Man spake to him:—"My Son,
To-morrow thou wilt leave me: with full heart
I look upon thee, for thou art the same
That wert a promise to me ere thy birth,
And all thy life hast been my daily joy.
I will relate to thee some little part
Of our two histories; 'twill do thee good
When thou art from me, even if I should touch
On things thou canst not know of.—After thou
First cam'st into the world—as oft befalls   340
To new-born infants—thou didst sleep away
Two days, and blessings from thy Father's tongue
Then fell upon thee. Day by day passed on,
And still I loved thee with increasing love.
Never to living ear came sweeter sounds
Than when I heard thee by our own fireside

First uttering, without words, a natural tune;
While thou, a feeding babe, didst in thy joy
Sing at thy Mother's breast. Month followed month,
And in the open fields my life was passed   350
And on the mountains; else I think that thou
Hadst been brought up upon thy Father's knees.
But we were playmates, Luke: among these hills,
As well thou knowest, in us the old and young
Have played together, nor with me didst thou
Lack any pleasure which a boy can know."
Luke had a manly heart; but at these words
He sobbed aloud. The old Man grasped his hand,
And said, "Nay, do not take it so—I see
That these are things of which I need not speak.   360
—Even to the utmost I have been to thee
A kind and a good Father: and herein
I but repay a gift which I myself
Received at others' hands; for, though now old
Beyond the common life of man, I still
Remember them who loved me in my youth.
Both of them sleep together: here they lived,
As all their Forefathers had done; and when
At length their time was come, they were not loth
To give their bodies to the family mould.   370
I wished that thou should'st live the life they lived:
But, 'tis a long time to look back, my Son,
And see so little gain from threescore years.
These fields were burthened when they came to me;
Till I was forty years of age, not more
Than half of my inheritance was mine.
I toiled and toiled; God blessed me in my work,
And till these three weeks past the land was free.
—It looks as if it never could endure
Another Master. Heaven forgive me, Luke,   380
If I judge ill for thee, but it seems good
That thou should'st go."
                          At this the old Man paused;
Then, pointing to the stones near which they stood,

Thus, after a short silence, he resumed:
"This was a work for us; and now, my Son,
It is a work for me. But, lay one stone—
Here, lay it for me, Luke, with thine own hands.
Nay, Boy, be of good hope;—we both may live
To see a better day. At eighty-four
I still am strong and hale;—do thou thy part;   390
I will do mine.—I will begin again
With many tasks that were resigned to thee:
Up to the heights, and in among the storms,
Will I without thee go again, and do
All works which I was wont to do alone,
Before I knew thy face.—Heaven bless thee, Boy!
Thy heart these two weeks has been beating fast
With many hopes; it should be so—yes—yes—
I knew that thou could'st never have a wish
To leave me, Luke: thou hast been bound to me   400
Only by links of love: when thou art gone,
What will be left to us!—But, I forget
My purposes. Lay now the corner-stone,
As I requested; and hereafter, Luke,
When thou art gone away, should evil men
Be thy companions, think of me, my Son,
And of this moment; hither turn thy thoughts,
And God will strengthen thee: amid all fear
And all temptation, Luke, I pray that thou
May'st bear in mind the life thy Fathers lived,   410
Who, being innocent, did for that cause
Bestir them in good deeds. Now, fare thee well—
When thou return'st, thou in this place wilt see
A work which is not here: a covenant
'Twill be between us; but, whatever fate
Befall thee, I shall love thee to the last,
And bear thy memory with me to the grave."
   The Shepherd ended here; and Luke stooped down,
And, as his Father had requested, laid
The first stone of the Sheepfold. At the sight   420
The old Man's grief broke from him; to his heart

He pressed his Son, he kissed him and wept;
And to the house together they returned.
—Hushed was that House in peace, or seeming peace,
Ere the night fell:—with morrow's dawn the Boy
Began his journey, and when he had reached
The public way, he put on a bold face;
And all the neighbours, as he passed their doors,
Came forth with wishes and with farewell prayers,
That followed him till he was out of sight.   430

    A good report did from their Kinsman come,
Of Luke and his well-doing: and the Boy
Wrote loving letters, full of wondrous news,
Which, as the Housewife phrased it, were throughout
"The prettiest letters that were ever seen."
Both parents read them with rejoicing hearts.
So, many months passed on: and once again
The Shepherd went about his daily work
With confident and cheerful thoughts; and now
Sometimes when he could find a leisure hour   440
He to that valley took his way, and there
Wrought at the Sheepfold. Meantime Luke began
To slacken in his duty; and, at length,
He in the dissolute city gave himself
To evil courses: ignominy and shame
Fell on him, so that he was driven at last
To seek a hiding-place beyond the seas.

    There is a comfort in the strength of love;
'Twill make a thing endurable, which else
Would overset the brain, or break the heart: 450
I have conversed with more than one who well
Remember the old Man, and what he was
Years after he had heard this heavy news.
His bodily frame had been from youth to age
Of an unusual strength. Among the rocks
He went, and still looked up to sun and cloud,
And listened to the wind; and, as before,
Performed all kinds of labour for his sheep,
And for the land, his small inheritance.
And to that hollow dell from time to time   460

Did he repair, to build the Fold of which
His flock had need. 'Tis not forgotten yet
The pity which was then in every heart
For the old Man—and 'tis believed by all
That many and many a day he thither went,
And never lifted up a single stone.

    There, by the Sheepfold, sometimes was he seen
Sitting alone, or with his faithful Dog,
Then old, beside him, lying at his feet.
The length of full seven years, from time to time,   470
He at the building of this Sheepfold wrought,
And left the work unfinished when he died.
Three years, or little more, did Isabel
Survive her Husband: at her death the estate
Was sold, and went into a stranger's hand.
The Cottage which was named the EVENING STAR
Is gone—the ploughshare has been through the ground
On which it stood; great changes have been wrought
In all the neighbourhood:—yet the oak is left
That grew beside their door; and the remains   480
Of the unfinished Sheepfold may be seen
Beside the boisterous brook of Greenhead Ghyll.

THE PET-LAMB

A PASTORAL

The dew was falling fast, the stars began to blink;
I heard a voice; it said, "Drink, pretty creature, drink!"
And, looking o'er the hedge, before me I espied
A snow-white mountain-lamb with a Maiden at its side.

Nor sheep nor kine were near; the lamb was all alone,
And by a slender cord was tethered to a stone;
With one knee on the grass did the little Maiden kneel,
While to that mountain-lamb she gave its evening meal.

The lamb, while from her hand he thus his supper took,
Seemed to feast with head and ears; and his tail with pleasure shook.   10

"Drink, pretty creature, drink," she said in such a tone
That I almost received her heart into my own.

'Twas little Barbara Lewthwaite, a child of beauty rare!
I watched them with delight, they were a lovely pair.
Now with her empty can the Maiden turned away:
But ere ten yards were gone her footsteps did she stay.

Right towards the lamb she looked; and from a shady place
I unobserved could see the workings of her face:
If Nature to her tongue could measured numbers bring,
Thus, thought I, to her lamb that little Maid might sing: 20

"What ails thee, young One? what? Why pull so at thy cord?
Is it not well with thee? well both for bed and board?
Thy plot of grass is soft, and green as grass can be;
Rest, little young One, rest; what is 't that aileth thee?

"What is it thou wouldst seek? What is wanting to thy heart?
Thy limbs are they not strong? And beautiful thou art:
This grass is tender grass; these flowers they have no peers;
And that green corn all day is rustling in thy ears!

"If the sun be shining hot, do but stretch thy woollen chain,
This beech is standing by, its covert thou canst gain;   30
For rain and mountain-storms! the like thou need'st not fear,
The rain and storm are things that scarcely can come here.

"Rest, little young One, rest; thou hast forgot the day
When my father found thee first in places far away;
Many flocks were on the hills, but thou wert owned by none,
And thy mother from thy side for evermore was gone.

"He took thee in his arms, and in pity brought thee home:
A blessèd day for thee! then whither wouldst thou roam?
A faithful nurse thou hast; the dam that did thee yean
Upon the mountain-tops no kinder could have been.   40

"Thou know'st that twice a day I have brought thee in this can
Fresh water from the brook, as clear as ever ran;
And twice in the day, when the ground is wet with dew,
I bring thee draughts of milk, warm milk it is and new.

"Thy limbs will shortly be twice as stout as they are now,
Then I 'll yoke thee to my cart like a pony in the plough;
My playmate thou shalt be; and when the wind is cold
Our hearth shall be thy bed, our house shall be thy fold.

"It will not, will not rest!—Poor creature, can it be
That 'tis thy mother's heart which is working so in thee? 50
Things that I know not of belike to thee are dear,
And dreams of things which thou canst neither see nor hear.

"Alas, the mountain-tops that look so green and fair!
I've heard of fearful winds and darkness that come there;
The little brooks that seem all pastime and all play,
When they are angry, roar like lions for their prey.

"Here thou need'st not dread the raven in the sky;
Night and day thou art safe,—our cottage is hard by.
Why bleat so after me? Why pull so at thy chain?
Sleep—and at break of day I will come to thee again!" 60

—As homeward through the lane I went with lazy feet,
This song to myself did I oftentimes repeat;
And it seemed, as I retraced the ballad line by line,
That but half of it was hers, and one half of it was *mine*.

Again, and once again, did I repeat the song;
"Nay," said I, "more than half to the damsel must belong,
For she looked with such a look and she spake with such a tone,
That I almost received her heart into my own."

THE WATERFALL AND THE EGLANTINE

I

"Begone, thou fond presumptuous Elf,"
Exclaimed an angry Voice,
"Nor dare to thrust thy foolish self
Between me and my choice!"
A small Cascade fresh swoln with snows
Thus threatened a poor Briar-rose,
That, all bespattered with his foam,

And dancing high and dancing low,
Was living, as a child might know,
In an unhappy home.   10

II

"Dost thou presume my course to block?
Off, off! or, puny Thing!
I'll hurl thee headlong with the rock
To which thy fibres cling."
The Flood was tyrannous and strong;
The patient Briar suffered long,
Nor did he utter groan or sigh,
Hoping the danger would be past;
But, seeing no relief, at last,
He ventured to reply.   20

III

"Ah!" said the Briar, "blame me not;
Why should we dwell in strife?
We who in this sequestered spot
Once lived a happy life!
You stirred me on my rocky bed—
What pleasure through my veins you spread
The summer long, from day to day,
My leaves you freshened and bedewed;
Nor was it common gratitude
That did your cares repay.   30

IV

"When spring came on with bud and bell,
Among these rocks did I
Before you hang my wreaths to tell
That gentle days were nigh!
And in the sultry summer hours,
I sheltered you with leaves and flowers;
And in my leaves—now shed and gone,
The linnet lodged, and for us two
Chanted his pretty songs, when you
Had little voice or none.   40

V

"But now proud thoughts are in your breast—
What grief is mine you see,
Ah! would you think, even yet how blest
Together we might be!
Though of both leaf and flower bereft,
Some ornaments to me are left—
Rich store of scarlet hips is mine,
With which I, in my humble way,
Would deck you many a winter day,
A happy Eglantine!"   50

VI

What more he said I cannot tell,
The Torrent down the rocky dell
Came thundering loud and fast;
I listened, nor aught else could hear;
The Briar quaked—and much I fear
Those accents were his last.

THE OAK AND THE BROOM

A PASTORAL

I

His simple truths did Andrew glean
Beside the babbling rills;
A careful student he had been
Among the woods and hills.
One winter's night, when through the trees
The wind was roaring, on his knees
His youngest born did Andrew hold:
And while the rest, a ruddy quire,
Were seated round their blazing fire,
This Tale the Shepherd told.   10

II

"I saw a crag, a lofty stone
As ever tempest beat!

Out of its head an Oak had grown,
A Broom out of its feet.
The time was March, a cheerful noon—
The thaw-wind, with the breath of June,
Breathed gently from the warm south-west:
When, in a voice sedate with age,
This Oak, a giant and a sage,
His neighbour thus addressed:— 20

III

" 'Eight weary weeks, through rock and clay,
Along this mountain's edge,
The Frost hath wrought both night and day,
Wedge driving after wedge.
Look up! and think, above your head
What trouble, surely, will be bred;
Last night I heard a crash—'tis true,
The splinters took another road—
I see them yonder—what a load
For such a Thing as you! 30

IV

" 'You are preparing as before,
To deck your slender shape;
And yet, just three years back—no more—
You had a strange escape:
Down from yon cliff a fragment broke;
It thundered down, with fire and smoke,
And hitherward pursued its way;
This ponderous block was caught by me,
And o'er your head, as you may see,
'T is hanging to this day! 40

V

" 'If breeze or bird to this rough steep
Your kind's first seed did bear;
The breeze had better been asleep,
The bird caught in a snare:
For you and your green twigs decoy

The little witless shepherd-boy
To come and slumber in your bower;
And, trust me, on some sultry noon,
Both you and he, Heaven knows how soon!
Will perish in one hour. 50

VI

" 'From me this friendly warning take'—
The Broom began to doze,
And thus, to keep herself awake,
Did gently interpose:
'My thanks for your discourse are due;
That more than what you say is true,
I know, and I have known it long;
Frail is the bond by which we hold
Our being, whether young or old,
Wise, foolish, weak, or strong. 60

VII

" 'Disasters, do the best we can,
Will reach both great and small;
And he is oft the wisest man,
Who is not wise at all.
For me, why should I wish to roam?
This spot is my paternal home,
It is my pleasant heritage;
My father many a happy year,
Spread here his careless blossoms, here
Attained a good old age. 70

VIII

" 'Even such as his may be my lot.
What cause have I to haunt
My heart with terrors? Am I not
In truth a favoured plant!
On me such bounty Summer pours,
That I am covered o'er with flowers;
And, when the Frost is in the sky,
My branches are so fresh and gay

That you might look at me and say,
This Plant can never die.   80

IX

" 'The butterfly, all green and gold,
To me hath often flown,
Here in my blossoms to behold
Wings lovely as his own.
When grass is chill with rain or dew,
Beneath my shade, the mother-ewe
Lies with her infant lamb; I see
The love they to each other make,
And the sweet joy which they partake,
It is a joy to me.'   90

X

"Her voice was blithe, her heart was light:
The Broom might have pursued
Her speech, until the stars of night
Their journey had renewed;
But in the branches of the oak
Two ravens now began to croak
Their nuptial song, a gladsome air;
And to her own green bower the breeze
That instant brought two stripling bees
To rest, or murmur there.   100

XI

"One night, my Children! from the north
There came a furious blast;
At break of day I ventured forth,
And near the cliff I passed.
The storm had fallen upon the Oak,
And struck him with a mighty stroke,
And whirled, and whirled him far away;
And, in one hospitable cleft,
The little careless Broom was left
To live for many a day."   110

HART-LEAP WELL

PART FIRST

The Knight had ridden down from Wensley Moor
With the slow motion of a summer's cloud,
And now, as he approached a vassal's door,
"Bring forth another horse!" he cried aloud.

"Another horse!"—That shout the vassal heard
And saddled his best Steed, a comely grey;
Sir Walter mounted him; he was the third
Which he had mounted on that glorious day.

Joy sparkled in the prancing courser's eyes;
The horse and horseman are a happy pair;   10
But, though Sir Walter like a falcon flies,
There is a doleful silence in the air.

A rout this morning left Sir Walter's Hall,
That as they galloped made the echoes roar;
But horse and man are vanished, one and all;
Such race, I think, was never seen before.

Sir Walter, restless as a veering wind,
Calls to the few tired dogs that yet remain:
Blanch, Swift, and Music, noblest of their kind,
Follow, and up the weary mountain strain.   20

The knight hallooed, he cheered and chid them on
With suppliant gestures and upbraidings stern;
But breath and eyesight fail; and, one by one,
The dogs are stretched among the mountain fern.

Where is the throng, the tumult of the race?
The bugles that so joyfully were blown?
—This chase it looks not like an earthly chase;
Sir Walter and the Hart are left alone.

The poor Hart toils along the mountainside;
I will not stop to tell how far he fled,   30
Nor will I mention by what death he died;
But now the Knight beholds him lying dead.

Dismounting, then, he leaned against a thorn;
He had no follower, dog, nor man, nor boy:
He neither cracked his whip, nor blew his horn,
But gazed upon the spoil with silent joy.

Close to the thorn on which Sir Walter leaned,
Stood his dumb partner in this glorious feat;
Weak as a lamb the hour that it is yeaned;
And white with foam as if with cleaving sleet.   40

Upon his side the Hart was lying stretched:
His nostril touched a spring beneath a hill,
And with the last deep groan his breath had fetched
The waters of the spring were trembling still.

And now, too happy for repose or rest,
(Never had living man such joyful lot!)
Sir Walter walked all round, north, south, and west,
And gazed and gazed upon that darling spot.

And climbing up the hill—(it was at least
Four roods of sheer ascent) Sir Walter found   50
Three several hoof-marks which the hunted Beast
Had left imprinted on the grassy ground.

Sir Walter wiped his face, and cried, "Till now
Such sight was never seen by human eyes:
Three leaps have borne him from this lofty brow,
Down to the very fountain where he lies.

"I'll build a pleasure-house upon this spot,
And a small arbour, made for rural joy;
'Twill be the traveller's shed, the pilgrim's cot,
A place of love for damsels that are coy."   60

"A cunning artist will I have to frame
A basin for that fountain in the dell!
And they who do make mention of the same,
From this day forth, shall call it HART-LEAP WELL.

"And, gallant Stag! to make thy praises known,
Another monument shall here be raised;

Three several pillars, each a rough-hewn stone,
And planted where thy hoofs the turf have grazed.

"And, in the summer-time when days are long,
I will come hither with my Paramour;
And with the dancers and the minstrel's song
We will make merry in that pleasant bower.

"Till the foundations of the mountains fail
My mansion with its arbour shall endure;—
The joy of them who till the fields of Swale,
And them who dwell among the woods of Ure!"

Then home he went, and left the Hart, stone-dead,
With breathless nostrils stretched above the spring,
—Soon did the Knight perform what he had said;
And far and wide the fame thereof did ring.

Ere thrice the Moon into her port had steered,
A cup of stone received the living well;
Three pillars of rude stone Sir Walter reared,
And built a house of pleasure in the dell.

And near the fountain, flowers of stature tall
With trailing plants and trees were intertwined,—
Which soon composed a little sylvan hall,
A leafy shelter from the sun and wind.

And thither, when the summer days were long,
Sir Walter led his wondering Paramour;
And with the dancers and the minstrel's song
Made merriment within that pleasant bower

The Knight, Sir Walter, died in course of time,
And his bones lie in his paternal vale.—
But there is matter for a second rhyme,
And I to this would add another tale.

PART SECOND

The moving accident is not my trade;
To freeze the blood I have no ready arts:

'Tis my delight, alone in summer shade,
To pipe a simple song for thinking hearts.

As I from Hawes to Richmond did repair,
It chanced that I saw standing in a dell
Three aspens at three corners of a square;
And one, not four yards distant, near a well.

What this imported I could ill divine:
And, pulling now the rein my horse to stop,   10
I saw three pillars standing in a line,—
The last stone-pillar on a dark hill-top.

The trees were grey, with neither arms nor head;
Half wasted the square mound of tawny green;
So that you just might say, as then I said,
"Here in old time the hand of man hath been."

I looked upon the hill both far and near,
More doleful place did never eye survey;
It seemed as if the spring-time came not here,
And Nature here were willing to decay.   20

I stood in various thoughts and fancies lost,
When one, who was in shepherd's garb attired,
Came up the hollow:—him did I accost,
And what this place might be I then inquired.

The Shepherd stopped, and that same story told
Which in my former rhyme I have rehearsed.
"A jolly place," said he, "in times of old!
But something ails it now: the spot is curst.

"You see these lifeless stumps of aspen wood—
Some say that they are beeches, others elms—   30
These were the bower; and here a mansion stood,
The finest palace of a hundred realms!

"The arbour does its own condition tell;
You see the stones, the fountain, and the stream;
But as to the great Lodge! you might as well
Hunt half a day for a forgotten dream.

"There's neither dog nor heifer, horse nor sheep,
Will wet his lips within that cup of stone;
And oftentimes, when all are fast asleep,
This water doth send forth a dolorous groan.   40

"Some say that here a murder has been done,
And blood cries out for blood: but, for my part,
I've guessed, when I've been sitting in the sun,
That it was all for that unhappy Hart.

"What thoughts must through the creature's brain have past!
Even from the topmost stone, upon the steep,
Are but three bounds—and look, Sir, at this last—
O Master! it has been a cruel leap.

"For thirteen hours he ran a desperate race;
And in my simple mind we cannot tell   50
What cause the Hart might have to love this place,
And come and make his deathbed near the well.

"Here on the grass perhaps asleep he sank,
Lulled by the fountain in the summer-tide;
This water was perhaps the first he drank
When he had wandered from his mother's side.

"In April here beneath the flowering thorn
He heard the birds their morning carols sing;
And he, perhaps, for aught we know, was born
Not half a furlong from that self-same spring.   60

"Now, here is neither grass nor pleasant shade;
The sun on drearier hollow never shone;
So will it be, as I have often said,
Till trees, and stones, and fountain, all are gone."

"Grey-headed Shepherd, thou hast spoken well;
Small difference lies between thy creed and mine:
This Beast not unobserved by Nature fell;
His death was mourned by sympathy divine.

"The Being, that is in the clouds and air,
That is in the green leaves among the groves,   70

Maintains a deep and reverential care
For the unoffending creatures whom he loves.

"The pleasure-house is dust:—behind, before,
This is no common waste, no common gloom;
But Nature, in due course of time, once more
Shall here put on her beauty and her bloom.

"She leaves these objects to a slow decay,
That what we are, and have been, may be known;
But at the coming of the milder day,
These monuments shall all be overgrown.   80

"One lesson, Shepherd, let us two divide,
Taught both by what she shows, and what conceals;
Never to blend our pleasure or our pride
With sorrow of the meanest thing that feels."

THE CHILDLESS FATHER

"Up, Timothy, up with your staff and away!
Not a soul in the village this morning will stay;
The hare has just started from Hamilton's grounds,
And Skiddaw is glad with the cry of the hounds."

—Of coats and of jackets grey, scarlet, and green,
On the slopes of the pastures all colours were seen;
With their comely blue aprons, and caps white as snow,
The girls on the hills made a holiday show.

Fresh sprigs of green box-wood, not six months before,
Filled the funeral basin at Timothy's door;
A coffin through Timothy's threshold had past;
One Child did it bear, and that Child was his last.

Now fast up the dell came the noise and the fray,
The horse and the horn, and the hark! hark away!
Old Timothy took up his staff, and he shut
With a leisurely motion the door of his hut.

Perhaps to himself at that moment he said:
"The key I must take, for my Ellen is dead."

But of this in my ears not word did he speak;
And he went to the chase with a tear on his cheek.

1802–1807

THE SPARROW'S NEST

Behold, within the leafy shade,
Those bright blue eggs together laid!
On me the chance-discovered sight
Gleamed like a vision of delight.
I started—seeming to espy
The home and sheltered bed,
The Sparrow's dwelling, which, hard by
My Father's house, in wet or dry
My sister Emmeline and I
  Together visited.

She looked at it and seemed to fear it;
Dreading, tho' wishing, to be near it:
Such heart was in her, being then
A little Prattler among men.
The Blessing of my later years
Was with me when a boy:
She gave me eyes, she gave me ears;
And humble cares, and delicate fears;
A heart, the fountain of sweet tears;
  And love, and thought, and joy.

THE SAILOR'S MOTHER

One morning (raw it was and wet—
A foggy day in winter time)
A Woman on the road I met,
Not old, though something past her prime:
Majestic in her person, tall and straight;
And like a Roman matron's was her mien and gait.

The ancient spirit is not dead;
Old times, thought I, are breathing there;
Proud was I that my country bred
Such strength, a dignity so fair: 10
She begged an alms, like one in poor estate;
I looked at her again, nor did my pride abate.

When from these lofty thoughts I woke,
"What is it," said I. "that you bear,
Beneath the covert of your Cloak,
Protected from this cold damp air?"
She answered, soon as she the question heard,
"A simple burthen, Sir, a little Singing-bird."

And, thus continuing, she said,
"I had a Son, who many a day   20
Sailed on the seas, but he is dead;
In Denmark he was cast away:
And I have travelled weary miles to see
If aught which he had owned might still remain for me.

"The bird and cage they both were his:
'Twas my Son's bird; and neat and trim
He kept it: many voyages
The singing-bird had gone with him;
When last he sailed, he left the bird behind;
From bodings, as might be, that hung upon his mind.   30

"He to a fellow-lodger's care
Had left it, to be watched and fed,
And pipe its song in safety;—there
I found it when my Son was dead;
And now, God help me for my little wit!
I bear it with me, Sir;—he took so much delight in it."

ALICE FELL

OR, POVERTY

The post-boy drove with fierce career,
For threatening clouds the moon had drowned;
When, as we hurried on, my ear
Was smitten with a startling sound.

As if the wind blew many ways,
I heard the sound,   and more and more,
It seemed to follow with the chaise,
And still I heard it as before.

At length I to the boy called out;
He stopped his horses at the word,   10
But neither cry, nor voice, nor shout,
Nor aught else like it, could be heard.

The boy then smacked his whip, and fast
The horses scampered through the rain;
But, hearing soon upon the blast
The cry, I bade him halt again.

Forthwith alighting on the ground,
"Whence comes," said I, "this piteous moan?"
And there a little Girl I found,
Sitting behind the chaise alone.   20

"My cloak!" no other word she spake,
But loud and bitterly she wept,
As if her innocent heart would break;
And down from off her seat she leapt.

"What ails you, child?"—she sobbed "Look here!"
I saw it in the wheel entangled,
A weather-beaten rag as e'er
From any garden scare-crow dangled.

There, twisted between nave and spoke,
It hung, nor could at once be freed;   30
But our joint pains unloosed the cloak,
A miserable rag indeed!

"And whither are you going, child,
To-night along these lonesome ways?"
"To Durham," answered she, half wild—
"Then come with me into the chaise."

Insensible to all relief
Sat the poor girl, and forth did send
Sob after sob, as if her grief
Could never, never have an end.   40

"My child, in Durham do you dwell?"
She checked herself in her distress,
And said, "My name is Alice Fell;
I'm fatherless and motherless.

"And I to Durham, Sir, belong."
Again, as if the thought would choke
Her very heart, her grief grew strong;
And all was for her tattered cloak!

The chaise drove on; our journey's end
Was nigh; and, sitting by my side,   50
As if she had lost her only friend
She wept, nor would be pacified.

Up to the tavern-door we post;
Of Alice and her grief I told;
And I gave money to the host,
To buy a new cloak for the old.

"And let it be of duffil grey,
As warm a cloak as man can sell!"
Proud creature was she the next day,
The little orphan, Alice Fell!   60

TO A BUTTERFLY

Stay near me—do not take thy flight!
A little longer stay in sight!
Much converse do I find in thee,
Historian of my infancy!

Float near me; do not yet depart!
Dead times revive in thee:
Thou bring'st, gay creature as thou art!
A solemn image to my heart,
My father's family!

Oh! pleasant, pleasant were the days,
The time, when, in our childish plays,
My sister Emmeline and I
Together chased the butterfly!
A very hunter did I rush
Upon the prey:—with leaps and springs
I followed on from brake to bush;
But she, God love her, feared to brush
The dust from off its wings.

"MY HEART LEAPS UP WHEN I BEHOLD"

My heart leaps up when I behold
 A rainbow in the sky:
So was it when my life began;
So is it now I am a man;
So be it when I shall grow old,
 Or let me die!
The Child is father of the Man;
And I could wish my days to be
Bound each to each by natural piety.

"AMONG ALL LOVELY THINGS MY LOVE HAD BEEN"

Among all lovely things my Love had been;
Had noted well the stars, all flowers that grew
About her home; but she had never seen
A glow-worm, never one, and this I knew.

While riding near her home one stormy night
A single glow-worm did I chance to espy;
I gave a fervent welcome to the sight,
And from my horse I leapt; great joy had I.

Upon a leaf the glow-worm did I lay,
To bear it with me through the stormy night:
And, as before, it shone without dismay;
Albeit putting forth a fainter light.

When to the dwelling of my Love I came,
I went into the orchard quietly;
And left the glow-worm, blessing it by name,
Laid safely by itself, beneath a tree.

The whole next day, I hoped, and hoped with fear;
At night the glow-worm shone beneath the tree;
I led my Lucy to the spot, "Look here,"
Oh! joy it was for her, and joy for me!

WRITTEN IN MARCH

WHILE RESTING ON THE BRIDGE AT THE FOOT OF
BROTHER'S WATER

The Cock is crowing,
The stream is flowing,
The small birds twitter,
The lake doth glitter,
The green field sleeps in the sun;
The oldest and youngest
Are at work with the strongest;
The cattle are grazing,
Their heads never raising;
There are forty feeding like one!

Like an army defeated
The snow hath retreated,
And now doth fare ill
On the top of the bare hill;
The ploughboy is whooping—anon—anon:
There's joy in the mountains;
There's life in the fountains;
Small clouds are sailing,

Blue sky prevailing;
The rain is over and gone!

To a Butterfly

I've watched you now a full half-hour,
Self-poised upon that yellow flower;
And, little Butterfly! indeed
I know not if you sleep or feed.
How motionless!—not frozen seas
More motionless! and then
What joy awaits you, when the breeze
Hath found you out among the trees,
And calls you forth again!

This plot of orchard-ground is ours;
My trees they are, my sister's flowers;
Here rest your wings when they are weary;
Here lodge as in a sanctuary!
Come often to us, fear no wrong;
Sit near us on the bough!
We'll talk of sunshine and of song,
And summer days, when we were young;
Sweet childish days, that were as long
As twenty days are now.

To the Small Celandine

Pansies, lilies, kingcups, daisies,
Let them live upon their praises;
Long as there's a sun that sets,
Primroses will have their glory;
Long as there are violets,
They will have a place in story:
There's a flower that shall be mine,
'Tis the little Celandine.

Eyes of some men travel far
For the finding of a star;

10

Up and down the heavens they go,
Men that keep a mighty rout!
I'm as great as they, I trow,
Since the day I found thee out,
Little Flower!—I'll make a stir,
Like a sage astronomer.

Modest, yet withal an Elf
Bold, and lavish of thyself;
Since we needs must first have met
I have seen thee, high and low,   20
Thirty years or more, and yet
'Twas a face I did not know;
Thou hast now, go where I may,
Fifty greetings in a day.

Ere a leaf is on a bush,
In the time before the thrush
Has a thought about her nest,
Thou wilt come with half a call,
Spreading out thy glossy breast
Like a careless Prodigal;   30
Telling tales about the sun,
When we've little warmth, or none.

Poets, vain men in their mood!
Travel with the multitude:
Never heed them; I aver
That they all are wanton wooers;
But the thrifty cottager,
Who stirs little out of doors,
Joys to spy thee near her home;
Spring is coming, Thou art come!   40

Comfort have thou of thy merit,
Kindly, unassuming Spirit!
Careless of thy neighbourhood,
Thou dost show thy pleasant face
On the moor, and in the wood,
In the lane;—there's not a place,

Howsoever mean it be,
But 'tis good enough for thee.

Ill befall the yellow flowers,
Children of the flaring hours!   50
Buttercups, that will be seen,
Whether we will see or no;
Others, too, of lofty mien;
They have done as worldlings do,
Taken praise that should be thine,
Little, humble Celandine!

Prophet of delight and mirth,
Ill-requited upon earth;
Herald of a mighty band,
Of a joyous train ensuing,   60
Serving at my heart's command,
Tasks that are no tasks renewing,
I will sing, as doth behove,
Hymns in praise of what I love!

RESOLUTION AND INDEPENDENCE

I

There was a roaring in the wind all night;
The rain came heavily and fell in floods;
But now the sun is rising calm and bright;
The birds are singing in the distant woods;
Over his own sweet voice the Stock-dove broods;
The Jay makes answer as the Magpie chatters;
And all the air is filled with pleasant noise of waters.

II

All things that love the sun are out of doors;
The sky rejoices in the morning's birth;
The grass is bright with rain-drops;—on the moors   10
The hare is running races in her mirth;
And with her feet she from the plashy earth

Raises a mist, that, glittering in the sun,
Runs with her all the way, wherever she doth run.

III

I was a Traveller then upon the moor,
I saw the hare that raced about with joy;
I heard the woods and distant waters roar;
Or heard them not, as happy as a boy:
The pleasant season did my heart employ:
My old remembrances went from me wholly;   20
And all the ways of men, so vain and melancholy.

IV

But, as it sometimes chanceth, from the might
Of joy in minds that can no further go,
As high as we have mounted in delight
In our dejection do we sink as low;
To me that morning did it happen so;
And fears and fancies thick upon me came;
Dim sadness—and blind thoughts, I knew not, nor could name.

V

I heard the sky-lark warbling in the sky;
And I bethought me of the playful hare: 30
Even such a happy Child of earth am I;
Even as these blissful creatures do I fare;
Far from the world I walk, and from all care;
But there may come another day to me—
Solitude, pain of heart, distress, and poverty.

VI

My whole life I have lived in pleasant thought,
As if life's business were a summer mood;
As if all needful things would come unsought
To genial faith, still rich in genial good;
But how can He expect that others should   40
Build for him, sow for him, and at his call
Love him, who for himself will take no heed at all?

VII

I thought of Chatterton, the marvellous Boy,
The sleepless Soul that perished in his pride:

Of Him who walked in glory and in joy
Following his plough, along the mountainside:
By our own spirits are we deified:
We Poets in our youth begin in gladness;
But thereof come in the end despondency and madness.

VIII

Now, whether it were by peculiar grace,   50
A leading from above, a something given,
Yet it befell, that, in this lonely place,
When I with these untoward thoughts had striven,
Beside a pool bare to the eye of heaven
I saw a Man before me unawares:
The oldest man he seemed that ever wore grey hairs.

IX

As a huge stone is sometimes seen to lie
Couched on the bald top of an eminence;
Wonder to all who do the same espy,
By what means it could thither come, and whence;   60
So that it seems a thing endued with sense:
Like a sea-beast crawled forth, that on a shelf
Of rock or sand reposeth, there to sun itself;

X

Such seemed this Man, not all alive nor dead,
Nor all asleep—in his extreme old age:
His body was bent double, feet and head
Coming together in life's pilgrimage;
As if some dire constraint of pain, or rage
Of sickness felt by him in times long past,
A more than human weight upon his frame had cast.   70

XI

Himself he propped, limbs, body, and pale face,
Upon a long grey staff of shaven wood:
And, still as I drew near with gentle pace,
Upon the margin of that moorish flood
Motionless as a cloud the old Man stood,
That heareth not the loud winds when they call
And moveth all together, if it move at all.

XII

At length, himself unsettling, he the pond
Stirred with his staff, and fixedly did look
Upon the muddy water, which he conned,   80
As if he had been reading in a book:
And now a stranger's privilege I took;
And, drawing to his side, to him did say,
"This morning gives us promise of a glorious day."

XIII

A gentle answer did the old Man make,
In courteous speech which forth he slowly drew:
And him with further words I thus bespake,
"What occupation do you there pursue?
This is a lonesome place for one like you."
Ere he replied, a flash of mild surprise   90
Broke from the sable orbs of his yet-vivid eyes,

XIV

His words came feebly, from a feeble chest,
But each in solemn order followed each,
With something of a lofty utterance drest—
Choice word and measured phrase, above the reach
Of ordinary men; a stately speech;
Such as grave Livers do in Scotland use,
Religious men, who give to God and man their dues.

XV

He told, that to these waters he had come
To gather leeches, being old and poor: 100
Employment hazardous and wearisome!
And he had many hardships to endure:
From pond to pond he roamed, from moor to moor;
Housing, with God's good help, by choice or chance,
And in this way he gained an honest maintenance.

XVI

The old Man still stood talking by my side;
But now his voice to me was like a stream
Scarce heard; nor word from word could I divide;

And the whole body of the Man did seem
Like one whom I had met with in a dream;
Or like a man from some far region sent,
To give me human strength, by apt admonishment.   110

XVII

My former thoughts returned: the fear that kills;
And hope that is unwilling to be fed;
Cold, pain, and labour, and all fleshly ills;
And mighty Poets in their misery dead.
—Perplexed, and longing to be comforted,
My question eagerly did I renew,
"How is it that you live, and what is it you do?"

XVIII

He with a smile did then his words repeat;   120
And said, that, gathering leeches, far and wide
He travelled; stirring thus above his feet
The waters of the pools where they abide.
"Once I could meet with them on every side;
But they have dwindled long by slow decay;
Yet still I persevere, and find them where I may."

XIX

While he was talking thus, the lonely place,
The old Man's shape, and speech—all troubled me:
In my mind's eye I seemed to see him pace
About the weary moors continually,   130
Wandering about alone and silently.
While I these thoughts within myself pursued,
He, having made a pause, the same discourse renewed.

X

And soon with this he other matter blended,
Cheerfully uttered, with demeanour kind,
But stately in the main; and when he ended,
I could have laughed myself to scorn to find
In that decrepit Man so firm a mind.
"God," said I, "be my help and stay secure;
I'll think of the Leech-gatherer on the lonely moor!"   140

"I Grieved for Buonaparté"

I grieved for Buonaparté, with a vain
And an unthinking grief! The tenderest mood
Of that Man's mind—what can it be? what food
Fed his first hopes? what knowledge could *he* gain?
'Tis not in battles that from youth we train
The Governor who must be wise and good,
And temper with the sternness of the brain
Thoughts motherly, and meek as womanhood.
Wisdom doth live with children round her knees:
Books, leisure, perfect freedom, and the talk
Man holds with week-day man in the hourly walk
Of the mind's business: these are the degrees
By which true Sway doth mount; this is the stalk
True Power doth grow on; and her rights are these.

A Farewell

Farewell, thou little Nook of mountain-ground,
Thou rocky corner in the lowest stair
Of that magnificent temple which doth bound
One side of our whole vale with grandeur rare;
Sweet garden-orchard, eminently fair,
The loveliest spot that man hath ever found,
Farewell!—we leave thee to Heaven's peaceful care,
Thee, and the Cottage which thou dost surround.

Our boat is safely anchored by the shore,
And there will safely ride when we are gone;   10
The flowering shrubs that deck our humble door
Will prosper, though untended and alone:
Fields, goods, and far-off chattels we have none:
These narrow bounds contain our private store
Of things earth makes, and sun doth shine upon;
Here are they in our sight—we have no more.
Sunshine and shower be with you, bud and bell!
For two months now in vain we shall be sought:
We leave you here in solitude to dwell

With these our latest gifts of tender thought;
Thou, like the morning, in thy saffron coat,
Bright gowan, and marsh-marigold, farewell!
Whom from the borders of the Lake we brought,
And placed together near our rocky Well.

We go for One to whom ye will be dear;
And she will prize this Bower, this Indian shed,
Our own contrivance, Building without peer!
—A gentle Maid, whose heart is lowly bred,
Whose pleasures are in wild fields gathered,
With joyousness, and with a thoughtful cheer,
Will come to you; to you herself will wed;
And love the blessed life that we lead here.
Dear Spot! which we have watched with tender heed,
Bringing thee chosen plants and blossoms blown
Among the distant mountains, flower and weed,
Which thou hast taken to thee as thy own,
Making all kindness registered and known;
Thou for our sakes, though Nature's child indeed,
Fair in thyself and beautiful alone,
Hast taken gifts which thou dost little need.

And O most constant, yet most fickle Place,
Thou hast thy wayward moods, as thou dost show
To them who look not daily on thy face;
Who, being loved, in love no bounds dost know,
And say'st, when we forsake thee, "Let them go!"
Thou easy-hearted Thing, with thy wild race
Of weeds and flowers, till we return be slow,
And travel with the year at a soft pace.

Help us to tell Her tales of years gone by,
And this sweet spring, the best beloved and best;
Joy will be flown in its mortality;
Something must stay to tell us of the rest.
Here, thronged with primroses, the steep rock's breast
Glittered at evening like a starry sky;
And in this bush our sparrow built her nest,
Of which I sang one song that will not die.

20

30

40

50

O happy Garden! whose seclusion deep
Hath been so friendly to industrious hours;
And to soft slumbers, that did gently sleep
Our spirits, carrying with them dreams of flowers,   60
And wild notes warbled among leafy bowers;
Two burning months let summer overleap,
And, coming back with Her who will be ours,
Into thy bosom we again shall creep.

COMPOSED UPON WESTMINSTER BRIDGE,

SEPT. 3, 1802

Earth has not anything to show more fair:
Dull would he be of soul who could pass by
A sight so touching in its majesty:
This City now doth, like a garment, wear
The beauty of the morning; silent, bare,
Ships, towers, domes, theatres, and temples lie
Open unto the fields, and to the sky;
All bright and glittering in the smokeless air.
Never did sun more beautifully steep
In his first splendour, valley, rock, or hill;
Ne'er saw I, never felt, a calm so deep!
The river glideth at his own sweet will:
Dear God! the very houses seem asleep;
And all that mighty heart is lying still!

COMPOSED BY THE SEA-SIDE, NEAR CALAIS,

AUGUST, 1802

Fair Star of evening, Splendour of the west,
Star of my Country!—on the horizon's brink
Thou hangest, stooping, as might seem, to sink
On England's bosom; yet well pleased to rest,
Meanwhile, and be to her a glorious crest
Conspicuous to the Nations. Thou, I think,

Should'st be my Country's emblem; and should'st wink,
Bright Star! with laughter on her banners, drest
In thy fresh beauty. There! that dusky spot
Beneath thee, that is England; there she lies.
Blessings be on you both! one hope, one lot,
One life, one glory!—I, with many a fear
For my dear Country, many heartfelt sighs,
Among men who do not love her, linger here.

CALAIS, AUGUST, 1802

Is it a reed that's shaken by the wind,
Or what is it that ye go forth to see?
Lords, lawyers, statesmen, squires of low degree,
Men known, and men unknown, sick, lame, and blind,
Post forward all, like creatures of one kind,
With first-fruit offerings crowd to bend the knee
In France, before the new-born Majesty.
'Tis ever thus. Ye men of prostrate mind,
A seemly reverence may be paid to power;
But that's a loyal virtue, never sown
In haste, nor springing with a transient shower:
When truth, when sense, when liberty were flown,
What hardship had it been to wait an hour?
Shame on you, feeble Heads, to slavery prone!

"IT IS A BEAUTEOUS EVENING, CALM AND FREE"

It is a beauteous evening, calm and free,
The holy time is quiet as a Nun
Breathless with adoration; the broad sun
Is sinking down in its tranquillity;
The gentleness of heaven broods o'er the Sea:
Listen! the mighty Being is awake,
And doth with his eternal motion make
A sound like thunder—everlastingly.
Dear Child! dear Girl! that walkest with me here,

If thou appear untouched by solemn thought,
Thy nature is not therefore less divine:
Thou liest in Abraham's bosom all the year;
And worship'st at the Temple's inner shrine,
God being with thee when we know it not.

ON THE EXTINCTION OF THE VENETIAN REPUBLIC

Once did She hold the gorgeous east in fee;
And was the safeguard of the west: the worth
Of Venice did not fall below her birth,
Venice, the eldest Child of Liberty.
She was a maiden City, bright and free;
No guile seduced, no force could violate;
And, when she took unto herself a Mate,
She must espouse the everlasting Sea.
And what if she had seen those glories fade,
Those titles vanish, and that strength decay;
Yet shall some tribute of regret be paid
When her long life hath reached its final day:
Men are we, and must grieve when even the Shade
Of that which once was great, is passed away.

TO TOUSSAINT L'OUVERTURE

Toussaint, the most unhappy man of men!
Whether the whistling Rustic tend his plough
Within thy hearing, or thy head be now
Pillowed in some deep dungeon's earless den;—
O miserable Chieftain! where and when
Wilt thou find patience? Yet die not; do thou
Wear rather in thy bonds a cheerful brow:
Though fallen thyself, never to rise again,
Live, and take comfort. Thou hast left behind
Powers that will work for thee; air, earth, and skies;
There's not a breathing of the common wind
That will forget thee; thou hast great allies;

Thy friends are exultations, agonies,
And love, and man's unconquerable mind.

COMPOSED IN THE VALLEY NEAR DOVER, ON THE DAY OF LANDING

Here, on our native soil, we breathe once more.
The cock that crows, the smoke that curls, that sound
Of bells; those boys who in yon meadow-ground
In white-sleeved shirts are playing; and the roar
Of the waves breaking on the chalky shore;—
All, all are English. Oft have I looked round
With joy in Kent's green vales; but never found
Myself so satisfied in heart before.
Europe is yet in bonds; but let that pass,
Thought for another moment. Thou art free,
My Country! and 'tis joy enough and pride
For one hour's perfect bliss, to tread the grass
Of England once again, and hear and see,
With such a dear Companion at my side.

NEAR DOVER, SEPTEMBER, 1802

Inland, within a hollow vale, I stood;
And saw, while sea was calm and air was clear,
The coast of France—the coast of France how near!
Drawn almost into frightful neighbourhood.
I shrunk; for verily the barrier flood
Was like a lake, or river bright and fair,
A span of waters; yet what power is there!
What mightiness for evil and for good!
Even so doth God protect us if we be
Virtuous and wise. Winds blow, and waters roll,
Strength to the brave, and Power, and Deity;
Yet in themselves are nothing! One decree
Spake laws to *them,* and said that by the soul
Only, the Nations shall be great and free.

In London, September, 1802

O Friend! I know not which way I must look
For comfort, being, as I am, opprest,
To think that now our life is only drest
For show; mean handy-work of craftsman, cook,
Or groom!—We must run glittering like a brook
In the open sunshine, or we are unblest:
The wealthiest man among us is the best:
No grandeur now in nature or in book
Delights us. Rapine, avarice, expense,
This is idolatry; and these we adore:
Plain living and high thinking are no more:
The homely beauty of the good old cause
Is gone; our peace, our fearful innocence,
And pure religion breathing household laws.

London, 1802

Milton! thou should'st be living at this hour:
England hath need of thee: she is a fen
Of stagnant waters: altar, sword, and pen,
Fireside, the heroic wealth of hall and bower,
Have forfeited their ancient English dower
Of inward happiness. We are selfish men;
Oh! raise us up, return to us again;
And give us manners, virtue, freedom, power.
Thy soul was like a Star, and dwelt apart:
Thou hadst a voice whose sound was like the sea:
Pure as the naked heavens, majestic, free,
So didst thou travel on life's common way,
In cheerful godliness; and yet thy heart
The lowliest duties on herself did lay.

"England! The Time Is Come When Thou Should'st Wean"

England! the time is come when thou should'st wean
Thy heart from its emasculating food;

The truth should now be better understood;
Old things have been unsettled; we have seen
Fair seed-time, better harvest might have been
But for thy trespasses; and, at this day,
If for Greece, Egypt, India, Africa,
Aught good were destined, thou would'st step between.
England! all nations in this charge agree:
But worse, more ignorant in love and hate,
Far—far more abject, is thine Enemy:
Therefore the wise pray for thee, though the freight
Of thy offences be a heavy weight:
Oh grief that Earth's best hopes rest all with Thee!

"Great Men Have Been Among Us"

Great men have been among us; hands that penned
And tongues that uttered wisdom—better none:
The later Sidney, Marvell, Harrington,
Young Vane, and others who called Milton friend.
These moralists could act and comprehend:
They knew how genuine glory was put on;
Taught us how rightfully a nation shone
In splendour: what strength was, that would not bend
But in magnanimous meekness. France, 'tis strange,
Hath brought forth for no such souls as we had then.
Perpetual emptiness! unceasing change!
No single volume paramount, no code,
No master spirit, no determined road;
But equally a want of books and men!

"It Is Not to Be Thought of That the Flood"

It is not to be thought of that the Flood
Of British freedom, which, to the open sea
Of the world's praise, from dark antiquity
Hath flowed, "with pomp of waters, unwithstood."
Roused though it be full often to a mood
Which spurns the check of salutary bands.

That this most famous Stream in bogs and sands
Should perish; and to evil and to good
Be lost for ever. In our halls is hung
Armoury of the invincible Knights of old:
We must be free or die, who speak the tongue
That Shakespeare spake; the faith and morals hold
Which Milton held.—In everything we are sprung
Of Earth's first blood, have titles manifold.

"When I Have Borne in Memory"

When I have borne in memory what has tamed
Great Nations, how ennobling thoughts depart
When men change swords for ledgers, and desert
The student's bower for gold, some fears unnamed
I had, my Country!—am I to be blamed?
Now, when I think of thee, and what thou art,
Verily, in the bottom of my heart,
Of those unfilial fears I am ashamed.
For dearly must we prize thee; we who find
In thee a bulwark for the cause of men:
And I by my affection was beguiled:
What wonder if a Poet now and then,
Among the many movements of his mind,
Felt for thee as a lover or a child!

Stanzas

written in my pocket-copy of thomson's "castle of indolence"

Within our happy Castle there dwelt One
Whom without blame I may not overlook;
For never sun or living creature shone
Who more devout enjoyment with us took:
Here on his hours he hung as on a book,
On his own time here would he float away,

As doth a fly upon a summer brook;
But go to-morrow, or belike to-day,
Seek for him,—he is fled; and whither none can say.

Thus often would he leave our peaceful home,   10
And find elsewhere his business or delight;
Out of our Valley's limits did he roam:
Full many a time, upon a stormy night,
His voice came to us from the neighbouring height:
Oft could we see him driving in full view
At mid-day when the sun was shining bright;
What ill was on him, what he had to do,
A mighty wonder bred among our quiet crew.

Ah! piteous sight it was to see this Man
When he came back to us, a withered flower,—   20
Or like a sinful creature, pale and wan.
Down would he sit; and without strength or power
Look at the common grass from hour to hour:
And oftentimes, how long I fear to say,
Where apple-trees in blossom made a bower,
Retired in that sunshiny shade he lay;
And, like a naked Indian, slept himself away.

Great wonder to our gentle tribe it was
Whenever from our Valley he withdrew;
For happier soul no living creature has   30
Than he had, being here the long day through.
Some thought he was a lover, and did woo:
Some thought far worse of him, and judged him wrong;
But verse was what he had been wedded to;
And his own mind did like a tempest strong
Come to him thus, and drove the weary Wight along.

With him there often walked in friendly guise,
Or lay upon the moss by brook or tree,
A noticeable Man with large gray eyes,
And a pale face that seemed undoubtedly   40
As if a blooming face it ought to be;
Heavy his low-hung lip did oft appear,

Deprest by weight of musing Phantasy;
Profound his forehead was, though not severe;
Yet some did think that he had little business here.

Sweet heaven forfend! his was a lawful right;
Noisy he was, and gamesome as a boy;
His limbs would toss about him with delight
Like branches when strong winds the trees annoy.
Nor lacked his calmer hours device or toy   50
To banish listlessness and irksome care;
He would have taught you how you might employ
Yourself; and many did to him repair,—
And certes not in vain; he had inventions rare.

Expedients, too, of simplest sort he tried:
Long blades of grass, plucked round him as he lay,
Made, to his ear attentively applied,
A pipe on which the wind would deftly play;
Glasses he had, that little things display,
The beetle panoplied in gems and gold,   60
A mailèd angel on a battle-day;
The mysteries that cups of flowers enfold,
And all the gorgeous sights which fairies do behold.

He would entice that other Man to hear
His music, and to view his imagery:
And, sooth, these two were each to the other dear:
No livelier love in such a place could be:
There did they dwell—from earthly labour free,
As happy spirits as were ever seen;
If but a bird, to keep them company,   70
Or butterfly sate down, they were, I ween,
As pleased as if the same had been a Maiden-queen.

To H. C.

SIX YEARS OLD

O thou! whose fancies from afar are brought;
Who of thy words dost make a mock apparel,
And fittest to unutterable thought
The breeze-like motion and the self-born carol;

Thou faery voyager! that dost float
In such clear water, that thy boat
May rather seem
To brood on air than on an earthly stream;
Suspended in a stream as clear as sky,
Where earth and heaven do make one imagery;   10
O blessed vision! happy child!
Thou art so exquisitely wild,
I think of thee with many fears
For what may be thy lot in future years.

   I thought of times when Pain might be thy guest,
Lord of thy house and hospitality;
And Grief, uneasy lover! never rest
But when she sate within the touch of thee.
O too industrious folly!
O vain and ceaseless melancholy!   20
Nature will either end thee quite;
Or, lengthening out thy season of delight,
Preserve for thee, by individual right,
A young lamb's heart among the full-grown flocks.
What hast thou to do with sorrow,
Or the injuries of to-morrow?
Thou art a dew-drop, which the morn brings forth,
Ill fitted to sustain unkindly shocks,
Or to be trailed along the soiling earth;
A gem that glitters while it lives,   30
And no forewarning gives;
But, at the touch of wrong, without a strife
Slips in a moment out of life.

THE GREEN LINNET

Beneath these fruit-tree boughs that shed
Their snow-white blossoms on my head,
With brightest sunshine round me spread
    Of spring's unclouded weather,
In this sequestered nook how sweet
To sit upon my orchard-seat!
And birds and flowers once more to greet,
    My last year's friends together.

One have I marked, the happiest guest
In all this covert of the blest: 10
Hail to Thee, far above the rest
    In joy of voice and pinion!
Thou, Linnet! in thy green array,
Presiding Spirit here to-day,
Dost lead the revels of the May;
    And this is thy dominion.

While birds, and butterflies, and flowers,
Make all one band of paramours,
Thou, ranging up and down the bowers,
    Art sole in thy employment: 20
A life, a Presence like the Air,
Scattering thy gladness without care,
Too blest with any one to pair;
    Thyself thy own enjoyment.

Amid yon tuft of hazel trees,
That twinkle to the gusty breeze,
Behold him perched in ecstasies,
    Yet seeming still to hover;
There! where the flutter of his wings
Upon his back and body flings   30
Shadows and sunny glimmerings,
    That cover him all over.

My dazzled sight he oft deceives,
A Brother of the dancing leaves;
Then flits, and from the cottage-eaves
    Pours forth his song in gushes;
As if by that exulting strain
He mocked and treated with disdain
The voiceless Form he chose to feign,
    While fluttering in the bushes.   40

YEW-TREES

There is a Yew-tree, pride of Lorton Vale,
Which to this day stands single, in the midst

Of its own darkness, as it stood of yore;
Not loth to furnish weapons for the bands
Of Umfraville or Percy ere they marched
To Scotland's heaths; or those that crossed the sea
And drew their sounding bows at Azincour,
Perhaps at earlier Crecy, or Poictiers.
Of vast circumference and gloom profound
This solitary Tree! a living thing   10
Produced too slowly ever to decay;
Of form and aspect too magnificent
To be destroyed. But worthier still of note
Are those fraternal Four of Borrowdale,
Joined in one solemn and capacious grove;
Huge trunks! and each particular trunk a growth
Of intertwisted fibres serpentine
Up-coiling, and inveterately convolved;
Nor uninformed with Phantasy, and looks
That threaten the profane;—a pillared shade,   20
Upon whose grassless floor of red-brown hue,
By sheddings from the pining umbrage tinged
Perennially—beneath whose sable roof
Of boughs, as if for festal purpose, decked
With unrejoicing berries—ghostly Shapes
May meet at noontide; Fear and trembling Hope,
Silence and Foresight; Death the Skeleton
And Time the Shadow;—there to celebrate,
As in a natural temple scattered o'er
With altars undisturbed of mossy stone,   30
United worship; or in mute repose
To lie, and listen to the mountain flood
Murmuring from Glaramara's inmost caves.

STEPPING WESTWARD

"What, you are stepping westward?"—"Yea."
—'Twould be a *wildish* destiny,
If we, who thus together roam
In a strange Land, and far from home,

Were in this place the guests of Chance:
Yet who would stop, or fear to advance,
Though home or shelter he had none,
With such a sky to lead him on?

The dewy ground was dark and cold;
Behind, all gloomy to behold;
And stepping westward seemed to be
A kind of *heavenly* destiny:
I liked the greeting; 't was a sound
Of something without place or bound;
And seemed to give me spiritual right
To travel through that region bright.

The voice was soft, and she who spake
Was walking by her native lake:
The salutation had to me
The very sound of courtesy:
Its power was felt; and while my eye
Was fixed upon the glowing Sky,
The echo of the voice enwrought
A human sweetness with the thought
Of travelling through the world that lay
Before me in my endless way.

THE SOLITARY REAPER

Behold her, single in the field,
Yon solitary Highland Lass!
Reaping and singing by herself;
Stop here, or gently pass!
Alone she cuts and binds the grain,
And sings a melancholy strain;
O listen! for the Vale profound
Is overflowing with the sound.

No Nightingale did ever chaunt
More welcome notes to weary bands
Of travellers in some shady haunt,
Among Arabian sands:

10

A voice so thrilling ne'er was heard
In spring-time from the Cuckoo-bird,
Breaking the silence of the seas
Among the farthest Hebrides.

Will no one tell me what she sings?—
Perhaps the plaintive numbers flow
For old, unhappy, far-off things,
And battles long ago: 20
Or is it some more humble lay,
Familiar matter of to-day?
Some natural sorrow, loss, or pain,
That has been, and may be again?

Whate'er the theme, the Maiden sang
As if her song could have no ending;
I saw her singing at her work,
And o'er the sickle bending;—
I listened, motionless and still;
And, as I mounted up the hill   30
The music in my heart I bore,
Long after it was heard no more.

YARROW UNVISITED

From Stirling castle we had seen
That mazy Forth unravelled;
Had trod the banks of Clyde, and Tay,
And with the Tweed had travelled;
And when we came to Clovenford,
Then said my "*winsome Marrow*,"
"Whate'er betide, we'll turn aside,
And see the Braes of Yarrow."

"Let Yarrow folk, *frae* Selkirk town,
Who have been buying, selling,   10
Go back to Yarrow, 'tis their own;
Each maiden to her dwelling!
On Yarrow's banks let herons feed,
Hares couch, and rabbits burrow!

But we will downward with the Tweed,
Nor turn aside to Yarrow.

"There's Galla Water, Leader Haughs,
Both lying right before us;
And Dryborough, where with chiming Tweed
The lintwhites sing in chorus;   20
There's pleasant Tiviot-dale, a land
Made blithe with plough and harrow:
Why throw away a needful day
To go in search of Yarrow?

"What's Yarrow but a river bare,
That glides the dark hills under?
There are a thousand such elsewhere
As worthy of your wonder."
—Strange words they seemed of slight and scorn
My True-love sighed for sorrow;   30
And looked me in the face, to think
I thus could speak of Yarrow!

"Oh! green," said I, "are Yarrow's holms,
And sweet is Yarrow flowing!
Fair hangs the apple frae the rock,
But we will leave it growing.
O'er hilly path, and open Strath,
We'll wander Scotland thorough;
But, though so near, we will not turn
Into the dale of Yarrow.   40

"Let beeves and home-bred kine partake
The sweets of Burn-mill meadow;
The swan on still St. Mary's Lake
Float double, swan and shadow!
We will not see them; will not go,
To-day, nor yet to-morrow,
Enough if in our hearts we know
There's such a place as Yarrow.

"Be Yarrow stream unseen, unknown!
It must, or we shall rue it: 50

We have a vision of our own;
Ah! why should we undo it?
The treasured dreams of times long past,
We 'll keep them, winsome Marrow!
For when we 're there, although 'tis fair,
'Twill be another Yarrow!

"If Care with freezing years should come,
And wandering seem but folly,—
Should we be loth to stir from home,
And yet be melancholy;
Should life be dull, and spirits low,
'Twill soothe us in our sorrow,
That earth has something yet to show,
The bonny holms of Yarrow!"

60

OCTOBER, 1803

These times strike monied worldlings with dismay:
Even rich men, brave by nature, taint the air
With words of apprehension and despair:
While tens of thousands, thinking on the affray,
Men unto whom sufficient for the day
And minds not stinted or untilled are given,
Sound, healthy, children of the God of heaven,
Are cheerful as the rising sun in May.
What do we gather hence but firmer faith
That every gift of noble origin
Is breathed upon by Hope's perpetual breath;
That virtue and the faculties within
Are vital,—and that riches are akin
To fear, to change, to cowardice, and death?

TO THE MEN OF KENT

OCTOBER, 1803

Vanguard of Liberty, ye men of Kent,
Ye children of a Soil that doth advance
Her haughty brow against the coast of France,
Now is the time to prove your hardiment!
To France be words of invitation sent!
They from their fields can see the countenance
Of your fierce war, may ken the glittering lance
And hear you shouting forth your brave intent.
Left single, in bold parley, ye, of yore,
Did from the Norman win a gallant wreath;
Confirmed the charters that were yours before;—
No parleying now! In Britain is one breath;
We all are with you now from shore to shore:—
Ye men of Kent, 'tis victory or death!

IN THE PASS OF KILLICRANKY

AN INVASION BEING EXPECTED, OCTOBER, 1803.

Six thousand veterans practised in war's game,
Tried men, at Killicranky were arrayed
Against an equal host that wore the plaid,
Shepherds and herdsmen.—Like a whirlwind came
The Highlanders, the slaughter spread like flame;
And Garry, thundering down his mountain-road,
Was stopped, and could not breathe beneath the load
Of the dead bodies.—'Twas a day of shame
For them whom precept and the pedantry
Of cold mechanic battle do enslave.
O for a single hour of that Dundee,
Who on that day the word of onset gave!
Like conquest would the Men of England see;
And her Foes find a like inglorious grave.

LINES ON THE EXPECTED INVASION, 1803

Come ye—who, if (which Heaven avert!) the Land
Were with herself at strife, would take your stand,
Like gallant Falkland, by the Monarch's side,
And, like Montrose, make Loyalty your pride—
Come ye—who, not less zealous, might display
Banners at enmity with regal sway,
And, like the Pyms and Miltons of that day,
Think that a State would live in sounder health
If Kingship bowed its head to Commonwealth—
Ye too—whom no discreditable fear
Would keep, perhaps with many a fruitless tear,
Uncertain what to choose and how to steer—
And ye—who might mistake for sober sense
And wise reserve the plea of indolence—
Come ye—whate'er your creed—O waken all,
Whate'er your temper, at your Country's call;
Resolving (this a free-born Nation can)
To have one Soul, and perish to a man,
Or save this honoured Land from every Lord
But British reason and the British sword.

TO THE CUCKOO

O blithe New-comer! I have heard,
I hear thee and rejoice.
O Cuckoo! shall I call thee Bird,
Or but a wandering Voice?

While I am lying on the grass
Thy twofold shout I hear,
From hill to hill it seems to pass,
At once far off, and near.
Though babbling only to the Vale,
Of sunshine and of flowers,   10

Thou bringest unto me a tale
Of visionary hours.

Thrice welcome, darling of the Spring!
Even yet thou art to me
No bird, but an invisible thing,
A voice, a mystery;

The same whom in my school-boy days
I listened to; that Cry
Which made me look a thousand ways
In bush, and tree, and sky.   20

To seek thee did I often rove
Through woods and on the green;
And thou wert still a hope, a love;
Still longed for, never seen.

And I can listen to thee yet;
Can lie upon the plain
And listen, till I do beget
That golden time again.

O blessèd Bird! the earth we pace
Again appears to be   30
An unsubstantial, faery place;
That is fit home for Thee!

"SHE WAS A PHANTOM OF DELIGHT"

She was a Phantom of delight
When first she gleamed upon my sight;
A lovely Apparition, sent
To be a moment's ornament;
Her eyes as stars of Twilight fair;

Like Twilight's, too, her dusky hair;
But all things else about her drawn
From May-time and the cheerful Dawn;
A dancing Shape, an Image gay,
To haunt, to startle, and way-lay.   10

I saw her upon nearer view,
A Spirit, yet a Woman too!
Her household motions light and free,
And steps of virgin-liberty;
A countenance in which did meet
Sweet records, promises as sweet;
A Creature not too bright or good
For human nature's daily food;
For transient sorrows, simple wiles,
Praise, blame, love, kisses, tears, and smiles.   20

And now I see with eye serene
The very pulse of the machine;
A Being breathing thoughtful breath,
A Traveller between life and death;
The reason firm, the temperate will,
Endurance, foresight, strength, and skill;
A perfect Woman, nobly planned,
To warn, to comfort, and command;
And yet a Spirit still, and bright
With something of angelic light.   30

"I WANDERED LONELY AS A CLOUD"

I wandered lonely as a cloud
That floats on high o'er vales and hills,
When all at once I saw a crowd,
A host, of golden daffodils;
Beside the lake, beneath the trees,
Fluttering and dancing in the breeze.
Continuous as the stars that shine
And twinkle on the milky way,
They stretched in never-ending line
Along the margin of a bay:
Ten thousand saw I at a glance,
Tossing their heads in sprightly dance.

The waves beside them danced; but they
Out-did the sparkling waves in glee:

A poet could not but be gay,
In such a jocund company:
I gazed—and gazed—but little thought
What wealth the show to me had brought:

For oft, when on my couch I lie,
In vacant or in pensive mood,
They flash upon that inward eye
Which is the bliss of solitude;
And then my heart with pleasure fills,
And dances with the daffodils.

THE AFFLICTION OF MARGARET

I

Where art thou, my beloved Son,
Where art thou, worse to me than dead?
Oh find me, prosperous or undone!
Or, if the grave be now thy bed,
Why am I ignorant of the same
That I may rest; and neither blame
Nor sorrow may attend thy name?

II

Seven years, alas! to have received
No tidings of an only child;
To have despaired, have hoped, believed,   10
And been for evermore beguiled;
Sometimes with thoughts of very bliss!
I catch at them, and then I miss;
Was ever darkness like to this?

III

He was among the prime in worth,
An object beauteous to behold;
Well born, well bred; I sent him forth
Ingenuous, innocent, and bold:
If things ensued that wanted grace,
As hath been said, they were not base;   20
And never blush was on my face.

IV

Ah! little doth the young one dream,
When full of play and childish cares,
What power is in his wildest scream,
Heard by his mother unawares!
He knows it not, he cannot guess:
Years to a mother bring distress;
But do not make her love the less.

V

Neglect me! no, I suffered long
From that ill thought; and, being blind,   30
Said, "Pride shall help me in my wrong;
Kind mother have I been, as kind
As ever breathed:" and that is true;
I 've wet my path with tears like dew,
Weeping for him when no one knew.

VI

My Son, if thou be humbled, poor,
Hopeless of honour and of gain,
Oh! do not dread thy mother's door;
Think not of me with grief and pain:
I now can see with better eyes;   40
And worldly grandeur I despise,
And fortune with her gifts and lies.

VII

Alas! the fowls of heaven have wings,
And blasts of heaven will aid their flight;
They mount—how short a voyage brings
The wanderers back to their delight!
Chains tie us down by land and sea;
And wishes, vain as mine, may be
All that is left to comfort thee.

VIII

Perhaps some dungeon hears thee groan,   50
Maimed, mangled by inhuman men;
Or thou upon a desert thrown
Inheritest the lion's den;

Or hast been summoned to the deep,
Thou, thou and all thy mates, to keep
An incommunicable sleep.

IX

I look for ghosts; but none will force
Their way to me: 'tis falsely said
That there was ever intercourse
Between the living and the dead;   **60**
For, surely, then I should have sight
Of him I wait for day and night,
With love and longings infinite.

X

My apprehensions come in crowds;
I dread the rustling of the grass;
The very shadows of the clouds
Have power to shake me as they pass:
I question things and do not find
One that will answer to my mind;
And all the world appears unkind.   **70**

XI

Beyond participation lie
My troubles, and beyond relief:
If any chance to heave a sigh,
They pity me and not my grief.
Then come to me my son, or send
Some tidings that my woes may end;
I have no other earthly friend!

THE SMALL CELANDINE

There is a Flower, the lesser Celandine,
That shrinks, like many more, from cold and rain;
And, the first moment that the sun may shine,
    Bright as the sun himself, 'tis out again!

When hailstones have been falling, swarm on swarm,
Or blasts the green field and the trees distrest,

Oft have I seen it muffled up from harm,
In close self-shelter, like a Thing at rest.

But lately, one rough day, this Flower I passed
And recognised it, though an altered form,
Now standing forth an offering to the blast,
And buffeted at will by rain and storm.

I stopped, and said with inly-muttered voice,
"It doth not love the shower, nor seek the cold:
This neither is its courage nor its choice,
But its necessity in being old.

"The sunshine may not cheer it, nor the dew;
It cannot help itself in its decay;
Stiff in its members, withered, changed of hue."
And, in my spleen, I smiled that it was grey.

To be a Prodigal's Favourite—then, worse truth,
A Miser's Pensioner—behold our lot!
O Man, that from thy fair and shining youth
Age might but take the things Youth needed not!

ODE TO DUTY

Stern Daughter of the Voice of God!
O Duty! if that name thou love
Who art a light to guide, a rod
To check the erring, and reprove;
Thou, who art victory and law
When empty terrors overawe;
From vain temptations dost set free;
And calm'st the weary strife of frail humanity!

There are who ask not if thine eye
Be on them; who, in love and truth,
Where no misgiving is, rely
Upon the genial sense of youth:
Glad Hearts! without reproach or blot
Who do thy work, and know it not:

10

Oh! if through confidence misplaced
They fail, thy saving arms, dread Power! around them cast.

Serene will be our days and bright,
And happy will our nature be,
When love is an unerring light,
And joy its own security. 20
And they a blissful course may hold
Even now, who, not unwisely bold,
Live in the spirit of this creed;
Yet seek thy firm support, according to their need.

I, loving freedom, and untried;
No sport of every random gust,
Yet being to myself a guide,
Too blindly have reposed my trust:
And oft, when in my heart was heard
Thy timely mandate, I deferred 30
The task, in smoother walks to stray;
But thee I now would serve more strictly, if I may.
Through no disturbance of my soul,
Or strong compunction in me wrought,
I supplicate for thy control;
But in the quietness of thought:
Me this unchartered freedom tires;
I feel the weight of chance-desires:
My hopes no more must change their name,
I long for a repose that ever is the same. 40

Stern Lawgiver! yet thou dost wear
The Godhead's most benignant grace;
Nor know we anything so fair
As is the smile upon thy face:
Flowers laugh before thee on their beds
And fragrance in thy footing treads;
Thou dost preserve the stars from wrong;
And the most ancient heavens, through Thee, are fresh and
    strong.

To humbler functions, awful Power!
I call thee: I myself commend 50

Unto thy guidance from this hour;
Oh, let my weakness have an end!
Give unto me, made lowly wise,
The spirit of self-sacrifice;
The confidence of reason give;
And in the light of truth thy Bondman let me live!

"WHEN TO THE ATTRACTIONS OF THE BUSY WORLD"

When, to the attractions of the busy world,
Preferring studious leisure, I had chosen
A habitation in this peaceful Vale,
Sharp season followed of continual storm
In deepest winter; and, from week to week,
Pathway, and lane, and public road, were clogged
With frequent showers of snow. Upon a hill
At a short distance from my cottage, stands
A stately Fir-grove, whither I was wont
To hasten, for I found, beneath the roof   10
Of that perennial shade, a cloistral place
Of refuge, with an unincumbered floor.
Here, in safe covert, on the shallow snow,
And, sometimes, on a speck of visible earth,
The redbreast near me hopped; nor was I loth
To sympathise with vulgar coppice birds
That, for protection from the nipping blast,
Hither repaired.—A single beech-tree grew
Within this grove of firs! and, on the fork
Of that one beech, appeared a thrush's nest;   20
A last year's nest, conspicuously built
At such small elevation from the ground
As gave sure sign that they, who in that house
Of nature and of love had made their home
Amid the fir-trees, all the summer long
Dwelt in a tranquil spot. And oftentimes,
A few sheep, stragglers from some mountain-flock,
Would watch my motions with suspicious stare,

From the remotest outskirts of the grove,—
Some nook where they had made their final stand,   30
Huddling together from two fears—the fear
Of me and of the storm. Full many an hour
Here did I lose. But in this grove the trees
Had been so thickly planted, and had thriven
In such perplexed and intricate array;
That vainly did I seek, beneath their stems
A length of open space, where to and fro
My feet might move without concern or care;
And, baffled thus, though earth from day to day
Was fettered, and the air by storm disturbed,   40
I ceased the shelter to frequent,—and prized,
Less than I wished to prize, that calm recess.
    The snows dissolved, and genial Spring returned
To clothe the fields with verdure. Other haunts
Meanwhile were mine; till, one bright April day,
By chance retiring from the glare of noon
To this forsaken covert, there I found
A hoary pathway traced between the trees,
And winding on with such an easy line
Along a natural opening, that I stood   50
Much wondering how I could have sought in vain
For what was now so obvious. To abide,
For an allotted interval of ease,
Under my cottage-roof, had gladly come
From the wild sea a cherished Visitant;
And with the sight of this same path—begun,
Begun and ended, in the shady grove,
Pleasant conviction flashed upon my mind
That, to this opportune recess allured,
He had surveyed it with a finer eye,   60
A heart more wakeful; and had worn the track
By pacing here, unwearied and alone,
In that habitual restlessness of foot
That haunts the Sailor measuring o'er and o'er
His short domain upon the vessel's deck,
While she pursues her course through the dreary sea.
    When thou hadst quitted Esthwaite's pleasant shore,

And taken thy first leave of those green hills
And rocks that were the play-ground of thy youth,
Year followed year, my Brother! and we two,   70
Conversing not, knew little in what mould
Each other's mind was fashioned; and at length,
When once again we met in Grasmere Vale,
Between us there was little other bond
Than common feelings of fraternal love.
But thou, a Schoolboy, to the sea hadst carried
Undying recollections! Nature there
Was with thee; she, who loved us both, she still
Was with thee; and even so didst thou become
A *silent* Poet; from the solitude   80
Of the vast sea didst bring a watchful heart
Still couchant, an inevitable ear,
And an eye practised like a blind man's touch.
—Back to the joyless Ocean thou art gone;
Nor from this vestige of thy musing hours
Could I withhold thy honoured name,—and now
I love the fir-grove with a perfect love.
Thither do I withdraw when cloudless suns
Shine hot, or wind blows troublesome and strong;
And there I sit at evening, when the steep   90
Of Silver-how, and Grasmere's peaceful lake,
And one green island, gleam between the stems
Of the dark firs, a visionary scene!
And, while I gaze upon the spectacle
Of clouded splendour, on this dream-like sight
Of solemn loveliness, I think on thee,
My Brother, and on all which thou hast lost.
Nor seldom, if I rightly guess, while Thou,
Muttering the verses which I muttered first
Among the mountains, through the midnight watch   100
Art pacing thoughtfully the vessel's deck
In some far region, here, while o'er my head,
At every impulse of the moving breeze,
The fir-grove murmurs with a sea-like sound,
Alone I tread this path;—for aught I know,
Timing my steps to thine; and, with a store

Of undistinguishable sympathies,
Mingling most earnest wishes for the day
When we, and others whom we love, shall meet
A second time, in Grasmere's happy Vale.　　　　　**110**

ELEGIAC STANZAS

SUGGESTED BY A PICTURE OF PEELE CASTLE, IN A STORM, PAINTED BY SIR GEORGE BEAUMONT

I was thy neighbour once, thou rugged Pile!
Four summer weeks I dwelt in sight of thee:
I saw thee every day; and all the while
Thy Form was sleeping on a glassy sea.

So pure the sky, so quiet was the air!
So like, so very like, was day to day!
Whene'er I looked, thy Image still was there;
It trembled, but it never passed away.

How perfect was the calm! it seemed no sleep;
No mood, which season takes away, or brings:　　　**10**
I could have fancied that the mighty Deep
Was even the gentlest of all gentle Things.

Ah! THEN, if mine had been the Painter's hand,
To express what then I saw; and add the gleam,
The light that never was, on sea or land,
The consecration, and the Poet's dream;

I would have planted thee, thou hoary Pile
Amid a world how different from this!
Beside a sea that could not cease to smile;
On tranquil land, beneath a sky of bliss.　　　　**20**

Thou shouldst have seemed a treasure-house divine
Of peaceful years; a chronicle of heaven;—
Of all the sunbeams that did ever shine
The very sweetest had to thee been given.

A Picture had it been of lasting ease,
Elysian quiet, without toil or strife;

No motion but the moving tide, a breeze,
Or merely silent Nature's breathing life.

Such, in the fond illusion of my heart,
Such Picture would I at that time have made: 30
And seen the soul of truth in every part,
A stedfast pace that might not be betrayed.

So once it would have been,—'tis so no more;
I have submitted to a new control:
A power is gone, which nothing can restore;
A deep distress hath humanised my Soul.

Not for a moment could I now behold
A smiling sea, and be what I have been:
The feeling of my loss will ne'er be old;
This, which I know, I speak with mind serene.   40

Then, Beaumont, Friend! who would have been the Friend,
If he had lived, of Him whom I deplore,
This work of thine I blame not, but commend;
This sea in anger, and that dismal shore.

O 'tis a passionate Work!—yet wise and well,
Well chosen is the spirit that is here;
That Hulk which labours in the deadly swell,
This rueful sky, this pageantry of fear!

And this huge Castle, standing here sublime,
I love to see the look with which it braves,   50
Cased in the unfeeling armour of old time,
The lightning, the fierce wind, and trampling waves.

Farewell, farewell the heart that lives alone,
Housed in a dream, at distance from the Kind!
Such happiness, wherever it be known,
Is to be pitied; for 'tis surely blind.

But welcome fortitude, and patient cheer,
And frequent sights of what is to be borne!
Such sights, or worse, as are before me here.—
Not without hope we suffer and we mourn.   60

TO A YOUNG LADY

WHO HAD BEEN REPROACHED FOR TAKING
LONG WALKS IN THE COUNTRY

Dear Child of Nature, let them rail!
—There is a nest in a green dale,
A harbour and a hold;
Where thou, a Wife and Friend, shalt see
Thy own heart-stirring days, and be
A light to young and old.

There, healthy as a shepherd boy,
And treading among flowers of joy
Which at no season fade,
Thou, while thy babes around thee cling,
Shalt show us how divine a thing
A Woman may be made.

Thy thoughts and feelings shall not die,
Nor leave thee, when grey hairs are nigh,
A melancholy slave;
But an old age serene and bright,
And lovely as a Lapland night,
Shall lead thee to thy grave.

THE WAGGONER

CANTO FIRST

'Tis spent—this burning day of June!
Soft darkness o'er its latest gleams is stealing;
The buzzing dor-hawk, round and round, is wheeling,—
That solitary bird
Is all that can be heard
In silence deeper far than that of deepest noon!
    Confiding Glow-worms, 'tis a night
Propitious to your earth-born light!
But, where the scattered stars are seen
In hazy straits the clouds between,   10
Each, in his station twinkling not,

Seems changed into a pallid spot.
The mountains against heaven's grave weight
Rise up, and grow to wondrous height.
The air, as in a lion's den,
Is close and hot;—and now and then
Comes a tired and sultry breeze
With a haunting and a panting,
Like the stifling of disease;
But the dews allay the heat,   20
And the silence makes it sweet.
Hush, there is some one on the stir!
'Tis Benjamin the Waggoner;
Who long hath trod this toilsome way,
Companion of the night and day.
That far-off tinkling's drowsy cheer,
Mixed with a faint yet grating sound
In a moment lost and found,
The Wain announces—by whose side
Along the banks of Rydal Mere   30
He paces on, a trusty Guide,—
Listen! you can scarcely hear!
Hither he his course is bending;—
Now he leaves the lower ground,
And up the craggy hill ascending
Many a stop and stay he makes,
Many a breathing-fit he takes;—
Steep the way and wearisome,
Yet all the while his whip is dumb!

The Horses have worked with right good-will,   40
And so have gained the top of the hill;
He was patient, they were strong,
And now they smoothly glide along,
Recovering breath, and pleased to win
The praises of mild Benjamin.
Heaven shield him from mishap and snare!
But why so early with this prayer?—
Is it for threatenings in the sky?
Or for some other danger nigh?
No; none is near him yet, though he   50

Be one of much infirmity;
For at the bottom of the brow,
Where once the DOVE and OLIVE-BOUGH
Offered a greeting of good ale
To all who entered Grasmere Vale;
And called on him who must depart
To leave it with a jovial heart;
There, where the DOVE and OLIVE-BOUGH
Once hung, a Poet harbours now,
A simple water-drinking Bard;   60
Why need our Hero then (though frail
His best resolves) be on his guard?
He marches by, secure and bold;
Yet while he thinks on times of old,
It seems that all looks wondrous cold;
He shrugs his shoulders, shakes his head,
And, for the honest folk within,
It is a doubt with Benjamin
Whether they be alive or dead!

   Here is no danger,—none at all!   70
Beyond his wish he walks secure;
But pass a mile—and *then* for trial,—
Then for the pride of self-denial;
If he resist that tempting door,
Which with such friendly voice will call;
If he resist those casement panes,
And that bright gleam which thence will fall
Upon his Leaders' bells and manes,
Inviting him with cheerful lure:
For still, though all be dark elsewhere,   80
Some shining notice will be *there,*
Of open house and ready fare.

   The place to Benjamin right well
Is known, and by as strong a spell
As used to be that sign of love
And hope—the OLIVE-BOUGH and DOVE;
He knows it to his cost, good Man!
Who does not know the famous SWAN?
Object uncouth! and yet our boast,

For it was planted by the Host; 90
His own conceit the figure planned,
'Twas coloured all by his own hand;
And that frail Child of thirsty clay,
Of whom I sing this rustic lay,
Could tell with self-dissatisfaction
Quaint stories of the bird's attraction!
    Well! that is past—and in despite
Of open door and shining light.
And now the conqueror essays
The long ascent of Dunmail-raise; 100
And with his team is gentle here
As when he clomb from Rydal Mere;
His whip they do not dread—his voice
They only hear it to rejoice.
To stand or go is at *their* pleasure;
Their efforts and their time they measure
By generous pride within the breast;
And, while they strain, and while they rest,
He thus pursues his thoughts at leisure.
    Now I am fairly safe to-night— 110
And with proud cause my heart is light:
I trespassed lately worse than ever—
But Heaven has blest a good endeavour;
And, to my soul's content, I find
The evil One is left behind.
Yes, let my master fume and fret,
Here am I—with my horses yet!
My jolly team, he finds that ye
Will work for nobody but me!
Full proof of this the Country gained; 120
It knows how ye were vexed and strained,
And forced unworthy stripes to bear,
When trusted to another's care.
Here was it—on this rugged slope,
Which now ye climb with heart and hope,
I saw you, between rage and fear,
Plunge, and fling back a spiteful ear,
And ever more and more confused,

As ye were more and more abused:
As chance would have it, passing by   130
I saw you in that jeopardy:
A word from me was like a charm:
Ye pulled together with one mind;
And your huge burthen, safe from harm,
Moved like a vessel in the wind!
—Yes, without me, up hills so high
'Tis vain to strive for mastery.
Then grieve not, jolly team! though tough
The road we travel, steep, and rough;
Though Rydal-heights and Dunmail-raise,   140
And all their fellow banks and braes,
Full often make you stretch and strain,
And halt for breath and halt again,
Yet to their sturdiness 'tis owing
That side by side we still are going!
    While Benjamin in earnest mood
His meditations thus pursued,
A storm, which had been smothered long,
Was growing inwardly more strong;
And, in its struggles to get free,   150
Was busily employed as he.
The thunder had begun to growl—
He heard not, too intent of soul;
The air was now without a breath—
He marked not that 't was still as death.
But soon large rain-drops on his head
Fell with the weight of drops of lead;—
He starts—and takes, at the admonition,
A sage survey of his condition.
The road is black before his eyes,   160
Glimmering faintly where it lies;
Black is the sky—and every hill,
Up to the sky, is blacker still—
Sky, hill, and dale, one dismal room,
Hung round and overhung with gloom;
Save that above a single height
Is to be seen a lurid light,

Above Helm-crag—a streak half dead,
A burning of portentous red;
And near that lurid light, full well   170
The ASTROLOGER, sage Sidrophel,
Where at his desk and book he sits,
Puzzling aloft his curious wits;
He whose domain is held in common
With no one but the ANCIENT WOMAN,
Cowering beside her rifted cell,
As if intent on magic spell;—
Dread pair, that, spite of wind and weather,
Still sit upon Helm-crag together!

  The ASTROLOGER was not unseen   180
By solitary Benjamin;
But total darkness came anon,
And he and everything was gone:
And suddenly a ruffling breeze,
(That would have rocked the sounding trees
Had aught of sylvan growth been there)
Swept through the Hollow long and bare:
The rain rushed down—the road was battered,
As with the force of billows shattered;
The horses are dismayed, nor know   190
Whether they should stand or go;
And Benjamin is groping near them,
Sees nothing, and can scarcely hear them.
He is astounded,—wonder not,—
With such a charge in such a spot;
Astounded in the mountain gap
With thunder-peals, clap after clap,
Close-treading on the silent flashes—
And somewhere, as he thinks, by crashes
Among the rocks; with weight of rain,   200
And sullen motions long and slow,
That to a dreary distance go—
Till, breaking in upon the dying strain,
A rending o'er his head begins the fray again.
  Meanwhile, uncertain what to do,
And oftentimes compelled to halt,

The horses cautiously pursue
Their way, without mishap or fault;
And now have reached that pile of stones,
Heaped over brave King Dunmail's bones;   210
His who had once supreme command,
Last king of rocky Cumberland;
His bones, and those of all his Power
Slain here in a disastrous hour!

    When, passing through this narrow strait,
Stony, and dark, and desolate,
Benjamin can faintly hear
A voice that comes from some one near,
A female voice:—"Whoe'er you be,
Stop," it exclaimed, "and pity me!"   220
And, less in pity than in wonder,
Amid the darkness and the thunder,
The Waggoner, with prompt command,
Summons his horses to a stand.

    While, with increasing agitation,
The Woman urged her supplication,
In rueful words, with sobs between—
The voice of tears that fell unseen;
There came a flash—a startling glare,
And all Seat-Sandal was laid bare!   230
'Tis not a time for nice suggestion,
And Benjamin, without a question,
Taking her for some way-worn rover,
Said, "Mount, and get you under cover!"

    Another voice, in tone as hoarse
As a swoln brook with rugged course,
Cried out, "Good brother, why so fast?
I 've had a glimpse of you—*avast!*
Or, since it suits you to be civil,
Take her at once—for good and evil!"   240
    "It is my Husband," softly said
The Woman, as if half-afraid:
By this time she was snug within,
Through help of honest Benjamin;
She and her Babe, which to her breast

With thankfulness the Mother pressed;
And now the same strong voice more near
Said cordially, "My Friend, what cheer?
Rough doings these! as God's my judge
The sky owes somebody a grudge!   250
We 've had in half an hour or less
A twelvemonth's terror and distress!"
    Then Benjamin entreats the Man
Would mount, too, quickly as he can:
The Sailor—Sailor now no more,
But such he had been heretofore—
To courteous Benjamin replied,
"Go you your way, and mind not me;
For I must have, whate'er betide,
My Ass and fifty things beside,—   260
Go, and I 'll follow speedily!"
    The Waggon moves—and with its load
Descends along the sloping road;
And the rough Sailor instantly
Turns to a little tent hard by:
For when, at closing-in of day,
The family had come that way,
Green pasture and the soft warm air
Tempted them to settle there.—
Green is the grass for beast to graze,   270
Around the stones of Dunmail-raise!
    The Sailor gathers up his bed,
Takes down the canvas overhead;
And, after farewell to the place,
A parting word—though not of grace,
Pursues, with Ass and all his store,
The way the Waggon went before.

CANTO SECOND

If Wytheburn's modest House of prayer,
As lowly as the lowliest dwelling,
Had, with its belfry's humble stock,
A little pair that hang in air,
Been mistress also of a clock,

(And one, too, not in crazy plight)
Twelve strokes that clock would have been telling
Under the brow of old Helvellyn—
Its bead-roll of midnight,
Then, when the Hero of my tale   10
Was passing by, and, down the vale
(The vale now silent, hushed I ween
As if a storm had never been)
Proceeding with a mind at ease;
While the old Familiar of the seas,
Intent to use his utmost haste,
Gained ground upon the Waggon fast,
And gives another lusty cheer;
For spite of rumbling of the wheels,
A welcome greeting he can hear;—   20
It is a fiddle in its glee
Dinning from the CHERRY TREE!

    Thence the sound—the light is there—
As Benjamin is now aware,
Who, to his inward thoughts confined,
Had almost reached the festive door,
When, startled by the Sailor's roar,
He hears a sound and sees a light,
And in a moment calls to mind
That 'tis the village MERRY-NIGHT!   30

    Although before in no dejection,
At this insidious recollection
His heart with sudden joy is filled,—
His ears are by the music thrilled,
His eyes take pleasure in the road
Glittering before him bright and broad;
And Benjamin is wet and cold,
And there are reasons manifold
That make the good, tow'rds which he's yearning,
Look fairly like a lawful earning.   40

    Nor has thought time to come and go,
To vibrate between yes and no;
For, cries the Sailor, "Glorious chance
That blew us hither!—let him dance,

Who can or will!—my honest soul,
Our treat shall be a friendly bowl!"
He draws him to the door—"Come in,
Come, come," cries he to Benjamin!
And Benjamin—ah, woe is me!
Gave the word—the horses heard   50
And halted, though reluctantly.
      "Blithe souls and lightsome hearts have we,
Feasting at the CHERRY TREE!"
This was the outside proclamation,
This was the inside salutation;
What bustling—jostling—high and low!
A universal overflow!
What tankards foaming from the tap!
What store of cakes in every lap!
What thumping—stumping—overhead!   60
The thunder had not been more busy:
With such a stir you would have said,
This little place may well be dizzy!
'Tis who can dance with greatest vigour—
'Tis what can be most prompt and eager;
As if it heard the fiddle's call,
The pewter clatters on the wall;
The very bacon shows its feeling,
Swinging from the smoky ceiling!
      A steaming bowl, a blazing fire,   70
What greater good can heart desire?
'Twere worth a wise man's while to try
The utmost anger of the sky:
To *seek* for thoughts of a gloomy cast,
If such the bright amends at last.
Now should you say I judge amiss,
The CHERRY TREE shows proof of this;
For soon of all the happy there,
Our Travellers are the happiest pair;
All care with Benjamin is gone—   80
A Cæsar past the Rubicon!
He thinks not of his long, long strife;—
The Sailor, Man by nature gay,

Hath no resolves to throw away;
And he hath now forgot his Wife,
Hath quite forgotten her—or may be
Thinks her the luckiest soul on earth,
Within that warm and peaceful berth,
   Under cover,
   Terror over,   90
Sleeping by her sleeping Baby,
 With bowl that sped from hand to hand,
The gladdest of the gladsome band,
Amid their own delight and fun,
They hear—when every dance is done,
When every whirling bout is o'er—
The fiddle's *squeak*—that call to bliss,
Ever followed by a kiss;
They envy not the happy lot,
But enjoy their own the more!   100
 While thus our jocund Travellers fare,
Up springs the Sailor from his chair—
Limps (for I might have told before
That he was lame) across the floor—
Is gone—returns—and with a prize;
With what?—a Ship of lusty size;
A gallant stately Man-of-war,
Fixed on a smoothly-sliding car.
Surprise to all, but most surprise
To Benjamin, who rubs his eyes,   110
Not knowing that he had befriended
A Man so gloriously attended!
 "This," cries the Sailor, "a Third-rate is—
Stand back, and you shall see her gratis!
This was the Flag-ship at the Nile,
The Vanguard—you may smirk and smile,
But pretty Maid, if you look near,
You 'll find you 've much in little here!
A nobler ship did never swim,
And you shall see her in full trim: 120
I 'll set, my friends, to do you honour,
Set every inch of sail upon her."

So said, so done; and masts, sails, yards,
He names them all; and interlards
His speech with uncouth terms of art,
Accomplished in the showman's part;
And then, as from a sudden check,
Cries out—" 'Tis there, the quarter-deck
On which brave Admiral Nelson stood—
A sight that would have roused your blood! 130
One eye he had, which, bright as ten,
Burned like a fire among his men;
Let this be land, and that be sea,
Here lay the French—and *thus* came we!"
   Hushed was by this the fiddle's sound,
The dancers all were gathered round,
And, such the stillness of the house,
You might have heard a nibbling mouse;
While, borrowing helps where'er he may,
The Sailor through the story runs 140
Of ships to ships and guns to guns;
And does his utmost to display
The dismal conflict, and the might
And terror of that marvellous night!
"A bowl, a bowl of double measure,"
Cries Benjamin, "a draught of length,
To Nelson, England's pride and treasure
Her bulwark and her tower of strength!"
When Benjamin had seized the bowl,
The mastiff, from beneath the waggon, 150
Where he lay, watchful as a dragon,
Rattled his chain;—'t was all in vain,
For Benjamin, triumphant soul!
He heard the monitory growl;
Heard—and in opposition quaffed
A deep, determined, desperate draught!
Nor did the battered Tar forget,
Or flinch from what he deemed his debt:
Then, like a hero crowned with laurel,
Back to her place the ship he led; 160
Wheeled her back in full apparel;

And so, flag flying at mast head,
Re-yoked her to the Ass:—anon,
Cries Benjamin, "We must be gone."
Thus, after two hours' hearty stay,
Again behold them on their way!

CANTO THIRD

Right gladly had the horses stirred,
When they the wished-for greeting heard,
The whip's loud notice from the door,
That they were free to move once more.
You think, those doings must have bred
In them disheartening doubts and dread;
No, not a horse of all the eight,
Although it be a moonless night,
Fears either for himself or freight;
For this they know (and let it hide,   10
In part, the offences of their guide)
That Benjamin, with clouded brains,
Is worth the best with all their pains;
And, if they had a prayer to make,
The prayer would be that they may take
With him whatever comes in course,
The better fortune or the worse;
That no one else may have business near them,
And, drunk or sober, he may steer them.
    So, forth in dauntless mood they fare,   20
And with them goes the guardian pair.
    Now, heroes, for the true commotion,
The triumph of your late devotion
Can aught on earth impede delight,
Still mounting to a higher height;
And higher still—a greedy flight!
Can any low-born care pursue her?
Can any mortal clog come to her?
No notion have they—not a thought,
That is from joyless regions brought!   30
And, while they coast the silent lake,
Their inspiration I partake;

Share their empyreal spirits—yea,
With their enraptured vision, see—
O fancy—what a jubilee!
What shifting pictures—clad in gleams
Of colour bright as feverish dreams!
Earth, spangled sky, and lake serene,
Involved and restless all—a scene
Pregnant with mutual exaltation,   40
Rich change, and multiplied creation!
This sight to me the Muse imparts;—
And then, what kindness in their hearts!
What tears of rapture, what vow-making,
Profound entreaties, and hand-shaking!
What solemn, vacant, interlacing,
As if they'd fall asleep embracing!
Then, in the turbulence of glee,
And in the excess of amity,
Says Benjamin, "That Ass of thine,   50
He spoils thy sport, and hinders mine:
If he were tethered to the waggon,
He'd drag as well what he is dragging,
And we, as brother should with brother,
Might trudge it alongside each other!"

Forthwith, obedient to command,
The horses made a quiet stand;
And to the waggon's skirts was tied
The Creature, by the Mastiff's side,
The Mastiff wondering, and perplext   60
With dread of what will happen next;
And thinking it but sorry cheer,
To have such company so near!

This new arrangement made, the Wain
Through the still night proceeds again;
No Moon hath risen her light to lend;
But indistinctly may be kenned
The VANGUARD, following close behind,
Sails spread, as if to catch the wind!
"Thy wife and child are snug and warm,   70
Thy ship will travel without harm;

I like," said Benjamin, "her shape and stature:
And this of mine—this bulky creature
Of which I have the steering—this,
Seen fairly, is not much amiss!
We want your streamers, friend, you know;
But, altogether as we go,
We make a kind of handsome show!
Among these hills, from first to last,
We 've weathered many a furious blast; 80
Hard passage forcing on, with head
Against the storm, and canvas spread.
I hate a boaster; but to thee
Will say 't, who know'st both land and sea,
The unluckiest hulk that stems the brine
Is hardly worse beset than mine,
When cross-winds on her quarter beat;
And, fairly lifted from my feet,
I stagger onward—heaven knows how;
But not so pleasantly as now: 90
Poor pilot I, by snows confounded,
And many a foundrous pit surrounded!
Yet here we are, by night and day
Grinding through rough and smooth our way;
Through foul and fair our task fulfilling;
And long shall be so yet—God willing!"
      "Ay," said the Tar, "through fair and foul—
But save us from yon screeching owl!"
That instant was begun a fray
Which called their thoughts another way: 100
The mastiff, ill-conditioned carl!
What must he do but growl and snarl,
Still more and more dissatisfied
With the meek comrade at his side!
Till, not incensed though put to proof,
The Ass, uplifting a hind hoof,
Salutes the Mastiff on the head;
And so were better manners bred,
And all was calmed and quieted.
      "Yon screech-owl," says the Sailor, turning 110

Back to his former cause of mourning,
"Yon owl!—pray God that all be well!
'Tis worse than any funeral bell;
As sure as I 've the gift of sight,
We shall be meeting ghosts to-night!"
—Said Benjamin, "This whip shall lay
A thousand, if they cross our way.
I know that Wanton's noisy station,
I know him and his occupation;
The jolly bird hath learned his cheer   120
Upon the banks of Windermere;
Where a tribe of them make merry,
Mocking the Man that keeps the ferry;
Hallooing from an open throat,
Like travellers shouting for a boat.
—The tricks he learned at Windermere
This vagrant owl is playing here—
That is the worst of his employment:
He's at the top of his enjoyment!"

     This explanation stilled the alarm,   130
Cured the foreboder like a charm,
This, and the manner, and the voice,
Summoned the Sailor to rejoice;
His heart is up—he fears no evil
From life or death, from man or devil;
He wheels—and, making many stops,
Brandished his crutch against the mountain tops;
And, while he talked of blows and scars,
Benjamin, among the stars,
Beheld a dancing—and a glancing;   140
Such retreating and advancing
As, I ween, was never seen
In bloodiest battle since the days of Mars!

CANTO FOURTH

Thus they, with freaks of proud delight,
Beguile the remnant of the night;
And many a snatch of jovial song
Regales them as they wind along;

While to the music, from on high,
The echoes make a glad reply.—
But the sage Muse the revel heeds
No farther than her story needs;
Nor will she servilely attend
The loitering journey to its end.   10
—Blithe spirits of her own impel
The Muse, who scents the morning air,
To take of this transported pair
A brief and unreproved farewell;
To quit the slow-paced waggon's side,
And wander down yon hawthorn dell,
With murmuring Greta for her guide.
—There doth she ken the awful form
Of Raven-crag—black as a storm—
Glimmering through the twilight pale;   20
And Ghimmer-crag, his tall twin brother,
Each peering forth to meet the other:—
And, while she roves through St. John's Vale,
Along the smooth unpathwayed plain,
By sheep-track or through cottage lane,
Where no disturbance comes to intrude
Upon the pensive solitude,
Her unsuspecting eye, perchance,
With the rude shepherd's favoured glance,
Beholds the faeries in array,   30
Whose party-coloured garments gay
The silent company betray:
Red, green, and blue; a moment's sight!
For Skiddaw-top with rosy light
Is touched—and all the band take flight.
—Fly also, Muse! and from the dell
Mount to the ridge of Nathdale Fell;
Thence, look thou forth o'er wood and lawn
Hoar with the frost-like dews of dawn;
Across yon meadowy bottom look,   40
Where close fogs hide their parent brook;
And see, beyond that hamlet small,
The ruined towers of Threlkeld-hall,

Lurking in a double shade,
By trees and lingering twilight made!
There, at Blencathara's rugged feet,
Sir Lancelot gave a safe retreat
To noble Clifford; from annoy
Concealed the persecuted boy,
Well pleased in rustic garb to feed   50
His flock, and pipe on shepherd's reed
Among this multitude of hills,
Crags, woodlands, waterfalls, and rills;
Which soon the morning shall enfold,
From east to west, in ample vest
Of massy gloom and radiance bold.

    The mists, that o'er the streamlet's bed
Hung low, begin to rise and spread;
Even while I speak, their skirts of grey
Are smitten by a silver ray;   60
And lo!—up Castrigg's naked steep
(Where, smoothly urged, the vapours sweep
Along—and scatter and divide,
Like fleecy clouds self-multiplied)
The stately waggon is ascending,
With faithful Benjamin attending,
Apparent now beside his team—
Now lost amid a glittering steam:
And with him goes his Sailor-friend,
By this time near their journey's end;   70
And, after their high-minded riot,
Sickening into thoughtful quiet;
As if the morning's pleasant hour
Had for their joys a killing power.
And, sooth, for Benjamin a vein
Is opened of still deeper pain
As if his heart by notes were stung
From out the lowly hedge-rows flung;
As if the Warbler lost in light
Reproved his soarings of the night,   80
In strains of rapture pure and holy
Upbraided his distempered folly.

Drooping is he, his step is dull;
But the horses stretch and pull;
With increasing vigour climb,
Eager to repair lost time;
Whether, by their own desert,
Knowing what cause there is for shame,
They are labouring to avert
As much as may be of the blame,   90
Which, they foresee, must soon alight
Upon *his* head, whom, in despite
Of all his failings, they love best;
Whether for him they are distrest,
Or, by length of fasting roused,
Are impatient to be housed:
Up against the hill they strain
Tugging at the iron chain,
Tugging all with might and main,
Last and foremost, every horse   100
To the utmost of his force!
And the smoke and respiration,
Rising like an exhalation,
Blend with the mist—a moving shroud—
To form an undissolving cloud;
Which, with slant ray, the merry sun
Takes delight to play upon.
Never golden-haired Apollo,
Pleased some favourite chief to follow
Through accidents of peace or war,   110
In a perilous moment threw
Around the object of his care
Veil of such celestial hue;
Interposed so bright a screen—
Him and his enemies between!
Alas! what boots it?—who can hide,
When the malicious Fates are bent
On working out an ill intent?
Can destiny be turned aside?
No—sad progress of my story!   120

Benjamin, this outward glory
Cannot shield thee from thy Master,
Who from Keswick has pricked forth,
Sour and surly as the north;
And, in fear of some disaster,
Comes to give what help he may,
And to hear what thou canst say;
If, as needs he must forebode,
Thou hast been loitering on the road!
His fears, his doubts, may now take flight—   130
The wished-for object is in sight;
Yet, trust the Muse, it rather hath
Stirred him up to livelier wrath:
Which he stifles, moody man!
With all the patience that he can;
To the end that, at your meeting,
He may give thee decent greeting.
   There he is—resolved to stop,
Till the waggon gains the top;
But stop he cannot—must advance: 140
Him Benjamin, with lucky glance,
Espies—and instantly is ready,
Self-collected, poised, and steady:
And, to be the better seen,
Issues from his radiant shroud,
From his close-attending cloud,
With careless air and open mien.
Erect his port, and firm his going;
So struts yon cock that now is crowing;
And the morning light in grace   150
Strikes upon his lifted face,
Hurrying the pallid hue away
That might his trespasses betray.
But what can all avail to clear him,
Or what need of explanation,
Parley or interrogation?
For the Master sees, alas!
That unhappy Figure near him,

Limping o'er the dewy grass,
Where the road it fringes, sweet,   160
Soft and cool to way-worn feet;
And, O indignity! an Ass,
By his noble Mastiff's side,
Tethered to the waggon's tail:
And the ship, in all her pride,
Following after in full sail!
Not to speak of babe and mother;
Who, contented with each other,
And snug as birds in leafy arbour,
Find, within, a blessed harbour!   170
   With eager eyes the Master pries;
Looks in and out, and through and through;
Says nothing—till at last he spies
A wound upon the Mastiff's head,
A wound, where plainly might be read
What feats an Ass's hoof can do!
But drop the rest:—this aggravation,
This complicated provocation,
A hoard of grievances unsealed;
All past forgiveness it repealed;   180
And thus, and through distempered blood
On both sides, Benjamin the good,
The patient, and the tender-hearted,
Was from his team and waggon parted;
When duty of that day was o'er,
Laid down his whip—and served no more.—
Nor could the waggon long survive,
Which Benjamin had ceased to drive:
It lingered on;—guide after guide
Ambitiously the office tried;   190
But each unmanageable hill
Called for *his* patience and *his* skill;—
And sure it is, that through this night,
And what the morning brought to light,
Two losses had we to sustain,
We lost both WAGGONER and WAIN!

Accept, O Friend, for praise or blame,
The gift of this adventurous song;
A record which I dared to frame,
Though timid scruples checked me long;
They checked me—and I left the theme
Untouched—in spite of many a gleam
Of fancy which thereon was shed,
Like pleasant sunbeams shifting still
Upon the side of a distant hill:
But Nature might not be gainsaid;   10
For what I have and what I miss
I sing of these;—it makes my bliss!
Nor is it I who play the part,
But a shy spirit in my heart,
That comes and goes—will sometimes leap
From hiding-places ten years deep;
Or haunts me with familiar face,
Returning, like a ghost unlaid,
Until the debt I owe be paid.
Forgive me, then; for I had been   20
On friendly terms with this Machine:
In him, while he was wont to trace
Our roads, through many a long year's space,
A living almanack had we;
We had a speaking diary,
That in this uneventful place
Gave to the days a mark and name
By which we knew them when they came.
—Yes, I, and all about me here,
Through all the changes of the year,   30
Had seen him through the mountains go,
In pomp of mist or pomp of snow,
Majestically huge and slow:
Or, with a milder grace adorning
The landscape of a summer's morning;
While Grasmere smoothed her liquid plain
The moving image to detain;

And mighty Fairfield, with a chime
Of echoes, to his march kept time;
When little other business stirred,   40
And little other sound was heard;
In that delicious hour of balm,
Stillness, solitude, and calm,
While yet the valley is arrayed,
On this side with a sober shade;
On that is prodigally bright—
Crag, lawn, and wood—with rosy light.
—But most of all, thou Lordly Wain!
I wish to have thee here again,
When windows flap and chimney roars,   50
And all is dismal out of doors;
And, sitting by my fire, I see
Eight sorry carts, no less a train;
Unworthy successors of thee,
Come straggling through the wind and rain!
And oft, as they pass slowly on,
Beneath my windows, one by one,
See, perched upon the naked height
The summit of a cumbrous freight,
A single traveller—and there   60
Another; then perhaps a pair—
The lame, the sickly, and the old;
Men, women, heartless with the cold;
And babes in wet and starveling plight;
Which once, be weather as it might,
Had still a nest within a nest,
Thy shelter—and their mother's breast!
Then most of all, then far the most,
Do I regret what we have lost;
Am grieved for that unhappy sin   70
Which robbed us of good Benjamin;
And of his stately Charge, which none
Could keep alive when He was gone!

FRENCH REVOLUTION

AS IT APPEARED TO ENTHUSIASTS AT ITS COMMENCEMENT.
REPRINTED FROM THE FRIEND

Oh! pleasant exercise of hope and joy!
For mighty were the auxiliars which then stood
Upon our side, we who were strong in love!
Bliss was it in that dawn to be alive,
But to be young was very heaven!—Oh! times,
In which the meagre, stale, forbidding ways
Of custom, law, and statute, took at once
The attraction of a country in romance!
When Reason seemed the most to assert her rights,
When most intent on making of herself   10
A prime Enchantress—to assist the work,
Which then was going forward in her name!
Not favoured spots alone, but the whole earth,
The beauty wore of promise, that which sets
(As at some moment might not be unfelt
Among the bowers of paradise itself)
The budding rose above the rose full blown.
What temper at the prospect did not wake
To happiness unthought of? The inert
Were roused, and lively natures rapt away!   20
They who had fed their childhood upon dreams,
The playfellows of fancy, who had made
All powers of swiftness, subtilty, and strength
Their ministers,—who in lordly wise had stirred
Among the grandest objects of the sense,
And dealt with whatsoever they found there
As if they within some lurking right
To wield it;—they, too, who, of gentle mood,
Had watched all gentle motions, and to these
Had fitted their own thoughts, schemers more mild,   30
And in the region of their peaceful selves;—
Now was it that both found, the meek and lofty
Did both find, helpers to their heart's desire,

And stuff at hand, plastic as they could wish;
Were called upon to exercise their skill,
Not in Utopia, subterranean fields,
Or some secreted island, Heaven knows where!
But in the very world, which is the world
Of all of us,—the place where in the end
We find our happiness, or not at all!   40

CHARACTER OF THE HAPPY WARRIOR

Who is the happy Warrior? Who is he
That every man in arms should wish to be?
—It is the generous Spirit, who, when brought
Among the tasks of real life, hath wrought
Upon the plan that pleased his boyish thought:
Whose high endeavours are an inward light
That makes the path before him always bright:
Who, with a natural instinct to discern
What knowledge can perform, is diligent to learn;
Abides by this resolve, and stops not there,   10
But makes his moral being his prime care;
Who, doomed to go in company with Pain,
And Fear, and Bloodshed, miserable train!
Turns his necessity to glorious gain;
In face of these doth exercise a power
Which is our human nature's highest dower;
Controls them and subdues, transmutes, bereaves
Of their bad influence, and their good receives:
By objects, which might force the soul to abate
Her feeling, rendered more compassionate;   20
Is placable—because occasions rise
So often that demand such sacrifice;
More skilful in self-knowledge, even more pure,
As tempted more; more able to endure,
As more exposed to suffering and distress;

Thence, also, more alive to tenderness.
—'Tis he whose law is reason; who depends
Upon that law as on the best of friends;
Whence, in a state where men are tempted still
To evil for a guard against worse ill,   30
And what in quality or act is best
Doth seldom on a right foundation rest,
He labours good on good to fix, and owes
To virtue every triumph that he knows:
—Who, if he rise to station of command,
Rises by open means; and there will stand
On honourable terms, or else retire,
And in himself possess his own desire;
Who comprehends his trust, and to the same
Keeps faithful with a singleness of aim;   40
And therefore does not stoop, nor lie in wait
For wealth, or honours, or for worldly state;
Whom they must follow; on whose head must fall,
Like showers of manna, if they come at all:
Whose powers shed round him in the common strife,
Or mild concerns of ordinary life,
A constant influence, a peculiar grace;
But who, if he be called upon to face
Some awful moment to which Heaven has joined
Great issues, good or bad for human kind,   50
Is happy as a Lover; and attired
With sudden brightness, like a Man inspired;
And, through the heat of conflict, keeps the law
In calmness made, and sees what he foresaw;
Or if an unexpected call succeed,
Come when it will, is equal to the need:
—He who, though thus endued as with a sense
And faculty for storm and turbulence,
Is yet a Soul whose master-bias leans
To homefelt pleasures and to gentle scenes;   60
Sweet images! which, wheresoe'er he be,
Are at his heart; and such fidelity
It is his darling passion to approve;
More brave for this, that he hath much to love:—

'Tis, finally, the Man, who, lifted high,
Conspicuous object in a Nation's eye,
Or left unthought-of in obscurity,—
Who, with a toward or untoward lot,
Prosperous or adverse, to his wish or not—
Plays, in the many games of life, that one   70
Where what he most doth value must be won:
Whom neither shape of danger can dismay,
Nor thought of tender happiness betray;
Who, not content that former worth stand fast,
Looks forward, persevering to the last,
From well to better, daily self-surpast:
Who, whether praise of him must walk the earth
For ever, and to noble deeds give birth,
Or he must fall, to sleep without his fame,
And leave a dead unprofitable name—   80
Finds comfort in himself and in his cause;
And, while the mortal mist is gathering, draws
His breath in confidence of Heaven's applause:
This is the happy Warrior; this is He
That every Man in arms should wish to be.

STAR-GAZERS

What crowd is this? what have we here! we must not pass it by;
A Telescope upon its frame, and pointed to the sky:
Long is it as a barber's pole, or mast of little boat,
Some little pleasure-skiff, that doth on Thames's water float.

The Showman chooses well his place, 'tis Leicester's busy Square;
And is as happy in his night, for the heavens are blue and fair;
Calm, though impatient, is the crowd; each stands ready with the
     fee,
And envies him that's looking;—what an insight must it be!

Yet, Showman, where can lie the cause? Shall thy Implement have
     blame,
A boaster, that when he is tried, fails, and is put to shame?   10

Or is it good as others are, and be their eyes in fault?
Their eyes, or minds? or, finally, is yon resplendent vault?

Is nothing of that radiant pomp so good as we have here?
Or gives a thing but small delight that never can be dear?
The silver moon with all her vales, and hills of mightiest fame,
Doth she betray us when they're seen? or are they but a name?

Or is it rather that Conceit rapacious is and strong,
And bounty never yields so much but it seems to do her wrong?
Or is it, that when human Souls a journey long have had
And are returned into themselves, they cannot but be sad?   20

Or must we be constrained to think that these Spectators rude,
Poor in estate, of manners base, men of the multitude,
Have souls which never yet have risen, and therefore prostrate lie?
No, no, this cannot be;—men thirst for power and majesty!
Does, then, a deep and earnest thought the blissful mind employ
Of him who gazes, or has gazed? a grave and steady joy,
That doth reject all show of pride, admits no outward sign,
Because not of this noisy world, but silent and divine!

Whatever be the cause, 'tis sure that they who pry and pore
Seem to meet with little gain, seem less happy than before: 30
One after One they take their turn, nor have I one espied
That doth not slackly go away, as if dissatisfied.

"NUNS FRET NOT AT THEIR CONVENT'S NARROW ROOM"

Nuns fret not at their convent's narrow room;
And hermits are contented with their cells;
And students with their pensive citadels;
Maids at the wheel, the weaver at his loom,
Sit blithe and happy; bees that soar for bloom,
High as the highest Peak of Furness-fells,
Will murmur by the hour in foxglove bells:
In truth the prison, into which we doom
Ourselves, no prison is: and hence for me,

In sundry moods, 'twas pastime to be bound
Within the Sonnet's scanty plot of ground;
Pleased if some Souls (for such there needs must be)
Who have felt the weight of too much liberty,
Should find brief solace there, as I have found.

PERSONAL TALK

I

I am not One who much or oft delight
To season my fireside with personal talk.—
Of friends, who live within an easy walk,
Or neighbours, daily, weekly, in my sight:
And, for my chance-acquaintance, ladies bright,
Sons, mothers, maidens withering on the stalk,
These all wear out of me, like Forms, with chalk
Painted on rich men's floors, for one feast-night.
Better than such discourse doth silence long,
Long, barren silence, square with my desire;   10
To sit without emotion, hope, or aim,
In the loved presence of my cottage-fire,
And listen to the flapping of the flame,
Or kettle whispering its faint undersong.

II

"Yet life," you say, "is life; we have seen and see,
And with a living pleasure we describe;
And fits of sprightly malice do but bribe
The languid mind into activity.
Sound sense, and love itself, and mirth and glee
Are fostered by the comment and the gibe."   20
Even be it so; yet still among your tribe,
Our daily world's true Worldlings, rank not me!
Children are blest, and powerful; their world lies
More justly balanced; partly at their feet,
And part far from them: sweetest melodies
Are those that are by distance made more sweet;
Whose mind is but the mind of his own eyes,
He is a Slave; the meanest we can meet!

III

Wings have we,—and as far as we can go,
We may find pleasure: wilderness and wood,   30
Blank ocean and mere sky, support that mood
Which with the lofty sanctifies the low.
Dreams, books, are each a world; and books, we know,
Are a substantial world, both pure and good:
Round these, with tendrils strong as flesh and blood,
Our pastime and our happiness will grow.
There find I personal themes, a plenteous store,
Matter wherein right voluble I am,
To which I listen with a ready ear;
Two shall be named, pre-eminently dear,—   40
The gentle Lady married to the Moor;
And heavenly Una with her milk-white Lamb.

IV

Nor can I not believe but that hereby
Great gains are mine; for thus I live remote
From evil-speaking; rancour, never sought,
Comes to me not; malignant truth, or lie.
Hence have I genial seasons, hence have I
Smooth passions, smooth discourse, and joyous thought:
And thus from day to day my little boat
Rocks in its harbour, lodging peaceably.   50
Blessings be with them—and eternal praise,
Who gave us nobler loves, and nobler cares—
The Poets, who on earth have made us heirs
Of truth and pure delight by heavenly lays!
Oh! might my name be numbered among theirs,
Then gladly would I end my mortal days.

"THE WORLD IS TOO MUCH WITH US; LATE AND SOON"

The world is too much with us; late and soon,
Getting and spending, we lay waste our powers:
Little we see in Nature that is ours;
We have given our hearts away, a sordid boon!

The Sea that bares her bosom to the moon;
The winds that will be howling at all hours,
And are up-gathered now like sleeping flowers;
For this, for everything, we are out of tune;
It moves us not.—Great God! I 'd rather be
A Pagan suckled in a creed outworn;
So might I, standing on this pleasant lea,
Have glimpses that would make me less forlorn;
Have sight of Proteus rising from the sea;
Or hear old Triton blow his wreathèd horn.

"WITH SHIPS THE SEA WAS SPRINKLED FAR AND NIGH"

With Ships the sea was sprinkled far and nigh,
Like stars in heaven, and joyously it showed;
Some lying fast at anchor in the road,
Some veering up and down, one knew not why.
A goodly Vessel did I then espy
Come like a giant from a haven broad;
And lustily along the bay she strode,
Her tackling rich, and of apparel high.
This Ship was nought to me, nor I to her,
Yet I pursued her with a Lover's look;
This Ship to all the rest did I prefer:
When will she turn, and whither? She will brook
No tarrying; where She comes the winds must stir:
On went She, and due north her journey took.

"WHERE LIES THE LAND TO WHICH YON SHIP MUST GO?"

Where lies the Land to which yon Ship must go?
Fresh as a lark mounting at break of day,
Festively she puts forth in trim array;
Is she for tropic suns, or polar snow?
What boots the inquiry?—Neither friend nor foe
She cares for; let her travel where she may,

She finds familiar names, a beaten way
Ever before her, and a wind to blow.
Yet still I ask, what haven is her mark?
And, almost as it was when ships were rare,
(From time to time, like Pilgrims, here and there
Crossing the waters) doubt, and something dark,
Of the old Sea some reverential fear,
Is with me at thy farewell, joyous Bark!

TO SLEEP

O gentle Sleep! do they belong to thee,
These twinklings of oblivion? Thou dost love
To sit in meekness, like the brooding Dove,
A captive never wishing to be free.
This tiresome night, O Sleep! thou art to me
A Fly, that up and down himself doth shove
Upon a fretful rivulet, now above
Now on the water vexed with mockery.
I have no pain that calls for patience, no;
Hence am I cross and peevish as a child:
Am pleased by fits to have thee for my foe,
Yet ever willing to be reconciled:
O gentle Creature! do not use me so,
But once and deeply let me be beguiled.

TO SLEEP

A flock of sheep that leisurely pass by,
One after one; the sound of rain, and bees
Murmuring; the fall of rivers, winds and seas,
Smooth fields, white sheets of water, and pure sky;
I have thought of all by turns, and yet do lie
Sleepless! and soon the small birds' melodies
Must hear, first uttered from my orchard trees;
And the first cuckoo's melancholy cry.
Even thus last night, and two nights more, I lay,
And could not win thee, Sleep! by any stealth:

So do not let me wear to-night away:
Without Thee what is all the morning's wealth?
Come, blessed barrier between day and day,
Dear mother of fresh thoughts and joyous health!

To Sleep

Fond words have oft been spoken to thee, Sleep!
And thou hast had thy store of tenderest names;
The very sweetest, Fancy culls or frames,
When thankfulness of heart is strong and deep!
Dear Bosom-child we call thee, that dost steep
In rich reward all suffering; Balm that tames
All anguish; Saint that evil thoughts and aims
Takest away, and into souls dost creep,
Like to a breeze from heaven. Shall I alone,
I surely not a man ungently made,
Call thee worst Tyrant by which Flesh is crost?
Perverse, self-willed to own and to disown,
Mere slave of them who never for thee prayed,
Still last to come where thou art wanted most!

To the Memory of Raisley Calvert

Calvert! it must not be unheard by them
Who may respect my name, that I to thee
Owed many years of early liberty.
This care was thine when sickness did condemn
Thy youth to hopeless wasting, root and stem—
That I, if frugal and severe, might stray
Where'er I liked; and finally array
My temples with the Muse's diadem.
Hence, if in freedom I have loved the truth;
If there be aught of pure, or good, or great,
In my past verse; or shall be, in the lays
Of higher mood, which now I meditate;—
It gladdens me, O worthy, short-lived, Youth!
To think how much of this will be thy praise.

"METHOUGHT I SAW THE FOOTSTEPS OF A THRONE"

Methought I saw the footsteps of a throne
Which mists and vapours from mine eyes did shroud—
Nor view of who might sit thereon allowed;
But all the steps and ground about were strown
With sights the ruefullest that flesh and bone
Ever put on; a miserable crowd,
Sick, hale, old, young, who cried before that cloud,
"Thou art our king, O Death! to thee we groan."
Those steps I clomb; the mists before me gave
Smooth way; and I beheld the face of one
Sleeping alone within a mossy cave,
With her face up to heaven; that seemed to have
Pleasing remembrance of a thought foregone;
A lovely Beauty in a summer grave!

NOVEMBER, 1806

Another year!—another deadly blow!
Another mighty Empire overthrown!
And We are left, or shall be left, alone;
The last that dare to struggle with the Foe.
'Tis well! from this day forward we shall know
That in ourselves our safety must be sought;
That by our own right hands it must be wrought;
That we must stand unpropped, or be laid low.
O dastard whom such foretaste doth not cheer!
We shall exult, if they who rule the land
Be men who hold its many blessings dear,
Wise, upright, valiant; not a servile band,
Who are to judge of danger which they fear,
And honour which they do not understand.

ODE
INTIMATIONS OF IMMORTALITY FROM RECOLLECTIONS OF EARLY CHILDHOOD

I

There was a time when meadow, grove, and stream,
The earth, and every common sight,
  To me did seem
  Apparelled in celestial light,
The glory and the freshness of a dream.
It is not now as it hath been of yore;—
  Turn wheresoe'er I may,
   By night or day,
The things which I have seen I now can see no more.

II

  The Rainbow comes and goes,   10
  And lovely is the Rose,
  The Moon doth with delight
Look round her when the heavens are bare,
  Waters on a starry night
  Are beautiful and fair;
  The sunshine is a glorious birth;
  But yet I know, where'er I go,
That there hath past away a glory from the earth.

III

Now, while the birds thus sing a joyous song,
  And while the young lambs bound   20
  As to the tabor's sound,
To me alone there came a thought of grief:
A timely utterance gave that thought relief,
  And I again am strong:
The cataracts blow their trumpets from the steep;
No more shall grief of mine the season wrong;
I hear the Echoes through the mountains throng,
The Winds come to me from the fields of sleep,
  And all the earth is gay;
   Land and sea   30

Give themselves up to jollity,
   And with the heart of May
Doth every Beast keep holiday;—
   Thou Child of Joy,
Shout round me, let me hear thy shouts, thou happy
   Shepherd-boy!

IV

Ye blessèd Creatures, I have heard the call
   Ye to each other make; I see
The heavens laugh with you in your jubilee;
   My heart is at your festival,
   My head hath its coronal,   40
The fulness of your bliss, I feel—I feel it all.
   Oh evil day! if I were sullen
   While Earth herself is adorning,
      This sweet May-morning,
   And the Children are culling
      On every side,
In a thousand valleys far and wide,
Fresh flowers; while the sun shines warm,
And the Babe leaps up on his Mother's arm:—   50
   I hear, I hear, with joy I hear!
   —But there's a Tree, of many, one,
A single Field which I have looked upon,
Both of them speak of something that is gone:
   The Pansy at my feet
   Doth the same tale repeat:
Whither is fled the visionary gleam?
Where is it now, the glory and the dream?

V

Our birth is but a sleep and a forgetting;
The Soul that rises with us, our life's Star,   60
   Hath had elsewhere its setting,
      And cometh from afar:
   Not in entire forgetfulness,
   And not in utter nakedness,
But trailing clouds of glory do we come
   From God, who is our home:

Heaven lies about us in our infancy!
Shades of the prison-house begin to close
   Upon the growing Boy,
But He beholds the light, and whence it flows,   70
   He sees it in his joy;
The Youth, who daily farther from the east
   Must travel, still is Nature's Priest,
   And by the vision splendid
   Is on his way attended;
At length the Man perceives it die away,
And fade into the light of common day.

VI

Earth fills her lap with pleasures of her own;
Yearnings she hath in her own natural kind,
And, even with something of a Mother's mind,   80
   And no unworthy aim,
   The homely Nurse doth all she can
To make her Foster-child, her Inmate Man,
   Forget the glories he hath known,
And that imperial palace whence he came.

VII

Behold the Child among his new-born blisses,
A six years' Darling of a pigmy size!
See, where 'mid work of his own hand he lies,
Fretted by sallies of his mother's kisses,
With light upon him from his father's eyes!   90
See, at his feet, some little plan or chart,
Some fragment from his dream of human life,
Shaped by himself with newly-learned art;
   A wedding or a festival,
   A mourning or a funeral;
     And this hath now his heart,
   And unto this he frames his song:
     Then will he fit his tongue
To dialogues of business, love, or strife;
   But it will not be long   100
   Ere this be thrown aside,
   And with new joy and pride

The little Actor cons another part;
Filling from time to time his "humorous stage"
With all the Persons, down to palsied Age,
That Life brings with her in her equipage;
    As if his whole vocation
    Were endless imitation.

VIII

Thou, whose exterior semblance doth belie
    Thy Soul's immensity;   110
Thou best Philosopher, who yet dost keep
Thy heritage, thou Eye among the blind,
That, deaf and silent, read'st the eternal deep,
Haunted for ever by the eternal mind,—
    Mighty Prophet! Seer blest!
    On whom those truths do rest,
Which we are toiling all our lives to find,
In darkness lost, the darkness of the grave;
Thou, over whom thy Immortality
Broods like the Day, a Master o'er a Slave,   120
A Presence which is not to be put by;
Thou little Child, yet glorious in the might
Of heaven-born freedom on thy being's height,
Why with such earnest pains dost thou provoke
The years to bring the inevitable yoke,
Thus blindly with thy blessedness at strife?
Full soon thy Soul shall have her earthly freight,
And custom lie upon thee with a weight,
Heavy as frost, and deep almost as life!

IX

    O joy! that in our embers   130
    Is something that doth live,
    That nature yet remembers
    What was so fugitive!
The thought of our past years in me doth breed
Perpetual benediction: not indeed
For that which is most worthy to be blest—
Delight and liberty, the simple creed
Of Childhood, whether busy or at rest,

With new-fledged hope still fluttering in his breast:—
    Not for these I raise   **140**
    The song of thanks and praise;
  But for those obstinate questionings
  Of sense and outward things,
  Fallings from us, vanishings;
  Blank misgivings of a Creature
Moving about in worlds not realised,
High instincts before which our mortal Nature
Did tremble like a guilty Thing surprised:
    But for those first affections,
    Those shadowy recollections,   **150**
  Which, be they what they may,
Are yet the fountain light of all our day,
Are yet a master light of all our seeing;
  Uphold us, cherish, and have power to make
Our noisy years seem moments in the being
Of the eternal Silence: truths that wake,
    To perish never;
Which neither listlessness, nor mad endeavour,
    Nor Man nor Boy,
Nor all that is at enmity with joy,   **160**
Can utterly abolish or destroy!
    Hence in a season of calm weather
    Though inland far we be,
Our Souls have sight of that immortal sea
    Which brought us hither,
    Can in a moment travel thither,
And see the Children sport upon the shore,
And hear the mighty waters rolling evermore.

                X

Then sing, ye Birds, sing, sing a joyous song!
    And let the young Lambs bound   **170**
    As to the tabor's sound!
We in thought will join your throng,
    Ye that pipe and ye that play,
    Ye that through your hearts to-day

Feel the gladness of the May!
What though the radiance which was once so bright
Be now for ever taken from my sight,
 Though nothing can bring back the hour
Of splendour in the grass, of glory in the flower;
 We will grieve not, rather find
 Strength in what remains behind;
 In the primal sympathy
 Which having been must ever be;
 In the soothing thoughts that spring
 Out of human suffering;
 In the faith that looks through death,
In years that bring the philosophic mind.

XI

And O, ye Fountains, Meadows, Hills, and Groves,
Forebode not any severing of our loves!
Yet in my heart of hearts I feel your might;
I only have relinquished one delight
To live beneath your more habitual sway.
I love the Brooks which down their channels fret,
Even more than when I tripped lightly as they;
The innocent brightness of a new-born Day
 Is lovely yet;
The Clouds that gather round the setting sun
Do take a sober colouring from an eye
That hath kept watch o'er man's mortality;
Another race hath been, and other palms are won.
Thanks to the human heart by which we live,
Thanks to its tenderness, its joys, and fears,
To me the meanest flower that blows can give
Thoughts that do often lie too deep for tears.

180

190

200

THOUGHT OF A BRITON ON THE SUBJUGATION OF SWITZERLAND

Two Voices are there; one is of the sea,
One of the mountains; each a mighty Voice:
In both from age to age thou didst rejoice,
They were thy chosen music, Liberty!
There came a Tyrant, and with holy glee
Thou fought'st against him; but hast vainly striven:
Thou from thy Alpine holds at length art driven,
Where not a torrent murmurs heard by thee.
Of one deep bliss thine ear hath been bereft:
Then cleave, O cleave to that which still is left;
For, high-souled Maid, what sorrow would it be
That Mountain floods should thunder as before,
And Ocean bellow from his rocky shore,
And neither awful Voice be heard by thee!

"THOUGH NARROW BE THAT OLD MAN'S CARES"

Though narrow be that old Man's cares, and near,
The poor old Man is greater than he seems:
For he hath waking empire, wide as dreams;
An ample sovereignty of eye and ear.
Rich are his walks with supernatural cheer;
The region of his inner spirit teems
With vital sounds and monitory gleams
Of high astonishment and pleasing fear.
He the seven birds hath seen, that never part,
Seen the SEVEN WHISTLERS in their nightly rounds,
And counted them: and oftentimes will start—
For overhead are sweeping GABRIEL'S HOUNDS
Doomed, with their impious Lord, the flying Hart
To chase for ever, on aërial grounds!

SONG AT THE FEAST OF BROUGHAM CASTLE

UPON THE RESTORATION OF LORD CLIFFORD, THE SHEPHERD, TO THE ESTATES AND HONOURS OF HIS ANCESTORS

High in the breathless Hall the Minstrel sate,
And Emont's murmur mingled with the Song.—
The words of ancient time I thus translate,
A festal strain that hath been silent long:—
"From town to town, from tower to tower,
The red rose is a gladsome flower.
Her thirty years of winter past,
The red rose is revived at last;
She lifts her head for endless spring,
For everlasting blossoming: 10
Both roses flourish, red and white:
In love and sisterly delight
The two that were at strife are blended,
And all old troubles now are ended.—
Joy! joy to both! but most to her
Who is the flower of Lancaster!
Behold her now She smiles to-day
On this great throng, this bright array!
Fair greeting doth she send to all
From every corner of the hall;   20
But chiefly from above the board
Where sits in state our rightful Lord,
A Clifford to his own restored!

    They came with banner, spear, and shield,
And it was proved in Bosworth-field.
Not long the Avenger was withstood—
Earth helped him with the cry of blood:
St. George was for us, and the might
Of blessed Angels crowned the right.
Loud voice the Land has uttered forth,   30
We loudest in the faithful north:
Our fields rejoice, our mountains ring,
Our streams proclaim a welcoming;

Our strong-abodes and castles see
The glory of their loyalty.
   How glad is Skipton at this hour—
Though lonely, a deserted Tower;
Knight, squire, and yeoman, page and groom:
We have them at the feast of Brough'm.
How glad Pendragon—though the sleep   **40**
Of years be on her!—She shall reap
A taste of this great pleasure, viewing
As in a dream her own renewing.
Rejoiced is Brough, right glad I deem
Beside her little humble stream;
And she that keepeth watch and ward
Her statelier Eden's course to guard;
They both are happy at this hour,
Though each is but a lonely Tower:—
But here is perfect joy and pride   **50**
For one fair House by Emont's side,
This day, distinguished without peer
To see her Master and to cheer—
Him, and his Lady-mother dear!
   Oh! it was a time forlorn
When the fatherless was born—
Give her wings that she may fly,
Or she sees her infant die!
Swords that are with slaughter wild
Hunt the Mother and the Child.   **60**
Who will take them from the light?
—Yonder is a man in sight—
Yonder is a house—but where?
No, they must not enter there.
To the caves, and to the brooks,
To the clouds of heaven she looks;
She is speechless, but her eyes
Pray in ghostly agonies.
Blissful Mary, Mother mild,
Maid and Mother undefiled,   **70**
Save a Mother and her Child!
   Now Who is he that bounds with joy

On Carrock's side, a Shepherd-boy?
No thoughts hath he but thoughts that pass
Light as the wind along the grass.
Can this be He who hither came
In secret, like a smothered flame?
O'er whom such thankful tears were shed
For shelter, and a poor man's bread!
God loves the Child; and God hath willed   80
That those dear words should be fulfilled,
The Lady's words, when forced away,
The last she to her Babe did say:
'My own, my own, thy Fellow-guest
I may not be; but rest thee, rest,
For lowly shepherd's life is best!'
  Alas! when evil men are strong
No life is good, no pleasure long.
The Boy must part from Mosedale's groves,
And leave Blencathara's rugged coves,   90
And quit the flowers that summer brings
To Glenderamakin's lofty springs;
Must vanish, and his careless cheer
Be turned to heaviness and fear.
—Give Sir Lancelot Threlkeld praise!
Hear it, good man, old in days!
Thou tree of covert and of rest
For this young Bird that is distrest;
Among thy branches safe he lay,
And he was free to sport and play,   100
When falcons were abroad for prey,
  A recreant harp, that sings of fear
And heaviness in Clifford's ear!
I said, when evil men are strong,
No life is good, no pleasure long,
A weak and cowardly untruth!
Our Clifford was a happy Youth,
And thankful through a weary time,
That brought him up to manhood's prime.
—Again he wanders forth at will,   110
And tends a flock from hill to hill:

His garb is humble; ne'er was seen
Such garb with such a noble mien;
Among the shepherd grooms no mate
Hath he, a Child of strength and state!
Yet lacks not friends for simple glee,
Nor yet for higher sympathy.
To his side the fallow-deer
Came, and rested without fear;
The eagle, lord of land and sea,　　　　　　　　　　120
Stooped down to pay him fealty;
And both the undying fish that swim
Through Bowscale-tarn did wait on him;
The pair were servants of his eye
In their immortality;
And glancing, gleaming, dark or bright,
Moved to and fro, for his delight
He knew the rocks which Angels haunt
Upon the mountains visitant;
He hath kenned them taking wing:　　　　　　　　130
And into caves where Faeries sing
He hath entered; and been told
By Voices how men lived of old.
Among the heavens his eye can see
The face of thing that is to be;
And, if that men report him right,
His tongue could whisper words of might.
—Now another day is come,
Fitter hope, and nobler doom;
He hath thrown aside his crook,　　　　　　　　　140
And hath buried deep his book;
Armour rusting in his halls
On the blood of Clifford calls;—
'Quell the Scot,' exclaims the Lance—
Bear me to the heart of France,
Is the longing of the Shield—
Tell thy name, thou trembling Field;
Field of death, where'er thou be,
Groan thou with our victory!
Happy day, and mighty hour,　　　　　　　　　　150

When our Shepherd, in his power,
Mailed and horsed, with lance and sword,
To his ancestors restored
Like a re-appearing Star,
Like a glory from afar,
First shall head the flock of war!"

Alas! the impassioned minstrel did not know
How, by Heaven's grace, this Clifford's heart was framed,
How he, long forced in humble walks to go,
Was softened into feeling, soothed, and tamed.   160

Love had he found in huts where poor men lie;
His daily teachers had been woods and rills,
The silence that is in the starry sky,
The sleep that is among the lonely hills.
In him the savage virtue of the Race,
Revenge, and all ferocious thoughts were dead:
Nor did he change; but kept in lofty place
The wisdom which adversity had bred.
Glad were the vales, and every cottage hearth;
The Shepherd-lord was honoured more and more;   170
And, ages after he was laid in earth,
"The good Lord Clifford" was the name he bore.

THE WHITE DOE OF RYLSTONE

OR, THE FATE OF THE NORTONS

CANTO FIRST

From Bolton's old monastic tower
The bells ring loud with gladsome power;
The sun shines bright; the fields are gay
With people in their best array
Of stole and doublet, hood and scarf,
Along the banks of crystal Wharf,
Through the Vale retired and lowly,
Trooping to that summons holy.
And, up among the moorlands, see
What sprinklings of blithe company!   10

Of lasses and of shepherd grooms,
That down the steep hills force their way,
Like cattle through the budded brooms;
Path, or no path, what care they?
And thus in joyous mood they hie
To Bolton's mouldering Priory.

    What would they there?—Full fifty years
That sumptuous Pile, with all its peers,
Too harshly hath been doomed to taste
The bitterness of wrong and waste: 20
Its courts are ravaged; but the tower
Is standing with a voice of power,
That ancient voice which wont to call
To mass or some high festival;
And in the shattered fabric's heart
Remaineth one protected part;
A Chapel, like a wild-bird's nest,
Closely embowered and trimly drest;
And thither young and old repair,
This Sabbath-day, for praise and prayer.   30

    Fast the churchyard fills;—anon
Look again, and they all are gone;
The cluster round the porch, and the folk
Who sate in the shade of the Prior's Oak!
And scarcely have they disappeared
Ere the prelusive hymn is heard:—
With one consent the people rejoice,
Filling the church with a lofty voice!
They sing a service which they feel:
For 'tis the sunrise now of zeal;   40
Of a pure faith the vernal prime—
In great Eliza's golden time.

    A moment ends the fervent din,
And all is hushed, without and within;
For though the priest, more tranquilly,
Recites the holy liturgy,
The only voice which you can hear
Is the river murmuring near.
—When soft!—the dusky trees between,

And down the path through the open green,   50
Where is no living thing to be seen;
And through yon gateway, where is found,
Beneath the arch with ivy bound,
Free entrance to the churchyard ground—
Comes gliding in with lovely gleam,
Comes gliding in serene and slow,
Soft and silent as a dream,
A solitary Doe!
White she is as lily of June,
And beauteous as the silver moon   60
When out of sight the clouds are driven
And she is left alone in heaven;
Or like a ship some gentle day
In sunshine sailing far away,
A glittering ship, that hath the plain
Of ocean for her own domain.

    Lie silent in your graves, ye dead!
Lie quiet in your churchyard bed!
Ye living, tend your holy cares;
Ye multitude, pursue your prayers;   70
And blame not me if my heart and sight
Are occupied with one delight!
'T is a work for sabbath hours
If I with this bright Creature go:
Whether she be of forest bowers,
From the bowers of earth below;
Or a Spirit for one day given,
A pledge of grace from purest heaven.

    What harmonious pensive changes
Wait upon her as she ranges   80
Round and through this Pile of state
Overthrown and desolate!
Now a step or two her way
Leads through space of open day,
Where the enamoured sunny light
Brightens her that was so bright;
Now doth a delicate shadow fall,
Falls upon her like a breath,

From some lofty arch or wall,
As she passes underneath: 90
Now some gloomy nook partakes
Of the glory that she makes,—
High-ribbed vault of stone, or cell,
With perfect cunning framed as well
Of stone, and ivy, and the spread
Of the elder's bushy head;
Some jealous and forbidding cell,
That doth the living stars repel.
And where no flower hath leave to dwell.
　　The presence of this wandering Doe   100
Fills many a damp obscure recess
With lustre of a saintly show;
And, reappearing, she no less
Sheds on the flowers that round her blow
A more than sunny liveliness.
But say, among these holy places,
Which thus assiduously she paces,
Comes she with a votary's task,
Rite to perform, or boon to ask?
Fair Pilgrim! harbours she a sense   110
Of sorrow, or of reverence?
Can she be grieved for quire or shrine,
Crushed as if by wrath divine?
For what survives of house where God
Was worshipped, or where Man abode;
For old magnificence undone;
Or for the gentler work begun
By Nature, softening and concealing,
And busy with a hand of healing?
Mourns she for lordly chamber's hearth   120
That to the sapling ash gives birth;
For dormitory's length laid bare
Where the wild rose blossoms fair;
Or altar, whence the cross was rent,
Now rich with mossy ornament?
—She sees a warrior carved in stone,
Among the thick weeds, stretched alone;

A warrior, with his shield of pride
Cleaving humbly to his side,
And hands in resignation prest,   130
Palm to palm, on his tranquil breast;
As little she regards the sight
As a common creature might:
If she be doomed to inward care,
Or service, it must lie elsewhere.
—But hers are eyes serenely bright,
And on she moves—with pace how light!
Nor spares to stoop her head, and taste
The dewy turf with flowers bestrown;
And thus she fares, until at last   140
Beside the ridge of a grassy grave
In quietness she lays her down;
Gentle as a weary wave
Sinks, when the summer breeze hath died
Against an anchored vessel's side;
Even so, without distress, doth she
Lie down in peace, and lovingly.
    The day is placid in its going,
To a lingering motion bound,
Like the crystal stream now flowing   150
With its softest summer sound:
So the balmy minutes pass,
While this radiant Creature lies
Couched upon the dewy grass,
Pensively with downcast eyes.
—But now again the people raise
With awful cheer a voice of praise;
It is the last, the parting song;
And from the temple forth they throng,
And quickly spread themselves abroad,   160
While each pursues his several road.
But some—a variegated band
Of middle-aged, and old, and young,
And little children by the hand
Upon their leading mothers hung—
With mute obeisance gladly paid

Turn towards the spot, where, full in view,
The white Doe, to her service true,
Her sabbath couch has made.
    It was a solitary mound;   170
Which two spears' length of level ground
Did from all other graves divide:
As if in some respect of pride;
Or melancholy's sickly mood,
Still shy of human neighbourhood;
Or guilt, that humbly would express
A penitential loneliness.
    "Look, there she is, my Child! draw near;
She fears not, wherefore should we fear?
She means no harm;"—but still the Boy,   180
To whom the words were softly said,
Hung back, and smiled, and blushed for joy,
A shame-faced blush of glowing red!
Again the Mother whispered low,
"Now you have seen the famous Doe;
From Rylstone she hath found her way
Over the hills this sabbath day;
Her work, whate'er it be, is done,
And she will depart when we are gone;
Thus doth she keep, from year to year,   190
Her sabbath morning, foul or fair."
    Bright was the Creature, as in dreams
The Boy had seen her, yea, more bright;
But is she truly what she seems?
He asks with insecure delight,
Asks of himself, and doubts,—and still
The doubt returns against his will:
Though he, and all the standers-by,
Could tell a tragic history
Of facts divulged, wherein appear   200
Substantial motive, reason clear,
Why thus the milk-white Doe is found
Couchant beside that lonely mound;
And why she duly loves to pace
The circuit of this hallowed place.

Nor to the Child's inquiring mind
Is such perplexity confined:
For, spite of sober Truth that sees
A world of fixed remembrances
Which to this mystery belong,   210
If, undeceived, my skill can trace
The characters of every face,
There lack not strange delusion here,
Conjecture vague, and idle fear,
And superstitious fancies strong,
Which do the gentle Creature wrong.
    That bearded, staff-supported Sire—
Who in his boyhood often fed
Full cheerily on convent-bread
And heard old tales by the convent-fire,   220
And to his grave will go with scars,
Relics of long and distant wars—
That Old Man, studious to expound
The spectacle, is mounting high
To days of dim antiquity;
When Lady Aäliza mourned
Her Son, and felt in her despair
The pang of unavailing prayer;
Her Son in Wharf's abysses drowned,
The noble Boy of Egremound.   230
From which affliction—when the grace
Of God had in her heart found place—
A pious structure, fair to see,
Rose up, this stately Priory!
The Lady's work;—but now laid low;
To the grief of her soul that doth come and go,
In the beautiful form of this innocent Doe:
Which, though seemingly doomed in its breast to sustain
A softened remembrance of sorrow and pain,
Is spotless, and holy, and gentle, and bright;   240
And glides o'er the earth like an angel of light.
    Pass, pass who will, yon chantry door;
And, through the chink in the fractured floor
Look down, and see a griesly sight;

A vault where the bodies are buried upright!
There, face by face, and hand by hand,
The Claphams and Mauleverers stand;
And, in his place, among son and sire,
Is John de Clapham, that fierce Esquire,
A valiant man and a name of dread   250
In the ruthless wars of the White and Red;
Who dragged Earl Pembroke from Banbury church
And smote off his head on the stones of the porch!
Look down among them, if you dare;
Oft does the White Doe loiter there,
Prying into the darksome rent;
Nor can it be with good intent:
So thinks that Dame of haughty air,
Who hath a Page her book to hold,
And wears a frontlet edged with gold.   260
Harsh thoughts with her high mood agree—
Who counts among her ancestry
Earl Pembroke, slain so impiously!
     That slender Youth, a scholar pale,
From Oxford come to his native vale,
He also hath his own conceit:
It is, thinks he, the gracious Fairy,
Who loved the Shepherd-lord to meet
In his wanderings solitary:
Wild notes she in his hearing sang,   270
A song of Nature's hidden powers;
That whistled like the wind, and rang
Among the rocks and holly bowers.
'Twas said that She all shapes could wear;
And oftentimes before him stood,
Amid the trees of some thick wood,
In semblance of a lady fair;
And taught him signs, and showed him sights,
In Craven's dens, on Cumbrian heights;
When under cloud of fear he lay,   280
A shepherd clad in homely grey;
Nor left him at his later day.
And hence, when he, with spear and shield,

Rode full of years to Flodden-field,
His eye could see the hidden spring,
And how the current was to flow;
The fatal end of Scotland's King,
And all that hopeless overthrow.
But not in wars did he delight,
This Clifford wished for worthier might;   290
Nor in broad pomp, or courtly state;
Him his own thoughts did elevate,—
Most happy in the shy recess
Of Barden's lowly quietness.
And choice of studious friends had he
Of Bolton's dear fraternity;
Who, standing on this old church tower,
In many a calm propitious hour,
Perused, with him, the starry sky;
Or, in their cells, with him did pry   300
For other lore,—by keen desire
Urged to close toil with chemic fire;
In quest belike of transmutations
Rich as the mine's most bright creations.
But they and their good works are fled,
And all is now disquieted—
And peace is none, for living or dead!
    Ah, pensive Scholar, think not so,
But look again at the radiant Doe!
What quiet watch she seems to keep,   310
Alone, beside that grassy heap!
Why mention other thoughts unmeet
For vision so composed and sweet?
While stand the people in a ring,
Gazing, doubting, questioning;
Yea, many overcome in spite
Of recollections clear and bright;
Which yet do unto some impart
An undisturbed repose of heart.
And all the assembly own a law   320
Of orderly respect and awe;
But see—they vanish one by one,

And last, the Doe herself is gone.
  Harp! we have been full long beguiled
By vague thoughts, lured by fancies wild;
To which, with no reluctant strings,
Thou hast attuned thy murmurings;
And now before this Pile we stand
In solitude, and utter peace:
But, Harp! thy murmurs may not cease—   330
A Spirit, with his angelic wings,
In soft and breeze-like visitings,
Has touched thee—and a Spirit's hand:
A voice is with us—a command
To chant, in strains of heavenly glory,
A tale of tears, a mortal story!

CANTO SECOND

The Harp in lowliness obeyed;
And first we sang of the greenwood shade
And a solitary Maid;
Beginning, where the song must end,
With her, and with her sylvan Friend;
The Friend who stood before her sight,
Her only unextinguished light;
Her last companion in a dearth
Of love, upon a hopeless earth.
  For She it was—this Maid, who wrought   10
Meekly, with foreboding thought,
In vermeil colours and in gold
An unblest work; which, standing by,
Her Father did with joy behold,—
Exulting in its imagery;
A Banner, fashioned to fulfil
Too perfectly his headstrong will:
For on this Banner had her hand
Embroidered (such her Sire's command)
The sacred Cross; and figured there   20
The five dear wounds our Lord did bear;
Full soon to be uplifted high,
And float in rueful company!

It was the time when England's Queen
Twelve years had reigned, a Sovereign dread;
Nor yet the restless crown had been
Disturbed upon her virgin head;
But now the inly-working North
Was ripe to send its thousands forth,
A potent vassalage, to fight   30
In Pércy's and in Neville's right,
Two Earls fast leagued in discontent,
Who gave their wishes open vent;
And boldly urged a general plea,
The rites of ancient piety
To be triumphantly restored,
By the stern justice of the sword!
And that same Banner, on whose breast
The blameless Lady had exprest
Memorials chosen to give life   40
And sunshine to a dangerous strife;
That Banner, waiting for the Call,
Stood quietly in Rylstone-hall.

It came; and Francis Norton said,
"O Father! rise not in this fray—
The hairs are white upon your head;
Dear Father, hear me when I say
It is for you too late a day!
Bethink you of your own good name:
A just and gracious Queen have we,   50
A pure religion, and the claim
Of peace on our humanity.—
'T is meet that I endure your scorn;
I am your son, your eldest born;
But not for lordship or for land,
My Father, do I clasp your knees;
The Banner touch not, stay your hand,
This multitude of men disband,
And live at home in blameless ease;
For these my brethren's sake, for me;   60
And, most of all, for Emily!"
Tumultuous noises filled the hall;

And scarcely could the Father hear
That name—pronounced with a dying fall—
The name of his only Daughter dear,
As on the banner which stood near
He glanced a look of holy pride,
And his moist eyes were glorified;
Then did he seize the staff, and say:
"Thou, Richard, bear'st thy father's name,   70
Keep thou this ensign till the day
When I of thee require the same:
Thy place be on my better hand;—
And seven as true as thou, I see,
Will cleave to this good cause and me."
He spake, and eight brave sons straightway
All followed him, a gallant band!

    Thus, with his sons, when forth he came
The sight was hailed with loud acclaim
And din of arms and minstrelsy,   80
From all his warlike tenantry,
All horsed and harnessed with him to ride,—
A voice to which the hills replied!

    But Francis, in the vacant hall,
Stood silent under dreary weight,—
A phantasm, in which roof and wall
Shook, tottered, swam before his sight;
A phantasm like a dream of night!
Thus overwhelmed, and desolate,
He found his way to a postern-gate;   90
And, when he waked, his languid eye
Was on the calm and silent sky;
With air about him breathing sweet,
And earth's green grass beneath his feet;
Nor did he fail ere long to hear
A sound of military cheer,
Faint—but it reached that sheltered spot;
He heard, and it disturbed him not.

    There stood he, leaning on a lance
Which he had grasped unknowingly,   100
Had blindly grasped in that strong trance,

That dimness of heart-agony;
There stood he, cleansed from the despair
And sorrow of his fruitless prayer.
The past he calmly hath reviewed:
But where will be the fortitude
Of this brave man, when he shall see
That Form beneath the spreading tree,
And know that it is Emily?

He saw her where in open view   110
She sate beneath the spreading yew—
Her head upon her lap, concealing
In solitude her bitter feeling:
"Might ever son *command* a sire,
The act were justified to-day."
This to himself—and to the Maid,
Whom now he had approached, he said—
"Gone are they,—they have their desire;
And I with thee one hour will stay,
To give thee comfort if I may."   120

She heard, but looked not up, nor spake;
And sorrow moved him to partake
Her silence; then his thoughts turned round,
And fervent words a passage found.

"Gone are they, bravely, though misled;
With a dear Father at their head!
The Sons obey a natural lord;
The Father had given solemn word
To noble Percy; and a force
Still stronger, bends him to his course.   130
This said, our tears to-day may fall
As at an innocent funeral.
In deep and awful channel runs
This sympathy of Sire and Sons;
Untried our Brothers have been loved
With heart by simple nature moved;
And now their faithfulness is proved:
For faithful we must call them, bearing
That soul of conscientious daring.
—There were they all in circle—there   140

Stood Richard, Ambrose, Christopher,
John with a sword that will not fail,
And Marmaduke in fearless mail,
And those bright Twins were side by side;
And there, by fresh hopes beautified,
Stood He, whose arm yet lacks the power
Of man, our youngest, fairest flower!
I, by the right of eldest born,
And in a second father's place,
Presumed to grapple with their scorn,   150
And meet their pity face to face;
Yea, trusting in God's holy aid,
I to my Father knelt and prayed;
And one, the pensive Marmaduke,
Methought, was yielding inwardly,
And would have laid his purpose by,
But for a glance of his Father's eye,
Which I myself could scarcely brook.
      Then be we, each and all, forgiven!
Thou, chiefly thou, my Sister dear,   160
Whose pangs are registered in heaven—
The stifled sigh, the hidden tear,
And smiles, that dared to take their place,
Meek filial smiles, upon thy face,
As that unhallowed Banner grew
Beneath a loving old Man's view.
Thy part is done—thy painful part;
Be thou then satisfied in heart!
A further, though far easier, task
Than thine hath been, my duties ask;   170
With theirs my efforts cannot blend,
I cannot for such cause contend;
Their aims I utterly forswear;
But I in body will be there.
Unarmed and naked will I go,
Be at their side, come weal or woe:
On kind occasions I may wait,
See, hear, obstruct, or mitigate.
Bare breast I take and an empty hand."

Therewith he threw away the lance,   180
Which he had grasped in that strong trance,
Spurned it, like something that would stand
Between him and the pure intent
Of love on which his soul was bent.
  "For thee, for thee, is left the sense
Of trial past without offence
To God or man; such innocence,
Such consolation, and the excess
Of an unmerited distress;
In that thy very strength must lie.   190
—O Sister, I could prophesy!
The time is come that rings the knell
Of all we loved, and loved so well:
Hope nothing, if I thus may speak
To thee, a woman, and thence weak:
Hope nothing, I repeat; for we
Are doomed to perish utterly:
'Tis meet that thou with me divide
The thought while I am by thy side,
Acknowledging a grace in this,   200
A comfort in the dark abyss,
But look not for me when I am gone,
And be no farther wrought upon:
Farewell all wishes, all debate,
All prayers for this cause, or for that!
Weep, if that aid thee; but depend
Upon no help of outward friend;
Espouse thy doom at once, and cleave
To fortitude without reprieve.
For we must fall, both we and ours—   210
This Mansion and these pleasant bowers,
Walks, pools, and arbours, homestead, hall—
Our fate is theirs, will reach them all;
The young horse must forsake his manger,
And learn to glory in a Stranger;
The hawk forget his perch; the hound
Be parted from his ancient ground:
The blast will sweep us all away—

One desolation, one decay!
And even this Creature!" which words saying,   220
He pointed to a lovely Doe,
A few steps distant, feeding, straying;
Fair creature, and more white than snow!
"Even she will to her peaceful woods
Return, and to her murmuring floods,
And be in heart and soul the same
She was before she hither came;
Ere she had learned to love us all,
Herself beloved in Rylstone-hall.
—But thou, my Sister, doomed to be   230
The last leaf on a blasted tree;
If not in vain we breathed the breath
Together of a purer faith;
If hand in hand we have been led,
And thou, (O happy thought this day!)
Not seldom foremost in the way;
If on one thought our minds have fed,
And we have in one meaning read;
If, when at home our private weal
Hath suffered from the shock of zeal,   240
Together we have learned to prize
Forbearance and self-sacrifice;
If we like combatants have fared,
And for this issue been prepared;
If thou art beautiful, and youth
And thought endue thee with all truth—
Be strong;—be worthy of the grace
Of God, and fill thy destined place:
A Soul, by force of sorrows high,
Uplifted to the purest sky   250
Of undisturbed humanity!"
    He ended,—or she heard no more;
He led her from the yew-tree shade,
And at the mansion's silent door,
He kissed the consecrated Maid;
And down the valley then pursued,
Alone, the armèd Multitude.

CANTO THIRD

Now joy for you who from the towers
Of Brancepeth look in doubt and fear,
Telling melancholy hours!
Proclaim it, let your Master hear
That Norton with his band is near!
The watchmen from their station high
Pronounced the word,—and the Earls descry,
Well-pleased, the armèd Company
Marching down the banks of Were.
    Said fearless Norton to the pair   10
Gone forth to greet him on the plain—
"This meeting, noble Lords! looks fair,
I bring with me a goodly train;
Their hearts are with you: hill and dale
Have helped us: Ure we crossed, and Swale,
And horse and harness followed—see
The best part of their Yeomanry!
—Stand forth, my Sons!—these eight are mine,
Whom to this service I commend;
Which way soe'er our fate incline,   20
These will be faithful to the end;
They are my all"—voice failed him here—
"My all save one, a Daughter dear!
Whom I have left, Love's mildest birth,
The meekest Child on this blessed earth.
I had—but these are by my side,
These Eight, and this is a day of pride!
The time is ripe. With festive din
Lo! how the people are flocking in,—
Like hungry fowl to the feeder's hand   30
When snow lies heavy upon the land."
    He spake bare truth; for far and near
From every side came noisy swarms
Of Peasants in their homely gear;
And, mixed with these, to Brancepeth came
Grave Gentry of estate and name,
And Captains known for worth in arms
And prayed the Earls in self-defence

To rise, and prove their innocence.—
"Rise, noble Earls, put forth your might   40
For holy Church, and the People's right!"
     The Norton fixed, at this demand,
His eye upon Northumberland,
And said; "The Minds of Men will own
No loyal rest while England's Crown
Remains without an Heir, the bait
Of strife and factions desperate;
Who, paying deadly hate in kind
Through all things else, in this can find
A mutual hope, a common mind;   50
And plot, and pant to overwhelm
All ancient honour in the realm.
—Brave Earls! to whose heroic veins
Our noblest blood is given in trust,
To you a suffering State complains,
And ye must raise her from the dust.
With wishes of still bolder scope
On you we look, with dearest hope;
Even for our Altars—for the prize,
In Heaven, of life that never dies;   60
For the old and holy Church we mourn,
And must in joy to her return.
Behold!"—and from his Son whose stand
Was on his right, from that guardian hand
He took the Banner, and unfurled
The precious folds—"behold," said he,
"The ransom of a sinful world;
Let this your preservation be;
The wounds of hands and feet and side,
And the sacred Cross on which Jesus died.   70
—This bring I from an ancient hearth,
These Records wrought in pledge of love
By hands of no ignoble birth,
A Maid o'er whom the blessed Dove
Vouchsafed in gentleness to brood
While she the holy work pursued."
"Uplift the Standard!" was the cry

From all the listeners that stood round,
"Plant it,—by this we live or die."
The Norton ceased not for that sound,   80
But said; "The prayer which ye have heard,
Much-injured Earls! by these preferred,
Is offered to the Saints, the sigh
Of tens of thousands, secretly."
"Uplift it!" cried once more the Band,
And then a thoughtful pause ensued:
"Uplift it!" said Northumberland
Whereat, from all the multitude
Who saw the Banner reared on high
In all its dread emblazonry,   90
A voice of uttermost joy brake out:
The transport was rolled down the river of Were,
And Durham, the time-honoured Durham, did hear,
And the towers of Saint Cuthbert were stirred by the shout!
      Now was the North in arms:—they shine
In warlike trim from Tweed to Tyne,
At Percy's voice: and Neville sees
His Followers gathering in from Tees,
From Were, and all the little rills
Concealed among the forked hills—   100
Seven hundred Knights, Retainers all
Of Neville, at their Master's call
Had sate together in Raby Hall!
Such strength that Earldom held of yore;
Nor wanted at this time rich store
Of well-appointed chivalry.
—Not loth the sleepy lance to wield,
And greet the old paternal shield,
They heard the summons;—and, furthermore,
Horsemen and Foot of each degree,   110
Unbound by pledge of fealty,
Appeared, with free and open hate
Of novelties in Church and State;
Knight, burgher, yeoman, and esquire;
And Romish priest, in priest's attire.
And thus, in arms, a zealous Band

Proceeding under joint command,
To Durham first their course they bear;
And in Saint Cuthbert's ancient seat
Sang mass,—and tore the book of prayer,—   120
And trod the bible beneath their feet.
   Thence marching southward smooth and free
"They mustered their host at Wetherby,
Full sixteen thousand fair to see,"
The Choicest Warriors of the North!
But none for beauty and for worth
Like those eight Sons—who, in a ring,
(Ripe men, or blooming in life's spring)
Each with a lance, erect and tall,
A falchion, and a buckler small,   130
Stood by their Sire, on Clifford-moor,
To guard the Standard which he bore.
On foot they girt their Father round;
And so will keep the appointed ground
Where'er their march: no steed will he
Henceforth bestride;—triumphantly,
He stands upon the grassy sod,
Trusting himself to the earth, and God.
Rare sight to embolden and inspire!
Proud was the field of Sons and Sire;   140
Of him the most; and, sooth to say,
No shape of man in all the array
So graced the sunshine of that day.
The monumental pomp of age
Was with this goodly Personage;
A stature undepressed in size,
Unbent, which rather seemed to rise,
In open victory o'er the weight
Of seventy years, to loftier height;
Magnific limbs of withered state;   150
A face to fear and venerate;
Eyes dark and strong; and on his head
Bright locks of silver hair, thick spread,
Which a brown morion half-concealed,
Light as a hunter's of the field;

And thus, with girdle round his waist,
Whereon the Banner-staff might rest
At need, he stood, advancing high
The glittering, floating Pageantry.
     Who sees him?—thousands see, and One   160
With unparticipated gaze;
Who, 'mong those thousands, friend hath none,
And treads in solitary ways.
He, following wheresoe'er he might,
Hath watched the Banner from afar,
As shepherds watch a lonely star,
Or mariners the distant light
That guides them through a stormy night.
And now, upon a chosen plot
Of rising ground, yon heathy spot!   170
He takes alone his far-off stand,
With breast unmailed, unweaponed hand.
Bold is his aspect; but his eye
Is pregnant with anxiety,
While, like a tutelary Power,
He there stands fixed from hour to hour:
Yet sometimes in more humble guise,
Upon the turf-clad height he lies
Stretched, herdsman-like, as if to bask
In sunshine were his only task,   180
Or by his mantle's help to find
A shelter from the nipping wind:
And thus, with short oblivion blest,
His weary spirits gather rest.
Again he lifts his eyes; and lo!
The pageant glancing to and fro;
And hope is wakened by the sight,
He thence may learn, ere fall of night,
Which way the tide is doomed to flow.
     To London were the Chieftains bent;   190
But what avails the bold intent?
A Royal army is gone forth
To quell the RISING OF THE NORTH;
They march with Dudley at their head,

And, in seven days' space, will to York be led!—
Can such a mighty Host be raised
Thus suddenly, and brought so near?
The Earls upon each other gazed,
And Neville's cheek grew pale with fear;   200
For, with a high and valiant name,
He bore a heart of timid frame;
And bold if both had been, yet they
"Against so many may not stay."
Back therefore will they hie to seize
A strong Hold on the banks of Tees;
There wait a favourable hour,
Until Lord Dacre with his power
From Naworth come; and Howard's aid
Be with them openly displayed.
 While through the Host, from man to man,   210
A rumour of this purpose ran,
The Standard trusting to the care
Of him who heretofore did bear
That charge, impatient Norton sought
The Chieftains to unfold his thought,
And thus abruptly spake;—"We yield
(And can it be?) an unfought field!—
How oft has strength, the strength of heaven,
To few triumphantly been given!
Still do our very children boast   220
Of mitred Thurston—what a Host
He conquered!—Saw we not the Plain
(And flying shall behold again)
Where faith was proved?—while to battle moved
The Standard, on the Sacred Wain
That bore it, compassed round by a bold
Fraternity of Barons old;
And with those grey-haired champions stood,
Under the saintly ensigns three,
The infant heir of Mowbray's blood—   230
All confident of victory!—
Shall Percy blush, then, for his name?
Must Westmoreland be asked with shame

Whose were the numbers, where the loss,
In that other day of Neville's Cross?
When the Prior of Durham with holy hand
Raised, as the Vision gave command,
Saint Cuthbert's Relic—far and near
Kenned on the point of a lofty spear;
While the Monks prayed in Maiden's Bower   240
To God descending in his power.
Less would not at our need be due
To us, who war against the Untrue;—
The delegates of Heaven we rise,
Convoked the impious to chastise:
We, we, the sanctities of old
Would re-establish and uphold:
Be warned"—His zeal the Chiefs confounded,
But word was given, and the trumpet sounded:
Back through the melancholy Host   250
Went Norton, and resumed his post.
Alas! thought he, and have I borne
This Banner raised with joyful pride,
This hope of all posterity,
By those dread symbols sanctified;
Thus to become at once the scorn
Of babbling winds as they go by,
A spot of shame to the sun's bright eye,
To the light clouds of mockery!
—"Even these poor eight of mine would stem—"   260
Half to himself, and half to them
He spake—"would stem, or quell a force
Ten times their number, man and horse:
This by their own unaided might,
Without their father in their sight,
Without the Cause for which they fight;
A Cause, which on a needful day
Would breed us thousands brave as they."
—So speaking, he his reverend head
Raised towards that Imagery once more: 270
But the familiar prospect shed
Despondency unfelt before:

A shock of intimations vain,
Dismay, and superstitious pain,
Fell on him, with the sudden thought
Of her by whom the work was wrought:—
Oh wherefore was her countenance bright
With love divine and gentle light?
She would not, could not, disobey,
But her Faith leaned another way.   280
Ill tears she wept; I saw them fall,
I overheard her as she spake
Sad words to that mute Animal,
The White Doe, in the hawthorn brake;
She steeped, but not for Jesu's sake,
This Cross in tears: by her, and One
Unworthier far we are undone—
Her recreant Brother—he prevailed
Over that tender Spirit—assailed
Too oft, alas! by her whose head   290
In the cold grave hath long been laid:
She first, in reason's dawn beguiled
Her docile, unsuspecting Child:
Far back—far back my mind must go
To reach the well-spring of this woe!

    While thus he brooded, music sweet
Of border tunes was played to cheer
The footsteps of a quick retreat;
But Norton lingered in the rear,
Stung with sharp thoughts; and ere the last   300
From his distracted brain was cast,
Before his Father, Francis stood,
And spake in firm and earnest mood.

  "Though here I bend a suppliant knee
In reverence, and unarmed, I bear
In your indignant thoughts my share;
Am grieved this backward march to see
So careless and disorderly.
I scorn your Chiefs—men who would lead,
And yet want courage at their need: 310
Then look at them with open eyes!

Deserve they further sacrifice?—
If—when they shrink, nor dare oppose
In open field their gathering foes,
(And fast, from this decisive day,
Yon multitude must melt away;)
If now I ask a grace not claimed
While ground was left for hope; unblamed
Be an endeavour that can do
No injury to them or you.   320
My Father! I would help to find
A place of shelter, till the rage
Of cruel men do like the wind
Exhaust itself and sink to rest;
Be Brother now to Brother joined!
Admit me in the equipage
Of your misfortunes, that at least,
Whatever fate remain behind,
I may bear witness in my breast
To your nobility of mind!"   330
    "Thou Enemy, my bane and blight!
Oh! bold to fight the Coward's fight
Against all good"—but why declare,
At length, the issue of a prayer
Which love had prompted, yielding scope
Too free to one bright moment's hope?
Suffice it that the Son, who strove
With fruitless effort to allay
That passion, prudently gave way;
Nor did he turn aside to prove   340
His Brothers' wisdom or their love—
But calmly from the spot withdrew;
His best endeavours to renew,
    Should e'er a kindlier time ensue.

CANTO FOURTH

'Tis night: in silence looking down,
The Moon, from cloudless ether, sees
A Camp, and a beleaguered Town,
And Castle, like a stately crown

On the steep rocks of winding Trees;—
And southward far, with moor between,
Hill-top, and flood, and forest green,
The bright Moon sees that valley small
Where Rylstone's old sequestered Hall
A venerable image yields   10
Of quiet to the neighbouring fields;
While from one pillared chimney breathes
The smoke, and mounts in silver wreaths.
—The courts are hushed;—for timely sleep
The greyhounds to their kennel creep;
The peacock in the broad ash tree
Aloft is roosted for the night,
He who in proud prosperity
Of colours manifold and bright
Walked round, affronting the daylight;   20
And higher still, above the bower
Where he is perched, from yon lone Tower
The hall-clock in the clear moonshine
With glittering finger points at nine.
   Ah! who could think that sadness here
Hath any sway? or pain, or fear?
A soft and lulling sound is heard
Of streams inaudible by day;
The garden pool's dark surface, stirred
By the night insects in their play,   30
Breaks into dimples small and bright;
A thousand, thousand rings of light
That shape themselves and disappear
Almost as soon as seen:—and lo!
Not distant far, the milk-white Doe—
The same who quietly was feeding
On the green herb, and nothing heeding,
When Francis, uttering to the Maid
His last words in the yew-tree shade,
Involved whate'er by love was brought   40
Out of his heart, or crossed his thought,
Or chance presented to his eye,
In one sad sweep of destiny—

The same fair Creature, who hath found
Her way into forbidden ground;
Where now—within this spacious plot
For pleasure made, a goodly spot,
With lawns and beds of flowers, and shades
Of trellis-work in long arcades,
And cirque and crescent framed by wall   50
Of close-clips foliage green and tall,
Converging walks, and fountains gay,
And terraces in trim array—
Beneath yon cypress spiring high,
With pine and cedar spreading wide
Their darksome boughs on either side,
In open moonlight doth she lie;
Happy as others of her kind,
That, far from human neighbourhood,
Range unrestricted as the wind,   60
Through park, or chase, or savage wood.

     But see the consecrated Maid
Emerging from a cedar shade
To open moonshine, where the Doe
Beneath the cypress-spire is laid;
Like a patch of April snow—
Upon a bed of herbage green,
Lingering in a woody glade
Or behind a rocky screen—
Lonely relic! which, if seen   70
By the shepherd, is passed by
With an inattentive eye.
Nor more regard doth She bestow
Upon the uncomplaining Doe
Now couched at ease, though oft this day
Not unperplexed nor free from pain,
When she had tried, and tried in vain,
Approaching in her gentle way,
To win some look of love, or gain
Encouragement to sport or play—   80
Attempts which still the heart-sick Maid
Rejected, or with slight repaid.

Yet Emily is soothed;—the breeze
Came fraught with kindly sympathies.
As she approached yon rustic Shed
Hung with late-flowering woodbine, spread
Along the walls and overhead,
The fragrance of the breathing flowers
Revived a memory of those hours
When here, in this remote alcove,   90
(While from the pendent woodbine came
Like odours, sweet as if the same)
A fondly-anxious Mother strove
To teach her salutary fears
And mysteries above her years.
Yes, she is soothed: an Image faint,
And yet not faint—a presence bright
Returns to her—that blessed Saint
Who with mild looks and language mild
Instructed here her darling Child,   100
While yet a prattler on the knee,
To worship in simplicity
The invisible God, and take for guide
The faith reformed and purified.
    'Tis flown—the Vision, and the sense
Of that beguiling influence,
"But oh! thou Angel from above,
Mute Spirit of maternal love,
That stood'st before my eyes, more clear
Than ghosts are fabled to appear   110
Sent upon embassies of fear;
As thou thy presence hast to me
Vouchsafed, in radiant ministry
Descend on Francis; nor forbear
To greet him with a voice, and say;—
'If hope be a rejected stay,
'Do thou, my christian Son, beware
'Of that most lamentable snare,
'The self-reliance of despair!' "
    Then from within the embowered retreat   120
Where she had found a grateful seat

Perturbed she issues. She will go!
Herself will follow to the war,
And clasp her Father's knees;—ah, no!
She meets the insuperable bar,
The injunction by her Brother laid;
His parting charge—but ill obeyed—
That interdicted all debate,
All prayer for this cause or for that;
All efforts that would turn aside   130
The headstrong current of their fate:
Her duty is to stand and wait;
In resignation to abide
The shock, AND FINALLY SECURE
O'ER PAIN AND GRIEF A TRIUMPH PURE.
—She feels it, and her pangs are checked.
But now, as silently she paced
The turf, and thought by thought was chased,
Came One who, with sedate respect,
Approached, and, greeting her, thus spake;   140
"An old man's privilege I take:
Dark is the time—a woeful day!
Dear daughter of affliction, say
How can I serve you? point the way."

      "Rights have you, and may well be bold;
You with my Father have grown old
In friendship—strive—for his sake go—
Turn from us all the coming woe:
This would I beg; but on my mind
A passive stillness is enjoined.   150
On you, if room for mortal aid
Be left, is no restriction laid;
You not forbidden to recline
With hope upon the Will divine."

      "Hope," said the old Man, "must abide
With all of us, whate'er betide.
In Craven's Wilds is many a den,
To shelter persecuted men:
Far under ground is many a cave,
Where they might lie as in the grave,   160

Until this storm hath ceased to rave:
Or let them cross the River Tweed,
And be at once from peril freed!"
    "Ah tempt me not!" she faintly sighed;
"I will not counsel nor exhort,
With my condition satisfied;
But you, at least, may make report
Of what befalls;—be this your task—
This may be done;—'tis all I ask!"
    She spake—and from the Lady's sight   170
The Sire, unconscious of his age,
Departed promptly as a Page
Bound on some errand of delight.
—The noble Francis—wise as brave,
Thought he, may want not skill to save.
With hopes in tenderness concealed,
Unarmed he followed to the field;
Him will I seek: the insurgent Powers
Are now besieging Barnard's Towers,—
"Grant that the Moon which shines this night   180
May guide them in a prudent flight!"
    But quick the turns of chance and change,
And knowledge has a narrow range;
Whence idle fears, and needless pain,
And wishes blind, and efforts vain.—
The Moon may shine, but cannot be
Their guide in flight—already she
Hath witnessed their captivity.
She saw the desperate assault
Upon that hostile castle made;—   190
But dark and dismal is the vault
Where Norton and his sons are laid!
Disastrous issue!—he had said
"This night yon faithless Towers must yield,
Or we for ever quit the field.
—Neville is utterly dismayed,
For promise fails of Howard's aid;
And Dacre to our call replies
That *he* is unprepared to rise.

My heart is sick;—this weary pause   200
Must needs be fatal to our cause.
The breach is open—on the wall,
This night, the Banner shall be planted!"
—'Twas done: his Sons were with him—all;
They belt him round with hearts undaunted
And others follow;—Sire and Son
Leap down into the court;—" 'Tis won"—
They shout aloud—but Heaven decreed
That with their joyful shout should close
The triumph of a desperate deed   210
Which struck with terror friends and foes!
The friend shrinks back—the foe recoils
From Norton and his filial band;
But they, now caught within the toils,
Against a thousand cannot stand;—
The foe from numbers courage drew,
And overpowered that gallant few.
"A rescue for the Standard!" cried
The Father from within the walls;
But, see, the sacred Standard falls!—   220
Confusion through the Camp spread wide:
Some fled; and some their fears detained:
But ere the Moon had sunk to rest
In her pale chambers of the west,
Of that rash levy nought remained.

CANTO FIFTH

High on a point of rugged ground
Among the wastes of Rylstone Fell
Above the loftiest ridge or mound
Where foresters or shepherds dwell,
An edifice of warlike frame
Stands single—Norton Tower its name—
It fronts all quarters, and looks round
O'er path and road, and plain and dell,
Dark moor, and gleam of pool and stream,
Upon a prospect without bound.   10
    The summit of this bold ascent—

Though bleak and bare, and seldom free
As Pendle-hill or Pennygent
From wind, or frost, or vapours wet—
Had often heard the sound of glee
When there the youthful Nortons met,
To practise games and archery:
How proud and happy they! the crowd
Of Lookers-on how pleased and proud!
And from the scorching noon-tide sun,   20
From showers, or when the prize was won,
They to the Tower withdrew, and there
Would mirth run round, with generous fare;
And the stern old Lord of Rylstone-hall
Was happiest, proudest, of them all!

But now, his Child, with anguish pale,
Upon the height walks to and fro;
'Tis well that she hath heard the tale,
Received the bitterness of woe:
For she *had* hoped, had hoped and feared,   30
Such rights did feeble nature claim;
And oft her steps had hither steered,
Though not unconscious of self-blame;
For she her brother's charge revered,
His farewell words; and by the same,
Yea by her brother's very name,
Had, in her solitude, been cheered.

Beside the lonely watch-tower stood
That grey-haired Man of gentle blood,
Who with her Father had grown old   40
In friendship; rival hunters they,
And fellow warriors in their day;
To Rylstone he the tidings brought;
Then on this height the Maid had sought,
And, gently as he could, had told
The end of that dire Tragedy,
Which it had been his lot to see.

To him the Lady turned; "You said
That Francis lives, *he* is not dead?"
"Your noble brother hath been spared;   50

To take his life they have not dared;
On him and on his high endeavour
The light of praise shall shine for ever!
Nor did he (such Heaven's will) in vain
His solitary course maintain;
Not vainly struggled in the might
Of duty, seeing with clear sight;
He was their comfort to the last,
Their joy till every pang was past.

    I witnessed when to York they came—   60
What, Lady, if their feet were tied;
They might deserve a good Man's blame;
But marks of infamy and shame—
These were their triumph, these their pride,
Nor wanted 'mid the pressing crowd
Deep feeling, that found utterance loud,
'Lo, Francis comes,' there were who cried,
'A Prisoner once, but now set free!
'Tis well, for he the worst defied
Through force of natural piety;   70
He rose not in this quarrel; he,
For concord's sake and England's good,
Suit to his Brothers often made
With tears, and of his Father prayed—
And when he had in vain withstood
Their purpose—then did he divide,
He parted from them; but at their side
Now walks in unanimity.
Then peace to cruelty and scorn,
While to the prison they are borne,   80
Peace, peace to all indignity!'

    And so in Prison were they laid—
Oh hear me, hear me, gentle Maid,
For I am come with power to bless,
By scattering gleams, through your distress,
Of a redeeming happiness.
Me did a reverent pity move
And privilege of ancient love;
And, in your service, making bold,

Entrance I gained to that stronghold.   90
   Your Father gave me cordial greeting;
But to his purposes, that burned
Within him, instantly returned:
He was commanding and entreating,
And said—'We need not stop, my Son!
Thoughts press, and time is hurrying on'—
And so to Francis he renewed
His words, more calmly thus pursued.

   'Might this our enterprise have sped,
Change wide and deep the Land had seen,   100
A renovation from the dead,
A spring-tide of immortal green:
The darksome altars would have blazed
Like stars when clouds are rolled away;
Salvation to all eyes that gazed,
Once more the Rood had been upraised
To spread its arms, and stand for aye.
Then, then—had I survived to see
New life in Bolton Priory;
The voice restored, the eye of Truth   110
Re-opened that inspired my youth;
To see her in her pomp arrayed—
This Banner (for such vow I made)
Should on the consecrated breast
Of that same Temple have found rest:
I would myself have hung it high,
Fit offering of glad victory!

   A shadow of such thought remains
To cheer this sad and pensive time;
A solemn fancy yet sustains   120
One feeble Being—bids me climb
Even to the last—one effort more
To attest my Faith, if not restore.

   Hear then,' said he, 'while I impart,
My Son, the last wish of my heart.
The Banner strive thou to regain;
And, if the endeavour prove not vain,
Bear it—to whom if not to thee

Shall I this lonely thought consign?—
Bear it to Bolton Priory,   130
And lay it on Saint Mary's shrine;
To wither in the sun and breeze
'Mid those decaying sanctities.
There let at least the gift be laid,
The testimony there displayed;
Bold proof that with no selfish aim,
But for lost Faith and Christ's dear name,
I helmeted a brow though white,
And took a place in all men's sight;
Yea offered up this noble Brood,   140
This fair unrivalled Brotherhood,
And turned away from thee, my Son!
And left—but be the rest unsaid,
The name untouched, the tear unshed;—
My wish is known, and I have done:
Now promise, grant this one request,
This dying prayer, and be thou blest!'
    Then Francis answered—'Trust thy Son,
For, with God's will, it shall be done!'—
    The pledge obtained, the solemn word   150
Thus scarcely given, a noise was heard,
And Officers appeared in state
To lead the prisoners to their fate.
They rose, oh! wherefore should I fear
To tell, or, Lady, you to hear?
They rose—embraces none were given—
They stood like trees when earth and heaven
Are calm; they knew each other's worth,
And reverently the Band went forth.
They met, when they had reached the door,   160
One with profane and harsh intent
Placed there—that he might go before
And, with that rueful Banner borne
Aloft in sign of taunting scorn,
Conduct them to their punishment:
So cruel Sussex, unrestrained
By human feeling, had ordained.

The unhappy Banner Francis saw,
And, with a look of calm command
Inspiring universal awe, 170
He took it from the soldier's hand;
And all the people that stood round
Confirmed the deed in peace profound.
—High transport did the Father shed
Upon his Son—and they were led,
Led on, and yielded up their breath;
Together died, a happy death!—
But Francis, soon as he had braved
That insult, and the Banner saved,
Athwart the unresisting tide 180
Of the spectators occupied
In admiration or dismay,
Bore instantly his Charge away."

    These things, which thus had in the sight
And hearing passed of Him who stood
With Emily, on the Watch-tower height,
In Rylstone's woeful neighbourhood,
He told; and oftentimes with voice
Of power to comfort or rejoice;
For deepest sorrows that aspire, 190
Go high, no transport ever higher.
"Yes—God is rich in mercy," said
The old Man to the silent Maid,
"Yet, Lady! shines, through this black night,
One star of aspect heavenly bright;
Your Brother lives—he lives—is come
Perhaps already to his home;
Then let us leave this dreary place."
She yielded, and with gentle pace,
Though without one uplifted look, 200
To Rylstone-hall her way she took.

CANTO SIXTH

Why comes not Francis?—From the doleful City
He fled,—and, in his flight, could hear
The death-sounds of the Minster-bell:

That sullen stroke pronounced farewell
To Marmaduke, cut off from pity!
To Ambrose that! and then a knell
For him, the sweet half-open Flower!
For all—all dying in one hour!
—Why comes not Francis? Thoughts of love
Should bear him to his Sister dear   10
With the fleet motion of a dove;
Yea, like a heavenly messenger
Of speediest wing, should he appear.
Why comes he not?—for westward fast
Along the plain of York he past;
Reckless of what impels or leads,
Unchecked he hurries on;—nor heeds
The sorrow, through the Villages,
Spread by triumphant cruelties
Of vengeful military force,   20
And punishment without remorse.
He marked not, heard not, as he fled,
All but the suffering heart was dead
For him abandoned to blank awe,
To vacancy, and horror strong:
And the first object which he saw,
With conscious sight, as he swept along—
It was the Banner in his hand!
He felt—and made a sudden stand.

He looked about like one betrayed: 30
What hath he done? what promise made?
Oh weak, weak moment! to what end
Can such a vain oblation tend,
And he the Bearer?—Can he go
Carrying this instrument of woe,
And find, find anywhere, a right
To excuse him in his Country's sight?
No; will not all men deem the change
A downward course, perverse and strange?
Here is it;—but how? when? must she,   40
The unoffending Emily,
Again this piteous object see?

Such conflict long did he maintain,
Nor liberty nor rest could gain:
His own life into danger brought
By this sad burden—even that thought,
Exciting self-suspicion strong
Swayed the brave man to his wrong.
And how—unless it were the sense
Of all-disposing Providence,   50
Its will unquestionably shown—
How has the Banner clung so fast
To a palsied, and unconscious hand;
Clung to the hand to which it passed
Without impediment? And why,
But that Heaven's purpose might be known,
Doth now no hindrance meet his eye,
No intervention, to withstand
Fulfilment of a Father's prayer
Breathed to a Son forgiven, and blest   60
When all resentments were at rest,
And life in death laid the heart bare?—
Then, like a spectre sweeping by,
Rushed through his mind the prophecy
Of utter desolation made
To Emily in the yew-tree shade:
He sighed, submitting will and power
To the stern embrace of that grasping hour.
"No choice is left, the dead is mine—
Dead are they, dead!—and I will go,   70
And, for their sakes, come weal or woe,
Will lay the Relic on the shrine."
So forward with a steady will
He went, and traversed plain and hill;
And up the vale of Wharf his way
Pursued;—and, at the dawn of day,
Attained a summit whence his eyes
Could see the Tower of Bolton rise.
There Francis for a moment's space
Made halt—but hark! a noise behind   80
Of horsemen at an eager pace!

He heard, and with misgiving mind.
—'Tis Sir George Bowes who leads the Band:
They come, by cruel Sussex sent;
Who, when the Nortons from the hand
Of death had drunk their punishment,
Bethought him, angry and ashamed,
How Francis, with the Banner claimed
As his own charge, had disappeared,
By all the standers-by revered.   90
His whole bold carriage (which had quelled
Thus far the Opposer, and repelled
All censure, enterprise so bright
That even bad men had vainly striven
Against that overcoming light)
Was then reviewed, and prompt word given
That to what place soever fled
He should be seized, alive or dead.

    The troop of horse have gained the height
Where Francis stood in open sight.   100
They hem him round—"Behold the proof,"
They cried, "the Ensign in his hand!
He did not arm, he walked aloof!
For why?—to save his Father's land;—
Worst Traitor of them all is he,
A Traitor dark and cowardly!"

    "I am no Traitor," Francis said,
"Though this unhappy freight I bear;
And must not part with. But beware;—
Err not by hasty zeal misled,   110
Nor do a suffering Spirit wrong,
Whose self-reproaches are too strong!"
At this he from the beaten road
Retreated towards a brake of thorn,
That like a place of vantage showed;
And there stood bravely, though forlorn.
In self-defence with warlike brow
He stood,—nor weaponless was now;
He from a Soldier's hand had snatched
A spear,—and, so protected, watched   120

The Assailants, turning round and round;
But from behind with treacherous wound
A Spearman brought him to the ground.
The guardian lance, as Francis fell,
Dropped from him; but his other hand
The Banner clenched; till, from out the Band,
One, the most eager for the prize,
Rushed in; and—while, O grief to tell!
A glimmering sense still left, with eyes
Unclosed the noble Francis lay—   130
Seized it, as hunters seize their prey;
But not before the warm life-blood
Had tinged more deeply, as it flowed,
The wounds the broidered Banner showed,
Thy fatal work, O Maiden, innocent as good!

    Proudly the Horsemen bore away
The Standard; and where Francis lay
There was he left alone, unwept,
And for two days unnoticed slept.
For at that time bewildering fear   140
Possessed the country, far and near;
But, on the third day, passing by
One of the Norton Tenantry
Espied the uncovered Corse; the Man
Shrunk as he recognised the face,
And to the nearest homesteads ran
And called the people to the place.
—How desolate is Rylstone-hall!
This was the instant thought of all;
And if the lonely Lady there   150
Should be; to her they cannot bear
This weight of anguish and despair.
So, when upon sad thoughts had prest
Thoughts sadder still, they deemed it best
That, if the Priest should yield assent
And no one hinder their intent,
Then, they, for Christian pity's sake,
In holy ground a grave would make;
And straightway buried he should be

In the Churchyard of the Priory.   160
    Apart, some little space, was made
The grave where Francis must be laid.
In no confusion or neglect
This did they,—but in pure respect
That he was born of gentle blood;
And that there was no neighbourhood
Of kindred for him in that ground:
So to the Churchyard they are bound,
Bearing the body on a bier;
And psalms they sing—a holy sound   170
That hill and vale with sadness hear.
    But Emily hath raised her head,
And is again disquieted;
She must behold!—so many gone,
Where is the solitary One?
And forth from Rylstone-hall stepped she,—
To seek her Brother forth she went,
And tremblingly her course she bent
Toward Bolton's ruined Priory.
She comes, and in the vale hath heard   180
The funeral dirge;—she sees the knot
Of people, sees them in one spot—
And darting like a wounded bird
She reached the grave, and with her breast
Upon the ground received the rest,—
The consummation, the whole ruth
And sorrow of this final truth!

CANTO SEVENTH

"Powers there are
That touch each other to the quick — in modes
Which the gross world no sense hath to perceive,
No soul to dream of."

Thou Spirit, whose angelic hand
Was to the harp a strong command,
Called the submissive strings to wake
In glory for this Maiden's sake,

Say, Spirit! whither hath she fled
To hide her poor afflicted head?
What mighty forest in its gloom
Enfolds her?—is a rifted tomb
Within the wilderness her seat?
Some island which the wild waves beat—   10
Is that the Sufferer's last retreat?
Or some aspiring rock, that shrouds
Its perilous front in mists and clouds?
High-climbing rock, low sunless dale,
Sea, desert, what do these avail?
Oh take her anguish and her fears
Into a deep recess of years!

'Tis done;—despoil and desolation
O'er Rylstone's fair domain have blown;
Pools, terraces, and walks are sown   20
With weeds; the bowers are overthrown,
Or have given way to slow mutation,
While, in their ancient habitation
The Norton name hath been unknown.
The lordly Mansion of its pride
Is stripped; the ravage hath spread wide
Through park and field, a perishing
That mocks the gladness of the Spring!
And, with this silent gloom agreeing,
Appears a joyless human Being,   30
Of aspect such as if the waste
Were under her dominion placed.
Upon a primrose bank, her throne
Of quietness, she sits alone;
Among the ruins of a wood,
Erewhile a covert bright and green,
And where full many a brave tree stood,
That used to spread its boughs, and ring
With the sweet bird's carolling,
Behold her, like a virgin Queen,   40
Neglecting in imperial state
These outward images of fate,
And carrying inward a serene

And perfect sway, through many a thought
Of chance and change, that hath been brought
To the subjection of a holy,
Though stern and rigorous, melancholy!
The like authority, with grace
Of awfulness, is in her face,—
There hath she fixed it; yet it seems   50
To o'ershadow by no native right
That face, which cannot lose the gleams,
Lose utterly the tender gleams,
Of gentleness and meek delight,
And loving-kindness ever bright:
Such is her sovereign mien:—her dress
(A vest with woollen cincture tied,
A hood of mountain-wool undyed)
Is homely,—fashioned to express
A wandering Pilgrim's humbleness.   60
      And she *hath* wandered, long and far,
Beneath the light of sun and star;
Hath roamed in trouble and in grief,
Driven forward like a withered leaf,
Yea like a ship at random blown
To distant places and unknown.
But now she dares to seek a haven
Among her native wilds of Craven;
Hath seen again her Father's roof,
And put her fortitude to proof;   70
The mighty sorrow hath been borne,
And she is thoroughly forlorn:
Her soul doth in itself stand fast,
Sustained by memory of the past
And strength of Reason; held above
The infirmities of mortal love;
Undaunted, lofty, calm, and stable,
And awfully impenetrable.
      And so—beneath a mouldered tree,
A self-surviving leafless oak   80
By unregarded age from stroke
Of ravage saved—sate Emily.

There did she rest, with head reclined,
Herself most like a stately flower,
(Such have I seen) whom chance of birth
Hath separated from its kind,
To live and die in a shady bower,
Single on the gladsome earth.
    When, with a noise like distant thunder,
A troop of deer came sweeping by;   90
And, suddenly, behold a wonder!
For One, among those rushing deer,
A single One, in mid career
Hath stopped, and fixed her large full eye
Upon the Lady Emily;
A Doe most beautiful, clear-white,
A radiant creature, silver-bright!
    Thus checked, a little while it stayed;
A little thoughtful pause it made;
And then advanced with stealth-like pace,   100
Drew softly near her, and more near—
Looked round—but saw no cause for fear;
So to her feet the Creature came,
And laid its head upon her knee,
And looked into the Lady's face,
A look of pure benignity,
And fond unclouded memory.
It is, thought Emily, the same,
The very Doe of other years!—
The pleading look the Lady viewed,   110
And, by her gushing thoughts subdued,
She melted into tears—
A flood of tears, that flowed apace,
Upon the happy Creature's face.
    Oh, moment ever blest! O Pair
Beloved of Heaven, Heaven's chosen care,
This was for you a precious greeting;
And may it prove a fruitful meeting!
Joined are they, and the sylvan Doe
Can she depart? can she forego   120
The Lady, once her playful peer,

And now her sainted Mistress dear?
And will not Emily receive
This lovely chronicler of things
Long past, delights and sorrowings?
Lone Sufferer! will not she believe
The promise in that speaking face;
And welcome, as a gift of grace,
The saddest thought the Creature brings?
    That day, the first of a re-union   130
Which was to teem with high communion,
That day of balmy April weather,
They tarried in the wood together.
And when, ere fall of evening dew,
She from her sylvan haunt withdrew,
The White Doe tracked with faithful pace
The Lady to her dwelling-place;
That nook where, on paternal ground,
A habitation she had found,
The Master of whose humble board   140
Once owned her Father for his Lord;
A hut, by tufted trees defended,
Where Rylstone brook with Wharf is blended.
    When Emily by morning light
Went forth, the Doe stood there in sight.
She shrunk:—with one frail shock of pain
Received and followed by a prayer,
She saw the Creature once again;
Shun will she not, she feels, will bear;—
But, wheresoever she looked round,   150
All now was trouble-haunted ground;
And therefore now she deems it good
Once more this restless neighbourhood
To leave.—Unwooed, yet unforbidden,
The White Doe followed up the vale,
Up to another cottage, hidden
In the deep fork of Amerdale;
And there may Emily restore
Herself, in spots unseen before.
    —Why tell of mossy rock, or tree,   160

By lurking Dernbrook's pathless side,
Haunts of a strengthening amity
That calmed her, cheered, and fortified?
For she hath ventured now to read
Of time, and place, and thought, and deed—
Endless history that lies
In her silent Follower's eyes;
Who with a power like human reason
Discerns the favourable season,
Skilled to approach or to retire,—   170
From looks conceiving her desire;
From look, deportment, voice, or mien,
That vary to the heart within.
If she too passionately wreathed
Her arms, or over-deeply breathed,
Walked quick or slowly, every mood
In its degree was understood;
Then well may their accord be true,
And kindliest intercourse ensue.
—Oh! surely 't was a gentle rousing   180
When she by sudden glimpse espied
The White Doe on the mountain browsing,
Or in the meadow wandered wide!
How pleased, when down the Straggler sank
Beside her, on some sunny bank!
How soothed, when in thick bower enclosed,
They, like a nested pair, reposed!
Fair Vision! when it crossed the Maid
Within some rocky cavern laid,
The dark cave's portal gliding by,   190
White as whitest cloud on high
Floating through the azure sky.
—What now is left for pain or fear?
That Presence, dearer and more dear,
While they, side by side, were straying,
And the shepherd's pipe was playing,
Did now a very gladness yield
At morning to the dewy field,
And with a deeper peace endued

The hour of moonlight solitude.   200
   With her Companion, in such frame
Of mind, to Rylstone back she came;
And, ranging through the wasted groves,
Received the memory of old loves,
Undisturbed and undistrest,
Into a soul which now was blest
With a soft spring-day of holy,
Mild, and grateful melancholy:
Not sunless gloom or unenlightened,
But by tender fancies brightened.   210
   When the bells of Rylstone played
Their sabbath music—"𝕲𝖔𝖉 𝖚𝖘 𝖆𝖞𝖉𝖊!"
That was the sound they seemed to speak;
Inscriptive legend which I ween
May on those holy bells be seen,
That legend and her Grandsire's name;
And oftentimes the Lady meek
Had in her childhood read the same;
Words which she slighted at that day;
But now, when such sad change was wrought,   220
And of that lonely name she thought—
The bells of Rylstone seemed to say,
While she sate listening in the shade,
With vocal music, "𝕲𝖔𝖉 𝖚𝖘 𝖆𝖞𝖉𝖊;"
And all the hills were glad to bear
Their part in this effectual prayer.
   Nor lacked she Reason's firmest power;
But with the White Doe at her side
Up would she climb to Norton Tower,
And thence look round her far and wide,   230
Her fate there measuring;—all is stilled,—
The weak One hath subdued her heart;
Behold the prophecy fulfilled,
Fulfilled, and she sustains her part!
But here her Brother's words have failed;
Here hath a milder doom prevailed;
That she, of him and all bereft,
Hath yet, this faithful Partner left;

This one Associate, that disproves
His words, remains for her, and loves.   240
If tears are shed, they do not fall
For loss of him—for one, or all;
Yet, sometimes, sometimes doth she weep
Moved gently in her soul's soft sleep;
A few tears down her cheek descend
For this her last and living Friend.

    Bless, tender Hearts, their mutual lot,
And bless for both this savage spot;
Which Emily doth sacred hold
For reasons dear and manifold—   250
Here hath she, here before her sight,
Close to the summit of this height,
The grassy rock-encircled Pound
In which the Creature first was found.
So beautiful the timid Thrall
(A spotless Youngling white as foam)
Her youngest Brother brought it home;
The youngest, then a lusty boy,
Bore it, or led, to Rylstone-hall
With heart brimful of pride and joy!   260

    But most to Bolton's sacred Pile,
On favouring nights, she loved to go;
There ranged through cloister, court, and aisle,
Attended by the soft-paced Doe;
Nor feared she in the still moonshine
To look upon Saint Mary's shrine;
Nor on the lonely turf that showed
Where Francis slept in his last abode.
For that she came; there oft she sate
Forlorn, but not disconsolate: 270
And, when she from the abyss returned
Of thought, she neither shrunk nor mourned;
Was happy that she lived to greet
Her mute Companion as it lay
In love and pity at her feet;
How happy in its turn to meet
The recognition! the mild glance

Beamed from that gracious countenance;
Communication, like the ray
Of a new morning, to the nature   280
And prospects of the inferior Creature!
   A mortal Song we sing, by dower
Encouraged of celestial power;
Power which the viewless Spirit shed
By whom we were first visited;
Whose voice we heard, whose hand and wings
Swept like a breeze the conscious strings,
When, left in solitude, erewhile
We stood before this ruined Pile,
And, quitting unsubstantial dreams,   290
Sang in this Presence kindred themes;
Distress and desolation spread
Through human hearts, and pleasure dead,—
Dead—but to live again on earth,
A second and yet nobler birth;
Dire overthrow, and yet how high
The re-ascent in sanctity!
From fair to fairer; day by day
A more divine and loftier way!
Even such this blessèd Pilgrim trod,   300
By sorrow lifted towards her God;
Uplifted to the purest sky
Of undisturbed mortality.
Her own thoughts loved she; and could bend
A dear look to her lowly Friend;
There stopped; her thirst was satisfied
With what this innocent spring supplied:
Her sanction inwardly she bore,
And stood apart from human cares:
But to the world returned no more,   310
Although with no unwilling mind
Help did she give at need, and joined
The Wharfdale peasants in their prayers.
At length, thus faintly, faintly tied
To earth, she was set free, and died.
Thy soul, exalted Emily,

Maid of the blasted family,
Rose to the God from whom it came!
—In Rylstone Church her mortal frame
Was buried by her Mother's side.   320
　Most glorious sunset! and a ray
Survives—the twilight of this day—
In that fair Creature whom the fields
Support, and whom the forest shields;
Who, having filled a holy place,
Partakes, in her degree, Heaven's grace;
And bears a memory and a mind
Raised far above the law of kind;
Haunting the spots with lonely cheer
Which her dear Mistress once held dear: 330
Loves most what Emily loved most—
The enclosure of this churchyard ground;
Here wanders like a gliding ghost,
And every sabbath here is found;
Comes with the people when the bells
Are heard among the moorland dells,
Finds entrance through yon arch, where way
Lies open on the sabbath-day;
Here walks amid the mournful waste
Of prostrate altars, shrines defaced,   340
And floors encumbered with rich show
Of fret-work imagery laid low;
Paces softly, or makes halt,
By fractured cell, or tomb, or vault;
By plate of monumental brass
Dim-gleaming among weeds and grass,
And sculptured Forms of Warriors brave:
But chiefly by that single grave,
That one sequestered hillock green,
The pensive visitant is seen.   350
There doth the gentle Creature lie
With those adversities unmoved;
Calm spectacle, by earth and sky
In their benignity approved!
And aye, methinks, this hoary Pile,

Subdued by outrage and decay,
Looks down upon her with a smile,
A gracious smile, that seems to say—
"Thou, thou art not a Child of Time,
But Daughter of the Eternal Prime!"

360

1814

THE EXCURSION

PREFACE

It may be proper to state whence the poem, of which "The Excursion" is a part, derives its Title of "The Recluse."—Several years ago, when the Author retired to his native mountains, with the hope of being enabled to construct a literary Work that might live, it was a reasonable thing that he should take a review of his own mind, and examine how far Nature and Education had qualified him for such employment. As subsidiary to this preparation, he undertook to record, in verse, the origin and progress of his own powers, as far as he was acquainted with them. That Work,[1] addressed to a dear Friend, most distinguished for his knowledge and genius, and to whom the Author's Intellect is deeply indebted, has been long finished; and the result of the investigation which gave rise to it was a determination to compose a philosophical poem, containing views of Man, Nature, and Society; and to be entitled, "The Recluse"; as having for its principal subject the sensations and opinions of a poet living in retirement.—The preparatory poem is biographical, and conducts the history of the Author's mind to the point when he was emboldened to hope that his faculties were sufficiently matured for entering upon the arduous labour which he had proposed to himself; and the two Works have the same kind of relation to each other, if he may so express himself, as the ante-chapel has to the body of a Gothic church. Continuing this allusion, he may be permitted to add, that his minor Pieces, which have been long before the Public, when they shall be properly arranged, will be found by the attentive Reader to have such connection with the main Work as may give them claim to be likened to the little cells, oratories, and sepulchral recesses, ordinarily included in those edifices.

---

1. "The Prelude."

The Author would not have deemed himself justified in saying, upon this occasion, so much of performances either unfinished or unpublished, if he had not thought that the labour bestowed by him upon what he has heretofore and now laid before the Public entitled him to candid attention for such a statement as he thinks necessary to throw light upon his endeavours to please and, he would hope, to benefit his countrymen.— Nothing further need be added, than that the first and third parts of "The Recluse" will consist chiefly of meditations in the Author's own person; and that in the intermediate part ("The Excursion") the intervention of characters speaking is employed, and something of a dramatic form adopted.

It is not the Author's intention formally to announce a system; it was more animating to him to proceed in a different course; and if he shall succeed in conveying to the mind clear thoughts, lively images, and strong feelings, the Reader will have no difficulty in extracting the system for himself. And in the meantime the following passage, taken from the conclusion of the first book of "The Recluse" may be acceptable as a kind of *Prospectus* of the design and scope of the whole Poem.

[See "The Recluse," pages 399–402, lines 754–860.]

BOOK FIRST
THE WANDERER

Argument

A summer forenoon—The Author reaches a ruined Cottage upon a Common, and there meets with a revered friend, the Wanderer, of whose education and course of life he gives an account—The Wanderer, while resting under the shade of the Trees that surround the Cottage, relates the History of its last Inhabitant.

> 'T was summer, and the sun had mounted high:
> Southward the landscape indistinctly glared
> Through a pale steam; but all the northern downs,
> In clearest air ascending, showed far off
> A surface dappled o'er with shadows flung
> From brooding clouds; shadows that lay in spots
> Determined and unmoved, with steady beams
> Of bright and pleasant sunshine interposed;

To him most pleasant who on soft cool moss
Extends his careless limbs along the front   10
Of some huge cave, whose rocky ceiling casts
A twilight of its own, an ample shade,
Where the wren warbles, while the dreaming man,
Half conscious of the soothing melody,
With side-long eye looks out upon the scene,
By power of that impending covert, thrown
To finer distance. Mine was at that hour
Far other lot, yet with good hope that soon
Under a shade as grateful I should find
Rest, and be welcomed there to livelier joy.   20
Across a bare wide Common I was toiling
With languid steps that by the slippery turf
Were baffled; nor could my weak arm disperse
The host of insects gathering round my face,
And ever with me as I paced along.

Upon that open moorland stood a grove,
The wished-for port to which my course was bound.
Thither I came, and there, amid the gloom
Spread by a brotherhood of lofty elms,
Appeared a roofless Hut; four naked walls   30
That stared upon each other!—I looked round,
And to my wish and to my hope espied
The Friend I sought; a Man of reverend age,
But stout and hale, for travel unimpaired.
There was he seen upon the cottage-bench,
Recumbent in the shade, as if asleep;
An iron-pointed staff lay at his side.

Him had I marked the day before—alone
And stationed in the public way, with face
Turned toward the sun then setting, while that staff   40
Afforded, to the figure of the man
Detained for contemplation or repose,
Graceful support; his countenance as he stood
Was hidden from my view, and he remained
Unrecognised; but, stricken by the sight,
With slackened footsteps I advanced, and soon

A glad congratulation we exchanged
At such unthought-of meeting.—For the night
We parted, nothing willingly; and now
He by appointment waited for me here,   50
Under the covert of these clustering elms.

We were tried Friends: amid a pleasant vale,
In the antique market-village where was passed
My school-time, an apartment he had owned,
To which at intervals the Wanderer drew.
And found a kind of home or harbour there.
He loved me; from a swarm of rosy boys
Singled out me, as he in sport would say,
For my grave looks, too thoughtful for my years.
As I grew up, it was my best delight   60
To be his chosen comrade. Many a time,
On holidays, we rambled through the woods:
We sate—we walked; he pleased me with report
Of things which he had seen; and often touched
Abstrusest matter, reasonings of the mind
Turned inward; or at my request would sing
Old songs, the product of his native hills;
A skilful distribution of sweet sounds,
Feeding the soul; and eagerly imbibed
As cool refreshing water, by the care   70
Of the industrious husbandman, diffused
Through a parched meadow-ground, in time of drought.
Still deeper welcome found his pure discourse;
How precious, when in riper days I learned
To weigh with care his words, and to rejoice
In the plain presence of his dignity!

Oh! many are the Poets that are sown
By Nature; men endowed with highest gifts,
The vision and the faculty divine;
Yet wanting the accomplishment of verse,   80
(Which, in the docile season of their youth,
It was denied them to acquire, through lack
Of culture and the inspiring aid of books,
Or haply by a temper too severe,

Or a nice backwardness afraid of shame)
Nor having e'er, as life advanced, been led
By circumstance to take unto the height
The measure of themselves, these favoured Beings,
All but a scattered few, live out their time,
Husbanding that which they possess within,   90
And go to the grave, unthought of. Strongest minds
Are often those of whom the noisy world
Hears least; else surely this Man had not left
His graces unrevealed and unproclaimed.
But, as the mind was filled with inward light,
So not without distinction had he lived,
Beloved and honoured—far as he was known.
And some small portion of his eloquent speech,
And something that may serve to set in view
The feeling pleasures of his loneliness,   100
His observations, and the thoughts his mind
Had dealt with—I will here record in verse;
Which, if with truth it correspond, and sink
Or rise as venerable Nature leads,
The high and tender Muses shall accept
With gracious smile, deliberately pleased,
And listening Time reward with sacred praise.

    Among the hills of Athol he was born;
Where, on a small hereditary farm,
An unproductive slip of rugged ground,   110
His Parents, with their numerous offspring, dwelt;
A virtuous household, though exceeding poor!
Pure livers were they all, austere and grave,
And fearing God; the very children taught
Stern self-respect, a reverence for God's word,
And an habitual piety, maintained
With strictness scarcely known on English ground.

    From his sixth year, the Boy of whom I speak,
In summer, tended cattle on the hills;
But, through the inclement and the perilous days   120
Of long-continuing winter, he repaired,

Equipped with satchel, to a school, that stood
Sole building on a mountain's dreary edge,
Remote from view of city spire, or sound
Of minster clock! From that bleak tenement
He, many an evening, to his distant home
In solitude returning, saw the hills
Grow larger in the darkness; all alone
Beheld the stars come out above his head,
And travelled through the wood, with no one near   130
To whom he might confess the things he saw.

So the foundations of his mind were laid.
In such communion, not from terror free,
While yet a child, and long before his time,
Had he perceived the presence and the power
Of greatness; and deep feelings had impressed
So vividly great objects that they lay
Upon his mind like substances, whose presence
Perplexed the bodily sense. He had received
A precious gift; for, as he grew in years,   140
With these impressions would he still compare
All his remembrances, thoughts, shapes, and forms;
And, being still unsatisfied with aught
Of dimmer character, he thence attained
An active power to fasten images
Upon his brain; and on their pictured lines
Intensely brooded, even till they acquired
The liveliness of dreams. Nor did he fail,
While yet a child, with a child's eagerness
Incessantly to turn his ear and eye   150
On all things which the moving seasons brought
To feed such appetite—nor this alone
Appeased his yearning:—in the after-day
Of boyhood, many an hour in caves forlorn,
And 'mid the hollow depths of naked crags
He sate, and even in their fixed lineaments,
Or from the power of a peculiar eye,
Or by creative feeling overborne,

Or by predominance of thought oppressed,
Even in their fixed and steady lineaments   160
He traced an ebbing and a flowing mind,
Expression ever varying!

                Thus informed,
He had small need of books; for many a tale
Traditionary, round the mountains hung,
And many a legend, peopling the dark woods,
Nourished Imagination in her growth,
And gave the Mind that apprehensive power
By which she is made quick to recognise
The moral properties and scope of things.
But eagerly he read, and read again,   ·   170
Whate'er the minister's old shelf supplied;
The life and death of martyrs, who sustained,
With will inflexible, those fearful pangs
Triumphantly displayed in records left
Of persecution, and the Covenant—times
Whose echo rings through Scotland to this hour!
And there, by lucky hap, had been preserved
A straggling volume, torn and incomplete,
That left half-told the preternatural tale,
Romance of giants, chronicle of fiends,   180
Profuse in garniture of wooden cuts
Strange and uncouth; dire faces, figures dire,
Sharp-kneed, sharp-elbowed, and lean-ankled too,
With long and ghostly shanks—forms which once seen
Could never be forgotten!

                In his heart,
Where Fear sate thus, a cherished visitant,
Was wanting yet the pure delight of love
By sound diffused, or by the breathing air,
Or by the silent looks of happy things,
Or flowing from the universal face   190
Of earth and sky. But he had felt the power
Of Nature, and already was prepared,
By his intense conceptions, to receive
Deeply the lesson deep of love which he,

Whom Nature, by whatever means, has taught
To feel intensely, cannot but receive.

   Such was the Boy—but for the growing Youth
What soul was his, when, from the naked top
Of some bold headland, he beheld the sun
Rise up, and bathe the world in light! He looked—   200
Ocean and earth, the solid frame of earth
And ocean's liquid mass, in gladness lay
Beneath him:—Far and wide the clouds were touched,
And in their silent faces could be read
Unutterable love. Sound needed none,
Nor any voice of joy; his spirit drank
The spectacle: sensation, soul, and form,
All melted into him; they swallowed up
His animal being; in them did he live,
And by them did he live; they were his life.   210
In such access of mind, in such high hour
Of visitation from the living God,
Thought was not; in enjoyment it expired.
No thanks he breathed, he proffered no request;
Rapt into still communion that transcends
The imperfect offices of prayer and praise,
His mind was a thanksgiving to the power
That made him; it was blessedness and love!

   A Herdsman on the lonely mountain tops,
Such intercourse was his, and in this sort   220
Was his existence oftentimes *possessed*.
O then how beautiful, how bright, appeared
The written promise! Early had he learned
To reverence the volume that displays
The mystery, the life which cannot die;
But in the mountains did he *feel* his faith.
All things, responsive to the writing, there
Breathed immortality, revolving life,
And greatness still revolving; infinite:
There littleness was not; the least of things   230
Seemed infinite; and there his spirit shaped
Her prospects, nor did he believe,—he *saw*.

What wonder if his being thus became
Sublime and comprehensive! Low desires,
Low thoughts had there no place; yet was his heart
Lowly; for he was meek in gratitude,
Oft as he called those ecstasies to mind,
And whence they flowed; and from them he acquired
Wisdom, which works through patience; thence he learned
In oft-recurring hours of sober thought   240
To look on Nature with a humble heart.
Self-questioned where it did not understand,
And with a superstitious eye of love.

   So passed the time; yet to the nearest town
He duly went with what small overplus
His earnings might supply, and brought away
The book that most had tempted his desires
While at the stall he read. Among the hills
He gazed upon that mighty orb of song,
The divine Milton. Lore of different kind,   250
The annual sayings of a toilsome life,
His Schoolmaster supplied; books that explain
The purer elements of truth involved
In lines and numbers, and, by charm severe,
(Especially perceived where nature droops
And feeling is suppressed) preserve the mind
Busy in solitude and poverty.
These occupations oftentimes deceived
The listless hours, while in the hollow vale,
Hollow and green, he lay on the green turf   260
In pensive idleness. What could he do,
Thus daily thirsting, in that lonesome life,
With blind endeavours? Yet, still uppermost,
Nature was at his heart as if he felt,
Though yet he knew not how, a wasting power
In all things that from her sweet influence
Might tend to wean him. Therefore with her hues,
Her forms, and with the spirit of her forms,
He clothed the nakedness of austere truth.
While yet he lingered in the rudiments   270

Of science, and among her simplest laws,
His triangles—they were the stars of heaven,
The silent stars! Oft did he take delight
To measure the altitude of some tall crag
That is the eagle's birth-place, or some peak
Familiar with forgotten years, that shows,
Inscribed upon its visionary sides,
The history of many a winter storm,
Or obscure records of the path of fire.

And thus before his eighteenth year was told,   280
Accumulated feelings pressed his heart
With still increasing weight; he was o'erpowered
By Nature; by the turbulence subdued
Of his own mind; by mystery and hope,
And the first virgin passion of a soul
Communing with the glorious universe.
Full often wished he that the winds might rage
When they were silent: far more fondly now
Than in his earlier season did he love
Tempestuous nights—the conflict and the sounds   290
That live in darkness. From his intellect
And from the stillness of abstracted thought
He asked repose; and, failing oft to win
The peace required, he scanned the laws of light
Amid the roar of torrents, where they send
From hollow clefts up to the clearer air
A cloud of mist that, smitten by the sun,
Varies its rainbow hues. But vainly thus,
And vainly by all other means, he strove
To mitigate the fever of his heart.   300

In dreams, in study, and in ardent thought,
Thus was he reared; much wanting to assist
The growth of intellect, yet gaining more,
And every moral feeling of his soul
Strengthened and braced, by breathing in content
The keen, the wholesome, air of poverty,
And drinking from the well of homely life.
—But, from past liberty, and tried restraints,

He now was summoned to select the course
Of humble industry that promised best   310
To yield him no unworthy maintenance.
Urged by his Mother, he essayed to teach
A village-school—but wandering thoughts were then
A misery to him; and the Youth resigned
A task he was unable to perform.

That stern yet kindly Spirit, who constrains
The Savoyard to quit his naked rocks,
The free-born Swiss to leave his narrow vales,
(Spirit attached to regions mountainous
Like their own stedfast clouds) did not impel   320
His restless mind to look abroad with hope.
—An irksome drudgery seems it to plod on,
Through hot and dusty ways, or pelting storm,
A vagrant Merchant under a heavy load,
Bent as he moves, and needing frequent rest;
Yet do such travellers find their own delight;
And their hard service, deemed debasing now,
Gained merited respect in simpler times;
When squire, and priest, and they who round them dwelt
In rustic sequestration—all dependent   330
Upon the PEDLAR'S toil—supplied their wants,
Or pleased their fancies, with the wares he brought.
Not ignorant was the Youth that still no few
Of his adventurous countrymen were led
By perseverance in this track of life
To competence and ease:—to him it offered
Attractions manifold;—and this he chose.
—His Parents on the enterprise bestowed
Their farewell benediction, but with hearts
Foreboding evil. From his native hills   340
He wandered far; much did he see of men,
Their manners, their enjoyments, and pursuits,
Their passions and their feelings; chiefly those
Essential and eternal in the heart,
That, 'mid the simpler forms of rural life,
Exist more simple in their elements,

And speak a plainer language. In the woods,
A lone Enthusiast, and among the fields,
Itinerant in this labour, he had passed
The better portion of his time; and there   350
Spontaneously had his affections thriven
Amid the bounties of the year, the peace
And liberty of nature; there he kept
In solitude and solitary thought
His mind in a just equipoise of love.
Serene it was, unclouded by the cares
Of ordinary life; unvexed, unwarped
By partial bondage. In his steady course,
No piteous revolutions had he felt,
No wild varieties of joy and grief.   360
Unoccupied by sorrow of its own,
His heart lay open; and, by nature tuned
And constant disposition of his thoughts
To sympathy with man, he was alive
To all that was enjoyed where'er he went,
And all that was endured; for, in himself
Happy, and quiet in his cheerfulness,
He had no painful pressure from without
That made him turn aside from wretchedness
With coward fears. He could *afford* to suffer 370
With those whom he saw suffer. Hence it came
That in our best experience he was rich,
And in the wisdom of our daily life.
For hence, minutely, in his various rounds,
He had observed the progress and decay
Of many minds, of minds and bodies too;
The history of many families;
How they had prospered; how they were o'erthrown
By passion or mischance, or such misrule
Among the unthinking masters of the earth 380
As makes the nations groan.
         This active course
He followed till provision for his wants
Had been obtained;—the Wanderer then resolved
To pass the remnant of his days, untasked

With needless services, from hardship free.
His calling laid aside, he lived at ease:
But still he loved to pace the public roads
And the wild paths; and, by the summer's warmth
Invited, often would he leave his home
And journey far, revisiting the scenes   390
That to his memory were most endeared.
—Vigorous in health, of hopeful spirits, undamped
By worldly-mindedness or anxious care;
Observant, studious, thoughtful, and refreshed
By knowledge gathered up from day to day;
Thus had he lived a long and innocent life.

    The Scottish Church, both on himself and those
With whom from childhood he grew up, had held
The strong hand of her purity; and still
Had watched him with an unrelenting eye.   400
This he remembered in his riper age
With gratitude, and reverential thoughts.
But by the native vigour of his mind,
By his habitual wanderings out of doors,
By loneliness, and goodness, and kind works,
Whate'er, in docile childhood or in youth,
He had imbibed of fear or darker thought
Was melted all away; so true was this,
That sometimes his religion seemed to me
Self-taught, as of a dreamer in the woods;   410
Who to the model of his own pure heart
Shaped his belief, as grace divine inspired,
And human reason dictated with awe.
—And surely never did there live on earth
A man of kindlier nature. The rough sports
And teasing ways of children vexed not him;
Indulgent listener was he to the tongue
Of garrulous age; nor did the sick man's tale,
To his fraternal sympathy addressed,
Obtain reluctant hearing.   420
                    Plain his garb;
Such as might suit a rustic Sire, prepared

For Sabbath duties; yet he was a man
Whom no one could have passed without remark.
Active and nervous was his gait; his limbs
And his whole figure breathed intelligence.
Time had compressed the freshness of his cheek
Into a narrower circle of deep red,
But had not tamed his eye; that, under brows
Shaggy and grey, had meanings which it brought
From years of youth; which, like a Being made   430
Of many Beings, he had wondrous skill
To blend with knowledge of the years to come,
Human, or such as lie beyond the grave.

    So was He framed; and such his course of life
Who now, with no appendage but a staff,
The prized memorial of relinquished toils,
Upon that cottage-bench reposed his limbs,
Screened from the sun. Supine the Wanderer lay,
His eyes as if in drowsiness half shut,
The shadows of the breezy elms above   440
Dappling his face. He had not heard the sound
Of my approaching steps, and in the shade
Unnoticed did I stand some minutes' space.
At length I hailed him, seeing that his hat
Was moist with water-drops, as if the brim
Had newly scooped a running stream. He rose,
And ere our lively greeting into peace
Had settled, " 'Tis," said I, "a burning day:
My lips are parched with thirst, but you, it seems
Have somewhere found relief." He, at the word,   450
Pointing towards a sweet-briar, bade me climb
The fence where that aspiring shrub looked out
Upon the public way. It was a plot
Of garden ground run wild, its matted weeds
Marked with the steps of those, whom, as they passed,
The gooseberry trees that shot in long lank slips,
Or currants, hanging from their leafless stems,
In scanty strings, had tempted to o'erleap
The broken wall. I looked around, and there,

Where two tall hedge-rows of thick alder boughs   460
Joined in a cold damp nook, espied a well
Shrouded with willow-flowers and plumy fern.
My thirst I slaked, and, from the cheerless spot
Withdrawing, straightway to the shade returned
Where sate the old Man on the cottage bench,
And, while, beside him, with uncovered head,
I yet was standing, freely to respire,
And cool my temples in the fanning air,
Thus did he speak. "I see around me here
Things which you cannot see: we die, my Friend,   470
Nor we alone, but that which each man loved
And prized in his peculiar nook of earth
Dies with him, or is changed; and very soon
Even of the good is no memorial left.
—The Poets, in their elegies and songs
Lamenting the departed, call the groves.
They call upon the hills and streams, to mourn,
And senseless rocks; nor idly; for they speak,
In these their invocations, with a voice
Obedient to the strong creative power   480
Of human passion. Sympathies there are
More tranquil, yet perhaps of kindred birth,
That steal upon the meditative mind,
And grow with thought. Beside yon spring I stood,
And eyed its waters till we seemed to feel
One sadness, they and I. For them a bond
Of brotherhood is broken: time has been
When, every day, the touch of human hand
Dislodged the natural sleep that binds them up
In mortal stillness; and they ministered   490
To human comfort. Stooping down to drink,
Upon the slimy foot-stone I espied
The useless fragment of a wooden bowl,
Green with the moss of years, and subject only
To the soft handling of the elements:
There let it lie—how foolish are such thoughts!
Forgive them;—never—never did my steps
Approach this door but she who dwelt within

A daughter's welcome gave me, and I loved her
As my own child. Oh, Sir! the good die first,   500
And they whose hearts are dry as summer dust
Burn to the socket. Many a passenger
Hath blessed poor Margaret for her gentle looks,
When she upheld the cool refreshment drawn
From that forsaken spring; and no one came
But he was welcome; no one went away
But that it seemed she loved him. She is dead,
The light extinguished of her lonely hut,
The hut itself abandoned to decay,
And she forgotten in the quiet grave.   510

    I speak," continued he, "of One whose stock
Of virtues bloomed beneath this lonely roof.
She was a Woman of a steady mind,
Tender and deep in her excess of love;
Not speaking much, pleased rather with the joy
Of her own thoughts: by some especial care
Her temper had been framed, as if to make
A Being, who by adding love to peace
Might live on earth a life of happiness.
Her wedded Partner lacked not on his side   520
The humble worth that satisfied her heart:
Frugal, affectionate, sober, and withal
Keenly industrious. She with pride would tell
That he was often seated at his loom,
In summer, ere the mower was abroad
Among the dewy grass,—in early spring,
Ere the last star had vanished.—They who passed
At evening, from behind the garden fence
Might hear his busy spade, which he would ply,
After his daily work, until the light   530
Had failed, and every leaf and flower were lost
In the dark hedges. So their days were spent
In peace and comfort; and a pretty boy
Was their best hope, next to the God in heaven.

    Not twenty years ago, but you I think
Can scarcely bear it now in mind, there came

Two blighting seasons, when the fields were left
With half a harvest. It pleased Heaven to add
A worse affliction in the plague of war:
This happy Land was stricken to the heart!   540
A Wanderer then among the cottages,
I, with my freight of winter raiment, saw
The hardships of that season: many rich
Sank down, as in a dream, among the poor;
And of the poor did many cease to be,
And their place knew them not. Meanwhile, abridged
Of daily comforts, gladly reconciled
To numerous self-denials, Margaret
Went struggling on through those calamitous years
With cheerful hope, until the second autumn,   550
When her life's Helpmate on a sick-bed lay,
Smitten with perilous fever. In disease
He lingered long; and, when his strength returned,
He found the little he had stored, to meet
The hour of accident or crippling age,
Was all consumed. A second infant now
Was added to the troubles of a time
Laden, for them and all of their degree,
With care and sorrow; shoals of artisans
From ill-requited labour turned adrift   560
Sought daily bread from public charity,
They, and their wives and children—happier far
Could they have lived as do the little birds
That peck along the hedge-rows, or the kite
That makes her dwelling on the mountain rocks!

       A sad reverse it was for him who long
Had filled with plenty, and possessed in peace,
This lonely Cottage. At the door he stood,
And whistled many a snatch of merry tunes
That had no mirth in them; or with his knife   570
Carved uncouth figures on the heads of sticks—
Then, not less idly, sought, through every nook
In house or garden, any casual work
Of use or ornament; and with a strange,

Amusing, yet uneasy, novelty,
He mingled, where he might, the various tasks
Of summer autumn, winter, and of spring.
But this endured not; his good humour soon
Became a weight in which no pleasure was:
And poverty brought on a petted mood   580
And a sore temper: day by day he drooped,
And he would leave his work—and to the town
Would turn without an errand his slack steps;
Or wander here and there among the fields.
One while he would speak lightly of his babes,
And with a cruel tongue: at other times
He tossed them with a false unnatural joy:
And 't was a rueful thing to see the looks
Of the poor innocent children. 'Every smile,'
Said Margaret to me, here beneath these trees,   590
'Made my heart bleed.' "

                      At this the Wanderer paused;
And, looking up to those enormous elms,
He said, " 'T is now the hour of deepest noon.
At this still season of repose and peace,
This hour when all things which are not at rest
Are cheerful; while this multitude of flies
With tuneful hum is filling all the air;
Why should a tear be on an old Man's cheek?
Why should we thus, with an untoward mind,
And in the weakness of humanity,   600
From natural wisdom turn our hearts away;
To natural comfort shut our eyes and ears;
And, feeding on disquiet, thus disturb
The calm of nature with our restless thoughts?"

He spake with somewhat of a solemn tone:
But, when he ended, there was in his face
Such easy cheerfulness, a look so mild,
That for a little time it stole away
All recollection; and that simple tale
Passed from my mind like a forgotten sound.   610

A while on trivial things we held discourse,
To me soon tasteless. In my own despite,
I thought of that poor Woman as of one
Whom I had known and loved. He had rehearsed
Her homely tale with such familiar power,
With such an active countenance, an eye
So busy, that the things of which he spake
Seemed present; and, attention now relaxed,
A heart-felt chillness crept along my veins;
I rose; and, having left the breezy shade,   620
Stood drinking comfort from the warmer sun,
That had not cheered me long—ere, looking round
Upon that tranquil Ruin, I returned,
And begged of the old Man that, for my sake,
He would resume his story.
                                    He replied,
"It were a wantonness, and would demand
Severe reproof, if we were men whose hearts
Could hold vain dalliance with the misery
Even of the dead; contented thence to draw
A momentary pleasure, never marked   630
By reason, barren of all future good.
But we have known that there is often found
In mournful thoughts, and always might be found,
A power to virtue friendly; were 't not so,
I am a dreamer among men, indeed
An idle dreamer! 'T is a common tale,
An ordinary sorrow of man's life,
A tale of silent suffering, hardly clothed
In bodily form.—But without further bidding
I will proceed.   640
                        While thus it fared with them,
To whom this cottage, till those hapless years,
Had been a blessèd home, it was my chance
To travel in a country far remote;
And when these lofty elms once more appeared,
What pleasant expectations lured me on
O'er the flat Common!—With quick step I reached
The threshold, lifted with light hand the latch;

But, when I entered, Margaret looked at me
A little while; then turned her head away
Speechless,—and, sitting down upon a chair,   650
Wept bitterly. I wist not what to do,
Nor how to speak to her. Poor Wretch! at last
She rose from off her seat, and then,—O Sir!
I cannot *tell* how she pronounced my name:—
With fervent love, and with a face of grief
Unutterably helpless, and a look
That seemed to cling upon me, she enquired
If I had seen her husband. As she spake
A strange surprise and fear came to my heart,
Nor had I power to answer ere she told   660
That he had disappeared—not two months gone.
He left his house: two wretched days had past,
And on the third, as wistfully she raised
Her head from off her pillow, to look forth,
Like one in trouble, for returning light,
Within her chamber-casement she espied
A folded paper, lying as if placed
To meet her waking eyes. This tremblingly
She opened—found no writing, but beheld
Pieces of money carefully enclosed,   670
Silver and gold. 'I shuddered at the sight,'
Said Margaret, 'for I knew it was his hand
That must have placed it there; and ere that day
Was ended, that long anxious day, I learned,
From one who by my husband had been sent
With the sad news, that he had joined a troop
Of soldiers, going to a distant land.
—He left me thus—he could not gather heart
To take a farewell of me; for he feared
That I should follow with my babes, and sink   680
Beneath the misery of that wandering life.'

    This tale did Margaret tell with many tears:
And, when she ended, I had little power
To give her comfort, and was glad to take
Such words of hope from her own mouth as served

To cheer us both. But long we had not talked
Ere we built up a pile of better thoughts,
And with a brighter eye she looked around
As if she had been shedding tears of joy.
We parted.—'Twas the time of early spring;   690
I left her busy with her garden tools;
And well remember, o'er that fence she looked,
And, while I paced along the foot-way path,
Called out, and sent a blessing after me,
With tender cheerfulness, and with a voice
That seemed the very sound of happy thoughts.

    I roved o'er many a hill and many a dale,
With my accustomed load; in heat and cold,
Through many a wood and many an open ground,
In sunshine and in shade, in wet and fair,   700
Drooping or blithe of heart, as might befall;
My best companions now the driving winds,
And now the 'trotting brooks' and whispering trees,
And now the music of my own sad steps,
With many a short-lived thought that passed between,
And disappeared.
              I journeyed back this way,
When, in the warmth of midsummer, the wheat
Was yellow; and the soft and bladed grass,
Springing afresh, had o'er the hay-field spread
Its tender verdure. At the door arrived,   710
I found that she was absent. In the shade,
Where now we sit, I waited her return.
Her cottage, then a cheerful object, wore
Its customary look,—only, it seemed,
The honeysuckle, crowding round the porch,
Hung down in heavier tufts; and that bright weed,
The yellow stone-crop, suffered to take root
Along the window's edge, profusely grew,
Blinding the lower panes. I turned aside,
And strolled into her garden. It appeared   720
To lag behind the season, and had lost
Its pride of neatness. Daisy-flowers and thrift

Had broken their trim border-lines, and straggled
O'er paths they used to deck: carnations, once
Prized for surpassing beauty, and no less
For the peculiar pains they had required,
Declined their languid heads, wanting support.
The cumbrous bind-weed, with its wreaths and bells,
Had twined about her two small rows of peas,
And dragged them to the earth.

                              Ere this an hour   730
Was wasted.—Back I turned my restless steps;
A stranger passed; and, guessing whom I sought,
He said that she was used to ramble far.—
The sun was sinking in the west; and now
I sate with sad impatience. From within
Her solitary infant cried aloud;
Then, like a blast that dies away self-stilled,
The voice was silent. From the bench I rose;
But neither could divert nor soothe my thoughts.
The spot, though fair, was very desolate—   740
The longer I remained, more desolate:
And, looking round me, now I first observed
The corner stones, on either side the porch,
With dull red stains discoloured, and stuck o'er
With tufts and hairs of wool, as if the sheep,
That fed upon the Common, thither came
Familiarly, and found a couching-place
Even at her threshold. Deeper shadows fell
From these tall elms; the cottage-clock struck eight;—
I turned, and saw her distant a few steps.   750
Her face was pale and thin—her figure, too,
Was changed. As she unlocked the door, she said,
'It grieves me you have waited here so long,
But, in good truth, I've wandered much of late;
And sometimes—to my shame I speak—have need
Of my best prayers to bring me back again.'
While on the board she spread our evening meal,
She told me—interrupting not the work
Which gave employment to her listless hands—
That she had parted with her elder child,   760

To a kind master on a distant farm
Now happily apprenticed.—'I perceive
You look at me, and you have cause; to-day
I have been travelling far; and many days
About the fields I wander, knowing this
Only, that what I seek I cannot find;
And so I waste my time: for I am changed;
And to myself,' said she, 'have done much wrong
And to this helpless infant. I have slept
Weeping, and weeping have I waked; my tears   770
Have flowed as if my body were not such
As others are; and I could never die.
But I am now in mind and in my heart
More easy; and I hope,' said she, 'that God
Will give me patience to endure the things
Which I behold at home.'
                  It would have grieved
Your very soul to see her. Sir, I feel
The story lingers in my heart; I fear
'Tis long and tedious; but my spirit clings
To that poor Woman:—so familiarly   780
Do I perceive her manners, and her look,
And presence; and so deeply do I feel
Her goodness, that, not seldom, in my walks
A momentary trance comes over me;
And to myself I seem to muse on One
By sorrow laid asleep; or borne away,
A human being destined to awake
To human life, or something very near
To human life, when he shall come again
For whom she suffered. Yes, it would have grieved   790
Your very soul to see her: evermore
Her eyelids drooped, her eyes downward were cast;
And, when she at her table gave me food,
She did not look at me. Her voice was low,
Her body was subdued. In every act
Pertaining to her house-affairs, appeared
The careless stillness of a thinking mind
Self-occupied; to which all outward things

Are like an idle matter. Still she sighed,
But yet no motion of the breast was seen,   800
No heaving of the heart. While by the fire
We sate together, sighs came on my ear,
I knew not how, and hardly whence they came.

    Ere my departure, to her care I gave,
For her son's use, some tokens of regard,
Which with a look of welcome she received;
And I exhorted her to place her trust
In God's good love, and seek his help by prayer.
I took my staff, and, when I kissed her babe,
·The tears stood in her eyes. I left her then   810
With the best hope and comfort I could give:
She thanked me for my wish;—but for my hope
It seemed she did not thank me.
                      I returned,
And took my rounds along this road again
When on its sunny bank the primrose flower
Peeped forth, to give an earnest of the Spring.
I found her sad and drooping: she had learned
No tidings of her husband; if he lived,
She knew not that he lived; if he were dead,
She knew not he was dead. She seemed the same   820
In person and appearance; but her house
Bespake a sleepy hand of negligence;
The floor was neither dry nor neat, the hearth
Was comfortless, and her small lot of books,
Which, in the cottage-window, heretofore
Had been piled up against the corner panes
In seemly order, now, with straggling leaves
Lay scattered here and there, open or shut,
As they had chanced to fall. Her infant Babe
Had from his Mother caught the trick of grief,   830
And sighed among its playthings. I withdrew,
And once again entering the garden saw,
More plainly still, that poverty and grief
Were now come nearer to her: weeds defaced
The hardened soil, and knots of withered grass:

No ridges there appeared of clear black mould,
No winter greenness; of her herbs and flowers,
It seemed the better part was gnawed away
Or trampled into earth; a chain of straw,
Which had been twined about the slender stem   840
Of a young apple-tree, lay at its root;
The bark was nibbled round by truant sheep.
—Margaret stood near, her infant in her arms,
And, noting that my eye was on the tree,
She said, 'I fear it will be dead and gone
Ere Robert come again.' When to the House
We had returned together, she enquired
If I had any hope:—but for her babe
And for her little orphan boy, she said,
She had no wish to live, that she must die   850
Of sorrow. Yet I saw the idle loom
Still in its place; his Sunday garments hung
Upon the self-same nail; his very staff
Stood undisturbed behind the door.

                    And when,
In bleak December, I retraced this way,
She told me that her little babe was dead,
And she was left alone. She now, released
From her maternal cares, had taken up
The employment common through these wilds, and gained,
By spinning hemp, a pittance for herself;   860
And for this end had hired a neighbour's boy
To give her needful help. That very time
Most willingly she put her work aside,
And walked with me along the miry road,
Heedless how far; and, in such piteous sort
That any heart had ached to hear her, begged
That, wheresoe'er I went, I still would ask
For him whom she had lost. We parted then—
Our final parting; for from that time forth
Did many seasons pass ere I returned   870
Into this tract again.

                  Nine tedious years;
From their first separation, nine long years,

She lingered in unquiet widowhood;
A Wife and Widow. Needs must it have been
A sore heart-wasting! I have heard, my Friend,
That in yon arbour oftentimes she sate
Alone, through half the vacant sabbath day;
And, if a dog passed by, she still would quit
The shade, and look abroad. On this old bench
For hours she sate; and evermore her eye   880
Was busy in the distance, shaping things
That made her heart beat quick. You see that path,
Now faint,—the grass has crept o'er its grey line;
There, to and fro, she paced through many a day
Of the warm summer, from a belt of hemp
That girt her waist, spinning the long-drawn thread
With backward steps. Yet ever as there passed
A man whose garments showed the soldier's red,
Or crippled mendicant in sailor's garb,
The little child who sate to turn the wheel   890
Ceased from his task; and she with faltering voice
Made many a fond enquiry; and when they,
Whose presence gave no comfort, were gone by,
Her heart was still more sad. And by yon gate,
That bars the traveller's road, she often stood,
And when a stranger horseman came, the latch
Would lift, and in his face look wistfully;
Most happy, if, from aught discovered there
Of tender feeling, she might dare repeat
The same sad question. Meanwhile her poor Hut   900
Sank to decay; for he was gone, whose hand,
At the first nipping of October frost,
Closed up each chink, and with fresh bands of straw
Chequered the green-grown thatch. And so she lived
Through the long winter, reckless and alone;
Until her house by frost, and thaw, and rain,
Was sapped; and while she slept, the nightly damps
Did chill her breast; and in the stormy day
Her tattered clothes were ruffled by the wind,
Even at the side of her own fire. Yet still   910
She loved this wretched spot, nor would for worlds

Have parted hence; and still that length of road,
And this rude bench, one torturing hope endeared,
Fast rooted at her heart: and here, my Friend,—
In sickness she remained; and here she died;
Last human tenant of these ruined walls!"
    The old Man ceased: he saw that I was moved;
From that low bench, rising instinctively
I turned aside in weakness, nor had power
To thank him for the tale which he had told.   920
I stood, and leaning o'er the garden wall
Reviewed that Woman's sufferings; and it seemed
To comfort me while with a brother's love
I blessed her in the impotence of grief.
Then towards the cottage I returned; and traced
Fondly, though with an interest more mild,
That secret spirit of humanity
Which, 'mid the calm oblivious tendencies
Of nature, 'mid her plants, and weeds, and flowers,
And silent overgrowings, still survived.   930
The old Man, noting this, resumed, and said,
"My Friend! enough to sorrow you have given,
The purposes of wisdom ask no more:
Nor more would she have craved as due to One
Who, in her worst distress, had ofttimes felt
The unbounded might of prayer; and learned, with soul
Fixed on the Cross, that consolation springs,
From sources deeper far than deepest pain,
For the meek Sufferer. Why then should we read
The forms of things with an unworthy eye?   940
She sleeps in the calm earth, and peace is here.
I well remember that those very plumes,
Those weeds, and the high spear-grass on that wall,
By mist and silent rain-drops silvered o'er,
As once I passed, into my heart conveyed
So still an image of tranquillity,
So calm and still, and looked so beautiful
Amid the uneasy thoughts which filled my mind,
That what we feel of sorrow and despair
From ruin and from change, and all the grief   950

That passing shows of Being leave behind,
Appeared an idle dream, that could maintain,
Nowhere, dominion o'er the enlightened spirit
Whose meditative sympathies repose
Upon the breast of Faith. I turned away,
And walked along my road in happiness."

He ceased. Ere long the sun declining shot
A slant and mellow radiance, which began
To fall upon us, while, beneath the trees,
We sate on that low bench: and now we felt,   960
Admonished thus, the sweet hour coming on.
A linnet warbled from those lofty elms,
A thrush sang loud, and other melodies,
At distance heard, peopled the milder air.
The old Man rose, and, with a sprightly mien
Of hopeful preparation, grasped his staff;
Together casting then a farewell look
Upon those silent walls, we left the shade;
And, ere the stars were visible, had reached
A village-inn,—our evening resting-place.   970

LAODAMIA

"With sacrifice before the rising morn
Vows have I made by fruitless hope inspired;
And from the infernal Gods, 'mid shades forlorn
Of night, my slaughtered Lord have I required:
Celestial pity I again implore;—
Restore him to my sight—great Jove, restore!"

So speaking, and by fervent tone endowed
With faith, the Suppliant heavenward lifts her hands;
While, like the sun emerging from a cloud,
Her countenance brightens—and her eye expands;   10
Her bosom heaves and spreads, her stature grows;
And she expects the issue in repose.

O terror! what hath she perceived?—O joy!
What doth she look on?—whom doth she behold?

Her Hero slain upon the beach of Troy?
His vital presence? his corporeal mould?
It is—if sense deceive her not—'tis He!
And a God leads him, wingèd Mercury!

Mild Hermes spake—and touched her with his wand
That calms all fear; "Such grace hath crowned thy prayer,　　**20**
Laodamía! that at Jove's command
Thy Husband walks the paths of upper air:
He comes to tarry with thee three hours' space;
Accept the gift, behold him face to face!"

Forth sprang the impassioned Queen her Lord to clasp;
Again that consummation she essayed;
But unsubstantial Form eludes her grasp
As often as that eager grasp was made.
The Phantom parts—but parts to re-unite,
And re-assume his place before her sight.　　**30**

"Protesiláus, lo! thy guide is gone!
Confirm, I pray, the vision with thy voice:
This is our palace,—yonder is thy throne;
Speak, and the floor thou tread'st on will rejoice.
Not to appal me have the gods bestowed
This precious boon; and blest a sad abode."

"Great Jove, Laodamía! doth not leave
His gifts imperfect:—Spectre though I be,
I am not sent to scare thee or deceive;
But in reward of thy fidelity.　　**40**
And something also did my worth obtain;
For fearless virtue bringeth boundless gain.
"Thou knowest, the Delphic oracle foretold
That the first Greek who touched the Trojan strand
Should die; but me the threat could not withhold:
A generous cause a victim did demand;
And forth I leapt upon the sandy plain;
A self-devoted chief—by Hector slain."

"Supreme of Heroes—bravest, noblest, best!
Thy matchless courage I bewail no more,　　**50**

Which then, when tens of thousands were deprest
By doubt, propelled thee to the fatal shore:
Thou found'st—and I forgive thee—here thou art—
A nobler counsellor than my poor heart.

"But thou, though capable of sternest deed,
Wert kind as resolute, and good as brave;
And he, whose power restores thee, hath decreed
Thou should'st elude the malice of the grave:
Redundant are thy locks, thy lips as fair
As when their breath enriched Thessalian air.   **60**

"No Spectre greets me,—no vain Shadow this;
Come, blooming Hero, place thee by my side!
Give, on this well-known couch, one nuptial kiss
To me, this day, a second time thy bride!"
Jove frowned in heaven: the conscious Parcæ threw
Upon those roseate lips a Stygian hue.

"This visage tells thee that my doom is past:
Nor should the change be mourned, even if the joys
Of sense were able to return as fast
And surely as they vanish. Earth destroys   **70**
Those raptures duly—Erebus disdains:
Calm pleasures there abide—majestic pains.

"Be taught, O faithful Consort, to control
Rebellious passion: for the Gods approve
The depth, and not the tumult, of the soul:
A fervent, not ungovernable, love.
Thy transports moderate; and meekly mourn
When I depart, for brief is my sojourn—"

"Ah, wherefore?—Did not Hercules by force
Wrest from the guardian Monster of the tomb   **80**
Alcestis, a reanimated corse,
Given back to dwell on earth in vernal bloom?
Medea's spells dispersed the weight of years,
And Æson stood a youth 'mid youthful peers.

"The Gods to us are merciful—and they
Yet further may relent: for mightier far

Than strength of nerve and sinew, or the sway
Of magic potent over sun and star,
Is love, though oft to agony distrest,
And though his favourite seat be feeble woman's breast.　　90

"But if thou goest, I follow——" "Peace!" he said,——
She looked upon him and was calmed and cheered;
The ghastly colour from his lips had fled;
In his deportment, shape, and mien, appeared
Elysian beauty, melancholy grace,
Brought from a pensive though a happy place.

He spake of love, such love as Spirits feel
In worlds whose course is equable and pure;
No fears to beat away——no strife to heal——
The past unsighed for, and the future sure;　　100
Spake of heroic arts in graver mood
Revived, with finer harmony pursued;

Of all that is most beauteous——imaged there
In happier beauty; more pellucid streams.
An ampler ether, a diviner air,
And fields invested with purpureal gleams;
Climes which the sun, who sheds the brightest day
Earth knows, is all unworthy to survey.

Yet there the Soul shall enter which hath earned
That privilege by virtue.——"Ill," said he,　　110
"The end of man's existence I discerned,
Who from ignoble games and revelry
Could draw, when we had parted, vain delight,
While tears were thy best pastime, day and night;

"And while my youthful peers before my eyes
(Each hero following his peculiar bent)
Prepared themselves for glorious enterprise
By martial sports,——or, seated in the tent,
Chieftains and kings in council were detained;
What time the fleet at Aulis lay enchained.　　120

"The wished-for wind was given:——I then revolved
The oracle, upon the silent sea;

And, if no worthier led the way, resolved
That, of a thousand vessels, mine should be
The foremost prow in pressing to the strand,—
Mine the first blood that tinged the Trojan sand.

"Yet bitter, oft-times bitter, was the pang
When of thy loss I thought, belovèd Wife!
On thee too fondly did my memory hang,
And on the joys we shared in mortal life,—   130
The paths which we had trod—these fountains, flowers,
My new-planned cities, and unfinished towers.

"But should suspense permit the Foe to cry,
'Behold they tremble!—haughty their array,
Yet of their number no one dares to die?',
In soul I swept the indignity away:
Old frailties then recurred:—but lofty thought,
In act embodied, my deliverance wrought.

"And Thou, though strong in love, art all too weak
In reason, in self-government too slow;   140
I counsel thee by fortitude to seek
Our blest re-union in the shades below.
The invisible world with thee hath sympathised;
Be thy affections raised and solemnised.

"Learn, by a mortal yearning, to ascend—
Seeking a higher object. Love was given,
Encouraged, sanctioned, chiefly for that end;
For this the passion to excess was driven—
That self might be annulled: her bondage prove
The fetters of a dream, opposed to love."——   150

Aloud she shrieked! for Hermes re-appears!
Round the dear Shade she would have clung—'tis vain:
The hours are past—too brief had they been years;
And him no mortal effort can detain:
Swift, toward the realms that know not earthly day,
He through the portal takes his silent way,
And on the palace-floor a lifeless corse She lay.

Thus, all in vain exhorted and reproved,
She perished; and, as for a wilful crime,
By the just Gods whom no weak pity moved,   160
Was doomed to wear out her appointed time,
Apart from happy Ghosts, that gather flowers
Of blissful quiet 'mid unfading bowers.

—Yet tears to human suffering are due;
And mortal hopes defeated and o'erthrown
Are mourned by man, and not by man alone,
As fondly he believes.—Upon the side
Of Hellespont (such faith was entertained)
A knot of spiry trees for ages grew
From out the tomb of him for whom she died;   170
And ever, when such stature they had gained
That Ilium's walls were subject to their view,
The trees' tall summits withered at the sight;
A constant interchange of growth and blight!

YARROW VISITED

SEPTEMBER, 1814

And is this—Yarrow?—*This* the Stream
Of which my fancy cherished,
So faithfully, a waking dream?
An image that hath perished!
O that some Minstrel's harp were near,
To utter notes of gladness,
And chase this silence from the air,
That fills my heart with sadness!

Yet why?—a silvery current flows
With uncontrolled meanderings;   10
Nor have these eyes by greener hills
Been soothed, in all my wanderings.
And, through her depths, Saint Mary's Lake
Is visibly delighted;

For not a feature of those hills
Is in the mirror slighted.

A blue sky bends o'er Yarrow vale,
Save where that pearly whiteness
Is round the rising sun diffused,
A tender hazy brightness; 20
Mild dawn of promise! that excludes
All profitless dejection;
Though not unwilling here to admit
A pensive recollection.

Where was it that the famous Flower
Of Yarrow Vale lay bleeding?
His bed perchance was yon smooth mound
On which the herd is feeding:
And haply from this crystal pool,
Now peaceful as the morning, 30
The Water-wraith ascended thrice—
And gave his doleful warning.

Delicious is the Lay that sings
The haunts of happy Lovers,
The path that leads them to the grove,
The leafy grove that covers:
And Pity sanctifies the Verse
That paints, by strength of sorrow,
The unconquerable strength of love;
Bear witness, rueful Yarrow! 40

But thou, that didst appear so fair
To fond imagination,
Dost rival in the light of day
Her delicate creation:
Meek loveliness is round thee spread,
A softness still and holy;
The grace of forest charms decayed,
And pastoral melancholy.

That region left, the vale unfolds
Rich groves of lofty stature, 50

With Yarrow winding through the pomp
Of cultivated nature;
And, rising from those lofty groves,
Behold a Ruin hoary!
The shattered front of Newark's Towers,
Renowned in Border story.

Fair scenes for childhood's opening bloom,
For sportive youth to stray in;
For manhood to enjoy his strength;
And age to wear away in!   60
Yon cottage seems a bower of bliss,
A covert for protection
Of tender thoughts, that nestle there—
The brood of chaste affection.
How sweet, on this autumnal day,
The wild-wood fruits to gather,
And on my True-love's forehead plant
A crest of blooming heather!
And what if I enwreathed my own!
'T were no offence to reason;   70
The sober Hills thus deck their brows
To meet the wintry season.

I see—but not by sight alone,
Loved Yarrow, have I won thee;
A ray of fancy still survives—
Her sunshine plays upon thee!
Thy ever-youthful waters keep
A course of lively pleasure;
And gladsome notes my lips can breathe,
Accordant to the measure.   80

The vapours linger round the Heights,
They melt, and soon must vanish;
One hour is theirs, nor more is mine—
Sad thought which I would banish,
But that I know, where'er I go,
Thy genuine image, Yarrow!

Will dwell with me—to heighten joy,
And cheer my mind in sorrow.

1815

"SURPRISED BY JOY—IMPATIENT AS THE WIND"

Surprised by joy—impatient as the Wind
I turned to share the transport—Oh! with whom
But Thee, deep buried in the silent tomb,
That spot which no vicissitude can find?
Love, faithful love, recalled thee to my mind—
But how could I forget thee? Through what power,
Even for the least division of an hour,
Have I been so beguiled as to be blind
To my most grievous loss?—That thought's return
Was the worst pang that sorrow ever bore,
Save one, one only, when I stood forlorn,
Knowing my heart's best treasure was no more;
That neither present time, nor years unborn
Could to my sight that heavenly face restore.

1817–1833

ODE TO LYCORIS. MAY, 1817

I

An age hath been when Earth was proud
Of lustre too intense
To be sustained; and Mortals bowed
The front in self-defence.
Who *then*, if Dian's crescent gleamed,
Or Cupid's sparkling arrow streamed,
While on the wing the Urchin played,
Could fearlessly approach the shade?
—Enough for one soft vernal day,

If I, a bard of ebbing time,   10
And nurtured in a fickle clime,
May haunt this hornèd bay;
Whose amorous water multiplies
The flitting halcyon's vivid dyes;
And smooths her liquid breast—to show
These swan-like specks of mountain snow,
White as the pair that slid along the plains
Of heaven, when Venus held the reins!

II

In youth we love the darksome lawn
Brushed by the owlet's wing;   20
Then, Twilight is preferred to Dawn,
And Autumn to the Spring.
Sad fancies do we then affect,
In luxury of disrespect
To our own prodigal excess
Of too familiar happiness.
Lycoris (if such name befit
Thee, thee my life's celestial sign!)
When Nature marks the year's decline,
Be ours to welcome it;   30
Pleased with the harvest hope that runs
Before the path of milder suns;
Pleased while the sylvan world displays
Its ripeness to the feeding gaze;
Pleased when the sullen winds resound the knell
Of the resplendent miracle.

III

But something whispers to my heart
That, as we downward tend,
Lycoris! life requires an *art*
To which our souls must bend;   40
A skill—to balance and supply;
And, ere the flowing fount be dry,
As soon it must, a sense to sip,
Or drink, with no fastidious lip.
Then welcome, above all, the Guest

Whose smiles, diffused o'er land and sea,
Seem to recall the Deity
Of youth into the breast:
May pensive Autumn ne'er present
A claim to her disparagement!   50
While blossoms and the budding spray
Inspire us in our own decay;
Still, as we nearer draw to life's dark goal
Be hopeful Spring the favourite of the Soul!

COMPOSED UPON AN EVENING OF EXTRAORDINARY SPLENDOUR AND BEAUTY

I

Had this effulgence disappeared
With flying haste, I might have sent,
Among the speechless clouds, a look
Of blank astonishment;
But 'tis endued with power to stay,
And sanctify one closing day,
That frail Mortality may see—
What is?—ah no, but what *can* be!
Time was when field and watery cove
With modulated echoes rang,   10
While choirs of fervent Angels sang
Their vespers in the grove;
Or, crowning, star-like, each some sovereign height,
Warbled, for heaven above and earth below,
Strains suitable to both.—Such holy rite,
Methinks, if audibly repeated now
From hill or valley, could not move
Sublimer transport, purer love,
Than doth this silent spectacle—the gleam—
The shadow—and the peace supreme!   20

II

No sound is uttered,—but a deep
And solemn harmony pervades
The hollow vale from steep to steep,
And penetrates the glades.
Far-distant images draw nigh,
Called forth by wondrous potency
Of beamy radiance, that imbues
Whate'er it strikes, with gem-like hues!
In vision exquisitely clear,
Herds range along the mountain side;   30
And glistening antlers are descried;
And gilded flocks appear.
Thine is the tranquil hour, purpureal Eve!
But long as god-like wish, or hope divine,
Informs my spirit, ne'er can I believe
That this magnificence is wholly thine!
—From worlds not quickened by the sun
A portion of the gift is won;
An intermingling of Heaven's pomp is spread
On ground which British shepherds tread!   40

III

And, if there be whom broken ties
Afflict, or injuries assail,
Yon hazy ridges to their eyes
Present a glorious scale,
Climbing suffused with sunny air,
To stop—no record hath told where!
And tempting Fancy to ascend,
And with immortal Spirits blend!
—Wings at my shoulders seem to play;
But, rooted here, I stand and gaze   50
On those bright steps that heavenward raise
Their practicable way.
Come forth, ye drooping old men, look abroad,
And see to what fair countries ye are bound!
And if some traveller, weary of his road,

Hath slept since noon-tide on the grassy ground,
Ye Genii! to his covert speed;
And wake him with such gentle heed
As may attune his soul to meet the dower
Bestowed on this transcendent hour!   60

IV

Such hues from their celestial Urn
Were wont to stream before mine eye,
Where'er it wandered in the morn
Of blissful infancy.
This glimpse of glory, why renewed?
Nay, rather speak with gratitude;
For, if a vestige of those gleams
Survived, 'twas only in my dreams.
Dread Power! whom peace and calmness serve
No less than Nature's threatening voice,   70
If aught unworthy be my choice,
From THEE if I would swerve;
Oh, let thy grace remind me of the light
Full early lost, and fruitlessly deplored;
Which, at this moment, on my waking sight
Appears to shine, by miracle restored;
My soul, though yet confined to earth,
Rejoices in a second birth!
—'Tis past, the visionary splendour fades;
And night approaches with her shades.   80

THE RIVER DUDDON

A SERIES OF SONNETS

I

Not envying Latian shades—if yet they throw
A grateful coolness round that crystal Spring,
Blandusia, prattling as when long ago

The Sabine Bard was moved her praise to sing;
Careless of flowers that in perennial blow
Round the moist marge of Persian fountains cling;
Heedless of Alpine torrents thundering
Through ice-built arches radiant as heaven's bow;
I seek the birthplace of a native Stream.—
All hail, ye mountains! hail, thou morning light!
Better to breathe at large on this clear height
Than toil in needless sleep from dream to dream:
Pure flow the verse, pure, vigorous, free, and bright,
For Duddon, long-loved Duddon, is my theme!

II

Child of the clouds! remote from every taint
Of sordid industry thy lot is cast;
Thine are the honours of the lofty waste
Not seldom, when with heat the valleys faint,
Thy handmaid Frost with spangled tissue quaint
Thy cradle decks;—to chant thy birth, thou hast
No meaner Poet than the whistling Blast,
And Desolation is thy Patron-saint!
She guards thee, ruthless Power! who would not spare
Those mighty forests, once the bison's screen,
Where stalked the huge deer to his shaggy lair
Through paths and alleys roofed with darkest green;
Thousands of years before the silent air
Was pierced by whizzing shaft of hunter keen!

III

How shall I paint thee?—Be this naked stone
My seat, while I give way to such intent;
Pleased could my verse, a speaking monument,
Make to the eyes of men thy features known.
But as of all those tripping lambs not one
Outruns his fellows, so hath Nature lent
To thy beginning nought that doth present
Peculiar ground for hope to build upon.
To dignify the spot that gives thee birth,
No sign of hoar Antiquity's esteem
Appears, and none of modern Fortune's care;

Yet thou thyself hast round thee shed a gleam
Of brilliant moss, instinct with freshness rare;
Prompt offering to thy Foster-mother Earth!

IV

Take, cradled Nursling of the mountain, take
This parting glance, no negligent adieu!
A Protean change seems wrought while I pursue
The curves, a loosely-scattered chain doth make;
Or rather thou appear'st a glistering snake,
Silent, and to the gazer's eye untrue,
Thridding with sinuous lapse the rushes, through
Dwarf willows gliding, and by ferny brake.
Starts from a dizzy steep the undaunted Rill
Robed instantly in garb of snow-white foam;
And laughing dares the Adventurer, who hath clomb
So high, a rival purpose to fulfil;
Else let the dastard backward wend, and roam,
Seeking less bold achievement, where he will!

V

Sole listener, Duddon! to the breeze that played
With thy clear voice, I caught the fitful sound
Wafted o'er sullen moss and craggy mound—
Unfruitful solitudes, that seemed to upbraid
The sun in heaven!—but now, to form a shade
For Thee, green alders have together wound
Their foliage; ashes flung their arms around;
And birch-trees risen in silver colonnade.
And thou hast also tempted here to rise,
'Mid sheltering pines, this Cottage rude and grey;
Whose ruddy children, by the mother's eyes
Carelessly watched, sport through the summer day,
Thy pleased associates:—light as endless May
On infant bosoms lonely Nature lies.

VI

FLOWERS

Ere yet our course was graced with social trees
It lacked not old remains of hawthorn bowers,

Where small birds warbled to their paramours;
And, earlier still, was heard the hum of bees;
I saw them ply their harmless robberies,
And caught the fragrance which the sundry flowers,
Fed by the stream with soft perpetual showers,
Plenteously yielded to the vagrant breeze.
There bloomed the strawberry of the wilderness;
The trembling eyebright showed her sapphire blue,
The thyme her purple, like the blush of Even;
And if the breath of some to no caress
Invited, forth they peeped so fair to view,
All kinds alike seemed favourites of Heaven.

VII

"Change me, some God, into that breathing rose!"
The love-sick Stripling fancifully sighs,
The envied flower beholding, as it lies
On Laura's breast, in exquisite repose;
Or he would pass into her bird, that throws
The darts of song from out its wiry cage;
Enraptured,—could he for himself engage
The thousandth part of what the Nymph bestows;
And what the little careless innocent
Ungraciously receives. Too daring choice!
There are whose calmer mind it would content
To be an unculled floweret of the glen,
Fearless of plough and scythe; or darkling wren
That tunes on Duddon's banks her slender voice.

VIII

What aspect bore the Man who roved or fled,
First of his tribe, to this dark fell—who first
In this pellucid Current slaked his thirst?
What hopes came with him? what designs were spread
Along his path? His unprotected bed
What dreams encompassed? Was the intruder nursed
In hideous usages, and rites accursed,
That thinned the living and disturbed the dead?
No voice replies;—both air and earth are mute;
And Thou, blue Streamlet, murmuring yield'st no more

Than a soft record, that, whatever fruit
Of ignorance thou might'st witness heretofore,
Thy function was to heal and to restore,
To soothe and cleanse, not madden and pollute!

IX
THE STEPPING-STONES

The struggling Rill insensibly is grown
Into a Brook of loud and stately march,
Crossed ever and anon by plank or arch;
And, for like use, lo! what might seem a zone
Chosen for ornament—stone matched with stone
In studied symmetry, with interspace
For the clear waters to pursue their race
Without restraint. How swiftly have they flown,
Succeeding—still succeeding! Here the Child
Puts, when the high-swoln Flood runs fierce and wild,
His budding courage to the proof; and here
Declining Manhood learns to note the sly
And sure encroachments of infirmity,
Thinking how fast time runs, life's end how near!

X
THE SAME SUBJECT

Not so that Pair whose youthful spirits dance
With prompt emotion, urging them to pass;
A sweet confusion checks the Shepherd-lass;
Blushing she eyes the dizzy flood askance;
To stop ashamed—too timid to advance;
She ventures once again—another pause!
His outstretched hand He tauntingly withdraws—
She sues for help with piteous utterance!
Chidden she chides again; the thrilling touch
Both feel, when he renews the wished-for aid:
Ah! if their fluttering hearts should stir too much,
Should beat too strongly, both may be betrayed.
The frolic Loves, who, from yon high rock, see
The struggle, clap their wings for victory!

XI
THE FAËRY CHASM

No fiction was it of the antique age:
A sky-blue stone, within this sunless cleft,
Is of the very footmarks unbereft
Which tiny Elves impressed;—on that smooth stage
Dancing with all their brilliant equipage
In secret revels—haply after theft
Of some sweet Babe—Flower stolen, and coarse Weed left
For the distracted Mother to assuage
Her grief with, as she might!—But, where, oh! where
Is traceable a vestige of the notes
That ruled those dances wild in character?—
Deep underground? Or in the upper air,
On the shrill wind of midnight? or where floats
O'er twilight fields the autumnal gossamer?

XII
HINTS FOR THE FANCY

On, loitering Muse—the swift Stream chides us—on!
Albeit his deep-worn channel doth immure
Objects immense portrayed in miniature,
Wild shapes for many a strange comparison!
Niagaras, Alpine passes, and anon
Abodes of Naiads, calm abysses pure,
Bright liquid mansions, fashioned to endure
When the broad oak drops, a leafless skeleton,
And the solidities of mortal pride,
Palace and tower, are crumbled into dust!—
The Bard who walks with Duddon for his guide,
Shall find such toys of fancy thickly set:
Turn from the sight, enamoured Muse—we must;
And, if thou canst, leave them without regret!

XIII
OPEN PROSPECT

Hail to the fields—with Dwellings sprinkled o'er,
And one small hamlet, under a green hill
Clustering, with barn and byre, and spouting mill!

A glance suffices;—should we wish for more,
Gay June would scorn us. But when bleak winds roar
Through the stiff lance-like shoots of pollard ash,
Dread swell of sound! loud as the gusts that lash
The matted forests of Ontario's shore
By wasteful steel unsmitten—then would I
Turn into port; and, reckless of the gale,
Reckless of angry Duddon sweeping by,
While the warm hearth exalts the mantling ale,
Laugh with the generous household heartily
At all the merry pranks of Donnerdale!

XIV

O mountain Stream! the Shepherd and his Cot
Are privileged Inmates of deep solitude;
Nor would the nicest Anchorite exclude
A field or two of brighter green, or plot
Of tillage-ground, that seemeth like a spot
Of stationary sunshine:—thou hast viewed
These only, Duddon! with their paths renewed
By fits and starts, yet this contents thee not.
Thee hath some awful Spirit impelled to leave,
Utterly to desert, the haunts of men.
Though simple thy companions were and few;
And through this wilderness a passage cleave
Attended but by thy own voice, save when
The clouds and fowls of the air thy way pursue!

XV

From this deep chasm, where quivering sunbeams play
Upon its loftiest crags, mine eyes behold
A gloomy NICHE, capacious, blank, and cold;
A concave free from shrubs and mosses grey;
In semblance fresh, as if, with dire affray,
Some Statue, placed amid these regions old
For tutelary service, thence had rolled,
Startling the flight of timid Yesterday!
Was it by mortals sculptured?—weary slaves
Of slow endeavour! or abruptly cast

Into rude shape by fire, with roaring blast
Tempestuously let loose from central caves?
Or fashioned by the turbulence of waves,
Then, when o'er highest hills the Deluge passed?

XVI
AMERICAN TRADITION

Such fruitless questions may not long beguile
Or plague the fancy 'mid the sculptured shows
Conspicuous yet where Oroonoko flows;
There would the Indian answer with a smile
Aimed at the White Man's ignorance, the while,
Of the GREAT WATERS telling how they rose,
Covered the plains, and, wandering where they chose,
Mounted through every intricate defile,
Triumphant—Inundation wide and deep,
O'er which his Fathers urged, to ridge and steep
Else unapproachable, their buoyant way;
And carved, on mural cliff's undreaded side,
Sun, moon, and stars, and beast of chase or prey;
Whate'er they sought, shunned, loved, or deified!

XVII
RETURN

A dark plume fetch me from yon blasted yew,
Perched on whose top the Danish Raven croaks;
Aloft, the imperial Bird of Rome invokes
Departed ages, shedding where he flew
Loose fragments of wild wailing, that bestrew
The clouds and thrill the chambers of the rocks;
And into silence hush the timorous flocks,
That, calmly couching while the nightly dew
Moistened each fleece, beneath the twinkling stars
Slept amid that lone Camp on Hardknot's height,
Whose Guardians bent the knee to Jove and Mars:
Or, near that mystic Round of Druid frame
Tardily sinking by its proper weight
Deep into patient Earth, from whose smooth breast it
    came!

XVIII
SEATHWAITE CHAPEL

Sacred Religion! "mother of form and fear,"
Dread arbitress of mutable respect,
New rites ordaining when the old are wrecked,
Or cease to please the fickle worshipper;
Mother of Love! (that name best suits thee here)
Mother of Love! for this deep vale, protect
Truth's holy lamp, pure source of bright effect,
Gifted to purge the vapoury atmosphere
That seeks to stifle it;—as in those days
When this low Pile a Gospel Teacher knew,
Whose good works formed an endless retinue:
A Pastor such as Chaucer's verse portrays;
Such as the heaven-taught skill of Herbert drew;
And tender Goldsmith crowned with deathless praise!

XIX
TRIBUTARY STREAM

My frame hath often trembled with delight
When hope presented some far-distant good,
That seemed from heaven descending, like the flood
Of yon pure waters, from their aëry height
Hurrying, with lordly Duddon to unite;
Who, 'mid a world of images imprest
On the calm depth of his transparent breast,
Appears to cherish most that Torrent white,
The fairest, softest, liveliest of them all!
And seldom hath ear listened to a tune
More lulling than the busy hum of Noon,
Swoln by that voice—whose murmur musical
Announces to the thirsty fields a boon
Dewy and fresh, till showers again shall fall.

XX
THE PLAIN OF DONNERDALE

The old inventive Poets, had they seen,
Or rather felt, the entrancement that detains
Thy waters, Duddon! 'mid these flowery plains—

The still repose, the liquid lapse serene,
Transferred to bowers imperishably green,
Had beautified Elysium! But these chains
Will soon be broken;—a rough course remains,
Rough as the past; where Thou, of placid mien,
Innocuous as a firstling of the flock,
And countenanced like a soft cerulean sky,
Shalt change thy temper; and, with many a shock
Given and received in mutual jeopardy,
Dance, like a Bacchanal, from rock to rock,
Tossing her frantic thyrsus wide and high!

XXI

Whence that low voice?—A whisper from the heart,
That told of days long past, when here I roved
With friends and kindred tenderly beloved;
Some who had early mandates to depart,
Yet are allowed to steal my path athwart
By Duddon's side; once more do we unite,
Once more, beneath the kind Earth's tranquil light,
And smothered joys into new being start.
From her unworthy seat, the cloudy stall
Of Time, breaks forth triumphant Memory
Her glistening tresses bound, yet light and free
As golden locks of birch, that rise and fall
On gales that breathe too gently to recall
Aught of the fading year's inclemency!

XXII
TRADITION

A love-lorn Maid, at some far-distant time,
Came to this hidden pool, whose depths surpass
In crystal clearness Dian's looking-glass;
And, gazing, saw that Rose, which from the prime
Derives its name, reflected, as the chime
Of echo doth reverberate some sweet sound:
The starry treasure from the blue profound
She longed to ravish;—shall she plunge, or climb
The humid precipice, and seize the guest

Of April, smiling high in upper air?
Desperate alternative! what fiend could dare
To prompt the thought?—Upon the steep rock's breast
The lonely Primrose yet renews its bloom,
Untouched memento of her hapless doom!

XXIII
SHEEP WASHING

Sad thoughts, avaunt!—partake we their blithe cheer
Who gathered in betimes the unshorn flock
To wash the fleece, where haply bands of rock,
Checking the stream, make a pool smooth and clear
As this we look on. Distant Mountains hear,
Hear and repeat, the turmoil that unites
Clamour of boys with innocent despites
Of barking dogs, and bleatings from strange fear.
And what if Duddon's spotless flood receive
Unwelcome mixtures as the uncouth noise
Thickens, the pastoral River will forgive
Such wrong; nor need *we* blame the licensed joys,
Though false to Nature's quiet equipoise:
Frank are the sports, the stains are fugitive.

XXIV
THE RESTING-PLACE

Mid-noon is past;—upon the sultry mead
No zephyr breathes, no cloud its shadow throws:
If we advance unstrengthened by repose,
Farewell the solace of the vagrant reed!
This Nook—with woodbine hung and straggling weed
Tempting recess as ever pilgrim chose,
Half grot, half arbour—proffers to enclose
Body and mind, from molestation freed,
In narrow compass—narrow as itself:
Or if the Fancy, too industrious Elf,
Be loth that we should breathe awhile exempt
From new incitements friendly to our task,
Here wants not stealthy prospect, that may tempt
Loose Idless to forego her wily mask.

XXV

Methinks 'twere no unprecedented feat
Should some benignant Minister of air
Lift, and encircle with a cloudy chair,
The One for whom my heart shall ever beat
With tenderest love;—or, if a safer seat
Atween his downy wings be furnished, there
Would lodge her, and the cherished burden bear
O'er hill and valley to this dim retreat!
Rough ways my steps have trod;—too rough and long
For her companionship; here dwells soft ease:
With sweets that she partakes not, some distaste
Mingles, and lurking consciousness of wrong;
Languish the flowers; the waters seem to waste
Their vocal charm; their sparklings cease to please.

XXVI

Return, Content! for fondly I pursued,
Even when a child, the Streams—unheard, unseen;
Through tangled woods, impending rocks between;
Or, free as air, with flying inquest viewed
The sullen reservoirs whence their bold brood—
Pure as the morning, fretful, boisterous, keen,
Green as the salt-sea billows, white and green—
Poured down the hills, a choral multitude!
Nor have I tracked their course for scanty gains;
They taught me random cares and truant joys,
That shield from mischief and preserve from stains
Vague minds, while men are growing out of boys;
Maturer Fancy owes to their rough noise
Impetuous thoughts that brook not servile reins.

XXVII

Fallen, and diffused into a shapeless heap,
Or quietly self-buried in earth's mould,
Is that embattled House, whose massy Keep,
Flung from yon cliff a shadow large and cold.
There dwelt the gay, the bountiful, the bold;
Till nightly lamentations, like the sweep
Of winds—though winds were silent—struck a deep

And lasting terror through that ancient Hold.
Its line of Warriors fled;—they shrunk when tried
By ghostly power:—but Time's unsparing hand
Hath plucked such foes, like weeds, from out the land;
And now, if men with men in peace abide,
All other strength the weakest may withstand,
All worse assaults may safely be defied.

XXVIII
JOURNEY RENEWED

I rose while yet the cattle, heat-opprest,
Crowded together under rustling trees
Brushed by the current of the water-breeze;
And for *their* sakes, and love of all that rest,
On Duddon's margin, in the sheltering nest;
For all the startled scaly tribes that slink
Into his coverts, and each fearless link
Of dancing insects forged upon his breast;
For these, and hopes and recollections worn
Close to the vital seat of human clay;
Glad meetings, tender partings, that upstay
The drooping mind of absence, by vows sworn
In his pure presence near the trysting thorn—
I thanked the Leader of my onward way.

XXIX

No record tells of lance opposed to lance,
Horse charging horse, 'mid these retired domains;
Tells that their turf drank purple from the veins
Of heroes fallen, or struggling to advance,
Till doubtful combat issued in a trance
Of victory, that struck through heart and reins
Even to the inmost seat of mortal pains,
And lightened o'er the pallid countenance.
Yet, to the loyal and the brave, who lie
In the blank earth, neglected and forlorn,
The passing Winds memorial tribute pay;
The Torrents chant their praise, inspiring scorn
Of power usurped; with proclamation high,
And glad acknowledgment, of lawful sway.

XXX

Who swerves from innocence, who makes divorce
Of that serene companion—a good name,
Recovers not his loss; but walks with shame,
With doubt, with fear, and haply with remorse:
And oft-times he—who, yielding to the force
Of chance-temptation, ere his journey end,
From chosen comrade turns, or faithful friend—
In vain shall rue the broken intercourse.
Not so with such as loosely wear the chain
That binds them, pleasant River! to thy side:—
Through the rough copse wheel thou with hasty stride;
I choose to saunter o'er the grassy plain,
Sure, when the separation has been tried,
That we, who part in love, shall meet again.

XXXI

The Kirk of Ulpha to the pilgrim's eye
Is welcome as a star, that doth present
Its shining forehead through the peaceful rent
Of a black cloud diffused o'er half the sky:
Or as a fruitful palm-tree towering high
O'er the parched waste beside an Arab's tent;
Or the Indian tree whose branches, downward bent,
Take root again, a boundless canopy.
How sweet were leisure! could it yield no more
Than 'mid that wave-washed Churchyard to recline,
From pastoral graves extracting thoughts divine;
Or there to pace, and mark the summits hoar
Of distant moonlit mountains faintly shine,
Soothed by the unseen River's gentle roar.

XXXII

Not hurled precipitous from steep to steep;
Lingering no more 'mid flower-enamelled lands
And blooming thickets; nor by rocky bands
Held; but in radiant progress toward the Deep
Where mightiest rivers into powerless sleep
Sink, and forget their nature—*now* expands
Majestic Duddon, over smooth flat sands

Gliding in silence with unfettered sweep!
Beneath an amber sky a region wide
Is opened round him:—hamlets, towers, and towns,
And blue-topped hills, behold him from afar;
In stately mien to sovereign Thames allied,
Spreading his bosom under Kentish downs,
With commerce freighted, or triumphant war.

XXXIII
CONCLUSION

But here no cannon thunders to the gale;
Upon the wave no haughty pendants cast
A crimson splendour: lowly is the mast
That rises here, and humbly spread, the sail;
While, less disturbed than in the narrow Vale
Through which with strange vicissitudes he passed,
The Wanderer seeks that receptacle vast
Where all his unambitious functions fail
And may thy Poet, cloud-born Stream! be free—
The sweets of earth contentedly resigned,
And each tumultuous working left behind
At seemly distance—to advance like Thee;
Prepared, in peace of heart, in calm of mind
And soul, to mingle with Eternity!

XXXIV
AFTER-THOUGHT

I thought of Thee, my partner and my guide,
As being past away.—Vain sympathies!
For, backward, Duddon, as I cast my eyes,
I see what was, and is, and will abide;
Still glides the Stream, and shall for ever glide;
The Form remains, the Function never dies;
While we, the brave, the mighty, and the wise,
We Men, who in our morn of youth defied
The elements, must vanish;—be it so!
Enough, if something from our hands have power
To live, and act, and serve the future hour;
And if, as toward the silent tomb we go,

Through love, through hope, and faith's transcendent dower,
We feel that we are greater than we know.

ECCLESIASTICAL SONNETS

IN SERIES

PART I

FROM THE INTRODUCTION OF CHRISTIANITY INTO BRITAIN, TO
THE CONSUMMATION OF THE PAPAL DOMINION

I
INTRODUCTION

I, who accompanied with faithful pace
Cerulean Duddon from his cloud-fed spring,
And loved with spirit ruled by his to sing
Of mountain quiet and boon nature's grace;
I, who essayed the nobler Stream to trace
Of Liberty, and smote the plausive string
Till the checked torrent, proudly triumphing,
Won for herself a lasting resting-place;
Now seek upon the heights of Time the source
Of a HOLY RIVER, on whose banks are found
Sweet pastoral flowers, and laurels that have crowned
Full oft the unworthy brow of lawless force;
And, for delight of him who tracks its course,
Immortal amaranth and palms abound.

III
TREPIDATION OF THE DRUIDS

Screams round the Arch-druid's brow the seamew—
　　white
As Menai's foam; and toward the mystic ring
Where Augurs stand, the Future questioning,
Slowly the cormorant aims her heavy flight,
Portending ruin to each baleful rite,
That, in the lapse of ages, hath crept o'er

Diluvian truths, and patriarchal lore.
Haughty the Bard: can these meek doctrines blight
His transports? wither his heroic strains?
But all shall be fulfilled;—the Julian spear
A way first opened; and, with Roman chains,
The tidings come of Jesus crucified;
They come—they spread—the weak, the suffering, hear;
Receive the faith, and in the hope abide.

IV

DRUIDICAL EXCOMMUNICATION

Mercy and Love have met thee on thy road,
Thou wretched Outcast, from the gift of fire
And food cut off by sacerdotal ire,
From every sympathy that Man bestowed!
Yet shall it claim our reverence, that to God,
Ancient of days! that to the eternal Sire,
These jealous Ministers of law aspire,
As to the one sole fount whence wisdom flowed,
Justice, and order. Tremblingly escaped,
As if with prescience of the coming storm,
That intimation when the stars were shaped;
And still, 'mid yon thick woods, the primal truth
Glimmers through many a superstitious form
That fills the Soul with unavailing ruth.

V

UNCERTAINTY

Darkness surrounds us; seeking, we are lost
On Snowdon's wilds, amid Brigantian coves,
Or where the solitary shepherd roves
Along the plain of Sarum, by the ghost
Of Time and shadows of Tradition, crost;
And where the boatman of the Western Isles
Slackens his course—to mark those holy piles
Which yet survive on bleak Iona's coast.
Nor these, nor monuments of eldest name,
Nor Taliesin's unforgotten lays,

Nor characters of Greek or Roman fame,
To an unquestionable Source have led;
Enough—if eyes, that sought the fountain-head
In vain, upon the growing Rill may gaze.

XXI
SECLUSION

Lance, shield, and sword relinquished, at his side
A bead-roll, in his hand a claspèd book,
Or staff more harmless than a shepherd's crook,
The war-worn Chieftain quits the world—to hide
His thin autumnal locks where Monks abide
In cloistered privacy. But not to dwell
In soft repose he comes: within his cell,
Round the decaying trunk of human pride,
At morn, and eve, and midnight's silent hour,
Do penitential cogitations cling;
Like ivy, round some ancient elm, they twine
In grisly folds and strictures serpentine;
Yet, while they strangle, a fair growth they bring,
For recompence—their own perennial bower.

XXII
CONTINUED

Methinks that to some vacant hermitage
My feet would rather turn—to some dry nook
Scooped out of living rock, and near a brook
Hurled down a mountain-cove from stage to stage,
Yet tempering, for my sight, its bustling rage
In the soft heaven of a translucent pool;
Thence creeping under sylvan arches cool,
Fit haunt of shapes whose glorious equipage
Would elevate my dreams. A beechen bowl,
A maple dish, my furniture should be;
Crisp, yellow leaves my bed; the hooting owl
My night-watch: nor should e'er the crested fowl
From thorp or vill his matins sound for me,
Tired of the world and all its industry.

XXX
CANUTE

A pleasant music floats along the Mere,
From Monks in Ely chanting service high,
While-as Canùte the King is rowing by:
"My Oarsmen," quoth the mighty King, "draw near,
That we the sweet song of the Monks may hear!"
He listens (all past conquests, and all schemes
Of future, vanishing like empty dreams)
Heart-touched, and haply not without a tear.
The Royal Minstrel, ere the choir is still,
While his free Barge skims the smooth flood along,
Gives to that rapture an accordant Rhyme.
O suffering Earth! be thankful: sternest clime
And rudest age are subject to the thrill
Of heaven-descended Piety and Song.

PART II

TO THE CLOSE OF THE TROUBLES IN THE REIGN OF CHARLES I

XXI
DISSOLUTION OF THE MONASTERIES

Threats come which no submission may assuage,
No sacrifice avert, no power dispute;
The tapers shall be quenched, the belfries mute,
And, 'mid their choirs unroofed by selfish rage.
The warbling wren shall find a leafy cage;
The gadding bramble hang her purple fruit;
And the green lizard and the gilded newt
Lead unmolested lives, and die of age.
The owl of evening and the woodland fox
For their abode the shrines of Waltham choose:
Proud Glastonbury can no more refuse
To stoop her head before these desperate shocks—
She whose high pomp displaced, as story tells,
Arimathean Joseph's wattled cells.

XXIV
SAINTS

Ye, too, must fly before a chasing hand,
Angels and Saints, in every hamlet mourned!
Ah! if the old idolatry be spurned,
Let not your radiant Shapes desert the Land:
Her adoration was not your demand,
The fond heart proffered it—the servile heart;
And therefore are ye summoned to depart,
Michael, and thou, St. George, whose flaming brand
The Dragon quelled; and valiant Margaret
Whose rival sword a like Opponent slew:
And rapt Cecilia, seraph-haunted Queen
Of harmony; and weeping Magdalene,
Who in the penitential desert met
Gales sweet as those that over Eden blew!

PART III

FROM THE RESTORATION TO THE PRESENT TIMES

I

I saw the figure of a lovely Maid
Seated alone beneath a darksome tree,
Whose fondly-overhanging canopy
Set off her brightness with a pleasing shade.
No Spirit was she; *that* my heart betrayed,
For she was one I loved exceedingly;
But while I gazed in tender reverie
(Or was it sleep that with my Fancy played?)
The bright corporeal presence—form and face—
Remaining still distinct grew thin and rare,
Like sunny mist;—at length the golden hair,
Shape, limbs, and heavenly features, keeping pace
Each with the other in a lingering race
Of dissolution, melted into air.

II
PATRIOTIC SYMPATHIES

Last night, without a voice, that Vision spake
Fear to my Soul, and sadness which might seem
Wholly dissevered from our present theme;
Yet, my belovèd Country! I partake
Of kindred agitations for thy sake;
Thou, too, dost visit oft my midnight dream;
Thy glory meets me with the earliest beam
Of light, which tells that Morning is awake.
If aught impair thy beauty or destroy,
Or but forebode destruction, I deplore
With filial love the sad vicissitude;
If thou hast fallen, and righteous Heaven restore
The prostrate, then my spring-time is renewed,
And sorrow bartered for exceeding joy.

XXXIV
MUTABILITY

From low to high doth dissolution climb,
And sink from high to low, along a scale
Of awful notes, whose concord shall not fail;
A musical but melancholy chime,
Which they can hear who meddle not with crime,
Nor avarice, nor over-anxious care.
Truth fails not; but her outward forms that bear
The longest date do melt like frosty rime,
That in the morning whitened hill and plain
And is no more; drop like the tower sublime
Of yesterday, which royally did wear
His crown of weeds, but could not even sustain
Some casual shout that broke the silent air,
Or the unimaginable touch of Time.

XXXVII
CONGRATULATION

Thus all things lead to Charity secured
BY THEM who blessed the soft and happy gale
That landward urged the great Deliverer's sail,
Till in the sunny bay his fleet was moored!

Propitious hour!—had we, like them, endured
Sore stress of apprehension, with a mind
Sickened by injuries, dreading worse designed,
From month to month trembling and unassured,
How had we then rejoiced! But we have felt,
As a loved substance, their futurity:
Good, which they dared not hope for, we have seen;
A State whose generous will through earth is dealt;
A State—which, balancing herself between
Licence and slavish order, dares be free.

XLVII
CONCLUSION

Why sleeps the future, as a snake enrolled,
Coil within coil, at noon-tide? For the WORD
Yields, if with unpresumptuous faith explored,
Power at whose touch the sluggard shall unfold
His drowsy rings. Look forth!—that Stream behold,
THAT STREAM upon whose bosom we have passed
Floating at ease while nations have effaced
Nations, and Death has gathered to his fold
Long lines of mighty Kings—look forth, my Soul!
(Nor in this vision be thou slow to trust)
The living Waters, less and less by guilt
Stained and polluted, brighten as they roll,
Till they have reached the eternal City—built
For the perfected Spirit of the just!

"SCORN NOT THE SONNET"

Scorn not the Sonnet; Critic, you have frowned,
Mindless of its just honours; with this key
Shakespeare unlocked his heart; the melody
Of this small lute gave ease to Petrarch's wound;
A thousand times this pipe did Tasso sound;
With it Camöens soothed an exile's grief;

The Sonnet glittered a gay myrtle leaf
Amidth cypress with which Dante crowned
His visionary brow: a glow-worm lamp,
It cheered mild Spenser, called from Faeryland
To struggle through dark ways; and, when a damp
Fell round the path of Milton, in his hand
The Thing became a trumpet; whence he blew
Soul-animating strains—alas, too few!

YARROW REVISITED

The gallant Youth, who may have gained,
    Or seeks, a "winsome Marrow,"
Was but an Infant in the lap
    When I first looked on Yarrow;
Once more, by Newark's Castle-gate
    Long left without a warder,
I stood, looked, listened, and with Thee,
    Great Minstrel of the Border!

Grave thoughts ruled wide on that sweet day,
    Their dignity installing   10
In gentle bosoms, while sere leaves
    Were on the bough, or falling;
But breezes played, and sunshine gleamed—
    The forest to embolden;
Reddened the fiery hues, and shot
    Transparence through the golden.

For busy thoughts the Stream flowed on
    In foamy agitation;
And slept in many a crystal pool
    For quiet contemplation: 20
No public and no private care
    The freeborn mind enthralling,

We made a day of happy hours,
  Our happy days recalling.

Brisk Youth appeared, the Morn of youth,
  With freaks of graceful folly,—
Life's temperate Noon, her sober Eve,
  Her Night not melancholy;
Past, present, future, all appeared
  In harmony united,   30
Like guests that meet, and some from far,
  By cordial love invited.

And if, as Yarrow, through the woods
  And down the meadow ranging,
Did meet us with unaltered face,
  Though we were changed and changing;
If, *then,* some natural shadows spread
  Our inward prospect over,
The soul's deep valley was not slow
  Its brightness to recover.   40

Eternal blessings on the Muse,
  And her divine employment!
The blameless Muse, who trains her Sons
  For hope and calm enjoyment;
Albeit sickness, lingering yet,
  Has o'er their pillow brooded;
And Care waylays their steps—a Sprite
  Not easily eluded.

For thee, O SCOTT! compelled to change
  Green Eildon-hill and Cheviot   50
For warm Vesuvio's vine-clad slopes;
  And leave thy Tweed and Tiviot
For mild Sorento's breezy waves;
  May classic Fancy, linking
With native Fancy her fresh aid,
  Preserve thy heart from sinking!

Oh! while they minister to thee,
　　Each vying with the other,
May Health return to mellow Age
　　With Strength, her venturous brother;　　**60**
And Tiber, and each brook and rill
　　Renowned in song and story,
With unimagined beauty shine,
　　Nor lose one ray of glory!

For Thou, upon a hundred streams,
　　By tales of love and sorrow,
Of faithful love, undaunted truth,
　　Hast shed the power of Yarrow;
And streams unknown, hills yet unseen,
　　Wherever they invite Thee,　　**70**
At parent Nature's grateful call,
　　With gladness must requite Thee.

A gracious welcome shall be thine,
　　Such looks of love and honour
As thy own Yarrow gave to me
　　When first I gazed upon her;
Beheld what I had feared to see,
　　Unwilling to surrender
Dreams treasured up from early days,
　　The holy and the tender.　　**80**

And what, for this frail world, were all
　　That mortals do or suffer,
Did no responsive harp, no pen,
　　Memorial tribute offer?
Yea, what were mighty Nature's self?
　　Her features, could they win us,
Unhelped by the poetic voice
　　That hourly speaks within us?

Nor deem that localised Romance
　　Plays false with our affections;　　**90**
Unsanctifies our tears—made sport
　　For fanciful dejections:

Ah, no! the visions of the past
    Sustain the heart in feeling
Life as she is—our changeful Life,
    With friends and kindred dealing.

Bear witness, Ye, whose thoughts that day
    In Yarrow's groves were centred;
Who through the silent portal arch
    Of mouldering Newark entered;   100
And clomb the winding stair that once
    Too timidly was mounted
By the "last Minstrel," (not the last!)
    Ere he his Tale recounted.

Flow on for ever, Yarrow Stream!
    Fulfil thy pensive duty,
Well pleased that future Bards should chant
    For simple hearts thy beauty;
To dream-light dear while yet unseen,
    Dear to the common sunshine,   110
And dearer still, as now I feel,
    To memory's shadowy moonshine!

"IF THOU INDEED DERIVE THY LIGHT FROM HEAVEN"

If thou indeed derive thy light from Heaven,
Then, to the measure of that heaven-born light,
Shine, Poet! in thy place, and be content:—
The stars pre-eminent in magnitude,
And they that from the zenith dart their beams,
(Visible though they be to half the earth,
Though half a sphere by conscious of their brightness)
Are yet of no diviner origin,
No purer essence, than the one that burns,

Like an untended watch-fire on the ridge
Of some dark mountain; or than those which seem
Humbly to hang, like twinkling winter lamps,
Among the branches of the leafless trees.
All are the undying offspring of one Sire:
Then, to the measure of the light vouchsafed,
Shine, Poet! in thy place, and be content.

"IF THIS GREAT WORLD OF JOY AND PAIN"

If this great world of joy and pain
    Revolve in one sure track;
If freedom, set, will rise again,
    And virtue, flown, come back;
Woe to the purblind crew who fill
    The heart with each day's care;
Nor gain, from past of future, skill
    To bear, and to forbear!

"MOST SWEET IT IS WITH UNUPLIFTED EYES"

Most sweet it is with unuplifted eyes
To pace the ground, if path be there or none,
While a fair region round the traveller lies
Which he forbears again to look upon;
Pleased rather with some soft ideal scene,
The work of Fancy, or some happy tone
Of meditation, slipping in between
The beauty coming and the beauty gone.
If Thought and Love desert us, from that day
Let us break off all commerce with the Muse:
With Thought and Love companions of our way,
Whate'er the senses take or may refuse,
The Mind's internal heaven shall shed her dews
Of inspiration on the humblest lay.

TO A CHILD

WRITTEN IN HER ALBUM

Small service is true service while it lasts:
Of humblest Friends, bright Creature! scorn not one:
The Daisy, by the shadow that it casts,
Protects the lingering dew-drop from the Sun.

Preface to the Second Edition of "Lyrical Ballads," 1800

The first Volume of these Poems has already been submitted to general perusal. It was published as an experiment, which, I hoped, might be of some use to ascertain how far, by fitting to metrical arrangement a selection of the real language of men in a state of vivid sensation, that sort of pleasure and that quantity of pleasure may be imparted, which a Poet may rationally endeavour to impart.

I had formed no very inaccurate estimate of the probable effect of those Poems: I flattered myself that they who should be pleased with them would read them with more than common pleasure: and, on the other hand, I was well aware, that by those who should dislike them they would be read with more than common dislike. The result has differed from my expectation in this only, that a greater number have been pleased than I ventured to hope I should please.

. . . .

Several of my Friends are anxious for the success of these Poems, from a belief that, if the views with which they were composed were indeed realised, a class of Poetry would be produced, well adapted to interest mankind permanently, and not unimportant in the quality and in the multiplicity of its moral relations: and on this account they have advised me to prefix a systematic defence of the theory upon which the Poems were written. But I was unwilling to undertake the task, knowing that on this occasion the Reader would look coldly upon my arguments, since I might be suspected of having been principally influenced by the selfish and foolish hope of *reasoning* him into an approbation of these particular Poems: and I was still more unwilling to undertake the task, because adequately to display the opinions, and fully to enforce the arguments, would require a space wholly disproportionate to a preface. For, to treat the subject with the clearness and coherence of which it is susceptible, it would be necessary to give a full account of the present state of the public taste in this country, and to determine how far this taste is healthy or depraved; which, again, could not be determined without pointing out in what manner language and the human mind act and re-act on each other, and without retracing the revolutions, not of literature alone, but likewise of society itself. I have therefore altogether declined to enter regularly upon this defence; yet I am sensible that there would be something like impropriety in abruptly obtruding upon the Public, without a few words of introduction, Poems so materially different from those upon which general approbation is at present bestowed.

It is supposed that by the act of writing in verse an Author makes a formal engagement that he will gratify certain known habits of association; that he not only thus apprises the Reader that certain classes of ideas and expressions will be found in his book, but that others will be carefully excluded. This exponent or symbol held forth by metrical language must in different eras of literature have excited very different expectations: for example, in the age of Catullus, Terence, and Lucretius, and that of Statius or Claudian; and in our own country, in the age of Shakespeare and Beaumont and Fletcher, and that of Donne and Cowley, or Dryden, or Pope. I will not take upon me to determine the exact import of the promise which, by the act of writing in verse, an Author in the present day makes to his reader; but it will undoubtedly appear to many persons that I have not fulfilled the terms of an engagement thus voluntarily contracted. They who have been accustomed to the gaudiness and inane phraseology of many modern writers, if they persist in reading this book to its conclusion, will, no doubt, frequently have to struggle with feelings of strangeness and awkwardness: they will look round for poetry, and will be induced to inquire by what species of courtesy these attempts can be permitted to assume that title. I hope, therefore, the reader will not censure me for attempting to state what I have proposed to myself to perform; and also (as far as the limits of a preface will permit) to explain some of the chief reasons which have determined me in the choice of my purpose: that at least he may be spared any unpleasant feeling of disappointment, and that I myself may be protected from one of the most dishonourable accusations which can be brought against an Author; namely, that of an indolence which prevents him from endeavouring to ascertain what is his duty, or, when his duty is ascertained, prevents him from performing it.

The principal object, then, proposed in these Poems, was to choose incidents and situations from common life, and to relate or describe them throughout, as far as was possible, in a selection of language really used by men, and, at the same time, to throw over them a certain colouring of imagination, whereby ordinary things should be presented to the mind in an unusual aspect; and further, and above all, to make these incidents and situations interesting by tracing in them, truly though not ostentatiously, the primary laws of our nature: chiefly, as far as regards the manner in which we associate ideas in a state of excitement. Humble and rustic life was generally chosen, because in that condition the essential passions of the heart find a better soil in which they can attain their maturity, are less under restraint, and speak a plainer and more emphatic language; because in that condition of life our elementary feelings co-exist in a state of greater simplicity, and, consequently, may be more accurately contemplated, and more forcibly communicated; because the manners of rural life germinate from those elementary feelings, and, from the necessary character of rural occupations, are more easily comprehended, and are more durable; and, lastly, because in that condition the passions of men are incorporated with the beautiful and permanent forms of nature. The language, too, of these men has been adopted (purified indeed from what appear to be its real defects, from all lasting and rational causes of dislike or disgust), because such men hourly communicate with the best objects from which the best part of language is originally derived; and because, from their rank in society and the sameness and narrow circle of their intercourse, being less under the influence of social vanity, they convey their feelings and notions in simple and unelaborated expressions. Accordingly, such a language, arising out of repeated experience and regular feelings, is a more permanent, and a far more philosophical language, than that which is frequently substituted for it by Poets, who think that they are conferring honour upon themselves and their art in proportion as they separate themselves from the sympathies of men, and indulge in arbitrary and capricious habits of expression, in order to furnish food for fickle tastes and fickle appetites of their own creation.[1]

1. It is worth while here to observe that the affecting parts of Chaucer are almost always expressed in language pure and universally intelligible even to this day.

I cannot, however, be insensible to the present outcry against the triviality and meanness, both of thought and language, which some of my contemporaries have occasionally introduced into their metrical compositions; and I acknowledge that this defect, where it exists, is more dishonourable to the Writer's own character than false refinement or arbitrary innovation, though I should contend at the same time that it is far less pernicious in the sum of its consequences. From such verses the Poems in these volumes will be found distinguished at least by one mark of difference, that each of them has a worthy *purpose*. Not that I always began to write with a distinct purpose formally conceived, but habits of meditation have, I trust, so prompted and regulated my feelings, that my descriptions of such objects as strongly excite those feelings will be found to carry along with them a *purpose*. If this opinion be erroneous, I can have little right to the name of a Poet. For all good poetry is the spontaneous overflow of powerful feelings: and though this be true, Poems to which any value can be attached were never produced on any variety of subjects but by a man who, being possessed of more than usual organic sensibility, had also thought long and deeply. For our continued influxes of feeling are modified and directed by our thoughts, which are indeed the representatives of all our past feelings; and as, by contemplating the relation of these general representatives to each other, we discover what is really important to men, so, by the repetition and continuance of this act, our feelings will be connected with important subjects, till at length, if we be originally possessed of much sensibility, such habits of mind will be produced that, by obeying blindly and mechanically the impulses of those habits, we shall describe objects, and utter sentiments, of such a nature, and in such connection with each other, that the understanding of the Reader must necessarily be in some degree enlightened, and his affection strengthened and purified.

It has been said that each of these Poems has a purpose. Another circumstance must be mentioned which distinguishes these Poems from the popular Poetry of the day; it is this, that the feeling therein developed gives importance to the action and situation, and not the action and situation to the feeling.

A sense of false modesty shall not prevent me from asserting that the Reader's attention is pointed to this mark of distinction, far less for the sake of these particular Poems than from the general importance of the subject. The subject is indeed important! For the human mind is capable of being excited without the application of gross and violent stimulants; and he must have a very faint perception of its beauty and dignity who does not know this, and who does not further know, that one being is elevated above another in proportion as he possesses this capability. It has therefore appeared to me, that to endeavour to produce or enlarge this capability is one of the best services in which, at any period, a Writer can be engaged; but this service, excellent at all times, is especially so at the present day. For a multitude of causes, unknown to former times, are now acting with a combined force to blunt the discriminating powers of the mind, and, unfitting it for all voluntary exertion, to reduce it to a state of almost savage torpor. The most effective of these causes are the great national events which are daily taking place, and the increasing accumulation of men in cities, where the uniformity of their occupations produces a craving for extraordinary incident which the rapid communication of intelligence hourly gratifies. To this tendency of life and manners the literature and theatrical exhibitions of the country have conformed themselves. The invaluable works of our elder writers, I had almost said the works of Shakespeare and Milton, are driven into neglect by frantic novels, sickly and stupid German Tragedies, and deluges of idle and extravagant stories in verse.—When I think upon this degrading thirst after outrageous stimulation, I am almost ashamed to have spoken of the feeble endeavour made in these volumes to counteract it; and, reflecting upon the magnitude of the general evil, I should be oppressed with no dishonourable melancholy, had I not a deep impression of certain inherent and indestructible qualities of the human mind, and likewise of certain powers in the great and permanent objects that act upon it, which are equally inherent and indestructible; and were there not added to this impression a belief that the time is approaching when the evil will be systematically opposed by men of greater powers, and with far more distinguished success.

Having dwelt thus long on the subjects and aim of these Poems, I shall request the Reader's permission to apprise him of a few circumstances relating to their *style*, in order, among other reasons, that he may not censure me for not having performed what I never attempted. The Reader will find that personifications of abstract ideas rarely occur in these volumes, and are utterly rejected as an ordinary device to elevate the style and raise it above prose. My purpose was to imitate, and, as far as is possible, to adopt the very language of men; and assuredly such personifications do not make any natural or regular part of that language. They are, indeed, a figure of speech occasionally prompted by passion, and I have made use of them as such; but have endeavoured utterly to reject them as a mechanical device of style, or as a family language which Writers in metre seem to lay claim to by prescription. I have wished to keep the Reader in the company of flesh and blood, persuaded that by so doing I shall interest him. Others who pursue a different track will interest him likewise; I do not interfere with their claim, but wish to prefer a claim of my own. There will also be found in these volumes little of what is usually called poetic diction; as much pains has been taken to avoid it as is ordinarily taken to produce it; this has been done for the reason already alleged, to bring my language near to the language of men; and further, because the pleasure which I have proposed to myself to impart is of a kind very different from that which is supposed by many persons to be the proper object of poetry. Without being culpably particular, I do not know how to give my Reader a more exact notion of the style in which it was my wish and intention to write, than by informing him that I have at all times endeavoured to look steadily at my subject; consequently there is, I hope, in these Poems little falsehood of description, and my ideas are expressed in language fitted to their respective importance. Something must have been gained by this practice, as it is friendly to one property of all good poetry, namely, good sense: but it has necessarily cut me off from a large portion of phrases and figures of speech which from father to son have long been regarded as the common inheritance of Poets. I have also thought it expedient to restrict myself still further, having abstained from the use of many expressions, in themselves proper and beautiful, but which have been foolishly repeated by bad Poets, till such feelings of disgust are connected with them as it is scarcely possible by any art of association to overpower.

If in a poem there should be found a series of lines, or even a single line, in which the language, though naturally arranged, and according to the strict laws of metre, does not differ from that of prose, there is a numerous class of critics, who, when they stumble upon these prosaisms, as they call them, imagine that they have made a notable discovery, and exult over the Poet as over a man ignorant of his own profession. Now these men would establish a canon of criticism which the Reader will conclude he must utterly reject, if he wishes to be pleased with these volumes. And it would be a most easy task to prove to him that not only the language of a large portion of every good poem, even of the most elevated character, must necessarily, except with reference to the metre, in no respect differ from that of good prose, but likewise that some of the most interesting parts of the best poems will be found to be strictly the language of prose when prose is well written. The truth of this assertion might be demonstrated by innumerable passages from almost all the poetical writings, even of Milton himself. To illustrate the subject in a general manner, I will here adduce a short composition of Gray, who was at the head of those who, by their reasonings, have attempted to widen the space of separation betwixt Prose and Metrical composition, and was more than any other man curiously elaborate in the structure of his own poetic diction.

> "In vain to me the smiling mornings shine,
> And reddening Phoebus lifts his golden fire;
> The birds in vain their amorous descant join,
> Or cheerful fields resume their green attire.
> These ears, alas! for other notes repine;
> *A different object do these eyes require;*
> *My lonely anguish melts no heart but mine;*
> *And in my breast the imperfect joys expire;*
> Yet morning smiles the busy race to cheer,
> And new-born pleasure brings to happier men;
> The fields to all their wonted tribute bear;
> To warm their little loves the birds complain.
> *I fruitless mourn to him that cannot hear,*
> *And weep the more because I weep in vain.*"

It will easily be perceived, that the only part of this Sonnet which is of any value is the lines printed in Italics; it is equally obvious that, except in the rhyme and in the use of the single word "fruitless" for fruitlessly, which is so far a defect, the language of these lines does in no respect differ from that of prose.

By the foregoing quotation it has been shown that the language of Prose may yet be well adapted to Poetry; and it was previously asserted that a large portion of the language of every good poem can in no respect differ from that of good Prose. We will go further. It may be safely affirmed that there neither is, nor can be, any *essential* difference between the language of prose and metrical composition. We are fond of tracing the resemblance between Poetry and Painting, and, accordingly, we call them Sisters: but where shall we find bonds of connection sufficiently strict to typify the affinity betwixt metrical and prose composition? They both speak by and to the same organs; the bodies in which both of them are clothed may be said to be of the same substance, their affections are kindred, and almost identical, not necessarily differing even in degree; Poetry[2] sheds no tears "such as Angels weep," but natural and human tears; she can boast of no celestial ichor that distinguishes her vital juices from those of Prose; the same human blood circulates through the veins of them both.

If it be affirmed that rhyme and metrical arrangement of themselves constitute a distinction which overturns what has just been said on the strict affinity of metrical language with that of Prose, and paves the way for other artificial distinctions which the mind voluntarily admits, I answer that the language of such Poetry as is here recommended is, as far as is possible, a selection of the language really spoken by men; that this selection, wherever it is made with true taste and feeling, will of itself form a distinction far greater than would at first be imagined, and will entirely separate the composition from the vulgarity and meanness of ordinary life; and, if metre be superadded thereto, I believe that a dissimilitude will be produced altogether sufficient for the gratification of a rational mind. What other distinction would we have? Whence is it to come? And where is it to exist? Not, surely, where the Poet speaks through the mouths of his characters: it cannot be necessary here, either for elevation of style, or any of its supposed ornaments; for, if the Poet's subject be judiciously chosen, it will naturally, and upon fit occasion, lead him to passions, the language of which, if selected truly and judiciously, must necessarily be dignified and variegated, and alive with metaphors and figures. I forbear to speak of an incongruity which would shock the intelligent Reader, should the Poet interweave any foreign splendour of his own wish that which the passion naturally suggests: it is sufficient to say that such addition is unnecessary. And, surely, it is more probable that those passages, which with propriety abound with metaphors and figures, will have their due effect if, upon other occasions where the passions are of a milder character, the style also be subdued and temperate.

But, as the pleasure which I hope to give by the Poems now presented

---

2. I here use the word "Poetry" (though against my own judgment) as opposed to the word Prose, and synonymous with metrical composition. But much confusion has been introduced into criticism by this contradistinction of Poetry and Prose, instead of the more philosophical one of Poetry and Matter of Fact, or Science. The only strict antithesis to Prose is Metre; nor is this, in truth, a *strict* antithesis, because lines and passages of metre so naturally occur in writing prose, that it would be scarcely possible to avoid them, even were it desirable.

to the Reader must depend entirely on just notions upon this subject, and as it is in itself of high importance to our taste and moral feelings, I cannot content myself with these detached remarks. And if, in what I am about to say, it shall appear to some that my labour is unnecessary, and that I am like a man fighting a battle without enemies, such persons may be reminded that, whatever be the language outwardly holden by men, a practical faith in the opinions which I am wishing to establish is almost unknown. If my conclusions are admitted, and carried as far as they must be carried if admitted at all, our judgments concerning the works of the greatest Poets, both ancient and modern, will be far different from what they are at present, both when we praise and when we censure: and our moral feelings influencing and influenced by these judgments will, I believe, be corrected and purified.

Taking up the subject, then, upon general grounds, let me ask, what is meant by the word Poet? What is a Poet? To whom does he address himself? And what language is to be expected from him?—He is a man speaking to men: a man, it is true, endowed with more lively sensibility, more enthusiasm and tenderness, who has a greater knowledge of human nature, and a more comprehensive soul, than are supposed to be common among mankind; a man pleased with his own passions and volitions, and who rejoices more than other men in the spirit of life that is in him; delighting to contemplate similar volitions and passions as manifested in the goings-on of the Universe, and habitually impelled to create them where he does not find them. To these qualities he has added a disposition to be affected more than any other men by absent things as if they were present; an ability of conjuring up in himself passions, which are indeed far from being the same as those produced by real events, yet (especially in those parts of the general sympathy which are pleasing and delightful) do more nearly resemble the passions produced by real events than anything which, from the motions of their own minds merely, other men are accustomed to feel in themselves:—whence, and from practice, he has acquired a greater readiness and power in expressing what he thinks and feels, and especially those thoughts and feelings which, by his own choice, or from the structure of his own mind, arise in him without immediate external excitement.

But whatever portion of this faculty we may suppose even the greatest Poet to possess, there cannot be a doubt that the language which it will suggest to him must often, in liveliness and truth, fall short of that which is uttered by men in real life under the actual pressure of those passions, certain shadows of which the Poet thus produces, or feels to be produced, in himself.

However exalted a notion we would wish to cherish of the character of a Poet, it is obvious that, while he describes and imitates passions, his employment is in some degree mechanical compared with the freedom and power of real and substantial action and suffering. So that it will be the wish of the Poet to bring his feelings near to those of the persons whose feelings he describes, nay, for short spaces of time, perhaps, to let himself slip into an entire delusion, and even confound and identify his own feelings with theirs; modifying only the language which is thus suggested to him by a consideration that he describes for a particular purpose, that of giving pleasure. Here, then, he will apply the principle of selection which has been already insisted upon. He will depend upon this for removing what would otherwise be painful or disgusting in the passion; he will feel that there is no necessity to trick out or to elevate nature: and the more industriously he applies this principle the deeper will be his faith that no words, which *his* fancy or imagination can suggest, will be to be compared with those which are the emanations of reality and truth.

But it may be said by those who do not object to the general spirit of these remarks, that, as it is impossible for the Poet to produce upon all occasions language as exquisitely fitted for the passion as that which the real passion itself suggests, it is proper that he should consider himself as in the situation of a translator, who does not scruple to substitute excellences of another kind for those which are unattainable by him; and endeavours occasionally to surpass his original, in order to make some amends for the general inferiority to which he feels he must submit. But this would be to encourage idleness and unmanly despair. Further, it is the language of men who speak of what they do not understand; who talk of Poetry, as of a matter of amusement and idle pleasure; who will converse with us as gravely about a *taste* for Poetry, as they express it, as if it were a thing as indifferent as a taste for rope-dancing, or Frontiniac or Sherry. Aristotle, I have been told, has said, that Poetry is the most philosophic of all writing; it is so: its object is truth, not individual and local, but general and operative; not standing upon external testimony, but carried alive into the heart by passion; truth which is its own testimony, which gives competence and confidence to the tribunal to which it appeals, and receives them from the same tribunal. Poetry is the image of man and nature. The obstacles which stand in the way of the fidelity of the Biographer and Historian, and of their consequent utility, are incalculably greater than those which are to be encountered by the Poet who comprehends the dignity of his art. The Poet writes under one restriction only, namely, the necessity of giving immediate pleasure to a human Being possessed of that information which may be expected from him, not as a lawyer, a physician, a mariner, an astronomer, or a natural philosopher, but as a Man. Except this one restriction, there is no object standing between the Poet and the image of things; between this, and the Biographer and Historian, there are a thousand

Nor let this necessity of producing immediate pleasure be considered as a degradation of the Poet's art. It is far otherwise. It is an acknowledgment of the beauty of the universe, an acknowledgment the more sincere because not formal, but indirect; it is a task light and easy to him who looks at the world in the spirit of love: further, it is a homage paid to the native and naked dignity of man, to the grand elementary principle of pleasure, by which he knows, and feels, and lives, and moves. We have no sympathy but what is propagated by pleasure: I would not be misunderstood; but wherever we sympathise with pain, it will be found that the sympathy is produced and carried on by subtle combinations with pleasure. We have no knowledge, that is, no general principles drawn from the contemplation of particular facts, but what has been built up by pleasure, and exists in us by pleasure alone. The Man of science, the Chemist and Mathematician, whatever difficulties and disgusts they may have had to struggle with, know and feel this. However painful may be the objects with which the Anatomist's knowledge is connected, he feels that his knowledge is pleasure; and where he has no pleasure he has no knowledge. What then does the Poet? He considers man and the objects that surround him as acting and re-acting upon each other, so as to produce an infinite complexity of pain and pleasure; he considers man in his own nature and in his ordinary life as contemplating this with a certain quantity of immediate knowledge, with certain convictions, intuitions, and deductions, which from habit acquire the quality of intuitions; he considers him as looking upon this complex scene of ideas and sensations, and finding everywhere objects that immediately excite in him sympathies which, from the necessities of his nature, are accompanied by an overbalance of enjoyment.

To this knowledge which all men carry about with them, and to these sympathies in which, without any other discipline than that of our daily life, we are fitted to take delight, the Poet principally directs his attention.

He considers man and nature as essentially adapted to each other, and the mind of man as naturally the mirror of the fairest and most interesting properties of nature. And thus the Poet, prompted by this feeling of pleasure, which accompanies him through the whole course of his studies, converses with general nature, with affections akin to those which, through labour and length of time, the Man of science has raised up in himself, by conversing with those particular parts of nature which are the objects of his studies. The knowledge both of the Poet and the Man of science is pleasure; but the knowledge of the one cleaves to us as a necessary part of our existence, our natural and unalienable inheritance; the other is a personal and individual acquisition, slow to come to us, and by no habitual and direct sympathy connecting us with our fellow-beings. The Man of science seeks truth as a remote and unknown benefactor; he cherishes and loves it in his solitude: the Poet, singing a song in which all human beings join with him, rejoices in the presence of truth as our visible friend and hourly companion. Poetry is the breath and finer spirit of all knowledge; it is the impassioned expression which is in the countenance of all Science. Emphatically may it be said of the Poet, as Shakespeare hath said of man, "that he looks before and after." He is the rock of defence for human nature; an upholder and preserver, carrying everywhere with him relationship and love. In spite of difference of soil and climate, of language and manners, of laws and customs: in spite of things silently gone out of mind, and things violently destroyed; the Poet binds together by passion and knowledge the vast empire of human society, as it is spread over the whole earth and over all time. The objects of the Poet's thoughts are everywhere; though the eyes and senses of men are, it is true, his favourite guides, yet he will follow wheresoever he can find an atmosphere of sensation in which to move his wings. Poetry is the first and last of all knowledge—it is as immortal as the heart of man. If the labours of Men of science should ever create any material revolution, direct or indirect, in our condition, and in the impressions which we habitually receive, the Poet will sleep then no more than at present; he will be ready to follow the steps of the Man of science, not only in those general indirect effects, but he will be at his side, carrying sensation into the midst of the objects of the science itself. The remotest discoveries of the Chemist, the Botanist, or Mineralogist, will be as proper objects of the Poet's art as any upon which it can be employed, if the time should ever come when these things shall be familiar to us, and the relations under which they are contemplated by the followers of these respective sciences shall be manifestly and palpably material to us as enjoying and suffering beings. If the time should ever come when what is now called science, thus familiarised to men, shall be ready to put on, as it were, a form of flesh and blood, the Poet will lend his divine spirit to aid the transfiguration, and will welcome the Being thus produced as a dear and genuine inmate of the household of man.—It is not, then, to be supposed that any one, who holds that sublime notion of Poetry which I have attempted to convey, will break in upon the sanctity and truth of his pictures by transitory and accidental ornaments, and endeavour to excite admiration of himself by arts, the necessity of which must manifestly depend upon the assumed meanness of his subject.

What has been thus far said applies to Poetry in general, but especially to those parts of compositions where the Poet speaks through the mouths of his characters; and upon this point it appears to authorise the conclusion that there are few persons of good sense who would not allow that the dramatic parts of composition are defective in proportion as they deviate from the real language of nature, and are coloured by a diction of the Poet's own, either peculiar to him as an individual Poet or belonging simply to Poets in general; to a body of men who, from the circumstance of their compositions being in metre, it is expected will employ a particular language.

It is not, then, in the dramatic parts of composition that we look for this distinction of language; but still it may be proper and necessary where the Poet speaks to us in his own person and character. To this I answer by referring the Reader to the description before given of a Poet. Among the qualities there enumerated as principally conducing to form a Poet, is implied nothing differing in kind from other men, but only in degree. The sum of what was said is, that the Poet is chiefly distinguished from other men by a greater promptness to think and feel without immediate external excitement, and a greater power in expressing such thoughts and feelings as are produced in him in that manner. But these passions and thoughts and feelings are the general passions and thoughts and feelings of men. And with what are they connected? Undoubtedly with our moral sentiments and animal sensations, and with the causes which excite these; with the operations of the elements, and the appearances of the visible universe; with storm and sunshine, with the revolutions of the seasons, with cold and heat, with loss of friends and kindred, with injuries and resentments, gratitude and hope, with fear and sorrow. These, and the like, are the sensations and objects which the Poet describes, as they are the sensations of other men and the objects which interest them. The Poet thinks and feels in the spirit of human passions. How, then, can his language differ in any material degree from that of all other men who feel vividly and see clearly? It might be *proved* that it is impossible. But supposing that this were not the case, the Poet might then be allowed to use a peculiar language when expressing his feelings for his own gratification, or that of men like himself. But Poets do not write for Poets alone, but for men. Unless, therefore, we are advocates for that admiration which subsists upon ignorance, and that pleasure which arises from hearing what we do not understand, the Poet must descend from this supposed height; and, in order to excite rational sympathy, he must express himself as other men express themselves. To this it may be added, that while he is only selecting from the real language of men, or, which amounts to the same thing, composing accurately in the spirit of such selection, he is treading upon safe ground, and we know what we are to expect from him. Our feelings are the same with respect to metre; for, as it may be proper to remind the Reader, the distinction of metre is regular and uniform, and not, like that which is produced by what is usually called POETIC DICTION, arbitrary, and subject to infinite caprices, upon which no calculation whatever can be made. In the one case, the Reader is utterly at the mercy of the Poet, respecting what imagery or diction he may choose to connect with the passion; whereas, in the other, the metre obeys certain laws, to which the Poet and Reader both willingly submit because they are certain, and because no interference is made by them with the passion but such as the concurring testimony of ages has shown to heighten and improve the pleasure which co-exists with it.

It will now be proper to answer an obvious question, namely, Why, professing these opinions, have I written in verse? To this, in addition to such answer as is included in what has been already said, I reply, in the first place, Because, however I may have restricted myself, there is still left open to me what confessedly constitutes the most valuable object of all writing, whether in prose or verse; the great and universal passions of men, the most general and interesting of their occupations, and the entire world of nature before me—to supply endless combinations of forms and imagery. Now, supposing for a moment that whatever is interesting in these objects may be as vividly described in prose, why should I be condemned for attempting to superadd to such description the charm which, by the consent of all nations, is acknowledged to exist in metrical language? To this, by such as are yet unconvinced, it may be answered that a very small part of the pleasure given by Poetry depends upon the metre, and that it is injudicious to write in metre, unless it be accompanied with the other artificial distinctions of style with which metre is usually accompanied, and that, by such deviation, more will be lost from the shock which will thereby be given to the Reader's associations than will be counterbalanced by any pleasure which he can derive from the general power of numbers. In answer to those who still contend for the necessity of accompanying metre with certain appropriate colours of style in order to the accomplishment of its appropriate end, and who also, in my opinion, greatly underrate the power of metre in itself, it might, perhaps, as far as relates to these Volumes, have been almost sufficient to observe, that poems are extant, written upon more humble subjects, and in a still more naked and simple style, which have continued to give pleasure from generation to generation. Now, if nakedness and simplicity be a defect, the fact here mentioned affords a strong presumption that poems somewhat less naked and simple are capable of affording pleasure at the present day; and, what I wished *chiefly* to attempt, at present, was to justify myself for having written under the impression of this belief.

But various causes might be pointed out why, when the style is manly, and the subject of some importance, words metrically arranged will long continue to impart such a pleasure to mankind as he who proves the extent of that pleasure will be desirous to impart. The end of poetry is to produce excitement in co-existence with an overbalance of pleasure; but, by the supposition, excitement is an unusual and irregular state of the mind; ideas and feelings do not, in that state, succeed each other in accustomed order. If the words, however, by which this excitement is produced be in themselves powerful, or the images and feelings have an undue proportion of pain connected with them, there is some danger that the excitement may be carried beyond its proper bounds. Now the co-presence of something regular, something to which the mind has been accustomed in various moods and in a less excited state, cannot but have great efficacy in tempering and restraining the passion by an intertexture of ordinary feeling, and of feeling not strictly and necessarily connected with the passion. This is unquestionably true; and hence, though the opinion will at first appear paradoxical, from the tendency of metre to divest language, in a certain degree, of its reality, and thus to throw a sort of half-consciousness of unsubstantial existence over the whole composition, there can be little doubt but that more pathetic situations and sentiments, that is, those which have a greater proportion of pain connected with them, may be endured in metrical composition, especially in rhyme, than in prose. The metre of the old ballads is very artless, yet they contain many passages which would illustrate this opinion; and, I hope, if the following poems be attentively perused, similar instances will be found in them. This opinion may be further illustrated by appealing to the Reader's own experience of the reluctance with which he comes to the reperusal of the distressful parts of "Clarissa Harlowe," or the "Gamester"; while Shakespeare's writings, in the most pathetic scenes, never act upon us, as pathetic, beyond the bounds of pleasure—an effect which, in a much greater degree than might at first be imagined, is to be ascribed to small, but continual and regular impulses of pleasurable surprise from the metrical arrangement.—On the other hand (what it must be allowed will much more frequently happen), if the Poet's words should be incommensurate with the passion, and inadequate to raise the Reader to a height of desirable excitement, then (unless the Poet's choice of his metre has been grossly injudicious), in the feelings of pleasure which the Reader has been accustomed to connect with metre in general, and in the feeling, whether cheerful or melancholy, which he has been accustomed to connect with that particular movement of metre, there will be found something which will greatly contribute to impart passion to the words, and to effect the complex end which the Poet proposes to himself.

If I had undertaken a SYSTEMATIC defence of the theory here maintained, it would have been my duty to develop the various causes upon which the pleasure received from metrical language depends. Among the chief of these causes is to be reckoned a principle which must be well known to those who have made any of the Arts the object of accurate reflection; namely, the pleasure which the mind derives from the perception of similitude in dissimilitude. This principle is the great spring of the activity of our minds, and their chief feeder. From this principle, the direction of the sexual appetite, and all the passions connected with it, take their origin: it is the life of our ordinary conversation; and upon the accuracy with which similitude in dissimilitude, and dissimilitude in similitude, are perceived, depend our taste and our moral feelings. It would not be a useless employment to apply this principle to the consideration of metre, and to show that metre is hence enabled to afford much pleasure, and to point out in what manner that pleasure is produced. But my limits will not permit me to enter upon this subject, and I must content myself with a general summary.

I have said that poetry is the spontaneous overflow of powerful feelings: it takes its origin from emotion recollected in tranquillity; the emotion is contemplated till, by a species of re-action, the tranquillity gradually disappears, and an emotion, kindred to that which was before the subject of contemplation, is gradually produced, and does itself actually exist in the mind. In this mood successful composition generally begins, and in a mood similar to this it is carried on; but the emotion, of whatever kind, and in whatever degree, from various causes, is qualified by various pleasures, so that in describing any passions whatsoever, which are voluntarily described, the mind will, upon the whole, be in a state of enjoyment. If Nature be thus cautious to preserve in a state of enjoyment a being so employed, the Poet ought to profit by the lesson held forth to him, and ought especially to take care that, whatever passions he communicates to his Reader, those passions, if his Reader's mind be sound and vigorous, should always be accompanied with an over-balance of pleasure. Now the music of harmonious metrical language, the sense of difficulty overcome, and the blind association of pleasure which has been previously received from works of rhyme or metre of the same or similar construction, an indistinct perception perpetually renewed of language closely resembling that of real life, and yet, in the circumstance of metre, differing from it so widely—all these imperceptibly make up a complex feeling of delight, which is of the most important use in tempering the painful feeling always found intermingled with powerful descriptions of the deeper passions. This effect is always produced in pathetic and impassioned poetry; while, in lighter compositions, the ease and gracefulness with which the Poet manages his numbers are themselves confessedly a principal source of the gratification of the Reader. All that it is *necessary* to say, however, upon this subject, may be effected by affirming, what few persons will deny, that of two descriptions, either of passions, manners, or characters, each of them equally well executed, the one in prose and the other in verse, the verse will be read a hundred times where the prose is read once.

Having thus explained a few of my reasons for writing in verse, and why I have chosen subjects from common life, and endeavoured to bring my language near to the real language of men, if I have been too minute in pleading my own cause, I have at the same time been treating a subject of general interest; and for this reason a few words shall be added with reference solely to these particular poems, and to some defects which will probably be found in them. I am sensible that my associations must have sometimes been particular instead of general, and that, consequently, giving to things a false importance, I may have sometimes written upon unworthy subjects; but I am less apprehensive on this account, than that my language may frequently have suffered from those arbitrary connections of feelings and ideas with particular words and phrases from which no man can altogether protect himself. Hence I have no doubt that, in some instances, feelings, even of the ludicrous, may be given to my Readers by expressions which appeared to me tender and pathetic. Such faulty expressions, were I convinced they were faulty at present, and that they must necessarily continue to be so, I would willingly take all reasonable pains to correct. But it is dangerous to make these alterations on the simple authority of a few individuals, or even of certain classes of men; for where the understanding of an author is not convinced, or his feelings altered, this cannot be done without great injury to himself: for his own feelings are his stay and support; and, if he set them aside in one instance, he may be induced to repeat this act till his mind shall lose all confidence in itself, and become utterly debilitated. To this it may be added, that the critic ought never to forget that he is himself exposed to the same errors as the Poet, and, perhaps, in a much greater degree: for there can be no presumption in saying of most readers, that it is not probable they will be so well acquainted with the various stages of meaning through which words have passed, or with the fickleness or stability of the relations of particular ideas to each other; and, above all, since they are so much less interested in the subject, they may decide lightly and carelessly.

Long as the reader has been detained, I hope he will permit me to caution him against a mode of false criticism which has been applied to poetry, in which the language closely resembles that of life and nature. Such verses have been triumphed over in parodies, of which Dr. Johnson's stanza is a fair specimen:—

> "I put my hat upon my head
> And walked into the Strand,
> And there I met another man
> Whose hat was in his hand."

Immediately under these lines let us place one of the most justly-admired stanzas of the "Babes in the Wood."

> "These pretty Babes with hand in hand
> Went wandering up and down;

> But never more they saw the Man
> Approaching from the Town."

In both these stanzas the words, and the order of the words, in no respect differ from the most unimpassioned conversation. There are words in both, for example, "the Strand," and "the Town," connected with none but the most familiar ideas; yet the one stanza we admit as admirable, and the other as a fair example of the superlatively contemptible. Whence arises this difference? Not from the metre, not from the language, not from the order of the words; but the *matter* expressed in Dr. Johnson's stanza is contemptible. The proper method of treating trivial and simple verses, to which Dr. Johnson's stanza would be a fair parallelism, is not to say, this is a bad kind of poetry, or, this is not poetry; but, this wants sense; it is neither interesting in itself, nor can *lead* to anything interesting; the images neither originate in that sane state of feeling which arises out of thought, nor can excite thought or feeling in the Reader. This is the only sensible manner of dealing with such verses. Why trouble yourself about the species till you have previously decided upon the genus? Why take pains to prove that an ape is not a Newton, when it is self-evident that he is not a man?

One request I must make of my Reader, which is, that in judging these Poems he would decide by his own feelings genuinely, and not by reflection upon what will probably be the judgment of others. How common is it to hear a person say, I myself do not object to this style of composition, or this or that expression, but to such and such classes of people it will appear mean or ludicrous! This mode of criticism, so destructive of all sound unadulterated judgment, is almost universal: let the Reader then abide, independently, by his own feelings, and, if he finds himself affected, let him not suffer such conjectures to interfere with his pleasure.

If an Author, by any single composition, has impressed us with respect for his talents, it is useful to consider this as affording a presumption that on other occasions where we have been displeased he, nevertheless, may not have written ill or absurdly; and further, to give him so much credit for this one composition as may induce us to review what has displeased us with more care than we should otherwise have bestowed upon it. This is not only an act of justice, but, in our decisions upon poetry especially, may conduce, in a high degree, to the improvement of our own taste: for an *accurate* taste in poetry, and in all the other arts, as Sir Joshua Reynolds has observed, is an *acquired* talent, which can only be produced by thought and a long-continued intercourse with the best models of composition. This is mentioned, not with so ridiculous a purpose as to prevent the most inexperienced Reader from judging for himself (I have already said that I wish him to judge for himself), but merely to temper the rashness of decision, and to suggest that, if Poetry be a subject on which much time has not been bestowed, the judgment may be erroneous; and that, in many cases, it necessarily will be so.

Nothing would, I know, have so effectually contributed to further the end which I have in view, as to have shown of what kind the pleasure is, and how that pleasure is produced, which is confessedly produced by metrical composition essentially different from that which I have here endeavoured to recommend: for the Reader will say that he has been pleased by such composition; and what more can be done for him? The power of any art is limited; and he will suspect that, if it be proposed to furnish him with new friends, that can be only upon condition of his abandoning his old friends. Besides, as I have said, the Reader is himself conscious of the pleasure which he has received from such composition, composition to which he has peculiarly attached the endearing name of Poetry; and all men feel an habitual gratitude, and something of an honourable bigotry, for the objects which have long continued to please them: we not only wish to be pleased, but to be pleased in that particular way in which we have been accustomed to be pleased. There is in these feelings enough to resist a host of arguments; and I should be the less able to combat them successfully, as I am willing to allow that, in order entirely to enjoy the Poetry which I am recommending, it would be necessary to give up much of what is ordinarily enjoyed. But would my limits have permitted me to point out how this pleasure is produced, many obstacles might have been removed, and the Reader assisted in perceiving that the powers of language are not so limited as he may suppose; and that it is possible for poetry to give other enjoyments, of a purer, more lasting, and more exquisite nature. This part of the subject has not been altogether neglected, but it has not been so much my present aim to prove, that the interest excited by some other kinds of poetry is less vivid, and less worthy of the nobler powers of the mind, as to offer reasons for presuming that if my purpose were fulfilled, a species of poetry would be produced which is genuine poetry; in its nature well adapted to interest mankind permanently, and likewise important in the multiplicity and quality of its moral relations.

From what has been said, and from a perusal of the Poems, the Reader will be able clearly to perceive the object which I had in view: he will determine how far it has been attained, and, what is a much more important question, whether it be worth attaining: and upon the decision of these two questions will rest my claim to the approbation of the Public.

Appendix,
1802

Perhaps, as I have no right to expect that attentive perusal, without which, confined, as I have been, to the narrow limits of a preface, my meaning cannot be thoroughly understood, I am anxious to give an exact notion of the sense in which the phrase poetic diction has been used; and for this purpose, a few words shall here be added, concerning the origin and characteristics of the phraseology which I have condemned under that name.

The earliest poets of all nations generally wrote from passion excited by real events; they wrote naturally, and as men: feeling powerfully as they did, their language was daring, and figurative. In succeeding times, Poets, and Men ambitious of the fame of Poets, perceiving the influence of such language, and desirous of producing the same effect without being animated by the same passion, set themselves to a mechanical adoption of these figures of speech, and made use of them, sometimes with propriety, but much more frequently applied them to feelings and thoughts with which they had no natural connection whatsoever. A language was thus insensibly produced, differing materially from the real language of men in *any situation*. The Reader or Hearer of this distorted language found himself in a perturbed and unusual state of mind: when affected by the genuine language of passion he had been in a perturbed and unusual state of mind also: in both cases he was willing that his common judgment and understanding should be laid asleep, and he had no instinctive and infallible perception of the true to make him reject the false; the one served as a passport for the other. The emotion was in both cases delightful, and no wonder if he confounded the one with the other, and believed them both to be produced by the same or similar causes. Besides, the Poet spake to him in the character of a man to be looked up to, a man of genius and authority. Thus, and from a variety of other causes, this distorted language was received with admiration; and Poets, it is probable, who had before contented themselves for the most part with misapplying only expressions which at first had been dictated by real passion, carried the abuse still further, and introduced phrases composed apparently in the spirit of the original figurative language of passion, yet altogether of their own invention, and characterised by various degrees of wanton deviation from good sense and nature.

It is indeed true that the language of the earliest Poets was felt to differ materially from ordinary language, because it was the language of extraordinary occasions; but it was really spoken by men, language which the Poet himself had uttered when he had been affected by the events which he described, or which he had heard uttered by those around him. To this language it is probable that metre of some sort or other was early superadded. This separated the genuine language of Poetry still further from common life, so that whoever read or heard the poems of these earliest Poets felt himself moved in a way in which he had not been accustomed to be moved in real life, and by causes manifestly different from those which acted upon him in real life. This was the great temptation to all the corruptions which have followed: under the protection of this feeling succeeding Poets constructed a phraseology which had one thing, it is true, in common with the genuine language of poetry, namely, that it was not heard in ordinary conversation; that it was unusual. But the first Poets, as I have said, spake a language which, though unusual, was still the language of men. This circumstance, however, was disregarded by their successors; they found that they could please by easier means: they became proud of modes of expression which they themselves had invented, and which were uttered only by themselves. In process of time metre became a symbol or promise of this unusual language, and whoever took upon him to write in metre, according as he possessed more or less of true poetic genius, introduced less or more of this adulterated phraseology into his compositions, and the true and the false were inseparably interwoven until, the taste of men becoming gradually perverted, this language was received as a natural language, and at length, by the influence of books upon men, did to a certain degree really become so. Abuses of this kind were imported from one nation to another, and with the progress of refinement this diction became daily more and more corrupt, thrusting out of sight the plain humanities of nature by a motley masquerade of tricks, quaintnesses, hieroglyphics, and enigmas.

It would not be uninteresting to point out the causes of the pleasure given by this extravagant and absurd diction. It depends upon a great variety of causes, but upon none, perhaps, more than its influence in impressing a notion of the peculiarity and exaltation of the Poet's character, and in flattering the Reader's self-love by bringing him nearer to a sympathy with that character; an effect which is accomplished by unsettling ordinary habits of thinking, and thus assisting the Reader to approach to that perturbed and dizzy state of mind in which, if he does not find himself, he imagines that he is *balked* of a peculiar enjoyment which poetry can and ought to bestow.

The sonnet quoted from Gray in the Preface, except the lines printed in Italics, consists of little else but this diction, though not of the worst kind; and indeed, if one may be permitted to say so, it is far too common in the best writers, both ancient and modern. Perhaps in no way, by positive example, could more easily be given a notion of what I mean by the phrase *poetic diction* than by referring to a comparison between the metrical paraphrase which we have of passages in the Old and New Testament, and those passages as they exist, in our common Translation. See Pope's "Messiah" throughout; Prior's "Did sweeter sounds adorn my flowing tongue," etc. "Though I speak with the tongues of men and of angels," etc. 1st Corinthians, chap. xiii. By way of immediate example, take the following of Dr. Johnson:—

"Turn on the prudent Ant thy heedless eyes,
Observe her labours, Sluggard, and be wise;
No stern command, no monitory voice,
Prescribes her duties, or directs her choice;
Yet, timely provident, she hastes away
To snatch the blessings of a plenteous day;
When fruitful Summer loads the teeming plain,
She crops the harvest, and she stores the grain.
How long shall sloth usurp thy useless hours,
Unnerve thy vigour, and enchain thy powers?
While artful shades thy downy couch enclose,
And soft solicitation courts repose,
Amidst the drowsy charms of dull delight,
Year chases year with unremitted flight,

        Till Want now following, fraudulent and slow,
        Shall spring to seize thee, like an ambush'd foe."

From this hubbub of words pass to the original. "Go to the ant, thou sluggard; consider her ways, and be wise: which having no guide, overseer, or ruler, provideth her meat in the summer, and gathereth her food in the harvest. How long wilt thou sleep, O sluggard? when wilt thou arise out of thy sleep? Yet a little sleep, a little slumber, a little folding of the hands to sleep: so shall thy poverty come as one that travelleth, and thy want as an armed man." Proverbs, chap. vi.

One more quotation, and I have done. It is from Cowper's Verses supposed to be written by Alexander Selkirk:—

      "Religion! what treasure untold
      Resides in that heavenly word!
      More precious than silver and gold,
      Or all that this earth can afford.
      But the sound of the church-going bell
      These valleys and rocks never heard,
      Ne'er sighed at the sound of a knell,
      Or smiled when a sabbath appeared.

      Ye winds, that have made me your sport,
      Convey to this desolate shore
      Some cordial endearing report
      Of a land I must visit no more.
      My Friends, do they now and then send
      A wish or a thought after me?
      O tell me I yet have a friend,
      Though a friend I am never to see"

This passage is quoted as an instance of three different styles of composition. The first four lines are poorly expressed; some Critics would call the language prosaic; that fact is, it would be bad prose, so bad, that it is scarcely worse in metre. The epithet "church-going" applied to a bell, and that by so chaste a writer as Cowper, is an instance of the strange abuses which Poets have introduced into their language, till they and their Readers take them as matters of course, if they do not single them out expressly as objects of admiration. The two lines "Ne'er sighed at the sound," etc., are, in my opinion, an instance of the language of passion wrested from its proper use, and, from the mere circumstance of the composition being in metre, applied upon an occasion that does not justify such violent expressions; and I should condemn the passage, though perhaps few Readers will agree with me, as vicious poetic diction. The last stanza is throughout admirably expressed: it would be equally good whether in prose or verse, except that the Reader has an exquisite pleasure in seeing such natural language so naturally connected with metre. The beauty of this stanza tempts me to conclude with a principle which ought never to be lost sight of, and which has been my chief guide in all I have said,—namely, that in works *of imagination and sentiment,* for of these only have I been treating, in proportion as ideas and feelings are valuable, whether the composition be in prose or in verse, they require and exact one and the same language. Metre is but adventitious to composition, and the phraseology for which that passport is necessary, even where it may be graceful at all, will be little valued by the judicious.

NOTES

"An Evening Walk" (p. 3)

Composed 1788–89, when Wordsworth was a student at Cambridge; published in 1793, shortly after Wordsworth's return from France, by Joseph Johnson, publisher of the *Analytical Review* and works by Mary Wollstonecraft and William Godwin. In 1794, Wordsworth wrote to his friend William Matthews that he hoped that "these little things might shew that I could do something." In particular, painfully aware of his responsibilities toward Annette Vallon and their child, Anne Caroline Wordsworth (b. December 1792), Wordsworth hoped to convince his relatives to aid him in attaining the curacy that he had previously shunned. To Isabella Fenwick, a dear friend to whom Wordsworth dictated notes on all his published poems in the winter of 1842–43, Wordsworth claimed, "There is not an image in [the poem] which I have not observed; and now, in my seventy-third year, I recollect the time and place where most of them were noticed." Though grounded in observation, Wordsworth also stressed the poem's ideal quality: "the plan of it has not been confined to a particular walk or an individual place,—a proof (of which I was unconscious at the time) of my unwillingness to submit the poetic spirit to the chains of fact and real circumstance. The country is idealised rather than described in any one of its local aspects." The poem's broad use of allusion to works by Horace, John Milton, James Beattie, and James Thomson provides a record of Wordsworth's literary taste, and contributes to his idealized handling of the Lake District landscape.

l. 1 *dearest Friend:* Wordsworth's sister, Dorothy, from whom he had been separated since the death of their parents.
l. 3 *Derwent:* a river. Also see note, *The Prelude,* Book First, l. 270 (p. 699).
l. 4 *Lodore:* a waterfall.

l. 7 *rude:* rustic, primitive.

l. 9 *Winander sleeps:* "These lines are only applicable to the middle part of that lake...." Wordsworth's note.

l. 39 *deep-embattled clouds:* Charlotte Smith, "Written September 1791, during a remarkable thunder storm," 1. 3. Also, Beattie, *The Minstrel* II.xii.

l. 49 *intake:* "Mountain enclosure." Wordsworth's note.

l. 53 *huddling rill:* See Milton, "huddling brook," "Comus," l. 495.

l. 54 *ghyll:* deep cleft or hollow.

ll. 72–77 These lines set up an allusion to Horace, *Odes*, III.xiii, praising the Bandusian spring.

l. 112 *involved:* enveloped.

l. 133 *'green rings':* "Vivid rings of green." "Greenwood's *Poems on Shooting*." Wordsworth's note.

l. 135 "Down the rough slope the pond'rous waggon rings." "Beattie, *Minstrel*, I.xxxix." Wordsworth's note (in 1793 edition only).

l. 141 See *Paradise Lost*, II.477.

l. 146 *Sweetly ferocious:* "From *Dolcemente feroce*, Tasso's description of the cock." Wordsworth's note.

l. 147 *monarch:* cock.

l. 148 *nervous:* sinewy.

l. 163 *gulf profound:* See *Paradise Lost*, II.592.

l. 174 *aspire:* rise.

l. 175 *a 'prospect all on fire':* See Moses Browne, "Sunday Thoughts," III.143.

l. 188 *druid-stones:* monolithic rings of stones—not, however, left by the Druids.

l. 191 *Gives one bright glance:* "See Thomson, *Seasons, Summer,* ll. 1628–29." Wordsworth's note.

ll. 196–207 "See a description of an appearance of this kind in Clark's 'Survey of the Lakes,' accompanied by vouchers of its veracity, that may amuse the readers." Wordsworth's note.

ll. 214–15 Wordsworth called these lines to the attention of Isabella Fenwick: "This is feebly and imperfectly expressed, but I recollect distinctly the very spot where this first struck me. It was in the way between Hawkshead and Ambleside, and gave me extreme pleasure. The moment was important in my poetical history; for I date from it my consciousness of the infinite variety of natural appearances which had been unnoticed by the poets of any age or country, so far as I was acquainted with them; and I made a resolution to supply in some degree, the deficiency. I could not have been at that time, above fourteen years of age." Of the swans in lines 216–31, Wordsworth notes that the description was taken from "the daily opportunities I had of observing their habits, not as confined to the gentleman's park, but in a state of nature."

l. 233 *holms:* level stretches of ground by a river.

l. 237 *'by distance made more sweet':* William Collins, "The Passions: An Ode for Music," l. 60.

ll. 250–78 "These verses relate the catastrophe of a poor woman who was found dead on Stanemoor two years ago with two children whom she had in vain attempted to protect from the storm in the manner described." Wordsworth's note (1794).

l. 279 *Sweet are the sounds:* Oliver Goldsmith, "The Deserted Village," l. 113.

l. 280 *folding star:* Collins, "Ode to Evening," l. 21.

l. 291 "Alluding to this passage of Spenser—'Her angel's face / As the great eye of heaven shined bright, / And made a sunshine in that [the] shady place.'" Wordsworth's note (1793). *The Faerie Queene,* I. iii. 4.

l. 293 *paly:* pale, or somewhat pale.

l. 306 *wreck:* trace.

l. 313 *mere:* lake.

l. 315 *accordant:* responsive.

ll. 323–64 These lines describing the rising moon provide imagery for a similar passage in the concluding book of *The Prelude.* See *The Prelude* XIV.38–62.

l. 328 *Æther's bound:* upper limit of space.

l. 356 *rimy:* silver.

l. 357 *front:* face.

ll. 362–63 *by wreaths / Of charcoal-smoke:* Compare to "Tintern Abbey," ll. 17–18.

l. 374 See Beattie, *The Minstrel,* I.xxxix: "Thro' rustling corn the hare astonish'd springs."

"DESCRIPTIVE SKETCHES" (P. 13)

Based on an Alpine walking tour, undertaken with his friend, Robert Jones, during the long vacation, July–September, of 1790. The two friends traveled nearly three thousand miles, walking almost two thousand. Following this clandestine trip (undertaken without letting anyone know), Wordsworth returned to Cambridge and completed a B.A. degree in January 1791. "Descriptive Sketches" was largely composed 1791–92, when Wordsworth was in France, and provides ample evidence of his support of the French Revolution. The poem was quickly prepared for publication upon Wordsworth's return to England late in 1792. It was brought out by Joseph Johnson in 1793.

l. 21 *frowning:* presenting a gloomy aspect.

l. 24 *"and calls it luxury":* See Joseph Addison, *Cato,* I.iv.71.

l. 32 *Memnon's lyre:* "The lyre of Memnon is purported to have emitted melancholy or cheerful tones, as it was touched by the sun's evening or morning rays." Wordsworth's note.

l. 41 *crazing:* crushing, rendering infirm.

l. 53 *Chartreuse:* Carthusian monastery high in the Alps.

l. 55 *sober Reason:* Samuel Rogers, *Pleasures of Memory,* II.433.

l. 61 *thundering tube:* rifle.

l. 69 *viewless:* invisible, unseen.

l. 71 *"parting Genius":* Milton, "On the Morning of Christs Nativity," l. 186.

l. 72 *mystic streams of Life and Death:* "Names of rivers of the Chartreuse." Wordsworth's note.

l. 75 *Vallombre:* "Name of one of the valleys of the Chartreuse." Wordsworth's note.

l. 78 *Como:* lake in Italy.

ll. 99–100 See John Dyer, "Grongar Hill," ll. 51–52, "Rushing from the woods, the spires / Seem from hence ascending fires."

l. 111 *cots:* cottages.

l. 157 *her waters:* "The river along whose banks you descend in crossing the Alps by the Simplon Pass." Wordsworth's note.

l. 161 *undistinguished:* indistinct.

l. 200 *cells:* "The Catholic religion prevails here: these cells are, as is well known, very common in the Catholic countries, planted, like the Roman tombs, along the roadside." Wordsworth's note.

l. 202 *death-cross:* "Crosses commemorative of the deaths of travellers, by the fall of snow or other accidents, are very common along this dreadful road." Wordsworth's note.

l. 214 *wood-cottages:* wooden cottage.

l. 226 *romantic:* fabulous, fanciful, with no foundation in fact.

l. 248 *fond:* idle.

l. 263 *chamois:* small mammal, similar to a goat, inhabiting the upper Alpine reaches.

l. 269 *Spartan fife:* William Collins, "Ode to Liberty." l. 1.

l. 286 *Tell:* William Tell, Swiss patriot.

l. 287 *Marathonian:* Alludes to the battle of Marathon (490 B.C.), in which Athens defeated the Persians. In the *Encyclopaedia Britannica* (1797), Marathonians are noted to worship those who were slain in the battle.

ll. 293–302 Contain references to four famous battlegrounds and the heroes who died there: Seigneur de Bayard, French, died at Aosta, Italy, 1524; General James Wolfe, British, died on the Plains of Abraham, outside Quebec, 1759; Sir Philip Sidney died on Zutphen's plain, 1586; John Graham Viscount Dundee, Jacobite leader, died in the battle of Killiecrankie, Scotland, 1679.

l. 302 *"faint huzzas":* Robert Burns, "The Author's Earnest Cry and Prayer," l. xxix.

l. 316 *his:* the chamois hunter's.

l. 344 *close:* conclusion of a musical phrase, theme, or movement. Compare to Milton's "On the Morning of Christs Nativity," ll. 99–100: "The Air / prolongs each heav'nly close."

l. 348 chalets: "Summer huts for Swiss herdsmen." Wordsworth's note.

l. 355 *Deep that calls to Deep:* Psalms 42:7, "Deep calleth unto deep."

l. 359 sugh: "A scotch word expressive of the sound of the wind through the trees." Wordsworth's note.

l. 410 *awful:* awe-inspiring.

l. 418 *flageolet:* small pipe or recorder.

l. 448 *"the blessings he enjoys to guard":* Tobias Smollett, "To Leven Water," l. 28.

l. 452 *few in arms:* "Alluding to several battles which the Swiss in very small numbers have gained over their oppressors, the house of Austria; and in particular to one fought at Naeffels, near Glarus, where three hundred and fifty men are said to have defeated an army of between fifteen and twenty thousand Austrians. Scattered over the valley are to be found eleven stones, with this inscription, 1388, the year the battle was fought, marking out, as I was told upon the spot, the several places where the Austrians, attempting to make a stand, were repulsed anew." Wordsworth's note.

l. 472 *Pikes, of darkness:* "As Shreck-Horn, the pike of terror; Wetter-Horn, the pike of storm, etc. etc." Wordsworth's note. *Pike* means peak.

l. 475 *angel's smile all rosy red: Paradise Lost,* VIII. 618–19.

l. 520 *Batavia:* Holland.

l. 527 "The well-known effect of the famous air, called in French Ranz des Vaches, upon the Swiss troops." Wordsworth's note.

l. 534 *installed:* filled with.

l. 538 *confide:* put trust in.

l. 546 *Einsiedlen's wretched fane:* "This shrine is resorted to from a hope of relief, by multitudes from every corner of the Catholic world, labouring under mental or bodily afflictions." Wordsworth's note.

l. 560 *fountains:* "Rude fountains built and covered with sheds for the accommodation of the Pilgrims, in their ascent of the mountain." Wordsworth's note.

l. 588 "It is scarce necessary to observe that these lines were written before the emancipation of the Savoy." Wordsworth's note (1793 edition only). Savoy was annexed by France in November 1792.

l. 619 *Sourd:* "An insect so called, which emits a short, melancholy arz, heard at the close of the summer evenings, on the banks of the Loire." Wordsworth's note.

l. 631 See Milton, *Areopagitica,* "There be delights, there be recreations and jolly pastimes that will fetch the day about from sun to sun, and rock the tedious year as in a delightful dream."

"GUILT AND SORROW; OR, INCIDENTS UPON SALISBURY PLAIN" (P. 31)
Composed largely in 1793, at the commencement of England's war with France, and following a walking tour of the West Country in 1793. Wordsworth set out with William Calvert, but separated from his friend after a dangerous accident on the road, and crossed Salisbury Plain on his own. Before setting out on their tour,

Wordsworth and Calvert spent a month on the Isle of Wight, where they could see the naval and merchant vessels preparing for war. In 1793, Wordsworth had strong sympathies with the French and the French Revolution. The prospect of war filled him with apprehension, not least of all because it promised to make reunion with Annette Vallon and their daughter profoundly difficult. Wordsworth revised the poem in 1795 and 1799, titling it "Adventures on Salisbury Plain," and published stanzas XII–XXXIV and XXXVII–L in the 1798 volume of *Lyrical Ballads*, as "The Female Vagrant." Wordsworth continued to revise the poem, toning down its revolutionary fervor and removing statements critical of the British government, many of which would have been deemed seditious if published in the 1790s.

The poem is accurate in many of its descriptive details, although Wordsworth noted in the 1842 Advertisement to its publication that "of the features described as belonging to it, one or two are taken from other desolate parts of England." To Isabella Fenwick, moreover, Wordsworth remarked that the female vagrant's description of her sufferings "as a sailor's wife in America, and her condition of mind during her voyage home, were faithfully taken from the report made to me of her own case by a friend who had been subject to the same trials and affected in the same way."

In the Advertisement prefixed to the poem in 1842, Wordsworth describes the feeling of "melancholy forebodings" instilled in·him by seeing the fleets massing for war with France. "The American war was still fresh in memory. The struggle which was beginning, and which many thought would be brought to a speedy close by the irresistible arms of Great Britain being added to those of the allies, I was assured in my own mind would be of long continuance, and productive of distress and misery beyond all possible calculation. This conviction was pressed upon me by having been a witness, during a long residence in revolutionary France, of the spirit which prevailed in that country." The Advertisement also stresses Wordsworth's concern for the "calamities, principally those consequent upon war, to which, more that other classes men, the poor are subject." Moreover, in a 1795 letter to Francis Wrangham, Wordsworth describes the purpose of the poem as, in part, "to expose the vices of the penal law and the calamities of war as they affect individuals."

l. 16 *pendent:* hanging.

l. 39 *heaven's darkening cope:* overarching canopy or vault of heaven.

l. 41 *spreading thorn:* generally a hawthorn or white-thorn tree or bush.

l. 51 The male vagrant was pressed into service in the British navy during the American Revolution. This practice was considered to be among the most odious forms of government oppression.

l. 72 *murderer's fate:* death by hanging.

l. 91 *habitual phrensy:* prone to regular epileptic or delusional fits, for example.

ll. 112–13 *strange lines, in former days / Left by gigantic arms:* monolithic formations left by ancient inhabitants of the area (not the Druids, however).

l. 122 *wicker:* In *The Gallic Wars,* Caesar describes the Druids as having "gigantic images, the limbs of which made of wickerwork they fill with living men and set on fire, and the victims perish, encompassed with the flames." In the 1794 version of the poem, Wordsworth made an explicit connection between the barbaric rites of the Druids and the current war with France. Wordsworth was mistaken, however, in supposing the Druids to have left the ruins, or to have engaged in human sacrifice.

l. 149 *Spital:* shelter for travelers.

l. 169 *sped:* fared, succeeded.

l. 196 *to a natural sympathy resigned:* a natural sympathy taking root.

l. 212 *freaks:* frolics, fun.

l. 229 *substance:* property. Unable to produce sufficient yields from his land, the woman's father loses his "hereditary nook" to a wealthy neighbor. Wordsworth may have based this incident on a similar one with which he was familiar, which occurred at Calgarth on Windermere. Here, as in poems such as "The Last of the Flock" and "Michael," Wordsworth depicts the loss of property to small freeholders as a tragedy.

l. 274 *strain:* clasp tightly.

l. 283 *pestilential:* disease-laden.

l. 297 *devoted:* doomed.

l. 324 *Tempered:* uttered.

l. 325 *wain:* a cart.

l. 336 *main:* sea.

l. 401 *amazed:* bewildered.

l. 438 *ruth:* sorrow.

l. 493 *griding:* piercing.

l. 494 *amain:* with great energy or force.

l. 513 *correspondent:* corresponding, answering.

l. 525 *regale:* bestow.

l. 623 *essay:* attempt.

"LINES LEFT UPON A SEAT IN A YEW-TREE" (P. 51)

Composed early in 1797; published in *Lyrical Ballads* (1798). To Isabella Fenwick, Wordsworth noted: "The tree has disappeared, and the slip of Common on which it stood, that ran parallel to the lake, and lay open to it, has long been enclosed; so that the road has lost much of its attraction. This spot was my favourite walk in the evenings during the latter part of my school-time." The injunction against pride and the admonition to care for all living things with which the poem closes express criticism of William Godwin's elevation of reason over a more emotional, passionate response to the world, in his *An Enquiry Concerning Political Justice* (1793).

l. 8 *Who he was:* "The individual whose habits and character are here given, was a gentleman of the neighbourhood, a man of talent and learning who had been educated at one of our Universities, and returned to pass his time in seclusion on his own estate." (Wordsworth to Isabella Fenwick.)

"THE REVERIE OF POOR SUSAN" (P. 53)
First published in *Lyrical Ballads* (1800) as "Poor Susan." Wood, Lothbury, and Cheapside are streets in London's mercantile district. A concluding stanza was deleted from subsequent publication:

> Poor Outcast! Return—to receive thee once more
> The house of thy Father will open its door,
> And thou once again, in thy plain russet gown,
> May'st hear the thrush sing from a tree of its own.

"A NIGHT-PIECE" (P. 54)
Composed early in 1798, beginning the flurry of composition that would comprise most of Wordsworth's contributions to *Lyrical Ballads* (1798). The poem was not published until 1815, however. To Isabella Fenwick, Wordsworth recalled: "I distinctly recollect the very moment when I was struck, as described 'He looks up at the clouds, etc.'" Dorothy Wordsworth describes the same phenomenon in her journal entry for January 25, 1798.

"WE ARE SEVEN" (P. 54)
Composed in the spring of 1798; published in *Lyrical Ballads*. Wordsworth told Isabella Fenwick that he met the girl in the poem in 1793, in the vicinity of Goodrich Castle. He looked for traces of her on a trip to the region in 1841, but was unsuccessful, for he did not know her name. Of the poem's composition, Wordsworth recalled: "My friends will not deem it too trifling to relate that while walking to and fro I composed the last stanza first, having begun with the last line." In the 1802 version of the Preface to *Lyrical Ballads*, Wordsworth explained that the poem dealt with "the perplexity and obscurity which in childhood attend our notion of death, or rather our utter inability to admit that notion."

"ANECDOTE FOR FATHERS" (P. 57)
Composed in the spring of 1798; published in *Lyrical Ballads*. From 1798 to 1843, the poem was subtitled "Showing how the Practice of Lying may be taught." The boy in the poem is Basil Montagu, who had been the charge of Wordsworth and his sister, Dorothy, for three years.

l. 3 *cast in beauty's mould:* Bishop Percy, "The Children in the Wood," l. 20, "framed in beauty's mold."

l. 10 *Kilve:* village on the Bristol Channel, about a mile from Alfoxden.

l. 24 *Liswyn farm:* "Taken from a beautiful spot on the Wye." Wordsworth's note.

"THE THORN" (P. 58)

Composed early in 1798, among the first of the poems that would comprise Wordsworth's contributions to *Lyrical Ballads.* Wordsworth called attention to the poem in the Advertisement to the 1798 edition of *Lyrical Ballads:* "The poem of The Thorn, as the reader will soon discover, is not supposed to be spoken in the author's own person: the character of the loquacious narrator will sufficiently show itself in the course of the story." Wordsworth's comment provoked swift and harsh criticism of the narrator. Moreover, the poem became a central touchstone in discussions of the success or failure of Wordsworth's experiment in *Lyrical Ballads* to "ascertain how far the language of conversation in the middle and lower classes of society is adapted to the purposes of poetic pleasure," as he put it in the 1798 Advertisement. In the 1800 Preface, Wordsworth expanded on this point: "The principal object, then, proposed in these Poems, was to choose incidents and situations from common life, and to relate or describe them throughout, as far as was possible, in a selection of language really used by men, and, at the same time, to throw over them a certain colouring of imagination whereby ordinary things should be presented to the mind in an unusual aspect." Wordsworth further stressed the importance of "The Thorn" by appending a long note to the poem in the 1800 edition of *Lyrical Ballads,* describing the character of his loquacious narrator in exacting detail, and explaining a connection between poetry and passion made manifest in repetition.

This Poem ought to have been preceded by an introductory Poem, which I have been prevented from writing by never having felt myself in a mood when it was probable that I should write it well. The character which I have here introduced speaking is sufficiently common. The Reader will perhaps have a general notion of it, if he has even known a man, a Captain of a small trading vessel, for example, who being past the middle age of life, had retired upon an annuity or small independent income to some village or country town of which he was not a native, or in which he had not been accustomed to live. Such men, having little to do, become credulous and talkative from indolence; and from the same cause, and other predisposing causes by which it is probable that such men may have been affected, they are prone to superstition. On which account it appeared to me proper to select a character like this to exhibit some of the general laws by which superstition acts upon the mind. Superstitious men are almost always men of slow faculties and deep feelings; their minds are not loose, but adhesive; they have a reasonable share of imagination, by which word I mean the faculty which produces impressive effects out of simple elements; but they are utterly destitute of fancy, the power by which pleasure and surprise are excited by sudden varieties of situation and an accumulated imagery.

It was my wish in this poem to show the manner in which such men cleave to the same ideas; and to follow the turns of passion, always different, yet not palpably different, by which their conversation is swayed. I had two objects to attain; first, to represent a picture which should not be unimpressive, yet consistent with the character that should describe it; secondly, while I adhered to the style in which such persons describe, to take care that words, which in their minds are impregnated with passion, should likewise convey passion to Readers who are not accustomed to sympathize with men feeling in that manner or using such language. It seemed to me that this might be done by calling in the assistance of Lyrical and rapid Metre. It was necessary that the Poem, to be natural, should in reality move slowly; yet I hoped that, by the aid of the metre, to those who should at all enter into the spirit of the Poem, it would appear to move quickly. The Reader will have the kindness to excuse this note, as I am sensible that an introductory Poem is necessary to give this Poem its full effect.

Upon this occasion I will request permission to add a few words closely connected with "The Thorn" and many other Poems in these volumes. There is a numerous class of readers who imagine that the same words cannot be repeated without tautology: this is a great error: virtual tautology is much oftener produced by using different words when the meaning is exactly the same. Words, a Poet's words more particularly, ought to be weighed in the balance of feeling, and not measured by the space which they occupy upon paper. For the Reader cannot be too often reminded that Poetry is passion: it is the history or science of feelings: now every man must know that an attempt is rarely made to communicate impassioned feelings without something of an accompanying consciousness of the inadequateness of our own powers, or the deficiencies of language. During such efforts there will be a craving in the mind, and as long as it is unsatisfied the speaker will cling to the same words, or words of the same character. There are also various other reasons why repetition and apparent tautology are frequently beauties of the highest kind. Among the chief of these reasons is the interest which the mind attaches to words, not only as symbols of the passion, but as things, active and efficient, which are of themselves part of the passion. And further, from a spirit of fondness, exultation, and gratitude, the mind luxuriates in the repetition of words which appear successfully to communicate its feelings. The truth of these remarks might be shown by innumerable passages from the Bible, and from the impassioned poetry of every nation. "Awake, awake, Deborah!" &c. Judges, chap. v, verses 125h, 27th, and part of 28th. See also the whole of that tumultuous and wonderful Poem.

In a letter to Sara Hutchinson (June 14, 1802), Wordsworth again defended his choice of narrator and narrative technique in "The Thorn": " 'The Thorn' is tedious to hundreds; and so is the *Idiot Boy* to hundreds. It is in the character of the old man to tell his story in a manner which an *impatient* reader must necessarily feel as tedious." Despite his stubborn affection for his narrator, Wordsworth revised the poem for subsequent publication, eliminating some of the passages that critics found most objectionable. In particular, he eliminated the narrator's claim in the concluding lines of stanza III to have measured the little pond "from side to side: / 'Tis three feet long, and two feet wide."

In the note to Isabella Fenwick, Wordsworth recalled the incident that motivated him to composition: "Arose out of my observing, on the ridge of Quantock Hill, on a stormy day, a thorn which I had often past, in calm and bright weather, without noticing it. I said to myself, 'Cannot I by some invention do as much to make this Thorn permanently an impressive object as the storm has made it to my eyes at this moment?' I began the poem accordingly, and composed it with great rapidity."

The poem bears close resemblance to Gottfried Bürger's ballad "The Lass of Fair Wone," which had been published in the *Monthly Magazine* in 1796. "The Thorn," together with "Goody Blake and Harry Gill," "The Idiot Boy," "The Complaint of a Forsaken Indian Woman," and "The Last of the Flock," demonstrates Wordsworth's interest in the poetic handling of "impassioned feelings" (Preface to *Lyrical Ballads*) or mental states bordering on pathology. Wordsworth's interest was shared by many of his contemporaries. As the playwright Joanna Baillie asked: "If man is an object of so much attention to man, engaged in the ordinary occurrences of life, how much more does he excite his curiosity and interest when placed in extraordinary situations of difficulty and distress?" (A Series of Plays in which it is attempted to delineate the stronger passions of the mind [1798]).

l. 105 *Martha Ray:* This was the name of the grandmother of Basil Montagu, Wordsworth's and Dorothy's young charge. She was an actress and the victim of a notorious murder, when she was shot by a rejected lover in 1779. Basil Montagu's father, Wordsworth's friend of the same name, was the illegitimate son of Martha Ray and the fourth earl of Sandwich.

"GOODY BLAKE AND HARRY GILL" (P. 66)

Composed in the spring of 1798; published in *Lyrical Ballads*. Wordsworth called attention to this poem in the Advertisement to the 1798 edition: "The tale of

Goody Blake and Harry Gill is founded on a well-authenticated fact which happened in Warwickshire." Wordsworth identified his source, however, noting that the incident was lifted from Erasmus Darwin's *Zoönomia* (1794–96). In the Preface to *Lyrical Ballads,* Wordsworth added: "I wished to draw attention to the truth that the power of the human imagination is sufficient to produce such changes even in our physical nature as might almost appear miraculous. The truth is an important one; the fact (for it is a fact) is a valuable illustration of it. And I have the satisfaction of knowing that it has been communicated to many hundreds of people who would never have heard of it, had it not been narrated as a Ballad, and in a more impressive metre than is usual in Ballads."

l. 6 *duffle:* coarse, thick woolen cloth.
l. 9 *July:* rhymes with "truly" in North Country dialect.
l. 39 canty: cheerful, in North Country dialect.

"HER EYES ARE WILD" (P. 69)
Composed in the spring of 1798; published in *Lyrical Ballads* with the title "The Mad Mother." Wordsworth told Isabella Fenwick that the poem's subject was told him by a "lady of Bristol, who had seen the poor creature." In the 1800 Preface to *Lyrical Ballads,* Wordsworth explained the purpose of this poem and "The Idiot Boy" as attempts to trace the "maternal passion through many of its more subtle windings."

l. 4 *main:* sea.
l. 11 *English tongue:* Wordsworth explained in an 1836 letter to John Kenyon: "Though she came from far, English was her native tongue.... While the distance removes her from us, the fact of her speaking our language brings us at once into close sympathy with her."
ll. 21–40 The woman describes a hallucinatory experience during which she sees her infant as a fiend, but she is restored to sanity as the child feeds at her breast. As in "Goody Blake and Harry Gill," Wordsworth draws on material from Darwin's *Zoönomia.* In the chapter devoted to "Diseases of Increased Volition," Darwin advises frequent nursing to alleviate postpartum depression.
l. 54 *hollow:* empty.

"SIMON LEE" (P. 73)
Composed in March of 1798; published in *Lyrical Ballads.* Wordsworth told Isabella Fenwick: "This old man had been huntsman to the Squires of Alfoxden, which, at the time we occupied [Alfoxden House], belonged to a minor. The old man's cottage stood upon the common, a little way from the entrance to Alfoxden Park. But it had disappeared.... The fact was as mentioned in the poem; and I

have, after an interval of 45 years, the image of the old man as fresh before my eyes as if I had seen him yesterday. The expression when the hounds were out, 'I dearly love their voices,' was word for word from his own lips." In the Preface to *Lyrical Ballads,* Wordsworth described the poem as an attempt to place the reader "in the way of receiving from ordinary moral sensations another and more salutary impression than we are accustomed to receive from them."

l. 1 *Cardigan:* a county in central Wales.
l. 25 *But, oh the heavy change:* Milton, "Lycidas," l. 37.
ll. 93–96 Robert Southey cited these lines in an 1816 *Quarterly Review* article on "The State of the Poor." "This is true radical reform.... The good man will not be deterred from persevering in good, though his attempts to benefit others should sometimes end in disappointment, or sometimes be ill-bestowed and unthankfully requited."

"LINES WRITTEN IN EARLY SPRING" (P. 75)
Composed in the spring of 1798; published in *Lyrical Ballads.* Wordsworth told Isabella Fenwick that the poem was "actually composed while I was sitting by the side of the brook that runs down from the Comb, in which stands the village of Alford, through the grounds of Alfoxden. It was a chosen resort of mine."

l. 1 *notes:* rhymes with "thoughts" in North Country dialect.

"TO MY SISTER" (P. 76)
Composed in March 1798; published in *Lyrical Ballads,* titled "Lines Written at a Small Distance from My House, and Sent, by My Little Boy to the Person to Whom They Are Addressed."

ll. 33–34 Compare to "Tintern Abbey," ll. 100–2: "A motion and a spirit, that impels / All thinking things, all objects of all thought, / And rolls through all things."

"'A WHIRL-BLAST FROM BEHIND THE HILL'" (P. 77)
Composed in March 1798 and published in *Lyrical Ballads.* Dorothy Wordsworth recorded in her journal on March 18, 1798: "On our return, sheltered under the hollies during a hailshower. The withered leaves danced with the hailstones. William wrote a description of the storm."

"EXPOSTULATION AND REPLY" (P. 78)
Composed in May 1798 and published in *Lyrical Ballads.* This poem and "The Tables Turned" are companion pieces. The friend with whom the speaker converses is William Hazlitt, who visited Wordsworth in 1798, and whose early admiration

for the poet would soon give way to sharp criticism of his ego and choice of lowly, overly prosaic, subjects for poetic composition. In the Advertisement to the 1798 edition of *Lyrical Ballads*, Wordsworth noted that the two poems arose "out of conversation with a friend who was somewhat unreasonably attached to modern books of moral philosophy."

"THE COMPLAINT OF A FORSAKEN INDIAN WOMAN" (P. 80)
Composed in the spring of 1798; published in *Lyrical Ballads*. As he recalled to Isabella Fenwick, Samuel Hearne's *A Journey from Prince of Wales's Fort in Hudson Bay to the Northern Ocean* (1795) supplied the idea and information for the poem.

ll. 3–6 "In the high northern latitudes, as [Hearne] informs us, when the northern lights vary their position in the air, they make a rustling and a crackling noise." Wordsworth's note.

"THE LAST OF THE FLOCK" (P. 82)
Composed in the spring of 1798; published in *Lyrical Ballads*. Wordsworth attested to the veracity of the incident to Isabella Fenwick, telling her that it "occurred in the village of Holford, close by Alfoxden."

"THE IDIOT BOY" (P. 85)
Composed in the spring of 1798; published in *Lyrical Ballads*. Wordsworth told Isabella Fenwick: "The last stanza—'The Cocks did crow to-whoo, to-whoo, And the sun did shine so cold'—was the foundation of the whole. The words were reported to me by my dear friend, Thomas Poole; but I have since heard the same repeated of other Idiots. Let me add that this long poem was composed in the groves of Alfoxden, almost extempore; not a word, I believe, being corrected, though one stanza was omitted. I mention this in gratitude to those happy moments, for, in truth, I never wrote anything with so much glee." The poem generated much hostile attention from critics. Wordsworth, however, defended the poem at length in a letter of June 7, 1802, to John Wilson. Like the narrator of "The Thorn," the subject of "The Idiot Boy" was deemed vulgar, tedious, and unpoetic. Wordsworth complained to Wilson that "People in our rank in life are perpetually falling into one sad mistake, namely, that of supposing that human nature and the persons they associate with are one and the same thing. Whom do we generally associate with? Gentlemen, persons of fortune, professional men, ladies, persons who can afford to buy or can easily procure books of half a guinea price, hot-pressed, and printed upon superfine paper. These persons are, it is true, a part of human nature, but we err lamentably if we suppose them to be fair representatives of the vast mass of human existence." It is the task of poets, Wordsworth continues, to "rectify men's feelings, to give them new compositions of feeling, to render their feelings more sane pure and permanent, in short, more

consonant to nature, that is, to eternal nature, and the great moving spirit of things." Of idiots, Wordsworth continues, the sublime expression of scripture, "their life is hidden with God," applies. "They are worshipped, probably from a feeling of this sort, in several parts of the East. Among the Alps where they are numerous, they are considered, I believe, as a blessing to the family to which they belong. I have indeed often looked upon the conduct of fathers and mothers of the lower classes of society towards Idiots as the great triumph of the human heart. It is there that we see the strength, disinterestedness, and grandeur of love." Finally, Wordsworth defends his picture of the idiot boy as having nothing "disgusting" in it. The boy "is not one of those who cannot articulate and such as are usually disgusting in their persons."

"LINES COMPOSED A FEW MILES ABOVE TINTERN ABBEY" (P. 99)
Composed in July 1798; published in *Lyrical Ballads*. Wordsworth wrote the poem immediately after visiting Tintern Abbey in early July 1798, on a walking tour with his sister, Dorothy, as they prepared to leave England for a stay in Germany. "I began it upon leaving Tintern, after crossing the Wye, and concluded it just as I was entering Bristol in the evening, after a ramble of four or five days, with my Sister. Not a line of it was altered, and not any part of written down till I reached Bristol," Wordsworth recalled to Isabella Fenwick. "Tintern Abbey" was hurried to the printer, and became the final poem in the 1798 edition of *Lyrical Ballads*.

"Tintern Abbey" conforms loosely to Wordsworth's biography. He had visited the abbey five years prior on his walking tour through Wales, shortly after returning from France. The same trip provided material for "Guilt and Sorrow." The years between 1793 and 1798, particularly 1793–95, moreover, were a difficult and unsettled time for Wordsworth. Wordsworth's unhappiness is reflected in his recollection of loneliness and the "dreary intercourse of daily life." His affirmation of subsequent healing and renewal of faith likewise conforms to biographical detail, and the role of Dorothy in his return to health and happiness is well documented. Some of the material in the poem departs from a narrow handling of Wordsworth's biography, however. For example, his suggestion in ll. 67–83 that he was a thoughtless boy for whom nature was all in all when he first came among these hills does not accurately describe the twenty-three-year-old Wordsworth who visited Tintern Abbey in 1793. Likewise, the depiction of Dorothy in the final stanza as an unformed youth obscures the fact that she was very much an adult as she stood beside her brother in 1798.

Wordsworth and Dorothy followed in the footsteps of William Gilpin's *Observations on the River Wye ... Made in the Summer of 1770*, which Wordsworth carried with him on the trip. He was also familiar with Richard Warner's *A Walk Through Wales, in August 1797*. The Wordsworths dined with Warner at the home of their mutual friend, James Losh, at Bath, immediately before setting out on their tour. Some of Wordsworth's description of the countryside around Tintern reflects

Gilpin's and Warner's handling of the same locale. However, Wordsworth's poem makes no mention of the many vagrants who had made the ruined abbey their residence and lived by begging from tourists, or of the production of iron and charcoal along the river, which darkened the sky with smoke and made a deafening racket. The poem also draws on literary sources. There are many verbal echoes of Charlotte Smith's meditative, blank verse poem, *The Emigrants* (1793). Conventions of topographical poetry established by William Cowper's *The Task*, Mark Akenside's *Pleasures of the Imagination*, and James Thomson's *The Seasons* shape Wordsworth's poem. "Tintern Abbey" contains several important allusions to Milton. For a full development of the poem's debt to literary tradition, see Mary Jacobus, " 'Tintern Abbey' and the Renewal of Tradition," in *Tradition and Experiment in Wordsworth's* Lyrical Ballads.

l. 4 *inland murmur:* "The river is not affected by the tides a few miles above Tintern." Wordsworth's note.

ll. 5–8 See Gilpin, "Many of the furnaces, on the banks of the river, consume charcoal, ... and the smoke, which is frequently seen issuing from the sides of the hills; and spreading its thin veil over a part of them, beautifully breaks their lines, and unites them with the sky."

l. 33 See Milton, Preface to *The Judgment of Martin Bucer Concerning Divorce*, "Whereby good men in the best portion of their lives."

l. 106 "This line has a close resemblance to an admirable line of Young's the exact expression of which I do not recollect." Wordsworth's note. See Edward Young, *Night Thoughts*, VI.417, 424 "Senses ... half create the wondrous world they see."

l. 113 *Suffer my genial spirits to decay:* Milton, *Samson Agonistes*, ll. 594–96. Samson laments his blindness compounded into "double darkness" by his despair. "So much I feel my genial spirits droop, / My hopes all flat: Nature within me seems / In all her functions weary of herself." *Genial* suggests conducive to growth, native, and creative.

l. 128 Milton, *Paradise Lost*, VII.26–27, "though fall'n on evil days, / On evil dayes though fall'n, and evil tongues."

"The Old Cumberland Beggar" (p. 103)

Composed in the spring of 1798; heavily revised for publication in the 1800 edition of *Lyrical Ballads*. To Isabella Fenwick, Wordsworth recalled: "Observed and with great benefit to my own heart, when I was a child: written at Racedown and Alfoxden in my twenty-eighth year. The political economists were about that time beginning their war upon mendacity in all its forms, and by implication, if not directly, on alms-giving also. This heartless process has been carried as far as it can go by the AMENDED poor-law bill [1834], though the inhumanity that prevails in this measure is somewhat disguised by the profession that one of its objects is to throw the poor upon the voluntary donations of their neighbours; that is, if rightly interpreted, to force them into a condition between relief in the Union poorhouse, and alms robbed of their Christian grace and spirit, as being *forced* rather from the benevolent than given by them; while the avaricious and selfish, and all in fact but the humane and charitable, are at liberty to keep all they possess from their distressed brethren." Wordsworth refers to the old man as one of a "class of Beggars" that will soon be extinct. "It consisted of poor, and, mostly, old and infirm persons, who confined themselves to a stated round in their neighbourhood, and had certain fixed days, on which, at different houses, they regularly received alms, sometimes in money, but mostly in provisions." This poem, together with "The Idiot Boy" and "The Last of the Flock," shows Wordsworth's suspicion of institutional responses to local hardship.

l. 116 *easy:* comfortable.

l. 123 *monitor:* reminder.

l. 179 HOUSE, *misnamed of* INDUSTRY: workhouse, set up to provide sustenance for the indigent in the late eighteenth century.

"ANIMAL TRANQUILLITY AND DECAY" (P. 108)
Composed in 1796 and 1797; published as "Old Man Travelling: Animal Tranquillity and Decay, A Sketch," in *Lyrical Ballads* (1798). Wordsworth deleted the six final lines from the poem in 1815:

> I asked him whither he was bound, and what
> The object of his journey: he replied
> That he was going many miles to take a last leave of his son, a mariner,
> Who from a sea-fight had been brought to Falmouth,
> And there was dying in an hospital.

PETER BELL (P. 109)
Composed in the spring of 1798. Wordsworth continued to revise and add to the poem until its eventual publication in 1819. The poem was much maligned by critics, who found its humble subject matter ludicrous and overburdened with significance. Its notoriety induced Percy Bysshe Shelley to compose an answering "Peter Bell the Third," before reading Wordsworth's poem. Shelley's notion was, as Mary Shelley put it, to show how "a man gifted, even as transcendently as the author of *Peter Bell,* with the highest qualities of genius, must, if he fostered such errors, be infected with dullness." To Isabella Fenwick, Wordsworth explained that the poem was "founded upon an anecdote, which I read in a newspaper, of an ass being found hanging his head over a canal in a wretched posture. Upon examination a dead body was found in the water and proved to be the body of its master. The countenance, gait, and figure of Peter, were taken from a wild rover with whom I walked from Builth, on the river Wye, downwards nearly as far

as the town of Hay.... In the woods of Alfoxden I used to take great delight in noticing the habits, tricks, and physiognomy of asses; and I have no doubt that I was thus put upon writing the poem out of liking for the creature that is so often dreadfully abused." *Peter Bell* forms a companion, albeit in an inveterately natural idiom, to Coleridge's supernatural *The Rime of the Ancient Mariner,* completed shortly before. Also see Coleridge's poem "Address to a Young Jack Ass," published in the *Morning Chronicle* in December 1794 and included in *Poems on Various Subjects* (1796). This poem brought derision on Coleridge, who was depicted as a braying jackass in *The Anti-Jacobin.*

EPIGRAPHS (P. 109)

l. 1 *What's in a* Name?: Shakespeare, *Romeo and Juliet.*
l. 2 Brutus will start a Spirit as soon as Cæsar!: Shakespeare, *Julius Caesar.*

PROLOGUE (P. 109)

l. 145 Compare to "Tintern Abbey," ll. 106–107, "Of eye, and ear,—both what they half create, / And what perceive ..."
l. 154 *Hippogriff:* a fabulous winged creature, like a griffin, but with body and hindquarters resembling those of a horse.

PART FIRST (P. 114)

l. 22 *Sarum:* Salisbury Plain.
l. 37 scars: deep, narrow valleys.
l. 46 *the Fleet:* prison ships for debtors.
l. 83 *Carl:* a base man.
l. 181 *Swale:* a river in Yorkshire.
l. 333 *Meet:* fit, appropriate.

PART SECOND (P. 124)

l. 63 *weal:* wealth.
l. 86 *plover:* a bird.
l. 87 *bittern:* a type of heron.
l. 181 *close:* deeply shaded.

PART THIRD (P. 130)

l. 23 *wight:* human being, person.
l. 26 *confound:* confuse, bewilder.
l. 55 *argument:* theme.
l. 62 *thridding:* threading.
l. 64 *anodyne:* anything that relieves pain.
l. 107 *Cotter:* peasant, cottager.

l. 139 *swimming:* dizzying.

l. 148 *planet-stricken:* stricken by the malign influence of an adverse planet; blasted; stricken with sudden fear or amazement.

l. 162 *kirk:* church.

l. 169 *troth:* loyalty.

l. 174 Genesis 35:18.

l. 188 *unsubstantial:* ghostly, hallucinatory.

l. 209 *Methodist:* Methodism, founded by John Wesley in 1738, had particular appeal for the rural and urban working classes, who felt disenfranchised by the Church of England. The movement grew rapidly throughout the eighteenth and nineteenth centuries. It was characterized by fervent belief, the possibility of personal redemption, and an interest in bettering social conditions.

l. 238 "The notion is very general that the cross on the back and shoulders of this Animal has the origin here alluded to." Wordsworth's note (1819).

l. 356 *self-involved:* absorbed in contemplation.

"THE SIMPLON PASS" (P. 142)

Perhaps composed in 1799 or 1804. Also in *The Prelude,* VI.621–40. First published in 1845. Based on Wordsworth's Alpine tour of 1790, which also provided material for "Descriptive Sketches."

"INFLUENCE OF NATURAL OBJECTS" (P. 142)

Composed in the winter of 1798, in Germany. Published in Coleridge's periodical, *The Friend,* December 28, 1809, as "Growth of Genius from the Influence of Natural Objects, on the Imagination in Boyhood, and Early Youth." Also in *The Prelude,* I.401–63.

"THERE WAS A BOY" (P. 144)

Composed in the winter of 1798, in Germany. Published in the second edition of *Lyrical Ballads* (1800). Also in *The Prelude,* V.364–97. The earliest drafts of the poem were written in first person. Of the last two lines, Coleridge wrote: "Had I met these lines running wild in the deserts of Arabia, I should have instantly screamed out, 'Wordsworth!'"

l. 2 *Winander:* Windermere, in the Lake District.

"NUTTING" (P. 145)

Composed in the winter of 1798, in Germany; published in *Lyrical Ballads* (1800).

l. 6 *wallet:* bag, satchel.

l. 9 *Tricked out:* dressed up; *weeds:* clothes.

" 'STRANGE FITS OF PASSION HAVE I KNOWN' "; " 'SHE DWELT AMONG THE UNTRODDEN WAYS' "; " 'I TRAVELLED AMONG UNKNOWN MEN' "; " 'THREE YEARS SHE GREW IN SUN AND SHOWER' "; " 'A SLUMBER DID MY SPIRIT SEAL' " (PP. 147–50)

These poems are known as the "Lucy poems." With the exception of " 'I Travelled Among Unknown Men' " (composed 1801), they were composed in the winter of 1798, in Germany, and published in the second edition of *Lyrical Ballads* (1800). Lucy is not identified, but a comment from Coleridge suggested that she was a figure for his sister, Dorothy, and the poems reflected Wordsworth's fears that he should lose her.

" 'STRANGE FITS OF PASSION HAVE I KNOWN' " (P. 147)

l. 15 *cot:* cottage.

" 'THREE YEARS SHE GREW IN SUN AND SHOWER' " (P. 148)

l. 18 *insensate:* inanimate.

"A POET'S EPITAPH" (P. 150)

Composed late in 1798 or early 1799, in Germany; published in *Lyrical Ballads* (1800).

l. 1 *Statist:* politician.
l. 9 *a Man of purple cheer:* a clergyman or doctor of divinity.
l. 18 *Philosopher:* natural scientist.
l. 19 *botanise:* collect, inventory, and sketch plant specimens.

"MATTHEW"; "THE TWO APRIL MORNINGS"; "THE FOUNTAIN" (PP. 152–55)

Composed in late 1798 or early 1799 and published in *Lyrical Ballads* (1800), these poems are known as the "Matthew poems." To Isabella Fenwick, Wordsworth noted: "This and other poems connected with Matthew would not gain by a literal detail of facts. Like the Wanderer in 'The Excursion', this School-master was made up of several both of his class and men of other occupations. I do not ask pardon for what there is of untruth in such verses, considered strictly as matters of fact. It is enough if, being true and consistent in spirit, they move and teach in a manner not unworthy of a Poet's calling."

"MATTHEW" (P. 152)

l. 6 *tablet:* stone tablet.
l. 9 *wreck:* record.

"THE FOUNTAIN" (P. 155)

l. 54 *approved:* proven good.

"LUCY GRAY" (P. 157)

Composed in late 1798 or early 1799, in Germany, and published in *Lyrical Ballads* (1800), this poem is not considered one of the "Lucy poems." Wordsworth told Isabella Fenwick that the poem was based on an account of a little girl lost and drowned in Halifax, Yorkshire. "The body however was found in the canal. The way in which the incident was treated and the spiritualizing of the character might furnish hints for contrasting the imaginative influences which I have endeavoured to throw over common life with [George] Crabbe's matter of fact style of treating subjects of the same kind."

"RUTH" (P. 159)

Composed in late 1798 or early 1799, in Germany. Published in *Lyrical Ballads* (1800).

l. 20 *casque:* helmet.

l. 26 *English tongue:* See "Her Eyes are Wild" (p. 69), l. 11.

l. 122 *tropic:* in the southern hemisphere.

l. 214 *Banks of Tone:* "The Tone is a river of Somersetshire at no great distance from the Quantock Hills. These hills, which are alluded to a few stanzas below, are extremely beautiful, and in most places richly covered with Coppice woods." Wordsworth's note (1800).

l. 254 *mould:* earth.

" 'BLEAK SEASON WAS IT, TURBULENT AND WILD' "; " 'ON NATURE'S INVITATION DO I COME' " (PP. 166, 167)

Composed sometime between 1800 and 1806; first published 1851. These poems were to have been included in *The Recluse* (p. 380).

" 'ON NATURE'S INVITATION DO I COME' " (P. 167)

l. 9 *only daughter of my parents:* Wordsworth's sister, Dorothy, with whom he shared a home from 1794 until her death, in 1855.

THE PRELUDE (1850) (P. 168)

Composed between 1799 and 1805; subsequently much revised; published posthumously in 1850. Wordsworth withheld publication until after his death because *The Recluse,* of which *The Prelude* was to have been a component, was never completed. Posthumous publication also extended the duration of copyright protection from which his heirs would benefit. Portions of *The Prelude* appeared in *Lyrical Ballads* ("The Simplon Pass," "There Was a Boy"), and in Coleridge's periodical, *The Friend* (Book XI.105–44). Wordsworth commented in 1805 on the length of the poem to his friend, George Beaumont: It is "a thing unprecedented in Literary history that a man should talk so much about himself.

It is not self-conceit, as you will know well, that has induced [me] to do this, but real humility; I began the work because I was unprepared to treat any more arduous subject and diffident of my own powers. Here at least I hoped that to a certain degree I should be sure of succeeding, as I had nothing to do but describe what I had felt and thought." The poem follows the poet's life from childhood up to about the time he began composition in 1798. In it, he traces the "dark inscrutable workmanship" (I.340–41) lodged in his interactions with nature and the social world that has formed him as a poet. The "Friend" to whom the poem is addressed is Coleridge, who heard Wordsworth read *The Prelude* over the course of several evenings in 1806. Coleridge's response is contained in his poem "To William Wordsworth: Lines Composed, for the Greater Part on the Night on which he Finished the Recitation of his Poem ... Concerning the Growth and History of his Own Mind," in which Coleridge effusively praises Wordsworth's power as a poet, the apprehension of which exacerbated his own dejected spirits.

BOOK FIRST (P. 168)

ll. 1–45 Known as the "glad preamble"; see Book Seventh, l. 4.

l. 14 *The earth is all before me: Paradise Lost*, XII. 646, "The world was all before them, where to choose / Their place of rest." Wordsworth sets up a comparison between his autobiographical poem of the growth of his mind as a poet and Milton's epic accounting of the ways of God to men. Beginning his poem where Milton left off helps Wordsworth to situate himself as Milton's heir and to suggest that *The Prelude* is a continuation of Milton's grand poem, but one that transposes Milton's epic into the dimensions of the poet's own mind.

l. 35 *correspondent breeze:* answering breeze.

l. 37 *redundant:* superabundant.

l. 38 *congenial:* creative.

l. 46 *Friend:* Coleridge.

ll. 71–72 *till choice was made / Of a known Vale:* the vale of Grasmere, where Wordsworth settled with Dorothy in 1799.

l. 96 *Æolian visitations:* Wordsworth compares his skill at poetic composition to the workings of an aeolian harp. The aeolian harp was a favored metaphor among the Romantic poets. It was a wind harp, whose strings sounded with the breeze. It suggested the dynamic interplay and cooperation between the poet's faculties and the impressions made on him or her by experience.

l. 120 *phantasies:* fancies, visions.

ll. 140–41 *mother dove / Sits brooding: Paradise Lost* I.20–21, of the Holy Spirit, "Dove-like satst brooding on the vast Abyss / And mad'st it pregnant."

l. 154 *external things:* learning, knowledge. Wordsworth begins to explore possible themes or topics for his poem.

l. 187 *Mithridates:* king of Pontus, who warred on Rome until his defeat by Pompey in 66 B.C.

l. 189 *Odin:* figure from Norse mythology.

l. 191 *Sertorius:* democratic governor of Spain, who opposed the Roman dictator Sulla. Sertorius was murdered in 72 B.C., and his followers escaped to the Canary Islands, the "Fortunate Isles" in line 192. Wordsworth found the accounts of Sertorius and Mithridates in Plutarch's *Lives.*

l. 206 *Frenchman:* "Dominique de Gougues, a French gentleman who went in 1568 to Florida to avenge the massacre of the French by the Spaniards there" (1850 note).

l. 212 *Gustavus:* Gustavus I of Sweden (1496–1560), who liberated his country from the Danish in 1520.

l. 214 *Wallace:* William Wallace (c. 1270–1305), Scottish hero who led opposition to English domination of Scotland. He was executed in 1305.

l. 225 *unsubstantial:* without substance; ethereal; of the mind.

l. 233 *Orphean lyre:* Referring to the lyre of Orpheus, given to him by Apollo, the god of poetry. Orpheus' song had the power to charm all listeners, and could make wild beasts, trees, and rocks follow its sound.

ll. 270–74 *Was it for this . . . dreams?* Wordsworth's question marks the beginning of his poem, for he turns, finally, to the theme and high argument that will engage his creative energies in this poem, namely the forces that have shaped him as a poet; *this* refers to the "listlessness" and "vain perplexity" of the preceding lines.

l. 270 *That one, the fairest of all rivers:* River Derwent, in the Lake District. This river flowed past Wordsworth's childhood home in Cockermouth. The scenes from childhood that follow were composed in late 1798, when Wordsworth was in Germany with his sister.

l. 275 *holms:* level stretches of ground by a river.

l. 282 *he:* the river.

l. 295 *Skiddaw:* a mountain north of the Lake District.

l. 304 *beloved Vale:* vale of Grasmere. See ll. 71–72 (p. 698).

l. 310 *springes:* traps, for birds.

l. 334 *amain:* at or with great speed.

l. 379 *instinct:* imbued.

l. 380 *I struck and struck again:* Also see *Peter Bell,* I.5. The boy is seated facing the stern of his skiff. As he moves away from the shore, he sees a distant peak emerging, as if with its own energy. Fleeing, the boy feels that the peak is following him. This episode dramatizes the dynamic and creative interplay between the mind and the world that is central to answering Wordsworth's question in line 270.

l. 435 *Confederate:* among friends.

l. 437 *The pack loud chiming:* game of "hare and hounds."

ll. 471–72 *Impressed, upon all forms, the characters / Of danger or desire:* nature stamps or prints an aspect of danger or desire on the objects of Wordsworth's boyish perceptions. Also see Book Sixth, ll. 632–40, and note to Book Sixth, l. 638 (p. 707).

l. 511 *with crosses and with cyphers:* tic-tac-toe.

l. 514 *snow-white deal:* wood of the Norway spruce.

l. 516 *loo or whist:* card games.

l. 521 *uncouth:* rough, childish.

l. 529 *knaves:* jacks.

l. 545 *extrinsic:* external or superficial. Wordsworth's concern is to sound the depth of the impressions left by nature on his mind. His memories and childish pleasures represent one level of his relationship with nature; they are the most visible part of a deeper relationship. The process of reflection that drives the composition of the poem allows Wordsworth to explore the more profound, but hidden, ways that nature has shaped the person that he has become and the poet he can be. He refers to the deep, shaping force of nature as "collateral impressions" in II.53.

l. 581 *vulgar:* physical; of the body.

l. 619 *fond:* foolish.

l. 640 *the road lies plain before me:* compare to Milton, *Paradise Lost* XII. 646, "The World was all before then,"; *theme:* subject matter for his poem.

BOOK SECOND (P. 185)

l. 78 *Sabine fare:* here, rustic. Sabine refers to the ancient Italians.

l. 98 *stud:* number of horses belonging to a single owner.

l. 103 *that large abbey:* Furness Abbey, twenty miles from Hawkshead.

l. 116 *chauntry:* chantry of the ruined abbey.

l. 201 *intervenient:* as a messenger.

l. 214 *succedaneum:* an inferior substitute.

ll. 216–17 *that false secondary power / By which we multiply distinctions:* scientific inquiry, which Wordsworth associates with descriptive enumeration of qualities and kinds, barren of the poetic, imaginative insight capable of seeing deep connections in the world and between the mind and the world. See also "The Tables Turned" (p. 79) for the "meddling" and murderous intellect.

l. 218 *puny boundaries:* enumerated qualities and kinds. Wordsworth suggests that the ways in which science objectively describes the world miss the subjective component that also creates the world of our perception.

l. 237 *Drinks in the feelings of his Mother's eye:* Wordsworth's language in this passage places the infant at the mother's breast, where the nursing infant can focus on the mother's face. This passage also suggests the primary and formative role of feeling in the development and growth of the child. Feeling precedes thinking, and what the child subsequently learns is grounded in a prior, feeling relationship with nature, whose first instance is the child's relationship with his mother.

l. 275 *chamois:* small hoofed mammal, similar to a goat, living in the high Alps.

ll. 276–79 *For now a trouble ... props of my affections:* Wordsworth may refer to the death of his mother, Ann, who died in 1778, when Wordsworth was seven years old. Following Ann Wordsworth's death, the Wordsworth children were split up among relatives. Wordsworth and Dorothy would not see each other again for nine years. In 1779, Wordsworth and his older brother, Richard (b. 1768), were sent to Hawkshead Grammar School.

l. 334 *Friend:* John Flemming, a classmate at Hawkshead.

l. 376 *transport:* elation.

BOOK THIRD (P. 198)

l. 8 *gown and tasselled cap:* The cap and gown were the normal garb of university students at the time.

l. 16 *Cam:* river running through the town of Cambridge.

ll. 38–39 *hair / Powdered like rimy trees:* Prior to the 1790s, when English dress was influenced by revolutionary practice in France, it was customary for both ladies and gentlemen to wear powder on their hair.

l. 46 *St. John:* one of the colleges at Cambridge. Wordsworth entered St. John's college on October 30, 1787.

ll. 74–75 Wordsworth was an undistinguished student at Cambridge. He admonishes himself for his indifferent efforts at university in *The Prelude,* VI.35–41 and 179–88.

ll. 77–83 Wordsworth alludes to his uncertainty about accepting the curacy for which his Cambridge education would prepare him, and on which his relatives had settled as his future work.

l. 333 *floating island:* For a description of this phenomenon see Wordsworth's *Guide Through the District of the Lakes.* "There occasionally appears above the surface of Derwent-Water, and always in the same place, a considerable tract of spongy ground covered with aquatic plants, which is called the Floating Island, but with more propriety might be named the Buoyant Island; and, on one of the pools near the lake of Esthwaite, may sometimes be seen a mossy Islet, with trees upon it, shifting about before the wind, a *lusus naturae* frequent on the great rivers of America, and not unknown in other parts of the world." The floating island also provided a subject for a poem by Dorothy Wordsworth, titled "Floating Island at Hawkshead, An Incident in the Schemes of Nature."

l. 476 *Bucer, Erasmus, Melancthon:* classical scholars of the Renaissance.

BOOK FOURTH (P. 215)

l. 3 *clomb:* climbed.

l. 12 *amain:* vigorously.

l. 14 *Charon:* Charon ferried the souls of the dead across the rivers Styx and Ancheron of the Greek underworld. In the context of friendly greetings and the release of summer vacation, Wordsworth's comparison of the ferryman to Charon is inept.

l. 21 *snow-white church:* Norman Church at Hawkshead, whitewashed.

ll. 28–39 Ann Tyson, with whom Wordsworth boarded while a student at Hawks-
head.

l. 54 *dimple:* ripple.

l. 57 *him:* i.e., the brook.

l. 104 *affecting private shades:* assuming the guise of.

l. 123 *passenger:* passerby.

l. 132 *regretted:* missed, longed for.

l. 182 *coppice:* copse, a small wood composed of hazel bushes.

l. 206 *filched:* stole.

l. 245 *fair Seven:* Pleiades, a constellation, also known as the "Seven Sisters."

l. 264 *shadow from the substance:* reflection on the water's surface from the object re-
flected.

l. 281 *gawds:* gaieties.

l. 288 *feeding pleasures:* pleasures that nourished the mind.

l. 297 *heartless:* discouraging, disheartening.

l. 302 *manners put to school:* the study of human behavior undertaken.

ll. 323–38 known as the "dedication episode."

l. 328 *Grain-tinctured:* scarlet; *empyrean:* the highest heaven, the sphere of the pure
element of fire. Wordsworth's word choices are Miltonic throughout the
passage.

l. 331 *Paradise Lost,* VIII.527–28, "fruits and flowers, / Walks, and the melody of
birds."

l. 339 The line should read: "Strange rendezvous my mind was at that time."

ll. 379–460 known as the "discharged soldier episode." These lines were drafted
in 1798, as Wordsworth was at work on the poems that he would contribute
to *Lyrical Ballads* (1798). It was a companion piece to "The Old Cumberland
Beggar."

BOOK FIFTH (P. 228)

l. 39 *adamantine:* incapable of being broken; having the qualities of adamant, a
stone.

l. 51 *studious friend:* Coleridge, probably.

ll. 56–139 Wordsworth's account of the dream of the Arab has been linked by
Jane Worthington Smyser (*Publications of the Modern Language Association of
America* 1956) to an account of a dream by the French philosopher René
Descartes in 1619. Smyser speculates that Coleridge described this dream
to Wordsworth. In Descartes's dream he sees a dictionary and a book of po-
etry. He is said to have understood it was a dream, and began to analyze it,
even before he awoke. The dictionary meant all the sciences gathered to-
gether, and the book of poetry to contain philosophy and wisdom joined
together. Wordsworth's dream contains many elements not present in
Descartes's, however.

ll. 60–61 Wordsworth is reading *Don Quixote,* by Cervantes.

ll. 65–67 Wordsworth studied mathematics and geometry at Hawkshead School and at Cambridge.

l. 75 *uncouth:* foreign or strange.

l. 87 *"Euclid's Elements":* Important Greek mathematical work of the third century B.C., which established the science of geometry.

l. 118 *Reckless:* without thought.

l. 172 *travelling back:* in memory toward composition of the poem.

l. 227 *an evil:* Wordsworth refers to educational schemes, such as those described in lines 295–345, which keep children under constant surveillance, as in lines 238–39.

l. 245 *prelibation:* an offering of the first fruits, or of the first taste. Wordsworth suggests that the "flower" of imaginative literature cannot be enjoyed until it has been put to didactic use.

ll. 256–57 Ann Wordsworth died in 1778. See note to Book Second, ll. 276–79 (pp. 700–2).

l. 295 *modern system:* refers to educational reform movements in which learning was to be carefully monitored to ensure rapid and rational progress. These efforts were predicated on John Locke's theory that the human mind at birth was a blank slate, and hence shaped by experience. If experience could be controlled and regularized, the reformers hypothesized, children could be freed from irrational fears and prejudices. For example, see Maria and Richard Lovell Edgeworth's *Practical Education* (1798).

l. 299 *model of a child:* compares the child to an automaton educated out of its childish nature.

ll. 307–9 Wordsworth's comments throughout the passage are ironic. He implies that fear, natural and supernatural, is part of the full round of human emotion and experience, and hence to be valued.

l. 310 *nice:* exaggeratedly refined or well-bred.

l. 327 *dimpling:* rippling; the surface of the water is "dimpled" by drops.

l. 328 Wordsworth places the blame on teachers' misguided notions.

ll. 341–44 *Fortunatus:* owner of the magic purse, who also had a hat that would transport him wherever he wanted to go; *Jack the Giant-killer:* rid the land of giants by virtue of a coat that made him invisible, shoes that gave him speed, and a magic sword; *St. George:* rescued *Sabra* from a dragon, and married her.

l. 348 *overbridged:* built a bridge of rational knowledge to the future bypassing error and misstep.

l. 349 *froward:* unruly.

l. 350 *they:* teachers.

l. 400 See Book Fourth, l. 22.

l. 409 *fatter:* richer.

ll. 418–19 *mysterious weight / Of pain, and doubt, and fear:* See also "Tintern Abbey" (p. 99), ll. 38–41, where Wordsworth describes the "burthen of the mystery."

The emotions Wordsworth describes are painful, but they also foster emotional maturity. In "Elegiac Stanzas, Suggested by a Picture of Peele Castle" (p. 484), sorrow, for example, humanizes the soul (l. 36).

ll. 426–59 known as the "drowned man episode." The man was James Jackson, a schoolmaster in the village of Sawrey, in the neighborhood of Hawkshead village. He was drowned on June 18, 1779. Wordsworth was at school at Hawkshead at the time.

l. 462 *Arabian tales: The Arabian Nights.* Wordsworth's defense of imaginative literature and supernatural tales recurs in *The Excursion,* Book First, ll. 170–85.

l. 503 *extravagate:* indulge, wander at large.

l. 512 *dubious:* indeterminate, between night and day.

ll. 536–38 Wordsworth compares childish reading to an isthmus, or land bridge, carrying him into mature understanding and taste. See Alexander Pope, *An Essay on Man,* II.3 "Plac'd on this isthmus of a middle state."

l. 561 *dear friend:* John Flemming.

l. 565 *conning:* learning by heart.

l. 571 *vulgar:* low.

l. 574 *inordinate:* unordered.

l. 605 Eight lines follow (ll. 606–13), which were deleted by accident in the first published edition of *The Prelude* (1850), the version printed in the current text.

> Thus far a scanty record is deduced
> Of what I owed to books in early life;
> Their later influence yet remains untold;
> But as this work was taking in my mind
> Proportions that seemed larger that had first
> Been meditated, I was indisposed
> To any further progress at a time
> When these acknowledgements were left unpaid.

BOOK SIXTH (P. 244)

l. 6 *Granta's cloisters:* Cambridge. Granta is a name for the River Cam.

ll. 28–29 Wordsworth alludes to his eventual disappointment of the desire of his maternal relatives, the Cooksons, that he take orders and enter the Church. Wordsworth here implies, however, that his decision not to leave Cambridge was the result more of cowardice than aversion from disappointing his relatives.

l. 48 *this very week:* the first week of April 1804.

l. 86 *Foot-bound:* without moving, as if bound to the spot.

l. 109 *classic niceties:* turns of phrase translated from Greek and Roman sources. Collecting phrases is akin to the robust interest in collecting fragments of classical architecture, for example.

l. 117 *geometric science:* See V.66–67, on Wordsworth's interest in geometry.

l. 121 *Indian:* Native American.

ll. 123, 125 *those abstractions; immaterial agents:* laws of geometry.

l. 133 *finite natures:* human nature, as opposed to the infinite wisdom of God or Nature.

ll. 142–54 The story is that of John Newton, captain of a slave vessel, who became curate of Olney and a close friend of the poet William Cowper. Newton recounts this experience in his *Authentic Narrative,* which Dorothy had copied into a notebook in 1798–99.

l. 173 *fits of spleen:* dejection, depression, in reference to the soon obsolete theory of the effects of bodily humors on determining health.

l. 178 *Redundancy:* abundance.

l. 180 *the Bard:* James Thomson, in *Castle of Indolence* (1748).

l. 186 *accidents:* by chance occurrence.

l. 199 *sole Sister:* Dorothy, from whom Wordsworth had been separated since the death of their mother in 1778.

l. 201 *Now:* summer of 1787.

ll. 204–5 *Emont:* a river that runs past the ruins of Brougham Castle, the "monastic castle" of line 205 (though there was nothing monastic about it).

l. 208 *Sidney:* Sir Philip Sidney had written his prose romance, *Arcadia,* for the pleasure of his sister. *Helvellyn; Cross-fell:* mountains visible from Brougham Castle.

l. 224 *Another maid:* Mary Hutchinson, whom Wordsworth married in 1802. She accompanied Wordsworth and Dorothy on their rambles during the summer vacation of 1787.

l. 233 *Border Beacon:* hill above Penrith.

l. 235 *fell:* wide, elevated stretch of waste- or pastureland; moorland ridge.

l. 240 Coleridge had left the Lake District in January 1804, and sailed for Malta in April. He hoped to improve his health and break his addiction to opium.

l. 251 *gales Etesian:* northwesterly Mediterranean winds.

ll. 266–67 Wordsworth refers to Coleridge's time as a student at Christ's Hospital, London, 1782–91. Coleridge spent most of his holidays in the city, for he was often unable to make the trip home to Devonshire. After graduating from Christ's Hospital, Coleridge went on to Jesus College, Cambridge, in 1791, missing Wordsworth by a year. Lines 266–74 contain allusions to Coleridge's "Sonnet: to the River Otter," "Frost at Midnight," and "Dejection: An Ode."

l. 281 *stormy course:* When at Cambridge, Coleridge became a Unitarian and spoke out in favor of radical reform and the French Revolution. He also contracted large debts, contemplated suicide, ran away to join the army, and planned to emigrate with Robert Southey to America, where the two hoped to found a utopian community. Coleridge left Cambridge in 1794 without a degree.

l. 287 *still:* always.

l. 288 *after-sojourn:* Coleridge's sojourn at Cambridge, which Wordsworth compares to his own.

l. 313 *airy wretchedness:* suggests Coleridge's inward bent toward philosophical speculation and fancy.

l. 314 *battened on:* grew fat upon.

l. 322 *third summer:* summer of 1790, when Wordsworth and Robert Jones set out, without notice to any of their relatives, on an ambitious Alpine walking tour. The tour formed material for "Descriptive Sketches" (composed 1791–92). See notes above (pp. 679–81).

l. 340 Wordsworth's trip took him through France just after the Revolution (1789), but before the commencement of violence.

l. 343 *white cliffs:* Dover.

l. 347 Wordsworth and Jones landed at Calais on July 13, 1790. July 14, 1789, was the day on which prisoners from the infamous Bastille prison were liberated, and King Louis XVI was forced to accede to a new constitution limiting his power. On July 14, 1790, there was a massive celebration throughout the country, the *Fête de la Fédération,* marking the anniversary of the Revolution.

l. 361 *umbrage:* foliage.

l. 389 *great spousals:* The metaphoric marriage between the king, Louis XVI, and the people of France, as the king swore fidelity to the new constitution.

l. 392 *vapoured:* boasted.

l. 397 Abraham entertains three angels who tell him (Genesis 18:1–15) that his wife, Sarah, though aged, will bear a son, Isaac.

l. 405 *forerunners in a glorious course:* the (English) Glorious Revolution of 1688. With the notable exception of Edmund Burke, who published his *Reflections on the Revolution in France,* in 1790, many in England believed that France was following in the peaceful footsteps of England's earlier revolution.

l. 418 *Convent of Chartreuse:* a Carthusian abbey in the Alps. The monks were expelled by the Revolutionaries in 1792, and the abbey was occupied by revolutionary forces. Wordsworth was not a witness to the expulsion. Here, as elsewhere in the poem, Wordsworth's account is in part an imaginative reconstruction, which departs from the strict details of Wordsworth's biography. On the imposition of present thoughts or modes of understanding onto an account of the past, see *The Prelude,* IV.256–76. Also see *The Prelude,* VI.237–39, where Wordsworth writes of his desire to plant Coleridge in a scene where he could not have been a participant.

l. 427 *frame of social being:* community.

l. 428 *bodied forth:* embodied; *ghostliness:* spirituality.

l. 439 *Life and Death:* rivers below the Grande Chartreuse.

l. 458 *sense:* sensuality; the body and its terrestrial form.

l. 464 *untransmuted shapes:* mountaintops, long unchanged.

l. 465 *Cerulean:* deep blue.

l. 480 *lawns:* open spaces between the woods; *Vallombre:* a valley near the monastery. Also see note to "Descriptive Sketches," l. 75 (p. 680).

l. 484 *cross of Jesus:* "Alluding crosses seen on the tops of the spiry rocks of the Chartreuse, which have every appearance of being inaccessible." Wordsworth's note (to "Descriptive Sketches").

l. 525 *Mont Blanc:* highest peak in the Alps.

l. 530 Wordsworth describes the glaciers of Chamouny, or Chamonix.

l. 549 *humour:* state of mind.

l. 552 *willow wreath:* Foliage of the willow was worn by forsaken lovers.

l. 563 Simplon Pass links France and Italy. In 1790, it was crossed by a mule track. Simplon Pass was later developed by Napoleon as a road, completed in 1807, for his troops to reach Italy.

ll. 595–616 Wordsworth's address to Imagination refers not to his thoughts at the time in 1790, but to his experience as he reflects on the experience in 1804. Reflection on past disappointment provides an occasion for Wordsworth to praise the present creative power that shapes his poem.

ll. 621–640 were published in 1845 as "The Simplon Pass." See p. 142.

l. 638 *great Apocalypse:* The passage suggests that the scenery bears the marks ("characters") of the biblical flood, which was taken to have shaped the morphology of all but the highest Alpine peaks. The scenery may also be read as an intimation of the next Apocalypse, foretold by St. John, in Revelations.

l. 652 *dimpling:* rippling.

l. 655 *Locarno's Lake:* lake at the town of Locarno, where Wordsworth and Jones stayed, before crossing to Lake Como.

l. 662 *Abyssinian:* refers to Milton's description of Abyssinia as the place where Paradise was mistakenly supposed to have been located, in *Paradise Lost*, IV.280–82.

l. 670 *While yet a youth:* refers to Wordsworth's earlier "Descriptive Sketches."

l. 764 *Brabant armies:* Belgian revolutionary troops; *on the fret:* eagerly anticipating.

l. 767 *social life:* adult life.

BOOK SEVENTH (P. 265)

l. *Six changeful years:* Writing in 1804, this refers incorrectly to the time elapsed since 1799, when Wordsworth wrote the "glad preamble." The beginnings of *The Prelude* were, however, six years prior, in the fall of 1798, when Wordsworth, isolated with Dorothy in Germany, began writing on his childhood memories.

l. 4 *glad preamble:* Book First, ll. 1–51.

l. 7 *Scafell:* a peak in the Lake District.

l. 15 *promised work:* The Prelude.

l. 44 *favourite grove:* the grove of firs in Ladywood, half a mile from Dove Cottage.

l. 57 *unfenced regions:* commons, as opposed to enclosed, privately owned land.

l. 65 *Three years:* Book Seventh describes Wordsworth's 1791 sojourn in London. He had made a previous visit in 1788.

l. 81 *Alcairo:* Cairo, mentioned with Babylon for its magnificence in *Paradise Lost,* I; *Persepolis:* capital of the Persian Empire, sacked by Alexander the Great in 331 B.C.

l. 112 Dick Whittington (d. 1423), three-time lord mayor of London.

ll. 121–41 These lines refer to famous tourist attractions in London. *Vauxhall* and *Ranelagh:* fashionable pleasure gardens on the Thames; *Whispering Gallery:* a walkway around the inside dome of St. Paul's Cathedral. The acoustics of the church allowed for a whisper from the floor below to be heard in the dome; *Westminster:* Westminster Abbey; *Giants of Guildhall:* carved wooden figures of Gog and Magog; *Bedlam:* Bethlehem hospital for the insane in Moorfields; *The Monument:* erected by Sir Christopher Wren in 1671–77, to commemorate the Great Fire of London in 1666; *Chamber of the Tower:* armory room, where one can see mail worn by the monarchs.

l. 174 *raree-show:* peep show, carried in a box.

l. 182 *thrilled:* pierced.

l. 193 *files of ballads:* printed ballads hung on strings for display; *dead walls:* walls without doors or windows.

l. 211 *hubbub:* alludes to the "hubbub wild" of Chaos in *Paradise Lost,* II.951.

l. 215 *frame of images:* statuettes.

l. 227 *Lascars:* East Indian sailors.

l. 243 *commissioned spirits:* spirits whose task was to cater to human desires.

ll. 244–47 Panoramas were eighteenth-century novelties. A spectator could view a large-scale image unfurled or displayed in the round. The spectator stood in the center. Wordsworth's comments in lines 229–315 describe modes of artistic production that reproduce or "ape" reality, as he puts it in lines 232–33, or that, as in the case of the stage productions of Jack the Giant-Killer (ll. 280–87), portray the fantastic as real.

l. 248 *mechanic artist:* model maker.

l. 267 *Sadler's Wells:* theater in the suburb of Islington that offered entertainment.

l. 280 *Jack the Giant-killer:* See note on Book Fifth, ll. 341–44 (p. 703).

ll. 283–84 From Milton's *Samson Agonistes,* ll. 87–89.

l. 297 *Maid of Buttermere:* Mary Robinson, of Buttermere, in the Lake District, was tricked into a bigamous marriage. A play based on her life was performed at Sadler's Wells in 1893. Her seducer, John Hatfield, was hanged in 1803.

l. 316 *memorial tribute:* a digression, memorializing Mary (see above). Mary later married a farmer.

l. 370 *fiery furnace:* a reference to Shadrach, Meshach, and Abednego, who had been cast by King Nebuchadnezzer into a fiery furnace but emerged unharmed (Daniel 3:23–26).

l. 379 *Mary:* Maid of Buttermere, again.

l. 389 This line should read: "Thrown in, that from humanity divorced."

ll. 390–91 The prostitute bears the "outward form" of humanity, yet her humanity is a facade; *twain:* two.

l. 406 *Siddons:* actress Sarah Siddons.

l. 409 *mean:* poor, rough.

ll. 413–33 These lines describe scenes and characters one could see onstage.

l. 512 *Genius of Burke:* Edmund Burke, conservative politician and author (1729–97). He was known to be an impressive orator and writer, and spoke out forcefully against the French Revolution. Wordsworth added this passage in praise of Burke in 1832. In 1791, at the time to which he refers in *The Prelude,* however, Wordsworth was critical of Burke.

l. 524 *systems built on abstract rights:* Burke argued against the notion that humans had innate and abstract rights. Rather, the rights of man were lodged in the traditions and customs of the land, and in divine right of the sovereign.

l. 533 Aeolus, classical god of winds, kept them chained in a cave.

l. 564 *Death of Abel:* popular poem by Salomen Gressner (1758); *the bard:* Edward Young, author of *Night Thoughts* (1742–45).

l. 568 *Morven:* name given by James Macpherson to the west coast of Scotland in his Ossian epics, *Fingal* and *Temora.* Doubts about the authenticity of the Ossian epics, purported by Macpherson to be translations of third-century Gaelic texts, were rampant from their publication in 1762 and 1763. A committee appointed in 1797 by the Highland Society issued a report in 1805 that declared the poems to be forgeries. The poems were based on sources from Gaelic balladry, but were largely composed by Macpherson.

l. 575 *conventicle:* place of worship for Protestant nonconformists.

l. 580 *strife of singularity:* effort to make a singular, fashionable impression.

l. 601 *foil:* The descriptions of vanity, depravity, poverty, and indifference that present themselves to the poet's eye in London create a foil against which images of tenderness, courage, integrity, or truth stand out.

l. 633 *second-sight:* visionary.

l. 644 *type:* emblem; anticipation or imperfect symbol.

l. 649 Compare the blind beggar to the figure of the Leech-gatherer in the 1802 "Resolution and Independence" (p. 449). In both instances, Wordsworth is admonished from another world.

l. 678 St. Bartholomew's fair was one of the largest of the London fairs. Wordsworth and Dorothy visited it in 1802.

l. 695 *roundabouts:* merry-go-rounds.

l. 700 *hurdy-gurdy:* a stringed instrument, resembling a lute or guitar.

l. 701 *salt-box:* a wooden box containing salt, rattled or beaten.

l. 703 *timbrel:* tambourine.

l. 715 *Promethean:* inventive. The Titan Prometheus was said to have fashioned humans out of clay. He also stole fire from the gods and gave it to humans, allowing for the development of civilization.

l. 716 The passage alludes to Milton's depiction of Hell in *Paradise Lost,* II.624–25.

l. 719 *mill:* factory.

l. 727 *differences:* perceived differences, appearances, which do not coalesce into a meaningful pattern.

BOOK EIGHTH (P. 285)

l. 1 *Helvellyn:* peak (3,118 feet) in the Lake District.

l. 21 *byre:* cowshed; *kine:* cattle.

l. 22 *cotes:* sheds for sheltering animals; *chaffering:* bargaining.

l. 32 *speech-maker:* barker.

l. 33 *raree-show:* peep show.

ll. 48–52 from "Malvern Hills," by Joseph Cottle (1798).

l. 55 *want:* lack.

l. 56 *circumambient:* encompassing, environing.

l. 74 Wordsworth had originally composed a section of fifty-five lines, which were included in the 1805 version of *The Prelude,* but cut from Book Eighth in 1838–39. The lines recount the seemingly miraculous appearance of two shepherds.

l. 76 *famed paradise:* Gehol (l. 77), pleasure gardens of the emperor of Gehol, called in Chinese the "paradise of innumerable trees."

l. 80 *China's stupendous mound:* Great Wall of China.

l. 89 *obsequious:* obedient, compliant.

l. 112 *transport:* elation.

l. 118 *all without regard:* without being noticed.

l. 121 *affections:* feelings.

l. 129 Saturn created the Golden Age in Latium (Italy) after being deposed by his son, Jupiter. Lines 129–44 contain examples of legendary literary pastoral scenes, to which the rustic pastoral setting of Wordsworth's Westmorland forms a contrast.

l. 133 *Arcadian:* Arcadia is the traditional setting of Greek and Latin pastoral.

l. 141 *false Ganymede:* Rosalind, from Shakespeare's *As You Like It.*

l. 142 *Perdita and Florizel:* from Shakespeare's *A Winter Tale,* heirs to the thrones of Bohemia and Sicilia, and king and queen of the sheep-shearing feast.

l. 144 *Spenser:* See, especially, "May," in *The Shepheard's Calendar.*

l. 152 *kirk-pillar:* church pillar.

l. 162 *substantial needs:* basic needs, for sustenance.

l. 172 Wordsworth composed eighty-nine lines, containing a story that illustrates the "tragedies of former time, / Hazards and strange escapes, of which the rocks / Immutable, and everflowing streams, / Where'er I roamed, were speaking monuments" (ll. 169–72). He deleted the lines, originally composed for "Michael" (1800) and incorporated into the 1805 version of *The Prelude*, in 1816–17. The tale narrates the journey of a shepherd and his son to retrieve a lost sheep. See *The Prelude* (1805), Book Eighth, ll. 222–311.

ll. 175–84 *Galesus* and *Clitumnus* are rivers in Calabria; *Adria* is the Adriatic coast of Italy; *Lucretilis* is the Latin name for Monte Gennaro, the hill above Horace's Sabine farm; *tutelary music:* music produced by Pan as guardian deity. These lines attest to Wordsworth's interest in and knowledge of Latin verse.

l. 185 *fold:* sheepfold.

l. 197 *rolling hut:* a small hut on wheels, allowing the shepherd to stay with his flock.

l. 200 *flageolet:* recorder or pipe.

l. 211 *Goslar:* the city in Germany where Wordsworth passed the winter of 1798–99, and began composition of *The Prelude*.

l. 215 *Hercynian forest:* Roman name for vast forests in western Germany.

l. 256 *native man:* human nature.

l. 266 Alludes to Thomson's *The Seasons,* III.725–27, where the mist magnifies the shepherd into a giant: "seen through the turbid air beyond the life / Objects appear, and, wildered, o'er the waste / The shepherd stalks gigantic."

ll. 285, 287 *Corin* and *Phyllis* are shepherd figures in Latin pastoral poetry; *coronal:* ring formed by dancers.

l. 288 *for the purposes of kind:* by nature.

l. 352 *viewless:* invisible.

l. 364 *circumfuse:* surround on all sides, to bathe in.

l. 382 *golden mean:* avoidance of excess in either direction.

l. 392 *obliquities:* aberration; error; deviation from the right path.

ll. 384–91; 402–6 Wordsworth's youthful attraction to pathos and pathos-ridden figures is evident in his early work. See, for example, the female vagrant passage in "An Evening Walk" (p. 3), ll. 239–300.

l. 455 *unconscious:* thoughtless, carefree.

l. 459 *Thurstonmere:* name for Conistonwater, a lake near Hawkshead.

l. 496 *temporal shapes:* worldly shapes, reality, as opposed to "idea, or abstraction of the kind" (l. 502).

l. 505 *Has been set forth:* In Book Third.

l. 506 *superficial life:* daily life and casual experience of the world.

l. 541 *thridded:* threaded through.

l. 547 *Mean:* roughshod.

l. 562 *Grotto of Antiparos:* a cave of vast dimension, on the Greek island Antiparos, hailed as a natural curiosity.

l. 564 *Yordas:* a cave near Ingleton in Yorkshire, much smaller than the Grotto of Antipos, however. Wordsworth and his brother, John, visited Yordas in 1800.

l. 580 *senseless mass:* meaningless, chaotic image.

l. 610 *punctual presence:* confined in space and time to a single point, *punctus.*

l. 614 *scattered wreck sublime:* in particular, the Druidic ruins and magalithic circles.

l. 620 *their:* ungrammatical pronoun, due to cutting of plural antecedent, "Events," in lines 772–73 in the 1805 *Prelude.*

ll. 660–64 These lines reproduce *Paradise Lost,* XI.203–7. In 1804, Wordsworth enclosed lines 663–64 in quotation marks to signal his allusion.

BOOK NINTH (P. 304)

l. 28 *Scarcely was a year thus spent:* Wordsworth actually spent only four months in London in 1791.

l. 36 *script and staff:* In *Memoirs* I, p. 14 (1847), Wordsworth recalled: "We went staff in hand, and carrying each his needments tied up in a pocket handkerchief."

l. 40 *pleasant town:* Orléans, where Wordsworth stayed briefly from December 1791 to January or February 1792, and where he met Annette Vallon.

ll. 45–49 These lines refer to places in Paris associated with the Revolution: *the field of Mars:* place where the *Fête de la Fédération* had been held, July 14, 1790; *suburbs of St. Anthony:* Faubourg St. Antonie, the militant working-class district next to the Bastille; *Mount Martre:* Revolutionary meeting place; *Dome of Geneviève:* The Panthéon, where the Comte de Mirabeau, the great Revolutionary statesman and orator, was buried. Voltaire and Rousseau were reburied in the same spot; *National Synod:* meeting place of the National Assembly; *the Jacobins:* Jacobin Club, meeting place of the radical Jacobins, who would wrest power from the more moderate Girondins in 1793.

l. 51 *Toss like a ship at anchor:* though turbulent and momentous, the Revolution was still peaceful in 1790.

l. 58 *hubbub wild:* see Milton's description of Chaos in *Paradise Lost,* II.951.

l. 77 *Magdalene of Le Brun:* painting by Charles Le Brun.

l. 97 *master pamphlets of the day:* Edmund Burke's *Reflections on the Revolution in France* and responses to it, such as Thomas Paine's *The Rights of Man,* Part I, and James Mackintosh's *Vinciciae Gallicae.*

l. 102 *organs:* instruments.

ll. 107–10 After an initial period of violence, the Revolution continued peacefully until the massacre of Royalist prisoners in August 1792. The Reign of Terror began in July 1793.

l. 117 *punctilio:* nice point of behavior, ceremony; petty formality.

l. 123 *patriot:* supporter of the Revolution.

l. 129 *chivalry:* nobility, aristocracy.

l. 132 *One:* Michel Beaupuis. A long passage on Beaupuis begins in line 287.

l. 176 *Carra, Gorsas:* Carra and Gorsas were deputies of the National Assembly. They were associated with the Girondins, who also had Wordsworth's sympathies. Both were influential journalists, and executed by Robespierre on October 7 and 31, 1793, respectively. Wordsworth later claimed to have been present in Paris for the execution of Gorsas. Traveling to France in 1793 would have been a very risky and difficult undertaking, for France and England were at war. If Wordsworth made such a trip, it was probably to join Annette Vallon and see their daughter, Anne Caroline Wordsworth.

l. 188 By April 1792, more than half the 9,000 French army officers had deserted to join the émigrés, the "band of emigrants in arms" (l. 183), who were preparing to attack the Revolutionary forces and to restore France to its pre-Revolutionary state.

l. 266 France declared war against Austria on April 20, 1792.

l. 287 This marks the beginning of a long passage devoted to Michel Beaupuy, a man for whom Wordsworth had enduring respect and affection. Beaupuy died in battle in October 1796. See lines 424–27.

l. 288 *mould:* cast, mold.

l. 295 *sensibly,* in a way apparent to the senses.

l. 318 *Complacently:* with enjoyment.

ll. 332–33 *a sounder judgment/Than later days allowed:* Wordsworth refers to his emotional distress in 1793–95.

ll. 392–93 *Rotha, Gretta,* and *Derwent* are rivers in the Lake District.

l. 398 *nature:* human nature.

l. 409 *Dion:* Pupil of Plato and a model of the philosopher-king, deposed Dionysis, tyrant of Syracuse, the "Sicilian Tyrant" (l. 415), in 357 B.C.

l. 412 *Eudemus* and *Timonides:* Eudemus Cyprian and Timonides Leucadian, who supported Dion in his liberation of Sicily, and sailed in the two vessels of line 414.

l. 416 *Zacynthus:* Ionian island of Zante.

ll. 450, 452 *Angelica, Erminia:* heroines of two famous Italian romantic epics, Lucovico Ariosto's *Orlando Furioso* and Torquato Tasso's *Gerusalemme Liberata.*

ll. 464–78 Wordsworth voices his sorrow over the destruction of the abbeys and churches. See also comments on the Grande Chartreuse in "Descriptive Sketches," ll. 53–79, and *The Prelude,* Book Sixth, ll. 418–35.

l. 466 *roofless pile:* ruin.

l. 481 *Romorentin:* small town in the Loire region.

l. 491 *Chambord:* château in the Loire valley, built by Francis I.

l. 546 Wordsworth refers to the tale of the lovers Vaudracour and Julia, recounted in lines 556–935 in the 1805 version of *The Prelude,* and published as a separate poem in 1820. Wordsworth deleted the tale from *The Prelude* in 1832. It is possible that Beaupuy, the "Patriot friend" (l. 547) told this story to Wordsworth, and the events recounted may have occurred at Blois, where Wordsworth had moved, early in 1792, to be close to Annette, who, by March, would be pregnant. In the tale of the lovers, Julia conceives a child out of wedlock by Vaudracour. The lovers wish to marry, but Vaudracour's father refuses to provide money that would make the union possible, and even puts his son under a warrant of arrest, which, when executed, results in the death of one of the assailants at Vaudracour's hand. Julia is eventually sent to a convent. The child, who cannot accompany its mother, remains with Vaudracour, and soon dies. From that time, Vaudracour "never uttered a word/To any living" (ll. 912–13), and in the 1850 version, he is reduced to insanity, "an imbecile mind" (l. 585).

The story of Vaudracour and Julia is often taken to be an oblique handling of Wordsworth's affair with Annette Vallon. Like Vaudracour, for example, Wordsworth's relatives prevented him from marrying his mistress, when they refused to aid him in attaining the curacy that he had earlier spurned. Without money and without occupation, Wordsworth would have been without means to marry and bring Annette to England. The declaration of war in 1793 posed another severe impediment. If Wordsworth returned to France in 1793, as he may have done (see note to l. 176, above), he was certainly unable to see Annette, and the two did not meet again until 1802, during the peace of Amiens, when travel between the countries became possible. Wordsworth married Mary Hutchinson later that same year.

l. 555 *love-knot:* ribbon tied in a particular way and worn as a sign of love.

BOOK TENTH (P. 320)

l. 12 *The King had fallen:* Louis XVI was deposed on August 10, 1792. France was invaded by Austrian and Prussian troops, who sought to restore him to the throne, on August 19. After the battle at Valmy, the invaders retreated, and the threat to the Republic was, thus, rendered "innocuous" (l. 16).

l. 19 *Agra and Lahore:* refers to *Paradise Lost,* XI.391.

l. 41 France became a republic, abandoning the constitutional monarchy declared in 1798, on September 22, 1792.

l. 57 These lines refer to the massacre by the Swiss guard in 1792 of some four hundred attackers on the Tuileries, Louis XVI's residence in Paris. The Swiss guard were massacred in their turn by the attackers when Louis ordered them to lay down their arms. The bodies of the dead were burned at the Place de Carrousel, a square in front of the Tuileries. Louis was executed on January 21, 1793.

l. 73 *September massacres:* massacre of prisoners in Paris suspected of being Royalist sympathizers, by an angry mob, September 2–6, 1792.

l. 87 *"Sleep no more":* See *Macbeth,* II.ii.35–36.

l. 101 *Maximilian Robespierre:* Robespierre was denounced by Jean-Baptiste Louvet as a would-be dictator in October 1792, in the National Convention. Louvet published a pamphlet, which these lines suggest Wordsworth must have seen. Robespierre seized control of the Revolutionary government in July 1793, inaugurating the Reign of Terror.

l. 127 *arbitrement:* arbitration.

ll. 198, 199, 200 *Harmodius* and *Aristogiton:* Athenian noblemen who died leading a rebellion against the tyrant Hippias of Athens in 514 B.C.; *Brutus* played an important part in the assassination of Caesar in 44 B.C.

l. 212 *impious crests:* factions vying for power.

ll. 224–25 Wordsworth is circumspect about the real circumstances prompting his return, the need for money to support himself, Annette, and their expected child.

l. 230 Wordsworth refers to his sympathy for the moderate Girondins, almost all of whom, like Wordsworth's acquaintances among their number, Gorsas and Carra, were executed in 1793; *haply:* perhaps.

l. 245 A Society for the Abolition of the Slave Trade had been founded in 1787. A bill to prohibit the trade in slaves under the British flag was passed in 1792 by the House of Commons, but rejected by the House of Lords. The slave trade was outlawed in 1807.

ll. 268–99 These lines describe the mental crisis Wordsworth suffered upon his return to England in the late fall of 1792 and which was exacerbated by the declarations of war by France and England in February 1793. Wordsworth was beset with worries about money, and had doubts about the course his future life would take; he did not settle decisively on poetry as his life's work, his sole "office upon earth" (XI.347), until early 1797. His ardent sympathies with the aims of the French Revolution, sustained even in the face of mounting violence in France, put him at odds with the prevailing sentiments in England. In 1793, in the guise of "A Republican," Wordsworth composed his "Letter to the Bishop of Llandaff," in which he spoke out passionately against monarchy and aristocracy. In the political climate of the day, this pamphlet could well have come under scrutiny for sedition or even treason, and its author could have faced deportation to Australia or execution. The "Letter," however, remained unpublished, probably due to Joseph Johnson's apprehensions about the consequences of publication both to author and publisher. Wordsworth's crisis was deepened by his separation from Annette and their daughter, Anne Caroline, born shortly after his departure from France in search of funds, and war between the two countries meant protracted separation between the lovers. Wordsworth's life continued unsettled until he took up residence with Dorothy at Racedown Lodge in 1795.

ll. 315–30 These lines describe Wordsworth's observation of the navel fleet at Portsmouth preparing for war, during the month he passed on the Isle of Wight in 1793, prior to embarking on the walking tour that would take him across Salisbury Plain.

l. 373 *front:* face; *amain:* vigorously.

l. 381 *wife of Roland:* major influence behind the Girondins. She was imprisoned in

June 1793, and executed in November. Wordsworth praises her composure at the hour of her death, and refers to her final words: "Oh Liberty, what crimes are committed in thy name."

l. 430 *second love:* love of humankind.

l. 491 Wordsworth traveled through France in the early days of the Revolution, on his walking tour through the Alps with Robert Jones in 1790. See also "Descriptive Sketches."

l. 502 As the Revolution became ever more radical and far-reaching in its aims, it turned against religious expression and practice.

l. 507 *King Lear,* III.ii.16: "I tax not you, you elements, with unkindness."

l. 515 *Leven's ample estuary:* estuary of the river Leven in the Lake District.

l. 520 *Creatures:* creations.

l. 521 *consistory:* council.

l. 522 *seraphs:* highest order of angels.

l. 523 *empyrean:* highest heaven.

l. 526 *fulgent:* shining, brilliant. Wordsworth's word choices are consistently Miltonic throughout this passage, as Wordsworth glances back to the happiness of childhood from the perspective of distress in 1793.

l. 534 *honoured teacher:* the Reverend William Taylor, headmaster of Hawkshead Grammar School, where Wordsworth was a pupil from 1779–83. Taylor died in 1786, at the age of thirty-two.

l. 536 *elegy of Gray:* Thomas Gray's "Elegy Written in a Country Churchyard," published in 1750.

ll. 548–52 Although the strictures of a classical education such as Wordsworth received at Hawkshead limited the curriculum to the study and translation of Greek and Latin texts, Taylor encouraged his students to read works by contemporary poets, such as Gray, Collins, and Thomson.

l. 573 Robespierre was executed on July 28, 1794. His death was reported in England on August 16.

l. 585 *Augean stable:* Hercules cleansed the stables of King Augeas by diverting the rivers Alpheus and Peneus.

l. 586 *their own helper:* the guillotine, preferred method of execution in France.

ll. 595–603 These lines recapitulate II.94–137. Line 603 repeats verbatim II.137.

BOOK ELEVENTH (P. 336)

In 1832 Wordsworth divided what had been Book Tenth in the 1805 version of *The Prelude* into Books Tenth and Eleventh of the 1850 version.

l. 2 *milder face:* The Reign of Terror came to a close with the execution of Robespierre in July 1784.

l. 10 *heartless:* disheartening.

ll. 18–21 Wordsworth believed at the time that the "great, universal, irresistible"

(l. 17) success of the Revolution of France would lead to a second but peaceful incarnation of its principles in England.

l. 24 *same in quality:* Wordsworth describes his conviction that his opposition to England's war with France was, in quality, the same as his love of his country and its deep and historic commitment to liberty.

l. 25 *two spirits:* France and England. France is "the better," of line 26, and England "the worse," of lines 24–25. Wordsworth recalls his belief in 1794 that war between England and France would only strengthen France's resolve and hence further the Revolution.

l. 38 *tower:* Tower of Babel.

ll. 52–73 This passage alludes to the repressive measures taken by the government in England to suppress any expression of disagreement with its principles and actions, and to prevent what it feared as the spread of radicalism and Jacobinism in England. Parliament passed the Two Acts, and suspended *habeas corpus* in 1794. Wordsworth and Coleridge themselves came under the scrutiny of the Home Office in 1797, when a spy was sent to observe their activities. In chapter ten of the *Biographia Literaria,* Coleridge lightheartedly spoofed this attempt on the part of the government to gather information on the two men, supposed to be in league with the French, by imagining that the friends' discussions of the philosopher Spinoza would have been reported to the Home Office as the radicals' talk of "Spy Nozy."

ll. 74–172 These lines recap events and Wordsworth's feeling in 1792, when he was in residence in France, prior to the degeneration of the Revolution into violent infighting.

ll. 105–44 These lines were published in 1809 in Coleridge's periodical, *The Friend,* titled "French Revolution, as it appeared to Enthusiasts at its Commencement." The final lines of the passage gave proof to those among the second generation of Romantic writers, such as Percy Bysshe Shelly, that Wordsworth's early idealism had lapsed into resigned acceptance of things as they are.

l. 106 *auxiliars:* helpers

l. 122 *temper:* temperament.

l. 124 *rapt away:* enraptured.

l. 136 *'both':* refers to the two tempers described in lines 125–35, one of lofty and wild imagination (ll. 125–32) and the other more sedate (ll. 132–35).

l. 138 *plastic:* malleable.

l. 153 *active partisan:* supporter of the Revolution.

l. 175 England declared war on France on February 11, 1793.

l. 208 France began aggressive campaigns against Spain, Italy, and Belgium. This was a departure from the renunciation of conquest of foreign territory, put forth in the constitution of May 1790.

ll. 225–26 *promised to abstract the hopes of Man / Out of his feelings:* Wordsworth criticizes in retrospect the work of William Godwin, in *An Enquiry Concerning Political Justice* (1793), for its reliance on reason, the "purer element" of line 227, as a fulcrum on which the perfection of humankind could be based. Lines 235–44 draw on language from Wordsworth's play *The Borderers* (completed 1797), in which he gave expression to his growing distance from Godwin, the second edition of whose *Political Justice* Wordsworth was reading in the spring of 1796.

l. 297 *titles:* deeds to ownership, entitlement.

l. 303 *in fine:* in the end.

l. 328 *abstract science:* mathematics and geometry.

l. 359 This line should read: "And rivet down the gains of France, a Pope."

l. 360 Napoleon was named emperor in May 1804. In December, he brought Pope Pius VII to Paris to crown him. Wordsworth's statements reflect pervasive English anti-Catholicism.

l. 369 *gewgaw:* toy.

l. 375 *thy ear:* Wordsworth read the earliest version of his completed *Prelude* to Coleridge at Christmastime 1806. Coleridge responded with his poem "To William Wordsworth" in 1807 (published 1817).

l. 376 In the fall of 1804, Coleridge was in Sicily, as he returned to England from his stay in Malta. Wordsworth considered Sicily to be a region tainted by endemic superstition and ignorance, in sad contrast with its glory during classical times.

l. 379 *Timoleon:* established a democratic regime in Syracuse, after deposing the tyrant Dionysius in 343 B.C.

l. 387 *now:* 1804.

l. 396 *sanative:* healthful.

l. 400 In 1804, Britain was alone in mounting armed opposition to French aggression.

l. 420 *Enna:* Where Proserpine was kidnapped by Pluto, as she gathered flowers. See *Paradise Lost,* IV.268–71.

ll. 434, 435 *Empedocles:* poet and philosopher; *Archimedes:* mathematician.

l. 437 *Theocritus:* pastoral poet, c. 310–250 B.C.

ll. 443–49 These lines refer to Theocritus' *Idyll,* VII.78–83, relating the story of Comates.

l. 465 *Arethuse:* spring at Syracuse, often named in classical pastoral poetry.

l. 468 *Thou gratulatest:* you rejoice over.

l. 469 *votary:* devotee, worshiper.

BOOK TWELFTH (P. 348)

Book Twelfth corresponds to Book Eleventh in the 1805 version of *The Prelude.*

l. 45 *intellectual:* spiritual.

l. 85 *those mysteries of being:* Wordsworth makes a contrast in his mature thought to the use of reason, by the radicals and revolutionaries, to underpin arguments about innate rights and equality.

l. 121 *insensible:* unresponsive.

l. 151 *a maid:* Mary Hutchinson. Wordsworth married Mary Hutchinson in October 1802. He had known her from childhood.

ll. 208–335 The first version of the "spots of time" passage was composed in the winter of 1799, when Wordsworth was in Germany. It was incorporated into the second book of the two-book *Prelude,* which was completed that year, and expanded into the twelve books of 1805.

l. 222 *outward sense:* the perceptual, observed world.

ll. 230–87 This passage recounts and embroiders on an experience that Wordsworth had at the age of five, when staying with his grandparents at Penrith.

l. 235 *bottom:* valley.

l. 236 *murderer:* The passage conflates two separate murder stories. Wordsworth probably did not see the letters that were said to have been carved into the turf at the spot.

l. 248 *common:* publicly held land.

l. 250 *beacon:* stone signal beacon, built in 1719 on the hill above Penrith.

l. 262 *loved one:* Mary Hutchinson, in 1787. Dorothy was also present on these journeys. See VI.190–251, for a handling of the same events and landscape.

ll. 287–335 These lines recount events in December 1783, when Wordsworth was a pupil with his brothers Richard and John at Hawkshead Grammar School. Their father, John Wordsworth, died on December 30, 1783.

Book Thirteenth (p. 357)

l. 22 *right reason:* Miltonic term for reason attuned to intellectual, moral, and religious truth stands in contradistinction to application of abstract reason, as discussed in Books Eleventh and Twelfth, and to use of pure reason in mathematical or geometric study.

l. 52 *intellectual:* spiritual.

l. 60 *sanguine:* hopeful.

l. 72 *statists:* politicians or political theorists.

l. 78 *"The Wealth of Nations":* Adam Smith's *Inquiry into the Nature and Causes of the Wealth of Nations* (1776).

l. 104 *My earliest notices:* earliest observations and memories.

ll. 111–12 *distinct regards/And truths of individual sympathy:* lived experience and observation of everyday life.

l. 157 *Bedlamites:* madmen, as might issue from Bethlehem (pronounced "Bedlam") Hospital for the Insane in London.

l. 158 *uncouth:* rough, of the laboring class.

l. 189 *vulgar:* common, ordinary.

ll. 199–200 *pre-occupy the ground/Of the affections:* consume all one's energies and affections, leaving no time or energy for anything else.

l. 212 *effeminately:* in a manner self-indulgent, weak, over-refined; as opposed to manly, which often connotes strength, vigor, and disciplined attention to drawing appropriate distinctions.

l. 233 *the task: The Recluse* (p. 380).

l. 238 *haply:* perhaps.

l. 239 *unadulterated:* uncorrupted.

l. 247 *miserable love:* unrequited love, for example.

l. 275 *them:* Refers to "words," of line 273.

l. 278 *unregarded:* unseen, hidden.

l. 294 *mean:* humble, low.

ll. 314–49 Wordsworth returns in memory to his solitary journey across Salisbury Plain (Sarum's Plain), in 1793. "Guilt and Sorrow," lines 109–26, contains much of the same imagery.

l. 323 *wold:* countryside.

l. 331 *sacrificial alter:* Wordsworth is mistaken in supposing that the Druids performed human sacrifice, and in attributing Stonehenge and other monolithic structures to the Druids.

l. 334 *monumental hillocks:* burial mounds.

l. 339 *divine:* conjecture (transitive verb).

l. 351 *obscurity:* distant reach.

l. 352 *monumental hints:* suggested by the monoliths on Salisbury Plain.

ll. 352–60 Wordsworth recalls the profound impression made on Coleridge by Wordsworth's "Adventures on Salisbury Plain," which Coleridge heard recited in 1795. The poem was later heavily revised into "Guilt and Sorrow" (1842). Coleridge records his response to Wordsworth's poem in Chapter 4 of the *Biographia Literaria,* where he classes the poem with "Tintern Abbey," and praises it in the highest of terms. In "Adventures," Coleridge perceived: "The union of deep feeling with profound thought; the fine balance of truth in observing, with the imaginative faculty in modifying the object observed; and above all the original gift of spreading the tone, the atmosphere, and with it the depth and height of the ideal world around forms, incidents, and situations, of which, for the common view, custom had bedimmed all the lustre, had dried up the sparkle and the dew drops."

l. 361 *partial:* prejudiced, biased by Coleridge's friendship with Wordsworth.

l. 362 Wordsworth and Coleridge were acquainted in 1795 but did not become close friends until 1797.

BOOK FOURTEENTH (P. 367)

The ascent of Mt. Snowdon, recounted in lines 1–129, was made by Wordsworth and his friend Robert Jones (with whom Wordsworth had hiked the Alps in 1790) while on a walking tour through Wales in 1791.

l. 3 *Cambria:* Wales.

l. 4 *Bethgelert's huts:* village at the southern foot of Snowden.

l. 22 *lurcher:* dog.

l. 66 *type:* distinguishing mark, sign, emblem. Wordsworth sees an image of the creative mind in the scene before him; also, by implication, the creative mind impresses (types) itself on the scene.

ll. 71–72 See Milton's description of the Holy Spirit, brooding over Chaos, in *Paradise Lost,* I.22–22. Wordsworth draws on the same imagery in *The Prelude,* I.140–41.

ll. 101–2 Compare to Wordsworth's note to "The Thorn," where he identifies the imagination as the "faculty which produces impressive effects out of simple elements."

l. 106 *sensible:* sense.

l. 132 *genuine liberty:* in contradistinction to the liberty based on abstract reason sought by the Revolutionaries.

l. 193 *feeding source:* source of nourishment.

l. 207 *intellectual:* spiritual.

l. 209 *Dividually:* separately.

l. 233 *elsewhere:* Wordsworth praises Dorothy in "Tintern Abbey," *The Prelude,* Books Sixth and Tenth, "Home at Grasmere" (the piece of writing that was to have been the first book of *The Recluse*), and many other poems.

ll. 245–46 See *Paradise Lost,* IX.490–91.

l. 350 *undomestic:* homeless.

L 354 *Cambrian:* Welsh; Wales was the home of Robert Jones.

l. 355 *Calvert:* Raisley Calvert, brother of Wordsworth's friend William Calvert. Raisley died in 1795, and left a legacy to Wordsworth for the express purpose of freeing him to pursue poetry as his life's work. Raisley's confidence in Wordsworth's potential was important in shaping Wordsworth's emergent sense of himself as a poet. Also see "To the Memory of Raisley Calvert" (p. 518).

l. 387 *gratulant:* expressive of joy.

ll. 388–92 Wordsworth's question refers to his unfinished philosophical poem. *The Recluse,* to which *The Prelude* was to serve as an ancillary component. He remarked to Thomas De Quincey that *The Prelude* "will not be published these many years, and never during my lifetime, till I have finished a larger and more important work to which it is tributary" (March 1804).

ll. 400–7 These lines refer to the joint work of Wordsworth and Coleridge in the spring of 1798. Many of the poems were included in the 1798 edition of *Lyrical Ballads.*

l. 400 *bright-eyed Mariner:* from Coleridge's *The Rime of the Ancient Mariner.*

l. 401 *Lady Christabel:* from Coleridge's poem "Christabel," composed 1797–1801, published 1816.

ll. 404–6 These lines refer to "The Idiot Boy."

l. 407 "The Thorn."

l. 419 *private grief:* the death of Wordsworth's brother John in February 1805.

THE RECLUSE (p. 380)

The Recluse was the title of Wordsworth's projected philosophical poem of epic dimension on Man, Nature, and Human Life (l. 754). Wordsworth first spoke of his intention to write such a poem in March 1798, and the project was enthusiastically endorsed by Coleridge. Wordsworth composed *The Prelude* and *The Excursion* as parts of *The Recluse.* Wordsworth continued to refer to *The Recluse* throughout his life, but he never completed the poem itself. "Home at Grasmere," which was intended as the first book of Part I of *The Recluse,* was begun in 1800, with work continuing through 1806. It was first published in 1888. The poem describes the journey of Wordsworth and his sister, Dorothy, in 1799, to settle at Dove Cottage, in Grasmere, after their return from Germany, and Wordsworth's hope for a new life there.

l. 3 *With paradise before him:* Compare to *Paradise Lost,* XII.646.

l. 79 *only Daughter of my Parents:* Dorothy Wordsworth, who would reside with her brother until her death.

l. 153 Wordsworth describes his and Dorothy's journey into Grasmere in December 1799.

l. 184 *prelusive:* serving as a prelude.

l. 266 *deadly tube:* rifle.

l. 267 *haply:* perhaps.

l. 318 *awful:* awe-inspiring.

l. 334 *bield:* shelter.

l. 481 *lawns:* open ground.

l. 506 *brute:* ass.

l. 548 *whelps:* pups; young of various wild animals.

l. 655 *Pilgrim of the Sea:* John Wordsworth.

l. 658 *Sisters of our hearts:* Mary and Sara Hutchinson; Mary and Wordsworth married in 1802.

l. 659 *Brother of our hearts:* Coleridge.

ll. 754–860 These lines were published in 1814, with *The Excursion,* as the Prospectus to *The Recluse.* They represent one of Wordsworth's most extended statements of his highest aspirations as a poet and articulation of the means and ends of poetry itself. The lines are explicitly Miltonic, and Wordsworth's allusions suggest his confidence that his own projected work in *The Recluse* will both continue and surpass Milton's work.

l. 776 *numerous:* metrical; see *Paradise Lost,* V.150.

l. 776 *"fit audience let me find though few":* This line echoes *Paradise Lost,* VII.30–31.

l. 778 *Urania:* The muse to whom Milton made appeal in *Paradise Lost.*

l. 787 *empyreal thrones:* thrones of highest heaven. See *Paradise Lost,* II.430.

l. 788 *Chaos:* the primal region out of which God, by means of the Holy Spirit, created the world. See *Paradise Lost,* Book I.

l. 789 *Erebus:* place of darkness between earth and Hades in Greek myth; also, the first child of Chaos, in Hesiod's *Theogony.*

ll. 792–94 Wordsworth elevates the mind of man into an appropriate subject for epic, and casts his own endeavor to look into his mind and that of human-kind as itself heroic.

ll. 799–824 Compare to *Paradise Lost,* I.14–16.

l. 824 *high argument: Paradise Lost,* I.24.

l. 839 *metropolitan:* belonging to or constituting the home country; ruling.

l. 850 *transitory Being:* Wordsworth himself.

"THE BROTHERS" (P. 402)

Begun in December 1799, completed in early 1800, and published in Volume 2 of *Lyrical Ballads* (1800). Wordsworth wrote of the poem: "This poem was intended to be the concluding poem of a series of pastorals, the scene of which was laid among the mountains of Cumberland and Westmorland. I mention this to apologise for the abruptness with which the poem begins." Wordsworth men-tioned the poem in the 1802 version of the Preface to *Lyrical Ballads.*

l. 16 *homely:* simple; *Ennerdale:* vale in the Lake District.

l. 65 "This description of the Calenture [a tropical fever, ll. 54–65] is sketched from an imperfect recollection of an admirable one in prose, by Mr. Gilbert, author of the Hurricane." Wordsworth's note.

ll. 143–45 "The impressive circumstance here described, actually took place some years ago in this country, upon an eminence called Kidstow Pike, one of the highest of the mountains that surround Hawes-water. The summit of the Pike was stricken by lightning; and every trace of one of the fountains disappeared, while the other continued to flow as before." Wordsworth's note (note to 1800–05 editions).

l. 267 *piety:* filial responsibility.

"MICHAEL" (P. 414)

Composed late in 1800; published in Volume 2 of *Lyrical Ballads* (1800), where it formed the final work in the volume. To Isabella Fenwick, Wordsworth remarked: "The character and circumstances of Luke were taken from a family to whom had belonged, many years before, the house we lived in at Town-end, along with some fields and woodlands on the eastern shore of Grasmere. The name of the Evening Star was not in fact given to this house but to another on the same side of the val-ley more to the north." Wordsworth commented on the poem in a letter to Thomas Poole (April 9, 1801). "I have attempted to give a picture of a man, of strong mind and lively sensibility, agitated by two of the most powerful affections of the human heart; the paternal affection, and the love of property, *landed* property, including the feelings of inheritance, home, and personal and family independence." He made a similar point in a letter to Charles James Fox (January 14, 1801), to whom he sent a copy of *Lyrical Ballads* (1800). Wordsworth comments that the "most calamitous effect, which has followed the measures which have lately been pursued in this country, is a rapid decay of the domestic affections among the lower orders of society." This decay has been produced, Wordsworth argues, by forces tending to decrease the value of labor. In "The Brothers" and "Michael," Wordsworth tells Fox that he has "attempted to draw a picture of the domestic affections as I know they exist amongst a class of men who are now almost confined to the North of England. They are small independent proprietors of land here called statesmen, men of respectable education who daily labour on their own little properties.... Their little tract of land serves as a kind of permanent rallying point for their domestic feelings, as a tablet upon which they are written which makes them objects of memory in a thousand instances when they would otherwise be forgotten."

l. 2 *Greenhead Ghyll:* located at the east end of Grasmere. A ghyll is a steep, narrow valley.
l. 11 *kites:* birds of prey.
l. 28 *careless:* taking little interest in.
l. 35 *rude:* of simple subject matter.
l. 111 *uncouth:* rustic.
l. 169 *Clipping Tree:* "Clipping is the word used in the north of England for shearing." Wordsworth's note.
ll. 210–11 *bound/In surety for his brother's son:* Michael has pledged his property as collateral, allowing his nephew to borrow money.
l. 217 *substance:* personal worth.
l. 252 *repair this loss:* repay the debt.
l. 324 *Sheepfold:* "A sheepfold in these mountains is an unroofed building of stone walls, with different divisions. It is generally placed by the side of a brook." Wordsworth's note. (1802–05).

"THE PET-LAMB" (P. 427)
Composed 1800; published in *Lyrical Ballads* (1800).

l. 5 *kine:* cattle.
l. 13 *Barbara Lewthwaite:* To Isabella Fenwick, Wordsworth remarked: "Barbara Lewthwaite, now [1842] living at Ambleside, though much changed as to beauty, was one of two most lovely sisters.... Barbara Lewthwaite was not in fact the child whom I had seen and overheard as engaged in the poem. I chose the name for reasons implied above."

"THE WATERFALL AND THE EGLANTINE" (P. 429)
Composed in 1800; published in *Lyrical Ballads* (1800).

l. 1 *fond:* foolish.
l. 14 *fibres:* small roots.

"THE OAK AND THE BROOM" (P. 431)
Composed in 1800; published in *Lyrical Ballads* (1800).

"HART-LEAP WELL" (P. 435)
Composed in 1800; published in *Lyrical Ballads* (1800). To Isabella Fenwick, Wordsworth recalled: "The first eight stanzas were composed extempore one winter evening in the cottage; when, after having tired myself with labouring at an awkward passage in 'The Brothers', I started with a sudden impulse to this to get rid of the other, and finished it in a day or two. My sister and I had past the place a few weeks before in our wild winter journey from Sockburn on the banks of the Tees to Grasmere. A peasant whom we met near the spot told us the story so far as concerned the name of the well, and the hart, and pointed out the stones. Both the stones and the well are objects that may easily be missed; the tradition by this time may be extinct in the neighbourhood: the man who related it to us was very old."

l. 33 *thorn:* thorn tree or bush, probably a hawthorn.
l. 59 *cot:* cottage.
l. 97 *moving accident:* See *Othello,* I.iii.135.

"THE CHILDLESS FATHER" (P. 440)
Composed in 1800; published in *Lyrical Ballads* (1800). To Isabella Fenwick, Wordsworth remarked: "When I was a child at Cockermouth, no funeral took place without a basin filled with sprigs of boxwood being placed upon a table covered with a white clothe in front of the house. The huntings on foot, in which the old man is supposed to join as here described, were of common, almost habitual, occurrence in our vales when I was a boy; and the people took much delight in them. They are now less frequent."

"THE SPARROW'S NEST" (P. 441)
Probably composed in 1802; published in 1807, in *Poems, in Two Volumes.*

l. 9 *Emmeline:* Dorothy Wordsworth.

"THE SAILOR'S MOTHER" (P. 441)
Composed in 1802; published in 1807, in *Poems, in Two Volumes.* Wordsworth told Isabella Fenwick: "I met this woman near the Wishing-Gate, on the high-road

that then led from Grasmere to Ambleside. Her appearance was exactly as here described, and such was her account, nearly to the letter."

"ALICE FELL: OR, POVERTY" (P. 443)
Composed in 1802; published in 1807, in *Poems, in Two Volumes.* Wordsworth told Isabella Fenwick that the poem was written at the request of Mr. Graham of Glasgow. "The incident happened to himself, and he urged me to put it into verse for humanity's sake. The humbleness, meanness if you like, of the subject, together with the homely mode of treating it, brought upon me a world of ridicule by the small critics, so that in policy I excluded it from many editions of my poems, till it was restored at the request of my son-in-law, Edward Quillinan." Dorothy records some of the same circumstances in her journal entry for February 16, 1802.

l. 57 *duffil grey:* coarse, thick woolen cloth.

"TO A BUTTERFLY" (P. 444)
Composed in 1802; published in 1807, in *Poems, in Two Volumes.*

l. 12 *Emmeline:* Dorothy Wordsworth.

" 'MY HEART LEAPS UP WHEN I BEHOLD' " (P. 445)
Composed in 1802; published in 1807, in *Poems, in Two Volumes.*

ll. 7–9 Wordsworth used these lines in 1815 as an epigraph to "Intimations of Immortality" (p. 520), which Wordsworth began the day after its composition.

" 'AMONG ALL LOVELY THINGS MY LOVE HAD BEEN' " (P. 445)
Composed in 1802; published in 1807, in *Poems, in Two Volumes.* Never reprinted in any subsequent collection by Wordsworth. The poem was untitled in 1807, but Dorothy referred to it as "The Glow-Worm," in her journal.

"WRITTEN IN MARCH" (P. 446)
Composed in 1802; published in 1807, in *Poems, in Two Volumes.* See Dorothy's journal (April 16, 1802) for a description of the circumstances of composition and the setting.

"TO A BUTTERFLY" (P. 447)
Composed in 1802; published in 1807, in *Poems, in Two Volumes.*

"TO THE SMALL CELANDINE" (P. 447)
Composed in 1802; published in 1807, in *Poems, in Two Volumes.*

"Resolution and Independence" (p. 449)

Composed in 1802; published in 1807, in *Poems, in Two Volumes.* To Isabella Fenwick, Wordsworth noted: "This old man I met a few hundred yards from my cottage at Town-End, Grasmere; and the account of him is taken from his own mouth. I was in the state of feeling described in the beginning of the poem, while crossing over Barton Fell from Mr. Clarkson's, at the foot of Ullswater, towards Askam. The image of the hare I then observed on the ridge of the Fell." Dorothy recorded the circumstances of the meeting in her journal (October 3, 1800). "When William and I returned from accompanying Jones, we met an old man almost double. He had on a coat, thrown over his shoulders above his waistcoat and coat. Under this he carried a bundle, and had an apron on and a nightcap. His face was interesting. He had dark eyes and a long nose. John, who afterwards met him at Wythburn, took him for a Jew. He was of Scotch parents, but he had been born in the army. He had had a wife, and 'a good woman, and it pleased God to bless us with ten children'. All these were dead but one, of whom he had not heard for many years, a sailor. His trade was to gather leeches, but now leeches are scarce, and he had not the strength for it. He lived by begging, and was making his way to Carlisle, where he should buy a few godly books to sell. He said leeches were very scarce, partly owing to the dry season, but many years they have been scarce. He supposed it owing to their being much sought after, that they did not breed fast and were of slow growth. Leeches were formerly 2s. 6d. [per] 100; now they are 30s."

For the Preface to *Poems* (1815), Wordsworth used the description of the old man in stanzas IX and X to illustrate the imagination "employed upon images in a conjunction by which they modify each other." In the lines cited, Wordsworth writes "the conferring, the abstracting, and the modifying powers of the Imagination, immediately and mediately acting, are all brought into conjunction. The stone is endowed with something of the power of life to approximate it to the sea-beast; and the sea-beast stripped of some of its vital qualities to assimilate it to the stone; which intermediate image is thus treated for the purpose of bringing the original image, that of the stone, to a nearer resemblance to the figure and condition of the aged Man; who is divested of so much of the indications of life and motion as to bring him to the point where the two objects unite and coalesce in just comparison."

ll. 1–49 "A young Poet in the midst of the happiness of Nature is described as overwhelmed by the thought of the miserable reverses which have befallen the happiest of all men, viz. Poets—I think of this till I am so deeply impressed by it, that I consider the manner in which I was rescued from my dejection and despair almost as an interposition of Providence." Wordsworth's note.

l. 39 *genial:* cheerful and creative.

l. 43 *Chatterton:* Thomas Chatteron (1752–70) poisoned himself at the age of seventeen. Compare Wordsworth's poem to Chatterton's "Excellent Ballade of Charitie."

l. 45 *Him:* Robert Burns.

" 'I GRIEVED FOR BUONAPARTÉ' " (P. 454)
Composed in 1802; published on September 16, 1802, in the *Morning Post.*

"A FAREWELL" (P. 454)
Composed in 1802; published in 1814.

l. 1 *little Nook of mountain-ground:* Dove Cottage, in Grasmere.

l. 22 *bright gowan:* globeflower.

l. 25 *one:* Mary Hutchinson.

l. 56 *one song:* "The Sparrow's Nest" (p. 441).

"COMPOSED UPON WESTMINSTER BRIDGE" (P. 456)
Composed in 1802; published in 1807, in *Poems, in Two Volumes.* Wordsworth told Isabella Fenwick that the sonnet was composed "on the roof of a coach on my way to France Sept. 1802." Wordsworth and his sister, Dorothy, were traveling to France during the peace of Amiens, 1802. He wanted to see Annette Vallon and his daughter, Anne Caroline Wordsworth (whom he had never met), prior to his marriage to Mary Hutchinson. Wordsworth used the occasion of this trip to generate subject matter for a number of sonnets commenting on England.

"COMPOSED BY THE SEA-SIDE, NEAR CALAIS" (P. 456)
Published in the *Morning Post,* January 13, 1803.

ll. 1–2 See Matthew 11:7.

ll. 3–7 Napoleon was made first consul for life on August 2, 1802.

" 'IT IS A BEAUTEOUS EVENING, CALM AND FREE' " (P. 457)
Composed in 1802; published in 1807, in *Poems, in Two Volumes.* Wordsworth told Isabella Fenwick that the poem was composed on the beach near Calais. Dorothy records events during the same time: "The weather was very hot. We walked by the seashore almost every evening with Annette and Caroline, or William and I alone."

l. 9 *Dear Child:* Anne Caroline Wordsworth, Wordsworth's daughter by Annette Vallon, born 1792.

l. 12 *Abraham's bosom:* See Luke 16:22.

"ON THE EXTINCTION OF THE VENETIAN REPUBLIC" (P. 458)
Composed in 1802; published in 1807, in *Poems, in Two Volumes.*

ll. 1–2 Venice had been a bulwark against Turkish invasion of Europe, and an important commercial center for the trade in products from the East.
l. 8 *espouse the everlasting Sea:* The doge of Venice wed his city to the Adriatic Sea in an annual ceremony.
l. 12 *final day:* Napoleon had crushed the Venetian Republic in 1797.

"TO TOUSSAINT L'OUVERTURE" (P. 458)
Composed in 1802; published in the *Morning Post,* February 2, 1803. François Dominique Toussaint-Louverture, the son of a black slave in Haiti, led a slave rebellion, which resulted in the abolition of slavery in Haiti in 1793, and served as governor of the island, designated as a protectorate of France. Napoleon reestablished slavery in 1802, and imprisoned Toussaint in Paris, where he died in 1803.

"COMPOSED IN THE VALLEY NEAR DOVER, ON THE DAY OF LANDING" (P. 459)
Composed in 1802; published in 1807, in *Poems, in Two Volumes.*

"NEVER DOVER, SEPTEMBER, 1802" (P. 459)
Composed in 1802; published in 1807, in *Poems, in Two Volumes.*

"IN LONDON, SEPTEMBER, 1802" (P. 460)
Composed in 1802; published in 1807, in *Poems, in Two Volumes.* Wordsworth told Isabella Fenwick that, upon his return from France in 1802, he was struck by "the vanity and parade of our own country, especially in great towns and cities, as contrasted with the quiet, and I may say the desolation, that the revolution had produced in France. This must be borne in mind, or else the reader may think that in this and the succeeding sonnets I have exaggerated the mischief engendered and fostered among us by undisturbed wealth."

l. 1 *Friend:* Coleridge.

"LONDON, 1802" (P. 460)
Composed in 1802; published in 1807, in *Poems, in Two Volumes.*

" 'ENGLAND! THE TIME IS COME WHEN THOU SHOULDS'T WEAN' " (P. 460)
Composed in 1802; published in 1807, in *Poems, in Two Volumes.*

" 'GREAT MEN HAVE BEEN AMONG US' " (P. 461)
Composed in 1802; published in 1807, in *Poems, in Two Volumes.*

ll. 3–4 *Sidney:* Algernon Sidney (1622–83); *Marvell:* Andrew Marvell (1621–78); *Harrington:* James Harrington (1611–77); *Vane:* Sir Henry Vane the Younger (1613–62). The men named were active in the Commonwealth.

" 'IT IS NOT TO BE THOUGHT OF THAT THE FLOOD' " (P. 461)
Composed in 1802; published in the *Morning Post* on April 16, 1803.

l. 4 Samuel Daniel's *Civil Wars,* II.7.

" 'WHEN I HAVE BORNE IN MEMORY' " (P. 462)
Composed in 1802; published in the *Morning Post* on September 17, 1803, titled "England."

"STANZAS" (P. 462)
Composed in 1802; published in 1815. The first four stanzas refer to Wordsworth, the last four to Coleridge.

l. 58 *deftly:* softly, in North Country dialect.

"TO H. C." (P. 464)
Composed in 1802; published in 1807. H. C. is Hartley Coleridge, Coleridge's eldest son.

"THE GREEN LINNET" (P. 465)
Composed in 1802; published in 1807.

"YEW-TREES" (P. 466)
Begun in 1804 (ll. 1–13), completed by 1814; published in 1815.

"STEPPING WESTWARD" (P. 467)
Composed in 1805; published in 1807; subsequently included in "Memorials of a Tour in Scotland, 1803." Dorothy Wordsworth records: "We met two neatly dressed women, without hats, who had probably been taking their Sunday evening's walk. One of them said to us in a friendly, soft tone of voice, 'What! You are stepping westward?' I cannot describe how affecting this simple expression was in that remote place, with the western sky in front, *yet* glowing with the departed sun. William wrote this poem long after in remembrance of his feelings and mine."

"THE SOLITARY REAPER" (P. 468)
Composed in 1805; published in 1807; subsequently included in "Memorials of a Tour in Scotland, 1803." In the 1807 edition, Wordsworth noted that the subject

was suggested by "a beautiful sentence in a MS Tour in Scotland written by a friend, the last line being taken from it *verbatim.*" The friend was Thomas Wilkinson, and his *Tours to the British Mountains* was published in 1824.

"YARROW UNVISITED" (P. 469)

Composed in 1803 and, possibly, 1804; published in 1807; subsequently included in "Memorials of a Tour in Scotland, 1803." Wordsworth sent a copy of this poem to his friend Walter Scott. The river Yarrow was a popular subject for poetry, and Wordsworth's poem makes use of several Scottish ballads: "The Braes of Yarrow," by William Hamilton, and the "Leader Haugh," by Nicol Burne. See also "Yarrow Visited" (p. 613) and "Yarrow Revisited" (p. 642).

l. 6 Marrow: companion.
l. 37 *Strath:* a wide valley.

"OCTOBER, 1803"; "TO THE MEN OF KENT, OCTOBER, 1803"; "IN THE PASS OF KILLICRANKY"; AND "LINES ON THE EXPECTED INVASION, 1803" (PP. 471–73)

An invasion of England by the French was expected in 1803, following the dissolution of the Peace of Amiens. Like the sonnets of 1802, these sonnets attest to Wordsworth's growing sense of himself as a national poet, ready to intervene in defense of England under stress of its war with France. On his return home from his Scottish tour in the summer of 1803, Wordsworth joined the Grasmere Volunteers, under the command of Lord Lowther. In a letter of October 9, 1803, Dorothy wrote of her brother: "surely there never was a more determined hater of the French nor one more willing to do his utmost to destroy them if they really do come."

"LINES ON THE EXPECTED INVASION, 1803" (P. 473)

l. 3 *Falkland:* Lucius Cary, Second Viscount Falkland (c. 1610–43)
l. 4 *Montrose:* James Graham, First Marquis of Montrose (1612–30). Falkland and Montrose remained loyal to Charles I.
l. 7 *Pyms:* John Pym (1584–1643), like Milton, was a Republican.

"TO THE CUCKOO" (P. 473)

Composed in 1802; published in 1807, in *Poems, in Two Volumes.* In the Preface to the 1815 edition of *Poems,* and in the *Guide to the Lakes,* Wordsworth comments on the imaginative resonance created by the sound of the cuckoo's call.

" 'SHE WAS A PHANTOM OF DELIGHT' " (P. 474)

The subject of the poem is Wordsworth's wife, Mary. To Isabella Fenwick, Wordsworth commented: "The germ of this poem was four lines composed as part of the verses on the Highland Girl. Though beginning in this way, it was written from my heart, as is sufficiently obvious."

l. 22 *machine:* human creature; here, Mary. The word does not carry the connotation of mechanical or machinelike.

" 'I WANDERED LONELY AS A CLOUD' " (P. 475)

Composed between 1804 and 1807; published in 1807, included among "Moods of My Own Mind." The subject of the poem is described in Dorothy's journal entry for April 15, 1802: "I never saw daffodils so beautiful. They grew among the mossy stones about and about them; some rested their heads upon these stones as on a pillow for weariness; and the rest tossed and reeled and danced, and seemed as if they verily laughed with the wind that blew upon them over the lake; they looked so gay, ever glancing, ever changing." The poem was criticized after its appearance in 1807 as demonstrating introspection carried to an exceptional degree, which Coleridge would later term "mental bombast," "thoughts and images too great for the subject," in the context of his critical comments on "Intimations of Immortality," in the *Biographia Literaria.* Poems such as "I Wandered Lonely as a Cloud," and the other poems included in "Moods of My Own Mind," fueled a consensus that Wordsworth's poetry, particularly in its choice of insignificant subjects, indulged its author's ego and abused its readers' patience. As William Hazlitt, one of Wordsworth's most vociferous critics, would put it in 1816, "Mr. Wordsworth would persuade you that the most insignificant objects are interesting in themselves, because he is interested in them" (*Round Table,* "On the Character of Rousseau"). Other poems in this volume included in "Moods of My Own Mind" are "The Sparrow's Nest," "To a Butterfly," "My Heart Leaps Up When I Behold," "Written in March," "To a Butterfly," "To the Cuckoo," and "The Small Celandine."

ll. 7–12 These lines were added in 1815.

ll. 21–22 These lines were written by Mary Wordsworth. To Isabella Fenwick, Wordsworth identified them as "the two best lines" in the poem.

"THE AFFLICTION OF MARGARET" (P. 476)

Composed between 1800 and 1807. The note to Isabella Fenwick places it in 1804, and links it to the well-known story of a widow living in Penrith. Coleridge praised it in the *Biographia Literaria* as a "most affecting composition," which could not be read without the shedding of tears.

"THE SMALL CELANDINE" (P. 478)

Possibly composed in 1803 or 1804; published in 1807, in *Poems, in Two Volumes.*

"ODE TO DUTY" (P. 479)

Largely composed in 1804, about the same time that Wordsworth was at work on "Intimations of Immortality." In the note to Isabella Fenwick, Wordsworth drew attention to similarities between his poem, Gray's "Ode to Adversity," and Horace's "Ode to Fortune." In 1807, line 40 was followed by an additional stanza:

> Yet not the less would I throughout
> Still act according to the voice
> Of my own wish; and feel past doubt
> That my submissiveness was choice:
> Not seeking in the school of pride
> For 'precepts over dignified.'
> Denial and restraint I prize
> No farther than they breed a second Will more wise.

" 'WHEN TO THE ATTRACTIONS OF THE BUSY WORLD' " (P. 481)

Largely composed in 1800, but revised through 1815, when it was first published. To Isabella Fenwick, Wordsworth noted that the fir grove still existed, and was a "favourite haunt" when Wordsworth and his family lived at Town-End, in Grasmere. The poem celebrates Wordsworth's love of his brother John Wordsworth, who visited the Wordsworths at Grasmere, in January 1800. John died at sea in 1805, when the ship whose command he accepted in 1800, the *Earl of Abergavenny*, sank.

l. 55 *cherished Visitant:* John Wordsworth.

l. 67 *Esthwaite's pleasant shore:* Hawkshead School, where Wordsworth and his brothers Richard and John were students.

"ELEGIAC STANZAS" (P. 484)

Composed in 1806; published in 1807. The poem is an elegy for John Wordsworth (died 1805, at sea).

l. 1 *rugged Pile:* Peele Castle, in North Lancashire. Wordsworth visited the region in 1794.

l. 42 *deplore:* mourn.

"TO A YOUNG LADY" (P. 486)

Composed in 1802; published in the *Morning Post,* February 12, 1802. The young lady has been variously identified as Dorothy Wordsworth or Joanna Hutchinson, one of Mary Hutchinson's sisters.

THE WAGGONER (P. 486)

Composed in 1806; published in 1819. Wordsworth claimed that the characters and story were from fact. The poem was published on the heels of *Peter Bell,* also composed many years prior, in hopes of capitalizing on the popular reception of that poem.

CANTO FIRST (P. 486)

l. 26 Compare to Gray's "Elegy Written in a Country Churchyard," line 8: "And drowsy tinklings lull the distant folds."

l. 53 DOVE *and* OLIVE-BOUGH: Dove Cottage, once an inn.

l. 88 SWAN: an inn near Grasmere.

l. 210 *Dunmail:* the last king of Cumberland, supposed to be buried under a pile of stones by the road from Grasmere to Keswick.

CANTO SECOND (P. 493)

l. 6 *crazy:* damaged.

l. 42 *vibrate:* vacillate.

l. 115 *at the Nile:* Admiral Nelson fought the French at the Battle of the Nile, 1798.

CANTO THIRD (P. 498)

l. 28 Wordsworth supplied about forty-five lines of verse in an 1836 note that he had held back from inclusion in the poem at the time of its publication.

l. 92 *foundrous:* likely to cause to stick fast or break down.

CANTO FOURTH (P. 501)

l. 21 *Ghimmer-crag:* "The crag of the ewe lamb." Wordsworth's note.

l. 123 *pricked:* ridden.

l. 159 *heartless:* disheartened.

"FRENCH REVOLUTION" (P. 509)

These lines were excerpted from *The Prelude* (1850), XI.105–44.

"CHARACTER OF THE HAPPY WARRIOR" (P. 510)

Wordsworth recalled to Isabella Fenwick that the poem was written shortly after hearing of the death of Lord Nelson (October 21, 1805).

l. 63 *approve:* demonstrate.

"STAR-GAZERS" (P. 512)

l. 21 *rude:* unpolished, unlearned.

" 'NUNS FRET NOT AT THEIR CONVENT'S NARROW ROOM' " (P. 513)

Composed in 1802; published in 1807, in *Poems, in Two Volumes.*

l. 6 *Furness-fells:* hills west of Lake Windermere.

"PERSONAL TALK" (P. 514)
Composed between 1802 and 1804; published in 1807, in *Poems, in Two Volumes.*

l. 7 *Forms:* lines drawn on the floor to guide dancers.
l. 41 *The gentle Lady:* Desdemona, in *Othello.*
l. 42 *Una:* Heroine of Spenser's *The Faerie Queene,* Book I.

"'THE WORLD IS TOO MUCH WITH US; LATE AND SOON'" (P. 515)
Composed between 1802 and 1804; published in 1807, in *Poems, in Two Volumes.*

l. 11 *pleasant lea:* See Spenser's "Colin Clouts Come Home Againe," line 283.
l. 13 *Proteus:* sea god, in Homer, the servant of Poseidon. Echoes *Paradise Lost,* III.603–604.
l. 14 *Triton:* merman of Greek mythology, who blows on a conch.

"'WITH SHIPS THE SEA WAS SPRINKLED FAR AND NIGH'" (P. 516)
Composed between 1802 and 1804; published in 1807, in *Poems, in Two Volumes.*

"'WHERE LIES THE LAND TO WHICH YON SHIP MUST GO?'" (P. 516)
Composed between 1802 and 1804; published in 1807, in *Poems, in Two Volumes.*

"TO SLEEP" (PP. 517–18)
Three sonnets titled "To Sleep" were composed in 1802, and published in 1807, in *Poems, in Two Volumes.*

"TO THE MEMORY OF RAISLEY CALVERT"
Composed in 1802; published in 1807, in *Poems, in Two Volumes.* Raisley Calvert died in 1795, leaving Wordsworth a legacy of £900. See note to *The Prelude,* XIV.355 (p. 720).

"'METHOUGHT I SAW THE FOOTSTEPS OF A THRONE'" (P. 519)
Composed in 1802; published in 1807, in *Poems, in Two Volumes.*

"NOVEMBER, 1806" (P. 519)
Composed late in 1806 or early in 1807; published in 1807, in *Poems, in Two Volumes.*

l. 2 *mighty Empire overthrown:* Prussia, defeated by Napoleon, at the Battle of Jena, October 14, 1806.
l. 3 *We are left, or shall be left, alone:* In 1806, England had become the sole remaining European nation to oppose Napoleon's wars of conquest.

"ODE. INTIMATIONS OF IMMORTALITY FROM RECOLLECTIONS OF EARLY CHILDHOOD" (P. 520)

Composed between 1802 and 1804; published in 1807, in *Poems, in Two Volumes.* Wordsworth's work at the poem was divided into two phases. The first four stanzas, concluding with the question "Whither is fled the visionary gleam?," were written in 1802, probably on the day following his composition of "My Heart Leaps Up When I Behold." The remainder was completed in 1804. The poem forms a rejoinder and companion piece to Coleridge's more pessimistic response to Wordsworth's question about the departure of visionary gleam, "Dejection: An Ode," written in April 1802 and published on Wordsworth's wedding day, October 4, 1802. To Isabella Fenwick, Wordsworth described the Intimations Ode as resting in part on "particular feelings or experiences of my own mind.... Nothing was more difficult for me in childhood than to admit the notion of death as a state applicable to my own being. I have said elsewhere—

> 'A simple child,
> That lightly draws its breath,
> And feels its life in every limb,
> What should it know of death!'

But it was not so much from [feelings] of animal vivacity that my difficulty came as from a sense of the indomitableness of the spirit within me. I used to brood over the stories of Enoch and Elijah, and almost to persuade myself that, whatever might become of others, I should be translated, in something of the same way, to heaven. With a feeling congenial to this, I was often unable to think of external things as having external existence, and I communed with all that I saw as something not apart from, but inherent in, my own immaterial nature. Many times while going to school have I grasped at a wall or tree to recall myself from this abyss of idealism to the reality." Wordsworth continues, noting that the poem's description of vivid childhood experience as intimating a prior state of existence should not be taken as expressing the poet's belief in a doctrine of reincarnation. The poem was harshly criticized by Wordsworth's early readers. Francis Jeffrey, in his *Edinburgh Review* article on the 1807 *Poems, in Two Volumes,* called the ode "beyond all doubt the most illegible and unintelligible part of the [1807 *Poems*]." Coleridge also objected to many aspects of the poem in his *Biographia Literaria,* Chapter 22, censuring the poem's description of the child-philosopher in stanzas VII and VIII. The syntax of the passage is "faulty and equivocal," Coleridge writes. "We will merely ask, what does all this mean? In what sense is a child of that age a *philosopher*? In what sense does he *read* 'the eternal deep'? In what sense is he declared to be *'for ever haunted by the Supreme Being'*? Or so inspired as to deserve the splendid titles of a *mighty prophet,* a *blessed seer*? By reflection? By knowledge? By conscious intuition? Or by any form or modification of consciousness? ... Children at this age give us no such information of themselves; and at what time were we dipt in the Lethe, which has produced such utter oblivion of a state so godlike?" Coleridge continues: "In what sense can the magnificent attributes, above quoted, be appropriated to a *child*, which would not make them equally suitable to a *bee*, or a *dog*, or a *field of corn*; or even to a ship, or to the wind and waves that propel it? The omnipresent Spirit works equally in *them*, as in the child; and the child is equally unconscious of it as they." Wordsworth considered the Intimations Ode as one of the most important of his works, and gave it the final spot in each of the various editions of his collected poetry.

l. 21 *tabor:* small drum.
l. 23 *timely utterance:* refers to Wordsworth's own poem, "My Heart Leaps Up" (p. 445).
l. 86 *the Child:* Hartley Coleridge.
l. 103 *cons:* learns by heart.
l. 120 In the original version, four lines followed, deleted in 1815, in response to criticism by Coleridge, who found their image of lying awake in the grave frightful:

> To whom the grave
> Is but a lonely bed without the sense of sight
> Of day or the warm light,
> A place of thought where we in waiting lie.

l. 132 *nature:* human nature.
ll. 203–4 These lines echo Thomas Gray's "Ode on the Pleasure Arising from Vicissitude," ll. 49–52:

> The meanest floweret of the vale,
> The simplest note that swells the gale,
> The common sun, the air, the skies
> To him are opening Paradise.

"THOUGHT OF A BRITON ON THE SUBJUGATION OF SWITZERLAND" (P. 526)
Composed in 1806 or 1807; published in 1807, in *Poems, in Two Volumes*. Coleridge thought this sonnet "one of the noblest Sonnets in our language" (*The Friend*), and, in a letter of September 27, 1808, Wordsworth referred to it as "being the best I had written."

" 'THOUGH NARROW BE THAT OLD MAN'S CARES' " (P. 526)
Composed in 1806 or early 1807; published in 1807, in *Poems, in Two Volumes*.

"SONG AT THE FEAST OF BROUGHAM CASTLE" (P. 527)
Composed in 1806 or 1807; published in 1807, in *Poems, in Two Volumes*. In a long note appended to the poem in 1807, Wordsworth detailed the historical events

behind its subject, the Wars of the Roses, which involved the Houses of Lancaster and York, from 1455 to 1485.

l. 6 *red rose:* emblem of the House of Lancaster. The white rose was the emblem of the House of York.

l. 7 *thirty years:* 1455–85, the Wars of the Roses.

l. 13 *the two . . . are blended:* The Houses of Lancaster and York were joined through the marriage in 1486 of Henry VII to Elizabeth of York.

l. 122 *the undying fish:* "It is imagined by the people of the Country that there are two immortal Fish, Inhabitants of this Tarn, which lies in the mountains not far from Threlkeld." Wordsworth's note.

THE WHITE DOE OF RYLSTONE (P. 531)

Composed 1807–08; published in 1815. The poem's subject was drawn from local lore, and was informed by Wordsworth's reading among poetry and history of the Lake District. Sources include *The History and Antiquities of the Counties of Westmorland and Cumberland,* by Joseph Nicolson and Richard Burn; *The History and Antiquities of the Deanery of Craven,* by Dr. Thomas Dunham Whitaker; and the ballad, "The Rising of the North," included in Thomas Percy's *Reliques of Ancient English Poetry* (1765). The poem tells the story of the Nortons in the unsuccessful rising of the North, in 1569. Wordsworth provided copious notes to the historical, geographical, and literary sources of the poem.

Following shortly upon Walter Scott's enormously popular and remunerative *Lay of the Last Minstrel,* Wordsworth may have hoped to undertake and publish something that would be well received by reviewers—who had sharply criticized his 1807 *Poems, in Two Volumes*—and by readers. In his comments to Isabella Fenwick, however, Wordsworth called comparisons between *The White Doe* and the *Lay of the Last Minstrel* "inconsiderate," and differentiated between his own and Scott's methods and ends: "Sir Walter pursued the customary and very natural course of conducting an action, presenting various turns of fortune, to some outstanding point on which the mind might rest as a termination or catastrophe. The course I attempted to pursue is entirely different. Everything that is attempted by the principal personages in 'The White Doe' fails, so far as its object is external and substantial. So far as it is moral and spiritual it succeeds." Wordsworth went to London in 1808 to negotiate for publication with Longman, and with Coleridge's intervention, Longman finally agreed to Wordsworth's terms. Wordsworth, however, soon withdrew the poem from Longman, and published nothing more until 1814, when *The Excursion* appeared.

CANTO FIRST (P. 531)

l. 6 *Wharf:* the river running beside Bolton Abbey.

l. 18 *Pile:* ruin.

l. 36 *prelusive:* serving as a prelude to.

l. 203 *couchant:* resting.

l. 244 *griesly:* grisly.

l. 260 *frontlet:* an ornament or band worn on the forehead.

l. 268 *Shepherd-lord:* "Song at the Feast of Brougham Castle, upon the Restoration of Lord Clifford, the Shepherd, to the Estates and Honours of his Ancestors." "To that Poem is annexed an account of this personage, chiefly extracted from Burns and Nicholson's History of Cumberland and Westmorland." Wordsworth's note.

l. 294 *Barden:* Barden Tower, two miles from Bolton Priory.

Canto Second (p. 540)

l. 3 *solitary Maid:* Emily.

l. 5 *sylvan Friend:* the white doe.

l. 24 *England's Queen:* Queen Elizabeth.

l. 31 *Percy:* Thomas Percy, Seventh Earl of Northumberland; *Neville:* Earl of Westmorland.

Canto Third (p. 547)

l. 2 *Brancepeth:* "Brancepeth Castle stands near the river Were, a few miles from the city of Durham. It formerly belonged to the Nevilles, Earls of Westmorland. See Dr. Percy's account." Wordsworth's note.

ll. 45–46 *England's Crown / Remains without an Heir:* Queen Elizabeth never married and thus never produced an heir. The uncertainty of succession was one of the factors that prompted the uprising of the North.

l. 74 *blessed Dove:* Holy Spirit.

l. 94 *Saint Cuthburt:* Durham Cathedral.

l. 130 *falchion:* sword.

l. 194 *Dudley:* Ambrose Dudley, Earl of Warwick (c. 1528–90).

l. 207 *Dacre:* Leonard Dacre (d. 1573), one of the leaders of the rebellion.

l. 208 *Howard:* Thomas Howard, Fourth Duke of Norfolk (1536–72.)

l. 221 *Thurston:* "See the Historians for the account of this memorable battle, usually denominated the Battle of the Standard." Wordsworth's note.

l. 235 *that other day:* Henry Percy defeated the Scottish at the Battle of Neville's Cross in 1346.

Canto Fourth (p. 555)

l. 50 *cirque and crescent:* trelliswork circlets and crescents.

l. 132 Her duty is to stand and wait: Compare to Milton's "Sonnet: On His Blindness," l. 14, "They also serve who only stand and wait."

CANTO FIFTH (P. 561)

l. 76 *divide:* separate.

l. 106 *Rood:* crucifix

CANTO SIXTH (P. 566)

l. 33 *oblation:* an offering or sacrifice.

l. 83 *Sir George Bowes:* (1527–80) provost marshal.

l. 144 *Corse:* corpse.

CANTO SEVENTH (P. 571)

Epigraph: Added in 1837, taken from Wordsworth's poem (completed 1827) "Address to Kilchurn Castle," ll. 6–9.

l. 284 *viewless:* invisible.

THE EXCURSION (P. 581)

The Excursion, published in 1814, is a long dramatic poem, structured as an ongoing conversation between three principle speakers: the Wanderer, the Solitary, and the Author. It is divided into nine books, amounting to nearly 9,000 lines of verse. As Wordsworth explains in the 1814 head note to the poem (pp. 581–82), *The Excursion* was intended to form a portion of *The Recluse,* Wordsworth's epic philosophical poem. The central portion of *The Recluse,* which would have consisted of first-person meditations on "Man, Nature, and Society," however, was never completed.

The portion of *The Excursion* here reproduced, Book First, "The Wanderer," was largely completed between 1797 and 1799. The sketch of the Wanderer's history (ll. 108–433) draws heavily on Wordsworth's own biography and interests. In the lengthy comments Wordsworth provided to Isabella Fenwick, he described the character of the Wanderer as "chiefly an idea of what I fancied my own character might have become in his circumstances." However, many components of the Wanderer's character were based on persons of Wordsworth's acquaintance or knowledge. See Wordsworth's note to "Matthew" (p. 696). The tale of Margaret (ll. 434–970) was initially completed as a separate poem in 1797, and titled "The Ruined Cottage." Its concern with tracing the destitution of one of England's rural inhabitants forms a piece with other poems from the same period, such as the "Female Vagrant" portion of "Guilt and Sorrow"; the discharged soldier episode, which was included in *The Prelude,* IV.339–460; and many of the shorter works that were included in *Lyrical Ballads,* such as "The Thorn," "Her Eyes Are Wild," "Simon Lee," and "The Old Cumberland Beggar."

The Excursion was reviled by the second generation Romantic writers, such as the Shelleys, Leigh Hunt, and Byron, and sharply criticized by William Hazlitt in

The Examiner and by Francis Jeffrey, Wordsworth's old nemesis, in the *Edinburgh Review*. It was well received by readers, however, and did much to restore both Wordsworth's confidence and reputation.

BOOK FIRST (P. 582)

ll. 77–80 *Poets . . . Yet wanting the accomplishment of verse:* Compare to Gray's "Elegy Written in a Country Churchyard," l. 59, "Some mute inglorious Milton, here may rest"; also, Wordsworth's "When to the Attractions of the Busy World" (p. 481), ll. 79–80, where John Wordsworth is described as a "*silent* Poet."

l. 85 *nice backwardness:* exaggerated diffidence.

ll. 253–54 *purer elements . . . lines and numbers:* mathematics, geometry.

l. 347 *speak a plainer language:* Compare to Preface to *Lyrical Ballads,* p. 651; "Humble and rustic life was generally chosen, because in that condition the essential passions of the heart find a better soil in which they can attain their maturity, are less under restraint, and speak a plainer and more emphatic language."

l. 384 *untasked:* without work, in retirement.

ll. 500–2 *the good die first . . . Burn to the socket:* Percy Bysshe Shelley included these lines in the Advertisement to his early work *Alastor,* published in 1815.

l. 539 *plague of war:* England's war with France, declared in 1793.

ll. 632–35 *found / In mournful thoughts . . . A power to virtue friendly:* Compare to "Intimations of Immortality," ll. 180–87, in particular, "soothing thoughts that spring / Out of human suffering" (ll. 184–85).

"LAODAMIA" (P. 608)

Published in 1815. Wordsworth derives his story of Laodamia and Protesilaus from the *Aeneid,* Book VI, the *Heroides,* Book XIII, by Ovid, and *Iphigenia in Aulis,* by Eruipides.

l. 3 *infernal Gods:* gods of the underworld.

l. 4 *slaughtered Lord:* Protesilaus.

l. 6 *Jove:* king of the gods.

l. 12 *issue:* return of Protesilaus from the underworld.

l. 16 *corporeal mould:* earthly form.

l. 26 *essayed:* attempted.

l. 27 *unsubstantial Form:* ethereal, ghostly.

l. 59 *redundant:* full, superabundant.

l. 61 *vain:* mere.

l. 65 *conscious Parcæ:* The Fates, conscious of what was transpiring.

l. 71 *Erebus:* region through which the Shades pass on the way to Hades.

l. 77 *Thy transports moderate:* Laodamia is counseled to suppress her enthusiasms.

ll. 79–82 Hercules successfully wrestled with Death for the return to life of Alcestis, to join her husband, Admetus.

ll. 83–84 *Æson:* Jason's father, Aeson, was revived by Medea's spells.

l. 106 *purpureal:* purple.

l. 157 *corse:* corpse.

ll. 158–63 These lines were revised to their present form in 1845. The edition of 1815–20 read:

> Ah, judge her gently who so deeply loved!
> Her, who, in reason's spite, yet without crime,
> Was in a trance of passion thus removed;
> Delivered from the galling yoke of time
> And these frail elements—to gather flowers
> Of blissful quiet 'mid unfading bowers.

In a version of 1827, Wordsworth described Laodamia as "not without crime" and "doomed to wander in a grosser clime." In a letter to his nephew, John Wordsworth, Wordsworth described his revisions to this portion of the poem: "As first written the heroine was dismissed to happiness in Elysium. To what purpose then the mission of Protesilaus? He exhorts her to moderate her passion; the exhortation is fruitless, and no punishment follows."

l. 169 *spiry trees:* "For the account of these long-lived trees, see Pliny's *Natural History,* lib. xvi. Cap. 44; and for the features in the character of Protesilaus see the 'Iphigenia in Aulis' of Euripides. Virgil places the Shade of Laodamia in a mournful region among unhappy Lovers." Wordsworth's note.

"YARROW VISITED" (P. 613)
In a letter to R. P. Gillies (November 23, 1814), Wordsworth wrote: "Second parts, if much inferior to the first, are always disgusting, and as I had succeeded in *Yarrow Unvisited,* I was anxious that there should be no falling off; but that was unavoidable, perhaps, from the subject, as imagination almost always transcends reality." Also see "Yarrow Revisited" (p. 642).

ll. 25–26 *famous flower ... lay bleeding:* See the Scottish ballad "The Dowie Dens of Yarrow," where a slain knight is compared to a fair flower: "A fairer flower I never saw / Then the lad I loved in Yarrow."

ll. 41–48 Wordsworth remarked in a letter to Charles Lamb (April 28, 1815) that "no lovelier stanza can be found in the wide world of poetry."

l. 61 *bower of bliss:* Edmund Spenser's *The Faerie Queene,* II.xii.42.

" 'SURPRISED BY JOY—IMPATIENT AS THE WIND' " (P. 616)
The remembrance in this poem is of Wordsworth's daughter Catherine, who died at the age of three, in 1812.

"ODE TO LYCORIS. MAY, 1817" (P. 616)

The title is drawn from Virgil's tenth Eclogue, in which the poet consoles his friend Gallus for the disappearance of the beautiful shepherdess Lycoris. To Isabella Fenwick, Wordsworth explained that "this poem originated in the four last lines of the first stanza. Those specks of snow, reflected in the lake and so transferred, as it were, to the subaqueous sky, reminded me of the swans which the fancy of the ancient classic poets yoked to the car of Venus. Hence the tenor of the whole first stanza, and the name of Lycoris, which—with some readers who think mythology and classical allusion too far-fetched and therefore more or less unnatural and affected   will tend to unrealize the sentiment that pervades these verses. But surely one who has written so much in verse as I have done may be allowed to retrace his steps in the regions of fancy which delighted him in his boyhood, when he first became acquainted with the Greek and Roman Poets.... No doubt the hackneyed and lifeless use into which mythology fell towards the close of the 17th century, and which continued through the 18th, disgusted the general reader with all allusion to it in modern verse; and though, in deference to this disgust, and also in a measure participate in it, I abstained in my earlier writings from all introduction of pagan fable, surely, even in its humble form, it may ally itself with real sentiment, as I can truly affirm it did in the present case."

l. 4 *front:* forehead.

"COMPOSED UPON AN EVENING OF EXTRAORDINARY SPLENDOUR AND BEAUTY" (P. 618)

Probably composed in 1817. Published in 1820. Wordsworth noted that the poem was "felt and in a great measure composed upon the little mount in front of our abode at Rydal."

l. 49 *Wings at my shoulders seem to play:* "In these lines I am under obligation to the exquisite picture of 'Jacob's Dream', by Mr. Alstone [*sic*], now in America." Wordsworth's note. Washington Allston was an American painter.

l. 80 "The multiplication of mountain-ridges, described at the commencement of the third Stanza of this Ode as a kind of Jacob's Ladder, leading to Heaven, is produced either by watery vapours, or sunny haze;—in the present instance by the latter cause. Allusions to the Ode entitled "Intimations of Immortality" pervade the last Stanza of the foregoing poem." Wordsworth's note.

THE RIVER DUDDON (P. 620)

Published in 1820. The thirty-four sonnets gathered in this sequence were composed between 1806 and 1820, and follow the river Duddon from its source, which Wordsworth imagines "near the noted Shire-stones placed at the meeting-point of the counties, Westmorland, Cumberland, and Lancashire," to its meeting with the sea. Wordsworth provided a lengthy note to Isabella Fenwick on the sequence. "This series of Sonnets was the growth of many years;—the one which stands the 14th was the first produced; and others were added upon occasional visits to the Stream, or as recollections of the scenes upon its banks awakened a wish to describe them. In this manner I had proceeded insensibly, without perceiving that I was trespassing upon ground pre-occupied, at least as far as intention went, by Mr. Coleridge; who, more than twenty years ago, used to speak of writing a rural Poem, to be entitled 'The Brook,' of which he has given a sketch in a recent publication [see *Biographia Literaria,* chapter 10]. But a particular subject cannot, I think, much interfere with a general one; and I have been further kept from encroaching upon any right Mr. C. may still wish to exercise, by the restriction which the frame of the Sonnet imposed upon me, narrowing unavoidably the range of thought, and precluding, though not without its advantages, many graces to which a freer movement of verse would naturally have led." The sequence was lauded by reviewers in 1820. In the *European Magazine,* for example, Wordsworth was hailed as "beyond all comparison the most truly sublime, the most touchingly pathetic, the most delightfully simple, the most profoundly philosophical, of all the poetical spirits of the age." Wordsworth prefaced the sequence with a verse dedication to his brother Christopher, who had been appointed master of Trinity College, Cambridge, "To the Rev. Dr. Wordsworth."

I

l. 4 *Sabine Bard:* Horace.
l. 5 *careless of:* indifferent to.

II

l. 11 *huge deer:* "The deer alluded to is the Leigh, a gigantic species long since extinct." Wordsworth's note.

III

l. 14 *Foster-mother Earth:* Compare to "Intimations of Immortality," stanza VI.

VI, "FLOWERS"

ll. 9–10 *There bloomed the strawberry . . . sapphire blue:* "These two lines are in a great measure taken from 'The Beauties of Spring, a Juvenile Poem,' by the Rev Joseph Sympson. He was native of Cumberland, and was educated at Hawkshead school: his poems are little known, but they contain passages of splendid description; and the versification of his 'Vision of Alfred' is harmonious and animated." Wordworth's note.

XIII, "Open Prospect"
l. 3 *byre:* barn or cowshed.

XIV
Composed in 1804; published in 1807.

l. 3 *nicest:* most exacting.
l. 9 *awful:* awe-inspiring.

XV
l. 11 *rude:* rough.

XVI, "American Tradition"
"See Humboldt's Personal Narrative." Wordsworth's note. Alexander von Humboldt published his *Personal Narrative of Travels to the Equinoctial Regions of the New Continent* in 1814.

l. 2 *sculptured shows:* rock paintings, described by Humbolt.

XVII, "Return"
Wordsworth appended a long note to this sonnet in which he included an extract from Green's *Guide to the Lakes* (Vol. 1, pp. 98–100), and describes various other approaches to the Duddon than that followed by the sonnet sequence, as well as further description of the countryside and its points of interest.

l. 2 *Danish Raven:* flag of the ancient Danes.
l. 3 *imperial Bird of Rome:* the eagle.
l. 10 *that lone Camp:* "The Roman fort here alluded to, called by the country people "Hardknot Castle" is most impressively situated half-way down the hill on the right of the road, that descends from Hardknow into Eskdale." Wordsworth's note.
l. 12 *mystic Round:* "The Druidical Circle is about half a mile to the left of the road ascending Stone-side from the vale of Duddon: the country people call it *Sunken Church.*" Wordsworth's note.

XVIII, "Seathwaite Chapel"
l. 10 *Gospel Teacher:* the Reverend Robert Walker, whose character is detailed at length in Wordsworth's notes.
l. 13 *skill of Herbert:* See George Herbert's *The Temple* (1633), for example.
l. 14 *tender Goldsmith:* See Oliver Goldsmith, *The Deserted Village,* ll. 137–92.

XX, "The Plain of Donnerdale"

l. 10 *cerulean:* deep blue.

l. 13 *Bacchanal:* a follower of Bacchus, god of wine.

l. 14 *thyrsus:* vine-covered staff, topped by a pine-cone, carried by a Bacchanal.

XXIV, "The Resting-Place"

l. 4 *solace of the vagrant reed:* sonnet-writing, pursued as the poet follows the path of the river.

XXVI

Composed in 1803–04.

l. 12 *men are growing out of boys:* Compare to "the child is father of the man," in "My Heart Leaps Up When I Behold" (p. 445).

XXVII

Composed between 1815 and 1819; not published with the original sequence; inserted in 1827. Of this poem, Wordsworth noted to Isabella Fenwick that it refers to the traditional lore of the countryside, which held that the original Rydal Hall was "deserted from the superstitious fear here described."

XXIX

l. 10 *blank earth:* without memorial.

XXX

l. 4 *haply:* perhaps.

XXXIII, "Conclusion"

l. 2 *haughty pendants:* flags, banners.

XXXIV, "After-thought"

l. 7 This line is a translation of Moschus' *Lament for Bion,* l. 102. Wordsworth noted: "The allusion to the Greek poet will be obvious to the Classical reader."

Ecclesiastical Sonnets (p. 635)

This sonnet sequence, published in 1822 as *Ecclesiastical Sketches,* tells the history of the Anglican Church, in 102 sonnets, from its earliest roots in the native beliefs of the island, through the coming of Christianity and the reformation. The sequence concludes in the present day, and was written under pressure of current events. Wordsworth was particularly concerned about efforts to give Roman Catholics rights of full participation in the public and political life of the country. Wordsworth believed that this reform would weaken England's character as a Protestant nation. Robert Southey's massive *Book of the Church* (published in 1824) took up the same subject matter as Wordsworth's sonnets.

Ecclesiastical Sonnets represents a stark reversal in Wordsworth's religious and political beliefs. In 1793, Wordsworth inveighed against the intertwined forces of monarchy, aristocracy, and established religion in his unpublished "Letter to the Bishop of Llandaff." As late as 1812, he told Henry Crabb Robinson that he had no need of a redeemer. But, in 1822, Wordsworth was eager to defend the Church of England as a bulwark against what he perceived as impending anarchy and cultural dissolution in the country.

Part I

I, Introduction

ll. 1–2 refers to the *River Duddon* sequence

ll. 5–6 *nobler Stream to trace / Of Liberty:* "Poems Dedicated to National Independence and Liberty," a section of the 1815 edition of poems, including a number of poems collected in this volume, in particular, the political sonnets of 1802–04 printed above.

III, Trepidation of the Druids

l. 1 *seamew—white:* "This water-fowl was, among the Druids, an emblem of those traditions connected with the Deluge that made an important part of their mysteries. The Cormorant was a bird of bad omen." Wordsworth's note.

l. 2 *Menai:* a strait in Wales.

l. 10 *Julian:* Roman emperor, A.D. 361–63.

IV, Druidical Excommunication

l. 6 *Ancient of days:* Daniel 7:9.

V, Uncertainty

l. 2 *Brigantian coves:* The Brigants were Celtic hill dwellers in Northern England, who successfully resisted Roman conquest.

l. 4 *Sarum:* Salisbury Plain, site of Stonehenge.

l. 7 *holy piles:* ruined churches; in particular, the temple of Classerniss.

l. 8 *Iona's coast:* island off the west coast of Scotland, site of an early Christian settlement.

l. 10 *Taliesin's unforgotten lays:* fourteenth-century poems attributed to a sixth-century Welsh bard, celebrating his people's struggle against the Germans.

XXII, Seclusion—Continued

l. 13 *thorp or vill:* homestead or small house.

XXX, CANUTE
King Canute II (c. 994–1035), king of England and Denmark, author of the ballad "Merie sangen the Muneches binen Ely."

PART II

XXI, DISSOLUTION OF THE MONASTERIES
Henry VIII disolved the monasteries in 1536.

ll. 11–14 These lines allude to the belief of Roman Catholic writers that Joseph of Arimathea and his companions brought Christianity into Britain, and built a rustic church at Glastonbury.

XXIV, SAINTS
l. 6 *fond heart:* foolish heart.
l. 9 *Margaret:* St. Margaret, virgin and martyr of the third century, supposed to have killed a dragon with a cross.

PART III

I
To Isabella Fenwick, Wordsworth remarked: "When I came to this part of the series I had the dream described in this Sonnet. The figure was that of my daughter, and the whole passed exactly as here represented."

XXXVII, CONGRATULATION
l. 3 *Deliverer's sail:* refers to William III, whose ships landed at Torbay, November 5, 1688.
ll. 5–6 "See Burnet, who is unusually animated on this subject; the east wind, so anxiously expected and prayed for, was called the 'Protestant wind.'" Wordsworth's note.
l. 10 *futurity:* the consequences of those acts, their future.

XLVII, CONCLUSION
l. 14 Compare to Hebrews 12:23, "to the spirits of just men made perfect."

" 'SCORN NOT THE SONNET' " (P. 641)
Possibly composed in 1827. Published in 1827; included in "Miscellaneous Sonnets."

"YARROW REVISITED" (P. 642)
Wordsworth recalled the circumstances of this poem to Isabella Fenwick. "In the autumn of 1831, my daughter and I set off from Rydal to visit Sir Walter Scott

before his departure for Italy.... How sadly changed did I find him from the man I had seen so healthy, gay, and hopeful, a few years before, when he said at the inn at Paterdale, in my presence, his daughter Anne also being there, with Mr. Lockhart, my own wife and daughter, and Mr. Quillinan,—'I mean to live till I am eighty, and shall write as long as I live.' . . . On Tuesday morning Sir Walter Scott accompanied us and most of the party to Newark Castle on the Yarrow. When we alighted from the carriages he walked pretty stoutly, and had great pleasure in revisiting those his favourite haunts. Of that excursion the verses 'Yarrow revisited' are a memorial." Wordsworth first made Scott's acquaintance in 1803, on the journey that gave rise to "Yarrow Unvisited" (p. 469). Also see "Yarrow Visited" (p. 613).

l. 2 *"winsome Marrow"*: companion; see William Hamilton's "The Braes of Yarrow" (1724), l. 2. Also see note to "Yarrow Unvisited," l. 6 (p. 731).
l. 8 *Great Minstrel of the Border*: Sir Walter Scott.

" 'IF THOU INDEED DERIVE THY LIGHT FROM HEAVEN' " (P. 645)
Possibly composed as early as 1813; published in 1827. Wordsworth set this poem at the head of his collected poems of 1845, where it served as a preface.

" 'IF THIS GREAT WORLD OF JOY AND PAIN' " (P. 646)
Composed December 5, 1833; published in 1835.

" 'MOST SWEET IT IS WITH UNUPLIFTED EYES' "
From *Poems Composed or Suggested During a Tour, in the Summer of 1833*, a sequence of forty-eight poems, of which this is XLVIII. Wordsworth was accompanied by Henry Crabb Robinson and his son, John Wordsworth.

"TO A CHILD" (P. 647)
The child was Rotha Quillinan, Wordsworth's goddaughter.

INDEX OF TITLES

Index of First Lines

THE MODERN LIBRARY EDITORIAL BOARD

Maya Angelou
·
Daniel J. Boorstin
·
A. S. Byatt
·
Caleb Carr
·
Christopher Cerf
·
Ron Chernow
·
Shelby Foote
·
Stephen Jay Gould
·
Vartan Gregorian
·
Richard Howard
·
Charles Johnson
·
Jon Krakauer
·
Edmund Morris
·
Joyce Carol Oates
·
Elaine Pagels
·
John Richardson
·
Salman Rushdie
·
Oliver Sacks
·
Arthur Schlesinger, Jr.
·
Carolyn See
·
William Styron
·
Gore Vidal

MODERN LIBRARY IS ONLINE AT
WWW.MODERNLIBRARY.COM

MODERN LIBRARY ONLINE IS YOUR GUIDE
TO CLASSIC LITERATURE ON THE WEB

THE MODERN LIBRARY E-NEWSLETTER

Our free e-mail newsletter is sent to subscribers, and features sample chapters, interviews with and essays by our authors, upcoming books, special promotions, announcements, and news.

To subscribe to the Modern Library e-newsletter, send a blank e-mail to: sub_modernlibrary@info.randomhouse.com or visit www.modernlibrary.com

THE MODERN LIBRARY WEBSITE

Check out the Modern Library website at
www.modernlibrary.com for:

• The Modern Library e-newsletter
• A list of our current and upcoming titles and series
• Reading Group Guides and exclusive author spotlights
• Special features with information on the classics and other paperback series
• Excerpts from new releases and other titles
• A list of our e-books and information on where to buy them
• The Modern Library Editorial Board's 100 Best Novels and 100 Best Nonfiction Books of the Twentieth Century written in the English language
• News and announcements

Questions? E-mail us at modernlibrary@randomhouse.com. For questions about examination or desk copies, please visit the Random House Academic Resources site at
www.randomhouse.com/academic

NO LONGER PROPERTY OF
THE QUEENS LIBRARY.
SALE OF THIS ITEM
SUPPORTED THE LIBRARY